WHAT ARE WE
FIGHTING FOR?

ALSO BY JOANNA RUSS

Nonfiction

Magic Mommas, Trembling Sisters, Puritans and Perverts

To Write like a Woman

How to Suppress Women's Writing

Fiction

The Other Side of the Moon

The Adventures of Alyx

The Zanzibar Cat

Extra(Ordinary) People

On Strike against God

The Two of Them

Kittatinny

We Who Are About To

The Female Man

And Chaos Died

Picnic on Paradise

JOANNA RUSS

WHAT ARE WE FIGHTING FOR?

*Sex, Race, Class, and
the Future of Feminism*

ST. MARTIN'S PRESS ✹ NEW YORK

Library of Congress Cataloging-in-Publication Data

Russ, Joanna, date
    What are we fighting for?: sex, race, class, and the
future of feminism / Joanna Russ. —1st ed.
        p.   cm.
    Includes bibliographical references.
    ISBN 0–312–15198–5
    1. Feminist theory—Evaluation. 2. Feminist
criticism. 3. Racism. 4. Social classes. 5. Social
conflict. I. Title.
HQ1190.R87   1998
305.42'01—dc20   96–36688

Design by Songhee Kim

First edition: March 1998

10 9 8 7 6 5 4 3 2 1

This book is dedicated to Susan Koppelman, feminist scholar, fellow disabled person, very dear friend, fellow Ashkenazy, a totally fine human being, and a real mensch. *So she should have something nice to read.*

This book is heavily indebted to Clara Fraser, whose lifetime socialist radicalism, commitment to bettering the world, political risk-taking, challenging of existing institutions, feminism, and Ashkenazy-American common sense challenged me to write it. She is a founding member of Radical Women, which, with the Freedom Socialist Party, has combined feminism and socialism for twenty-nine years of organizing and speaking out. Thank you, all of you.

Contents

Introduction /xiii

Acknowledgments /xvii

1. ADVANCING BACKWARD /1

2. WHO'S ON FIRST, WHAT'S ON SECOND, AND I DON'T
KNOW'S ON THIRD: FREUD TO DINNERSTEIN TO CHODOROW
TO EVERYBODY /18

3. MOMMY, WHERE DO BABY THEORIES COME FROM? /48

4. FOR WOMEN ONLY: OR, WHAT IS THAT MAN DOING
UNDER MY SEAT? /84

5. SHE WASN'T, SHE ISN'T, SHE DIDN'T, SHE DOESN'T, AND
WHY DO YOU KEEP ON BRINGING IT UP? /104

6. I THEE WED, SO WATCH IT: THE WOMAN JOB /126

7. WHY WE WOMEN, SLOPPY CREATURES THAT WE ARE, CAN
NEVER FIND ANYTHING IN OUR POCKETBOOKS /154

8. SEEING RED: MY LIFE IS HARDER BECAUSE
YOURS IS EASIER /184

9. "A SOCIALIST FEMINIST IS A WOMAN WHO GOES TO TWICE
AS MANY MEETINGS" /211

10. IS LABOR LABOR? /236

11. LOOKING BACKWARD (AND FORWARD?) /265

12. "THERE IS A VILLAGE / OVER / THAT HILL" /292

13. "O.K., MOMMA, WHO THE HELL AM I?" /317

14. "COALITION WORK IS NOT DONE IN YOUR HOME" /336

15. SO . . . /366

LEFTOVERS

1. THE DAILY CORRUPTION OF THESE
SWEET SMALL BOYS /381

2. SCALING THE OFFICE BUILDING /411

3. HOME THOUGHTS FROM A
(WHOLE LOT OF) BROAD(S) /420

4. COMPARING NOTES /429

Bibliography /439

Index /459

Introduction

When I was learning how to write school papers in the 1940s, we were told to begin by stating what we wished to "prove," then to continue by "proving" it, and then to conclude by "summarizing our proofs."

When I went to college in the 1950s and learned to write scholarly essays, I found, unsurprisingly, that they followed exactly the same structure I had been taught in elementary school.

I assumed—although I preferred stories and novels to "papers" any day— that the barrenness of the Q.E.D.s lay in the factual world, not in the technique itself or its application to everything outside of mathematics and pure logic. In those places I found tautological Q.E.D.s (restating the same thing in different words, basically) so much more delicious than factual ones that I became the despair of my Philosophy 101 teacher. ("Why do you keep doing that?" he said. I said, "They're so beautiful.")

Although the aesthetic satisfaction of the syllogistic form still attracts me, I'm no longer sure that it can handle much more complexity than that of a shopping list, let alone social criticism or the reconceptualization (or "breaking set") feminists have been calling the *click!* phenomenon for some two decades now.

Anyway, I could no more have written this book in the form of a Q.E.D. than I can fly by wiggling my fingers. As marxists and feminists have been saying for a long time, *knowledge is a social construction;* when it happened, how it happened, whose interests it serves, who developed it, and how they did so are all a crucial part of what it is. So are the unexpressed assumptions that theories employ, the persons they are implicitly addressed to, and the particular sort of language in which they are written or spoken. Syllogistic logic ignores all of this.

This book began as a short (hah, *short!*) paper for the National Women's Studies Association Conference in Seattle in May 1985, one never delivered. It still bears some of the marks of its origin, in particular the academic, feminist audience I originally expected to deliver it to, but what with Dale Spender and Jeanette Silveira and Clara Fraser (and Radical Women) it grew and grew and grew and lo! the smallish newt, originally entitled "Reactionary Feminism," became a many-headed, fire-breathing dragon, tentatively entitled *Putting It All Together: Feminist Conversations about Sex, Class, and Race.* Of course the above title is a misnomer, since the book is far from "putting it all together," but I hope that here and there in this newly titled book there may be some frail bridges from one little bit of all of it to another little bit of all of it and that somebody, someday, may find these useful.

In short, I discovered the book as I wrote it, so that instead of imposing on my material the kind of unity that makes you believe that the author knew it all along (I certainly didn't), I've tried to keep that process of discovery intact. This is the form in which I have always worked, whether in fiction or nonfiction: to start with whatever is most personally important to me (feminism in this case) and then attempt to follow out the four-dimensional, misty, half-glimpsed, supercomplicated, overdetermined network in which my first preoccupation is suddenly visible as only one knotted strand. "Reactionary Feminism" began with developments in feminism, especially in academic feminism, moved to some of the theories such developments have used, then to a consideration of just what has messed us all up, then to a possible cause of the mess-up, then to the cause's further manifestations, and then to the forces preventing us from doing something about the cause of the mess-up in the first place.

Put that way it all sounds very logical. It wasn't—except that if everything is related to everything else (which I believe) then you can start anywhere, and (*if* you attend carefully to your own experience and everything you know) you will find yourself forced to broaden your inquiry to include as much of everything else as you possibly can.[1]

There is another source for some of the attitudes in this book (if not for its ideas), and that is a source not usually taken seriously. I mean science fiction.

I began reading science fiction in the 1950s and got from it a message that didn't exist anywhere else then in my world. Explicit sometimes in the detachable ideas, implicit in the gimmicks, peeking out from behind often intolerably class-bigoted, racist, and sexist characterizations, somehow surviving the usual America-the-empire-is-good plots, most fully expressed in the strange life-forms and strange, strange, wonderfully strange landscapes, was the message:

Things can be really different.

Despite the "foreclosed futures" of most science fiction (the phrase is Teresa Neilsen-Hayden's, in conversation), the message persists. I remember popularized science of the 1950s presenting biological evolution as a grand Mystery Play of aspiration and struggle upward that finally culminated in . . . well, us. But then came the silly, frivolous, lurid, "crazy" voice of science fiction: *Evolution hasn't stopped. And it may be continuing somewhere else on Earth in other than our own species.* (Or our own culture or our own kind of people . . .)

Readers surprised by my capitalization of "Human" throughout this book can refer this habit to science fiction. We may not, by the way, be the only sapient beings in the galaxy—in fact the odds are heavily against such an occurrence—which probability sometimes gave me inexplicable comfort in the midst of the combined horrors of adolescence and the ghastliness of growing up to the tune of "Love and marriage / Go together like a horse and carriage," illegal abortion, and all the other viciousness we endured because we *were* young. There seem to be plenty of folks now who find that smothering, coercive, conformist, witch-hunting, red-baiting era an object of nostalgia.

They can have it.

I remember remarking, "Even if we don't know what electrons are doing, it's a comfort to know that *they* know, don't you think?" and suddenly realizing that all the other teenagers in the Westinghouse Science Talent Search for 1953 (there were four of us "girls" out of twenty-odd finalists, all wearing the nylon net evening gowns of the period that scratched, made you sweat, and didn't turn when you did) found what I had said totally inexplicable.

And that experience too is part of the following book.

INTRODUCTION: NOTE

1. According to Dale Spender, Mary Wollstonecraft's feminist classic *Vindication of the Rights of Woman* "almost without exception [has been] described as poorly written, rambling, difficult to read. . . . I could [also] quote some of the comments which abound on the deficiencies of [Margaret] Fuller's style" (Dale Spender, *Women of Ideas: What Men Have Done to Them* [London: Routledge and Kegan Paul,

1982], 147). It's my impression that feminist documents have often been described as lacking in logical construction or badly written. Perhaps there really is a feminist style—or at least a radicals' style—arising out of the attempt not to gather new facts (which is not in itself a political goal) but to make a different kind of sense of what is already extremely obvious. Or this style may have something to do with a sense that everything is interconnected, and this sense may be something women really do feel more forcefully than men, at least within the European cultural tradition. In 1975, at a woman's bookstore in Boulder, Colorado, Marilyn Hacker and Suzanne Juhasz, both poets, spent an evening arguing that there was such a woman's style, while I, a fictioneer, argued that there wasn't. Somewhere in the early writings of the women's liberation movement is a reference to a visual test for "field-independence" (keeping a line projected on a screen vertical in a darkened room) that complains that the men tested were found "field-*independent*" while the women's results were (mis)called "field-*dependent*." This sensitivity to context may be what Hacker and Juhasz were talking about and what has led critics, almost all of them male, to find *Vindication* and *Woman in the Nineteenth Century* (Margaret Fuller's great feminist book) badly written. See Joanna Russ, *How to Suppress Women's Writing* (Austin: University of Texas Press, 1983).

On the other hand, they may very likely have simply been hostile to the emphasis and content of the works, i.e., their feminism.

A c k n o w l e d g m e n t s

Current scholarly practice in the humanities divides thinking into two kinds: "original" ideas, which are presented as one's own private property, and others' "original" ideas, which function both as appeals to authority and as a sign of loyalty to the system by which the idea producer sits on a usually slim heap of idea property with intellectual rifle at the ready to repel burglars.

The above is not an intellectual system but a commercial one,[1] and it has had the same effect on intellectual production as on every other: the encouragement of superficiality and pettiness in the continual attempt to invent something "new," the deference to the authority of Great Men [sic], and that planned obsolescence whose other name is fashion.

For quite a while now, the humanities have been imitating the form of the sciences without their content. In the physical sciences, it's often possible to cite objectively replicable experiments or observations upon which other researchers can build, but there is, I think quite obviously, no such thing operative in literature or politics that (insofar as they don't present actual new documents or facts) are addressed by subjectivities to subjectivities. There are few basic ideas in any field, and those that occur tend to do so to many people simultaneously, while such "ideas," rather than the discovery of new facts, are apt to be shifts in the field's unexamined assumptions, "re-seeings" that make new sense out of what's already known.

Nor is what I have just said anything but an illustration of itself, these ideas about ideas having been common property for some time now!

In the following work, almost nothing is solely my own. In the ever changing flux of information exchange (so inadequately described by the limp oversimplification "influence"), how can anybody locate "my ideas" and "your ideas"? There are books and books, endless conversations with feminist friends, letters, more books, recommendations of books, articles exchanged, chance remarks that take root and proliferate, offhand observations, painfully expensive long-distance calls that mingle personal news with political speculation, the effect of illnesses (major), the effect of a worsening economic situation on neighbors, friends, and lovers, exchanged chapters of unpublished books that contain glancing bibliographical references that lead to more books, lost pamphlets, meditations on why they got lost, articles glimpsed in (endless) doctors' offices—and much, much more.

Although original ideas don't originate in any one place or with one person—and why should being "first" be more crucial than being fully worked through or given vivid and beautiful expression, unless we're talking about commercial patents?—work does.

So if I want credit, it's not for my "ideas" but for typing the first draft of this monster (several times), searching on my hands and knees while ill amid messes of slippery slips of paper for the elusive quotation whose siren song has led me to ransack every book in the house twice, hurting my back, muttering to myself for months, being perpetually exhausted, eating badly, being obsessed, weighing words, trying out the rhythms of every word and every phrase, scribbling happily at night and tearing up (appalled) in the morning, getting headaches from endless attempts to put everything in the context of everything else (psychology, technology, ecology, history, class, sex, color, ideology—but never mind!)—and then condensing all of it—and then expanding it again—and not seeing friends—but everyone who's ever written anything knows all about the process.

And since I do want my *work* recognized (for good or ill), I must honor the same claim in others' efforts. If I don't, the whole system collapses. But that isn't ownership. Rather, it's the celebration of all Human effort.

Precisely because it's impossible to divide intellectual synthesis into "what-I-own and what-you-own," I wish to indicate here something of the webwork of collegial thinking, talking, and reading from which this work arose. Add what's below to the dedication and acknowledgment above.

My knowledge of the systematic burial of previous feminist movements in the last three centuries in England and the United States I owe largely to Dale Spender's *Women of Ideas: What Men Have Done to Them.* That book was the spark that ignited the long train of thinking that resulted in this book. I owe a great deal to the author's other works also, especially *Man-Made Language* and *Invisible Women.* Spender's work gives me hope that the straightforward, hard-hitting feminism of fifteen years ago may be in for a revival.

To Jeanette Silveira I'm indebted for her article in *Lesbian Ethics,* "Why Men Oppress Women," in which she extends the marxist analysis of class to the class of women via population control.

To Patricia Frazer Lamb I'm indebted—as always—for a long untiring friendship, years of encouragement, and the endless hammering out of ideas about our oppression as women (and everything else in the cosmos). This book is not dedicated to her only because there's another one coming (I hope) that is.

What I have learned about socialism in the last twenty years comes especially from Clara Fraser, socialist, feminist, the moving spirit behind Radical Women, and worker for a just society to whom I wish to express my immense obligation and my gratitude.

To Christine Delphy I'm indebted for her *Close to Home.*

Of course, my use of the ideas generated by this webwork of help and information is my own.

Since our language has few ways of indicating relationships other than those of owning (which is hardly an accident), that "my own" will have to stand.

Nevertheless, there's little in here that I do own, despite the presence of the copyright (on which the publisher insists as a condition of printing and distributing what lies herein). Even that is meant, as *I* see it, to prevent you from stealing paragraphs and pages, not ideas. If folks take up "my ideas" as "their ideas," what more can any thinker want? They're not my ideas, anyway. As far as I'm concerned, even the sentences and the paragraphs are public property—but because it's unlikely that the publisher will take such a view, I suggest that you check with her, him, them, or it before you reprint wholesale. You have my permission to "steal" ideas right now.

Meanwhile: plunder, plunder.

Use, use.

Enjoy, enjoy.

ACKNOWLEDGMENTS: NOTE

1. Mary O'Brien has pointed out that the use of the scholarly footnote in Europe parallels the rise of capitalism. Property in ideas necessitates acknowledging others' property in their ideas as well as insisting that one's own ideas are one's own property. See Dale Spender, *Women of Ideas: What Men Have Done to Them* (London: Routledge and Kegan Paul, 1982), 46.

Author's Note: We've all been taught, if we've had literary educations, that there's something silly about italicizing, something *overdone* and *ridiculous.* Women in the

U.S. dominant culture use more inflection and more emphasis in speaking than men do—or at least we are supposed to—and it is the male monotone that is normative for speech. Italics in print show that whoever is speaking is hysterical, foolish, or (in the case of men) "effeminate." I have seen reviewers condemn the italicization of many other women writers besides, for example, Helen Gurley Brown, whose "house" use of emphasis in *Cosmopolitan* does seem to me mechanical and forced. I've therefore avoided emphasis and inflection in my own work quite automatically in the past but have let them flow freely in this book. See Sally McConnell-Ginet, "Intonation in a Man's World," *Signs* 3:3 (1978), 541–59.

O N E

ADVANCING BACKWARD

Whatever happened to male supremacy?
 Women's oppression?
 The women's *liberation* movement?
 Matilda Joslyn Gage?
 Who?

Gage's name not only belongs in the above list, it sheds light on it. Although Mary Daly has paid tribute to Gage in *Gyn/Ecology*,[1] I don't remember seeing Gage's name much anywhere else in the last fifteen years of U.S. feminism.[2] It was Dale Spender's *Women of Ideas* that provided me with knowledge about this White nineteenth-century lady who lived all her life in a small upstate New York town (the location moved me to immediate sympathy with her; I've lived there and know the isolation and the awful winters) and who published her "chief life-work," *Woman, Church and State,* in 1893. One of the most brilliant theorists of feminism in the United States, Gage was also part of a feminist movement that in numbers and sheer duration equaled or surpassed our own. Similarly it was *Women of Ideas* that—after fifteen years of studying everything I could find about feminism—first gave me positive and detailed knowledge about the splendidly effective tactics of Christabel Pankhurst, whom a male contemporary called the greatest political strategist who ever lived.[3]

Many feminists have suspected that women's achievements in general and previous feminist movements in particular have been edited out of official history, but only in Spender's book have I found that suspicion substantiated by an accumulation of evidence (more than eighty cases) that didn't allow me to say, "Oh, sure, we all know that," but instead, *"Omigod, I didn't know it was that bad."*

Far from having no history, we have a mass of brilliant and inspiring action and theory behind us but—like every feminist movement before us—we have been forced by the obliteration of that thought and action from the official record to spend enormous amounts of time and energy fighting the psychological consequences of thinking ourselves the first and only pioneers. Nor are the problems psychological only. We suffer also from the consequences of not knowing what techniques work in what situations, and our theoretical ignorance, combined with our practical lack of techniques and the psychological burden of isolation, makes us work many times as hard and as long as we would otherwise have to do.[4]

Nor are the above circumstances the most appalling part of recognizing these repeated erasures of our history. To me, what is worse is seeing these erasures take place right now.

Consider, for example, the disappearance and noncollection of so many radical texts that fueled rebellion in the 1970s.[5] Consider the disappearance of phrases (and concepts) like "male supremacy," "women's oppression," "women's liberation," and their replacement by evasions like "women's new role" in what has become "the women's movement," a phrase so vague that it can include (and in my recent experience has included) everything from learning to read the tarot to discussing summer vacations.[6] Similarly what used to be called "woman-battering" and "the rape of children" has become "family violence" (let's be democratic: maybe there *are* little girls and boys who beat and rape their fathers), and the feminist-aroused consciousness of the battery and rape practiced on children has been twisted by the Right and the mass media into a whipped-up horror at adult homosexual men having consensual relations with male "children" of sixteen and seventeen.[7] In some quarters, feminism has become a counterculture rather than a political analysis of society with its corresponding plan for ending male hegemony. In others, the crucial idea that all women's experiences are equally valid has been supplanted by the new and totally muddling idea that all women's opinions are equally valid, a piece of mystification that accepts almost anything any woman says or does as "feminist" merely because it was a woman who said it or did it. We can also find, in some quarters, instead of the idea that men as a class exploit and oppress the class of women, the astonishingly simpleminded substitution that women are naturally good and men naturally bad, especially in sexual matters, so that "feminist revolution" means women having to behave in the way mandated by the worst kind of sexism: completely preoccupied with personal relations, incapable of public action, anti-intellectual, naturally nurturant, specialized in loving, incapable of selfishness or anger, and totally altruistic.

There is also the absence of consciousness-raising and the proliferation of a class of feminist—or at least female—therapists, who now take money for teaching us (if we are lucky) what we used to teach each other.[8]

Aside from the above, what seem to me really ominous are two signs often taken as positive: that the caricaturing of feminism and feminists has significantly lessened in the past few years (as of this writing), and that more and more women are willing to call themselves feminist, even if their position on the issues certainly doesn't match anything those of us who were active in the 1970s consider feminist.

First, *caricature stops when confrontation stops.* When the air no longer rings with horrid tales of ball-breaking dykes, man-hating neurotics, vicious and parasitic wives, and the rest of the tiny train of male-imagined phantoms, that's not because feminism has influenced patriarchy but because patriarchy has influenced feminism almost out of existence. Redefining "feminism" to mean anything having to do with women (or anything having to do sympathetically with women) without the context of the explicit political analysis that ignited the subject in the early 1970s may meet with less direct opposition—but try speaking about "exploitation" and "oppression" and you will be met with the same attacks, the same mockery, and the same snide complaints with which we are all so dismally familiar.[9] Or at best you will be faced with the nervousness that signals: *I'm willing to assume that we're all friends again, but only as long as you pretend that the whole issue is a dead letter and never, never bring it up again.*

Second, *feminism is something you do, not something you are.* Women who say "I'm not a feminist" and proceed to do feminist work are allies no matter what they call themselves. Those who call themselves "feminists" and don't substantiate that claim by their actions are another story entirely. In the last few years, I've heard accounts of women who wander into conferences on "women" or "women's studies" beatifically ignorant of any feminist theory and without feminist awareness of even the most rudimentary kind. Sometimes, they even say they've been sent by their (male) superiors on the presumption that other women will be "nicer" to them than men or because women's studies is assumed to be so much less demanding than the rest of academia.[10] Less heartbreaking—but often troubling—are those publications that call themselves "feminist" while sturdily refusing to define that highly variable term, those (much worse) that want to celebrate women and women's work without bringing up anything as nasty as sexism,[11] and (sharks among the dolphins) plain old sexist crap now being advertised in the company of work that, however problematic one branch or other of the feminist movement may find it, is still not an attack on the very idea that feminism means something.[12]

Examples: *Ms.* in June 1985 published a cover story entitled "Secrets of

Long-lasting Marriages," in which the examples were all legal, heterosexual, and White. Other issues of about the same vintage had low-calorie recipes for those of us who just happened to want to be thin out of our own spontaneous and quirky individual preferences—not that such desires have anything to do with coercive social standards, heaven to Matilda Joslyn, no!—and a book review a few years ago in which the belittlement and slander described in *Women of Ideas* was in full force.[13] (Let me make it clear that I am talking about the mass-market *Ms.* of the 1980s, not its reincarnation as a no-advertisement, non–mass-slick publication in the 1990s.)

Another example: Hilary Cosell, in the August 1985 *Ladies Home Journal*, proposed as a solution to women's double-job dilemma the idea of the "double career" first advanced in the 1950s. It was not much of an advance then and is totally reactionary now.[14]

I'm hardly the only feminist disaffected with such stuff. Adrienne Rich writes, "With the academization of Women's Studies . . . how easily, in a society turning Rightward, feminism can blur into female enclave, how feminist affirmation of women can slide into mere idealism."[15] Bell hooks states:

> Currently feminism seems to be a term without any clear sig-
> nificance . . . but another prepackaged role . . . a lifestyle
> choice. . . . Emphasis on identity and lifestyle is appealing be-
> cause it creates a false sense that one is engaged in praxis. . . .[16]

Barbara Haber locates the major problem in "the turning away from . . . a . . . critique of the family and relationships between women and men, the political consequence of which has been the fragmentation of struggles related to the family into an array of seemingly isolated issues."[17] Barbara Macdonald, in a speech at the National Women's Studies Association conference in Seattle in May 1985 sharply criticized ageism among young feminists, stating that its cause—here she agrees with Haber—was the abandonment of a radical critique of the family:

> Feminism has moved away from a position in which we rec-
> ognized that [the] family is [the] building block of patriarchy.
> . . . Mainstream feminists have moved back to reaffirming the
> notion that . . . family is a safe and wholesome place to be. Rad-
> ical feminists have affirmed [the] family as the source of our
> cultures . . . [this] coincides with a reactionary administration's
> push back to family values.[18]

Here is Ellen Willis, reviewing Betty Friedan's *Second Stage:*

> [There is] the current trend toward mindless sentimentality about the family . . . [and the often feminist demand that we] abandon our abrasive habit of analyzing and criticizing it. . . . [There is also] cultural feminism . . . escape from the influence of corrupt "male" values and the reassertion of superior "female" values . . . the equation of feminism with lesbianism or with an alternative women's culture or simply with female bonding. Such assumptions have also become popular in the peace and ecology movements . . . [and] form the basis of the antipornography movement. . . . [This is] no intellectual basis for a concrete antisexist politics . . . [and it] reinforces oppressive cultural stereotypes.[19]

Judith Stacey, another critic, talks about feminism's "crisis of confidence" and what she calls "the new conservative feminism," giving as her examples Jean Bethke Elshtain and the later work of Betty Friedan, noting that Elshtain's work has received wide circulation and "instantaneous recognition within the academy." Citing the "germinal insight of feminist thought" to be " 'woman' is a *social* category," Stacey says, "it is this form of sexual politics in particular that new conservative feminists reject in an attempt to avoid all forms of direct struggle against male domination." Such thought is "pro-family," "affirms gender differentiation and celebrates traditionally feminine qualities, particularly those associated with mothering," and believes that "struggle against male domination detracts from political agendas they consider more important."

Stacey goes on to observe that Elshtain declares the family to be universal and laces her writing with "romantic affirmations of heterosexual union." Stacey states dryly about Friedan's third book *(The Second Stage)* that its "central objective . . . appears to be that of making the world safe, and more livable, for dual-career coparenting couples." Stacey finds two consequences of what she calls "conservative feminism" to be the most serious: "the loss of a sex/gender theory" and "the disappearance of a feminist critique of the family."[20]

Nor do the yuppie successes of some women delight these critics. Clara Ehrlich writes:

> Women need to know (and are increasingly prevented from finding out) that feminism is *not* about dressing for success, or becoming a corporate executive, or gaining elective office; it is *not* being able to share a two career marriage and take skiing vacations and spend huge amounts of time with your husband

and two lovely children because you have a domestic worker, who makes all this possible for you.[21]

Clara Fraser, socialist and feminist, speaks of the "establishment's" attempt to make feminism into "lifestyle and personal aggrandizement, devoid of political impact" and describes women executives, managers, and bureaucrats who are vicious opponents of women workers "although their careers exist by dint of the feminist movement, and . . . who expect to receive our support and our gratitude because they are 'role models'!"[22]

Nor is academia exempt from such charges. Adrienne Rich describes women's studies programs as "the dutiful daughter of the white, patriarchal university—a daughter who threw tantrums and played the tomboy when she was younger but who has now learned to wear a dress and speak almost as nicely as Daddy wanted her to."[23] And here is Nina Baym, literary critic, stating:

> Feminist [literary] theory addresses an audience of prestigious male academics and attempts to win its respect. It succeeds . . . only when it ignores or dismisses the earlier paths of feminist literary study as "naive" and grounds its own theories in those currently in vogue.[24]

But it's not only literary theory or women's studies that does this. Julia Penelope says about feminist theory in general:

> Instead of having a "home" of our own, we now have cramped rooms rented to us by xtians, freudians, marxists, socialists, etc. . . . [There has been a shift from feminist issues to issues] validated because men have prioritized them as REAL ISSUES . . . [like] nuclear energy and racism.[25]

Two years ago, as of this writing, I met in my university classes a young single mother who was attending school full-time, working full-time, and raising a two-year-old in isolation. The child's father criticized her way of raising the baby, "helped" by occasional visits that left the boy hyperactive and crying, and provided sparse, erratic financial help from a salary three times hers. I asked her if her predicament had been discussed in her women's studies class. Her answer made it clear to me just how far the living women's studies programs of the early 1970s had become merely another academic specialty: "Oh, no," she said. "We just learned statistics."

And here are some more personal communications from feminists I know:

Men are more or less consciously diluting or debasing the meaning of feminism and . . . some women at least are recognizing from the emotional atmosphere that feminism is somehow threatening to men. In what they mistakenly believe is self-protection, they either say to their (liberal) male associates that feminism is *not really* threatening (because I'm one and your faithful servant) or to their (conservative) male associates that it *is* really threatening (and I'm certainly not one).[26]

In the past few years I have noticed . . . [some] tendencies in feminist groups.

a) A willingness to compromise to get a proposal (or whatever) passed. (Compromising often means being silent about lesbianism or using a unisex title instead of "women's" or "feminist.")

b) An adoption of yuppie values: upward mobility rather than social consciousness. Personal goals, not political action.

c) An obsession with appearance and weight and babies. (I was in a women's reading group that used to discuss women's lit . . . but then shifted to discussing diets and babies more than books.)

d) Women's centers offering sessions on assertiveness, fitness, time management, etc., not on political issues.

e) Every woman in the group is so pressured by her own job that she seldom has time to get together to talk to other women. (Tactic: Keep her too busy to cause trouble!)

f) Women are wearing dresses and makeup again. At least where I live, they are!

g) I also have noted women's studies speakers using male authorities. (To gain "respectability"? to get tenure or promotion?)[27]

The uneasy feeling many of us have [is] that the movement is being co-opted. I had some young students read *Sisterhood Is Powerful* last semester and they really noticed the difference— said they wished they'd been around then.[28]

[In a] continuing education for women Introduction to Women's Studies college-credit class I taught last summer . . . the first day of class I had each woman respond to the question of what is feminism. Almost every woman said she was a feminist but had a very limited concept of what feminism was all about. Almost no one saw feminism as the impetus to a radical reordering of society. It came out something closer to equal pay for equal work.[29]

In a women's group:

> Ideas that had been freely developed and articulated years be-fore all of a sudden became suspect, too risky, too strong, too angry, too threatening to half the women in the [women's] group. . . . Half the women in the group are talking about where they buy their meat, having rummage sales, telling and retelling labor and delivery stories, nesting, getting reinvolved in their marriages, establishing new and of course time-consuming and exclusive relationships with men, etc. . . . You suggest that women withdraw their support from the patriarchy. This con-cept is absolutely abhorrent to these women. They say the time for such action is over. They say it is no longer fashionable. . . . They look at me like I have 2 heads and say that I am para-noid.[30]

And Hester Eisenstein sums up the process that resulted in all the effects listed above:

> The feminist attack on sex roles was taken up by social scientists and the media, and the analysis of power in sexual politics became diffused. Instead, the emphasis moved to what was wrong with women and how they required resocialization in order to compete on an equal basis with men.[31]

Of course women's liberation is not the only radical movement that has been treated in this way. Radical movements are always the victims of at-tempted premature burial, but in at least some other cases, when the victim is forced into the grave, yelling, and the evildoers rain stones from above, a few appalled onlookers recognize the outrage, share their anger, and try to pass the knowledge of the crime on to future generations. What is so frightening to me about the feminist tradition we know—or rather, don't know—is that the identical oblivion overtook nineteenth-century feminists, nineteenth-century antifeminist women, the work of feminist authors like Gage, and those raw, immensely radical pamphlets of the late 1960s. It's not that this society has brought its heaviest guns to bear against feminist thinking and acting—the obliteration of other groups' lives and histories (like that of American Indians and Black Americans, to name only two examples) has been much more publicly violent—but that women's lives and feminist history have both shown the same peculiar exploitation and oppression occurring *in isolation*. Particularly disturbing to me and others is the resemblance between the current turning away from feminism as a radical political analysis and what happened to English and American feminism after World War I. Ann Oakley notes a "general wave of antifeminism that swept Europe after 1918." She writes:

> The majority [of suffragettes] gave up pursuit of the franchise or women's advancement for war work, and a minority repudiated the war and continued to work for women's issues. . . . [Of these many] wanted to use their political power for . . . general humanitarian causes . . . like the promotion of international understanding and the improvement of health education in which they saw a need for the *special* contribution women might make.

As an example Oakley quotes *British Woman's Life* (February 1920): "The sex is returning to the deep, very deep sea of femininity from which her newly acquired power can be more effectively wielded."[32]

The change from radical politics to valorizing "femininity," the insistence that "femininity" is power, the turn to "general humanitarian issues," the insistence that women as women are somehow naturally suited to issues like peace and nurturance,[33] the illusion that women have all the power they need or all the success they need (Linda Tschirhart Sanford and Mary Ellen Donovan note "the myth that women today are 'making it' in great numbers"[34]) mark both eras. As Elizabeth Abbott wrote in 1927: "The issue is not between 'old' and 'new' feminism. There is no such thing as 'new' feminism, just as there is no such thing as 'new' freedom. There is freedom; and there is tyranny. The issue is between feminism . . . and that which is *not* feminism."[35]

The conspiracy of belittlement, caricature, and dismissal that turned the century-long suffrage movement in England and the United States into a bad joke has certainly been turned against "women's lib." Nevertheless, the high feminism of the 1960s and 1970s is still too recent, as of this writing, to be dismissed entirely. There is too much evidence of it still in the culture, from TV jokes, to T-shirts, to articles in women's magazines, to feminist magazines and journals, to "feminist therapists," to women's peace organizations that, though they often accept the patriarchal stereotype of women as naturally peaceful and loving, just as often call their daring and extremely unfeminine activities "feminist." There are even still women who declare, shuddering, that *they* aren't "women's libbers." Most youngsters, even in the comparatively sophisticated environments of university communities, undoubtedly believe that "women's lib" was a bunch of hairy-legged, ugly crazies who burned their bras and are now thoroughly antiquated. But in serious intellectual circles, whether feminist or not, there's still considerable consciousness of feminism as a political force and a body of knowledge and theory. Inside academia or out, whether as demonstrations, community activities, popular books, scholarly articles, rap groups, and so on, feminism persists.

It does not, however, persist unchanged.

All of us have had to respond to the changed economic and political conditions of the last decade. What do you do when you feel that somehow your favorable historical moment has passed, that people don't like you any more, that your friends now consider your "obsessions" passé, that attacks are hitting you not only personally but economically (and this at a time when jobs are scarce and money tight), and that the freedom, conviction, support, and energy that sustained you are somehow gone? (The following is not a list of Things To Do but rather Things To Be Wary Of.)

You can abandon your politics quietly, hoping nobody will notice. You can abandon them loudly, misrepresenting your own history and declaring that it was all a big mistake, as in Cosell's essay.

You can cling to your politics in a way that puts the primary focus of your energies on the form set for them by specific historical circumstances while allowing their basic principles to take a backseat. In short, you can make your politics into a cult.[36]

You can declare that the problems your politics existed to solve are now solved and isn't it wonderful.

You can go backwards while declaring that you're going forwards, as in the essay by Cosell.

Or you can turn from the analysis of objective oppression—matters like poverty, exploitation, powerlessness, coercion, violence, and propaganda—to an emphasis on the psychology of the oppressed group, *seen not as the psychology of oppression but as something unique to the group by virtue of its special "nature."* This will enable you to withdraw your attention from attempts to mend matters by political activity to a concentration on the culture of the oppressed, seen not as a product of specific historical conditions but as an absolute value produced by the special aforesaid psychology. You can then declare the area of "culture" (so defined) and "psychology" (thus conceptualized) as *the area within which the real struggle for liberation must occur.*

This doesn't work, of course. The attempt to claim worth for an oppressed group by praising the psychology it's always supposed to have had and the activities to which it's always been restricted leads right back to the oppression everyone in the group was trying to get out of in the first place. The position of "you-say-it's-bad-but-we-say-it's-good-therefore-we'll-change-everything-by-retreating-right-back-into-it" may at first salve the lack of self-esteem generated by oppression, but it does not deal with the oppression itself. This oppression continues and goes right on undermining everybody's happiness and self-esteem. Eventually people notice that what used to make them feel good doesn't anymore, and having no clear idea of what's causing such a deprivation—since they're certainly continuing to follow the program that made them feel so much better in the first place—they turn and rend one another, and you have the whole dreary catalog of accusations, betrayals, factionalization, and ultimate loss of hope with which all oppressed groups are so dreadfully familiar. The only way oppressed people can reclaim their damaged self-esteem is by struggling against those responsible for their actual, objective, material oppression. Struggling with each other will not do. Attempting to make the group a haven where one can ignore the deprivation and devaluation enforced on the "outside" leads to the suppression of anger and conflict and falsifies the genuineness of whatever interchange is going on; the result is again the mysterious fading away of what at first seemed to make everything all right.[37]

The attempt to substitute for the uncompromising radicalism of the feminism of the late 1960s and early 1970s an account of women that sees us as a group with a "unique" psychology and "special" needs, possessors of an already existing "culture" that needs only to be recognized, is about to land a great many of us in the tar pit where (so to speak) our bones will be found in a hundred years or so and confused, not unreasonably, with those of the dinosaurs—who also hadn't enough sense to trot onto drier and safer ground.

As Dale Spender has shown for the British feminism of the nineteenth century, open belittlement is never enough to obliterate feminism from the public record.

It must be replaced.

And lo! the name of Freud led all the rest.

NOTES

1. Mary Daly, *Gyn/Ecology: The Metaethics of Radical Feminism* (Boston: Beacon Press, 1978), 216–22.

2. Gage was the mother-in-law of L. Frank Baum, creator of the *Oz* books. Susan Koppelman discovered this interesting fact and communicated it to me in the summer of 1985, speculating that the strong female figures of the *Oz* world (quite

a gynocentric one) owe their existence to Gage's witty and feminist influence. She also suggested that some of them may even be portraits of Gage, a very en-Gage-ing idea.

3. Dale Spender, *Women of Ideas: What Men Have Done to Them* (London: Routledge and Kegan Paul, 1982), 588.

4. Spender calls our existence as women in a patriarchy one of "interruptions and silences" (ibid., 14).

5. I have tried in vain, for example, to find copies of Margaret Adams's "The Compassion Trap" (1971) and Anselma dell'Olio's piece on trashing. I'd appreciate information about either.

6. A women's resource center I attended in the last few years listed these phrases among the topics selected for one of its rap groups. When I mentioned consciousness-raising, some replies were, "I come here to get away from thinking about all that," "We don't want therapy," and, angriest of all, "I don't need politics; I have a happy life."

7. At the 24–25 July 1985 hearings of Attorney General Meese's Commission on Pornography, the Justice Department called pornography "one of the nation's most significant domestic issues of the decade." According to reporter Pam Dorries, who also testified before the commission, "Testimony by law enforcement officials, right-wing and religious groups . . . led to a confusing moralistic conflation of child pornography, pedophilia, adult pornography, child abuse, homosexuality and moral degeneracy. Pornography and those who purchase or view it were described as 'sexual filth' " (*Gay Community News,* 14 August 1985). Whatever the polarization among feminists and whatever our bitterness toward each other (which leads Dorries to put quotation marks around "pornography victims" in her article), it's clear that the issue is being exploited by the Right.

8. In such a one-on-one, therapeutic situation, even though some of the experts do have real and very useful expertise, the focus is inevitably on coping with our low standard of living, our imposed conflicts, our enforced lack of self-esteem, our deprivations and persistent "failures" by some kind of individual repair work. Once a class of people earn their living this way, they are naturally resistant to being told that they're profiting from oppression. They also have (as we all do) a vested interest in believing that the work they're doing is useful and important. They also have a vested interest in not noticing or dealing with the recent very striking trend toward the *medicalization* of all sorts of "problems" whose roots are largely economic and political: drug abuse, alcoholism, woman-battering, rape, the rape and battery of children, and so on. It's hardly a coincidence that the rising number of empty hospital beds has coincided with the "discovery" that these and everything else are "medical" problems.

9. When this book was only a wee paper of forty pages, I sent it to a small, supposedly feminist press. It was returned with anonymously scribbled comments in

the margin, one of which was, "Does she know that her heroine, Dale Spender, is living with a *man?*" (I did.) Such stupid stuff is feminist-baiting, no matter who does it.

10. My information comes from Susan Koppelman.

11. A good example is the first issue of *Belles Lettres: A Review of Books by Women,* which turned up in my mailbox in May 1985. (Later issues got better, partly because I and other older feminists complained vigorously.) A picture of a very conventionally pretty and "feminine" Lou Andreas Salomé was on the front cover, while such works as Meridel LeSueur's *I Hear Men Talking, Cuentos: Stories by Latinas,* and *Lesbian Nuns* were reviewed without the slightest reference to class, racism, homophobia, or organized religion. Then there are the groups who believe that women are important and deserve more than before but have no clear idea why women haven't gotten it before and don't want to know. In the 1970s, such a group held an open meeting to establish a woman's building and art gallery only to be told by a friend of mine that they'd shackled themselves to an unrealistically high rental. They got angry at hearing this; their response was, "But we deserve the best." In a few months, they were unable to pay their rent, and the place and the group both folded.

12. One of these Blue Meanies popped up in an advertisement in the Harper and Row Women's Studies catalog for 1985. The author, Edward Shorter, we were told, "shows that contrary to the 'conventional wisdom' of women's history, women occupied an inferior social position because they were victimized by gynecological disease, unwanted pregnancies, and children" (page 11 of the catalog). Erna Olafson, reviewing the book, says the following:

> Shorter's argument is flawed at every point. Historians of medicine have shown that in the course of the nineteenth century, a higher living standard along with improvements in diet, hygiene, and public health were more instrumental in improving the health and longevity of Europeans than was medical science. . . . Even Shorter notes that tuberculosis claimed more female victims of all ages than did childbearing and that it afflicted women more often than men. . . . Others have noted, however, *that when women began to earn wages and feed themselves, they lived longer (Signs,* 11:1 [1985], 194, italics added).

I remember an argument of my own in the early 1970s with a beastly little male twit who held the surreal theory that the reason women had never been a force in politics in the history of the world was that our voices were too soft and faint to carry far in addressing groups of men. The sheer looniness of this fantasy (had he never heard Wagnerian sopranos?) is even more unnerving than the bigotry involved.

13. The June 1985 *Ms.* is issue xiii: 12. In the December 1984 issue of *Ms.,*

Marion Meade, reviewing various biographies, called poet Louise Bogan savage and irrational (an effective way of killing anybody's interest in her) and declared that Bogan's depressions were caused by her mother's promiscuity; she also called the unmarried state of the first woman accepted to the medical faculty of Harvard (in 1919, mind you) a "mystery" and made another "mystery" out of Elizabeth Cady Stanton not preventing her seven pregnancies in an age when reliable contraception was rare in the United States and the abortifacient most commonly used was lead poisoning. The reviewer seemed also unaware that during that period in Stanton's life a husband's customary and legal control over his wife, including sexual access to her, was absolute. The reviewer even quoted Susan Anthony's angry letter to Stanton that makes it clear that Anthony's only notion of avoiding pregnancy (probably a common one) was abstinence. I later found critical comments about some of the same biographies in *Women of Ideas,* which leads me to believe that Meade was simply and uncritically repeating the opinions of the biographers themselves. Keeping the young ignorant of the past is a great way to prevent them from dealing with the present. As Audre Lorde puts it, "The 'generation gap' is an important social tool for any repressive society" (Audre Lorde, *Sister Outsider: Essays and Speeches* [Trumansburg, NY: Crossing Press, 1984], 117).

14. Cosell's essay (abstracted from a book of hers) speaks to the difficulties of the double workday by maintaining that "women" were mistaken to "choose" having "careers" (which the vast majority of U.S. women didn't and don't have; they have jobs) and not mentioning the divorce rate, women's poverty as a sex, the economic depression, and the increasing necessity for families to have a double income to avoid poverty (Hillary Cosell, "Did We Have the Wrong Dreams?" *Ladies Home Journal,* April 1985, 92–94, 168–171).

15. Adrienne Rich, *Blood, Bread, and Poetry: Selected Prose, 1979–1985* (New York: Norton, 1986), xiii.

16. bell hooks, *Feminist Theory from Margin to Center* (Boston: South End Press, 1984), 48, 28.

17. Barbara Haber, "Is Personal Life Still a Political Issue?" *Feminist Studies* 5:3 (1979), 420.

18. Barbara Macdonald, "On Ageism in the Women's Movement," *Sojourner,* August 1985.

19. Ellen Willis, "Betty Friedan's 'Second Stage': A Step Backward," *Nation,* 14 November 1981, 494–96.

20. Judith Stacey, "The New Conservative Feminism," *Feminist Studies* 9:3 (1983), 560–62, 571, 572.

21. In Lydia Sargent, ed., *Women and Revolution: A Discussion of the Unhappy Marriage of Marxism and Feminism* (Boston: South End Press, 1981), 130.

22. Clara Fraser, letter to author, 24 April 1985.

23. Quoted in Cheris Kramarae and Paula A. Treichler, *A Feminist Dictionary* (Boston: Pandora, 1985), 504.

24. Ibid., 448.

25. Julia Penelope, "The Mystery of Lesbians," *Lesbian Ethics* 1:2 (1985), 32, 40. Penelope's irony, I take it, is directed not at stating that racism and the dangers of nuclear energy aren't issues but at their being unconnected to structural analysis that would link them with sexism.

26. Barbara Hillyer, letter to author, 14 March 1985.

27. Marty Knepper, letter to author, 1985.

28. Barbara White, letter to author, 1 January 1985.

29. Annette van Dyke, letter to author, 25 March 1985.

30. Lois Neville, letter to author, 8 March 1985.

31. Hester Eisenstein, *Contemporary Feminist Thought* (Boston: G. K. Hall, 1983), 140.

32. Ann Oakley, *Subject Women* (New York: Pantheon, 1981), 23, 22, 21. Italics added.

33. Bell hooks criticizes this trend as well:

> By equating militarism and patriarchy, women who advocate feminism . . . suggest that to be male is synonymous with strength, aggression, and the will to dominate and do violence to others; to be female is synonymous with weakness, passivity, and the will to nourish and affirm the lives of others. Such dualistic thinking reinforces the cultural basis of sexism. . . . This is a "dangerous perspective" [says Leslie Cagan] . . . because it focuses on women's biology "and tends to reinforce the sexist notion that womanhood equals motherhood" (hooks, *Feminist Theory,* 126–27).

I agree. It's possible to see many women's special interest in ending war as (among other things) a result of the *investment* in labor, time, and emotion that they make in raising children, but the antiwar movement in general, as far as I know, does not seem to do this.

34. Linda Tschirhart Sanford and Mary Ellen Donovan, *Women and Self-Esteem* (New York: Anchor/Doubleday, 1984), 211.

35. Sheila Jeffreys, *The Spinster and Her Enemies: Feminism and Sexuality, 1880–1930* (London: Pandora, 1985), 154.

36. For example, avoiding the word "women," which quite a few feminists do, and replacing it by other spellings like "womon" or "wimmen" can be effective as consciousness-raising or guerrilla theater. It can also become the kind of irritating point of doctrinal purity that led a *Gay Community News* writer, in a piece of tongue-in-cheek fiction published a few years ago, to invent and use the nonserious plural "wymeen."

37. JoAnn Loulan points out that in a love relationship frowned on by an oppressive world, the desire to make the twosome a haven of peace and security

can lead to avoiding conflict because those involved fear to risk their one secure retreat by expressing emotions like anger and disappointment. The result, alas, is that such a relationship loses its spontaneity and reality and the partners become distant from one another, thus making impossible the very security and good feeling the relationship was supposed to provide in the first place (JoAnn Loulan, *Lesbian Life* [San Francisco: Spinsters Ink, 1984], 143–46). Such a dynamic isn't limited to lesbian relationships, of course, or to twosomes; the group dynamic I'm describing here seems to me to follow the same pattern.

Author's Note: An inaccurate and, I think, even sexist view of feminism has emerged in the early 1990s, one which credits World Wars I and II with being the genesis of feminism in the United States, despite the obvious, long-term effects of industrialization on Europe and North America throughout the nineteenth and twentieth centuries. (See Chapter XI.) This view (which was presented in a feminist television special, "A Century of Women," in June 1994) ignores both the intense feminism of the First Wave during the nineteenth century and the very savage political and economic repression that followed both wars, a repression that was entirely effective, as some feminists recall it. "Patriotic" freedom for women was illusory and lasted only as long as their labor was needed. Thus Marielouise Jansen-Jurreit writes of the trade-off made by a great portion of "the bourgeois women's movement" in Germany "at the outbreak of the First World War" in which this part of the women's movement identified with a "chauvinistic image of women derived from Tacitus" that promised not only freedom but *conflict-free freedom,* won not against opposition by men and the state but with the blessing of both. (Marielouise Jansen-Jurriet, *Sexism: The Male Monopoly on History and Thought,* trans. Verne Moberg [New York: Farrar, Straus and Giroux, 1982], 40).

Ray Strachey, describing the end of the First World War in England, wrote in 1928:

> Thousands upon thousands of women workers were dismissed and found no work to do. . . . Everyone assumed . . . that they would go quietly back to their homes . . . [but] this was impossible. The war had enormously increased the number of surplus women, so that very nearly one woman in every three had to be self-supporting; it had broken up innumerable homes and brought into existence a great class of 'new poor'. . . . [as] prices were nearly double what they had been in 1914. . . . All these facts were forgotten. Public opinion assumed that all women could still be supported by men and that if they went on working it was from a sort of deliberate wickedness. The tone of the Press swung, all in a moment, from extravagant praise to the opposite extreme, and

the very same people who had been heroines and saviours of their country a few months before were now parasites, blacklegs and limpets. Employers were implored to turn them out as passionately as they had been implored to employ them.

Oakley adds, having quoted Strachey (above): "The labour movement responded sympathetically when an unemployed ex-serviceman in Bristol smashed the windows of tramcars and attacked conductresses in protest against women's employment in the public services" (Oakley, *Subject Women*, 20).

Although, says Margolis of the United States, "a survey of women war workers in 1945 indicated that 61 percent intended to remain in the job market" and "only 600,000 women voluntarily retired from the labor force":

Under the Selective Service Act veterans were given priority over war workers for jobs, and . . . many women were fired, especially those who had worked in heavy industry. As a result, 60 percent of all wartime employees thrown out of work in the first months after V-E day were females, and by November 1946 two million women had been dismissed from their wartime jobs. In addition to reimposing bans on hiring married women, many employers changed age requirements and fired women over 45; men . . . could remain . . . until age 65. . . . Women's layoff rate was 75 percent higher than men's (Maxine L. Margolis, *Mothers and Such: Views of American Women and Why They Changed* [Berkeley: University of California Press, 1984], 216).

As an adolescent and young adult during the late 1940s and 1950s I cannot remember the war producing anything politically that could remotely be called feminist, nor did the New Left women I knew in the 1960s ever cite their mothers or their mothers' lives as in any way an inspiration for anything feminist except as Horrible Examples they were reacting against. The new conventional wisdom described here (feminism caused by two world wars) is, I suspect, a way of reestablishing male agency as the cause of female rebellion, obliterating both female agency and the long-term social changes that (in the long run) made European feminism a twin of both industrial capitalism and its other product, socialism. This view strikes me as a way of "domesticating" the last twenty-odd years of feminism, making them more "respectable" and acceptable. After all, now that it's all right for "women" to have "jobs," it's necessary to present the change as part of some inevitable form of "progress," caused by events supposedly beyond the women's own control—or possibly anybody's control.

T W O

WHO'S ON FIRST, WHAT'S ON SECOND, AND I DON'T KNOW'S ON THIRD: FREUD TO DINNERSTEIN TO CHODOROW TO EVERYBODY

Some years ago at a Modern Language Association annual convention,[1] I ran into a student of mine who'd been in one of the earliest women's studies classes I had taught. Then a blond, bejeaned, braless free spirit, she had metamorphosed into an upwardly aspiring young academic professional in heels, hose, makeup, success dress, and some very new—or very old—ideas.

As we chatted, she told me enthusiastically that sexism, far from being rooted in male privilege or power, had its real cause in the collective unconscious and that all our efforts to change women's position would fail until we learned how to affect the collective unconscious, a process that might take centuries. I blew up, called her a traitor, snarled, "Forever, if we're lucky!" and took off to avoid colleaguicide. Her astonished, "But Freud—but Jung—but Lacan—" borne on the air-conditioning of the hotel in which the conference took place remains with me still.[2]

Since then we've had Dorothy Dinnerstein, whose *The Mermaid and the Minotaur* (1976) locates the cause of patriarchy in children being raised by women during infancy and early childhood; Nancy Chodorow's *The Reproduction of Mothering* (1978), which assimilates the freudian theory of object relations to essentially the same cause; and, more recently, Janice Radway's *Reading the Romance* (1984), which uses Chodorow's theory to come to the same conclusions.

In this tradition, which has appeared lately in many places in academia, belongs Carol Gilligan's assumption that women's values are embedded in the depths of women's personalities; women's egos are "discovered" (or rather asserted) to have flexible boundaries (which can change to "weak" in the twinkling of an eye), and women want to have babies because we wish to reproduce the triadic nature of our early situation in the family.[3] Chodorow and Radway further assure us that women's altruism, low self-esteem, dependency, and craving for nurturance from men stem from our early relationships with our mothers.

Lest I be misunderstood, I want to make it clear at this point that I don't wish to indict all these authors equally. Dinnerstein's account seems to me to be passionately sincere and her observations and anecdotal material sharp, deeply felt, and to the point. Although the book was published in 1976, its preface states that Dinnerstein outlined its first nine chapters "years before" and tried out the book's ideas on Rutgers undergraduates as early as 1966. The preface also states briefly, "Keeping *au courant* is not my style: newspapers, magazines, and especially TV are phenomena of which very little goes a long way with me; the same is true of meetings, conferences, and workshops."[4]

Her bibliography of fifty-one books and a few articles lists only eight feminist titles, all of them printed by well-known trade publishers: Simone de Beauvoir's *The Second Sex* (1953); Shulamith Firestone's *The Dialectic of Sex* (1970); Betty Friedan's *The Feminine Mystique* (1963); Germaine Greer's *The Female Eunuch* (1970); Elizabeth Janeway's *Man's World, Woman's Place* (1971); *Sisterhood Is Powerful* (1970), the anthology of early women's liberation movement articles edited by Robin Morgan; and one essay each by Joan Bamberger and Marge Piercy. Conspicuously absent from this list (according to *my* list!) are Phyllis Chesler's *Women and Madness* (1972), Eva Figes's *Patriarchal Attitudes* (1970), Kate Millet's *The Prostitution Papers* (1971), Elizabeth Gould Davis's *The First Sex* (1971), Engels's *The Origin of the Family, Private Property, and the State,* Juliet Mitchell's *Woman's Estate* (1971), and Adrienne Rich's "When We Dead Awaken" (1971).[5] There is no early anthology besides Morgan's. I have also in my bookcase Betty Roszak and Theodore Roszak's *Masculine/Feminine* (1969), Leslie Tanner's *Voices from Women's Liberation* (1971), Elsie Adams and Mary Louise Briscoe's *Up Against the Wall, Mother . . .* (1971), Vivian Gornick and Barbara K. Moran's *Woman in Sexist Society* (1971), and the collectively edited *Liberation Now!* (1971). Nor does Dinnerstein use books published by small presses. Pamphlets from the early days—many of them more radical than anything written since—are also absent,[6] and although Woolf's *Orlando* (1928) is the last item in Dinnerstein's bibliography, Woolf's *A Room of One's Own* (1929) and *Three Guineas* (1938) either didn't strike Dinnerstein as relevant to her own enterprise or were unknown to her.

There is no lesbian presence in *The Mermaid and the Minotaur,* no socialist presence, and nothing about racism. As Dinnerstein writes, "I *believe* in reading unsystematically and taking notes erratically. Any effort to form a rational policy about what to take in, out of the inhuman flood of printed human utterance that pours over us daily feels to me like a self-deluded exercise in pseudomastery." I share Dinnerstein's exasperation with pseudo-scientific standards of "scholarship" that demand "mastery" of what absolutely anybody has ever said about a particular subject—and the subject "women" is all of Human history. Nonetheless, what one does read and take notes on is determined by one's definition of what's important about one's subject. In her preface to *The Mermaid and the Minotaur,* Dinnerstein says "the intellectual tradition out of which this account grows includes the Gestalt research tradition in which the laboratory-experimental side of my identity as a psychologist is rooted." The other main intellectual source she cites is "psychoanalytic thought" and adds, "Feminist preoccupations with Freud's patriarchal bias, with his failure to jump with alacrity right out of his male Victorian skin, seem to me wildly ungrateful. The conceptual tool that he has put into our hands is a revolutionary one."[7] I would suggest that *The Mermaid and the Minotaur* is best understood (as is *The Feminine Mystique*) in the context of the early 1970s isolation of feminists from our past and from the work of other women. *The Feminine Mystique* was nonetheless written within the tradition of feminist radicalism—that is, the oppressed taking their own oppression and their own understanding of their oppression as primary and refusing to bow to any intellectual authority except their own precisely because, in a society corrupt enough to practice oppression, "intellectual traditions" are all too apt to be corrupt too. *The Mermaid and the Minotaur* was not. Some critics have commented on the narrow culture-color-class limits of Dinnerstein's book and its ahistoricity,[8] but I don't know if anyone has noticed how ahistorical is Dinnerstein's view of psychoanalysis itself. First (if you insist on using the periodicity of English history as a standard for Europe), Freud is not precisely a Victorian. In fact, much of his work was done in the twentieth century. To call him "Victorian" (Dinnerstein is hardly alone in this) is in popular parlance to remove him—very much against the factual evidence—from the context of the struggles of the suffragists, the "New Woman" in art and literature, the attempt of women to enter the trades and professions, and the rest of that huge feminist fight that was *in Freud's own time* preoccupying Europe. To think of Freud as active in the era of Christabel Pankhurst puts his "failure" to jump out of his "Victorian" skin in a very peculiar light. To consider that Freud was still intellectually active at the time of publication of Charlotte Perkins Gilman's *Women and Economics* (another book not in Dinnerstein's bibliography) makes Freud look perhaps even more reactionary. Feminists may not have been so "wildly ungrateful" after all.

I remember a talk delivered at Cornell University in the early 1970s in which we were told by a male professor from the Philosophy Department that merely listening to women was an unprecedented act in Freud's day and that Freud could not possibly have known anything about feminism.[9] At that time, the historical ignorance of the feminists in the audience was almost as total as that of the speaker, but we listened with deep cynicism nevertheless. *Nobody* could make us believe that fifty years after the publication of *Jane Eyre* (1847) and a whole decade after *A Doll's House* had electrified London theatergoers (1889) that anybody could be that dumb. (The date of Freud's famous address on "Femininity" is a very non-Victorian 1933.) As for the "revolutionary tool" put in our hands by the founder of psychoanalysis, how is it possible for Dinnerstein to trust any intellectual tool proceeding from a Human history she herself believes to be so thoroughly distorted by the infantile fear of women from which both women and men suffer?

Dinnerstein never does solve this logical problem—how to criticize a corrupt tradition from within—except by giving academic intellect, as traditionally defined, primacy over every other kind of understanding and psychoanalysis primacy over every other tradition of psychology. As I've said, I find Dinnerstein's account of specific misogynist abuses keenly felt and keenly observed, but I also find *The Mermaid and the Minotaur* an intellectually and politically reactionary work. Insofar as the book persuades readers that Dinnerstein's account of the cause of sexism is a true one, so far does it doom all of us to despair. As the author writes, "There is no way to feel so confident that this struggle can really turn the lethal tide . . . to fight what seems about to destroy everything earthly that you love—to fight it . . . intelligently, armed with your central resource, which is passionate curiosity—is for me the human way to live until you die."[10] These are brave words, but like Dinnerstein's central thesis, they reserve intelligent struggle for a tiny, educated elite. They also trust one or two culturally limited, class-biased, ahistorical theories (themselves produced by the woman-hating tradition Dinnerstein sees as about to destroy our planet) to save us if we are to be saved at all.

The fifteen-page bibliography of Nancy Chodorow's *Reproduction of Mothering* lists only seven books or essays that I can identify as part of the 1960s–70s feminist movement: "The Traffic in Women" by Gayle Rubin (1975); Jessie Bernard's *Future of Marriage* (1973); *Complaints and Disorders: The Sexual Politics of Sickness* by Ehrenreich and English (1973); Jo Freeman's essay "The Social Construction of the Second Sex" (1971); *Pronatalism: The Myth of Mom and Apple Pie*, edited by Ellen Peck and Judith Senderowitz (1974); and Adrienne Rich's *Of Woman Born* (1976). *The Origin of the Family, Private Property, and the State* is here, as is Marx's *Capital*; also present are Gilman's *Women and Economics* (1898) and Ruth Herschberger's *Adam's Rib* (1948). The remaining citations are heavily in the tradition of psychoanalysis with an admixture of anthropology and sociology.

Although Chodorow's preface states that *The Reproduction of Mothering* "owes its existence to the feminist movement and feminist community,"[11] Chodorow—like Dinnerstein—does not share the early women's liberation movement's analysis of the family as an institution central to the oppression of women. Nor does she take the view that men and women constitute socially constructed classes whose relation to one another is other than purely personal. Instead, *The Reproduction of Mothering* employs the basic assumptions of psychoanalysis: that "behind" behavior and reports of subjective experience, producing both, lies a metaphysical entity called "personality," that this Human core is essentially static, and that it is constructed by very early personal relations *and very early personal relations only*. Chodorow also assumes that the cause of present behavior is to be found in past (very early) personal relations *and nowhere else*.

This view of personal relations is what Jean-Paul Sartre has called essentialist: the idea that people behave the way they do because of an *essence* inside them (or in psychoanalytic terms a "core" personality formed very early in life) that causes them to do so. This view is summed up neatly by one of Chodorow's chapter headings (40) in which she quotes Harry Guntrip: "What we do at each developmental stage with bodily organs such as the mouth, anus and genital is determined by the quality of our personality and personal relations at each state, *rather than vice-versa*" (italics added). This view assumes that the symbolic, imaginative, time-binding dimension of Human life (what Guntrip calls "personality" and "personal relations") is logically and ontologically prior to all behavior. Although Freud himself was careful to propose specific neurological and physiological states as the basis of personality, his followers seem to have lost sight of such a necessity and speak (as above) as if "personal relations" and "personality" overrode everything, even the specialization of Human nerve endings for certain kinds of pain and pleasure. That is, physiology and neurology do not seem to make demands of their own or provide their own sensations. (If this is so and if personal relations are not based on specific sensory experiences of pleasure and pain, including concrete perceptual cues "hard-wired" into the infant's physiology, then surely there is no basis left for personal relations except telepathy. This view—the omnipotence of the psychic—is in fact the contrary of Freud's.) Even if psychoanalysts don't go to such extremes, there still remains the question of whether "personality" can be conceptualized as "lying behind" behavior (objectively observable) and experience (subjectively observable). Perhaps behavior and experience are *identical with* "personality"—in which case the very concept of "personality" is redundant and so does not belong in any system that purports to be a scientific description of anything.

Despite Chodorow's explicit allegiance to psychoanalytic assumptions like the above, much of what Chodorow says about her subject is not only unrelated to her psychoanalytic statements; it is in actual conflict with them. With scissors and tape one could easily produce a version of her book in which psychoanalysis would be entirely absent. For example, Chodorow suggests that it's not sons who spontaneously and libidinally sexualize their relations with their mothers but mothers who sexualize their relationships with their sons *because* women's relationships with men are so often sexually and emotionally unrewarding. She also notes that it's not daughters who spontaneously view themselves as nonseparate from their mothers but mothers who enforce this view on their daughters out of the mothers' own social, sexual, and emotional deprivation (like the old adage, "misery loves company"). She says that it's fathers, not mothers, who insist on forcing on their children our culture's heavily polarized gender definitions. Chodorow also states that although most women become "genitally heterosexual" (she does not distinguish between behavior and desire here, and neither does our culture), in a father-absent, father-seductive society they become so only superficially[12], a view that ties right in with Adrienne Rich's opinion that heterosexuality is so far from "natural" in most women that it must be forced upon them[13] by means of economic dependency, propaganda, and the threat of violence from men, against which heterosexual pairing is supposed to protect women.[14]

Chodorow also states that it may be the child's *isolation with one female caretaker* (an extremely recent social development) that produces the overwhelmingness of Mother and hence both sexes' rejection of women; that family patterning produces the kind of character structure (that is, the kind of behavior) that the economy requires; that many men's sexism is a defense against "powerlessness in the labor market"; that heterosexually coupled women may want babies so much because the rest of their lives are unsatisfying; and that taboos against homosexuality may be all that prevent women from turning to one another.[15]

To my mind, these unsystematized bits and pieces not only make more sense than the rest of the book, they have no necessary connection with the rest of the book. *The Reproduction of Mothering* strikes me as a classically feminist book badly hampered by a mass of psychoanalytic theory to which it's connected quite inorganically. What I find ominous is that in the feminist circles I know, Chodorow has not been cited for these insights but for their opposites: the belief that mother-rearing *inevitably* produces the gender differences we know; that women desire, bear, and rear children because of character traits *inevitably* produced by mother-rearing; and that women's "special" needs and "unique" psychology are somehow connected with the psychology of infancy and very early childhood.

The Reproduction of Mothering is a self-contradictory book. In considering it, I believe we must add to the chronic isolation of modern women from previous feminist movements the isolation of many women intellectuals from the women's liberation movement and their isolation from any kind of economic, political, or historical perspective on psychoanalysis itself, surely by now one of the most rigidly closed, self-validating systems of thought of the twentieth century.[16]

Janice Radway's *Reading the Romance* is another kettle of co-optation entirely. The book seems to have been written after the most minimal contact with other feminist work. Of 188 entries in Radway's bibliography, 14 (as far as I can judge) come directly out of the recent women's liberation movement. These are Betty Friedan's *The Feminine Mystique* (1963); Susan Griffin's *Pornography and Silence: Culture's Revenge against Nature* (1981); two essays by Heidi Hartmann, "The Unhappy Marriage of Marxism and Feminism" (1979) and "The Family as the Locus of Gender, Class, and Political Struggle" (1981); Molly Haskell's "The 2000 Year Old Misunderstanding" (*Ms.*, 1976); Helena Znaniecki's *Occupation Housewife* (1971); two essays from *Feminism and Materialism: Women and Modes of Productivity*, edited by Annette Kuhn and Annmarie Wolpe (1978); Kate Millett's *Sexual Politics* (1970); Juliet Mitchell's *Woman's Estate* (1971); and two books by Ann Oakley, *The Sociology of Women's Housework* and *Women's Work: The Housewife, Past and Present* (1974).

The bibliography also includes Simone de Beauvoir's *The Second Sex* (1952), two essays specifically about romances, and one about mother-daughter relationships (the three essays can be found in *Feminist Studies* [1978]).

The book's dedication to "My Husband Scott," who "has helped in so many ways at once practical and emotional" and whose "understanding, encouragement, and above all else, his interest" made the book possible,[17] may strike some as a witty role reversal—or simply as a "personal" statement having nothing to do with politics—but I remember all too well the kind of I'm-really-respectable credentials many feminists would advance in the early 1970s (so as not to appear "man-hating," "strident," or "too radical") to feel anything but resentment at Radway's statement. Apparently it's still all right to come to feminist conclusions (about other women, mind you) if one states one's love for a man (and often one's love for male children as well). This kind of statement to the reader, that the author's critique of sexist norms is purely academic and that she obeys them in her personal life, whatever she may say or do elsewhere, is dishonest and to my mind inexcusable.

Furthermore, I see the book as an appeal to academic orthodoxy, from its use of psychoanalysis to its very brief and mild indictment of capitalism, its enormous overblownness, and its exasperating imitation of the form of a scientific monograph.

Of course, none of the above is specific to Radway or Radway's book; this stuff is standard operating procedure in the academic humanities. Junior faculty are unlikely to get published—or promoted—or even listened to—unless their work follows such a standard line. What seems to me especially destructive is the humanities' blanket imitation of the form of scientific research without any of its content; viz. first we "survey the work in the field" (which outside matters of objective fact can mean nothing but the current climate of opinion), then we appeal to accepted work (which here can mean only the appeal to authority), and finally we come to a "conclusion" that is—as it must be—simply asserted and not "proved," since apart from some fairly small areas of historical fact, nothing outside the physical sciences can be anything more than an interpretation. The physical sciences may address objective fact and experimental observation, but other studies—from philosophy to literature to social criticism—are largely (and often only) the address of one subjectivity to another concerning the statements or behavior of other subjectivities.

Certainly there's such a thing as nonsyllogistic or "soft" evidence (what a sexist metaphor!), but the current form of nonscientific academic studies owes more to scientists' budgets and high status than to any rational intellectual considerations. (The connection between the "scientific" form given to nonscientific activity and the envy felt by humanists for scientific money and prestige was, I think, clearer—because newer—in the 1950s than it is today.)

What I find most daunting about *Reading the Romance* is that in six short years Chodorow's tentative conclusions have hardened into a reductive and reactive orthodoxy. As Radway puts it, "the desire for a heterosexual partner . . . seems to mask a covert and unconscious wish to regress to a state of infancy in order to experience again, but this time and completely without the slight withholding born of homophobia, that primary love the infant received at the breast and hands of the mother."[18]

One of the eeriest things about the above passage is just *whose* homophobia Radway means. The infant's? Surely not. The mother's fear that her feelings for her infant daughter are homosexual? A grotesque possibility. That of the adult woman remembering her own infancy (it's debatable, by the way, whether Human neurological development after birth makes such memory possible) and afraid that her own longing for nurturance violates homophobic taboos? Radway doesn't say. Nor does she suggest, as some feminists have, that female self-hatred, caused by sexism, can easily produce ambivalence toward infant daughters.

I find much in Radway's book that's useful, especially her emphasis on the lack of emotional reciprocity in patriarchal heterosexual relationships. She also does note romance's double function: to validate traditional marriage while providing an escape from its dissatisfactions. Nonetheless, to attribute the longings of a deprived and dissatisfied life to repressed infantile motives is obviously reactionary.

For one thing, it shifts the focus from what Phyllis Chesler calls our culture's enforcement of father-daughter incest as the model for women's compulsory heterosexuality to the inadequacies of the mother-daughter bond, an emphasis that seems to me a subtle way of blaming the victim.

It erases the economic and other institutional imperatives that lie behind women's attachment to men.

It obscures the direct and indirect contempt women must live with, the exclusion from what's valued in our society, the effect of the sexual double standard (Dorothy Dinnerstein speaks eloquently about the destructive effects of what she calls "feminine carnal muting" on Human self-esteem),[19] and the burden of internalized hatred that affects women.

It obscures the everyday, here-and-now lives of women in a patriarchy, which are quite enough to produce the psychology Radway describes,[20] in favor of events that are not only located in the distant past and safely "personal" *but which are produced by women's relations with other women and therefore not attributable to male misbehavior.*[21]

The theory does, of course, have some evidence going for it. It's true that Human beings learn more in their first few years of life than they will ever learn again (and that the ability to learn decreases with age). It is also true that most contemporary women in the United States (and even elsewhere) display attachment to men and a longing for nurturance and do not get such nurturance from women or believe they cannot. It's certainly true that childhood deprivation can produce lifelong psychological scarring. But the writers in the tradition I'm discussing assume a great deal more than that.

To recapitulate briefly the theories under question, crucial to the kind of thing Radway and others hypothesize is the conflict between fusion and individuation in infants and small children. Male children have an escape route from the fear of fusion with Mommy via their gender identity as males (different-from-mother), but female children, lacking this "solution," have much more trouble with the conflict, which persists into adult life and results in daughters' strong ambivalence toward mothers and adult women's wanting and needing more nurturance than men. Thus women's "solution" to the problem of leftover needs for nurturance and their consequent ambivalence toward their mothers (neither the male nor the female solution really works, of course) is to "become" their mothers by providing nurturance to others, i.e., men and children.

It's important to note at this point that *the psychology described here is supposed to be universal.* It is a description of *all women,* not a particular group of women or the women of a particular culture or historical period. Everywhere that infants and small children are taken care of by women and not by men—which means almost everywhere—this psychology is supposed to apply. Unfortunately (or fortunately, depending on your opinion of the theory), there are, at the very least, two groups of women who don't fit this theory, and one of them is quite vocal about it.

The nonvocal group (and the less important for the purposes of my argument) is that of nineteenth-century White European and North American ladies, whose ties with their mothers and other women remained strong, positive, and nurturant throughout their lives and whose relations with their husbands were considerably more emotionally distant than is the case today. This is true, at least, for those from whom we have letters, diaries, and novels.[22] The other group seems to me far more important for the theory under discussion. Out of what the editors of *Sage* call "Black mother-daughter relationships"[23] comes evidence that does not jibe with such theory. Gloria Joseph and Jill Lewis find the differences in mother-daughter relationships between White and Black women important enough to merit an entire chapter in *Common Differences.* Joseph, for example, speaks of

> the curious refrain among White women of *fear of becoming like their mothers* . . . [and] the way in which the White daughters said they feared their mothers [was] rarely mentioned by the Black daughters. . . . "I fear I might be like her. I want to be independent of her."

Lewis talks of the "odd contrast of the Black woman's respect and admiration for her mother and what she stands for, with the curious refrain among White women of *fear of becoming* like their mothers." Joseph says flatly: "It is misleading and invalid to discuss Black and White mother/daughter relationships within the framework of identical theories."[24]

Elsewhere Joseph addresses herself directly to the theories under consideration here:

> Consider the assumption of Nancy Chodorow in her very popular book, *The Reproduction of Mothering* . . . that the mothering role is the root cause of female dependence and the subordi-

nation to men. These findings are in direct contrast to the results of research conducted by Black women on Black
subjects.[25]

Nor do other women of color report the kind of experiences Joseph and
Lewis mention as typical of White women: fearing to be like one's mother
or fearing dependency on her (a fear due to deprivation of dependency in
childhood). Alice Walker defines "womanish" as

> a word our mothers used to describe, and to attempt to inhibit,
> strong, outrageous, or outspoken behavior when we were chil-
> dren. . . . A labeling that failed, for the most part, to keep us
> from acting "womanish" whenever we could, that is to say, *like
> our mothers themselves and other women we admired.*[26]

Bell hooks, commenting on White feminists' feeling that they have never
had enough support from other women, says: "When I entered my first
women's studies class in Stanford University in the early 1970s, white
women were reveling in the joy of being together. . . . *I had not known a life
where women had not been together.*[27]

Other feminists of color report ambivalence—or at least, outright anger—
at their mothers, but assign the cause to something quite concrete. Thus
Spring Redd describes her anger at her mother *and* her aunt *and* her grandmother in terms quite alien to those reported by the White women Joseph
and Lewis talk about. It was, she says, the power of the women in her family
to perpetuate the family's sexism, as the men in the family seemed to be
"merely figureheads" and the real decisions were made by her grandmother.[28] And, in an interview with Luisah Teish, Gloria Anzaldúa reports
similar perceptions: "I always felt when I was growing up that women had
the power, that women were strong and they *pretended* that they didn't have
it, that the men did; it was a *conspiracy.*"[29]

Why this difference? As far as Black women are concerned, Joseph's explanation deals with the kinds of lessons Black mothers teach their daughters. She cites Joyce Ladner writing in a 1979 issue of the *Urban Research
Review* (5:3, 3):

> Black females are socialized . . . to become strong, independent
> women who, because of precarious circumstances growing out
> of poverty and racism, might have to eventually become heads
> of their own households. Black mothers teach their female off-
> spring to perform adult tasks, such as household chores, when
> they are still in the preadolescent years.[30]

They also do this

> through oft-repeated comments such as: "Be independent and
> as financially independent as you possibly can"; "Get an educa-
> tion"; "Have self-respect or no one else will respect you"; "Don't
> trust any man"; "It takes two to make a marriage successful."[31]

Of her interviewees, when asked "the best way to succeed in life," 87.5
percent chose either "your own efforts" or "education," or a combination
of the two.[32]

Black mothers' messages to their daughters, according to Joseph, also
included messages about men that White mothers do not generally give
their daughters. Of her own 1979–80 nationwide survey of Black women,
she writes: "An overwhelming number of mothers (72 percent) gave their
daughters negative messages about men. . . . There was more romanticism
in the messages from the White mothers. "Marry for love" was a popular
response."[33] She also notes elsewhere in *Common Differences* that "the Black
woman's socialization process ceremoniously includes the parameter of a
distrust for men," referring readers to the book's chapters on mothers and
daughters.[34] There are other differences. Joseph points to Black daughters'
familiarity with "the circumstances within which their mothers existed and
raised their children and an empathy caused by understanding these situations." She observes:

> Black daughters learn at an early age that their mothers are
> not personally responsible for not being able, through their
> individual efforts, to make basic changes in their lives or the
> lives of their children. This recognition enables daughters in
> later life to be more appreciative, understanding, and forgiving
> of their mothers when they are unable to fulfill and meet the
> daughters' expectations and needs for material and emotional
> comforts.[35]

As Renita Weems puts it, "We knew that what our mothers were forced
to become was not what they had dreamed for themselves,"[36] and Merle
Woo speaks of her nonprivileged mother:

> A little ten-year-old Korean girl, being sent alone from Shanghai
> to the United States, in steerage with only one skimpy little
> dress, being sick and lonely on Angel Island for three months;
> then growing up in a "Home" run by white missionary women.
> Scrubbing floors on your hands and knees, hauling coal in

heavy metal buckets up three flights of stairs . . . putting hot bricks on your cheeks to deaden the pain from the terrible toothaches you always had. . . . Because of your life, because of the physical security you have always given me: my education, my full stomach, my clothed and starched back, my piano and dancing lessons—all those gifts you never received—I saw myself as having worth.[37]

Such affirmations, such teaching, and such empathy do not jibe either with the universal emotional female neediness stressed by Radway (who is, I assume, White), the conflict between fusion and individuation present in the tradition I've been discussing (which is White), or with the turn to men and heterosexuality as a way of solving such a conflict. Daughters whose mothers are strong, daughters who admire their mothers for being strong and who know clearly that the limits on their mothers' ability to nurture them came from outside the family, daughters taught to be independent, do not express the ambivalence about autonomy and its solution in mothering posited by Chodorow and others.

There are still more differences. Joseph (to whose work in this area I'm indebted) points out that in Black communities:

> Children seem to be less focused on the *adult* as the central figure for sustenance and guidance and seem more likely to seek help and support from agemates. . . . Socialization and learning . . . are not [all] supervised or controlled by adults. . . . [There are] patterns of communication and behavior extending far beyond the boundaries of the nuclear family or household.[38]

Joseph sees this pattern as originating in slavery and stresses that it did not parallel that of European immigrants. She also states briefly about her interviewees: "The class variable appeared to make a significant difference in responses about men and marriage. The [White] working-class women (mothers) gave responses that were more similar to the Black mothers' response."[39] The results? Daughters, says Joseph "overwhelmingly (94.5 percent) showed great respect for their mothers, despite difficulties that exist in the relationships."[40]

It seems clear to me that the presence or absence of the suffocatingly close nuclear family (a relatively new thing in history) coupled with the kind of dependency training given a group of daughters by their mothers, along with the mothers' own position in the world and the family, goes a long way toward explaining some daughters' ambivalence toward their mothers—their fear of becoming like their mothers or dependent on them—or others' respect for, admiration of, and wish to become like their mothers. White, professional-class feminists' comments on their ambivalence and their mothers' lives are legion. Here is Judith Arcana's:

> Men are objectified by most of our mothers as basic requirements, prerequisites, to living life as proper women. . . . We are taught to consider men brutal, insensitive, emotionally inadequate . . . requiring special handling like babies or convalescents; we are shown how to trick them, demonstrate false affection and/or sexual passion, trap them into giving us money and social security. . . . *A very small number of mothers did give their daughters advice. . . . to be independent.*"[41]

Is it any wonder that faced with such an expectation and such an example of adult womanhood and expecting also to be as separated from other women as the dominant culture insists we should be, a great many such women feel ambivalent about their mothers, dependent on men, and afraid of becoming like their mothers? Lewis says it flatly:

> The fear of becoming our mothers . . . is a fear of the specific conditions of motherhood and womanhood, which necessitate our oppression. . . . The fear stems from our knowledge that, through our relationship with our mothers, we are cyclically part of those conditions.[42]

Now, the results of infantile experience and psychology supposed to be common to all Human beings must fit all Human beings. I would submit here that the account of the mother-daughter bond and the psychology arising from it given by Dinnerstein, Chodorow, and Radway do not fit the experiences and behavior of all women. Since the psychology used by these theorists is supposed to be based on an account of Human infancy that is universal, timeless, and "built into" the entire Human species, we must conclude either that the women quoted above are not Human—a possibility I don't think psychoanalysis is ready to entertain nowadays, at least not publicly—or that they are lying (ditto), or that the theories discussed in this chapter are simply false.

I believe the theories to be false.

I will go further and maintain that the character traits, feelings, and behavior that are being offered to us in the three books I've discussed (and in the academic tradition derived from Dinnerstein and Chodorow) as "special" to women and due to the "unique" experience of women's infancy and early childhood are clearly and obviously similar, if not identical, to the character traits, emotions, and behavior manifested by every other oppressed group.[43]

In short, what is being offered to us as the special psychology of women is the psychology of oppression itself.

The horizontal hostility (what Marge Piercy calls the "carnage in the fish tank" and "the wrong anger"[44]) is similar.

The sense of devaluation and ambivalent longing for unconditional acceptance by one's "superiors" (that is, members of the oppressor class) are similar.

The love-hatred felt towards one's fellows is similar.[45]

The scapegoating of mothers—or any other part of or aspect of the group closest to the oppressed and onto whom the "bad" side of the group identity can be projected (ageism is very important here, as is the sexist devaluation of old women)—is the same. The idea that inadequate motherly love makes women oppressed is like the contention that it's pushy, vulgar Jews who give rise to Jew-hating, or that straights wouldn't hate homosexuals if it weren't for those flamboyant and disgusting queens, or that Black women are responsible for Black men's misery, or that Jewish women are ugly, overaggressive and at fault for the defects of Jewish men while Gentile women are beautiful, soft, and "know how to be women," and so on.

The attribution of enormous power to any member of the group who has "made it" and the endlessness of subsequent attacks and/or demands for help are the same.

The envy and hatred of those perceived as leaders—and the pride in them and love for them—are the same.

Some oppressed groups may manifest such a cluster of feelings and behavior more strikingly than others. For example, there are, of course, very great differences between predominantly nonurban American Indians, third-generation urbanized Black people whose grandparents came to the Northern cities to get jobs created by the war industries' need for workers in the 1940s, and third-generation Ashkenazy (of whom I'm one). People whose community structures are more intact live out a different situation than those whose community structures are less so, having been assimilated into or shattered by urban Anglo-American industrial civilization. The most "assimilated" (in the sense of having had their community structures shattered and their original culture erased by a world that oppresses, exploits, and despises them) may well exhibit the worst anomie. To the extent that members of such groups have been "culturally colonized"—that is, to the extent that no other values are available to them except the dominant ones—to that extent they may well be psychologically vulnerable, self-hating, and more likely to experience ambivalence toward their fellows.

In such a situation, self-hatred can become intense, and the practical as well as the emotional risk of trusting other members of the group can become considerable. To the degree that real community is absent, the members of the group will be isolated emotionally from one another.

When there's no possibility at all of "rising" out of one's class (or color, or ethnic group, or sex), oppression visited on the group from the outside will produce rage and some of this rage will be vented on other members of the group. At the same time, the very impossibility of leaving the group will make for group solidarity, and ambivalence and distrust may not reach the extremes that they can among groups less ghettoized. I believe it's when the possibility of "rising out of one's class" (or group) exists, with the enormous pressure it creates to renounce one's group or class identity and betray one's comembers (if only by letting them continue to be oppressed while one escapes their fate), that the ambivalence of group members toward each other and themselves reaches fever pitch. When the actual possibility of "rising out of one's class" coexists with the glimpsed possibility of rising *with* one's class—*as well as the continuing likelihood that both possibilities are rare or illusory*—then I think you *may* get the worst degree of rational and irrational mistrust: the denunciations and the bitter factionalizing that occur in Left groups; the constant accusations of betrayal and vituperative attacks in the women's liberation movement; the assertion that it's women who most hate and betray women; that it's those low-class Irish, or vulgar uneducated darkies, or pushy Jews who cause bigotry; that so-and-so isn't a real dyke, real Jew, real feminist, or hasn't got negritude; that lesbian practitioners of leather S/M who get chased by the police and beaten up by male punks are the *real* agents of the patriarchy,[46] that the real enemies of third-generation Jewish men (and all that prevents them from enjoying the fruits of the Gentile United States) are their Jewish mothers and wives; that mothers and daughters are inevitably enemies (and at the same time strongly bonded to each other); and the rest of the tragic mess Lorde calls "kitchen wars."[47] If White women show extreme lack of self-esteem and more need for unconditional love than other oppressed groups (I'm not sure we do), I don't believe for a moment that Mommy is the agent responsible. Living, many of us, in relatively recent isolation from people whose oppression is identical with ours, with no culture or community *as a group* to call upon, forced upon pain of considerable sanctions (ranging from guilt and discomfort, to losing custody of our children, to comparative poverty, to being beaten on the street or at home) to direct our affection and allegiance toward members of the very group that's oppressing ours, drafted into lifelong tending of other people's emotional and physical needs as our "mission" in life, and forced to draw upon that constant emotional and physical work as our primary source of self-esteem—

Well, if many such women's craving for love and the valorization provided by it seems (on the whole) rather extreme, if some women's "feminist" theories tend to blame other women for women's woes—

—Is that in any way the slightest bit surprising?

In the case of Radway (and others) theorizing that "women's" sense of emotional deprivation is caused by the mother-daughter bond (whether such a theory is qualified by adding "under patriarchal conditions" or not), the conditions that produce horizontal hostility are being reproduced, not analyzed. A situation that is being constantly reproduced in adulthood, instead of being understood as having causes outside personal relations, becomes projected *onto* personal relations and located in the past—where it joins with the enormous sexist chorus of "Blame Mommy" to produce what I would like to call "antitheory": theory that functions to direct attention away from the causes of oppression located outside the oppressed individual and toward the inadequacies in personal relations between oppressed individuals.

Theories that assign White women's feelings of not being nurtured or supported enough to the unmet needs of infancy also ignore the possibility that if most men, or at least White men, don't express women's need for nurturance, it may because many White men are afraid to do so. It may also be precisely because, at least in the dominant group, it is men who are the emotionally dependent sex, not women. There is, for example, the life-long emotional and practical work many women do to nurture many men, work that such theories serve to obscure. Such theories also obscure our society's attempt to mystify this situation by proclaiming that such women are more dependent than such men, more "emotional," less stable, less self-sufficient, more clinging, and unable to go it alone. Many men and women (including some feminists) believe in the patriarchal myth of the romantic male loner, while at the same time these men expect to be nurtured by these women and dislike women who refuse this obligation, expressing their disapproval in social behavior that ranges anywhere from loudly proclaimed neediness to jokes to curtness to carping to rage and even sometimes to murder. Such women are often held responsible for such men's happiness, convenience, and feelings of well-being without having the social power to produce this delightful result except through charm, tact, compassion, and emotional and sexual manipulation. To be held responsible for something without being given the power to produce it is at the very least unsettling; at the worst, it can be terrifying. "Women are nicer than men," said a (White) male colleague of mine, noticing that the secretaries always smiled at him (a matter of class as well, of course). Shulamith Firestone's "dream action" for the women's liberation movement in 1970 was *a smile boycott* to remove "that smile that's like a tic on the faces of every woman and adolescent girl."[48]

The raw, early days of the 1960s and early 1970s were full of analyses like the ones outlined above. Indeed, one early and quite interesting one— suggested at a panel on "Lesbian Identity" held at the Gay Academic Union conference in New York City on 29–30 November 1974 (I was there)— seems to point toward at least one theory of gender differentiation, a theory that constitutes (I think) a partial explanation of women's "mothering" and that takes into account both mothers' differential nurturing of girl and boy children and the structure of patriarchal marriage so responsible for women's feelings of neediness and the lack of fulfillment of those needs. I offer it not as any kind of comprehensive account but merely as an example of the direction in which such analyses could go, one consonant with the material I've already discussed.

At the panel several speakers (among them Karla Jay and Pam Oline) noted that girls in patriarchal societies continue living in what they called a "matrisociety" up to a fairly late age, usually puberty (at least), while their brothers are forced out of this gynocentric enclave within the larger patri- archal society at a much younger age, at five or even earlier. Even if boys and girls were treated identically within this enclave, which does not seem to be the case, seven or eight more years' exposure to its values, habits, and behavior would undoubtedly make a considerable difference, not only in the extent to which the values "take" but also to the emotional and other circumstances of the leave-taking and the emotional, social, and intellectual resources available to the leave-taker to deal with the whole process.

Nor is the process itself the same. If such boys are lured out of let's call it "matrisociety" at a very early age by promises of independence, power, and fatherly approval while simultaneously being forced out by fatherly punishment and intimidation, the resulting childish guilt and fear would have a very different effect from girls' much later temptation by association with powerful masculinity and the social coercion to exhibit heterosexual behavior.[49]

One piece of evidence that can be brought to bear on this sketch of a theory is that it seems to be fathers, by and large, who insist on treating girls and boys differently and who insist on gender differentiation in their children.[50] Another is the age at which girls have been required to leave their primary group of women and the degree to which they've been re- quired to isolate themselves from it. Both have changed drastically for women in the dominant culture during the last two centuries. Lesbian "crushes" that were expected to occur (if at all) at eleven or twelve in the 1950s as a sort of "trial flight" for the serious business of heterosexual coupling were expected to occur in the nineteenth century too—*but they were expected to occur as late as the early or even middle twenties.*[51] (The age of female puberty has gone down in the last century and a half but not that much.) Simultaneously, the intimacy expected between husband and wife has increased enormously as the isolation of the wife from other women (including her mother) has become almost total, certainly in middle-income White groups and in popular Anglo-American cultural expectations. For example, a story like Tess Slesinger's 1935 "Mother to Dinner" in which a White, middle-class, young wife's love is divided between her new husband and her mother (with her husband coming second) is written with surprising innocence and lack of "pathology," considering today's expectations and standards.[52]

To lay women's inadequate self-esteem and longing for affection at the feet of the mother-daughter bond is, as some feminists have suggested, to mistake the line foreman for the factory owner—or rather the line foreman for the elite of the international conglomerate that owns the factory and enforces whatever policies and conditions it wants. As Nancy Henley notes, "The real problem with 'slave psychology' is, after all, *slavery*."[53]

Is it too plain, base, and vulgar to suggest here that Human emotional dependency does not cease in adulthood and that therefore evidence of unfulfilled dependency needs in adults are not "special" needs left over from inadequate mothering in infancy? As Jean Baker Miller notes, the assumption that dependency needs must be infantile, that "people who need caretaking or nurturance from others are childish and immature," is the political result of devaluing nurturance and assigning it largely to women.[54] If men (at least White men) exhibit less in the area of dependency needs and seem more self-sufficient and generally more "mature" or "autonomous" than women (at least White women), that may be not because these men in general need less but because *they get more*—and from whom?[55]

Why, *from their women*, of course, women as diverse as lovers, clerks, employees, mothers, wives, colleagues, sisters, customers, daughters, and even women met by chance on the street![56]

I would like to propose here that women's "motherliness" can be explained as a matter of skills, behavior, *and values*, all of which can be learned. I would certainly accept that many or most women's fascination with their own infants may be explicable biologically—that is, via certain cues provided by infant behavior, shape, smell, and so on that most women find—by and large—attractive and gratifying. I would add to many women's response to this cluster of cues many men's responses also, judging from the effect I've seen puppies, kittens, and babies all have on my classes and on young adults in general, during my twenty years of teaching.[57]

(That such a response may be much intensified in some—or many—women by the process of giving birth is surely likely, but I agree with Dinnerstein that such a reaction to infants does not explain years of mothering behavior toward much older children or female "motherliness" in general.)

An account of Human behavior that included the effect of politics (including sex-class membership and its many consequences), the enormous plasticity of the Human brain and its capacity for learning, and Human biology, not in the sense of the popular sociobiologists' attributing each bit of extremely complex Human social behavior to a different "gene" or cluster of genes[58] but in the sense of the kind of basic needs described by Maslow or Harris,[59] would leave no room for psychoanalysis as such and would eliminate the necessity for appealing to it.

To sum up: concrete and rather obvious accounts of women's behavior derived from feminist politics have been replaced by accounts of a "special" psychology arising from the mother-daughter bond. This is not an intellectual phenomenon but a political one, and it represents not feminist progress but feminist reaction.[60]

APPENDIX

I considered adding an analysis of Juliet Mitchell's *Psychoanalysis and Feminism* (1974) to the text of this chapter but finally decided not to, as most of that book seems to me simply a recapitulation of psychoanalytic theory. For example, there is the assertion that the only alternative to freudian theory is a very narrowly conceived rationalism and that those who reject psychoanalysis "unconsciously deny the unconscious."[61] Mitchell calls Eysenck's 1930s outcome-of-therapy study "notorious" but does not say why, and she maintains that Freud "discovered" unconscious mental life, infantile sexuality, and the importance of sexuality, instead of hypothesizing (that is, proposing) them. She also calls Freud's attributing neurosis to sexual sources his "great initial *discovery*" and "*his discovery* of the omni-importance of sexual ideas" (italics mine). The book contains an extraordinarily snide attack on Wilhelm Reich (the author calls the federal prosecution, his jailing, and the burning of his books "petty prosecutions") and quotes Robinson's *The Sexual Radicals* to the effect that Reich's career was "hopelessly grandiose . . . [and] faded imperceptibly into farce."[62] The attack on Reich (which, if I recall properly, is not peculiar to Mitchell among psychoanalysts) undoubtedly has much to do with his class interests— Reich was a socialist who attempted to place psychoanalytic theory at the service of the working class and who emphasized social constraints on sexual expression, for example, climate of opinion, the presence or lack of privacy, the punishment visited on women for free sexual activity, and so on.

Mitchell writes badly in a way many psychoanalysts do;[63] that is, she shifts inconsistently from the literal level of discourse to the figurative and back again, apparently without awareness that she's doing so. The resulting self-contradictions make her work both hard to follow and impossible to disprove. Here is one Mitchellian self-contradiction in little: "Freud found that the incest and seduction that was being claimed *never in fact took place.* The *fact that,* as Freud himself was well aware, *actual paternal seduction or rape occurs not infrequently* has *nothing to do with* the essential concepts of psychoanalysis" (italics added). When we hear that the essential concepts of psychoanalytic "cure" are not concerned with anything like feeling better—well, I don't know what you conclude, but I concluded that such stuff was impervious to logic and decided to leave the book alone.[64]

I believe that Mitchell is attempting to make psychoanalysis into an analysis of patriarchal thinking rather than an example of it. Her contention that Freud had such an analysis in mind is not, I think, borne out by his work nor by what she calls Freud's "conservative realism," i.e., his moderate and conventional antifeminism. As in Chodorow's work, the feminism of the last chapter is unconnected to the rest of the book. Mitchell concludes that "the economic mode of capitalism" and "the ideological mode of patriarchy" remain independent of one another and that the "unconscious that Freud analyzed could thus be described as the domain of the production of . . . ideology." She also sees—most interestingly, if confusingly—a contradiction between "patriarchal law and the social organization of work—a contradiction held in check by the nuclear family."[65] (This account sounds almost like Faderman's and Katz's, although Mitchell doesn't elaborate on it.)

In short, like so many feminists, Mitchell can trace no clear connection between capitalism and patriarchy and has had recourse to psychoanalysis as a way of explaining the construction of patriarchy without investigating patriarchy's material existence and its material base. I also believe that the nuclear family (which didn't in fact reach the English or European working class until the last part of the nineteenth century) was a stopgap invention to contain the possibilities of women's freedom made available by the Industrial Revolution. (More of this later.) There is, however, it seems to me, no reason to attach such an idea to psychoanalysis itself, nor does Mitchell do so.

She is not the first or the only feminist to attach her feminism to some culturally acceptable "truth"—a truth that, in turn, manages to contain, limit, or destroy the feminism attached to it rather than the feminism transforming the patriarchal "truth" involved.

NOTES

1. The annual Modern Language Association convention comprises university and college teachers of English and all other modern languages. The last annual convention I attended in 1975 attracted more than eleven thousand such teachers, a fearful sight

2. My behavior was really abominable. (I think I might do it again, though.)

3. Sociologist Jessie Bernard lists such social reasons for women's deciding to have babies as the enormously coercive effects of pronatalism, the association of motherhood with adult status, competition with one's mother or other women, the desire to gain attention or get a man, a way to "escape from freedom" and fill up one's time, pressure from relatives and obstetricians, the need for company, a desire for power, the widespread assumption that childlessness is pathological, and so on (Jessie Bernard, *The Future of Motherhood* [New York: Dial Press, 1974], 19–56).

4. Dorothy Dinnerstein, *The Mermaid and the Minotaur: Sexual Arrangements and Human Malaise* (New York: Harper and Row, 1976) vii, viii.

5. I have tried to limit myself to titles Dinnerstein might reasonably have had access to before her own book went into print.

6. For example, there is *Woman and Her Mind: The Story of Daily Life* by Meredith Tax (1970), a Bread and Roses publication. Some of the offhand brilliancies in the pamphlet include statements that women "produce" themselves for male consumption (Tax lists on page 17 diets, makeup, curlers, depilatories, clothes, etc.), that "sex is not transcendent to women because it is a continuation of their work role" (19), and that the "anxiety, the false consciousness, and the sense of loss many men experience are common to oppressors in other situations" (19). The pamphlet is an analysis of consumerism as it applies to sexism. Such marxist perspectives and such daring analyses were not uncommon in the early days.

7. Dinnerstein, *Mermaid,* ix, xi.

8. I was not one of them, unfortunately. In a review in *Frontiers* in 1979 (IV:2), I praised the book to the skies. It's hard to recapture my reactions at the time, but I suspect that before that no one had, to my knowledge, treated the fact that White middle-income American children were brought up (and not just through early childhood) by Mother in relative isolation and related this phenomenon to sexism in general. Dinnerstein's thesis focused attention on this asymmetry in the position of the sexes and promised a strikingly easy (and mechanical) solution.

9. His main point was that it was a man's listening to women—a gentleman's listening to ladies, actually—that was unprecedented. Had ladies been listening to ladies? Had women been listening to women? Such eventualities did occur rather a lot by the 1880s and the 1890s in Europe and England. There is also the honorable history of socialist-feminist rapprochement earlier in the century.

10. Dinnerstein, *Mermaid,* viii.

11. Nancy Chodorow, *The Reproduction of Mothering: Psychoanalysis and the Sociology of Gender* (Berkeley: University of California Press, 1978), vii.

12. Ibid., 119, 168.

13. I'm talking here about what Ti-Grace Atkinson and others have called "the heterosexual institution," of which more later.

14. Unfortunately, recent research on the subject has presented considerable evidence that heterosexual pairing, far from protecting women against male violence, sometimes furnishes it. The family is supposed to be a place of special safety for women and children, but can be dangerous for both. See Del Martin's *Battered Wives* (1976); Andrea Dworkin's *Intercourse* (1987); Diana Russell's *The Secret Trauma* (1986), *The Politics of Rape* (1975), and *Crimes against Women* with Nicole Van de Ven (1976); and Florence's Rush's *The Best Kept Secret* (1980). A whole literature on child abuse and "incest" (a misnomer, since what children are actually subjected to is intimidation, coercion, and violence by adults or older children) has grown up in the last few years.

15. Chodorow, *Reproduction of Mothering*, 186–87, 190, 203–4.

16. You think not? Brace yourself for Chapter III!

17. Janice A. Radway, *Reading the Romance: Women, Patriarchy, and Popular Literature* (Chapel Hill: University of North Carolina Press, 1984), x.

18. Ibid., 145.

19. Dinnerstein writes:

> What the double standard hurts in women (to the extent that they genuinely, inwardly bow to it) is the animal center of self-respect: the brute sense of having a right to one's bodily feeling. . . . The burden of sensual self-abnegation imposed on women by the double standard . . . helps make women . . . humble, dependent, malleable. . . . The female burden of genital deprivation . . . sometimes cripples real interest in sexual interaction, but . . . it can deepen a woman's need for the emotional rewards of carnal contact. What it most reliably cripples is human pride (Dinnerstein, *Mermaid,* 73).

20. Bernard has this to say of the occupation of housewife: "It is extremely hard for one's self-esteem . . . to withstand such negative evaluation from the outside world. If it is acceptable when one is a member of the majority, it becomes difficult as a member of a [cultural] minority" (Jessie Bernard, *The Female World* [New York: Free Press, 1981], 245).

21. Hooks quotes Marlene Dixon: "A politics of psychological oppression . . . pit[s] individual against individual and . . . [mystifies] the social basis of exploitation" (bell hooks, *Feminist Theory from Margin to Center* [Boston: South End Press, 1984], 25).

22. See Judith Kegan Gardiner, "A Wake for Mother: The Maternal Deathbed in Women's Fiction (*Feminist Studies* 4:2 [1978]) for striking differences of this sort between nineteenth- and twentieth-century fiction written by White women in English.

23. See *Sage* 1:2 (1984), 25. Joyce A. Ladner and Ruby Morton Gourdine note that "mother-daughter relationships among Blacks is a little explored area of investigation" ("Intergenerational Teenage Motherhood: Some Preliminary Findings," *Sage* 1:2 [1984], 8).

24. Gloria Joseph and Jill Lewis, *Common Differences: Conflicts in Black and White Feminist Perspectives* (New York: Anchor, 1981), 128, 125, 83.

25. Gloria Joseph, "Black Mothers and Daughters: Traditional and New Populations," *Sage* 1:2 (1984), 17.

26. In Laura Lederer, ed., *Take Back the Night: Women on Pornography* (New York: Morrow, 1980), 100. Italics added.

27. hooks, *Feminist Theory*, 11.

28. In Barbara Smith, ed., *Home Girls: A Black Feminist Anthology* (New York: Kitchen Table Women of Color Press, 1983), 54.

29. Cherríe Moraga and Gloria Anzaldúa, eds., *This Bridge Called My Back: Writings by Radical Women of Color* (Watertown, MA: Persephone Press, 1981), 227.

30. Joseph and Lewis, *Common Differences*, 95.

31. Ibid., 106. This statement contrasts strikingly with the common—or is it just White?—idea that the primary responsibility for making a marriage work is the woman's.

32. Ibid., 107.

33. Ibid., 125.

34. Ibid., 29.

35. Ibid., 96.

36. Renita Weems, "Breaking the Silence between Mothers and Daughters," *Sage* 1:2 (1984), 27.

37. Moraga and Anzaldúa, *This Bridge*, 141–42.

38. Joseph and Lewis, *Common Differences*, 91, quoting Sara Lightfoot.

39. Ibid., 90, 125. Although I could not find much evidence connecting differences in the mother-daughter bond itself with class, there is one thing that does appear to depend directly on class and that is *mother-blaming*. Judith Arcana, interviewing families for two of her books (1979 and 1986), "found that class . . . was a major factor in mother-blaming. . . . [It] increases with moves into the middle class" (*Sojourner*, August 1987, 22). Lillian Rubin, in her study of the working-class family, found that working-class women do not blame their mothers in the way that middle-class daughters do theirs. Like the Black women interviewed by Joseph, Rubin says:

> [Working-class children are often] "lonely and scared" or
> both. But the child in the working-class family understands

that often there's nothing his [sic] parents can do about it. They're stuck just as he is . . . they know that father works two jobs to keep a roof over their heads and food on the table; that mother does dull, demeaning and exhausting work just to help make ends meet. When the father gets drunk or violent; when the mother "takes it," joins the father in his behavior or . . . simply runs away, a child's condemnation doesn't come easily. . . . Children in such families sense the adults' frustration and helplessness (Lillian Breslow Rubin, *Worlds of Pain: Life in the Working-Class Family* [New York: Basic Books, 1976], 27).

Arcana points to mother-blaming as a technique used by minority men who hope to become assimilated into the majority culture. She cites Jewish-American men since World War II (see Portnoy and his famous *Complaint*) and Black men "for several decades now. . . . The men of both . . . groups are encouraged by the cultural majority" (*Sojourner*, August 1987, 23). Alice Walker also notes the belief of some Black men that they are somehow less Black, more "assimilated" than Black women (in Laura Lederer, ed., *Take Back the Night: Women on Pornography* [New York: Morrow, 1980], 99). The work of psychologically oriented middle-class professionals like Chodorow unfortunately fits right in with this tradition, as Arcana notes, citing both Dinnerstein and Chodorow for "subtle but potent . . . mother-blaming" (*Sojourner*, August 1987, 23).

    40. Joseph and Lewis, *Common Differences*, 79.

    41. Judith Arcana, *Our Mother's Daughters* (Berkeley: Shameless Hussy Press, 1979), 46–48. Italics added.

    42. Joseph and Lewis, *Common Differences*, 139–140.

    43. In *The Nature of Prejudice* Gordon Allport lists as "traits due to victimization":

> [O]bsessive concern and suspicion, cunning, strengthening in-group ties, prejudice against other groups, aggression and revolt, stealing, competitiveness, rebellion, enhanced striving, denial of membership in own group, withdrawal and passivity, clowning, self-hate, in-group aggression, sympathy with all victims, symbolic status striving and neuroticism (Allport, *The Nature of Prejudice* [Garden City, NY: Doubleday Anchor, 1958], 157).

Because women's job *as* women vis-à-vis men as prescribed by the dominant culture is to provide emotional support, physical services, and sexual expression, and because of our culture's omnipresent belief that "feminine" behavior is natural, the list may need some renaming. I think "self-hate," "sympathy with all victims," and "neuroticism" (whatever that is) may stand as they are. I would propose for "cunning" the emotional manipulation of men and the female deceitfulness men have complained about for centuries; for "strengthening in-group ties" the formation of the feminine "counteruniverse" that de Beauvoir describes in *The Second Sex;* for "prejudice" both class and racist bigotry and dislike of those "other," i.e., bad, women: career women, housewives, old women, "ugly" women, fat women. "Aggression and revolt" may be renamed shrewishness and nagging; for "stealing," we can say perhaps "fuzziness" about or sheer disregard of masculine rules; for "competitiveness," competition about "looks," children, housekeeping, or who has the best man; and for "perfectionism," the constant obligation to do everything for everybody and the guilt about not doing all jobs well—motherhood, housekeeping, professional work, and wifehood—that attacks so many women who work both in and outside the home. For "denial of membership in own group," I'd put identification with men and masculine standards; for "withdrawal and passivity," ordinary "feminine" passivity; for "clowning," both charm and pretended stupidity (or incompetence), for "in-group aggression," "cattiness," backbiting, and the treachery for which we're supposed to be famous; and for "status-striving," the acquisition of material possessions, the working for and being obsessed with "respectability." Ditto sexual virtue. Freud's "passivity," "envy," and "narcissism" fit perfectly into the above list.

In short, if many women feel emotionally deprived and treated badly, it's because we are.

Both that statement and the list of "feminine" characteristics above used to be feminist commonplaces.

44. Marge Piercy, *The Moon Is Always Female* (New York: Knopf, 1980), 22.

45. See Audre Lorde's "Eye to Eye: Black Women, Hatred, and Anger" in *Sister Outsider: Essays and Speeches* (Trumansburg, NY: Crossing Press, 1984) for an analysis of the effect of racism on such phenomena.

46. Pat Califia, self-described S/M lesbian, has been publicly protesting this last assessment since the late 1970s. Most but not all of her essays on the subject have appeared in *The Advocate.* Califia has written me that she tried to publish her work in feminist journals with no success except for one essay (Califia, letter to the author, 5 May 1980). Califia pulls no punches in her material, but most of them are directed at the institutions of church, state, and family, not at feminism. I find the controversy between the antipornography feminists and the pro-sex contingent (both self-named) to be a bitter tangle, part of the intergroup hostility to be expected from the oppressed.

47. Lorde, *Sister Outsider,* 48.

48. Shulamith Firestone, *The Dialectic of Sex* (New York: Morrow, 1970), 90.

49. Shulamith Firestone interprets the Oedipus complex in terms of power (ibid., 47–52) as does John Stoltenberg (Jon Snoddgrass ed., *For Men against Sexism* [Albion, CA: Times Change Press, 1977], 97–109).

50. Judith Arcana interviewed a group of men of various colors and classes,

asking them various questions about their parents. Most "said that their mothers had not subscribed to sex-role stereotyping; they couldn't recall even subtle, unspoken exhortation to be 'men' when they were boys." She adds, "Even those sons whose mothers do teach and encourage them to follow the rules" will learn how to be men from observing adult men, from older boys, and from the communications media that are dominated by men and that present "images men have made" (Arcana *Every Mother's Son* [Seattle: Seal Press, 1986], 117–19).

51. See Nancy Sahli, "Smashing: Women's Relationships before the Fall," *Chrysalis* 8 (1979) and Carroll Smith-Rosenberg, "The Female World of Love and Ritual: Relations between Women in Nineteenth-Century America," *Signs* I: 1 (1975), 1–29.

52. The story appears in *Between Mothers and Daughters: Stories across a Generation,* edited and with an introduction by Susan Koppelman (Old Westbury, NY: Feminist Press, 1985), on 141–60. Koppelman's fifteen years of research into the short stories written by women in the United States—she has found more than four thousand, most never collected in multi-author anthologies—has led her in this volume to call the relationship between mothers and daughters one of the crucially important themes of women's literature in the United States. Stories on this topic by women seldom appear in contemporary multi-author anthologies. In fact, stories by women seldom appear in such anthologies, and those that do are almost always atypical examples of the author's work.

53. Nancy M. Henley, *Body Politics: Power, Sex, and Non-Verbal Communication* (Englewood Cliffs, NJ: Prentice-Hall, 1977), 201.

54. Jean Baker Miller, "Psychoanalysis, Patriarchy, and Power: One Viewpoint on Women's Goals and Needs," *Chrysalis* 2 (1977), 19–20.

55. Thus say Luise Eichenbaum and Susie Orbach in *What Do Women Want* (New York: Coward McCann, 1983).

56. Early feminist writing often dealt with the psychological benefit men derived directly or indirectly from "street hassling" and its messages. These were that public space was male space, controlled by men; that men had the right to judge women's appearance; that women were not fully Human but in some sense decorative or inferior objects; that men were immune to the self-consciousness of being constantly "onstage"; and that women were interchangeable. Men's position as "superior" to women as a group is clearly reinforced by the *institution* of street hassling. See Gwenda Linda Blair's "Standing on the Corner . . ." (*Liberation* July/August, 1974), Pam McAllister's "Wolf Whistles and Warnings" (*Heresies* 6, 1978), Dana Densmore's pamphlet "Chivalry—the Iron Hand in the Velvet Glove" (1969), and especially Nancy Henley's *Body Politics* (1977).

One day in my early twenties in Manhattan I formed a hypothesis that the reason men did not bump into me in the street was that I made way for them so habitually that I had ceased to notice that I did so. I decided to test this notion by walking in a straight line. Three collisions and two "why don't you look where you're going"s later, I abandoned the project. Twenty years later I found similar observations in *Body Politics*. In Eugene, Oregon, researcher Fox [Jeanette Silveira] observed people passing on the sidewalk and noted who got out of whose way. In twelve out of nineteen mixed-sex encounters she observed, it was the woman who moved, in four cases both moved, and in three cases the man did (Henley, *Body Politics*, 40).

Similarly a student at Michigan State University made sidewalk observations in the Lansing, Michigan, area involving more than one hundred subjects. She found "that women tended to move out of the way more frequently than men did . . . also that women moved earlier in the encounter (and younger people also tended to yield to older)" (ibid).

57. I will never forget the sight of six or seven students in the 1970s grouped around a very young puppy, apparently the ward of one of the young men, who was cooing at it, starry-eyed, while the surrounding young men and women followed suit. Of course, neither women nor men then felt the pressure to insulate themselves against every motive but ambition for material success. Writer friend Samuel Delany, whom I asked about men's "maternal reactions to babies and toddlers" in 1976, wrote me that yes, boys and men yearned after babies and toddlers and that yes, such reactions "bothered" the male Humans in question, sometimes very much.

58. *Not in Our Genes: Biology, Ideology and Human Nature* by R. C. Lewontin, Steven Rose, and Leon J. Kamin (New York: Pantheon, 1984) deals with biological theory and its misuse by the Right and includes much material on popular sociobiology as the newest disguise for social darwinism. The volume is extremely useful both for defending radicals against such pseudoscientific theories as popular sociobiology (and equivalents in the area of sex and class) and in defending the scientific method against those radicals (I am particularly concerned with feminists) who, having found poison in their medicine cabinets, now wish to dump everything else in them out the window. The total effect of the book (like the effect of Spender's *Women of Ideas*) is to change bored and tired acceptance of clichéd truths (of course we all know that) to horror at the truly awful state of affairs revealed by the author (I didn't know it was that bad!).

59. In *Toward a Psychology of Being* (New York: Van Nostrand and Reinhold, 1968), Abraham Maslow proposed a theory of the "hierarchy" of Human needs and the "prepotency" of some over others. Briefly, the version of his theory I have in mind would go something like this: Physiological homeostasis constitutes the foundation of the Human satisfaction of needs, with some needs (like that for oxygen) being structurally prior to (Maslow called these "prepotent over") the need for water, which in turn is biologically prior to the need for food. Somewhere in between— the levels are by no means clear, as Maslow notes, and the interrelationships are complex—come those like the need for immediate physical safety. Ones like the Human need for community membership can be pursued only after the need for safety has been largely satisfied, and this need can be pursued only after the needs for salt, oxygen, and so on have been met. Maslow makes the point that no level of

need has to be satisfied 100 percent before proceeding to the next, but that satisfaction need only be *enough* to make such a progression possible. Certainly, the
"hierarchy" of needs—I would rename "hierarchy," I think much more accurately,
as a matter of logical and temporal *priorities*—is a useful idea in explaining how
Humans make choices between, for example, strangulation and self-expression, with
sufficient oxygen being a precondition of wanting or experiencing self-expression
(or anything else). Choices are often not that simple, of course, and Maslow does
recognize that needs that he places "high" in his hierarchy can become what he calls
"functionally autonomous." Or, as I would put it, a two-dimensional scheme isn't
sufficient to account for the interrelations of such needs; what's needed is at least a
three-dimensional model. I believe Maslow to have been badly hampered by his
language, which is very hierarchy-minded. Marvin Harris lists "a minimal set of
human bio-psychological selective principles" as follows:

> 1. People need to eat and will generally opt for diets that
> offer more rather than fewer calories, proteins and other nu-
> trients. 2. People cannot be totally inactive, but when con-
> fronted with a given task, they prefer to carry it out by
> expending less rather than more energy. 3. People are highly
> sexed and generally find reinforcing pleasure in sexual in-
> tercourse [sic]—more often from heterosexual intercourse.
> 4. People need love and affection in order to feel secure and
> happy, and other things being equal they will act to increase
> the love and affection which others give them (Marvin Har-
> ris, *Cultural Materialism: The Struggle for a Science of Culture*
> [New York: Random House, 1979], 63).

There are obvious difficulties with the above, but in general I would agree, adding
the qualifications that "most" be added to "people," that there are biological (and
variable) "ceilings" on all the above needs, that "sexual intercourse" must be taken
in the broad sense of arousal and orgasm, and that Maslow's "hierarchy of needs,"
which recognizes that the satisfaction of one human need often conflicts with the
satisfaction of another, be added to Harris's very minimal list.

60. That such theories spring from the reactionary temper of the times and
are not merely intellectual mistakes can be demonstrated by a look at Nancy Friday's
My Mother My Self (New York: Delacorte Press, 1979), a nonfeminist best-seller with
a psychoanalytic explanation for everything, which reads eerily like a caricature of
Chodorow's book. Friday's central and passionate contention is that heterosexuality
was providentially sent us (by whom she doesn't say) to save women from being
overwhelmed and smothered by their emotional attachment to their mothers. The
overwhelmingness of the bond that Friday complains of seems to consist of a sense
of being like Mom, a desire for her love and approval, and horror at the restrictions
of Mom's life. Friday is describing, without being aware of it, the ambivalence felt

by women growing up in a society that both separates women from one another and holds out the illusory possibility that allegiance to men will somehow provide the freedom Mom doesn't have. Zelda Fitzgerald, who wanted to live an exciting life and whose sexual escapades (mild by contemporary standards) expressed her desire to escape from the restrictions suffered by her mother's generation, has her parallel in students of mine who announce defensively that they're going to get married or move in with a boyfriend. After all, even though it violates the purity of their feminism (in their own naive opinion), it will open up to them the wonderful world of ideas, important friends, and adventures. It will also, they think, provide love and safety forever after. The "sexual revolution" of the 1960s was full of such young women. Somewhere in the early writings of the 1970s is a piece on that "sexual revolution" that concluded by saying after six months of such women's freedom, their mothers would've gone hoarse saying "I told you so." (I would appreciate news of who wrote the piece and where it can be found.) Friday's authority on psychology, psychoanalyst Richard C. Robertiello, also appears in Jonathan N. Katz's *Gay American History*. Katz reprints material from Robertiello's *Voyage From Lesbos* (1959) in which Robertiello writes of "curing" a lesbian patient of her homosexuality. Among other things, Katz quotes the following passage:

> I told Connie that it was important for her to realize that if she anticipated exploitation [from men] she would be more likely to get it. If a man sees that a woman doesn't trust him and, therefore, cannot love or respect him, he may then decide to exploit her since he feels no mutual love relationship is possible with her (Katz, *Gay American History: Lesbians and Gay Men in the U.S.A.* [New York: Avon, 1976], 288–89).

The above is pretty obviously a good example of blaming the victim. I recall a psychoanalytic therapy group of the 1960s in which a woman who'd gone to a singles dance in Manhattan (at the analysts' urging) reported having been almost raped by a man who took her home. His comment was that she must have known there was "something wrong" with the man; why (he said, until she burst into tears and ran out of the room) had she wanted to do that *to herself?*

61. Juliet Mitchell, *Psychoanalysis and Feminism* (New York: Pantheon, 1974), 12, 5.

62. Ibid., 340, 5, 48, 151.

63. Not Freud, as I recall.

64. Mitchell, *Psychoanalysis*, 9, 340.

65. Ibid., 433, 413.

T H R E E

MOMMY, WHERE DO BABY THEORIES
COME FROM?

But what if psychoanalytic theories are true?

If so, it would certainly be "wildly ungrateful" of us to refuse to use them.[1]

But what *is* "true"?

In talking about what's "true," what's "evidence," and what's "scientifically acceptable," those who do so draw on a body of rules for making science that were developed out of some earlier social rules for deciding which explanations of Human behavior and other phenomena were to be preferred over others. Briefly, the "scientific method" as I will understand it for the purposes of this chapter represents a historically decisive break with *some* previous standards in European culture (principally the absolute authority of theology and the ancient world) but not with all. The following list (which I'm doing from memory and which may therefore be incomplete) does not depart that radically from what most readers of this book would probably consider "common sense." Those who know, please bear with me. Here they are:

Falsifiability means that the theoretical system in question is capable of being disproved—that is, it is defined in such a way that evidence can conceivably be brought to bear against it. What isn't falsifiable isn't provable. Theories that explain everything are good for nothing.

Predictive power is important because a theory that can explain anything after it happens but can't predict what will happen is likewise useless.

Parsimony refers to a principle for choosing between theories: the one with fewer theoretical entities and few explanatory principles ("laws") is to be preferred to the one with more theoretical entities and more explanatory principles.

Widest applicability means that the theory that accounts for the larger number of observable phenomena is to be preferred to the theory that explains fewer.

Consistency with established knowledge means that a theory that fits in with established knowledge is to be preferred to one that doesn't.

Replicability means that the same results can be obtained from the same experimental conditions by more than one person at more than one time. Strictly speaking, replicability is a requirement of experimental evidence rather than a standard for judging theory. In studying Humans, replicability presents grave difficulties because experiments with Humans are often unethical (depending on the kind of experiment) and always difficult to do because of the enormous number of factors entering into Human behavior. The requirement of replicability can sometimes be satisfied indirectly, for example by statistical studies controlled for relevant factors (what's "relevant" can, of course, be a matter of dispute) such as age, sex, class, educational background, income, diet, and so on—to name some of the common measures used to "match" one sample of Human beings with another.

The requirement of the absence of unnecessary entities (in a theory, that is) is sometimes called Occam's razor after the fourteenth-century English thinker, William Occam, who asserted it. The requirement can be stated thus: "Do not multiply entities needlessly." If you disobey this "rule," you can create a new entity every time your theory gets in difficulty, create ever newer entities to take care of the further difficulties you get into, and so on forever.

None of the above means that knowledge must be quantifiable, or that proof must be syllogistic or mathematical, or that people must be treated like things. Nor does it imply an "objectivity" that ignores the bigotry of some scientists, the inescapability of observer bias, the contamination of much that passes for evidence, the ignoring of the undoubted fact that knowledge is a social product, and all that other *scientism* we've been treated to for the last century and a half about Human behavior. Nor is it possible in Human affairs to obtain the kind of "hard" evidence[2] that's possible in the physical sciences. Much evidence in support of theories concerning why people do what they do—or feel what they report they feel—will of necessity be suggestive rather than cut-and-dried, and more of it will be necessarily devoted to disproving theories than to proving them.[3]

Nor does the above list imply that objectivity and subjectivity are totally different, or that they are in conflict, or that consciousness is an illusion, or that "science" can prove or disprove values, or that as material complexity increases there is no qualitative change but merely a quantitative one, or that physical, chemical, biological, psychological, and social phenomena are organized in hierarchies. Such ideas have been historically determined by the specific historical conditions under which the scientific enterprise arose and the solidly material interests it served and still serves.

I'm not saying (by the way) that there's a "real" science we must rescue from historically accidental contaminations of it. The same historical forces that produced the part of scientific rule-making I would like to preserve here produced the other stuff too. As a *historical* enterprise, science was everything that it was. Nonetheless I believe that a great deal that was produced by those forces is worth keeping.

First, most of the above standards for theory-making seem to me the same as those that ordinary people have used quite matter-of-factly, both cross-culturally and transhistorically, in their everyday doings. Scientific rules largely represent a development out of such standards rather than a complete departure from them. What science does (when it's behaving in this way) is to sharpen and refine such standards, not contradict them.

Second, the successes of some parts of the scientific enterprise in the last two centuries have been so spectacular (both theoretically and practically) that they must be onto something. True, most of these successes have not been in the area of Human beings studying Human beings, but in what are called the "physical" sciences. I don't believe this is a good enough reason to foreclose completely on the potential of the whole scientific enterprise in other areas. (If we do, what standards remain to show us what to choose between competing interpretations in other areas?) I believe that so many feminists have found the actual content of so much supposed "scientific thinking" to be so poisonous, such an attack on their happiness and self-esteem, that many have thrown all of it away, quite understandably. (If the only alternative to throwing it all away were keeping it all, I would throw it all away too.) Politically motivated nonsense abounds, of course. There is also the confusion of science with technology and technology with the power of big business, as well as the use of "Science" as a validation for any doubtful enterprise from Pa Bell to atomic power plants.[4]

But back to psychoanalysis.

First of all, psychoanalysis (in common with some other theories of Human psychology) rests on certain assumptions that seem to me—and many others—to be problematic. It assumes that adult needs are "caused" almost exclusively by childhood experiences or by memories of such experiences. It assumes also that dependency needs, sexuality, and certain other issues need to be accounted for in a way that other needs and other issues don't, i.e., that the latter are "rational" and the former are not. It does not, in fact, distinguish between what is rational and present-oriented and what isn't, nor does it propose any clear way to distinguish the two. Moreover it contains no clear account of what distinguishes normal behavior from pathological. In general, it uses (quite uncritically) concepts that originated in physical medicine and that make sense when applied to notions of illness as an invasion from outside the organism by viruses, bacteria, poisons, or trauma but make much less reliable sense when they're broadened out and fuzzied up to include behavior or emotions.

Second, claiming "interpretative" status for psychoanalysis, as Nancy Chodorow and others do, will not wash; interpretations of Human behavior have always abounded and continue to do so today. Many of these are occult, or numerological or religious, and like religious exegeses of what the Bible *really* means, interpretations unsupported by other evidence can go on forever—and do. That is, as Chodorow stresses, "the evidential basis of psychoanalysis is clinical. It is drawn mainly from the psychoanalysis of adults and children, and consists in interpretations made by analysts of what is said in the analytic situation."[5] As many feminists have pointed out, interpretations of one person's behavior made by other persons whose livelihood depends upon believing in their own competence to make such interpretations and in the interpretive system they have been taught—upon which their livelihood also depends—are not, let us say, entirely trustworthy.[6] Furthermore, as most analysts were and are men and most analysands women, masculine bias is undoubtedly at work here as well as class bias and the quite natural Human tendency to find that years of experience only confirm the beliefs one started out with in the first place.[7] Nancy Henley notes that any interpretation of others' intentions or unconscious motives *by someone else who is an authority*

> fits in with the general pattern that subordinates (e.g. children, mental inmates) are often denied the right to state their own motives. This is part of the power of psychiatry [in general]: to ascribe motives that people don't claim for themselves. . . . If a message is "received" but the "sender" claims no intention of sending it (as happens often in psychoanalytic interpretation) can we nonetheless claim that it was sent, albeit unconsciously? Can we talk about *communication* in such a circumstance, especially when there is no known or accepted nonverbal code in the interacting community (except that code used by interpreting "experts")?[8]

Third, the assumption that the study of psychosis provides a key to normal infantile development, one made by early psychoanalysts, seems now to be a mistake.

Fourth, psychoanalysis itself is not all of a piece. Freud's ideas about the "defense mechanisms" are certainly widely accepted now, both in much of the popular culture of the United States and in most psychotherapy unrelated to psychoanalysis, but not the freudian theory of "object relations," the kind of thing meant by talk about "infantile sexuality," "the Oedipus complex," the "oral," "anal," and "genital" stages of development,[9] the "libido" theory, the erotic/mental adventures of the Human personality from infancy until about the age of five, and the continuing importance of such matters in adulthood. This psychoanalytic description of object relations goes far beyond simple assertions that Human beings often lie to themselves, bemuddle themselves, deny what others think is obvious, attribute their own feelings to others, and so on in an effort to deal with unpleasant mental states.[10]

Fifth—and this may come as a surprise to some of my readers, as it certainly did to me when I discovered it a few years ago—outside psychoanalysis itself, only one group in the United States now accepts psychoanalysis as established, unmodified truth: academic literary humanists. Among psychiatrists and psychologists, as Karen J. Winkler notes, "Freud's reputation is in serious decline," while it is on the rise among "literary and film critics, historians, anthropologists, and political scientists"—all folks devoted to explaining things after the fact (because they needn't predict anything), and all of them (shall we say?) rather creative in their interpretations of Human behavior.[11]

Here are some other opinions about psychoanalysis, all of them feminist. Naomi Weisstein states:

> What he [Freud] thought constituted evidence violated the most minimal conditions of scientific rigor. In *The Sexual Enlightenment of Children,* the classic document which is supposed to demonstrate empirically the existence of the castration complex and its connection to phobia, Freud based his analysis on the reports of the father of the little boy, himself in therapy and a devotee of Freudian theory. I don't really have to comment further on the contamination in this kind of evidence.

She goes on to talk about the problem of "interpretation" in psychoanalysis, i.e., the lack of any other kind of verification:

> There is nothing wrong with such an approach [interpretation based on clinical evidence] to theory *formulation:* a person is free to make up theories with any inspiration that works: divine revelation, intensive clinical practice, a random numbers table. However, he is not free to claim any validity for this theory until it has been tested and confirmed. . . . [The problem with a dis-

cipline] which rests its findings on insight, sensitivity and intuition, is that it can confirm for all time the biases that one started out with.[12]

And as for the reliability of clinical judgments, Weisstein has the following rather daunting tale to tell. Citing Hooker's "Male Homosexuality in the Rorschach" (1957) and Little and Schneidman's "Congruences among Interpretations of Psychological Test and Anamnestic Data" (1959), she presents the very disturbing evidence that clinicians in general

> cannot judge reliably [i.e., make the same judgments over time] nor can they judge consistently . . . [either in distinguishing] which set of stories was written by men and which by women . . . which of a whole battery of test results [are by homosexuals or heterosexuals and which] of a battery of clinical results *and* interviews [with questions like "do you have delusions" and "what are your symptoms"] are products of psychotics, neurotics, psychosomatics or normals.

Worse still, if clinicians assume sexuality "to be of fundamental importance in the deep dynamic of personality" (a concept we are told originated with Freud and that psychoanalysis has certainly kept) and yet they cannot spot "gross sexual deviance . . . what are [they] talking about when they . . . claim that the basis of paranoid psychosis is 'latent homosexual panic'? They can't identify what homosexual anything is."[13]

Shulamith Firestone lists six outcome-of-therapy studies for psychotherapy in general, one more than Weisstein does. The results were all disappointing; all confirmed that *the best kind of therapy for anyone was to leave them alone.* Psychoanalysis ranked lowest in effectiveness.[14]

Here is another comment on psychoanalysis (not psychotherapy in general) from the late Alice Sheldon, an experimental psychologist whose field was perception. She states:

> Among general psychologists Freud has never been much more than an object of curiosity because his theory . . . *cannot be falsified.* With it you can explain anything *post hoc* [after it happens] but you can predict nothing. A few feeble studies have attempted to pick out children being reared in a manner that should result in one of the Freudian pathologies, but nothing much came of it, as I recall. And that point about unfalsifiability is crucial. If you can't prove it false, you can't prove it true.[15]

One feminist historian, Ann Oakley, does cite a study that appears to disprove the psychoanalytic idea advanced by Chodorow and others that women's libidinal energies start by being attached to their mothers but then at some crucial point in childhood become attached to their fathers. Thus "Arthur Aron (1974) found in a study of Toronto couples that both men *and women* seek to repeat in marriage the early relationship they had with their mothers by choosing a mate who, like a mother, will combine loving care and considerate control."[16]

In connection with the scientific requirement of parsimony—don't invent entities needlessly and if you must, invent as few as possible—Elizabeth Janeway has this to say: "Some of Freud's more labyrinthine formulations . . . take on a pre-Copernican, epicyclical air."[17] Henley goes further in this connection, seeing unseen forces like "drives" as redundant in any psychological theory.[18]

There have been other criticisms of psychoanalytic theory, two in particular concentrating on what Freud certainly considered to be the crucial point both in his theory of the unconscious and his account of Human mental development. One is by a feminist, and one is by a biographer of Freud who appeared (at the time I corresponded with him) to be in the process of turning into a feminist.

In 1976, Florence Rush, a feminist and an expert on childhood sexual abuse, seriously challenged the historically and logically crucial doctrine of psychoanalysis: that adult women's reports of having been sexually abused by fathers or other adult male relatives during the women's childhood or adolescence were in fact fantasies. The freudian explanation of these fantasies hinges on the repressed incestuous desire for their fathers that all little girls supposedly experience as an inevitable part of the Human development of early childhood. Freud had originally believed his patients' reports. It was his later belief that such reports were *not* factual that led to his formulation of the idea of the unconscious and of the sequence of Human development in infancy and early childhood that constitutes his theory of Human object relations and its corollary, the drive theory. In her essay, Rush notes Freud's alarm at the sheer "number of fathers named by his patients as sexual molesters," his inferring "from some hysterical features in his brother and several sisters that even his father had been thus incriminated," his concern over a dream in which he himself "was feeling overly affectionate towards his daughter," and his refusal to believe that "perverted acts against children were so general" on the grounds that "it was hardly credible." Rush then goes on to characterize the shift from believing patients to not believing them as "a Freudian gaslight" and states that subsequent psychoanalysis and psychoanalysis-dominated psychiatry and psychology turned away "from any concrete reality" to the belief that "the psyche was considered capable of dominating the external world."

She sums up the psychoanalytic theory of Oedipal fantasy, which Freud first employed about his women patients and later established as the central doctrine of psychoanalysis for both sexes, as "foolproof emotional blackmail. If the victim incriminates the abuser, she also incriminates herself."[19]

What followed these very emphatic statements that the emperor was exposing his epidermis unprotected to the cold, cold winds of logic?

Nothing. Apparently the literary and intellectual establishment did not choose *Chrysalis,* the feminist periodical in which Rush's essay appeared, for its bedtime reading.

Then in 1984 another criticism of the fundamentals of psychoanalysis appeared, this one by a man, a psychoanalyst, and the former director of the Freud archives, Jeffrey Masson.[20] Although his resources allowed his work to be far more detailed and far better documented than Rush's, Masson's argument was essentially the same: Freud's theory of infantile sexuality and the Oedipus complex was unsubstantiated, part of a totally sealed system of belief impervious to evidence and especially destructive to women. Very briefly, according to Masson, Freud's first paper about the abuse of his female patients in childhood or adolescence by adult men (often their fathers) led to considerable social sanctions. In 1894, when Freud not only believed his patients but said so publicly, his monograph, although listed in the proceedings of the conference at which he presented it, was not accompanied by the usual summary and was deleted from the newspaper report of the conference. Nor was that all that happened. In the previous year Freud and his close friend the nose-and-throat specialist William Fliess had almost caused the death of a patient, Emma Eckstein, whom Freud had been treating. Fliess, with Freud's approval, had removed a bone in Eckstein's nose in order to control her masturbation (which European medicine then saw as an evil, as did Freud, who believed that masturbation led to neurosis). Fliess's surgery had subjected Eckstein to three life-threatening hemorrhages. Freud, at first horrified by what he and Fliess had put Eckstein through, *later decided that the hemorrhages had been produced by Eckstein herself as neurotic symptoms.*[21] Concurrently he made the change in theory that he and his followers both regard as the beginning of psychoanalysis. Freud stated later that this change of belief was "the beginning of psychoanalysis as a science, a therapy, and a profession."[22]

Masson's book, published by a major publisher, Farrar, Straus and Giroux, and excerpted before its publication in a major periodical, *Harper's,* was not met with the silence that greeted Weisstein and Rush. Indeed, it was widely reviewed. In the preface to the second (paperback) edition of the book, the author quotes from these reviews: "a vengeful outcast . . . perpetually adolescent . . . a kid . . . a charlatan . . . a master of seduction . . . a grave slander . . . comical and self-serving . . . pathetic and mean-spirited . . . intellectual terrorist . . . predator . . . sudden virulent anti-Freudianism," and so on.[23] In short, Masson's arguments were ignored, and discussions focused on the supposed pathology of his personality, just as women's arguments and achievements so often meet with no discussion but endless scurrilities directed at their supposed sexuality or their supposed lack of it.[24] Masson has written me that the only quarter from which he got support for his ideas was "the feminists," mentioning Florence Rush and Judith Herman by name.[25] In his preface to the second edition, Masson also gives credit to the feminist pioneers who have done research on the sexual abuse of children, including Diana Russell, Florence Rush, Judith Herman, and the "feminist literature of the 1970s."[26]

Masson also notes the bad effect on Freud's patients of what R. D. Laing has called "ascription" (insisting unilaterally on someone else's qualities, motives, or emotions) and that any theory or any psychotherapist who on principle believes a patient's memories of rape or incest to be fantasies "is in covert collusion with what made her ill in the first place." He notes as well that such ascriptions cause "the uncertainty of one's past [to] deepen and the sense of who one is [to be] undermined."[27] Of course, theories of Human psychology can't possibly (or can't yet) be subject to the kind of evidence that's common in the physical sciences. Much of the evidence in support of theories concerning why people behave as they do or feel what they report they feel will of necessity be somewhat suggestive rather than the hard-and-fast "proof" popularly supposed to exist in the physical sciences.[28] As in most scientific endeavors, much more activity will be devoted to disproving theories than to proving them. As Stephen Jay Gould says, scientific theory is always in long supply.[29] Nonetheless, a theory that rests on interpretation only, that can explain anything after the fact but can predict nothing, a theory to which evidence cannot apply, and that invents ever more entities as causal explanations for phenomena is not theory at all.

It is, to put it mildly, a mess.

Let me repeat this because it's important: any theory set up so that it *cannot be disproved* (that is, one that can explain away any evidence directed against it) is lousy theory, and a theory that invents new entities every time it encounters a difficulty is the same. If permitted to invent new entities ad lib, anyone can explain any phenomenon by a totally untestable speculation, "prove" that untestable speculation by another untestable speculation, and so on and so on for as long as they please.

Here is an actual historical example. Start by insisting that the planets revolve around the earth in perfect circles. This is not entirely unreasonable—after all, you can look up in the night sky and see them do it. But if you watch them night after night, you can also see them perform what is called "retrograde" motion—that is, they appear to move backwards in their orbits too. Circles will not do for *this* at all, so you invent further circles that you stick onto the first, simple, circular orbits. (These are called "epicycles.") As observations of the night sky get better and better, the epicycles get more and more complex until you end up with the pre-Copernican theory of heavenly motion, too complicated to be reasonable (the scientific requirement of parsimony) and too full of specially created entities to be a good theory (Occam's razor). This theory was in fact believed in medieval Europe. Why? *Because* the circle was the most perfect shape, a notion inherited from Greek geometers and held on to *because* their authority was considered absolute by a society whose ruling ideas (the ideas of the ruling class, that is) emphasized the sacredness of authority. There's another because: *because* the Earth had to be in the center of the universe, and everything above the moon had to be perfect. Why?

Because the church said so, and folks who questioned the authority of the church were likely to have highly unpleasant things happen to them,[30] just as those who question the truth of psychoanalysis today can be accused of expressing neurotic resistance to its truths—which takes care of *them*. (I don't mean to imply that those who offend the psychoanalytic establishment today face punishment of the same order as that endured by Michael Servetus and Galileo Galilei—unless, of course, the contemporary offender is poor, despised for reasons of color, believed to be mentally ill, young, desperate, rebellious, female, or otherwise socially vulnerable. Even then such people are much more likely to face the psychiatric establishment and not psychoanalysis. See Chesler [1972] and Smith and David [1975] or, for a fictional presentation of the same themes, Piercy's *Woman on the Edge of Time*.)

Note well: Anybody can explain anything in any terms whatever if permitted to add theoretical entities whenever he or she encounters a difficulty. Anybody can explain anything in any terms whatever if permitted to define theoretical entities so that they are unfalsifiable. And anybody can have a field day if permitted to explain away logical objections to a theory by citing the unconscious motivations of those who object.

Psychoanalysis from Freud's time on—and much of psychotherapy in general—adds theoretical entities whenever difficulties arise. These entities are unfalsifiable, and we all know the Catch-22 by which agreement with a psychological interpretation means that it's true and disagreement also means that it's true.

If I emphasize the field's lack of scientific status so very emphatically, it's because any theory of the sort I've described—one that rests on unfalsifiable assertions, a multiplication of theoretical entities to answer every difficulty, and what amounts to slander as a way of countering objections—*is perfectly designed for blaming the victim*. Rush and Masson actually see this as the original purpose of the psychoanalytic theory of object relations. This may not be as far-fetched as it sounds, and it may have little to do with Freud's individual motives and much to do with the time and place in which the fundamentals of psychoanalysis occurred.

The end of the nineteenth century in Europe was a time of enormous change, which included a massive reconceptualization of Human sexuality and its place in Human society. Freud's "discovery" of the importance of sexuality for Human personality, far from being unique, was part of what Jonathan Katz calls "a . . . general manufacture and distribution of hetero-sexuality." The idea that sexual suppression or abstinence caused various mental and somatic ills was quite common in the 1880s and 1890s. Katz comments on the eroticization of language that occurred in these decades: "to make love to," which had previously meant to court, came to mean to have sexual intercourse with; "orgy," which had meant only an uninhibited gathering, came to refer specifically to sexual activity; and "sex" itself, which "Victorians had used . . . to refer to the sexes (males and females) or "the sex" (females) now commonly came to have specific erotic reference . . . 'Sexology' by 1904 named the study of male-female marital and erotic re-lations . . . doctors now began to call *lack* of erotic feeling . . . an 'aberration' of the 'procreative sense.' "[31] Katz links the "discovery" that sexuality was crucial to personality with the shift from early capitalism to consumer cap-italism—and surely the recent spate of how-to books on sexual adjustment and sexual pleasure support the idea that the popularity of psychoanalysis in the United States can be seen as merely another incident in the conversion of sex and its accoutrements into a prime consumer good.

Moreover, as Katz and Lillian Faderman both note, the 1920s, the era in which psychoanalysis became popular in the United States, was—like the 1950s, in which psychoanalysis also bulked large in commercial culture—a period of political reaction, class persecution, individualist explanations, and antifeminist backlash.[32] Indeed, Firestone describes the "pseudo-liberated sexuality" of the "era of the flappers" as largely reactionary in actuality, whether or not it's gotten into our history books as "progress."[33]

It may therefore be significant that Freud's essay on "Femininity" was written in 1932, and his "Female Sexuality" was published in October 1931 and translated into English in 1932.[34]

Perhaps I can make the association of psychoanalysis with political re-action more vivid and more understandable by describing a parallel development in another set of theories about Human activity. One can't, of course, "prove" that one caused the other in the way that "hard" sciences prove things, but the association is suggestive and, I think, important. Moreover, the events I'm going to describe now took place in a field I know very well—that of the literary humanists, who are (many of them) so accepting of psychoanalysis that they too will be familiar with what happened.

The era was the 1930s, the Great Depression. People were living in rusted-out car bodies and orange-crate shacks. Citrus fruit was being sprayed with tar and chemicals to make it inedible while thousands starved. Women lived on rotten bananas, there were children with stick-thin legs, swollen bellies, and pellagra, and there was also an abundance of helplessness and despair about an economic system that seemed to have failed suddenly for no understandable reason.[35] Some people even thought socialist revolution was just around the corner.

It was in this atmosphere that a major intellectual development occurred in literary criticism in the United States, one that reached its height in the 1950s. It was—and still is—called "the New Criticism." Marjorie Perloff describes it as "almost 100% WASP, politically conservative and orthodox Christian."[36] Antipolitical, quietist, recognizing the working class as material for symbolism only, this theory was originated by White southern gentlemen who were totally opposed to the idea that art ought to change anything in the realm of reality. By the time I reached college in the 1950s, the New Criticism had moved from its original application to lyric poetry and was being used to "explicate" everything else, including drama and fiction. It was *the* dominant theory.

Adrienne Rich, who entered college in the late 1940s, a few years before I did, has this to say:

> The thirties, a decade of economic desperation, social unrest, war and also of affirmed political art, was receding behind the fogs of the Cold War, the selling of the nuclear family with the mother at home as its core, heightened activity by the FBI and CIA, a retreat by many artists from so-called "protest" art, witch-hunting among artists and intellectuals as well as in the State Department, anti-Semitism, scapegoating of homosexual men and lesbians.

Rich goes on to describe the many voices "warning North American artists against 'mixing politics with art' " and the "falsely mystical view of art that assumes a kind of supernatural possession by universal forces unrelated to questions of power and privilege" and says, "In the fifties and early sixties there was much shaking of heads if an artist was found 'meddling in politics'; art was mystical and universal, but the artist was also . . . irresponsible and emotional and politically naive."[37]

Marge Piercy, educated in the 1950s as I was, describes this climate of opinion and the effect it had on her (she was the "wrong" class, sex, ethnic group, and religion): "Even the lawns were Christian. . . . Human nature was a universal constant." She too links the politics of the era with the New Criticism:

> The concept of American classlessness was being pushed at the same time that critics like Lionel Trilling were calling for . . . literature *interior* to the world of the affluent. The defeat of marxist literary criticisms and theory meant rejection of the class struggle and somehow even of working-class experiences as a viable theme. . . . When characters who were not white, male, and affluent appeared . . . they were all image and mythology, when not comic relief. When a character was black, generally she represented something in the white writer's psyche.[38]

Not that the literary-critical New Criticism ever won in a fair fight over the social consciousness of the 1930s. What won was World War II and the reaction of the 1950s, which made it possible to reinvent history in order to belittle or obliterate a whole era of creative and intellectual achievement in the United States.[39] Along with the "proletarian novel," consciously American or even merely Western or Midwestern writers like Carl Sandburg, Sinclair Lewis, and Theodore Dreiser were relegated to second-rateness while the expatriate Hemingway, the expatriate Eliot, the expatriate James, the expatriate Pound, and the reactionary Faulkner became pillars of the literary canon.[40]

Why did all this happen, this turning away from the outward, the social, and the economic, this concentration on the odyssey of an individual male, White, well-to-do soul who somehow belonged everywhere and nowhere at once and whose only connections with people, places, and even nature, were often those of a tourist?

Rich says:

> In the McCarthy era there was a great deal of fear abroad. The writer Meridel LeSueur was blacklisted, hounded by the FBI, her books banned; she was dismissed from job after job—teaching, waitressing—because the FBI intimidated her students and employers. A daughter of Tillie Olsen recalls going with her

mother in the 1950s to the Salvation Army to buy heavy winter clothes because the family had reason to believe Leftists in the San Francisco Bay Area would be rounded up and taken to detention camps farther north.[41]

I have described the above as a sort of parallel to psychoanalysis, but I must confess now that I've not been entirely honest. The New Criticism was not just a parallel to psychoanalysis in its ignoring of dreadful public events and its concentration on the inner world of a small elite; psychoanalysis flourished right along with the New Criticism, at least in the kinds of humanistic literary studies I know all too well. In the 1950s, I learned them both as the *assumed* bases of literary criticism; in the 1970s and even the 1980s during my teaching, I met them again and again still being used that way in the work of students and colleagues.[42]

Psychoanalysis did not win in a fair intellectual fight either. It too owed its prevalence to the political and economic circumstances of the 1950s, which made it possible to shatter the U.S. Left. At that time Red-baiting was often done with appeals to "mental health" and "maturity" formulated in the terms of a depth psychology dominated by the idea of psychoanalysis. In the 1940s a psychoanalysis-dominated psychology was used to force women out of wartime jobs when returning male veterans wanted jobs. There was no attempt to create jobs for the men—or create jobs for the displaced women—nor were the jobs from which women were fired the usual part-time, badly paid "women's" jobs to which women of color and poor women (often the same women) had always been relegated.

My own experience in the 1950s and that of many of my age-mates was of the use of psychoanalysis-dominated psychology to enforce compulsory "femininity" and absence from the job market, as well as unswerving loyalty to even the most idiotic minutiae of patriarchal ideology and behavior. It is, I believe, from that direct experience of the 1950s and early 1960s that so much White, middle-class feminist criticism of psychoanalysis comes, from Alix Kates Shulman's *Burning Questions* to Betty Friedan's *The Feminine Mystique* to—well, here are some of them:

Oakley states that "Freudian theory . . . has undoubtedly been one of the . . . most influential reactionary ideologies affecting women in the last half century."[43]

In the late 1960s, Alice Rossi described

the pervasive permeation of psychoanalytic thinking throughout American society. Individual psychoanalysts vary widely among themselves, but when their theories are popularized by social scientists, marriage and family counselors, writers, social critics, pediatricians and mental health specialists, there emerges a common and conservative image of the woman's role. . . . The consequences of this acceptance of psychoanalytic ideas and conservatism in the social sciences in the United States have contributed very little since the 1930s to any lively intellectual dialogue on sex equality as a goal or the ways of implementing that goal. Second, they have provided a quasi-scientific underpinning to educators, marriage counselors, mass media and advertising researchers, who together have partly created and certainly reinforced the withdrawal of millions of young American women from the mainstream of thought and work in our society.[44]

Kay Keshod Hamod, one of the artists whose essays are included in *Working It Out,* describes the "five hundred mothers . . . I came to know" in her eight years of teaching as "first of all, made insecure by popular Freudianism . . . burdened by unwarranted anxiety and guilt. Most of these women were doing all that is humanly possible for their children; in some cases, they were sacrificing themselves heroically."[45] In the same collection Sara Ruddick describes herself as daunted, in college, by the "sexual demands of adult life" (she is actually describing the demands of the heterosexual institution, as presented in the 1950s). She says:

> Although Vassar was still a woman's college and had then a woman president, it was permeated by the myth of the sexual division . . . of adult life. The myth was expressed in Freudian language. . . . It was tacitly assumed in the domestic life-style—and in some instances in the explicit sexism—of an increasingly male faculty. It was expressed in the self-doubt and self-deception of the younger women faculty, who suffered from it most.[46]

What on earth are supposed feminist theorists doing cozying up to a theory that has such a lousy history, no claim to any kind of scientific truth, and such a persistent association with the worst kind of political reaction? It's certainly clear that by accepting an account of Human behavior that assigns to infancy and early childhood an overwhelmingly determinative role in what happens thereafter, one can easily ignore the uncomfortable area of social forces as mere epiphenomena having nothing to do with what *really* produces Human happiness or misery. As Christine Delphy puts it, far too many

> accept the extravagant claim of psychoanalysis to be, not a system of interpretation of subjectivity, but subjectivity itself. . . .

> They equate my criticism of psychoanalysis with a lack of in-
> terest in subjectivity, even though . . . I criticize psychoanalysis
> . . . precisely because . . . [of] its idealist and naturalist presup-
> positions.[47]

Nancy M. Henley also protests against what Delphy calls the "idealism" of
psychoanalysis (i.e., the idea that ideas have a life of their own and are the
prime causative agents in Human affairs):

> There has been in the United States a tendency . . . a prime
> example [of which] may be seen in Freudian psychoanalysis . . .
> to assume the Great American myth of the classless society [and
> therefore to] deny the social context and see human problems
> as internally caused.[48]

If today we see less emphasis in the mass media on psychoanalysis than
we used to, I believe that's because the Right's version of sociobiology has
in part replaced it, and because the assumptions of psychoanalysis, far from
being dead, have become diffused through the entire culture. Blaming
mother-headed families for the lifetimes of poverty and racist oppression
that produce inner-city ghetto riots is psychoanalysis-at-large, as is the recent explosion of books on psychological self-manipulation and the management of personal interaction, most of which assume a control over the
circumstances of one's life impossible to any but the very wealthy. They
also take for granted the psychoanalytic ideas that most difficulties in living
are caused not by social forces but by errors in thinking and feeling that
can be corrected by various kinds of psychological self-manipulation.[49] It
is, of course, no coincidence that such material has proliferated during an
era of political reaction and economic depression, an era that has also given
rise to a spate of books on how to profit from other people's failures, how
to consider nobody but yourself, how other people's suffering really doesn't
exist (or matter) because they "chose it," and all the other bash-thy-neighbor
handbooks.

What is most heartbreaking to me is what happens to the youngsters
whose education in feminism takes this form. Recently Susan Koppelman
sent me a copy of a paper about two stories, one of them mine, presented
by Elizabeth Hirsh at the Midwest Modern Language Association conference
in August 1984.[50] I am going to use some quotations from this paper as
Bad Examples, not because I think Hirsh a bad critic or stupid writer (I
don't), but because I think her education has been abysmal, and it is a
feminist education. It also frightens me that what this student (as she was at
the time) was obviously taught sounds as if it came out of a time machine:

literary tradition, Freud—and nothing else. Shades of the 1950s! Here is Hirsh's version of Hélène Cixous: "When women try to express themselves in patriarchal language, they can only stutter and err." And here is her version of Nancy Chodorow: "The female child has special difficulty in establishing definite ego boundaries." Now, what Chodorow actually said was that women's ego boundaries were more *flexible* than men's—and that men's were, by the way, pretty rigid. "Special difficulty" is a reactionary revision. (Later in her paper, the author goes further and mentions the girl's *"permeable"* ego boundaries.)[51] As for Freud, Hirsh later insists that Henry Ford's joke about the customer having any color car he wants as long as it's black (a joke that appears in the story she's writing about) "was undoubtedly lifted" from "Freud's book on wit." Well, it wasn't. I know. I wrote the story. I got the joke from my father, who owned a Model A Ford when I was a child (they came only in black too). Later Hirsh also insists that the car in question must be a "hearse" (!), having never ridden in a Model A, as I did, *or* a Model T Ford, as my mother did when she was a child. Nor does the author seem to know that information about Henry Ford can be found in all sorts of other places besides Freud's writings, e.g., United States history, the history of mass production, the history of the automobile, or the history of anti-Semitism.[52]

Another famous statement of Ford's that I used in my story was "History is bunk," which the author didn't appear to notice and doesn't mention.

What I find so disquieting about the paper is not its author's interpretation of my story (which in many ways matches mine) but that her theoretical background, like that of so many young literary critics, is so narrow. A combination of Freud, Chodorow, and Cixous is not enough equipment for the study of anything. My subjective impression of the paper is that its author, like so many other graduate students who could have served as her stand-ins in the above paragraphs, needs and wants feminist theory and that what she's been given or been able to find in this area is totally inadequate.

As Delphy puts it, "It is not a new temptation to explain the social by the psychological. On the contrary, it is as old as the hills." Thus we have in a recent review of a biography of Helene Deutsch, Carolyn Heilbrun's all-too-uncritical view of psychoanalysis. Heilbrun proposed that we preserve what Freud "discovered" about the unconscious and repression "while stripping away his simplistic and culture-bound views on women." And (as I've mentioned in another connection) *Ms.* reviewer Marion Meade assumed that a biographer's treatment of Louise Bogan must have been accurate when the author wrote that Bogan's lifelong depression was "caused by" her mother's promiscuity when Bogan was a child.[53] And here is a rather charming cherry for the top of the feminist psychoanalytic sundae, a statement by five authors, none of whom is a psychologist, psychoanalyst, psychiatrist, counselor, or therapist:

> Our mutual presence as female teachers and students creates a highly charged, fantasy-laden recapitulation of the mother/daughter nexus, that lifelong relationship imbued with a complex and contradictory dynamic of individuation and fusion, reminiscent of the infant's needs for separation and differentiation from the mother. . . . Powerlessness, rage and guilt conflate with longing, love and dependency just when our students are confronted by a woman professor, purveying at the same time the maternal breast and the authoritative word of the texts.[54]

It's not surprising that so much academic feminism has remained attached to psychoanalysis or has newly discovered it. For many, it is probably simply part of the intellectual landscape with which they are familiar. The lack of scientific education or scientific interest that is characteristic of the literary humanities in general guarantees for many that they will never be exposed to the recent developments in psychiatry, which constitute both an alternative to psychoanalysis and a critique of it. For others, it is simply the only *feminism* they have come across—and they need and want feminism. For still others, it provides something that will feed their intellectual appetite for rigor and complexity or (for those who don't have this particular motive) a way of thinking and feeling as if they were scientists without the difficulty of actually learning something hard. Science has such prestige and money that we all feel its pressure on us; as Marjorie Perloff notes, one of the motives leading people to the New Criticism in the early 1960s was that "criticism, so it seemed, had finally reached the sophistication and maturity of other fields *like physics.*" Also at work here may be the simple fact that female scholars and thinkers are to be found largely in the humanities, especially in fields like literature and psychology.[55] It's hardly surprising that those whose training and sensibility lie in the area of the expressive, the "personal," and the interior—as do those of most women socialized for the job of wife-and-mother, whether in academia or not—should assume the importance of the skills we know and avoid areas we find unfamiliar, intimidating, and often tabooed. But for many, it must also be an easy way to avoid the profound uneasiness of having to confront (and learn about) the hard money-and-power questions that lie at the bottom of all oppressions, with the fear they inevitably bring that if our opponents are as rich and as strong as all that, there is nothing we can do. Talk about psychology makes things sound manageable, especially to women. Talk about money and guns makes them sound difficult or impossible.[56]

Why on earth *do* women behave so strangely? Is the female nervous system functionally defective (as was believed by so many in the nineteenth century)? Are we hormonal cowards? (A more recent view.) Is it our early deprivation of mother-love that makes us so fragile? Or is it the terrible strain of telling our truths in a hostile language? Have our breasts run out of their invisible ink-milk?[57] Why have these thinkers bought the "mystifying idea," as Fox calls it in "Why Men Oppress Women" that " 'women's problems' are personal, psychological, emotional, private and non-economic"? Part of the answer may be the one she herself provides: "Even those of us who know better can fall into the trap [of] arguing that [these] factors are important *as a way of arguing that women's issues are important*."[58] It seems to me also (as I've said) that there is an obvious connection between economic depression, political reaction, and the retreat into what our society defines as "private life," especially among those feminists who blame infantile experience, the nature of language, or the collective unconscious.

Women who live in patriarchies are draftees, *as a class,* into the lifelong job of making men happy without the power to do the job and without enough emotional, sexual, and material reciprocity for themselves. Often they (like the men) blame the nature of their relationships or their own defective psychology for the sheer loneliness, insecurity, and endless competitive stress enforced on us all by advanced industrial capitalism.[59]

Let me repeat—for it cannot be repeated too often—that theories about women that concentrate on women's "unique" psychology or the oppressive centrality of language have a very clear and disastrous effect: they shift feminist effort from confronting those in power, who are, after all, *people,* to confronting something that is by its very nature nonconfrontable: the collective unconscious, language, or our own infantile psychology.

Is it too late in the day to point out a fact so gross and so obvious that enormous amounts of social pressure have been deployed around it in order to render it invisible—the fact that we face a mystification that could not work and does not work without the threat of force, from random violence to a vast mass of sexist propaganda, much of it called "culture" and "psychology," to the structure of institutions?

That it is *people* who exploit and oppress other *people*?

That in sexism it is *men as a group* who exploit and oppress *the group of women*?

As our most brilliant nineteenth-century theorist put it (I mean, *of course,* Matilda Joslyn Gage), what we call patriarchy is the arrangement by which women's resources are made available to men nonreciprocally. By resources

I mean concern, reproductive capacity, labor, sexual access, and the capacity for emotional support, as well as large amounts of underpaid labor and even larger amounts of totally unremunerated labor. Men have also stolen women's self-esteem, our sense of being normative, our right to our own ideas, and much more. By this I mean that many men's self-esteem *as men* is overblown precisely because many women's self-esteem *as women* is low; insofar as men are seen by women and see themselves as the important, intelligent, hardworking, competent, worthy *sex*, this is because our achievements *as a sex* have been belittled or obliterated, our work trivialized or rendered invisible, and our worth denied; men see themselves and are seen as centrally Human (in a species in which they do not even constitute a majority) precisely because we are seen and see ourselves as somehow not quite Human.[60]

What has happened to the above ideas—which used to be commonplaces of feminist theory in the early days? Inside the academy—but we've been through that. Outside, although many feminists have certainly held on to these early views, the lack of coherent theory has nonetheless caused much confusion. Different feminists have focused on so many different issues as the "cause" or central focus of patriarchy—it's violence against women; it's personal relations; no, it's the mass media; no, it's the idea of "femininity"; and so on—that quite often any sense of the connection of issues with one another has been lost.[61]

This is not to say a lot of important reform hasn't occurred in the 1970s and '80s. I don't mean to condemn "liberal" or "bourgeois" reforms here. They are crucial. But as Hester Eisenstein puts it, "The radical views . . . of the second wave made it possible for the less sweeping reforms of liberal or bourgeois feminism to make some headway" (Eisenstein, 1983, 137). *Liberals need radicals.*[62]

That's why the evasions of the original central premises of early feminist analysis are so destructive. I mean the ideas that men and women constitute *sex-classes* (the term is Dworkin's),[63] that the interests of these sex-classes are often opposed, that the "personal" is in large part produced by the "political," that the division between private and public life is a social construct, imposed by propaganda and force, that relegating women's experience of oppression to the "private" realm is itself oppressive and mystifying, that gender is a social construct, that the father-headed family is a social institution that functions to exploit and oppress women, that the social construction of "femininity" produces large benefits for somebody, that the work women do *as women* is unrecognized and unpaid, that such work is not "natural" but socially arranged, that male privilege, just like skin privilege and class privilege, exists whether or not individual men want it to, that such a state of affairs, although it hurts men, hurts women more,[64] and that feminist opposition to women's oppression is not based on altruism or the love of abstract justice but on our own anger and our own healthily selfish desires for a more happy life.[65]

To add a little of my own personal motivation to my own healthily selfish desire for a happy life, I am angry at academic colleagues whose work, supposedly feminist, leaves a deficit in the education of female students in my classes who are classically feminist in their perceptions, emotions, and preoccupations, and which deficit I find myself having to make up single-handed. I am sick to death of the lies of the mass media, I am sick of not having enough allies, and I want feminism to become ravingly radical once again. I even have a suggestion as to how to achieve this happy end.

We must all become crazy, man-hating separatists.

APPENDIX

In Chapter II, I mentioned briefly some alternatives to psychoanalysis. I'd like to add a little more on the subject. Although some psychoanalysts like Mitchell tend to see, as the only alternative to psychoanalysis, theories that suppose Human beings to be perfectly rational,[66] there are many other theories of Human psychology and behavior that make ample room for Human unreasonableness. Many feminist explanations for "irrational" behavior center on the internalization of the social and interpersonal forces that affect Human beings, or rather on the way beliefs, attitudes, and behavior that masquerade (so to speak) as intrapersonal are in fact the result of propaganda from the outside, or punishment or the threat of it, or a Human attempt to deal with a situation that has been deliberately mystified by the culture, i.e., that has been publicly assigned to the area of the intrapersonal when it's nothing of the sort.

Such "exposés" of the supposedly intrapersonal have been stressed by almost all feminist theorists *except* those oriented toward psychoanalysis. For example, says Rosalind Coward: "The war with fat . . . is a war conducted in highly emotive language . . . the *sexual* ideal of the slim, lithe, firm body is also a statement of [appetitive] self-denial."[67]

Other feminist writers have proposed that popular hatred of fat women[68] and hence so many women's guilt or fear about indulging their physical appetites for food do not spring from the psychology of the mother-daughter bond[69] but from the patriarchal condemnation of women who are "too big" in any way, a fear that has been expressed through the hatred of fat women only quite recently and only in some parts of the world.[70]

Some feminist theorists emphasize that mothers teach daughters not to have needs (shades of *Women, Church, and State!*), first, because it's women's job to attend to others' needs, a task interfered with by needs of one's own that are too clamorous, and second, because most women do not in fact get their emotional and sexual needs met as much as their men do. Others stress that much of what has been called "repressed" is actually *mystified*, that is, taken for granted, assumed, echoed by one's friends and family, the mass media, strangers encountered in the street, language, slang, advertising, the structure of work, the physical shapes of our cities and dwelling places, and so on. When this is true and one is in addition punished for noticing and commenting on such messages, what happens is not exactly repression but rather a response to immediate situations and to the fear of alienating others.

Christine Delphy gives an account of one such mystification: the socially enforced "truth" that having menstrual periods is a misfortune and a sign of female inferiority. Here a learned ("internalized") judgment is reinforced by objective material conditions because, she says,

> There are neither sanitary towels nor tampons in French public toilets . . . nowhere to change and nowhere to throw tampons or napkins. . . . The society is materially understood and made for a population without periods. . . . There are thus not one but *two* cultural interventions [attitudes *and* lack of facilities.][71]

In *Body Politics,* Nancy Henley studies many of the interpersonal social signals that are mystified so that they appear to be intrapsychic matters only. Among the many examples she cites are that women's dominance gestures (staring, unsolicited touching, or close approach) are either ignored, interpreted as sexual invitations (since women's body language is not supposed to include dominance gestures), or punished in some way; that some male gestures serve as threats toward women; and that "play" can signal actual male hostility, physical control over women, and female physical inferiority.[72]

Henley's work also includes the interpersonal "vocabulary" by which class differences, as well as sex-class differences, are expressed. For example, a writer acquaintance of mine, Syn Ferguson, recalls being criticized by one male boss at work while another defended her; both stood (one on each side of her) while she, seated in between at her typewriter, was unable to rise because they were so close. They talked over her head, both literally and figuratively.[73]

We are all surrounded by the massive mystification of our world, which those around us appear to accept and which we are punished, in one form or another, for questioning.

We are constantly rewarded or punished for particular kinds of behavior by those around us, a matter of import for a very gregarious species.[74]

Some of us are also subject to physiological malfunctions of the brain and central nervous system.

We are materially dependent on those around us and on extremely complex social institutions, a fact of which most of us are quite aware, whether or not we talk about it to ourselves or others in the terms used by social scientists, political radicals, or psychotherapists.

We all process a great deal of the above information very fast and not explicitly via "emotions," "reactions," intuitions, personal imagery, and "impulses" and in other ways that do not necessarily match the vocabulary we have available for discussing such things, in academia or anywhere else.

Where, in the facts outlined above, is there the slightest necessity for the psychoanalytic drive theory, which assigns to inevitable intrapsychic development (it's never clear if other species share this development) almost all of Human behavior? One witty early feminist stated that those who try to find out what Human "nature" is are looking for a needle in a haystack—and ignoring the haystack.[75] If the psychoanalytically minded mean by "irrational," anything except slow, verbalized, intellectually explicit, calculating *cognition,* then I must agree with them that most of Human mental life is not rational, but I would still maintain that our lightning-fast, largely "intuitive" mix of habit, learning, (possibly not explicit) beliefs, and emotion/impulse is—most of the time and with most people—reasonable and sensible, according to our lights.

Furthermore, interpretations of phenomena that stress what lies "beneath" or "behind" the "surface" of reality—I am talking here about depth psychology in general and a good deal more—have always been the property of conservative thinkers. Radicals of whatever stripe (at least in the European tradition I know) have rarely subscribed to the idea that truth lies under or behind the "surface" of phenomena or that it's mysterious or somehow in the depths of nature or the Human soul. On the contrary, they emphasize that *truth lies right on the surface of everyday life.* That is exactly why such an enormous apparatus of social coercion and mystification must be deployed around it to keep it "invisible." Without social coercion—behind which always lies the actuality and the threat of force—too many people will perceive such truths. There remains, of course, the problem of how, specifically, people "do" their not-knowing and not-perceiving: an inquiry for neurology. There remains the problem of what it feels like to do this: an inquiry for art. Do all Human beings exhibit the needs or desires outlined by Harris or Maslow? A problem for anthropology and history. Are there those who don't have them or have them to different degrees or exhibit different needs and desires? A problem for social psychology.

Massive mystification can be extremely difficult to combat. Here are some recent feminist comments about some of the various effects of mystifying the *status quo*. Barbara Du Bois writes about the difficulty of "holding on" to radical ideas:

> I'd be surprised if there is anyone who is doing feminist schol-
> arship who hasn't at some point wondered . . . whether she
> weren't perhaps "making it all up" . . . [due to] the conflict be-
> tween the ways we've been taught to see, know and judge reality
> and the beginnings of a different cosmos of values about what
> reality is and how it can be known.[76]

In this context, Sandra Boyner remarks on the origins of the professionalization of the academic disciplines, contrasting the reality of the process
with its professed aims, in terms that should, I think, make us all extremely
suspicious of *any* received truths in or outside our own profession:

> The rhetoric of objectivity came in academe in the nineteenth
> century, along with academic freedom and autonomy, in a pro-
> cess called "professionalization" . . . which promoted so-called
> objectivity . . . by limiting scholarship to experts who had sur-
> vived extensive training in theory, methods, professional ethics,
> and the work already completed by others. . . . [For example]
> the professionalization of economics [has been] convincingly
> described . . . as primarily the triumph of conservative views
> over more liberal ones.[77]

(I would add that those who become professionals must also be able to
afford long and expensive educations, which screens out just any non-
middle-class Tom, Dick, Jane, or Judith.)

And here is Catharine MacKinnon, on the anatomy of the mystification
and threats that can all too easily be seen as psychoanalytic "repression":

> Typically, employers, husbands, judges *and the victims them-*
> *selves* have understood and dismissed [sexual harassment at
> work] . . . as trivial, isolated and "personal" or as universal,
> "natural" or "biological." . . . *When an outrage has been so long*
> *repressed* [MacKinnon is clearly talking about the *social* and not
> the individual process here] *there will be few social codifications*
> *for its expression.* Depending on who is asking them and how,
> victims may initially say (and believe) that they are not victims,
> so near is denial to erasure. Women's consciousness erupts

through fissures in the socially knowable. Personal statements direct from daily life, in which we say more than we know, may be the primary form in which such experiences exist in social space. . . . Until 1976, lacking a term to express it, sexual harassment was literally unspeakable. . . . *The unnamed should not be mistaken for the nonexistent. Silence often speaks of pain and degradation so thorough that the situation cannot be conceived as other than it is.*[78]

The above points to the same kind of phenomenon psychoanalysis may be trying to explain, but it emphasizes the social dimension of it and assumes, as I do, that what most people think and feel, though not a matter of explicit calculation or the kind of awareness we tend to call "conscious," is nonetheless fairly rational.

The idea that truth, like the truths of psychology, resides in the *depths* of something (like Human personality) and is therefore hard to get at, is allied to an old, discreditable, and sexist tradition of European thought. Evelyn Fox Keller, tracing the social paradigms used to make and conceptualize science in the European tradition since Francis Bacon, finds that this model of knowing is that of a man "violating" or "penetrating" the female body of Nature, "unveiling" "her" to get at "her" "hidden" secrets. The psychoanalytic enterprise certainly follows the outlines of this model: an expert knower, usually male, a largely female clientele, and the "hidden" truth of her life or her symptoms, which must be interpreted or uncovered.

Here is one alternative model, Nature as a sibyl and stern taskmistress, from experimental psychologist Alice Sheldon:

> There is no greater thrill I've ever had than to stand bare-faced in front of Nature and say, "I think this is the way your creations work; tell me, am I right?" And Nature grumblingly and reluctantly makes you do—as I did—thirteen different paradigms of the god damned experiment before you get the thing without any uncontrolled variables and then finally says, in answer to your question, a clear-cut "Yes." That is the most thrilling moment I have ever had in my whole life.[79]

(Alice Sheldon, having to leave experimental psychology because of physical illness, made a second career for herself—actually her third or fourth— writing science fiction under the pen name of James Tiptree, Jr.)

Attachment to psychoanalytic theory may also come from the inaccurate notion that without these assumptions there will be no psychological theory at all. Such a belief is, I think, the result of decades of treating psychoanalysis in the United States as the only possible theory for psychology. As Stephen Jay Gould puts it:

> The idea of unilinear progress . . . suggests a false conception of how science develops. In this view, any science begins in the nothingness of ignorance and moves toward truth by gathering more and more information, constructing theories as facts ac cumulate. In such a world, debunking would be primarily negative, for it would only shuck some rotten apples from the barrel of accumulating knowledge. But the barrel of theory is always full: *sciences work with elaborated contexts for explaining facts from the very outset.*[80]

Thus, in a sense, most theory is always a case of too much, too soon. That is precisely what is wrong with closed systems like literal belief in the Bible—or contemporary belief in psychoanalysis.

NOTES

1. The words are Dinnerstein's (Dorothy Dinnerstein, *The Mermaid and the Minotaur: Sexual Arrangements and Human Malaise* [New York: Harper and Row, 1976], xi).

2. Note the sexist metaphor.

3. Most scientific activity is of this order.

4. Those who know, please forgive the great oversimplification of this whole discussion. There's much more to be said about the ontological status of scientific theory, of course. Recent feminist writing on the subject, from which I've drawn some of this chapter, include Ruth Bleier's *Science and Gender: A Critique of Biology and Its Theories on Women* (New York: Pergamon Press, 1984); Evelyn Fox Keller's *Reflections on Gender and Science* (New Haven: Yale University Press, 1985), which traces the basic paradigms that shaped and continue to shape science-making; Donna Haraway's "Animal Sociology and a Natural Economy of the Body Politic: I" (in Elizabeth Abel and Emily K. Abel, ed., *The Signs Reader* [Chicago: University of Chicago Press, 1983], 123–38); and Stephen Jay Gould's *The Mismeasure of Man* (New York: Norton, 1981), which traces the history of racism in science and the invention and misuse of the concept of the I.Q. Both Haraway and Keller attack what they call "the rupture between subject and object" (ibid., 125), the exclusion of certain elements from science because they are defined as female, and the denial that scientists have a subjectivity,—i.e., the ideology of "objectivity"—and in general the scientism long mistaken (they say) for science. Haraway proposes to criticize the paradigms of scientific research by conceptualizing the Human position in the world

as "involved in the satisfaction of needs and thus . . . labor." She calls this "Marxist humanism" (ibid., 127). Gould emphasizes the extreme difficulty of dealing with physical evidence and the necessity of being constantly aware of one's own subjectivity and one's assumptions.

5. Nancy Chodorow, *The Reproduction of Mothering: Psychoanalysis and the Sociology of Gender* (Berkeley: University of California Press, 1978), 41, 52.

6. See Phyllis Chesler, *Women and Madness* (New York: Doubleday, 1972), and Dorothy E. Smith and Sara J. David, eds., *Women Look at Psychiatry* (Vancouver: Press Gang Publishers, 1975).

7. Naomi Weisstein, " 'Kinder, Kuche, Kirche' as Scientific Law: Psychology Constructs the Female," in Robin Morgan, ed., *Sisterhood Is Powerful* (New York: Vintage Books, 1970), 205–20.

8. Nancy M. Henley, *Body Politics: Power, Sex, and Non-Verbal Communication* (Englewood Cliffs, NJ: Prentice-Hall, 1977), 16, 24.

9. One of the interesting things about contemporary psychoanalysis (at least in the United States) is its isolation from the physical sciences. An example: Psychoanalysts talk, at least in the popular media, as if adult Human orality were merely a residue of infantile and early childhood experience, apparently unaware that lips, tongue, and palate, put together, contain more sensory nerve endings than even the hands, which contain the second-most of any other area in the body. Thus adult Human emphasis on oral pleasure is solidly grounded in adult human neurology, for obvious evolutionary reasons.

10. Freud could hardly have been the first person in the world to notice such behavior.

11. Karen J. Winkler, "Scholars Prescribe Freud's 'Talk Cure,' " *Chronicle of Higher Education,* 22 October 1986, 4.

12. Weisstein in Morgan, *Sisterhood Is Powerful,* 209–10.

13. Ibid., 211.

14. Eysenck's study of "neurotics" was published in 1952. The improvement rate for psychoanalysis was 44 percent, for psychotherapy (undefined) 64 percent, and for nothing 72 percent. Weisstein says, "These findings have never been refuted." The older studies she cites are dated 1955 to 1963 (Weisstein in Morgan, *Sisterhood Is Powerful,* 212–14).

15. Alice Sheldon, letter to the author, 20 April 1985.

16. Ann Oakley, *Subject Women* (New York: Pantheon, 1981), 275. Italics added.

17. Elizabeth Janeway, *Between Myth and Morning: Women Awakening* (New York: Morrow, 1974), 105.

18. Henley, *Body Politics,* 24.

19. Florence Rush, "The Freudian Cover-Up," *Chrysalis* 2 (1976), 36–37, 45. The "gaslight" reference is to the 1944 film *Gaslight* in which a woman is led to believe she's going mad by her conniving husband. In its silliest—but quite com-

mon—form, at least in New York City in the 1960s among psychoanalysts, the idea that anything that happened to a person was really caused by that person. Helen Yalof, a playwright and friend of mine, wrote a play at the time in which the belief was satirized by the following bit of dialogue: "My psychoanalyst says that when a plane crashes, the accident is due to the combined death wish of all those on board the plane."

20. Jeffrey Masson, The Assault on Truth: Freud's Suppression of the Seduction Theory, 2d ed. (New York: Penguin, 1985).

21. How he thought she had done this or how anyone could physically produce such a hemorrhage voluntarily (even if unconsciously) is not clear.

22. Masson, Assault, xxvii.

23. Ibid., xvii.

24. See Dale Spender, Women of Ideas: What Men Have Done to Them (London: Routledge and Kegan Paul, 1982).

25. Jeffrey Masson, letter to the author, 18 July 1984.

26. Masson, Assault, xx–xxi.

27. Ibid., 191, 192.

28. The most recondite reaches of physics are getting to be like this. I remember a newspaper report on recent researches in nuclear physics to the effect that everyone agreed on what had been observed but it would take them years to agree on how to interpret the observations. This sort of thing makes one wonder if physics is not approaching some sort of epistemological limit, i.e., a limit on what Human beings can know due to our particular position as observers.

29. Gould, Mismeasure of Man, 321.

30. Galileo was put under house arrest for heresy during the last decades of his life, and Michael Servetus was burned for heresy. Nonetheless, the largest number of those tortured and executed in Europe were not men who propounded scientific heresy but those people, most of them women, who were "proved" to be witches. (Some were children.) Estimates range from the tens of thousands to the millions.

31. Jonathan Katz, Gay/Lesbian Almanac: A New Documentary (New York: Harper and Row, 1983), 153, 156, 141–42.

32. Lillian Faderman, Surpassing the Love of Men: Romantic Friendship and Love between Women from the Renaissance to the Present (New York: Morrow, 1981), 461–65. According to Spender in Women of Ideas, vigorous feminist activity persisted and feminists were numerous through the 1920s in England. Women of Ideas (604–88) treats Lady Rhondda, Cicely Hamilton, Elizabeth Robins, Winifred Holtby, Vera Brittain, Rebecca West, Ray Strachey, Dora Russell, and Virginia Woolf as among those feminist women active through the twenties and thirties and often beyond. On the other hand, what she chooses to call "feminist" for these decades is (usually) exactly the kind of work for peace and social welfare that has begun to replace feminism in the United States during the 1980s. According to Frederick J. Hoffman,

the 1920s also marked the beginning of the popularity of psychoanalytic thought in the United States (*Freudianism and the Literary Mind*, 2d ed. [Baton Rouge: Louisiana State University Press, 1957], 44–58).

33. Shulamith Firestone, *The Dialectic of Sex* (New York: Morrow, 1970), 25.

34. Juliet Mitchell, *Psychoanalysis and Feminism* (New York: Pantheon, 1974), 321; Janeway, *Between Myth*, 93. Ironically, the Nazis considered psychoanalysis to be "Jewish science." Many of its practitioners were Jews, as were many physicists who likewise fled to the United States and whose work was ultimately responsible for the creation of the atomic bomb.

35. Studs Terkel, *Hard Times: An Oral History of the Great Depression* (New York: Pantheon, 1970), 55, 272, 4; Kathy Kahn, *Hillbilly Women* (New York: Avon, 1974), 4–6.

36. Marjorie Perloff, " 'Theory' and the Creative Writing Classroom," *AWP Newsletter*, November/December 1987, 2.

37. Adrienne Rich, *Blood, Bread, and Poetry: Selected Prose, 1979–1985* (New York: Norton, 1986), 171, 178.

38. Marge Piercy, *Braided Lives* (New York: Summit Books, 1982), 115.

39. I'm indebted to Madelyn Arnold and Clara Fraser for enlightening me about this matter.

40. Our current taken-for-granted notion that "art" and "propaganda" are irreconcilable and that the former is superior to the latter (and that this has always been the case) comes directly from the "New Criticism," a literary theory discussed in this chapter. Nineteenth-century novelists (like Charles Dickens) would surely have found such a doctrine both strange and immoral. At the Modern Language Association annual convention in New York in 1975 or 1976, Judith Fetterley delivered a paper on the New Criticism that described it as literary "isometrics." It was a fine paper, and I'd appreciate any news about its whereabouts.

41. Rich, *Blood*, 179.

42. Marge Piercy's *Braided Lives* (New York: Summit Books, 1982) is a fictional re-creation of the 1950s. It's written about working-class characters, from a working-class point of view, by an author of working-class origins. It includes none of the emphasis on psychoanalysis I'm discussing here, which suggests that popular freudianism was a message received by or aimed at the middle class in the United States and largely ignored elsewhere.

43. Oakley, *Subject Women*, 26.

44. June Sochen, *The New Feminism in Twentieth-Century America* (Lexington, MA: D. C. Heath, 1971), 92.

45. Sara Ruddick and Pamela Daniels, eds., *Working It Out: 23 Women Writers, Artists, Scientists, and Scholars Talk about Their Lives and Work* (New York: Pantheon, 1977), 16.

46. Ibid., 134. The book is a heartbreaking one; again and again women tell

of their extremely strained and difficult "adjustment" to the demands of the period with no sense that they were cheated or oppressed.

My own memories of the 1950s include a friend's fiancé criticizing her walk, saying, "Joanna knows how to walk like a woman." (Both my friend and I were baffled.) The young man in question seemed sure not only of the rightness of his demand that she "walk like a woman" but of his competence to make such demands and such judgments. (So did many other young men.) I also remember anxiously gloomy, collegiate female discussions about whether or not we were having our orgasms in the right place and whether or not it was abnormal to want to be lawyers or writers or whatever. One friend of mine wanted to attend law school, but her parents gave tuition money to her brother (who didn't want to do so) and a pearl necklace to her as a sort of consolation prize; her brother used the money for something else, she worked as a secretary during the day, went to law school at night, ruined her eyesight, gave up . . . and married a lawyer.

I also remember, in 1959, reading some psychoanalytic tome that described the difficult path to feminine maturity (the giving up of the clitoris, the giving up of autonomy, the giving up of activity, the giving up of ambition) and stated that barely one woman in fifty actually reached . . . *normalcy*. To my mind no other single quotation can convey more vividly the illogical sexist looniness of that reactionary slum of a decade.

47. Christine Delphy, *Close to Home: A Materialist Analysis of Women's Oppression*, trans. Diana Leonard (Amherst, MA: University of Massachusetts Press, 1984), 172.

48. Henley, *Body Politics*, 210.

49. One might see some of these books as psychotherapy democratized, simplified, taken away from the esoteric, authoritative, and expensive experts, and transformed into an easy, cheap "how-to" for everyone. Of course, the phenomenon is double-edged; I believe that valuable information and techniques can be found in some of these books, principally in those theories based on the group experience of people who've been through it themselves like those presented in Alcoholics Anonymous or Adult Children of Alcoholics, and the literature associated with both.

50. O indefatigable!

51. Elizabeth Hirsh, "Writing the Self as (M)Other: Autobiographical Fictions by Joanna Russ and Rosellen Brown" (unpublished manuscript, 1984). I find Hélène Cixous's "The Laugh of the Medusa" (in Abel and Abel, *Signs*) moving and at times even inspiring. Nonetheless, Cixous's view (and that of some others) that women cannot express themselves in existing language but only by subverting existing language—or by inventing a totally new one—seems to me extreme. Hélène Vivienne Wenzel describes "écriture féminine" as perpetuating long-held sexist stereotypes of women and avoiding the demand for political power ("The Text as Body/Politics: An Appreciation of Monique Wittig's Writings in Context" *Feminist Studies* 7:2 [1981], 272–4). I agree.

Although some English-speaking feminists (like Dale Spender in *Man-Made Language*) have analyzed the biases in English and concluded that such biases have considerable influence over thought, such feminist theorists also believe that these biases can be corrected and that new, feminist-invented language (e.g., "sexual harassment," "sexism," and so on) is beginning to correct them. Only Cixous & Co. seem to find linguistic bias so extreme that women can't use existing language at all while remaining true to their own female experience.

Cixous's viewpoint (or that which many of her U.S. followers appear to regard as hers) seemed plausible to me (even Spender admits the bias of English) until I remembered the early days of the women's liberation movement and the forces that actually kept us from speaking up. These included the fear of losing our jobs (or losing the job of marriage), being publicly ridiculed, having friends desert us, and being insulted, threatened, or beaten up. There was also the ever-present terror *of having our socially imposed conviction that we were somehow always in the wrong (inadequate, stupid, crazy, third-rate, ineffectual, incompetent, and trivial) confirmed at last.* We shouted anyway. Interestingly, Cixous notes in "The Laugh of the Medusa" that English-speaking women writers have always done better than their French counterparts. It may be that the real villain in Cixous's scheme is not the French language itself but the language of "high" culture anywhere. Certainly in the United States, the most refractorily, zanily sexist language occurs at the "high culture" level of scholarship, philosophy, psychology, political theory, and other abstract theory. A country in which intellectuals receive virtually identical higher educations and in which an Académie still exists for the purpose of keeping language pure may be much more monolithic and suffocating than the rather more eclectic and various educational traditions of North America.

Focusing on language as the cause of sexism itself (which, by the way, *Man-Made Language* does not do) of course leads us away from the enormous area of intimidation, punishment, and social control that lies "behind" (or rather within and around) language.

52. Ford was the first in the United States to publish an English translation of that Jew-hating Czarist forgery *The Protocols of the Elders of Zion* (Elly Bulkin et al., *Yours in Struggle: Three Feminist Perspectives on Anti-Semitism and Racism* [Brooklyn, NY: Long Haul Press, 1984], 108).

53. Delphy, *Close to Home*, 192; Carolyn Heilbrun, "In Search of Authenticity," review of *Helene Deutsch: A Psychoanalyst's Life,* by Paul Roazen, and *The Female Autograph,* ed. Donna C. Stanton, in *Women's Review of Books* II:12 (1985), 12; Marion Meade, "The Unexamined Life: A Good Season for Biographies," *Ms.,* December 1984, 39.

54. Margo Culley and Catherine Portuges, eds., *Gendered Subjects: The Dynamics of Feminist Teaching* (Boston: Routledge and Kegan Paul, 1985), 16. Note the slippage from literal to figurative again. (Is it or isn't it? Only her unconscious knows for sure.) Such remarks also ignore the obvious social fact that college students are

suffering—among other things—from the longest period of artificially lengthened economic and social dependency in Human history. Some of them have been physically adult for as much as ten years, a fact radicals of the 1960s used to harp on quite a lot.

55. Perloff, " 'Theory,' " 3. Italics added. Is this phenomenon the result of higher education in the 1950s? I remember that during that era many college students who didn't know what they wanted to do ended up in English literature. Later in the sixties, in two places at which I taught, psychology had become the same catch-all field for those with no strong interests or ambitions. Of course, women were always shunted out of areas like engineering or physics and into literature and psychology. For example, I remember an acquaintance of mine, another Westinghouse Science Talent Search winner, changing her major from engineering physics (the most difficult course of study at Cornell in 1955) to psychology. When I asked her why, she shrugged and said, "Psychology is more feminine."

56. There is also another mistake at work, I think. This is the conviction that something that feels as old, ubiquitous, and "profound" as patriarchy must be explained by motives equally as "profound" and that an oppression that manifests itself—or seems to do so—largely in the writer's personal life must be attributable to personal causes, i.e., psychological ones. I have found several statements of this sort in my reading of the last two years; for example, Mitchell's insistence that "the longevity of the oppression of women *must* be based on something more than conspiracy, something more complicated than biological handicap [sic] and more durable than economic exploitation" (Mitchell, *Psychoanalysis*, 362). Batya Weinbaum, a socialist, makes a similar statement:

> I think, like others, that psychoanalysis can provide the missing link between the ideological superstructure . . . and the socio-economic base. . . . [Otherwise] I am left with the unpleasant task of recounting a depressing history, blow by blow, without a comprehending interpretation (Batya Weinbaum, *The Curious Courtship of Women's Liberation and Socialism* [Boston: South End Press, 1978], 64).

Socialist feminist Iris Young likewise states, "We need some account of gender. Such an account, I think, must be psychological" (in Lydia Sargent, ed., *Women and Revolution: A Discussion of the Unhappy Marriage of Marxism and Feminism* [Boston: South End Press, 1981], 54). As Delphy notes, these theorists are part of a large number who insist or assume "that the oppression suffered by women and exercised by men is psychological [and] . . . interpersonal" (Delphy, *Close to Home*, 113).

57. The phrase "white ink" is Cixous's in "The Laugh of the Medusa" (Abel and Abel, *Signs*, 285). It appears to be a pun on breast milk and (although translators Keith Cohen and Paula Cohen don't render it that way literally) *invisible* ink. Literal milk-writing becomes visible only when held near heat.

58. Fox [Jeanette Silveira], "Why Men Oppress Women," *Lesbian Ethics* I:1 (1984), 41. Italics added.

59. One of the persistent themes of the New Left in the 1960s was precisely this isolation of people in the United States from one another. Surely much male resistance to feminism is based, at least in part, on the desire for one last bastion of emotional support, self-esteem, relative leisure, and freedom from competition, all of which are very hard to find in a capitalist society outside the institution of the home and women's emotional and material services within it.

60. The ubiquity of this dulls us to its enormity. To my mind, Dorothy Sayers's essay "The Human-Not-Quite Human" is a classic feminist example of the strain such a situation can produce: attempting to be polite (!) while refuting abuse that is an attack on one's very existence as a Human being. That such arguments had to be made at all is, of course, grotesque (Betty Roszak and Theodore Roszak, eds., *Masculine/Feminine: Readings in Sexual Mythology and the Liberation of Women* [New York: Harper and Row, 1969], 116–22).

61. This statement could use a lot more amplification and documentation, but if I tried to provide it, this book wouldn't have been finished for more years. I do believe that I've had the feminist experience—decades of reading, arguing, teaching, administering, corresponding, and so on as of this writing—to make such a generalization. One example, which may make the point above clearer, if not better established, is (in my view) the current fight against pornography, insofar and only insofar as pornography is vaguely or circularly defined, treated as monolithic, and assigned total responsibility for producing patriarchal abuses.

62. Clever reformers would cultivate radicals, not shun them. Not only do radicals extend the area of what is possible, they also provide the intellectual vitality without which reform falters and dies. Clever radicals would remember that many reformist demands are in fact radical—that is, the system can't meet them without altering itself significantly or even without collapsing totally.

63. Andrea Dworkin, *Right-Wing Women* (New York: Perigee, 1983), 221.

64. I remember Judith Long Laws, a psychologist, saying bitterly in conversation in the early 1970s, "First you have to liberate the children because they're the future. Then you have to liberate the men because they suffer so. Then if there's any liberation left, you can go into the kitchen and eat it."

65. In April 1987, the feminist journal *Sojourner* carried in its letters column a paper war between a reader who believed feminism implies all good causes and therefore condemned nonvegetarian feminists and various other readers who made various objections to her stand. Nobody, as far as I recall, raised the point that feminism is a specific political cause whose foundation is collective self-interest. There are degrees of enlightenment in self-interest, of course, and I would wish the very highest degree of it on all feminists everywhere (and on everybody else too). Nonetheless, feminism is not identical with universal love, peace, the ecology movement, a celebration of female values, or any of the other things that seem to be using

the label nowadays. That is not to say that feminism is incompatible with any of these things either. What is so striking to me is that these substitute "feminisms" make no break with the characteristic patriarchal demand that women be altruistic *because they are women*. In *Women and Madness*, Phyllis Chesler calls such a break "risking winning"—that is, preferring one's own welfare before others' and women's before men's. In a society that posits self-aggrandizement as the only alternative to self sacrifice, such a choice is bound to be misunderstood. See my own "Power and Helplessness in the Women's Movement" (collected in *Magic Mommas, Trembling Sisters, Puritans and Perverts*, 1985).

66. For example, Mitchell criticizes Shulamith Firestone's reinterpretation of the "Oedipus complex" in terms of power relations within the family by stating that Firestone has rejected mental life altogether so that "every move a person makes is a sensible, conscious choice" (Mitchell, 1974, 347–48).

67. Rosalind Coward, *Female Desires: How They Are Sought, Bought, and Packaged* (New York: Grove Press, 1985), 43–45.

68. See Lisa Schoenfielder and Barb Wieser, eds., *Shadow on a Tightrope: Writings by Women on Fat Oppression* (Iowa City: Aunt Lute, 1983). As far as I know, fat liberation groups date back only through the 1980s; another I happen to know of is Fat Lip Theatre in (I believe) San Francisco.

69. Some feminists (like Mary Daly) have noted that mothers are the "forewomen" of patriarchy and that much transmitted from mother to daughter is not part of the inevitable relationship between them but rather comprises specific cultural lessons mothers believe they must teach their daughters if the latter are to survive. Such lessons are simply "the way it is" and serve a useful purpose (in patriarchal terms) by deflecting the daughters' rage against "the way it is" to the mother, who seems to be causing "the way it is." Mary Daly's phrase in *Gyn/Ecology* is "token torturers."

70. The famous beauty Lillian Russell was what we would today call obese. Quite a few writers have noted that the insistence on extreme thinness as part of female beauty began only a few decades ago in U.S. life. Some feminists have called this ideal a form of male impersonation and part of the backlash against the feminism of the last two decades. Many have noted the sudden and extraordinary increase in bulimia and anorexia among young women in recent years. Despite various attempts to explain these eating disorders purely intrapsychically, it is clear that changes in cultural ideals of female beauty have a lot to do with them. Naomi Wolf writes in her preface to the paperback edition of *The Beauty Myth:*

> Researchers at Wayne State University found that anorexia
> and bulimia were triggered, in women who had a biochem-
> ical predisposition to it, by simple dieting; caloric restriction
> resulted in biochemical changes in the brain which addicted
> women physiologically to anorexia and bulimia (Wolf, *The*

Beauty Myth: How Images of Beauty Are Used against Women
[New York: Anchor, 1992], 6).

Normal college men, volunteers, became hysterical, ritualistic, obsessive, and de-pressed, binged and vomited, and became terrified of the outside world and tense and irritable upon losing 25 percent of their original body weight—precisely the amount most women need to lose in order to fit the current beauty ideal, what Wolf calls "the Iron Maiden" (ibid., 196). I think this is life-saving knowledge, especially important in a country whose focus is so psychology-oriented; that's why I've in-cluded a reference here that breaks the rule I imposed on myself during the writing of this book, i.e., not to use any material published after 1988. (Without that rule, I'd never have finished the manuscript.)

71. Delphy, *Close to Home,* 195. Delphy adds that changing one such con-dition without changing both will be ineffective; thus "reevaluating" menstruation without changing the availability of menstrual technology will not work. It's not enough simply to decide that menstruation is okay. This decision must result in changes in behavior and in the outside world.

72. The examples are fascinating, as are Henley's many readings of physical arrangements in the workplace or overprivileged people's cavalier use of underpriv-ileged people's time. Her interpretations are backed up by experimental evidence of the simplest kind, work conventional psychology has apparently never thought to do. For example, male and female experimenters stared at people on the street and tallied their responses, finding that in general women avoided men's gaze, men gazed back at women who gazed at them, and men avoided other men's gazes with especial rigor. Henley's conclusion is that women in public experience a conflict between being aware of what the males around them are doing and averting their gazes (a woman's direct gaze, a dominance gesture, is often interpreted by men as a sexual invitation), so that "visual information may be a prize furtively caught in stolen glances" (Henley, *Body Politics,* 164–65). What would be dominance gestures in a man are usually interpreted as something quite different in women: "A touch, a stare, a closeness [of physical approach], a loosening of demeanor, even huskiness of the voice—are all perceived as sexiness in women" (ibid., 197). Henley empha-sizes that what may seem to be many women's timidity—and what a woman may even perceive in herself as an inexplicable backing off from a course of action—can actually be a response to interpersonal cues so well learned that it has become automatic. She notes the interpersonal threats some men use on women: "a hard squeeze of the upper arm, or of the hand, physical restraint (holding her back), stepping on the toe, or kicking the ankle surreptitiously when seated" (ibid., 149–50). I would add from my own observation examples like a direct stare, clenching of the fists, or thickening of the muscles of the neck. Henley's examples of mock play are women "swung painfully dizzy at square dances, chased . . . and thrown in water, carried, spanked, or dunked at a beach. . . . The message that comes through

to women in such physical displays is: you are so physically inferior that you can be played with like a toy. Males are the movers and powerful in life, females the puppets" (ibid., 150).

73. Syn Ferguson, letter to the author, 1986.

74. We do the same to others, of course.

75. I can't find where this remark came from and would appreciate learning its provenance.

76. Bowles and Klein, 1983, 113.

77. Ibid., 49–50.

78. Catharine MacKinnon, *Sexual Harassment of Working Women: A Case of Sex Discrimination* (New Haven: Yale University Press, 1979), 2, 28, xii. Italics added.

79. Quoted in Charles Platt, *Dream Makers: The Uncommon Men and Women Who Write Science Fiction,* vol. II (New York: Berkeley, 1983), 265.

80. Gould, *Mismeasure of Man,* 321.

F O U R

FOR WOMEN ONLY:
OR, WHAT IS THAT MAN
DOING UNDER MY SEAT?

But separatists are such terrible people.

If there's one thing on which many feminists of all other persuasions emphatically agree, it's the truth of that statement. I myself assumed for years that separatism was inexcusable and separatists grotesque and ill. (In the process, I alienated one separatist acquaintance completely and almost lost another.) I've gossiped about the idiotic zap actions of a separatist group in my area—well, I heard they did it, and I *heard* they were separatists— and condemned separatists' lack of political sense or common intelligence (let alone sanity), their physical ugliness, their pathological obesity,[1] how they ignored and dismissed issues of race and class,[2] their foolish biologism, their random violence against men (of which I had no evidence), their financial ease and their self-indulgence in being separatists at all (one was "self-indulgently" disabled and on welfare), their condemnation of women who have anything to do with men or boys (including sons), their irrational rage at men and their worse rage at nonseparatist women, their total failure to do anything political except attack other feminists, and so on. I remember how these orgies of self-congratulation—one can hardly call them conversations—emphasized our own bravery, our compassion (for men), and our refusal to "take the easy way out" by cutting ourselves off from men.[3]

Oddly enough, our criticisms of separatists, like almost all those I've heard (and I've informally heard a good deal more over the years than I can find in print), were vague about details like place, time, and the identity of the people involved.

Even odder, nobody I knew ever cited any published statements by separatists or written-down reports of their actions, things you could check and actually find out if they happened or not.

Even more odd than that, there seems to be far more spoken, informal criticism of separatism than anything published, and what has been published tends to be vague.

Oddest of all, the stereotype of The Separatist described above bears an extremely striking resemblance to another stereotype—and *that is the stereotype of The Feminist herself, as presented in the mass media of the 1970s and '80s.*[4]

Now that is too much oddness. I think it's pretty clear that feminist attacks on separatists and feminist horror stories about separatists are a form of scapegoating, just like the scapegoating of the "undesirables" of one's own sex or ethnic group described in Chapter II. Of course, political radicals of any kind are not born into an ethnic group[5] of political radicalism (though political radicalism can certainly be part of the tradition of some ethnic groups in the United States),[6] but the process of blaming the "bad" part of one's group for the oppression visited on the whole group seems awfully similar. Feminists, like other radicals, don't have available to them the sources of real or imagined support or reassurance that nonradicals have, and even though such reassurances and support may be illusory, they do keep people from getting scared.[7] We're afraid for our jobs, afraid of random male violence, afraid of the teenage boy down the block who's been writing "dyke" on our garage door (or might do so), afraid of the fellow worker who's been "teasing" us with his or her "jokes" about what he or she considers our "feminism." Or we're afraid of the extent of our own anger,[8] or what will happen if we cut ourselves off from male power and the help and support it seems to promise. Such fears need not be realistic; indeed, the kind of fear that produces scapegoating is unrealistic by definition—and like all unrealistic fears, it will grow in proportion to the length of time during which it remains untested.[9]

Is it surprising then that some of us try to draw a hard-and-fast distinction between Blameless Me, who couldn't possibly bring down such treatment on myself (because I don't deserve it) and Terrible Her, who does deserve it?[10] We haven't gone too far; *she* has. We aren't crazy; *she* is. We aren't angry or bad or out of control; *she* is. We don't hate men (the sin of sins); *she* does.[11] Don't punish us; punish *her*.

Alas, whatever impeccable distinctions we draw between those unacceptably nutso extremists over there and ourselves over here, the rest of the world pays little attention. In fact, it persists in confusing Blameless Me and Terrible Her, no matter how much we protest. Protesting may make us feel better, but it does little else. As Julia Penelope puts it: "When the neo-humanists and socialists among us urge 'unity' with sympathetic men, they're really saying they want to feel safe. When they talk about 'healing men,' they're really trying to protect the institution of Motherhood."[12] Moreover (needless to say), taking one's stand on the assertion "I'm not really as bad as she is, honest," does not put one in a position of strength or self-confidence. I am sorry to be such a *noodj* and will stop now.[13] Let's move on to something fresh, constructive, heartening, and politically creative: *separatism*. The real stuff.[14]

Here is separatism as actually defined by feminist separatists Katharine Hess, Jean Langford, and Kathy Ross:

> To us [separatism] means prioritising feminism. We want to distinguish clearly between men's interests and women's interests so that we can act in women's interests. . . . Men get material benefits from women's oppression: better pay, better working conditions, free labor in the household, more status, greater control over sexual relations, etcetera. . . . We may fight alongside (we do not say *with* men) in certain situations like the anti-Nazi and anti-initiative 13 marches in Seattle in the summer of 1978 but in these situations we insist on our political independence.*

Hess, Langford, and Ross go on to state what has now come to seem obvious to me but may not be so to some of my readers: that separatism is not spiritually per se, that it doesn't depend on women's supposedly superior biology, that it has nothing necessarily to do with terrorism, that it isn't fascism, that it's theoretically compatible with other analyses of exploitation and oppression applied to other groups, and that it is multi-issue and compatible with working in coalitions. Moreover, Hess, Langford, and Ross have a view of feminist reaction that matches those of many antiseparatists, for example:

> Cultural revolution is essential but . . . not enough. . . . The strong community base which is a valuable part of separatism . . . comes to be a substitute for a movement, instead of a support for it. And the services eventually usually become severed from any ideology. . . . Our little enclaves are totally defenseless. At any time the government can cut off funds and either release or lose control of citizen backlash. . . . Women are lim-

---

*Initiative 13 was a citywide initiative designed to limit the civil rights of lesbians and gay men. It failed.

ited in what they can do politically within a feminist business because of the pressure to make it financially, which invariably comes first. . . . No one is going to pay us to have a revolution.[15]

And here is separatist Julia Penelope's very similar definition:

[Separatism is the belief that] men, individually and collectively, oppress women, that every man benefits directly and indirectly . . . from the oppression of women, that . . . patriarchy is a social structure designed to perpetuate the subjugation of women and the dominance of men, and that all females must withdraw their energies from men and cease to nurture and take care of them if women's oppression is to cease.[16]

Elsewhere Penelope writes that separatism means putting women first[17] and adds that there are no male groups that make feminist issues an absolute priority. She also notes that successful coalitions require separatism—an important point, I think—"as the power base for political trade-offs." She observes that "separatist consciousness" has been crucial to groups like the Chicano family,[18] as does Sarah Lucia Hoagland, who points out that

when such a unit is a haven, it is a haven . . . not specifically because it is a certain structure called a family (no matter how varied that structure can be). Nor is the Black Church a haven because it is a church, i.e. xtian—rather, despite it. If such institutions are havens, it is because they are groups made up of people who are to some degree separatist and not assimilationist in their consciousness.[19]

And here is Dale Spender's surprisingly similar account of the Women's Social and Political Union, the party of the militant suffragettes in England at the end of the nineteenth and the beginning of the twentieth century. Their tactics advanced the fight for the vote more in a decade, says Spender, than had been all through the nineteenth century:

The source of much of this success (and later the basis of much of the criticism) was the WSPU insistence that all men be treated as members of *one* party. Among themselves in a male electorate with male members, men had decided that some would be more powerful than others, but as far as the WSPU was concerned, the means by which this hierarchy among men was arranged was *irrelevant* to women. . . . These "personal" issues among

men were of no account to women. . . . *The mileage lay in . . .*
refusing to adhere to male distinctions and treating all men the same.
. . . The divisions among men, so clearly prized by themselves, were
irrelevant to women.[20]

Spender goes on to describe the extraordinarily scurrilous and unprovable
personal attacks leveled at this particular group of suffragists, then and now
(hysteria, childishness, humorlessness, power lust, sexual frustration, fad-
dishness, stupidity, and craziness), their huge membership, which cut
across classes and parties, the enormous amount of money they received
from women everywhere, and the brutality with which they were treated
by the British government. Moreover, the WSPU did not allow men to join,
although it accepted them as allies.[21] Although Spender doesn't actually use
the word "separatist," the WSPU's tactic of treating all men in power as the
same certainly sounds like what the other feminists I've been quoting here
advocate.

Elsewhere Spender (a native of Australia who works in London) takes on
and settles to her satisfaction precisely those criticisms always brought to
bear against feminist separatism in the United States:

> *Portraying men as the enemy.* . . . Men . . . are not likely to en-
> courage women to call them the enemy and make male power
> a problem. . . . It is more in men's interest to argue for the *in-*
> *terdependence* of the sexes . . . [and] more likely that men will
> argue that women should understand, mediate, conciliate, ap-
> pease and endure rather than resist and confront. As no equiv-
> alent good manners are required in relation to race and class,
> as no similar concern is shown in these contexts to refrain from
> calling the oppressor the enemy, I see no good reason for mak-
> ing sex an exception.[22]

The last chapter of *Women of Ideas* is a plea for "active non-cooperation,"
which ends: "I want women . . . to refrain from cooperating with men, to
cease making our resources available to men who are likely to use against
us what they have taken. *I want men to be 'irrelevant' to our enterprise of*
constructing our own knowledge."[23]

Other well-known feminists have made public statements in favor of
separatism. For example, Mary Daly writes, "Separatism/separation is . . .
expanding room of our own, moving outside the realm of the War
State, War Stare" and "the primary intent of women who choose to be
present to each other . . . is not an invitation to men. It is an invitation to
our Selves."[24]

In *Woman's Estate*, Juliet Mitchell stated simply, "The reason for segregation [woman-only activities and organizations] is simply that we are (in this case) the oppressed people and around this we organize." In 1968, Marlene Dixon wrote of the similar refusal of many women's groups at the "first national gathering of militant women's groups since Seneca Falls . . . to utter *the ritualistic 'we don't hate men'* " (italics added). There were many such straightforward defenses of separatism in the early days of the women's liberation movement. Today I have had trouble finding such statements anywhere except in the work of avowed separatists like Hess, Langford, and Ross, who say simply, "Women-onliness . . . is not a shelter from reality, nor is it only a comfort. It is a political right and an organizational tool."[25]

But separatists do not get a good press, even within the women's movement. Penelope notes that "articles by Separatists are systematically rejected by mainstream 'feminist' magazines and newspapers." She asks why "we are expected to justify our insistence on putting wimmin first" and why our commitment is considered dubious if we're not working to liberate men as well.[26] She quotes Andrea Dworkin to the effect that women are "defined everywhere as evil when we act on our own self-interest," and so we "strive to be good by renouncing self-interest altogether." Norma Alarçon notes that "as Chicanas embrace feminism they are charged with betrayal. . . . Often great pains are taken to explain that our feminism assumes a humanistic nuance." Anna Lee, in "The Tired Old Question of Male Children," sketches the problems that occurs in lesbian communities when women-only events or spaces exclude male children (even if they do provide child care): the assumption that "one of our 'chores' is to [see that male children do not] become sexist," the impossibility of doing so, given the influence of the culture, the implicit belief that "wimmin [are] the cause of male failure or bad behavior," and the perpetuation of the "historical sexist pattern of assuming wimmin are responsible for something we have no power over." She also writes: "As a black womon I have seen sons taught passivity to enable them to survive in a world committed to lynching black males. . . . It hasn't made any difference in how those males treat wimmin."[27]

I have noted, in the feminist community to which I belong, the further assumptions that male children will be irremediably damaged by being excluded from those very few events and places that are women-only, the idea that children in general will be hurt by not having access to all adult spaces (although it's true that women with children are isolated from many adult spaces and activities in this country), and the assumption by some mothers of boy children that their boys deserve or need more than others' girls and that they themselves are more consequential than the mothers of girls.[28]

Here are some of the experiences I've had with feminist separatism:

After an all-women's dance in 1970 in the university in which I taught, male students pelted the women leaving the dance with threats, obscenities, and, in a few cases, rocks. The editor of the student newspaper, a young White man of well-to-do antecedents, printed an editorial that ignored the violence done the women and denounced them (the women) as bigoted, chauvinist, inhumane, and vicious, predicting that women would do incalculable harm to the feminist cause if they pursued such a woman-only policy because it would alienate men. (I arranged a meeting with him, but since his conversation consisted almost solely of "They *can't* keep me out!" I gave up any further attempt at communication.)

In 1970 or 1971, I had a further go at the subject, this time with a powerful and important academic colleague in another department, who insisted on lecturing to a women's studies class that was afraid to exclude him. I turned and left the classroom—after a good deal of provocation—while he kept repeating, "But you've *got* to talk to me!"[29]

In 1986, in a women's tavern, three gay men showed up one evening to publicize a gay benefit event. In full drag they were twice as large and twice as loud as anyone else there. It was a chore to get past them, as they located themselves right in the middle of the tavern, blocking traffic.[30] When I complained of their presence to one of the young women who worked there, she accused me of "intolerance," citing the men's bravery in appearing in public in the clothes they were wearing. She had a point, I think, but so did I. Several young lesbians had become the men's audience, reminding me that the starry-eyed look of admiration directed at men by women for no particular reason except their sex is not solely the province of heterosexual women.

Similarly, when I remarked on the presence of male-to-female transsexuals and male transvestites in space reserved specifically for women,[31] I was criticized by other women for my lack of "compassion." I was then told that these men had "become women" and that they had "no other place to go," although there's nothing to prevent transvestites and male-to-female transsexuals from organizing their own groups around their own histories and their own present situations, which are not ours, or from our acting as their allies, whether we admit them to certain of our groups or not. Again, very sexist assumptions lie behind such abandonment of woman-only spaces: that it's our job to take care of men, that we must accept into our space all who need help, whether their presence serves our ends or not, and that to place our own space and our own desires first is intolerant and unloving—a judgment that assumes our lives and characters have value only if we love and tolerate everybody else, that is, men.

Marilyn Frye, a feminist philosopher, writing in 1977, found separatism everywhere in the feminist movement: shelters for battered women, women's studies programs, women's bars, and women's communities. Although, she states, separatism is "vigorously obscured, trivialized, mystified, and outright denied by many feminist apologists . . . [it] is [also] embraced, explored, expanded and ramified." Frye finds (as I do) that:

> the [physical] exclusion of men is seen as a device whose use needs elaborate justification. . . . Only a small minority of men go crazy when an event is advertised to be for women only— just one man tried to crash our women-only Rape Speak-out, and only a few hid under the auditorium seats to try to spy on a woman-only meeting at a NOW convention in Philadelphia.[32]

Assuming a view of men's "parasitism" on women that strongly recalls Matilda Josyln Gage's, Frye locates the male terror of separatism (and, I would add, many women's terror of it as well) in the issue of men's access to women's resources. She speaks of "the panic, rage and hysteria generated in so many of them by the thought of being abandoned by women." Citing evidence from Jessie Bernard's *The Future of Marriage* (1975) and George Gilder's work, she states that men tend

> to fall into mental illness, petty crime, alcoholism, physical infirmity, chronic unemployment, drug addiction and neurosis when deprived of the care and companionship of a female mate or keeper . . . [while] women without male mates are significantly healthier and happier than women with male mates.[33]

Frye likewise maintains that those who fear and hate female separatism are onto something:

> The woman-only meeting is a fundamental challenge to the structure of power. . . . When those who control access have made you totally accessible, *your first acts of control must be denying access or must have denial of access as one of its aspects.*

Therefore (if I follow Frye's logic):

> All-woman groups, meetings, projects seem to be great things for causing controversy and confrontation. Many women are offended by them; many are afraid to be the one to announce the exclusion of men. . . . This is because conscious and delib-

erate exclusion of men by women, from anything, is blatant insubordination and generates in women fear of punishment and reprisal (fear which is often well-justified).[34]

Frye also notes that "contrary to the image of the separatist as cowardly escapist, hers is the life and program which inspires the greatest hostility, disparagement, insult and confrontation. . . . She is the [feminist] against whom economic sanctions operate most conclusively." If other feminists are afraid of separatism, if they disparage it, if they pick it out as the unacceptably extremist scapegoat of the feminist movement, the reason is not far to seek. *"We are afraid of what will happen to us when we really frighten them* [men]. This is not an irrational fear."[35]

I agree with the writers of *Feminismo Primero;* feminist separatism means putting women first, and it is crucial to any feminism. It is what Chesler calls "risking winning." As she says, "Women must begin to 'save' themselves and their daughters before they 'save' their husbands and their sons, before they 'save' the whole world." Such an act of self-love is not easy for most women. Jessie Bernard's account of women's lives emphasizes what she calls the love and duty ethos of the female world, and Carol Gilligan's account of women's morality stresses her female subjects' terror of what they call "selfishness" and their attempt *not* to treat others as well as they treat themselves but far, far better—that is, to act so that they will get absolutely nothing for themselves from their own actions and others will get everything.[36]

To go against the grain of such socialization—a socialization that is constantly reinforced—and to risk the disapproval one is bound to get from men and women both is a difficult business. I think it crucial to any feminist effort, however.

Such a stance—abandoning men to their own resources—has been criticized by both men and women as selfish, inhumane, and the result of rage or general immorality or even sheer craziness. *But what is so dreadful about abandoning men to their own resources?* Haven't they got any? Men as a group at every class level have relatively more disposable income than women, more command over institutions, more leisure, more immunity from sexual violence, and more control over community resources than women—and yet whenever any woman or group of women propose to use its own resources for its own ends, there is an enormous amount of shock and horror at such ghastly behavior. It's certainly true that most men control a great deal less property, money, and resources than élite men—and some men are sleeping in the streets—but such distinctions arise from other differences among them than their sex.[37]

Even in communities in which everyone is badly off, men's self-esteem, their access to resources, their representation of what is Human, their share of the world's work, their surprisingly common assumption that they could control half the people they meet by personal violence (given no other way),[38] and the very sense that they make of their lives and the Human dilemmas they face in common with all of us all are heavily influenced by the sex-class system (Andrea Dworkin's phrase), which is loaded in their favor *as men and against ours as women*. We may as well be self-loving—though in a capitalist society that assigns self-aggrandizement to men and self-abasement to women (and has a lot of trouble with self-love for anybody), true selfishness is not easy.[39]

The fear that men will be angry if you withdraw your resources from them is a realistic one. On the other hand, no one is unaffected by this society's misogyny.[40] To deal with such dislike consciously is better than attempting to bribe one's way past it, is better than trying to bribe it by giving up one's own concerns and thus rendering oneself politically and personally helpless.

The fear that feminism will suffer if we withdraw our resources from men is not realistic. For one thing, feminism has already suffered in the last ten years. For another, its future never was in masculine hands but in feminine ones, despite all those earnest fellows who have said, "If you do that, I won't support you." (Ask them what support they've actually given women recently, and the answer is apt to be little or none.)

Putting oneself first—and other women second—has one fine result. Freed of the halo of power, stripped of their socially assumed superiority, men and men's affairs lose much of their power to impress. As Carolyn Heilbrun puts it:

> The whole paraphernalia of stardom . . . falls away. They [antifeminist men] become no more than frightened individuals (perhaps just a little nastier and sillier than other people). . . . Once the pyrotechnics of power cease to dazzle . . . a kind of energy returns to frightened women.[41]

Nor will withdrawing our resources from men result in our becoming victims of personal male violence. As Susan Brownmiller has pointed out, male violence is usually directed at women at random.[42] Adherence to feminine "unselfishness" is therefore no protection. And for battery—see feminist work on the subject, starting with Erwin Pizzey's and Dale Martin's—it can't be avoided by behaving "well" since it's not motivated by women's behaving "badly." Certainly putting ourselves first gives us more hope of defending ourselves or escaping from male violence when we meet it—or working with institutions to make sure it stops.

Interviews with feminists used to begin, "Why do you hate men?" and we used to have to explain carefully that we didn't. Only then could we begin to make clear that the task of feminism was not to provide nurture for "everybody" or to guarantee an environment in which men would feel generous and comfortable. To abandon feminism for the "humanism" that tries to treat everybody identically,[43] thus ignoring the concrete realities of everyone's lives, is—to put it tactfully—just a teeny bit premature. To speak more bluntly, it's reactionary and always was. As Frye notes, *access is crucial in race/sex/class situations.*

As Henley notes, access to others' space, time, and bodies runs one way: parents touch growing children in order to control or guide them; children do not usually touch parents this way. Superiors in business touch subordinates casually, but subordinates don't usually touch superiors casually. Teachers touch students, but students don't touch teachers; men touch women casually, but women don't so touch men. (Access also goes down the medical and ability/disability hierarchy, as Susan Hannaford points out, and down the age hierarchy.) When women do touch men, the women's behavior is interpreted by both sexes as a sexual invitation. When a student touches a teacher, the touch is interpreted as invasive or a threat, and so on.[44]

Adrienne Rich has warned us all about the "intensive training all women go through in every society" to place our long-term and collective interests "second or last," about the female conviction that "women's self-determination and survival are secondary to the 'real' revolution," and of the belief in "selfless, sacrificial love as somehow redemptive." She calls such love an addiction. She adds that women's attempts to put ourselves and other women first will for a long time not be seen by men as "a new form of love. We will be told we are acting and speaking out of hatred; that we are becoming 'like them'; that they will perish emotionally without our constant care and attention."[45]

I agree. Nor do I think that women can "teach men to love." Such proposals are wishful thinking, whether they come from women or men. I believe that men will "learn to love" (whatever that means) when they must but not before, and that they will learn it when they have to deal with one another without our help. Anything else merely feeds into our current sexist setup where women and men are frozen into a perpetual "rescue" scenario[46] in which women provide the warmth and emotional support men need because men need not provide it for themselves or one another because women provide it, and so on.

What about those separatists who want to kill off all the men? Luckily, I know of nobody who's planning such a large project in the near future. I say "luckily" because I don't consider such an effort feasible and am worried about the punishment such quixotic behavior may bring down on those who attempt it. (And, I must in honesty add, on those meritorious, profeminist men they may accidentally or ignorantly attempt it upon.) Nonetheless, I will defend to the limit any feminist's right to state anything she pleases about the impossibility of women's ever being safe on this planet as long as men exist.

After all, the historical evidence is very largely—and tragically—on her side.[47]

I often sympathize with her.

I would certainly prefer to take her side than to support her opposite number, whose antiseparatism is merely a scapegoating of those who deserve serious attention, an expression of self-hatred, a nervous limitation placed on feminism, and something of an obsession in its own right.

After all, the real question, of course, is not whether women will practice separatism against men, but rather whether men will continue to practice it against women. European—if not world—history is full of statements by various influential gentlemen that women ought not to exist, that men ought to be able to get children without women,[48] that women are the devil's gateway,[49] that we are not adults and cannot be allowed civil rights, that we must continue to bear children even if it kills us,[50] that husbands ought to have absolute power over wives, that women ought to be ashamed of their existence, that women's and girls' lives are dispensable,[51] that God is a man, and on and on and on in a long, very long, far too long, centuries-long catalog of hatred and violence. In the face of such oppression (which even feminists don't usually like to dwell on, by the way; it's far too unpleasant), the conviction of a few separatists that men are a bad business altogether strikes me as rather mild and perhaps even justified. Surely it ought to provoke no reaction in the rest of us except, perhaps, a gloomy *I do hope they're mistaken.*

I would like to be proved wrong—about the men, I mean—but the only thing that will do that is the demonstration by large numbers of men that they are able and willing, publicly as well as privately, to support, advocate, and practice feminism, and that they will do so and continue to do so. Criticizing women for noticing our own oppression is purely and simply blaming the victim. For men who don't like separatism, the remedy is in your own hands: work publicly to make sexism nonexistent and its continuation forever impossible. Deeds, not words, as Christabel Pankhurst demanded of a British government that was always "in favor of" woman suffrage and never did anything about it. In the late 1960s, Dana Densmore got tired of the horror provoked by women putting women's interests first and wrote a pamphlet about it, in which she noted that the question "Why do you want to kill off all the men?" was feminist-baiting and meant "You'll have to kill me to change me." She wrote:

> If . . . men are innocent and well-meaning, then we will see that demonstrated in their response to our rejection of our role of victim and our criticism of the institutions that cast men into the role of oppressor. . . . They will probably be surprised at first, showing the signs of being forced to think completely new thoughts. . . . But, given encouragement, education, and demonstrations of how strongly we feel, they will declare themselves our allies.
>
> They will not continue to ridicule us (if indeed they ever did), they will not play dumb and demand that the same thing be explained over and over as if we had never said a word to them, they will not set themselves up as an "enemy." They will show respect for us as persons and for our cause as appropriate and legitimate.
>
> In fact, it turns out that men sort themselves out into allies and "enemies."[52]

Deeds, not words.

NOTES

1. Yes I did. I really did. Oh, shame. Oh, embarrassment.

2. Not that I and my fellow gossipers were doing anything about these issues ourselves at the time, of course.

3. None of us had much contact with men at the time either, but we never let that spoil the fine sweep of our condemnation of others.

4. Both of these stereotypes strongly resemble the stereotype of The Strong-Minded Woman of the late nineteenth century, i.e., the advocate of women's rights *and* The Spinster of the same period. See Sheila Jeffreys, *The Spinster and Her Enemies: Feminism and Sexuality, 1880–1930* (London: Pandora, 1985).

5. "Ethnic" is a word used in the United States to apply to everyone except White Christian people with northern European ancestors, who are supposed to be ethnos-free. Such an attitude is, of course, a sign of the cultural dominance of that particular group.

6. The example I'm most familiar with is that of the socialism that was such a strong presence among the Eastern European Jews (the Ashkenazy) who migrated to the United States at the end of the nineteenth and beginning of the twentieth

century. See Melanie Kaye/Kantrowitz and Irena Klepfisz, eds., *The Book of Dina: A Jewish Women's Anthology* (Montpelier, VT: Sinister Wisdom Books, 1986), especially Kaye/Kantrowitz's "radical tour" of New York's Lower East Side.

7. For example, a few years ago when the state of Washington decided to delay its employees' salaries for half a month, a woman at my workplace was forced temporarily to use food stamps. She reported, in shocked and outraged surprise, that she had been treated badly at a neighborhood store she had shopped at for years. She had assumed that she would never be treated like that because she was not like some mythical, irresponsible "them," *her* fantasized scapegoat.

8. To Patricia Frazer Lamb I'm indebted for the analysis that what many women fear is not that men will cease to love them but that they will be driven to the point at which they will cease to feel compassion or concern for men. I used to think that this fear meant only the fear of reprisal; now I think it may well be the fear that the values upon which one has depended and which have given moral meaning to one's life will finally be revealed to be lies or illusions. In such a world—a world of what some people call "naked power"—it is indeed better to curse god and die. There is the allied fear of finding huge numbers of people totally irredeemable and the shattering of the very possibility of Human community such a discovery must produce.

9. Testing such fears—even finding out how bad things really get—can produce the courage and common sense that a realistic estimate of catastrophe can give people. Those who have risked least are sometimes awed by what they think is the special courage of those who've experienced poverty, jail, illness, persecution, and so on. Such folks often assume some innate difference separates them from the "brave" ones and even use that assumption to defend themselves against having to take risks. That is, they excuse themselves by saying, "I'm not as brave as you are." As one acquaintance of mine who'd left her marriage said angrily to another who wanted to but wasn't "brave" enough, "I didn't leave my husband because I was brave. I became brave because I left him." Of course, I don't mean that if only one takes risks, all will be well. Those who've suffered don't become impervious to pain or fear, nor do they always discover that the risks they take have no consequences. I mean only that their judgments aren't distorted by the overblownness and confusion caused by untested, unrealistic fears. In this connection, cowardice can be thought of as fear beyond the demands of reality.

10. Robin Morgan has wittily entitled a volume of her collected feminist writings *Going Too Far: The Personal Chronicle of a Feminist* (New York: Random House, 1977).

11. To give an example, in the first formal consciousness-raising group I attended in 1970, one of the women declared that if there were a "man-hater" present, she would leave the room.

12. Julia Penelope, "The Mystery of Lesbians: II," *Lesbian Ethics* I:2 (1985), 42.

13. A *noodj* (Yiddish) is a nudger, a reminder-maker who makes a nuisance

of *noodj*self by constantly *noodj*ing you to do something, an urger, a gadfly. For example: "You said you'd clean up your room. I see dust balls under your bed the size of people." "Oh, Ma, I'll do it." "So do it." "Ma, do you have to *noodj* all the time?" "Only when the bed starts moving into the hall under the accumulated pressure of a billion dust balls." And so on.

14. Feminist theorizing about prepatriarchal societies has sometimes been greeted with the same horror as separatism for, I think, the same reasons. It is *going too far, claiming too much.* So has spirituality. An instance is an essay by Sally R. Binford ("Are Goddesses and Matriarchies Merely Figures of Feminist Imagination? Myths and Matriarchies," *Human Behavior,* May 1979) that is a blanket condemnation of feminist theorists who maintain that there were such things as prepatriarchal societies. The essay is vague about its facts and obviously redolent of the terror that critics will find such theories irrational, emotional, and foolish, that is, *like women.* It was Binford's essay that forced me to reconsider my own taken-for-granted, blanket prejudices against such theorizing, prejudices that proved to be unfounded. Like the you're-not-as-radical-as-I-am game, this I'm-not-as-extremist-as-you-are game hurts real people. I suggest that all of us—socialists, feminists, socialist-feminists, antiracists, peace activists, disability rights activists, and all sorts of other good folks—get together and invent, for the purpose of scapegoating, a group of alien sentient beings of dreadful beliefs and wretched behavior who live very, very, very, very, very, very, very far away (preferably in another galaxy). We can then proceed to be better than they with no harm done to anyone. For this purpose I suggest the "Glotologs," whose detestable sexism I've thoroughly condemned in an earlier book (see Joanna Russ, *How to Suppress Women's Writing* [Austin: University of Texas Press, 1983]). They have the enormous advantage of being completely imaginary, a very fine quality in a scapegoat.

15. Katherine Hess et al., eds., *Feminism First: An Essay on Lesbian Separatism,* trans. Helen Weber and Fabiola Rodríguez (Seattle: Tsunami Press, 1981), 59–60, 74–79.

16. Julia Penelope, "The Mystery of Lesbians," *Lesbian Ethics* 1:1 (1984), 29.

17. Ibid., 20.

18. Penelope, "Mystery II," 51, 65. Her reference is to Cherríe Moraga's description of the Chicano family as a source of love and shelter from racism (Moraga, *Loving in the War Years* [Boston: South End Press, 1983], 54; see also 110–11). Penelope makes the point that Moraga's specific examples are drawn from particular women in her family and not "the family" as an institution. As Clara Fraser has said, when families are good, the institution of "the family" is given the credit for it; when families fail, the people involved are blamed. Hardly anyone but some socialists and feminists give *people* the credit for making *institutions* work (conversation with the author, 1985 or 1986).

19. Sarah Lucia Hoagland, "Lesbian Ethics: Some Thought on Power in Our Interactions," *Lesbian Ethics* 2:1 (1986), 73.

20. Dale Spender, *Women of Ideas: What Men Have Done to Them* (London: Routledge and Kegan Paul, 1982), 570–71. Italics added to last sentence.

21. Ibid., 587–603. Also see Hess et al., *Feminism First,* on coalition work.

22. Spender, *Women of Ideas,* 16–17.

23. Ibid., 736–37.

24. Mary Daly, *Gyn/Ecology: The Metaethics of Radical Feminism* (Boston: Beacon Press, 1978), 380, xii. A phenomenon I called "woman-centeredness" in an earlier work (Russ, *How to Suppress,* 109) now strikes me as very consistent with the separatist theory I've been describing.

25. Juliet Mitchell, *Woman's Estate* (New York: Random House, 1971), 57; Edith Hoshino Altbach, ed., *From Feminism to Liberation* (Cambridge, MA: Schenkman, 1971), 53; Hess et al., *Feminism,* 94.

26. Penelope, "Mystery," 33, 19. This is another commonplace of the early 1970s. I remember endless justifications of women meeting "alone"—that is, without men—and the assumption that women without men in ordinary life were "alone" or "lonely." I believe it was humorist Kate Clinton who told in a performance of being approached in a restaurant by a man who asked why she and her companion were "alone." She answered, "We're not alone. We're with each other."

27. Penelope, "Mystery II," 41; Cherríe Moraga and Gloria Anzaldúa, eds., *This Bridge Called My Back: Writings by Radical Women of Color* (Watertown: MA: Persephone Press, 1981), 188; Anna Lee, "The Tired Old Question of Male Children," *Lesbian Ethics* 1:2 (1985), 106.

28. A few I've met are indeed the kind of people who use the consequentiality of their motherhood as a means to their own importance. Others are in painful conflict between their feminism and their unanalyzed belief that boys ought not to face the same kinds of self-muting or "realistic" hard lessons as girls. Donna Allegra comments on the latter: "The boy child has learned well / to cling and keep you there; Why have you shown him the way / to pull at the wings / and stop the wide stroke / of your lesbian angel / courage? / How can your daughters grow?" (in Dorothy E. Smith and Sarah J. David, eds., *Women Look at Psychiatry* [Vancouver: Press Gang Publishers, 1975], 167).

I've also seen feminist mothers of small children, overwhelmed by the burden of paid job and inadequate child care and suffering from the exclusion of mothers with infants and small children from so many adult spaces and events in this society, turn their anger not toward their childrens' fathers or fathers in general, or male friends or employers or the community in general, but toward women friends and feminist organizations. Even those who know that demanding child care from fathers, employers, and the community is crucial to feminist goals nonetheless expect more help from women than from any other source and blame other women if they don't get it.

29. This same White gentleman was infamous at the time for having stopped a man of color in the street (an absolute stranger to him) and demanding that the

man discuss racial discrimination with him. The man so addressed turned and walked away; the professor in question said for weeks (as I'm told he did about me) that he couldn't understand how such a person could possibly refuse to talk to him.

30. This particular behavior—blocking doorways and paths—is a Human habit, but few women have to be shouted at thrice or poked in the back (ditto) before they notice that somebody female is trying to get by.

31. In fact, these spaces were reserved *for lesbians,* a harder judgment to make about someone (usually) than his or her biological sex.

32. Marilyn Frye, *The Politics of Reality: Essays in Feminist Theory* (Trumansburg, NY: Crossing Press, 1983), 103–4.

33. Ibid., 99.

34. Ibid., 104, 103.

35. Ibid., 98, 107. Italics added.

36. Phyllis Chesler, *Women and Madness* (New York: Doubleday, 1972), 300, 301; Jessie Bernard, *The Female World* (New York: Free Press, 1981); Carol Gilligan, *In a Different Voice: Psychological Theory and Women's Development* (Cambridge: Harvard University Press, 1982). A writer friend, Syn Ferguson, once wrote me, saying that she'd been "running interference" for another woman worker in her workplace. She said at last she felt "good" and "right" in doing so, without the timidity and self-doubt she underwent when fighting for her own rights. She analyzed the issue as a feminist one and noted that others behaved much better toward her when she was working for someone else's welfare. Everywhere she went in the institutional structure she was met with praise and help. No one ever provided such praise and help when the interests she was fighting for, however justified, were her own.

37. For example, in communities so oppressed that young men own nothing but their muscles and their economic hopelessness, random male violence against women is not matched by similar widespread female terrorism against men. To reverse the class point: the security of Buckingham Palace apparently failed, a few years ago, to keep out an intruder who made his way to the bedroom of the Queen of England, Elizabeth II. The newspapers reported the intrusion as eccentric but harmless (he merely wanted to talk to her), but several feminist friends of mine immediately suspected—as I did—that the official story covered rape or attempted rape. As one friend of mine said, if *she's* not safe, what woman is? Of course, severe conflicts can occur in the situations of men to whom society holds out the promise of masculine privilege and who are then punished for their color or class. I'm not attempting to prove here that sexism is worse than class oppression or oppression due to color (or vice versa) but to lay out the gridwork of a sexism that "crosses" other distinctions bestowing privilege, immunity, oppression, or exploitation.

38. Hooks is right, of course, when she says that male terrorism against women is not a privilege but an expression of moral bankruptcy (bell hooks, *Feminist*

Theory from Margin to Center [Boston: South End Press, 1984], 75). Perhaps a better word than "privilege" (with its implication of luxury) is "immunity." There are certainly immunities that depend on class, color, or sex. I've personally met the idea that men dominate women as a group because individual men can knock individual women down. (The statement is never that some men can knock down some women some of the time; it is always absolute.) Twice professional, well-to-do White men have told me this, not that either of them actually practiced this rather odd principle of social interaction in his own life. Even odder, they invoked it only in connection with women, *never with other men.* Twice my novels have been reviewed by well-to-do White male persons who confidently stated that I didn't understand the nature of the real relations between the sexes and then advanced this astonishingly naive theory, although neither had gotten his position as a book reviewer in an important daily newspaper (let alone his place to live or his groceries) by beating up other men.

Male muscle matters, of course, especially in anomic situations (those on the social fringes, where there are no rules), but the really crucial factor seems to be community support. Men who enjoy this fantasy—and it is a fantasy—can't allow themselves to extend the necessary conditions of the fantasy to relations *between men*—that would be too frightening—which leads us to Phyllis Chesler's idea that one of the important functions of misogyny is to provide a class of people (women) who will absorb the male violence that would otherwise be directed by men *at other men.* When community support is given openly to men simply *as men,* when men's lives and doings are regarded as more important than women's, when women are dehumanized by such community values and tacit permission is given to men *as men* to terrorize and brutalize "their" women and some women in certain situations, with the knowledge that their community will support them, then there result appalling examples of brutality like the New Bedford rapes. Lynching is structurally a parallel phenomenon. See also Chesler's *About Men* (New York: Simon and Schuster, 1978) for male preoccupations with violence expected or feared from other men.

39. I take this to be a capitalist problem, not only a sexist one. Again and again, I'm struck with the dominant culture's positing self-aggrandizement and self-abasement as its only possibilities and the lack in the mass media and most churches and schools of any alternative, namely self-love. The assumption is always that putting oneself first puts everyone else nowhere.

40. See the chapter entitled "Fear and Loathing" in Germaine Greer, *The Female Eunuch* (New York: McGraw-Hill, 1971).

41. Carolyn Heilbrun, *Reinventing Womanhood* (New York: Norton, 1979), 206.

42. The rage provoked by separatism is another matter. At the moment no one seems to have recommendations for easy ways to neutralize or avoid such violence. There are recent cases of women fighting back in situations of personal violence and some even being acquitted for it. Again, what seems to me crucial isn't

even the personal ability to fight back one-to-one (desirable though that be) but the imposition of community sanctions. We need both.

43. Catharine MacKinnon notes that treating unequals as if they were equal is unequal treatment ("Feminism, Marxism, Method, and the State: An Agenda for Theory," *Signs*, 7:3, 1982).

44. Susan Hannaford, *Living Outside Inside: A Disabled Woman's Experience—Towards a Social and Political Perspective* (Berkeley: Canterbury Press, 1985); Nancy M. Henley, *Body Politics: Power, Sex, and Non-Verbal Communication* (Englewood Cliffs, NJ: Prentice-Hall, 1977), 109.

45. Adrienne Rich, *On Lies, Secrets, and Silence: Selected Prose, 1966–1978* (New York: Norton, 1979), 128, 122; *Of Woman Born* (New York: Norton, 1976), 217. Note the irony of a feminist with the radical commitment of Rich defending putting women first as a new form of love for men. Her later work does not contain statements of this sort.

46. "Rescue" in this sense doesn't describe a particular act (which may or may not be effective) or any situation in which one person needs the specific help that another can provide. Rather it describes a vicious circle in which one person is perpetually doing for another the kind of thing nobody in fact *can* do for another. Both partners are obsessed by their respective positions in a compulsive and self-perpetuating system. The "rescues" never work; the rescuee remains helpless and the rescuer obsessed by impossible control over the other person. Either or both parties strenuously resist any actual resolution of actual problems. Women do not have the power to "teach men to love" or to change their emotions in this way. Women who believe this stuff are either fearful of conflict with men or are trying to make the stereotyped relations of the sexes "work"—i.e., because women are the society's emotional experts, men will therefore need and value them. As Delphy has pointed out, merely standing patriarchal values on their heads and proclaiming the goodness of "feminine" values has no lasting effect either politically or personally. If women are to continue to be important to men because women can provide emotional support men can't provide for themselves, men must continue to be incapable of "loving." That is, women who attempt this project will have a vested interest in men's continuing emotional incapacity, just as men who wish to continue to "rescue" women economically (individually or as a class) have an important stake in keeping women poor.

47. See Marilyn French, *Beyond Power: On Women, Men, and Morals* (New York: Ballantine, 1986) for a massively comprehensive and cumulatively horrific record of woman-hating and woman-killing throughout a good deal of Human history. *Beyond Power*, like Spender's *Women of Ideas*, takes material that "everybody knows" (that is, all feminists know, sort of) and documents it to the point of I-didn't-know-it-was-that-bad.

48. This is from ancient Greece. I forget which cultural luminary of those great and glorious cultural ancestors of ours expressed this particular wish.

49. Tertullian? I forget. Another culture hero.

50. Luther, religious leader and certified Great Man.

51. See Madhu Kishwar and Ruth Vanita, eds., *In Search of Answers: Indian Women's Voices from Manushi* (London: Zed Books, 1984), for a contemporary version of this. Where poverty is extreme, girl children and women are starved and denied what medical care there is. In relatively wealthy countries, women must rely on a segregated, badly paid job market and medicine exploits both those women who pay (through such practices as unnecessary surgery and the covering up of the dangers of lucrative items like IUDs and breast-augmentation surgery) and those who can't (by ignoring their needs or using them in tests for contraceptive pills and so on). Race and class produce the same kinds of nasty phenomena, of course.

52. Dana Densmore, "Who Is Saying Men Are the Enemy?" (Pittsburgh: KNOW, Inc., 1970).

SHE WASN'T, SHE ISN'T, SHE DIDN'T, SHE DOESN'T, AND WHY DO YOU KEEP ON BRINGING IT UP?

Those who find the preceding chapter evasive are right; it is. Although some feminist separatism (like Spender's) does not rest on and is not involved with sexuality, most declared separatism is lesbian separatism, and, as one feminist told me in 1973, you can talk about lesbianism one night to one audience and feminism another night to another audience, but never put the two together in the same speech to the same audience, or the explosion will take off the roof of the hall.

But how can separatism possibly have anything to do with lesbians? Lesbians don't exist.

This striking—not to say staggering—not to say astonishing—truth may be gleaned from the most cursory inspection of our culture (not to mention that of a great many other countries) in which lesbian persons (except for a few books like this one, which is immediately suspect and weird for that very reason), are rare, grotesque, evil people, or really something else anyway, and are presented to us in the flesh (excuse the expression)[1] only in that grim, gray, gritty, constricted territory known as The Social Problem, an area so unpleasantly un-American that hardly a single advertisement for a single commercial product is located therein.[2]

Although to judge by books, movies, TV, ads, magazines, public behavior, and popular opinion in the United States, lesbians and lesbian experience are so rare as to be nonexistent, research in the area does not support this conclusion. In 1953, an era less liberal about sexual behavior than our own, Kinsey stated that a quarter of the female Human beings in his sample had recognized erotic responses to other females by age thirty and that overall some 30 to 40 percent of single women and 10 percent of married women were not entirely heterosexual. In 1977 Shere Hite reported that of the women who had answered her questionnaire, 4 percent reported themselves as bisexual, 8 percent preferred sex with women, 3 percent preferred themselves, and 1 percent would rather have no sex at all. Hite further observed "how frequently, *even though it was not specifically asked,* women mentioned that they might be interested in having sexual relations with another woman or at least were curious. Even more surprising results were observed in 1929 by Katherine Bement Davis in a study conducted among U.S. women "assumed to be 'normal' " and chosen for that reason. She

> found that 50.4% had experienced "intense emotional rela-
> tions" with other women . . . [and that] about half of those ex-
> periences were accompanied by sex or were "recognized as
> sexual in character". . . . Only 13.6% of those with lesbian ex-
> periences saw them as problematic.[3]

Nor is same-sex activity confined to the (presumably odd or corruptible) Human species. To cite Kinsey et al. again, other species do not confine themselves to heterosexual activity any more than Humans do, and those researchers who are not aware of this fact "have simply ignored the existence of sexual activity which is not reproductive." Female-female mounting is common in species like domestic cattle; Susan Cavin remarks ironically on the way such activity is so often rendered invisible by the language used to describe it, for example that such mounting signals the female's "receptivity" to the male. She also lists species in which female-female copulatory behavior has been observed: baboons, gibbons, chimpanzees, domestic cats, horses, lions, porcupines, elephants, bats, hyenas, raccoons, donkeys, porpoises, seagulls, cattle, rats, guinea pigs, goats, mice, rabbits, and apes.[4]

And yet lesbians and lesbian behavior don't exist.

One contemporary theorist, Paula Gunn Allen, a lesbian and a Laguna-Sioux–Lebanese-American, has (as she states) "read hundreds of books and articles dealing with American Indians." Her conclusions: "The Lesbian is to the American Indian what the Indian is to the American—invisible."[5]

Another, Evelyn Torton Beck, jokes about the total invisibility of lesbians in her community, Judaism: "This book is written by people who do not exist. I assure you, it's all very logical; we're not proscribed because we don't exist. If we existed, believe me, they'd be against us."[6]

Maureen Brady and Judith McDaniel, commenting on sixteen commercial press novels published between 1974 and 1979 that deal even minimally with lesbian characters or experiences, concluded that "these novels . . . distort, trivialize and betray lesbian experiences."[7] In the novels, lesbian existence is equated with sexlessness, woman-woman rape, a preoccupation with heterosexuality or bisexuality, sheer lack of time to think about the subject or do anything about it, regret for one's abnormal condition, and experimentation that was unpleasant and not repeated. (The fate suffered by the lesbian characters in the books includes decapitation, fifty years of loneliness after one brief affair, a nervous breakdown, addiction to drugs, and depression. Several, for no clear reason, return to heterosexuality.)

Cavin notes that polyandrous marriage—so rare on earth as to occur in only 4 out of 565 societies in a 1957 world sample—is constantly mentioned in anthropological discussions of marriage but that the numerically much more frequent woman-woman marriage "is rarely cited in world societal tables of marriage forms." When it is, it is averred to be only a property relation on no better evidence than that which can be used to prove that heterosexual marriage is also only a property relation. Elsewhere she notes that theorists of "original promiscuity" among Human beings ignore the possibility that such promiscuity included nonheterosexual behavior, despite findings like Kinsey's and observations of non-Human species, which clearly indicate that such behavior cannot be labeled either biologically abnormal or even very rare.[8]

Even in the area of feminist theory itself, where one might expect to find more commentary on the subject, consideration of lesbianism is very often absent. My reading in this area comprises some four hundred books and journals; I have found little or no reference to lesbianism or analyses of its importance to feminism in such well-known works as Marilyn French's *Beyond Power* (1986); Jessie Bernard's *The Female World* (1981), in which lesbians appear to have come into existence only with the advent of the women's liberation movement in the 1970s; Elizabeth Gould Davis's *The First Sex* (1971); Paula Giddings's *When and Where I Enter* (1984), which refers to lesbianism briefly as a phenomenon of the 1970s women's movement; Betty Friedan's *The Feminine Mystique* (1963); Germaine Greer's *The Female Eunuch* (1970); Nancy Chodorow's *The Reproduction of Mothering* (1978); Dorothy Dinnerstein's *The Mermaid and the Minotaur* (1976); Mary Daly's *Beyond God the Father* (1973)[9]; Eva Figes's *Patriarchal Attitudes* (1970); Carol Gilligan's *In a Different Voice* (1982)[10]; Jean Baker Miller's *Toward a New Psychology of Women* (1976); Juliet Mitchell's *Woman's Estate* (1971); Dale Spender's *Women of Ideas* (1982); Claudia Dreifus's *Seizing Our Bodies* (1977), which is a collection by various hands; Betty Roszak's and Theodore Roszak's *Masculine/Feminine* (1969), which is another; June Sochen's *The New Feminism* (1971), which is yet another; Mary Helen Washington's collections of short stories by Black women, *Black-Eyed Susans* (1975) and *Keeping the Faith* (1974); and Michele Wallace's *Black Macho and the Myth of the Superwoman* (1979).[11] Perhaps the most striking absence in modern feminist literature occurs in Carroll Smith-Rosenberg's pioneering essay "The Female World of Love and Ritual" (1975), which makes not the slightest suggestion that the passionately intense relationships between the nineteenth-century women described therein might have any resemblance to relationships we call by such a very pejorative name today. Smith-Rosenberg does not state that these relationships were *not* "lesbian," nor does she distinguish them from ones that were, nor does she deny that eroticism between women did not or might not or could not occur.

More evidence comes from Sheila Jeffreys, who comments unfavorably on many feminist historians' assumption that nineteenth-century women who were passionately and intensely committed to one another must nonetheless have been "devoid of genital expression" solely because they *were* nineteenth-century women and thus had to be sexually repressed.[12] Jeffreys notes that the distinction between the sensual and the erotic, which several writers try to make, "is very difficult to draw." Jeffreys also notes that Smith-Rosenberg's pioneering essay spends a great deal of time "explaining why women might find such friendships necessary . . . she implies that such expression between women needs more explanation than heterosexuality."[13]

I do not believe such absences to be merely coincidental. Whether writers leave the subject out because of their own ignorance, or because they consider it trivial, or because they judge it irrelevant, or because they're afraid of the effect it might have on their audiences, they do leave it out. And when the evidence of a subject's lesbian inclinations or behavior are too obvious to ignore, many of those writers who do bring the subject up also employ tortuous and illogical arguments to "prove" that it either didn't happen or couldn't have happened, and it doesn't really matter anyway. Thus Judith P. Hallett devotes a good many pages and some very involved reasoning to "prove" that Sappho was not a lesbian and that the evidence in her poetry that seems so clear—her invoking Aphrodite to aid her in a love affair with a woman, mourning for lost female lovers, and so on—doesn't "really" mean what it seems to mean.[14] Here are some more examples of what historian Lisa Duggan has dubbed "not-lesbian history":[15]

M. Carey Thomas, first dean of Bryn Mawr College, was a lesbian. The editor of Thomas's letters and journals, Mary Housepian Dobkin, was shocked to discover this. Her reaction was to dismiss Thomas's passionate relationships with women as "inconsequential"—*but also* to present a battery of (quite naive) arguments to prove that Thomas *could not* have been a lesbian: she never stated a wish to be a man, she found the idea of *heterosexual* intercourse repugnant (!), and she expressed a fear that public discussions of lesbianism would make life difficult for women who lived together. Leila J. Rupp (who reports on Dobkin's reaction) also comments on Arthur Schlesinger Jr.'s *New York Times* review of the Eleanor Roosevelt—Lorena Hickok letters in which Schlesinger, using the same illogic as Dobkin, called Eleanor Roosevelt's lesbianism of "stunning inconsequence" *and also* denied that it could possibly exist (an assertion the letters contradict) on the ground that Roosevelt and Lorena Hickok, whose letters span the years 1932–62, were "children of the Victorian age."[16]

The biographer of Lorena Hickok, Doris Faber, first reacted to her discovery of the subjects' passion for one another by wanting to remove the material from public access until the year 2000, wishing it had been destroyed or suppressed, expressing a reluctance to speculate about anyone's "private affairs," *and then* insisting that neither woman could really have been a you-know-what or have done anything about it.[17] Faber also states "the unfairness of using contemporary standards to characterize behavior from a different era" (that of the New Deal, World War II, and the Cold War!) and compared the supposedly platonic affair with E. M. Forster's *Maurice,* a novel she badly misinterprets.[18]

Anna Mary Wells, biographer of Jeannette Marks (president of Mount Holyoke College) and Mary E. Woolley (chairwoman of the English Department), who lived together for years, found similar evidence about her two subjects. Her reaction was to insist that the two women, because they were "Victorians" (here we go again), must therefore have been sexually naive, that they chose—on no evidence—to avoid "physical contact," *and also* that it was "impertinent" to try to discover the exact nature of the relationship. Considering "lesbian" or "homosexual" to be inexact and pejorative terms, Wells preferred what she called the exact and neutral "sexual deviation." When the Marks-Woolley papers were opened and the women's relationship discovered, the papers were immediately reclosed and an alumni meeting called at which some women asked why the papers had not simply been burned.[19]

Then there was the forty-year relationship between Mary Rozet Smith and Jane Addams of Hull House fame, called "spouse surrogates" by historian William O'Neill, who concluded that Addams (because she rejected marriage) never experienced life: "Life . . . eluded her." Blanche Wiesen Cook, whose essay on women's support networks is the one I'm citing here, notes a similar judgment made by Addams's biographer, Allen Davis. " 'It would be easy to misunderstand Addams' relationship with her earlier companion, Ellen Gates Starr,' " Davis writes, as " 'perversion' " because " 'the romantic words and the love letters' can be easily misinterpreted." Davis concludes " 'Whether or not these women were actually lesbians is essentially irrelevant.' " Cook comments:

> We are being told that, since Jane Addams was a conventional lady with pearls, her intense "romantic attachments" to other

women could not possibly be suspected of "perversion." As a
result, the perfectly ordinary nature of women's differing sexual
preferences has been denied expression. . . . Our prejudices are
such that it has been considered less critical—kinder even—to
label a woman "asexual" rather than "lesbian."

Cook's third example, Lillian Wald's biographer, Allen Reznick, states that
Wald " 'accepted female affection, even solicited it.' Then, he concludes,
she was too busy for social relations anyway."[20]

Similar arguments occur in Nancy Sahli's account of nineteenth-century
college women's flirtations with one another; again the author claims both
that the relationships were not sexual *and* that their sexuality or lack of it is
not the point. Noting that women were labeled sexual perverts in the late
nineteenth century in Europe and North America as a way of attacking female solidarity and women's refusal to obey the rules of gender (an acute
and feminist observation with which I emphatically agree), she asked, about
one particular woman who loved women, avoided men, dressed in male
clothing, and wrote "tender love-letters" to women, "Is this really homosexual behavior?" In a comment, I said that yes, it certainly was; Sahli's answer
was to wonder why I was so "concerned" and "eager" for her to "admit that
these 19th-century women were sexually motivated" and then to state
(again!) that contemporary definitions could not be used for past behavior.[21]

Another technique often used in not-lesbian history is the double standard of evidence. Some years ago I wrote an essay on the relation of Willa
Cather's lesbianism to certain anomalies in her fiction and sent it to a feminist journal. It was returned with complaints that I hadn't "proved" Cather's
lesbianism and with two separate statements that it was wrong to make
such "accusations" without proof.

Cather's lack of sexual interest in men, her long and profoundly important relationships with a least two women, her auctorial habit of writing
from a male point of view despite critics' condemnation, her profound depression at the marriage of Isabelle McClung, the first important relationship of her adult life, her dressing as a boy and cutting her hair short in
her teens, her assuming a male name at this time and her relishing male
parts in amateur theatricals, her mannish dress later on, her openly stating
her admiration of female beauty in her high school yearbook—all these
were not enough evidence for my critics. (The essay appeared elsewhere.)[22]

Of course, requiring such absolute proof—photographs perhaps?—for
establishing the heterosexuality of writers would result in most heterosexual
biographees being presumed homosexual, but for reasons that I hope are
obvious, such evidence is never required in the case of heterosexuality. Thus
male lovers are often alleged to have been involved in the lives of women

like Emily Dickinson or Mary E. Wilkins Freeman simply because it's assumed that every woman must have had her heterosexual romance, whether or not real evidence of such a romance exists.[23] The expectation (even by some lesbians and gay men) that lesbians and gay men will be strikingly visible *as such* conspires with the tendency of Human beings to hide behavior that will get them into trouble to reinforce the arranged, social invisibility of homosexuality. Thus Marilyn Young, an artist, describes her undergraduate admiration for a history professor "who shared a house with a woman colleague" and seemed "fulfilled" to her and her friends (this was the 1950s) without noting that such a ménage was very likely a lesbian one. She also states that her parents' fear that she might follow this teacher's example was only a fear that she might become a "spinster." Sometimes it's simply assumed that anyone who would engage in such rare and grotesquely dreadful behavior must be ill. Thus Jessie Bernard quotes without criticism a study by sociologist Robert Stoller, published in 1968, in which Stoller, reporting on three women who passed as men, finds it necessary to say they are "not clinically psychotic," as if such could be expected to be the case.[24]

The denial that lesbianism exists can also take the form of an insistence that women who are erotically attracted to women are nonetheless really in a primary relation to men. That is, they are on strike *against men,* disappointed or hurt *by men,* can't *get a man* (because they are ugly or timid or sexually repressed), or are afraid of the overwhelming nature of their attraction *to men* or are just afraid *of men.*[25] (Theories about male gay sexuality have been equally tortuous and illogical, citing everything from gay men's fear of men, to fear of committing symbolic incest with women, to fear of women, and so on.) Such theories, although they don't make homosexuality invisible, do make it impossible—by attributing to lesbian and gay male behavior every motive except a specifically erotic one.

Another way of expressing uneasiness about the subject while maintaining a liberal stance is to insist that while such experience exists, there is no real difference between it and heterosexual experience. Audre Lorde described just such a reaction to her lesbian love poetry by readers who insist it is identical with their own heterosexual experience because love is "universal." Lorde commented that the universalizing of any experience, particularly one so surrounded with taboo, robs it of its concreteness.[26]

It is also possible, while admitting that lesbianism is a civil rights issue, to deny the matter any other significance. Betty Friedan, who asserted in the early days of the women's liberation movement that lesbians were giving the women's movement a bad name and later changed her opinions markedly, is a good example, as is the whole feminist controversy of the 1970s about "the lavender menace."[27]

It is also possible, while admitting that the topic exists, to deny it rhetorically. Thus in *Coming of Age in Samoa* (1968), the otherwise liberal Margaret Mead states that the adolescent girls she interviewed for the book had equal amounts of lesbian and heterosexual experience, but this fact can be located only in a table at the back of the book; somehow it is never referred to in the text. Mead also never mentions homosexuality, female or male, without calling it "casual," although she states explicitly elsewhere in her text that heterosexuality too is casual for Samoans. Within a page of this assertion (the whole discussion occupies only two pages in the text), the author describes a very noncasual lesbian relationship between two girls whose "casual homosexual practices" accompany "one of the really important friendships in the whole group." Two lines later we read that "these casual homosexual relationships between girls never assumed any long-term importance" (except for the one that wasn't casual because it was really important!). Mead writes of one boy, "a real pervert . . . incapable of normal heterosexual response," whose "homosexual drive was strong enough to goad him into making advances to other boys" who rejected him. Although Mead elsewhere makes it plain that all Samoan men strike Westerners as "feminine" in appearance, she puzzles over this boy's "feminine . . . appearance," finally concluding that he is "*slightly* . . . feminine in appearance," that is, very like all other Samoan men.[28] The sheer illogic of this perverted boy's being both feminine and not feminine in appearance, whose "drives" "goad" him (a term not used of heterosexual activity in the text) and the girls who have a relationship that is simultaneously important and casual do not, I think, need any more comment from me.[29]

It is also possible simply to ignore lesbianism or homosexuality. For example, Sarah Orne Jewett, a nineteenth-century Yankee novelist and short story writer, was one of the many nineteenth-century women who lived in a "Boston marriage" (a woman-woman household) with another woman, Annie Fields, during most of her adult life. A contemporary feminist literary critic, Josephine Donovan, writes:

> Most Jewett scholars have erred . . . by omitting material or by ignoring the significance of her relationship with women. . . . Annie Fields herself . . . [did so] in her edition of the Jewett letters published in 1911. The decision to edit out intimate material was made, however, only at the urging of Mark Anthony DeWolfe Howe, an eminent but genteel Boston scholar, who later put forth a heavily edited version of Fields' journals. . . . According to Howe's daughter Helen . . . [Howe] particularly urged her to delete nicknames, an obvious sign of inti-

macy, arguing that otherwise "all sorts of people [will read] them wrong."

What people might have "read wrong" can be suggested by the following bit of poetry Jewett wrote to another woman. Donovan notes that Jewett's poems "have been available to researchers for more than forty years; none has chosen to pay attention." She then quotes the following:

> Do you remember, darling,
> A year ago today
> When we gave ourselves to each other
> Before you went away
> At the end of that pleasant summer weather
> Which we had spent by the sea together?[30]

Micaela di Leonardo lists other well-known nineteenth-century and twentieth-century women who formed "Boston marriages:" Mary Wilkins Freeman, Willa Cather, M. Cary Thomas (dean and then president of Bryn Mawr), Mary Woolley and Jeannette Marks (a couple), Jane Addams, and finally, Alice James, sister of the more famous Henry.[31]

To drive home the invisibility of the lesbian—which cannot be unconnected with other matters of social consequence—here is one last account of a more recent public figure whose feminism and lesbianism were both rendered invisible by the forces around her, both during her lifetime and after her tragically early death.[32]

Famous in the early 1960s, she planned to write a play about an African woman returning to her tribal village for her mother's funeral. Later the characters of the daughter and mother were transformed into an intellectual, Europeanized African man and his dead warrior father. She planned another play the same year, which was to be called *The Sign in Jenny Reed's Window*. Its protagonist she also transformed into a man. She noted her desire to write a full-length drama about Mary Wollstonecraft, wrote an essay in 1957 in which she said that *The Second Sex* "may well be the most important work of this century," and addressed such feminist topics as the politics of housework, pornography, dress and adornment, and the socialist position on women's status. In 1961 she wrote an essay that challenged psychoanalytic theories about women and another that attacked the view that women are responsible for provoking woman-battering. Later she criticized Strindberg for his woman-hating "propaganda," celebrated Black women's leadership in the civil rights struggle, declared in an interview that Black women were doubly oppressed as Blacks and as women and therefore doubly militant, and in a letter to that early, pioneering lesbian publication *The Ladder*, described the persecution facing the "married woman who would prefer emotional-physical relationships with other women" and who dared not leave her husband to form a union with another woman, especially since marriage was the way she earned her living.[33]

She was Lorraine Hansberry.

But of course she wasn't a lesbian. She was merely broad-minded.[34]

She couldn't have been a lesbian. She was married. (Like Virginia Woolf.)

Happily married. (So was Woolf. And Vita Sackville-West.)

You haven't proved it. (No comment.)

But she had children. (So did Audre Lorde, and so does Adrienne Rich.)

She didn't do anything about it, so she wasn't. (Norman Mailer has somewhere used this astonishing argument about D. H. Lawrence. It's seldom argued that because somebody wanted to Do It with a member of the other sex but didn't, he or she *wasn't heterosexual.*)

She couldn't have been a lesbian because she was such a good person. (I've had this argument applied to myself and been told of it by acquaintances whose declarations about their sexual preference were not believed either.)[35]

Unfortunately the prohibition against homosexuality is further linked (as in so many taboos) with a prohibition against discussing or knowing anything about the subject. Like J. Edgar Hoover's view of communism—all any good American needs to know is that it's evil—what we all learn about homosexuality isn't merely that it's bad but that we mustn't know anything about it, that asking for information is in and of itself depraved and culpable behavior, and that everybody knows all about the subject anyway. As with the "horrible and detestable crimes against nature" that still populate some states' law books, the anxiety about knowledge converges with the anxiety about the subject itself to produce a double taboo. The double injunction (against doing *and* knowing) results in assumptions that are vague, powerful, *and unlocatable,* so that the popular beliefs hiding behind the taboo in question become extremely difficult to challenge. Because of this peculiarly contentless anxiety that surrounds the subject, it becomes possible for well-meaning people to admit that homosexuality is neither bad, grotesque, nor evil—and *still* resist any attempt to identify it, talk about it, or attribute it to anyone, especially people they consider worthy of admiration. I believe much of the anxiety about homosexuality today is due to the peculiar nature of the doubly negative injunction directed against the subject. No matter, for example, what a gay speaker says, heterosexual audiences are sure that he or she is hiding something dreadful, although none of them has any clear (or even a common) idea of what that something is. When merely approaching a subject produces ever-increasing anxiety because of the taboo against knowing or discussing the topic, this anxiety is going to be attributed to the subject itself, and then the subject becomes not only forbidden behavior but the ostensible cause of an anxiety so pervasive and un-challengeable that one can easily believe that one's being confronted with absolute evil.[36] It's not the same with events that are clear *and clearly known,* even when they are upsetting, like the terrible things done to Human beings in the German death camps of World War II. These can be heart-wrenching, tragic, and sickening, but they don't carry the same atmosphere of the final, mind-blasting, unspeakable (but totally unimaginable) *secret* of ultimate evil. The evil there may be ultimate, all right, but it's all too specific and too plain.

Injunctions against knowing produce a situation in which no information can change people's minds, precisely because the real nature of the taboo is not being challenged. No matter how one argues that gay people do not molest children, do not attempt to "convert" adolescents, do not plot to take over the world, do not have special privileges, and are not the only people spreading AIDS,[37] somehow the impression remains that the real horror of homosexuality is not being addressed. Nor is this merely a matter or ignorance and naiveté: note please that the little woman (or man) who isn't there is not merely invisible. She is also punished.[38]

One of the ways she is punished, of course, is by having invisibility forced upon her. It's not happy or comfortable to be forced to lie, forced to remain silent about most of your personal life, forced to invent stories about an "acceptable" life so people won't wonder about you, forced (sometimes) to join in the baiting of others like yourself. "Silence is like starvation," says Cherríe Moraga, and Adrienne Rich calls invisibility "a dangerous and pain-ful condition." She describes the sensation of seeing the world described by those in authority—and not seeing oneself in it—as "psychic disequilib-rium, as if you looked into a mirror and saw nothing."[39]

For those who avoid expressing, or sometimes even recognizing, their erotic feelings until later in life, there is another punishment: the freezing of eroticism, the experiencing of much in one's life as somehow unreal, the confusion about what one really thinks and feels (see Cynthia Rich's article "Reflections on Eroticism"[40]), and the submission to what is experienced as a kind of rape, despite the good intentions of the man or men involved. Thus Adrienne Rich writes, "I do not know / if sex is an illusion / I do not know / who I was when I did those things / or who I said I was / Or whether I willed to feel / what I had read about / or who in fact was there with me."[41] Cynthia Rich calls the process "to grow up straightened" and com-ments on the distortion of feeling it produces.[42] Artist Betsy Damon de-scribes the way erotic energy is linked to the rest of Human personality and notes the effect of internalized homophobia on creativity, stating:

Do not for a minute imagine that art has to be explicit about sex or anything so simplistic. . . . A person must be able to put the full force of herself behind her work [which is prevented by] . . . fear of being seen as sexual, fear of the audience, fear of offending heterosexual friends, fear of retribution.[43]

Also speaking of internalized homophobia, Cherríe Moraga writes of her fears while growing up "that giving in to such desires would find me shot-up with bullets or drugs in a gutter somewhere."[44] And here is Jane Rule, describing a "phone call from a younger friend who says, 'My lover, ever since a political fight about tenure at her university eighteen months ago, has vomited every time we have made love, which has been no more than once every two months.' " Rule adds, about her own earlier life, "My lovers . . . returned to husbands, the church, celibate scholarship. . . . I slept, drank, masturbated through days to avoid writing and believed my will to defy these escapes and get back to work would finally kill me. It's not simply a story of the terrible fifties. I hear it all around me now."[45] I can recall a colleague who spoke glowingly of her closest friends, who'd known her from childhood—and added that of course she'd never told them she was a lesbian as they "wouldn't understand."[46] I have another colleague who couldn't say the word "lesbian" without dropping her voice to a whisper, even in her own home, even when the only people present were lesbians.

Such reactions may appear extreme, but here are some reports from those who eventually decided not to remain invisible: Barbara Smith burned all her journals in the second year of her marriage "because . . . I had no safe place for them away from my husband." Lesbians, even within feminist institutions like battered-women's shelters and women's studies programs, are fired if they're open or warned to stay hidden if they're not. Cherríe Moraga writes of fighting with her lover late at night in whispers "while the Latina who lives below us . . . is pounding on the ceiling. . . . My lover says, 'We are two women. We have no right to care so much about each other that the pain could keep us up.' 'These women—or *whatever* they are,' she [the woman one floor down] describes us to the lady next door the next morning." Julia Penelope describes the ostracism visited on her in her adolescence because of her "obviousness," her lack of "daintiness," and her unfeminine body type. Later came the violence of the police raids on gay bars that accompanied every election, the isolation and exhaustion of constantly having to cope with such unpredictable violence, the constant stares from people in the street, the condescension visited on her by most heterosexual feminists in the women's movement, and the constant risk of job, family ties, physical safety, housing, and for some even their sanity.[47]

Barbara Smith, describing a break-in and robbery in her and her lover's apartment, reports that the robber, knowing she was Black and a lesbian, painted obscenities on her walls which the two women scoured off—a detail they didn't report to the police, although they were terrified that the burglar might return.[48]

Jill Johnston's *Lesbian Nation* (1973) contains a long, vivid account of the effect lesbian invisibility had on her life and others' lives. It describes a social milieu—the sophisticated art life of Manhattan in the 1950s—in which lesbians were invisible *and* in which young heterosexual men felt it was their duty to break up any relationship between women that even seemed lesbian. Avoiding such men spelled professional disaster for any artist or writer, both of which Johnston was. She also describes many lesbian women's insistence that they were not "really" lesbian but only attracted to the right "person," an assumption that left such women's love relationships undefended against the enormous social advantages of a heterosexual pairing (to which one of the partners would often defect). She sums up the choices open to most lesbians before the gay rights movement: "an embittered angry bar dyke; a eunuch by default; or a partner in a fearfully tenacious dependent isolated remote declassé illegal and paranoid marriage. Or any sequential or simultaneous combination of these impossibilities."[49]

Of the lesbians I've known personally during the last twenty-five years, one was almost raped in her teens to "convert" her (the logic behind this sort of activity escapes both of us—convert her to what?); another had bricks smashed through the windows of her car; a third has been beaten up three times on the streets of supposedly tolerant San Francisco (for "looking lesbian"); a fourth, caught by a police raid in a gay bar at fifteen and disowned by her family, was committed to the back ward of a state mental hospital; a fifth, after a student in her high school declared (on no evidence) that she was a lesbian, was driven from both the job she'd had for twenty years and a house she had just bought with her lover of eighteen years, not through any official process but from constant harassment. A strong-willed friend of mine, who somewhere found the stubbornness to declare herself a lesbian at age eleven and stick to it, was constantly told by her family that she'd end up in the gutter and experienced constant pressure to date and marry from parents and therapists. Another friend, during the feminist 1970s, received a declaration of love from her female boss with terror—because she was terrified to think her lesbianism "showed"—and bolted out of the office. Her boss, terrified of disclosure, fired her. A young woman I know has been disowned by her family for being a lesbian, and her father has destroyed heirlooms she inherited from her mother and her snapshot albums and journals, so that every record of her childhood and adolescence is now lost to her. Then there was the love relationship between two lesbian friends of mine in the 1970s that broke up because of their isolation—there was no one to whom to reveal the stresses and strains, the quarrels and difficulties, inevitable in any pairing. The necessity for secrecy (they lived in a small town) kept them isolated, the isolation kept them from risking their relationship in open conflict, and the lack of open conflict eventually ruined the relationship. One of them was also a young mother, who carefully hid all her lesbian posters, books, and records each time her parents visited, in quite realistic fear of a custody battle. (Her mother and father had earlier threatened to commit her to a mental hospital when she'd dated a Black man in her teens.) I myself remember a convergence of fear, confusion, and an almost absolute lack of information, to the point that while I longed to buy the pulp lesbian novels I constantly saw at the bookstore near my home, I didn't dare because if I had, I might get so—well, so *something*—that I would go out and do something lesbian and that would be dreadful because I wasn't, you see.

I'm White. Barbara Smith describes both similar and dissimilar contradictions in Black lesbians' lives. Their community is homophobic, and "heterosexual privilege is usually the only privilege that Black women have." She adds, "even at this moment I am not convinced that one can write explicitly as a Black lesbian and live to tell about it."[50]

And then, while writing this chapter, I decided to relax with feminist news from around the world, in particular the burgeoning of feminists and feminism in so many different places. And there in the introduction to *Sisterhood Is Global* was the news that in Spain, India, and Iran, "floggings and executions of same-sex lovers are public events."[51]

Now that's not only god-awful, it's silly. A middle-aged woman who's lived eighteen quiet years with her lover; a teenager nuts about women and glowing at the sight of her first lesbian bar; another whom I know to be kind and concerned and full of bravery and goodwill; a middle-aged academic (myself) who spends most of her time typing and checking footnotes, surely an innocent occupation; a tiny, beautiful poet with sad, haunted eyes; a young mother whose little girl has inherited her pointed elfin nose and big ears; a twenty-five-year-old terrified she'll lose the job she's so proud of; a thirtyish novelist with a bravura taste in earrings; and all the other people I've been quoting in this chapter—how can we possibly be as dangerous as that?

On the other hand, maybe they're right. Maybe there *is* an unspoken horror connected with homosexuality, one that largely remains unaddressed by the gay rights movement. But I would maintain that it has nothing to do with lesbians and gay men. It's a horror of quite other dimensions, located in quite another social area.

And maybe it is this horror that makes us *really dangerous,* after all.

NOTES

1. Note how fast ordinary words and phrases become sexual puns when the talk is about lesbians or simply women in general. Early women's liberation speakers found that common New Left phrases like "we shall take to the streets," harmless when applied to students, men, workers, or "people," elicited ridicule when used in a feminist context to describe women. The sexualization of much of the English language when applied to women is described by Dale Spender in *Man-Made Language* (London: Routledge and Kegan Paul, 1980).

2. Gay men, while subject to the same kind of treatment, have always been more visible, partly because of men's greater freedom, mobility, and importance in patriarchal societies. As many lesbians have pointed out, gay men's more open persecution *as gay* is certainly balanced by lesbians' oppression *as women*. See Del Martin and Phyllis Lyon, *Lesbian/Woman* (New York: Glide Publications, 1972).

3. Lillian Faderman, *Surpassing the Love of Men: Romantic Friendship and Love between Women from the Renaissance to the Present* (New York: Morrow, 1981), 326.

4. Susan Cavin, *Lesbian Origins* (San Francisco: Ism Press, 1985), 258, 258–60.

5. Paula Gunn Allen, "Lesbians in American Indian Cultures," *Conditions* 7 (1981), 67.

6. Evelyn Torton Beck, ed., *Nice Jewish Girls: A Lesbian Anthology* (Watertown, MA: Persephone Press, 1982), xiii.

7. Maureen Brady and Judith McDaniel, "Lesbians in the Mainstream: Images of Lesbians in Recent Commercial Fiction," *Conditions* 6 (1980), 102.

8. Cavin, *Lesbian*, 130, 164.

9. Her later work is another matter entirely.

10. One might argue that the topic is irrelevant to Gilligan's conclusions, yet a comparison of heterosexual and homosexual women's ethics (like that of homosexual and heterosexual men) might have been as illuminating as a breakdown along lines of class, color, or age. Gilligan did none of these.

11. My memory of a few of these may not be entirely accurate. Nonetheless, I believe my conclusion to be correct in the main. Cheryl Clarke points out the omission of lesbian fiction from Washington's anthologies and notes that although Washington states her indebtedness to the work of Adrienne Rich and Barbara Smith in the introduction to *Midnight Birds,* she doesn't mention their openly declared lesbianism or use fiction by Smith or Lorde (in Barbara Smith, ed., *Home Girls: A Black Feminist Anthology* [New York: Kitchen Table Women of Color Press, 1983], 204). In Bernard there is a long and elaborate discussion of legal, heterosexual marriage but no indication that unions of any other kind exist. Bernard cites a 1978 study that lists a group of marital options presented to a group of college students for comment: "egalitarian marriage, five-year evaluation and renewal of marriage, long-term cohabitation, traditional marriage, child-free marriage with role reversal,

commune with shared sex, consensual extramarital sex, serial monogamy, spouse swapping, group marriage" (Jesse Bernard, *The Female World* [New York: Free Press, 1981], 159). Two striking omissions are celibate unions and homosexual ones. That is, marriage is assumed not only to be primarily about sex but about only one kind of sex. Bernard doesn't comment on these omissions.

12. Ignorance can have quite a different effect. Contemporary accounts of lesbian experience stress that while girls are warned about sex with boys, sometimes nobody warns them about sex with girls and that therefore sex with girls can be—for some girls—early, natural, and unrepressed. I have heard one such personal account; see also Rosemary Curb and Nancy Manahan, eds., *Lesbian Nuns: Breaking Silence* (Tallahassee: Naiad Press, 1985). Naiveté can be a protection. It's worth noting also that those who give accounts of nineteenth-century women as "only" kissing and embracing seem totally unaware of the sexual practice of "tribadism," which, in nineteenth-century France, at least, was thought to be such a characteristic lesbian sexual technique that it gave lesbianism its name. It is my opinion that such denials also underestimate the ingenuities of ignorance. I remember a young heterosexual friend of mine saying earnestly to me when we were both fifteen about her newly enjoyed experience, "It can't be what they warned me about. It feels too nice." The historians whose work I'm describing seem unaware of these possibilities.

13. Sheila Jeffreys, *The Spinster and Her Enemies: Feminism and Sexuality, 1880–1930* (London: Pandora, 1985), 104, 103.

14. Judith P. Hallett, "Sappho and Her Social Context: Sense and Sensuality," *Signs* 4:3 (1979), 447–64. *Signs* also provided a refutation by Eva Stehle Stigers that avoided either explaining away the obvious *or* assuming that poetry is always literally autobiographical. Of Sappho's supposed promiscuity, Stigers writes, "The same reasons . . . would, if applied to Emily Dickinson, conclude that she had died frequently" (*Signs* 4:3 [1979], 467).

15. In Jonathan Katz, *Gay/Lesbian Almanac: A New Documentary* (New York: Harper and Row, 1983), 10.

16. Leila J. Rupp, "Imagine My Surprise: Women's Relationships in Historical Perspective," *Frontiers* V:3 (1981), 61–70.

17. Such reluctance to handle historical figures' private lives almost never applies to heterosexual behavior. Biographers assume its importance to their subject and display little reluctance to mention it.

18. The novel does depict, as she says, a "pure [nongenital] affair" between two men but condemns it as exploitative, dishonest, and selfish on the part of the "pure" partner and has the other partner (its protagonist) leave for a thoroughly carnal love affair with another and better man, after emphatically stating his opinion of the "pure affair." Forster also emphasizes his hero's salvation from the conventional snobbishness, ignorance, and dishonest conventionality of his class precisely through the marginality forced on him by his homosexuality. Faber doesn't mention either theme.

19. Katz, *Gay/Lesbian,* 6; Rupp, "Imagine," 61–70. Blanche Wiesen Cook reports others suggested that "tales of lesbianism might decrease enrollment" to which an older alumna replied, "That's ridiculous! They worried about that when they agreed to end compulsory chapel" ("Female Support Networks and Political Activism: Lillian Wald, Crystal Eastman, Emma Goldman, *Chrysalis* 3 [1977], 46).

20. Cook, "Female Support," 46–47.

21. Nancy Sahli, "Smashing: Women's Relations Before the Fall," *Chrysalis* 8 (1979), 18; comment by Joanna Russ and reply by Sahli, *Chrysalis* 9 (1979), 6–7. The assertion that contemporary definitions cannot be used for past behavior seldom occurs when historians call fifteenth-century peasant revolts "class struggles" (though surely the term "class struggle" had not yet been invented) or, to use a less political example, when literary critics apply modern literary terms like "irony" to Chaucer's work. (Nor do we write about Chaucer in Middle English.) I believe lesbian-baiting to be at work here. As for Sahli's essay, I believe the author was caught between her accurate and very important feminist perception that the doctors of the 1880s and 1890s were attaching a "pejorative label . . . to behavior they found threatening" and the continuing power of the label "lesbian" to intimidate even feminists (or perhaps especially feminists).

22. At one college class, she leaned around the door, visible from the waist up, and the class assumed her to be a man; then she entered and proved to be a skirted being. The class laughed. During her college career she was befriended and "civilized" by a faculty couple who persuaded her to dress and behave in a more feminine manner (Monika Kehoe, ed., *Historical, Literary, and Erotic Aspects of Lesbianism* [New York: Haworth Press, 1986], 78).

23. Dolores Klaich points out that the 200 B.C.E. sculpture of two women in a tender embrace, picked by herself as the frontispiece for her book, *Woman + Woman,* was named (by the curators of the British Museum) "Women Gossiping" (Klaich, *Woman + Woman: Attitudes toward Lesbianism* [New York: Simon and Schuster, 1974], 9). Such sexist and heterosexist censoring of reality omits from possibility not only eroticism between women but even the possibility of women's feeling affection for one another and the possibility of female solidarity.

24. Sara Ruddick and Pamela Daniels, eds., *Working It Out: 23 Women Writers, Artists, Scientists, and Scholars Talk about Their Lives and Work* (New York: Pantheon, 1977), 219; Bernard, *Female World,* 221. Lesbian and gay people constantly experience such toe-stubbings. In the mid-1970s at an academic gathering late in the evening, only our host, myself, and two gay male professors were left, everyone else having gone home. One of my fellow guests spoke of his research on Gide and Gide's homosexuality, the other of Forster and his research on Forster's gayness, and I finally mentioned Emily Dickinson and her falling in love with various women. (The discussion was actually a spontaneous attempt to educate the host and see how much of our talk he would accept; gay people often "test" straight ones this way, while the latter are—almost always—unaware that such things are happening.) Our

host, who had nodded seriously through the men's accounts, found mine harder to believe. He removed his pipe from his mouth and said earnestly, "Oh, I don't think so." There was a glance of wordless communication between the rest of us. Our host, apparently unaware of it, of the commonness of homosexuals in literature and life (and the fact that there were three of them in his living room at that very moment), put his pipe back in his mouth and smoked placidly on. To be lesbian or gay is often to receive or send messages, abundantly clear to oneself and other gay persons, that are nonetheless totally opaque to the otherwise intelligent and reasonable heterosexual people in the same environment. Years ago at Cornell University, Allen Ginsberg recited "Walt Whitman at the Supermarket." (Whitman was cruising a stock boy.) A handful of men in the audience laughed; at the time I (and others) only wondered mildly what on earth was going on. The perceptions of oppressed groups is always sharper than that of their oppressors. I recall, for example, my Polish-Jewish grandmother exclaiming with ritual contempt, *"Goyische kopf!"* which means literally "Gentile head" and figuratively "Gentile stupidity."

25. Spender quotes Dora Russell, who finds lesbianism "reactionary" (i.e., reactive), "a response to male dominance, to an absence of power." Spender calls it a "choice," whereupon Russell says, "Aha . . . it's a strike. Now that I can understand" (Dale Spender, *There's Always Been a Women's Movement This Century* [London: Pandora, 1983], 116). Nope. The idea that women who relate primarily to other women are nonetheless really relating to men is on a par with all the other contradictions in popular belief about lesbians and gay men. On the one hand, homosexuality is exceedingly rare; on the other hand, it is also very common *and* it is increasing to a frightening extent. On the one hand, homosexuality is naturally repugnant to almost everyone and revolts all right-thinking people; on the other hand, it is also fearfully attractive, especially to the young, who will adopt it in a minute if given half a chance. On the one hand, women can truly be satisfied emotionally and physically only by men and the penis; on the other hand, if exposed to the slightest feminist or pro-lesbian messages, women will instantly refuse to marry, refuse to have children, and refuse to have anything to do with the very men to whom they are so naturally, inevitably, and overwhelmingly attracted. On the one hand, homosexuality is unnatural; on the other hand, if it isn't punished and suppressed, everyone will become homosexual. And so on.

26. In Mari Evans, ed., *Black Women Writers (1950–1980): A Critical Evaluation* (Garden City, NY: Anchor, 1984), 264. It's common for Human beings to assert that other people and their experiences are either just like one's own *or* totally different from one's own. Taking both positions alternately, or even simultaneously, is quite common. It takes time, experience, and humility, as well as pressure from the outside and a willingness to undergo some anxiety without avoiding the matter altogether, to learn the concrete and specific differences and likenesses that really exist between people or groups of people. Some recent attempts by gay people to win acceptance have taken the line "We are just like you except in bed." This is true

and false. It is equally true, and equally false, to say "We are like you in bed but nowhere else." The differences, including possible differences in erotic behavior, are concrete, like all differences between groups. I suspect that the first attempt by a majority to understand a minority or cultural minority is to insist that "they" are just like "us," that they must be treated identically with us, and that it's wrong and embarrassing to even notice or discuss any of the real differences that do exist. This disastrous misunderstanding omits far and away the most enormous difference between the two groups—oppression itself, with all its consequences. My White students, asked to deal with race, have often exhibited just such behavior, i.e., the whole area makes them so uncomfortable that they insist it doesn't exist.

27. I have not met in feminist circles (and doubt that anyone ever will) the contemporary assertion that gays, far from being persecuted, are receiving preferential treatment. The assertion appears to be a speciality of the Right, on a par with other contemporary Big Lies: that Christian White men are the most discriminated-against group in the United States, that the Holocaust never happened, that Christmas is a national holiday, and that ketchup (as ex-president Reagan assured us) is a vegetable. A few years ago a White male student in one of my writing classes told me that White men had fewer privileges than anyone in the United States. I asked him how he knew this and received the enlightening reply, "My father told me." (Teaching has its compensations.)

28. Margaret Mead, *Coming of Age in Samoa: A Psychological Study of Primitive Youth for Western Civilization* (New York: Laurel, 1968), 209, 114. Italics added.

29. I do *not* want to add ammunition to the attacks on Mead by Derek Freeman, whose book *Margaret Mead and Samoa: The Making and Unmaking of an Anthropological Myth* (1983) is called "a personal attack on Mead" by Bonnie A. Nardi and an attack on the "female liberation" of which she has long been a symbol (Nardi, "The Height of Her Powers: Margaret Mead's Samoa," *Feminist Studies* 10:2 [1984], 323–37). Rather I want to indicate the limits of that liberation at the time of the publication of Mead's *Coming of Age in Samoa* and the intellectual confusion resulting from those limits. Virginia Yans-McLaughlin also comments on Freeman's book, seeing in it "a much-needed Aesopian fable to justify belt tightening, budget cuts in federal and university support for the 'soft' sciences' and the humanities and replacement of the liberal philosophy of abundance and permissiveness with classical Republican virtues of morals, hard work, and authority." Yans-McLaughlin notes that media treatment of the book included "A dramatic front-page *New York Times* article (31 January 1983) . . . a flurry of follow-ups in *Time, Newsweek,* and *Science.*" The language used included "towering errors" of twentieth-century science, "ideological misrepresentation," and "wholesale self-deception." In short, there was a fuss. Some scholars, she adds, "merely wondered why anyone would want to review the long-deceased nature/nurture controversy or attack a fifty-year-old book" (Virginia Yans-McLaughlin, "Comment on the Freeman/Mead Controversy," *Signs* [10:3], 1985). Such is not my intention.

30. Josephine Donovan, "The Unpublished Love Poems of Sarah Orne Jewett," *Frontiers* IV:3 (1979), 27, 28.

31. Micaela di Leonardo, "Warrior Virgins and Boston Marriages: Spinsterhood in History and Culture," *Feminist Issues* 5:2 (1985), 51.

32. One of these forces was her husband's posthumous editing of her work. Like Leonard Woolf, who, Jane Marcus tells us, did not mention certain of his wife's radical and feminist writings (Marcus, "Art and Anger," *Feminist Studies* 4 [1978], 81), his intention may well have been to shield his wife's reputation—a telling comment on what would have happened to Hansberry's reputation had some of this material become public in the 1950s or 1960s.

33. Adrienne Rich, *Blood, Bread, and Poetry: Selected Prose, 1979–1985* (New York: Norton, 1986), 15–19, 59.

34. A friend of mine, having read my fantasy-for-children-of-all-ages, *Kittatinny,* in which a young woman goes off with a woman lover at the end of the book, was surprised when I told her I was a lesbian. She said she had believed I was merely broad-minded. Heterosexual writers who try to do justice to a nonbigoted view of homosexuality in their books do exist—and such activity is praiseworthy—but assuming that someone who writes personally of lesbianism is *not* a lesbian coincides too well with the all-too-prevalent view that nobody is a lesbian, or nobody admirable is a lesbian, or nobody is "really" a lesbian.

35. This sort of thing can happen, even more grotesquely, in the area of color. A light-skinned Black scholar I know once described, enraged, how a White male colleague at a conference she attended refused to believe her statement of her color. He said, "You're just saying that." In somewhat similar fashion, people whose disabilities are not immediately spottable (like mine) often meet folks who refuse to believe we're disabled, while people whose disabilities are perceptible often have to deal with folks who refuse to believe they're Human. See Jo Campling, ed., *Images of Ourselves: Women with Disabilities Talking* (London: Routledge and Kegan Paul, 1981); Susan Hannaford, *Living Outside Inside: A Disabled Woman's Experience—Towards a Social and Political Perspective* (Berkeley: Canterbury Press, 1985); and especially Susan E. Browne, Debra Connors, and Nanci Stern, eds., *With the Power of Each Breath: A Disabled Women's Anthology* (Pittsburgh: Cleis Press, 1985), for pioneering material by women who have disabilities.

36. I remember my own shock in my early thirties when two academic women I admired told me they were lovers. Eventually, my intense and totally nonspecific fear of some terrible thing they were likely to do, either to me or in front of me or *something,* ebbed, and I could perceive that no such horrid shock was going to happen because nothing erotic they could do could possibly be that terrible. In fact, my anxiety had no imaginable object. Similarly, a gay group I used to attend met in the basement of a Unitarian church. One night our nongay sponsor from the church met with us for twenty minutes; although he had waged a campaign against some of his colleagues for our use of the room, he nonetheless trembled and sweated

so badly that all of us were made very uncomfortable by our own awareness of his fear. Being gay can also coexist perfectly well with a terror of gayness and gay people. I still remember the forty-five minutes I spent in my car outside my first gay bar (it was women's night), too frightened, finally, to go in.

37. The unreason of these contentions has certainly been commented on by the gay rights movement. I have even seen letters to gay newspapers in which lesbians are lumped together with gay men as spreading AIDS to the "general population," despite the fact that (as of this writing) lesbians are the lowest risk group in the United States for the disease except for nuns. A few years ago our local gay press carried a letter from a woman who accused lesbians of "standing by your men," i.e., defending gay men from the charge of having infected the "general population" with AIDS. It was, apparently, impossible for the writer to understand clearly that we don't "have" men in this sense and that not having a man is precisely what being a lesbian is all about. (I have put "general population" in quotation marks above since using the phrase implies that gay men or lesbians are not part of the general population of this country, an obvious impossibility. What the letter writer meant—or should mean— is "the rest of the population." I consider this choice of phrase no accident; they do indeed think of us as not part of the population of this country.)

38. The invisibility can be breached to make scandalous accusations, of course. Thus advance coverage of a feminist conference in Hartford, Connecticut, by the *Hartford Courant* "was headlined 'Lesbian Housing for Women's Conference at UConn' and focused entirely on the arrangement for a 'lesbian section' of the dormitory. . . . Heavy emphasis was laid on alleged difficulties between lesbians and heterosexual women last year in Bloomington" (Rich, *Blood*, 76). What the news-paper account did not mention was the subject of the conference, which was racism. Smearing feminism by calling it "lesbian" or "only lesbian" is common; here (as I take it) the *Courant* both sensationalized and trivialized the conference and erased the subversiveness of its very explosive and dangerous subject, U.S. racism.

39. Cherríe Moraga, *Loving in the War Years* (Boston: South End Press, 1983), 52; Rich, *Blood*, 189. European fantasy and folktales (and the literary works derived therefrom) use the image of not having a reflection as a sign that one has lost one's soul. What is not present in a situation, a dialogue, an activity, or a mirror can convey a very strong social message. For the way in which people in the United States learn such messages about being gay, see Don Clark, *Living Gay* (Millbrae, CA: Celestial Arts, 1977).

40. Cynthia Rich, "Reflections on Eroticism," *Sinister Wisdom* 15 (1980), 59–63.

41. In Gloria Joseph and Jill Lewis, *Common Differences: Conflicts in Black and White Feminist Perspectives* (New York: Anchor, 1981), 256.

42. Rich, "Reflections," 60.

43. Betsy Damon, "From the Lesbian Issue Collective," *Heresies* 1 (1977), 2.

44. Moraga, *Loving*, 122.

45. Jane Rule, "Homophobia and Romantic Love," *Conditions* 3 (1978), 35, 36.

46. This kind of confused double-think happens all the time. Julia Penelope [Stanley] and Susan J. Wolfe coedited a collection of lesbian writing called *The Coming Out Stories* (1980). The book consisted of autobiographical essays by forty-one contributors; nineteen of these present evidence of real confusion—and this from women who later clearly identified themselves as lesbian. Either lesbians "don't exist"—so how can I be one?—or we/I can't "really" be lesbians, or "really" sexual, or sex between women isn't "real sex." With perhaps one exception, all the contributors describe either social pressure not to be lesbian or ignorance and social censorship so pervasive as to amount to the same thing. An older gay man in a gay church group I was in once boasted of his ability to get along with his straight friends, adding that "of course" they didn't know he was gay. Such friendships are illusions unless the straight friends (as sometimes happens) know the gay friend's "secret" perfectly well but don't reveal that they know, which makes yet another secret between them. Then there are friendships in which the straight friends (or relatives) tolerate the other person's gayness as long as they don't have to acknowledge it, talk about it, or face it. The ways of bigotry are many.

47. Smith, *Home Girls,* 171; Rich, *Blood,* 24; Moraga, *Loving,* 137; Julia Penelope, "The Mystery of Lesbians," *Lesbian Ethics* 1:1 (1984), 7–33, and "The Mystery of Lesbians: II," *Lesbian Ethics* 1:2 (1985), 26–67.

48. Smith, *Home Girls,* xlvi, xlvi–lvii.

49. Jill Johnston, *Lesbian Nation: The Feminist Solution* (New York: Simon and Schuster, 1973), 157.

50. Barbara Smith, *Toward a Black Feminist Criticism* (Brooklyn, NY: Out and Out Books, 1980), 16.

51. Robin Morgan, ed., *Sisterhood Is Global: The International Women's Movement Anthology* (New York: Anchor, 1984), 14.

S I X

I THEE WED, SO WATCH IT:
THE WOMAN JOB

To tell you why lesbians are so evil and dangerous, I must tell you something you may find surprising. Once upon a time, scarcely a century ago, there were no lesbians.

Of course there were women in North America and Europe (and elsewhere, actually) who fell in love with women, women who lusted after women, women who lived together in "Boston marriages," developed crushes (they called them "smashes") on other women,[1] walked in public with their arms around each other's waists, exchanged rings, wrote each other love letters, and so on. Such relationships were publicly recognized and considered perfectly all right. They were irrelevant to marriage (so Smith-Rosenberg describes her nineteenth-century American examples) because for most women in Europe and North America in the eighteenth and nineteenth centuries, marriage was an economic and social necessity. In fact, it was precisely this disconnection of marriage from personal female preference that made women's love for one another unthreatening and thus provided the freedom for what the eighteenth and nineteenth centuries called "romantic friendships" between women.[2]

That is, women might feel for one another whatever they liked, but without civil rights, social freedom, and the access to a living wage, these feelings were not a serious threat to marriage and hence not a threat to the status quo supported by it. When women (or at least ladies) were assumed to be "pure"—that is, not capable of carnal lust—such attachments between them were assumed to be nongenital also and hence not an infringement on male prerogative. But then something happened. Near the end of the nineteenth century, decades of feminist effort in England, Europe, and North America finally produced the possibility of middle-class women entering the professions and trades in comparatively large numbers,[3] access to higher education for the wives and daughters of educated men, social tolerance for women living alone without men, and even the claims of some such women to motherhood without husbands.[4] The result of all this activity was severe social dislocation, widespread female agitation for political and economic rights, much talk about "the new woman," and a considerable threat to those whose interests lay in keeping women in their place. To give just one example, so passionate was the fight for the vote in England that its advocates often called it merely "the Cause" and gave to it an enormous amount of work and money. Contributions to the Women's Social and Political Union alone, the party of the Pankhursts, rose from £3,000 in 1906–7 to £32,000 in 1909–10. This was from a constituency rarely wealthy in its own right or able to earn anything comparable to what was earned by its male counterparts in the same class. One WSPU demonstration in Hyde Park numbered 250,000 people.[5] England and the United States in this period also saw the highest proportion of never-married women in the history of both countries. Their numbers declined swiftly after World War I and were matched again only in the United States from the mid-1960s to the mid-1970s.[6] For those whose domestic or public interests lay in maintaining the status quo, it was necessary to find new ways to bind women to the service of men in general and to conventional marriage in particular, thus ensuring for the class of men sexual access to the class of women and access to the domestic, emotional, and badly underpaid (or unpaid) labor of that class. Feminists during this era were protesting not only their civil powerlessness and women's exclusion from the public world (between 1886 and 1892 the British Commons did not even debate women's suffrage) but also male sexual exploitation of women, child abuse and prostitution, prostitution, rape, battery and rape in marriage, the double standard of legal protection, and the sexual objectification of women. Englishwomen's rights in these matters may be judged by the reform of the 1884 Matrimonial Causes Act. It established—for the first time in British law—that a husband could *not* imprison a wife who refused him conjugal rights. United States custom may be judged by Victoria Woodhull's public protest against "the sexual crime . . . [of] sexual intercourse obtained by force" and "intercourse carried on habitually without perfect and reciprocal consummation."[7]

There are also feminist comments from that era that define marriage as equivalent to prostitution because of the economic coercion that forced women into both. For example, Olive Schreiner in *The Story of an African Farm*, originally published in 1883, has her heroine maintain, "A woman who has sold herself, even for a new ring and a new name, need hold her skirt aside for no creature in the street. They both earn their bread in one way."[8]

When economic constraint, ignorance, social custom, and the law grow less effective in keeping any subordinate class of people in its place, propaganda often steps in. Of those who responded to the threat posed by feminism to the traditional family and hence to the traditional social structure, one group—the medical profession—did so by reconceptualizing sexuality and marriage so thoroughly that any good Victorian, not to mention any good Puritan (as Jonathan Katz points out), would have found that institution not only unrecognizable but absolutely immoral. Such theorists of sexuality as Krafft-Ebing in Germany and later Havelock Ellis in England and even later the Dutch Van de Velde (whose book *Ideal Marriage* I found in my parents' bookcase and read when I was a teenager), were among those who participated in what we now call "the sex reform movement" and who gave the world the important social invention that is the subject of this chapter.

Ann Jones has called this new doctrine "an astonishingly powerful instrument for social control," one that "supplanted religion," "supplemented the law, so significantly weakened by feminist attacks," and obscured "the common social and political concerns all women shared." Between 1870 and 1920, says Jones, the United States divorce rate increased fifteen times, five times faster than the increase in the population as a whole, and "the number of married couples who had no children at all rose to almost one-third of all families."[9] Something obviously had to be done.

So it was. In her description of the sex reform movement, Jones concentrates on its advocates' insistence that maternity was woman's supreme function ("the prescribed number of children kept rising," she reports dryly), that sexual fulfillment was crucial, and that sexual fulfillment *meant* marrying and having babies.[10] I am going to concentrate on the prelude to babies. Consider the following ideas, all of which are still alive today:

Marriage is primarily an erotic institution. It is not primarily dynastic, economic, or a matter of binding communities together. Such motives would be heartless or suspect. Marriage is entirely personal. Marriage means love, and love means sex. A marriage license is a sex license.

"Sex" means heterosexual intercourse. Heterosexual penis-in-vagina intercourse is the "goal" and "real" function of erotic behavior and without it no "full" or "complete" or even simply "sexual" behavior has taken place. Without it, "nothing *really* happened." As Sanford and Donovan put it, "We . . . were taught that real sex begins when the penis penetrates the vagina. . . . Intercourse and sexual relations are one and the same."[11]

"Foreplay" is erotic activity distinct from that of heterosexual intercourse, and

its function is to get women to the point of desiring or allowing heterosexual intercourse. Orgasm attained by "foreplay" only is incomplete, inferior, or perverted. This is true even though many feminists of the last twenty years have contended that many women find heterosexual intercourse a difficult or impossible way to attain orgasm and that valuing it as the only "real" or "mature" sex is not favorable to women's pleasure in general. Other feminists note that other kinds of satisfying sex are possible with more than one kind of person and that no one has proved this fact less true for men than women. Anne Koedt noted early in the women's liberation movement that the psychoanalytic "double orgasm" was a social construct intended to benefit men. There is evidence for this contention. Linda Gordon notes that in the decades before the 1940s many doctors had observed and written "that the clitoris was the seat of all observable female sexual stimulation," but such knowledge did not affect the sexological assumptions as to heterosexual intercourse being the only "real" sex and women's orgasm during such activity as the only complete, real, normal satisfaction for all women.[12]

Women naturally desire and enjoy heterosexual intercourse. At the same time, it takes most women considerable time and sometimes even professional help to learn to desire and enjoy heterosexual intercourse. The sex reform movement explained away this rather obvious contradiction by referring to women's antisexual training, i.e., to what we today would call "inhibition." Shere Hite speculates as does Andrea Dworkin that much female inhibition may be due to the symbolic nature of the act in patriarchies and many women's attempt to resist male supremacy. Sheila Jeffreys reports such interpretations as widespread among feminist women and men in England in the period of the 1890s and 1900s.

Women who do not enjoy heterosexual intercourse, or (at least until recently) *those who don't come to orgasm by means of it, are frigid. Frigidity is abnormal, neurotic, and evidence of psychological illness (even if no other symptoms are present). It is also extremely common.* Women become frigid because they hate men (or hate men because they are frigid), because they fear sex, because they fear the strength of their desire for sex, because they masturbate, or because they don't, or because they refuse to submit to men, or any or all of the above.

Women who object to any male sexual behavior, or to male sexual exploitation of women, or to men's jokes about women, or to men's unsolicited advances or unsolicited touching, are prudes.[13] Prudes are frigid. (See above.) Sometimes women are prudes or frigid because they are lesbians or hate men—or vice versa.

The cure for frigidity or prudery is heterosexual intercourse. (That is, if you like it, you do it. If you don't like it, you do it anyway.)

Sexual motives constitute the core of the Human personality or (at the very least) are crucial to it. Elizabeth Wilson notes that "only in the mid-seventies [in Britain] did some feminists begin to question the idea that our sexuality expresses the core and center of our being." Feminists like Barbara Rush, Shulamith Firestone, and Linda Tschirhart Sanford and Mary Ellen Donovan have followed some of the radicals of the 1960s in noticing that Human needs for emotional warmth, intimacy, and a kindlier world have been channeled into a search for "sex," which has been simultaneously over-emphasized, trivialized, and commercialized. Katz makes the same point, speaking of "eroticism and intimacy as things plucked from a supermarket shelf," while Gordon describes "freer sexual standards" reaching large numbers of people in the United States of the 1920s as commercial importations via mass commercial culture. Anne Schaef finds the overestimation of sex and the sexualization of everything to be part of what she calls the "White Male System," noting that this system classifies people and situations according to sexuality, assumes that every relationship is sexual and that "everything we do and everyone we meet" has sexual significance, values orgasm but not sexual pleasure otherwise, and categorizes any protest against this view as "frigid" or "afraid of sex."[14]

There is an entity called heterosexuality. It is good, normal, and healthy, and it determines the heterosexual's whole personality.

There is an entity called homosexuality. It is evil, abnormal, and sick (or corrupt), and it determines the homosexual's whole personality.

Heterosexuals are those who have or wish to have heterosexual intercourse with persons of the opposite sex.[15]

Homosexuals are those who have or wish to have some substitute for heterosexual intercourse with persons of the same sex.

These two kinds of people are very different, and the line between them is sharp and unmistakable. (For the moment I won't go into this statement except to refer you to Katz's evidence that the construction of "homosexuals" and "heterosexuals" *as people* would not even have been understood a century or so before.)[16]

The sex reform movement, which was instrumental in inventing and popularizing the above, was the foe of Victorian repression and a great advance in Human affairs. Was it? Jeffreys presents considerable evidence that the sex reform movement did not work well, even on its own terms. Certainly the conditions it sought to remedy are still with us. For example, the movement's theorists expected that sexual pleasure within marriage for both partners would lead to the end of prostitution, as they explained men's resort to prostitutes as a response to "decent" women's antisexual attitudes and behavior. In 1976, sociologist Lillian Rubin attributed the relative inability of working-class women to enjoy heterosexual intercourse to the same causes.[17] And yet prostitution thrives—along with pornography—in our (presumably) less inhibited age. The reforms of the sex reform movement may look good when compared with the most reactionary social ideas of the period, but compare them, as historians generally fail to do, with the radical, feminist protests of the time and they show up rather badly. I agree with Jeffreys, Dworkin, Catharine MacKinnon, and one Mrs. Lucinda B. Chandler, who stated flatly in 1888, "When prostitution ceases inside marriage, it will disappear outside."[18] Many feminists, both in the last twenty years and at the end of the nineteenth century, have found male power over women in our society to be the villain here, not deficiencies in women's erotic education. Gordon describes 1930s marriage counseling in the United States (an advance, according to itself) as, at the very best, an attempt to "deflect or suppress challenges to male-defined sex" by stressing the evil of "domination" by the woman and the primacy of male rhythm in lovemaking, the psychological origin of women's difficulty in reaching orgasm by way of heterosexual intercourse, the supposed slowness and periodicity of women's desire as opposed to men's, and the necessity for women to suppress anger and resentment.[19] Late nineteenth-century feminists had a different recipe for sexual happiness: women's self-determination in all areas of life. To make the sex reform movement look good, historians must suppress the real radicalism of the period and its still revolutionary proposals.

If the sex reform movement was in fact not a great advance in women's happiness there is one thing it did very well: *it combated male fears of obsolescence.* After all, marriage—even if transformed into a consumer good (Katz's description)—was still by and large a consumer good that women "produced" by their domestic labor and men "consumed" by the provision of economic support. What in this arrangement (besides economic need) would lead women to marry? After all, for companionship women had each other, and for economic support, their own efforts. The social impossibility of living outside the family was fast disappearing. True, nineteenth-century ideology said that all women wanted children, but some women were declaring that they could very well do without children, while others (even more frighteningly) were asserting the right to have children without the obligation of having husbands at the same time. The brilliance of the sex reform movement lay in taking the one function men could still perform for women and women could not do for themselves or each other—heterosexual intercourse—and advertising it as fundamental to Human personality, fundamental to female physiological and physical health,[20] conditional on male dominance, and obtainable only through marriage. It is, of course, this last condition that is (and was) the weak link in the chain of social control. In fact, the arrangement of heterosexual-intercourse-obtainable-only-through-marriage began to break down pretty quickly, although I still remember the terror of young women in the 1950s (I was one) at the possibility of being "caught" in an unwed pregnancy and the furious fight for abortion rights in the 1960s and 1970s.

But the sex reform movement did not only attempt to find a function for men who faced this important kind of "unemployment." Nor did it only assign normalcy to a certain kind of sexual desire and behavior. *It also linked certain kinds of sexual desire and behavior with all other traditional female behavior and activity.* The "normal" woman, who is normal because she enjoys and wants heterosexual intercourse with men, is also the "good" woman who has committed herself to a lifetime of loyalty to men and work done for men, and she is the second woman *because* she is the first.

That is: why does a woman make herself sexually accessible to a man or men?

In this view, *because she is heterosexual.* (A reasonable view, certainly.)

Why does a woman make herself attractive to men and "feminine" with dress and cosmetics, which activity is often time-consuming, expensive, and uncomfortable?

Because she is heterosexual. (There are some arguments against this, like having to do it for many paid jobs, but let it stand.)

Why will a woman do so much for male attention and male approval?

Because she is heterosexual. (This argument is beginning to look a little odd.)

Why does a woman make available to men her emotional support and her sympathy? Why does she "love" men?

Because she is heterosexual. (And here we have the reason that women who challenge the traditional bounds of female behavior are always asked "Why do you hate men?" as if no third alternative were possible.)

Why does a woman marry?

Because she is heterosexual.

Why does a woman adopt men's perspectives, admire men's work, and respect (and stay off) men's territory?

Because she is heterosexual.

Why does a woman accept low wages, scrub floors and toilets, wash diapers and other people's clothes, shop, cook, save money on household expenses, defer to her husband, clean up after her husband, and so on?

Because she is heterosexual.

Now, that's absurd. Linking the desire to squeeze a handsome stranger's buttocks and tiptoe through the tulips with him to a lifetime of hard work and accommodation to male privilege is not logical.[21] Furthermore, it does not ensure the stability of any social arrangement based on it. It has not a single thing to do with liking or wanting or taking care of children. And it's currently in the process of breaking down in the United States and elsewhere with our rising divorce rate, the legalization of contraception and abortion, the gay liberation movement, feminism, the increasing poverty of women and children not in association with men and men's wages, fights for comparable pay, and the flight of many men, when they can afford it, from their end of the marriage bargain.[22] If the sex reformers' attempt to bind women to marriage, which is how Gordon describes the sex reform movement—Barbara Epstein calls it the "New Deal" of family life[23]—were not failing right and left, I would not be writing this book, and you would not be reading it. Nonetheless, we still confuse a desire for a particular erotic activity or a certain kind of partner with having a certain kind of personality, and we confuse that imagined personality with a lifetime of socially acceptable behavior. And it is precisely this social invention that feminists have been calling for some time now *compulsory heterosexuality* or *the heterosexual institution.*

Adrienne Rich, documenting the coercion of compulsory heterosexuality in women's lives and the punishment of would-be escapees,[24] makes it clear that women's participation in *the heterosexual institution* has never been voluntary and that social prescriptions in this direction suggest "that an enormous potential counterforce is having to be restrained."[25] If "heterosexuality," far from being merely a description of erotic behavior, marks a whole set of behaviors into which women are drafted by a combination of early training, economic coercion, propaganda, romantic idealization, lack of alternatives, social pressure, and promises of emotional and sexual fulfillment—

If such behavior serves to attach women to men and men's interests and secure for the *sex-class* of men (Dworkin's term) sexual access to the loyalty and labor of the *sex-class* of women—

If such an institution can allow no escapees among women and no laggards among men (for men are also compelled by the heterosexual institution to do what they don't want to do, and all men's lives are affected for the worse by it, though they are not hurt as much as women are)—

Then the punishment and enforced invisibility visited on The Little Woman Who Isn't There (and her gay male counterpart) have a clear social function. As the punishment visited on soldiers who go AWOL is intended not only to punish those soldiers who do it but (more important) to deter those soldiers who'd like to if only they could do so without getting punished, thus women who have gone AWOL from the heterosexual institution are punished, and the possibility of doing likewise is made frightening or unthinkable or both for other women. As Adrienne Rich notes, "the destruction of records and memorabilia and letters documenting the realities of lesbian existence must be taken very seriously as a means of keeping heterosexuality compulsory for women." Blanche Wiesen Cook expresses the same opinion: "In a hostile world in which women are not supposed to survive except in relation with and in service to men, entire communities of women were simply erased. History tends to bury what it seeks to reject." And as Smith puts it (about Toni Morrison's *Sula*), the danger in that book posed to a community by its one "promiscuous" woman "acts like the presence of lesbians everywhere *to expose the contradictions of supposedly 'normal' life.*"[26]

And contradictions there most certainly are.

A system of beliefs that uses delight in doing certain kinds of narrowly defined erotics with certain kinds of people to enforce upon a whole class of people a massive array of extra-erotic behavior is, as I have said, a very shaky system indeed. There is not, of course, the slightest necessary connection between lust and housework (if there were, men would be clamoring to vacuum floors), or lust and "feminine" self-effacement, or lust and the desire to be badly paid, or even lust and the desire to starve oneself in order to be "beautiful" in whatever grotesque, limited, expensive, time-consuming, and physically uncomfortable fashion manufacturers and advertisers (who, of course, profit immensely from this particular "expression" of "heterosexuality" among women) have invented to part us from our money this particular season. Nor is the connection as invariable as the heterosexual institution assumes it to be. If it were, men *as a class* would be deferring to, placating, submitting to, and admiring women *as a class,* and rape and violence directed at women would not exist. The heterosexual institution takes care of this contradiction by positing entirely different "natures" for men and women, which "natures" are then enforced on pain of social sanctions.[27]

Please note: when the specific desire for heterosexual intercourse—presumed to be the foundation of "heterosexuality" and hence the linchpin of the whole system—*is not there,* do we then hear that the woman in question *is not heterosexual?* Not when the woman in question engages in other socially approved "feminine" behavior. In fact, *her heterosexuality is assumed,* and we hear—if we hear anything—about her "frigidity" or her mate's "clumsiness" or any and every other possible cause except the one lack that ought to invalidate the whole system. Ann Landers, a popular columnist, once asked her female readers, "Would you be content to be held close and treated tenderly and forget about 'the act'? Reply YES or NO." On 14 and 15 January 1985, she published the results of her informal poll:

> Ann was forced to publish results she had not expected: "Seventy-two percent said YES, they would be content to be held close and treated tenderly and forget about the act. Of those 72 percent who said yes, 40 percent were under 40 years old. That

was the most surprising aspect of the survey. Ann received over
a hundred and thirty thousand responses.[28]

Similarly, in a different context, we hear that father-daughter incest has
harmed daughters only if the daughters fail to marry or if they are sexually
promiscuous. That is, failure to comply with the heterosexual institution or
to do so in a socially proper way is the "only conclusive evidence," say
Judith Herman and Lisa Hirschorn, surveying the professional literature on
father-daughter incest, accepted as proof that the daughter has been
harmed.[29] Indeed, women who do sex with men for their own pleasure—
"promiscuous" women, as popularly understood—and women who do sex
with men for their own economic profit—prostitutes—and women who
choose to do sex with women—"lesbians"—are all three condemned. (Even
more oddly, promiscuous women, who don't do sex for profit, are called
by the same condemning name as women who do: "whores"!) All three
kinds of women face random male violence and, at the very least, a double
standard of legal and communal treatment.[30] Like the masterless man of
medieval Europe, who owed fealty to no lord and thus posed a danger to
the feudal hierarchy, the manless woman—that is, the woman committed
to no man—is a danger to patriarchal hierarchy and is named and treated
as an enemy. A few recent Hollywood movies may have praised prostitutes
for being accessible sexually to men and for making no personal or emotional demands on them, but there are few popular films that admire women
who use and discard men erotically and financially or women who have no
use for men at all. Furthermore, as I've said, feminists have always noted
that it is extraordinarily difficult to define "prostitute" and "wife" in a way
that will make it clear what the sexual difference is between them, as both
exchange sexual services for material survival.[31] From Mary Wollstonecraft
to Olive Schreiner to Emma Goldman to Catharine MacKinnon, feminist
critics have pointed out that exchanging sexual access for economic support
is characteristic of both marriage and prostitution. (In fact, unless one takes
as one's standard lifelong monogamy, it is also impossible to draw a clear
line between promiscuity and nonpromiscuity. I remember promiscuity defined somewhere as more partners than the number the speaker has had.)

So far I think most feminists will agree: wanting to do sex of any sort at
all with a man or with men does not condemn a woman to a lifetime of
picking up socks. Neither does it mean she must accept the narrow, male-
oriented definition of what constitutes proper heterosexual behavior.
Nonetheless the nonlogical, historical link between The Woman Job and
Heterosexual Intercourse is recent enough still to be very strong. It's been
my experience that most heterosexual feminists, like most heterosexual
women, find it frightening to question the naturalness of women's attraction

to men, even more frightening to label women they admire "lesbian," and most frightening of all to be called "lesbian" themselves. Feminists of the late 1960s and early 1970s were aware of such fears. In "Notes of a Radical Lesbian," Martha Shelley described brave members of the early women's liberation movement who picketed the 1968 Miss America pageant as standing up intrepidly to those who called them "commies" and "tramps" but bursting into tears when they were called "lesbians." (The interchangeability of these labels—commies, indeed!—is strikingly illustrated by the epithets Shelley records.) Sidney Abbott and Barbara Love agree with Shelley in "Is Woman's Liberation a Lesbian Plot?" (note the title), and the authors of "The Woman Identified Woman" ("Radicalesbians") wrote, "When a woman hears this word tossed her way, she knows she is stepping out of line."[32]

Unfortunately, the early awareness I have given examples of above has not become general in feminist writing. If the last seventeen years have seen a change among feminists, it hasn't been in the direction of challenging the naturalness of heterosexuality or even, most of the time, in exploring the social construction of all sexuality. Feminists do not, as a group, support women's freedom to cross-dress or cross-behave—certainly they don't make this a major part of their activities—nor do they usually consider these freedoms to be important issues.[33] Rather, the drift of feminist activities in this area has been in publicly supporting the issue of lesbian (and gay) civil rights or in moderately renegotiating the terms of the heterosexual institution. Neither does the critique of the heterosexual institution that has recently surfaced among some feminist, lesbian thinkers inform most publicly visible feminism, nor is it linked with most public advocacy of gay rights, nor do most public advocates of gay rights link feminism with their activities. In both areas—feminism and gay rights—most activities, at best, advance the idea that "normal" is different for different people and that the same standards ought not to apply to everyone. This is surely better than accepting persecution from the majority as inevitable, but such a stand does not directly challenge the supposed naturalness of the heterosexual institution, and it leaves intact the idea that if women want to be erotic with men, they must accept all sorts of other behavior too, and their only real alternative is a different kind of sexuality. (I've even heard some lesbians say essentially the same thing, i.e., that straight women "deserve" what they get for associating sexually with men.)

The naturalness of any form of erotic behavior aside, the use of women's erotic interest in men to draft women into a lifetime fulfillment of The Woman Job has important results for women *as a class*. When female sexuality is forced to conform to a model that is not in women's interest and not of women's making, when this model assumes all women's sexual interest in men and all men's entitlement to sexual access to women, when the double standard of responsibility and consequence still generally prevails, when a display of "femininity" is required from women quite apart from their own particular erotic interest in a particular man or a particular situation, when intimacy and maintaining relationships remain largely women's business, when marriage or marriagelike arrangements remain women's assumed and only options (and still operate in women's best economic interests), then—as Rich points out—the whole area of heterosexuality becomes painful for many women, inadequate for many more, and questionable for all, even those who heartily fancy this particular sort of tulip-tiptoe for themselves.[34]

For one thing, women do not *choose* to marry or enter marriagelike arrangements at all. As Jessie Bernard describes the situation:

> Few women make a deliberate or conscious decision never to marry, if, in fact, one can even call entering marriage a decision when one considers all the pressure bearing down on young women to marry. It is so taken for granted . . . that almost everything in their world is based on that outcome.[35]

In the working class, writes Rubin:

> Getting married . . . probably still is the singularly acceptable way out of an oppressive family situation and into a respected social status. . . . Despite the fact that the models of marriage they see before them don't look like their cherished myths, their alternatives are often so slim and so terrible—a job they hate, more years under the oppressive parental roof—that working-class girls tend to . . . cling to their [romantic] fantasies with extraordinary tenacity.[36]

These fantasies, of course, are not ones they have created all by themselves. They have had a lot of help from the mass media. Writer Helena Maria Viramontes, for example, describes the mass media image of the "happy home" she tried to create as a compound of freshly ironed apron, soup, cupcakes, and a cherubic baby, although the reality never matched the ideal. Similarly, hooks found, both among her interviewees and in her perusal of *Essence* magazine, "an obsessive concern among black women with male-female relationships."[37] Even if the men in the girls' fantasies of marriage have only the "strangely insubstantial" or "symbolic significance" Oakley finds in one researcher's account of British schoolgirls' fantasies of married life—"economic providers, bestowers of status and marks of respectability"[38]—they remain necessary. Without dates or (later) sexual contacts with men, a woman is neither a "real woman" nor a socially acceptable one. One young woman whose disability had prevented her becoming involved with men said, "I sometimes feel like I'm not a member of the human race," while another, describing her single, "independent . . . energetic, well-satisfied" aunt, nonetheless noted her mother's reaction: " 'Poor thing,' said my mother, 'she's all *alone.*' "[39]

I myself remember a conversation among five or six old White women from the Northwest, all at least in their seventies, in the women's dressing room of a public swimming pool I used to go to. They emphatically stated that men were no use and no help, and if they had it to do over again, most of them would have children but would on no account marry. One old woman gleefully informed them that she never had married (the others said they envied her). A White woman of about forty then came out of a dressing room to ask wistfully, "But what about loneliness?" The old women laughed. (Sanford and Donovan cite a study in which four out of five people who "identified themselves as lonely were housewives.")[40] A younger White woman of about twenty-five then shot a very condescending look at me; what could they—old and not pretty—teach her?

In *Working It Out,* a volume of essays by women who are successful artists, scientists, and scholars, there are statements typical of the 1950s, when most of these women grew up, that make clear how little choice any of these White, well-to-do managerial professionals actually had (or thought they had) about marriage:

> The Woman's Life Plan . . . is to marry well, to bear and raise children. . . . Where I grew up, the Plan was so widely endorsed . . . that I had no need to articulate it, only to live it.

> When it was time to marry, I married. . . . It seemed the thing to do. Everyone was getting married.

> [My college peers] were engaged . . . happily planning to marry in the next year or so. . . . I felt futureless. . . . I got "involved," though not very happily, with a divinity student. I found a foothold, in other words, on the edge of a future.

> [I put myself] into marriage and motherhood . . . without understanding why.

> The pressure to succeed as a "girl" weighed heavy upon me; it took a long time to realize that the problem was not to find someone who wanted to marry me but to find someone I could give myself to wholeheartedly.

Marriage was something you did, like a long term paper, and
if you did it well, everything would work out fine.[41]

Although such attitudes were certainly more common and more taken
for granted in the 1950s than they are today, some of the women quoted
in *Working It Out* still find nothing unfortunate or even odd in the situations
they describe. Some propose fairly mild remedies like not committing oneself to marriage and children "prematurely" or establishing "their independence in some measure before marriage." One woman writes of her early
marriage to a professor, which stopped her own academic work, as she
believed it to be inconsistent with marriage. She writes, "I can remember
walking by the tennis courts on some outrageously sunny, cheerful day and
feeling so overwhelmed with self-hatred it made my skin crawl." Only a
small number of other contributors report such a vehemently negative reaction. More typical is the comment of one artist contributor whose husband refused to pay for household help: "If I required more money, it was
my responsibility to earn it. I have always been grateful to my husband for
taking a very specific and clear stand on this. He was not against me, not
an enemy, at any level." Another writes of her painter husband that "the
competition that inevitably exists in even the most loving relationship has
chipped at my strength." Such sad compromises recall Rubin's report on
the minimal qualities her "working-class interviewees ticked off most readily
when asked what they valued most in their husbands. . . . 'He's a steady
worker; he doesn't drink; he doesn't hit me.' "[42]

Nor is the female sexuality manifested in marriage or marriagelike relationships unconnected with the requirements of The Woman Job. In 1970,
Meredith Tax observed that men are, sexually, "consumers" of women who
create themselves as the "product" to be "consumed." British feminist Rosalind Coward notes that often women, believing their sexuality to exist for
their men and not for themselves, feel guilty about masturbation while men
do not, while Sanford and Donovan cite women who feel guilty at having
an orgasm before their man's (it's selfish) or believe that their own mastur-
bating is a sign of "weakness." These authors also go much further than I
do in assuming that almost all women's early sexual experiences are "unpleasant" or at least "unsatisfying" and in asserting that women learn "a
right way to have sex" that is "male-initiated and male dominant/female
submissive" from "parents' example, movies and romance novels."[43] In this
connection it is noteworthy to ponder the extra-erotic reasons Rubin's married interviewees give (along with their erotic ones) for participating in sex
with their husbands. They range from "caring and consideration" through
"a sense of duty . . . fear of losing their men" all the way to "resignation and
a sense of powerlessness." Some find the requirement that they experience

orgasm only "another demand in a life already too full of demands . . . her orgasm is for him, not for her." In such circumstances it's not likely that women will become acquainted with their own likes and desires. Linda Phelps maintains that

> the fantasies we [women] take in, the images that describe to us how to act, are male fantasies about females. In a male world, female sexuality is from the beginning unable to get a clear picture of itself. . . . [Women] neither relate to ourselves as self-directed persons nor to our partners as the objects of our desire, but to a false world of symbol and fantasy. . . . We experience our sexuality in symbolic terms at the expense of active physical involvement. . . . our physical experience has been denied and distorted for so long that most of us are not even aware of the sacrifice we have made. We are only uneasy that all is not well.[44]

Worse still, women's sexuality is also often supposed to be *something of which women are not aware,* a "sexuality which pervades their bodies almost as if in spite of themselves. . . . Young girls [especially] are often seen as expressing a [heterosexual] need even if the girl herself does not know it."[45] As MacKinnon describes sexual harassment in the workplace, a similar dynamic is at work; "no" is taken to mean "yes," and men often attribute sexual motives to women independently of or even in direct opposition to the women's expressed desires. Such attribution agrees with a basic assumption of the sex reform movement, which also attributed heterosexual desire to all women, despite many women's concurrent critique of just that attribution. As MacKinnon writes of her contemporary sample of cases, the woman who refused such attribution (then as now) "is accused of prudery, unnaturalness. . . . and lesbianism."[46]

In such an atmosphere it's not surprising, as Christine Delphy puts it, that for a woman to be oppressed in heterosexual relationships, it's not necessary for the man to be a voluntary oppressor; the heterosexual institution "precede[s] any particular relationship . . . [and] determines the very existence of the relationship." Women who call attention to these things are accused of complaining about the nature of sexuality itself. As Dworkin says, "Every complaint that a woman makes against the hostility of male dominance is taken to be a complaint against love." And Rubin calls this whole atmosphere, which she finds typical of the "sexual revolution" of the 1960s, "at once sexually permissive and coercive." If many women do not like sex, feminist critics say, it is "because of the politics of sexual oppression," because of the way in which heterosexuality has been institutionalized in our society, because of "a continuing double standard [in which] . . .

women's guilt feelings are not mere relics of a dead morality [but] . . . withdrawals from danger," and because, says Amber Hollibaugh, of "the extraordinary price women must pay to explore their own sexual questions, upbringings and experiences."[47]

In this connection, Nancy Henley cites a 1975 study which found that "touch that signified sexual desire to females was *opposed* to pleasantness, warmth, friendliness and playfulness," while for males in the same study "pleasantness, sexual desire and warmth/love formed a cluster," and MacKinnon found that a considerable number of women who had experienced sexual harassment on the job responded not only with anger and fear but with guilt as well. She adds that because "employed women are supposed to develop, and must demonstrate, regard for the man [their employer] as part of the job and since women are taught to identify men's evaluations of them . . . with their sexual attractiveness to men, as a major component of their *own* identities and sense of worth," confusion about a woman's responsibility for causing sexual harassment is often the result. It's hard not to conclude, with Coward, that only women's skill "at subordinating their own active needs"—that is, performing The Woman Job— keeps the whole system from breaking down. Daly goes even further, identifying "femininity" itself as a "man-made concept," as does Linda Strega, who says, "feminine behavior is . . . *masculine* to [sic] the extreme."[48]

With the enormous requirements of The Woman Job attached to heterosexuality, as well as operative within it, it's no wonder that a happy frolic among the flowers fares so badly in the lives of many women. Neither is it surprising that books like *The Hite Report* rouse the ire they do, nor that nonfeminist radicals refuse even to consider such alarming complaints about an institution they so very often confuse with nature. A recent debate between MacKinnon on the one hand and Rosalind Petchesky and Carol Joffe on the other illustrates what can happen when the feminist party to the debate (MacKinnon) views sexuality as part of the political-social realm while what MacKinnon calls the "liberal" parties view it as a private phenomenon that is somehow exempt from sex-class interests or any other social forces. In an exchange that strongly recalls the sex reform movement's treatment of feminist protest, Joffe condemns MacKinnon's analysis of the heterosexual institution as "puritanical" and denies her assertion that the heterosexual institution is oppressive to women by saying that "in the past few years" (but not before, presumably!) "birth control clinics have counseled young women to refuse unwanted sexual overtures." As MacKinnon describes it:

> I criticize sexuality as a sphere of inequality; they defend it as
> a sphere of equality. . . . Since when are . . . people acting under

conditions of inequality termed "autonomous"? . . . Who trivi-
alizes an analysis of the systematic disparity created by the powerful acting in their own interest as a "plot"? . . . Who treats
"negotiating" under unequal conditions as an exercise in freedom?[49]

That is, Joffe and Petchesky are using against MacKinnon's feminist analysis
precisely the kinds of specious accusations made by the political Right to
counter the sort of class analysis made by exactly such people as Joffe and
Petchesky themselves.

Nor is female disappointment at The Woman Job confined to the sexual.
The job includes giving emotional support to men, but like Rubin's interviewees who "know . . . that the dream is not being fulfilled . . . [they are]
married but feel lonely," women who provide emotional support as part of
their marital work often find themselves not getting enough of the same
sort of care. Bernard states that "most of [women's] intimate personal contacts are with other women. . . . Companionship with one's husband is minimal in many marriages." She quotes a 1974 study that "found that women
supplied emotional support to their husbands twice as often as they received
it in return." In another, she reports,

> American women were asked to specify the three persons they
> would most like to be with. The husband was mentioned by
> 64 percent . . . a girl friend (or woman friend) by 98 percent.
> It was estimated in one study [1972] that American married
> couples spend an average of twenty minutes a week in direct
> conversation with each other.[50]

With "little expectation of friendship or companionship" from their husbands," women's intimate communication is mostly feminine, "with daily
contact between the blue-collar woman and her mother or sisters." Sanford
and Donovan find a pattern of women's condemning themselves for "being
so emotionally demanding rather than condemning him for being so emotionally unresponsive," while Renita Weems writes, "eventually we [Black
women] learn it will be a Black woman that we turn to for comfort and
advice when that man fails to love us the way we want."[51] Pat Lamb's
Touchstones (1983) contains a vivid account of married women's reliance
on woman friends for the continuing emotional support of which women
get all too little from their husbands.

As MacKinnon notes, insofar as women's work *as women* is to create the
private realm *for men,* men's privacy is founded on women's lack of a gen-

uinely private life and men's leisure (of which more later) is founded on and requires women's lack of leisure. And, as many nineteenth-century feminists remarked, insofar as women make homes *for men,* in a sense women have no homes of their own.

If I do not here touch on rape and other male violence directed toward women as far too frequent conditions of The Woman Job, it's only because I am going to examine them later in another context. Instead I will join my voice with that of E. Noel Morgan, who argued in *The Freewoman* of 8 August 1912 that what we now call the heterosexual institution is a monopoly in Human affairs and ought to be abolished. She argued that

> a celibate class of women was necessary for the "task of raising the fair sex out of its subjection. . . . Wherever . . . the celibate class is practically non-existent, there the position of women socially, economically and intellectually is of a lower order.

In *Marriage as a Trade,* another early twentieth-century feminist, Cecily Hamilton, likewise described marriage as affording women subsistence wages *because it constituted a socially enforced monopoly* (this was in 1909). And "Christabel Pankhurst stated categorically that spinsterhood was a political decision."[52]

In short, the Little Woman Who Isn't There turns out to be a politically important person, not because all women ought to be lesbians (I am arguing nothing of the kind) but because heterosexuality as a personal erotic or affectional preference is absolutely different and distinct from the heterosexual institution, which is public and compulsory. The latter must be challenged and eradicated, and this process includes the achievement of female economic independence, the altering of law and custom, and an end to homophobic bigotry. The demystification of lesbian presence and lesbian visibility (and of course that of gay men) is an important part of this process. Describing the way in which such mystifications affect all women's choices, Rich has this to say:

> A young woman, entering her twenties in a blur of stereotypes and taboos, with a vague sense of anxiety centering around the word *lesbian,* is ill-equipped to think about herself, her feelings, her options, her relations with men *or* women. It is not only lesbian[s] . . . who should be calling for a recognition of their history and presence in the world; it is *all* women who want a more accurate map of the way social relations have been and are, as they try to imagine what might be.[53]

Such challenges have in fact been made. One very heartening instance of such protest was, for example, the speakout at Brown University on 2 May 1985, which connected sexual assault and other violence committed by men against women with racism, homophobia, and imperialism. Here is a report of the speakout from the *Gay Community News* of 1 June 1985. (I have cut moderately and rearranged some paragraphs.)

> Organizing began when Yuko Uchikawa, a Japanese student, became angered by harassment during Brown's "Spring Weekend." . . . [She] contacted a newly-formed women's support group . . . and word spread to the Third World Center, the Sarah Doyle Women's Center and the Lesbian Collective, a campus organization. Over 100 women met . . . [and] a steering committee of 14 was formed, including five women of color and two out lesbians. . . . Women of color . . . [met separately] at one point to discuss feeling pushed by men of color to prioritize race before gender. . . . Organizers of the speakout had anticipated a one-hour action with no more than 20 women addressing the audience. Instead over 120 rape and harassment survivors spoke in the cold rain from noon until 5 P.M., drawing connections between racist, sexist and homophobic violence. Many women were describing their experiences for the first time.
>
> Other women of color took issue with those men of color who had considered the planned speakout "a white women's issue." "Sexual assault is my issue," one speaker said. . . . "And the last time I looked down, I was Black."
>
> Melissa Walker, a Black activist [the women quoted are all Brown University students] . . . challenged both straight women and lesbians to "love men in a furious enough way to make them change. And if you don't love men, make them change anyway."
>
> Some women addressed the fraternity men standing on the sidelines, screaming . . . "Why didn't you help me [when I was assaulted]?" and "Don't make me hate you; you are supposed to be my friends."
>
> Male harassers at the speakout were quickly silenced when women quietly surrounded one perpetrator and later when the audience turned as a group and silently pointed at a small, leering crowd . . . the men stopped their harassment.

The report goes on to list demands presented to the university: stronger penalties for physical and verbal sexual violence; more representation of lesbians, gay men, and Third World students on the University Council of Student Affairs; the addition of "sexual orientation" to the university's nondiscrimination policy; free courses in self-defense; a weekly crime map and column publicizing racist violence and sexual assaults; a dusk-to-dawn vehicle escort service; and revocation of the charters of the two most offensive fraternities. All were granted except the addition of "sexual orientation" to the university's nondiscrimination policy. In addition, one fraternity's charter was revoked and the other had its housing rights withdrawn, though the reasons given said nothing about the speakout.

> The fraternities . . . responded to the speakout and the Dean's announcement [about meeting demands listed above] with continuing violence, blockading roads and smashing windows. One frat hung an effigy of the Women's Political Task Force Coordinator from a window, with the doll's breasts slashed.
>
> Brown's staff assistant for Women's Concerns, Kate Garrett, told GCN that . . . frat men "threw whole kegs of beer at a tree, yelling 'dyketree, dyketree,' and others marched to the home of . . . President Howard Swearer, chanting 'Howie is a homo.' . . . Men have been yelling both 'Sarah Doyle sucks cocks' and 'Sarah Doyle is all dykes.' "[54]
>
> Resnick noted that over the course of only three days of planning, straight women began to include lesbian issues as a matter of course, and white women brought up the necessity of a Third World perspective. . . . the Black Women's Political Task Force . . . is forming as a result of the speakout.
>
> Uchikawa concluded that she and others had taken action "because we think we can make changes. We want to make the school a less homophobic, sexist, racist, and less Eurocentric place. By working together and raising our voices, we will all be more culturally affluent."

Heartening words like Uchikawa's ought to end a book, and there was a time when I thought to end this book with the account given above. But in recent years (Clara Fraser's views have been central to this process), I have come to believe that the Brown University protesters—and many others as well—have left out of their feminist activism one crucial concern, the one that may well give us the key to all the others.

I refer to neither men's right to women's *love* or women's *lust* nor to men's right to women's *loyalty* but to a fourth activity/commodity that is usually taken for granted in the heterosexual institution, one not mentioned in the speakout at Brown (or at least in the *GNC* account of it)[55] possibly because the students *were* students and as yet relatively untouched by it.

I refer to women's *labor*.

APPENDIX

As far as I have been able to trace the history of contemporary U.S. feminism's naming of the heterosexual institution, it happened thus:

In 1968 Ti-Grace Atkinson stated that *[hetero]sexual intercourse* (as she put it) was a political institution that had been recently created to shore up the institution of marriage, which was dying.[56]

In 1971, according to Adrienne Rich, a lesbian feminist paper called *The Furies,* which had been founded that year, first declared that *heterosexuality* was an *institution.*[57]

Others have taken up the subject. Among them is hooks, who stated that "the feminist movement to eradicate *compulsory heterosexuality* . . . [is] central to efforts to end sexual oppression," while Ruth Bleier has analyzed "the *institutions and ideologies of heterosexuality*" as "the primary force in the maintenance of patriarchal rule." Delphy labels "the belief that there must be close and permanent relations between most females and most males at all times" as "the stronghold of patriarchal ideology [and] the basis of *heterosexual ideology.*" Sylvia Federici, emphasizing that female sexuality, which is supposed to be spontaneous and natural, is actually part of women's work, states, "They say it is love. We say it is unwaged work. They call it frigidity. We call it absenteeism." Rich, whose treatment of the subject is the longest and most systematic I've been able to find, calls the enforcement of the heterosexual institution a means of "assuring male right of physical, economic and emotional access" to women, thus restating Matilda Josyln Gage's formulation of a century before.[58] Her essay stresses women's unacknowledged lack of choice in deciding whether and under what conditions they will associate sexually or otherwise with men. She notes the existence of past rebels against marriage and heterosexuality, like the medieval Beguines and the Chinese marriage-resistance sisterhoods. She also observes that many women have been counted as heterosexual whose marriages indicate nothing about their sexual (or other) preferences precisely because their choices were not truly free.

It would seem reasonable to look to modern sexology for a critique of the heterosexual institution. I have not done this. As late as 1977, Carole Vance attended an annual sexological conference in a "major center of broadly based sex research in America," she says, one that is "highly influential and respected," only to find that, with its largely male staff and largely female supporting staff, it adhered to "heterosexist paradigms which were rarely analyzed or related to social structure. Basic questions about masculinity and femininity, the social construction of gender and the relations between subordinates and superordinates were not addressed." Vance describes such daunting movie cartoons as the one in which a pickle pursued a fleeing doughnut, rubbed "in and out" of her "hole," and ejaculated; another in which "God" created man with a penis and woman with breasts but no clitoris; and a third about a male partner who tied up an unspeaking female partner, beat her, threw her downstairs, and turned her into a typewriter upon which he pounded, and then penetrated her again when she was in a hospital bed "enclosed from head to foot in a body cast." The audience found the cartoons comic, but disapproved of—and walked out on—the film "In the Best Interests of the Children," which viewed lesbian mothers favorably. Vance also states that heterosexual sex was called "sex" throughout, that hierarchies of sexual activity from " 'foreplay' to 'real sex' " were strongly in evidence and unquestioned, that fellatio was described and depicted but not cunnilingus, that male sexual style was presented as "sex" with no possibility that there might be other styles, that anal intercourse was treated "in lectures only" and as "a strictly [male] homosexual activity," and that "transsexualism was assigned to family pathology or hormonal abnormality." She further reports that "monogamy, order and stability" were the conference's "prime goals." Most disturbing of all to her was the anti-intellectualism of the conference, its "atheoretical posture," its use of "white, middle-class norms" as universal, and its separation of feeling from thought.[59]

From the above account, it seems reasonable to assume that any recent changes in the field have arisen not as spontaneous reforms within the discipline but from feminist and other pressure manifesting itself largely from the outside. Similarly, theories that propose a continuum between "normal" heterosexual practice and the rape perpetrated by some men against women and children have come from feminists.

An important part of our legacy from the sex reform movement is the absolute disjunction between the two kinds of behavior, that is, the attribution of all rape solely to insanity or other kinds of individual pathology. Jeffreys calls this belief the "medical model" of male sexual exploitation and finds that it became the "dominant form of explanation" by the 1930s.[60] Feminists have been asserting the continuum between these two modes of behavior for the last twenty-five years, as did British feminists of the 1880s–1920s, pointing out men's power as a class over women as a class, the connection between rape and ordinary, male-dominant behavior, the assumption that women's "no" means "yes," and so on. Susan Brownmiller's *Against Our Will* (1975) argues that rape represents not individual pathology but rather terrorism against women as a class. Similarly, feminist works on battering take the position that the ordinary, everyday treatment of women as second-class citizens at the very least facilitates such acts, as does the law's and the community's turning away from the victims.

NOTES

1. Nancy Sahli, "Smashing: Women's Relationships before the Fall," *Chrysalis* 8 (1979).

2. For this chapter I have drawn largely on Lillian Faderman's *Surpassing the Love of Men: Romantic Friendship and Love between Women from the Renaissance to the Present* (New York: Morrow, 1981); Jonathan Katz's *Gay/Lesbian Almanac: A New Documentary* (New York: Harper and Row, 1983) and *Gay American History: Lesbians and Gay Men in the U.S.A.* (New York: Avon, 1976); and Sheila Jeffreys's *The Spinster and Her Enemies: Feminism and Sexuality, 1880–1930* (London: Pandora, 1985). Faderman is the pioneer, tracing love between women in England, Europe, and the United States from the sixteenth century to the present; Katz links the reconceptualization of sexuality and marriage with the shift from early capitalism, with its ideology of production, to late industrial or corporate capitalism, with its push toward consumption. Jeffreys, following Faderman, traces the vituperative campaign against the spinster in England from the 1880s to the 1930s. (See especially Faderman I:B and III:A.) One of Katz's interesting historical recoveries is that of the trial of two women charged before a colonial New England court with "lewd behavior . . . upon a bed" (*Gay/Lesbian*, 92–93).

3. Dale Spender (*Women of Ideas: What Men Have Done to Them* [London: Routledge and Kegan Paul, 1982], 559–66, 571–72) describes working-class women's participation in the British suffrage movement and feminist attempts to train working women in remunerative skilled trades like printing. Upper-class ladies' "social duties," productive of "good" marriages and consequent social position, were mandatory; Florence Nightingale's 1852 essay *Cassandra* (Old Westbury, NY: Feminist Press, 1979) describes a lady's social duties as sure to drive insane any woman of character and sense.

4. In England, one of these unwed mothers was Rebecca West, essayist, novelist, and turn-of-the-century feminist. Her lover, H. G. Wells, wrote a novel, *Ann Veronica,* that presented an unmarried mother sympathetically. It caused a scandal.

5. Spender, *Women of Ideas,* 577; Marielouise Jansen-Jurreit, *Sexism: The Male Monopoly on History and Thought,* translated by Verne Moberg (New York: Farrar, Straus and Giroux, 1982), 143.

6. In England the peak years were 1901–11, with 1911 the peak year for women in every age from twenty-five up who remained unmarried. (Jeffreys, *Spin-*

ster, 88.) In the United States the last two decades of the nineteenth century were the peak years for this phenomenon. (Jessie Bernard, *The Female World* [New York: Free Press, 1981], 114.) These statistics are matched in the United States only by the mid-1960s to mid-1970s, with a drastic decline in first-marriage rates and a divorce rate that doubled during the decade. (ibid., 175). In England adult women outnumbered adult men throughout the nineteenth century and well into the twentieth, a demographic event that may be related to the peculiar intensity and force of the British suffragist movement of that time. Jeffreys describes British feminist demands of the 1850s and 1860s as aimed at middle-class "surplus" women, dependent and without vocation (Jeffreys, *Spinster*, 87).

7. Ann Oakley, *Subject Women* (New York: Pantheon, 1981), 10; Jeffreys, *Spinster*, chaps. 1–4, 31; Johanna Jonston, *Mrs. Satan: The Incredible Saga of Victoria C. Woodhull* (New York: Popular Library, 1967), 185.

8. Olive Schreiner, *The Story of An African Farm* (New York: Modern Library, 1927), 225.

9. Ann Jones, *Women Who Kill* (New York: Holt, Rinehart and Winston, 1980), 262–63, 258.

10. Ibid., 259–60.

11. Linda Tschirhart Sanford and Mary Ellen Donovan, *Women and Self-Esteem* (New York: Penguin, 1985), 394. See also Andrea Dworkin, *Intercourse* (New York: Free Press, 1987), which explores the patriarchal meanings of heterosexual intercourse as revealed in samples of "classic" literature written by men in various countries during the last two centuries.

12. Fox [Jeanette Silveira], "Why Men Oppress Women," *Lesbian Ethics* I:1 (1984), 38; Koedt in Elsie Adams and Mary Briscoe, eds., *Up Against the Wall, Mother . : On Women's Liberation* (Beverly Hills: Glencoe Press, 1971), 237–245; Linda Gordon, *Woman's Body, Woman's Right: A Social History of Birth Control* (New York: Grossman, 1976), 378–79.

13. The earlier meaning of "prudery" signified the public ostentation of exaggeratedly correct sexual morality and behavior by women whose private activities might be quite different.

14. Elizabeth Wilson, "Forbidden Love," *Feminist Studies* 10:2 (1984), 217; Florence Rush, *The Best Kept Secret: Sexual Abuse of Children* (New York: McGraw-Hill, 1980), 191; Shulamith Firestone, *The Dialectic of Sex* (New York: Morrow, 1970), 147; Sanford and Donovan, *Women*, 387–88, 400; Katz, *Gay/Lesbian*, 171; Gordon *Woman's Body*, 201; Anne Wilson Schaef, *Women's Reality: An Emerging Female System in a White Male Society* (New York: Harper and Row, 1985), 46–50.

15. "Opposite what?" Samuel Delany, the novelist, once wrote in angry annoyance. Or, as Alice Sheldon put it, "the belief that men and women exist at opposite ends of an infinite number of bipolar dimensions . . . is a monstrous exercise in fluff" (*Khatru* 3–4 [November 1975], 35, 17).

16. In the seventeenth century in the North American eastern seaboard ter-

ritory that later became the United States, there was no such idea that feeling desire for someone of one's own sex made one into a different sort of person. Katz quotes from the 1650s journal of the Reverend Michael Wigglesworth, whose "filthy lust" for his male pupils at Harvard (sprung, he says, from "too much doting affection") made him not a sodomite—sodomy was a crime anyone could commit—but merely "a sinner." The distinction we make between heterosexual and homosexual personalities simply did not exist then (Katz, *Gay/Lesbian*, 47).

17. Lillian Breslow Rubin, *Worlds of Pain: Life in the Working-Class Family* (New York: Basic Books, 1976) 136–39.

18. Jeffreys, *Spinster*, 23.

19. Gordon, *Woman's Body*, 379–83.

20. Jeffreys quotes extensively to this effect. I'm reminded of a poem by W. H. Auden called "Miss Gee," in which a spinster gets her natural comeuppance by developing cancer. There were many other dumpings on women who did not have heterosexual intercourse with men in what was presented to me while a student in the 1950s as the great literature written in English from the 1920s through the 1950s.

21. See Joanna Russ, "*Amor Vincit Foeminam*: The Battle of the Sexes in Science Fiction" (*S.-F. Studies* 20 7:1 [1980], 2–14) for an account of science fiction stories that defeat female independence with forced heterosexual activity, ranging from a kiss in the 1930s to gang rape in the 1970s. The male authors who wrote these stories believed—or at least said—exactly what the sex reformers did: if voluntary heterosexuality causes female love, loyalty, and labor, then forced heterosexuality will cause them too, somehow.

22. See Barbara Ehrenreich, *The Hearts of Men: American Dreams and the Flight from Commitment* (Garden City, NY: Anchor/Doubleday, 1984).

23. Gordon, *Woman's Body*, 256; Epstein in Ann Snitow et al., *Powers of Desire: The Politics of Sexuality* (New York: Monthly Review Press, 1983), 119.

24. Contemporary additions to economic necessity include romantic idealization, social pressure, and promises of emotional fulfillment. Patricia Frazer Lamb has noted that often these promises of emotional intimacy, sexual fulfillment, and an exciting and happy work life go unfulfilled (Lamb, ed., *Touchstones: Letters between Two Women, 1953–1964* [New York: Harper and Row, 1983]).

25. Adrienne Rich, *Blood, Bread, and Poetry: Selected Prose, 1979–1985* (New York: Norton, 1986), 39.

26. Ibid., 52, Dorothy E. Smith, *Feminism and Marxism: A Place to Begin, a Way to Go* (Vancouver: New Star, 1977), 13.

27. See Katz for descriptions of when and how in the colonial United States the idea of the *hierarchy* of the sexes became transformed into the idea of a "natural" *opposition* between the sexes (Katz, *Gay/Lesbian*, 49–51). Two of his examples are especially striking. One is the absence of any accusation brought against a hated colonial ruler, Lord Cornbury (governor of New York and New Jersey), for his public

cross-dressing. No one even hinted that this eccentricity, which Lord Cornbury said he did in honor of Queen Anne, might be associated with illicit sexual behavior, though such accusations would surely have been made if such an association had occurred to Cornbury's many enemies (ibid., 49–50). The other is a 1629 case of "alleged hermaphroditism." Neighbors of one "Thomas/Thomasine Hall" brought Hall before a magistrate for a determination of Hall's sex. (Presumably the matter confused them.) The governor of Virginia declared "that Hall was a man and a woman.' The magistrate also ruled that Hall wear [both] 'man's apparel' *and* items of clothing that were traditional for women. . . . [This] decision contrasts with nineteenth-century American doctors' responses to alleged hermaphroditism, cross-dressing, and other forms of sexual crossing." Katz adds that by the nineteenth century "the categories man and woman" had become "mutually exclusive" (ibid., 50). Today, of course, the categories are still mutually exclusive, and individuals uncomfortable with their placement in one category can obtain surgery and hormonal treatments to put them in the other category, it being easier to "transsex" people physically than to change ideas about sex and gender.

28. David Grossvogel, *Dear Ann Landers: Our Intimate and Changing Dialogue with America's Best-Loved Confidante* (Chicago: Contemporary Books, 1987), 216.

29. In Elizabeth Abel and Emily K. Abel, eds., *The Signs Reader* (Chicago: University of Chicago Press, 1983), 261. Now that incest survivors have begun to speak out publicly, the picture has changed strikingly.

30. For example, Joan Nestle has written of her working-class mother bringing home

> boyfriends so that sex and her enjoyment of it were not se-
> crets. Respectable ladies did not speak to my mother. . . .
> Several times she was beaten by the man she brought home.
> . . . [once] she was beaten unconscious. . . . "I never allow
> anyone to bully me out of my sexual needs. Just like you,
> Joan, when in the fifties I took you to doctors to see if you
> were a lesbian [sic] and they called you freak and me whore"
> (Snitow, *Powers*, 469–70).

31. Catharine MacKinnon, *Sexual Harassment of Working Women: A Case of Sex Discrimination* (New Haven: Yale University Press, 1979), 174, 175.

32. Shelley in Robin Morgan, ed., *Sisterhood Is Powerful* (New York: Vintage Books, 1970), 308; Abbot and Love in Vivian Gornick and Barbara K. Moran, eds., *Woman in Sexist Society: Studies in Power and Powerlessness* (New York: NAL, 1971), 601–02; "Radicalesbians" in *Liberation Now! Writings from the Women's Liberation Movement* (New York: Dell, 1971), 288.

33. At the very least, cross-dressing and cross-behaving challenge the supposed naturalness of gender. At their most creative, these activities are a complex statement about mood, personality, identity, erotic feeling and interest, anger at

persecution or coercion, and so on. Statements of this sort are made largely by rearranging the terms provided by the dominant culture because of the culture's power and ubiquity and the extreme difficulty Human beings have in inventing anything that is completely new. Jokes, slang, and in-group signals and meanings are all developed by oppressed groups from the materials provided by their own particular, concrete situation. This kind of behavior can easily be seized on by those in the culturally dominant position to prove that the oppressed have an innate essence that "makes" them behave thus. Joan Nestle gives an example: At a 1982 conference, heterosexual women in her audience stated that they felt comfortable with femme-dressed Nestle but not with her butch-dressed lover. Nestle considered this uneasiness with the one and comfortableness with the other to be the transformation of "an erotic conversation" between her lover and herself *back into* a gender-stereotyped statement about the naturalness of femininity in women. Her response was to embrace her lover, saying, "Yes, but it's the two of us together that makes everything clear" (Carol Vance, ed., *Pleasure and Danger: Exploring Female Sexuality* [Boston: Routledge and Kegan Paul, 1984], 237).

34. Rich, *Blood,* 25.

35. Bernard, *Female,* 141.

36. Rubin, *Worlds of Pain,* 41.

37. Alma Gómez et al., eds., *Cuentos: Stories by Latinas* (New York: Kitchen Table Women of Color Press, 1983), 17–18; bell hooks, *Ain't I a Woman* (Boston: South End Press, 1981), 82.

38. Oakley, *Subject Women,* 237.

39. Sanford and Donovan, *Women,* 118; Sara Ruddick and Pamela Daniels, eds., *Working It Out: 23 Women Writers, Artists, Scientists, and Scholars Talk about Their Lives and Work* (New York: Pantheon, 1977), 308.

40. Sanford and Donovan, *Women,* 119–20.

41. Ruddick and Daniels, *Working,* 130, 201, 273, 318, 105, 255.

42. Ibid., 133, 138, 222–23, 286, 115; Rubin, *Worlds of Pain,* 93.

43. Rosalind Coward, *Female Desires: How They Are Sought, Bought, and Packaged* (New York: Grove Press, 1985), 194–95; Sanford and Donovan, *Women,* 394–95, 393.

44. Rubin, *Worlds of Pain,* 151–52; Phelps in Jo Freeman, ed., *Women: A Feminist Perspective,* 2d ed. (Palo Alto, CA: Mayfield, 1979), 23, 21, 24.

45. Coward, *Female Desires,* 42–43.

46. MacKinnon, *Sexual Harassment,* 51.

47. Christine Delphy, *Close to Home: A Materialist Analysis of Women's Oppression,* trans. Diana Leonard (Amherst, MA: University of Massachusetts Press, 1984), 116; Andrea Dworkin, *Right-Wing Women* (New York: Perigee, 1983), 212; Rubin, *Worlds of Pain,* 137; bell hooks, *Feminist Theory from Margin to Center* (Boston: South End Press, 1984), 55; Bernard, *Female,* 368; Gordon, *Woman's Body,* 407; Hollibaugh in Vance, *Pleasure,* 401.

48. Nancy M. Henley, *Body Politics: Power, Sex, and Non-Verbal Communication* (Englewood Cliffs, NJ: Prentice-Hall, 1977), 118; MacKinnon, *Sexual Harassment*, 47, 45; Coward, *Female Desires*, 131; Mary Daly *Gyn/Ecology: The Metaethics of Radical Feminism* (Boston: Beacon Press, 1978), 68; Linda Strega, "The Big Sellout: Lesbian Femininity," *Lesbian Ethics* 1:3 (1985), 83.

49. Rosalind Petchesky and Carol Joffe, "Abortion as 'Violence against Women': A Feminist Critique," *Radical America* 18 (1984). 2–3, Catharine Mac Kinnon, "Reply by MacKinnon," *Radical America* 18 (1984): 2–3.

50. Rubin, *Worlds of Pain*, 114; Bernard, *Female*, 163, 292, 10.

51. Bernard, *Female*, 10; Sanford and Donovan, *Women*, 121; Weems in Barbara Smith, ed., *Home Girls: A Black Feminist Anthology* (New York: Kitchen Table Women of Color Press, 1983), 100.

52. Quoted in Jeffreys, *Spinster*, 93, 89.

53. Rich, *Blood*, 200–1.

54. Note that challenges to male privilege produced *defenses of heterosexuality as such,* although the literal meanings of the fraternity members' statements were surely absurd. "The Sarah Doyle Women's Center is full of women who degrade themselves doing certain sexual acts with men" completely contradicts the statement "The Sarah Doyle Women's Center is full of women who do sexual acts only with women." Similarly, chanting "Howie is a homo" has no logical connection whatsoever with the presumed erotic life of President Swearer. He is a traitor to his sex-class and the women are uppity, that's all. *Therefore* they are not "normal." (Note also that the fraternities' members, fraternities being what they are, are probably also privileged in terms of class and color.)

55. I'm assuming that the *Gay Community News* did report the conference accurately. If there had been any material on class, they probably would have included it. They have done so in other reports of other events and activities.

56. Ti-Grace Atkinson, *Amazon Odyssey* (New York: Link Books, 1974), 12–23.

57. Rich, *Blood*, 25.

58. hooks, *Feminist Theory*, 150; Ruth Bleier, *Science and Gender: A Critique of Biology and Its Theories on Women* (New York: Pergamon Press, 1984), 182; Delphy, *Close to Home*, 180–81; Federici in Ellen Malos, ed., *The Politics of Housework* (London: Alison and Busby, 1980), 253; Rich, *Blood*, 50.

59. Carole S. Vance, "Gender Systems, Ideology, and Sex Research: An Anthropological Analysis," *Feminist Studies* 6:1 (Spring 1980), 130–32, 133–43.

60. Jeffreys, *Spinster*, 67.

SEVEN

WHY WE WOMEN, SLOPPY CREATURES THAT WE ARE, CAN NEVER FIND ANYTHING IN OUR POCKETBOOKS

Women have always worked, as an angry Mary Taylor wrote in the mid-1840s to her friend the novelist Charlotte Brontë.

Women have always been poor, wrote Virginia Woolf in *A Room of One's Own* in 1929.

Woman, said Matilda Joslyn Gage in 1873, *is the great unpaid laborer of the world.*[1]

Although Woolf may have been wrong in reading the female poverty of her own day into all of history, our three foresisters are right, not only for their own day but for ours as well. Women work and women are poor, both when we are paid for our work and when we are not. In fact, after reading the material from which I've drawn most of the information in this chapter, I began to think that women's poverty and women's work were absolutely the most important things there are to know about women. I will give you the information the way it hit me—although what I'm quoting here is a small part of what can be found (even in the same works) on the same subject. These are glimpses: portable, easily excerptable material, merely a sample of what exists. Nonetheless, I hope the following snippets will reproduce some of the effect of the original texts from which they come.[2]

What does it mean to say "Women are poor"? First of all, it means that women make up a disproportionate number of all the poor. Here are some figures:

> While 15 per cent of all families [in the United States] are headed by women, they account for half of all the poor families . . . and they include nearly one-quarter of all children aged 3 to 13.

[In the United States] of the 22 million people receiving food stamps in 1982, 85 per cent were women and their children. In 1982 women and their children also made up 93 per cent of the four million people receiving Aid to Families with Dependent Children.[3]

Second, it means that old women are more often poor than young ones: "Women predominate among the elderly . . . [which] is a group especially prone to . . . poverty."[4]

They are also more often poor than are old men —

Among those over 65 [in the U.S.] two-and-a-half times as many women as men live in poverty, according to Geraldine Ferraro, 1984 Democratic vice-presidential candidate. The rate for all elderly women is 20 per cent.[5]

—while in the United States, Black women are more likely to be poor than White ones—

As many as 41 per cent of all black families are supported by women alone and 54 per cent of these families are officially poor compared to 27 per cent of all white families maintained by women, 16 per cent of families headed by black men and 6 per cent of those headed by white men.[6]

—especially if they are old—

. . . one-half of black older women [in the United States] are poor.

Forty-one per cent of black women aged 65 or over lived in poverty [in the United States] in 1977 while 8% of white men in this age group were poor.[7]

—and unconnected to men. Most women unconnected to men are poor: "Eighty-five per cent of all old women [in the United States] who are single or widowed live near or below the poverty line."[8]

Meanwhile, figures from Britain reveal a similar picture. Ann Oakley, quoting research published in 1979, writes:

Women constitute a majority of the poor. . . . "More than half the poor were women and girls. . . . Women were at a disadvantage at most . . . ages. The proportion of women in poverty was higher than that of men at all ages except under fifteen. . . ." [In 1982] one of the findings reported by the Finer Committee on One-Parent Families was that . . . 50 per cent of fatherless families depended on supplementary benefits as against 10 per cent of motherless families.[9]

Why are women so poor? Perhaps it has something to do with women's wages. All the figures I have been able to find certainly support this idea. For example:

> In 1956 . . . [in the United States] the median earnings of women working full-time and year-round came to 63 per cent of men's earnings. By 1970 . . . women's earnings had tumbled to 59 per cent of men's. By 1974 . . . women's portion was down to 57 per cent. . . . In 1950 the median income of families headed by women had been 56 per cent of those with a husband as sole earner. By 1974 the income of the female-headed family had plummeted to 47 per cent of the modest bundle the male earner was taking home.

> In the U.S. in 1980 half the women of working age were in the labor force but only about half of them earned more than the minimum necessary to keep a family of two above the poverty line. This means that some 75 per cent of all American women aged 16 to 64 would be dependent on resources other than their own earned income if they had to support themselves and one other person.[10]

Nor are such figures anything but conservative. The official poverty line itself, Hilda Scott notes, is extremely low and is based on antiquated spending patterns. As she says:

> People in the US don't believe that a family of four can get along on an income of $9800, the 1982 poverty line for a family that size; they put the minimum at an average of $15,400, according to a Gallup Poll inquiry in January 1983 . . . this is almost exactly the U.S. Bureau of Labor Statistics' . . . "lower standard of living" threshold. By this standard not 34.4 million people but 55–60 million people in the US can be considered poor.[11]

Nor do other countries than ours present a cheerier picture:

[In Britain] 10 per cent of men and 23 per cent of women earn below the 'decency' threshold.

The average hourly industrial wage of women in Sweden has risen to 90 per cent of men's. In white-collar employment, however, women's salaries average only 70 per cent of what men are paid. In the OECD countries women's pay for *full-time, year-round* work ranges from an average of 57 per cent of men's in the US to 81 per cent in Sweden. It is 77 per cent in the Netherlands, 74 per cent in Austria, 73 per cent in France, 66 per cent in Canada, and 65 per cent in the UK.

In Israel as a whole, women's average hourly wages are 20 per cent lower than men's.

For the [then] Soviet Union . . . although female employment rates are exceptionally high, with almost all able-bodied women of working age in the workforce . . . where whole professions have become feminized, as teaching and medicine, they have lost status and the pay compares unfavorably with that of a skilled worker.

In 20 per cent of Hungarian families the woman's earnings are the main or only income. Yet 53 percent of women earn less than sufficient to maintain two people at the official subsistence level compared to 14 per cent of men.

In the iron ore mines [in India] women get 67 percent less than men in their minimum total pay packet. Women are . . . paid less than men for doing the same jobs.

It has been estimated that in India, among agricultural laborers, women are generally paid 40% to 60% of the male wage while they perform much more labor intensive tasks than men. . . . The disparity between the daily earnings of men and women belonging to agricultural labour households increased by approximately 50% between 1964–65 and 1974–75. The grading of certain jobs as "skilled" and therefore better paid is based . . . merely on the assumption that jobs performed by women are, by virtue of that fact alone, low value jobs.[12]

The above discrepancies can be explained only partly by pointing to pay inequities existing between *men* and *women* working at the same kind of job. Equally important are the pay inequities between women's *jobs* and men's *jobs,* what some call the "ghettoization" of women's jobs. My sources put it this way:

> [There is a] division of labor [by sex] within occupations.
>
> [There is a] female ghetto . . . of poorly paid work. . . . [In Britain and the United States] 80 per cent of women work in twenty-five job categories.[13]

Unfortunately for women's financial health as a sex-class, women's jobs pay considerably worse than men's. Hence the recent fights for women's entry into "nontraditional" jobs. Unfortunately this attack on "tradition" may itself be a tradition:

> In 1900 . . . most women in the paid labor force [in the United States] were in occupations disproportionately filled by women. Still true today.
>
> In 1900 . . . one occupation . . . accounted for nearly a third of the female labor force. Domestic service. Today there is one occupation that accounts for over a third. Clerical work.
>
> In 1900 most members of the female labor force could be found in agricultural, manufacturing or domestic service jobs. Today nearly two-thirds can be found in clerical, service or sales jobs. . . . The rate of occupational segregation by sex is exactly as great today. . . . as it was at the turn of the century, if not a little greater. . . . well over half of all women were in occupations in which at least two-thirds of the work force were female. Equally true right now.
>
> And that somewhere between 30 and 48 per cent were consistently employed in occupations in which *80 per cent or more* were female. Exactly the case right now.[14]

Louise Howe lists the 303 separate occupations in the 1900 United States Census, noting that women were reported employed in all but nine. Some of the jobs were: trapper, police officer, firefighter, detective, engineer, barber, chemist, accountant, teamster, steamfitter, undertaker, blacksmith, miner, tilemaker, and steelworker. There were many more.[15] And:

> In 1976 [in the United States] 60% of working women—up from 52% in 1962—were segregated into just four occupations: clerks, saleswomen, waitresses, and hairdressers.
>
> Married women [in the United States] in the eight elite profes-

sions (architect, college teacher, computer systems analyst, doctor, engineer, lawyer, mathematician, scientist) represented less than 1 per cent of all employed wives in 1979. Only "tiny numbers of women" reach upper levels of management.[16]

Nor is the picture substantially different in many other countries:

[In Britain] in 1977 only 13 per cent of employed women were skilled manual workers or held professional or managerial positions.

In 1968 the Swedish government announced the goal of sex-role equality. . . . Occupational segregation was first among the barriers between the sexes that were to come tumbling down. Yet fifteen years and much legislative activity later, with a record 75 per cent of women between 16 and 64 in the workforce, Sweden has one of the most segregated labor forces in Europe. Eighty per cent of women work in thirty job categories.

[Swedish men] have entered women's (paid) jobs in greater numbers than the reverse—the result being that women are deprived of work in a previously "female-intensive" labor category but still are unable to break the gender barrier in more rewarded employment areas.

In the strongly pro-equality [then] German Democratic Republic [women's] educational and training opportunities are far in advance of those . . . in the neighboring Federal Republic [with] accommodation [in day care] for 50 per cent of children under 3 and 90 per cent of those between 3 and 6. . . . In both Germanies women were grossly underrepresented in manufacturing (except in the conventionally female industries) in transportation and communications, and even more so in construction. . . . The concentration of women learning to be office workers, sales personnel, hairdressers and textile workers in the GDR approaches 100 per cent saturation [even though] the industrial workforce has been expanding [and] between 1955 and 1975 the male workforce grew by more than half a million.[17]

Such ghettoization is unfortunate for women's wages, because

[Where] women form the bulk of the labor force . . . pay is usually low. Unionization is usually nil or weak and . . . equal-pay-for-equal work laws are of little or no meaning since if women are competing with anyone for these jobs, they are competing with other women.

[Women's jobs] are labor-intensive. . . . What work in a typing pool and on an electronic components assembly line have in common is . . . [that] these operations require a relatively large number of people . . . [they are] difficult or expensive to mechanize. . . . Since productivity is low [per worker], labor costs must be kept low. . . . Labor-intensive jobs are reserved for women . . . just because women can be paid less.

[Thus] the ranks of construction tradeswomen [in the United States] shrank 24% last year [1982] . . . while the industry's total blue collar employment dropped just 4%. . . . job segregation will increase and opportunities for women diminish [because of] the introduction of the microchip into office work, which is overwhelmingly female. . . . Today office workers represent some kind of a new proletariat, with wages far lower than those in industry and few of the fringe benefits.

Claire, the supervisor, was demonstrating the new word-processing machines [in 1977]. . . .
    "It's really something, isn't it?" Claire marveled.
    In parallel rows young women, about half of them black, sat silently typing away. . . .
    "How many do you have working here?" . . .
    "As of this month, we're down to ten."
    "And just a few years ago there were how many?" . . .
    "Twenty-three."
    "And I bet you're getting out as much work as before."
    "Oh, yes. Probably more."

The potential reduction in clerical employment [1981] . . . [is] one-half or more. . . . [In a study made in Britain in 1980 one observer held that] the "protection" against unemployment that women "enjoyed" as a result of their willingness to work for low pay is evaporating, since it is just those low-level, repetitive jobs that can be computerized. Over a three-year period at American Telephone & Telegraph, 22,000 women lost jobs because of automation, while 13,000 new positions were obtained by men.[18]

"Ghettoized" in low-paying jobs, paid less than men for the same jobs, women are also more vulnerable than men to unemployment:

> Women are . . . the hardest hit by unemployment . . . even with the present pattern of lay-offs in the traditional male industries like steel, autos and engineering. During the world recession in the mid-1970s, women were reported to be 60 per cent of the unemployed in Italy, although less than one-quarter of the workforce. In Sweden, Belgium, France, West Germany, Austria and the US over half the unemployed were women [in 1979]. . . . Swedish female unemployment rates averaged 35 per cent higher than male for . . . 1963–1981. Official unemployment in the UK between 1974 and 1978 increased three times as fast for women as for men. . . . Everywhere youth unemployment figures are double or triple those of adults and young women are reported particularly likely to give up the search.[19]

And then there are the women who are poor because they must work part-time, usually because they are caring for children. Not only do fewer hours of work bring in less pay, the kinds of jobs that can be done part-time don't usually include jobs that pay well by the hour. As Howe puts it, very few jobs are available for "part-time managers . . . pilots, butchers [and] machinists."[20] Here are comments on the relation of motherhood to jobs:

> The social reality women have had to face is that motherhood and paid employment are objectively incompatible. . . . [In 1979 in Britain] 33% of new mothers interviewed returned to work, but of these only 4% returned to full-time work and 29% worked occasionally and/or on a part-time basis. . . .

> [In the US and Britain] mothers can't earn enough to support themselves and their children—or they can't get jobs compatible with child-rearing. Their longer dependence on inadequate state benefits penalizes them financially for motherhood.[21]

Part-time work is itself a problem: "Of Swedish women [in 1981] . . . more and more women work, fewer and fewer are able to support themselves, due to part-time work and lower pay."[22]

Nor is part-time work always as genuinely part-time as the use of that phrase would lead us to believe. Worth pondering are phenomena like the following:

In Britain *when overtime was included* [italics added] 54 per cent
. . . [of] women [employed part-time] were classified as "low-
paid" in 1980. . . .

[Women who work part-time] are women who are too old, too
untrained or too burdened with childcare to get other work.
They often put in a full working week but they do so at a time,
in a place, and for the kind of rates that lead their jobs to be
dismissed as "casual" part-time work.

Hiring on a temporary or casual basis is one of the oldest means
used by employers [in India] to evade laws which protect the
interest of labourers. Fifty-six per cent of all woman workers in
the mining industry are temporary, as against 21% of men. A
large number of these women are still "temporary" after five
years of service and some are "casual" workers after ten years
of continuous service. . . . [Often] not a single women holds
permanent status.[23]

(Of course such tactics are not used only in India. As I write this, hospitals
in the city in which I live and work in the United States have been listing
as "part-time" jobs that take thirty or even thirty-five hours a week—so that
they can avoid paying benefits like health insurance or pensions to the
employees who do them.)

If women's jobs are ghettoized and women's wages so low, why not
choose marriage, or marriage *and* a paid job, as a career instead? In fact
many women do, and it's not hard to find feminist statements to the effect
that for most women marriage is still their best career option. But this career,
The Woman Job, has other disadvantages besides the effect of compulsory
heterosexuality. Although it does provide many women with the space and
funding to bear and raise children, continuing to care for the children pays
a woman little or nothing if her "employer" "fires" her or if she "quits."
Take a look at only a few comments. Here is Scott's:

[A] slippery downward slope . . . awaits the nominally middle-
class woman when she loses her husband through separation
or divorce.

And Chesler's:

In 1983, the United States Census Bureau reported that in 1981,
of 4 million mothers supposed to receive child support payments, only 47 percent did; that mothers who received court-

ordered payments received about 55 percent of the amount due
. . . and that paternal child-support payments averaged $2,110
a year. . . . child support payments accounted for 13 percent of
the average income of fathers. . . . Fifteen percent of 17 million
divorced or separated women were awarded alimony. . . . 43
percent received the amount owed. The mean alimony payment
in 1981 was $3,000.[24]

Delphy says:

> In a study I was involved in, we found in one provincial
> [French] court that the ex-wife was awarded a *mean* of £10 per
> month per child. In general, courts in France [in the 1970s]
> will never instruct the ex-husband to pay more than one-third
> of his income to his ex-wife and children.[25]

Such statistics lead Delphy to argue that the situation existing for women
in the labor market "constitutes an objective incentive to marry," and so it
does. Women's wages are less than men's, even in nonghettoized jobs, and
many women are limited to part-time jobs (sometimes with full-time job
hours). Of course, there are many women whose jobs are necessary for their
own support or because they are the heads of families (their numbers are
increasing) or because their wages are necessary for a family in which they
are one of two wage-earners, but even when her man earns enough to
support a family, surely there is every incentive for a woman not to look
for work in a job market that is in every way less rewarding to her than it
is to him. But if she marries and does not "work" (a misnomer, as we will
see), she then faces other constraints and other problems. This "fourth (26.7
percent) of adult women [in the United States] who have no income of their
own" may find that they are poorer than their husbands. The reasons?
According to Scott:

> Many people who are 'indirectly' *not* in poverty by virtue of the
> chief breadwinner's status *are* poor in the sense that their own
> access to resources is limited."[26]

That is, says Jessie Bernard:

> Many nonemployed housewives at all income levels have felt
> especially degraded by the unilateral control of their monetary
> resources. There is a whole body of female lore dealing with
> when is the best time to ask for money; how to finagle bills and

charge accounts to disguise expenditures; how to save secretly out of household allowances.

Oakley states:

> Family-budget enquiries, especially among working-class couples, persistently show that many wives are kept in ignorance of their husbands' earnings [1973, 1971]. British husbands are notably less generous in this respect than others: 70 per cent of British husbands in one study did not tell their wives what they earned, compared with 40 per cent in West Germany and 1 per cent in the United States [1975]. . . . half of one sample of working wives had received no increase in their housekeeping money even though their husbands were earning more [1974]. In other words, mothers and children can be in poverty while husbands are not. . . . Less than half the pay rises men get [in middle-class marriages] are passed on to wives [Britain, 1977]. . . . "Sharing" one's income (via a joint bank account and joint cheque books) may fit the middle-class ethic of companionate marriage, but it, too, renders wives crucially dependent on husband's economic resources.

Smith notes:

> If he chooses to drink his wage with his buddies after work, it may jeopardize everything she's trying to keep going, but it's his wage. If he makes a down payment on a car they can't afford, or buys into a power boat with his friends, it may throw off all her careful calculations for next winter's clothing, but it's his wage. If his union calls a strike, she's going to pick up the tab in work she has to put in to make up what she can't use money to buy at the store, but it's his job and his wage, and it's not her business. It's not her business if his politics get him first fired and then blacklisted even if everything she's worked for, the kid's security, the household furnishings . . . go down the drain.

And here's Rubin:

> Observers . . . often point to the fact that so many women handle the family finances [in the United States] as evidence that

they wield a great deal of power and influence in the family.
. . . However . . . among [my] professional middle-class families, for example, where median income is at $22,000—a level
that allows for substantial discretionary spending—the figures
flip over almost perfectly; the *men* manage the money in three-
quarters of the families. Moreover, among those working-class
families where some discretion in spending exists, almost always the husband handles the money, or the wife pays the bills
while he makes the decisions. Conversely, in the few professional families where the women manage the money, almost
invariably they are families [in which] . . . incomes are still quite
low and the choices around spending are very limited. . . . Men
manage the money when there is enough of it so that the task
involves some real decision-making. Only then is the job worth
their while.[27]

Note, please, that inequality in marriage is not a monopoly of the working
class.[28] Rubin also notes:

Middle-class marriages [are not] so much more egalitarian [than
those of the working class] but the *ideology* of equality is more
strongly *asserted* there . . . [and] an ideology so strongly asserted tends to obscure the reality, leaving middle-class women
even more mystified than their working-class sisters about how
power is distributed in their marriages.[29]

Middle-class wives—or rather, the wives of middle-class men—also perform different tasks from those performed by working-class wives.[30] Such
differences in the job description do not necessarily imply more freedom.
Indeed, the necessity of presenting a certain sort of social image, for example, may require the kind of psychological self-manipulation not needed
for the working-class wife's more concrete job. Woolf, writing in the 1930s
about the economic dependency central to the life and education of young
Edwardian English ladies of well-to-do families (her own situation as a girl),
finds the "higher" class position quite intolerable. Speaking of how "the
daughters of educated men" rushed into war work when Britain entered
World War I, she wrote, "So profound was her unconscious loathing for
the education of the private house with its poverty, its hypocrisy, its immorality, its inanity, that she would undertake any task . . . that enabled
her to escape." Rubin's description of the working-class women she interviewed is strikingly similar:

There is, perhaps, no greater testimony to the deadening and deadly quality of the tasks of the housewife than the fact that so many women find pleasure in working at jobs that by almost any definition would be called alienated labor—low-status, low-paying, dead-end work made up of dull, routine tasks; work that often is considered too menial for men who are less-educated than these women.[31]

Moreover, whether women wish to enter the paid workforce or not, and whether they prefer marriage to paid work or not, an increasing number of women in the United States and England (and, I suspect, in all industrialized countries) *must* work for wages.[32] All my sources agree that this century has seen a steady increase in the number of women in the U.S. workforce. Obviously, 1940 was a watershed year; in that year (say most), U.S. women's participation in the labor force skyrocketed. But Jessie Bernard notes that female participation in the U.S. labor force rose "phenomenally after 1940" and adds that it rose "from 29.9 to almost 60 per cent, 59.61[,] in 1978." Paula Giddings states:

> Even in the woman-idealizing [U.S.] South, seven out of eight married women were working by 1940; the national proportion of such workers was six out of seven. The Women's Bureau under Mary Anderson conducted studies which showed that the great majority of women who worked in factories contributed at least 50 per cent to their families' income. Furthermore, more than half of all married women were employed in domestic and personal service or low-paying factory work.[33]

In Great Britain, according to Ann Oakley, the proportion of women in the labor force

> only began to rise dramatically in the late 1940s. . . . The jobs women took—whether new or old—tended to be those at the bottom of every scale: low paid, low status, unskilled. . . . In 1911, one in ten married women had a job; in 1951 one in five; in 1976, one in two. Two out of three employed women are now married.[34]

In Peggy Morton's words: "We are not talking about a group of workers that are peripheral to the economy, but a group which are central to the maintenance of labor-intensive manufacturing, and service and state sectors where low wages are a priority." For example, she adds that 75 percent of all U.S. clothing workers are women, 65 percent of workers in knitting mills, and 51 percent in leather products.[35] From the 1950s onward, women no longer formed only a reserve army of labor in the United States, i.e., workers pulled into paid jobs when there's a shortage of male workers and forced out when no longer needed.

Female labor is also what Louise Howe calls "quality labor at a low price," as employers can hire women who are "relatively well-educated . . . for much less than men who have received a comparable education."[36]

In short, women's poverty is highly attractive to women's employers and even more worth preserving than the poverty of poor men—which is why women tend to be so strongly located in labor-intensive work. Where there is "a very high degree of monopolisation and automation" and "huge investments in plant or equipment," there is also a small one in labor; thus "the need to control wages is not an absolute." In "labor-intensive" businesses, labor is a big cost; these are the industries in which women usually work. Peggy Morton writes that equal wages in *this* sector would make necessary "a transformation of the industry."[37]

Thus employers pay "women's jobs" less than "men's jobs"; thus men defend "men's jobs" against entry by women; thus women are given a strong economic motivation to marry and stay married, are punished economically for divorce, and as mothers are punished economically for bearing and raising children who are everybody's indispensable future. Thus husbands subsidize not only their wives' domestic activities (as most of them think) but also their wives' employers' activities, under the mistaken impression that they are protecting their own jobs and their own earning power. Strictly in terms of family income, it would be to most men's economic advantage to maximize their wives' earnings. Employers would not like such a change—it would cost them a good deal. Husbands should—but often don't. Why?

Because paid work is not the only work that women do.

"The dinners," wrote Woolf in 1929, "are cooked, the plates and cups are washed; the children sent to school and gone out in the world. Nothing remains at all. All has vanished. No biography or history has a word to say about it."[38] But some voices from the past do find their way into the present. In 1739, Mary Collier, an English working woman, described her fellows' labor in the field with a vivid picture of what feminists now call the *second shift* or *the double workday:*[39]

> When Harvest comes, into the Field we go,
> And help to reap the wheat as well as you;
> Or else we go the Ears of Corn to glean;
> No Labour scorning, be it e'er so mean. . . .

> To get a Living we so willing are,
> Our tender Babes unto the Field we bear,
> And wrap them in our Cloaths to keep them warm,
> While round about we gather up the Corn. . . .
>
> When Night comes on, unto our Home we go,
> Our Corn we carry, and our infant too;
> Weary indeed! but 'tis not worth our while
> Once to complain or rest at ev'ry Stile;
> We must make haste, for when we home are come,
> We find again our Work but just begun;
> So many things for our Attendance call,
> Had we ten Hands, we could employ them all.
> Our Children put to Bed with greatest Care. . . .
> You sup and go to Bed without Delay,
> And rest yourselves till the ensuing Day;
> While we, alas! but little sleep can have,
> Because our froward Children cry and rave;
> Yet without fail, soon as Day-light doth spring,
> We in the Field again our work begin
>
> . . . .

The poet goes on to describe working women's labor in the wintertime ("Hard labour we most chearfully pursue") with its laundress work, its dishwashing, its polishing of iron and brass, and its brewing. At one point Collier sarcastically addresses working men:

> Those mighty Troubles which perplex your Mind
> (Thistles before and Females come behind)
> Would vanish soon and quickly disappear
> Were you, like us, encumber'd thus with Care.

She then asks the working men what on earth they want of women—aren't the women working hard enough?[40]

The double workday was always a problem for women—if not for ladies—but in the last two generations or so, having been "democratized" in the industrial countries, it has become a problem for many ladies too, which may be why there's been so much feminist comment on it. Howe, writing of the United States in the mid-1970s, speaks of "young mothers slicing themselves into five pieces to get everything done," while Oakley tells us that a " 'good woman' in the 1970s is one who has two careers: one as a wage/salary earner, and one as a home-provider, which includes up-to-date knowledge of the techniques of child-rearing, meal-provision and sexual satisfaction."[41] Dale Spender maintains that women's work in the home produces men's leisure, and Scott calls the double workday "a high-wire balancing act."[42] Sanford and Donovan emphasize "the never-ending nature of women's work in the home" and how hard it is to tell when and whether such work is done. Smith notes the way men take such work for granted. Lee Comer even asserts that one of a wife's functions is to serve as "the container for the male worker's dehumanization. . . . A worker can punch his wife but not his boss!" (This is exactly Chesler's view of male violence against women.) Oakley, interviewing forty housewives in 1971, stressed the monotony of housework, its fragmentation, the time limits set on tasks by other tasks, its isolation, its structurelessness, and the contradictions of caring for house *and* children (who are neither clean nor tidy in their natural state). Jan Williams, Hazel Twort, and Ann Bachelli also speak of the housewife, the physical and emotional "crowding" in on her of her family's demands, the lack of time alone, the feeling of futility caused by the "compulsive circle" of maintenance work without closure or standards for people with whom one is leading a personal, not a "work," life.[43] After all, as Mariarosa Dalla Costa and Selma James notice, "If you are not paid by the hour, within certain limits, nobody cares how long it takes you to do your work" or how much work you have to do.[44] All this and a paid job into the bargain!

Here are some more voices, these from the anthology *Women and Disability:* "Ninety percent of women alcoholics are left by their husbands; 20 percent of men alcoholics are left by their wives (National Council on Alcoholism, 1980)." In one study, when men became disabled, their wives "helped them manage instrumentally and affectively their personal and professional endeavors. . . . Disabled women . . . have no wives."[45]

Barbara Macdonald and Cynthia Rich write:

> Dr. Monica Blumenthal, a geriatric psychiatrist . . . explained that right now there are a million Americans who require twenty-four-hour care. . . . It's a myth, she explained, that the aged are being cared for by their families. "It's almost always a girl, a female child. And my impression is that the family nominates one person. . . . The family usually abandons this one person and doesn't lend a hand any more." So the problem of the aged falls on the daughters—and the daughters-in-law.[46]

In a support group for disabled women that I have attended, one-third of the members were the only people available to care for other disabled spouses or parents. A woman who had multiple sclerosis, a disease subject to erratic recurrences, was caring for a husband who had just had a heart attack. Such situations are doubly stressful and many find a parallel in the situations of many women who belong to groups that are oppressed for reasons other than sex.

Here is Black psychotherapist Eleanor Johnson, describing a typical client of hers:

> She's come in to turn in her Mammy-badge after having allowed everyone to feed off her. Is that why she's so tired? Will she guard herself against me for fear of one more ounce of bottomless giving? Or will she fight me for caring since that's *her* lot, taking care of everyone but herself?[47]

Leghorn and Parker give examples of women's work:

> Women also produce a higher standard of living for their families. They make goods which in effect serve as luxury goods for families who would not be able to afford them if they had to buy them. . . . [thus they] bring the family's standard of living up . . . to the culturally defined minimum—that which is required either to meet social expectations (such as fashionable clothing or home decorations) or that which is required to survive economically within the cultural context (i.e. a car to get to work in Los Angeles, a bicycle for an African man working in a big town).

> Women everywhere also try to make ends meet by cutting down on expenses, which usually involves increasing domestic work. In industrialized countries comparison shopping must be done to counteract the effects of inflation. Women spend more time mending and washing clothes, and learning 16 new ways to make hamburgers. . . .

In short, as Rosalind Petchesky states, women thus "take over the state's job, smoothing the rough edges of the [economic] crisis and making it humanly endurable."[48]

As far as I can tell (although my knowledge is inadequate here), things do not seem to be fundamentally different outside the industrialized countries. Thus Robin Morgan writes, "The "two-job" burden is deplored by contributors from societies so different as China, Cuba, Egypt, Finland, Pakistan, Rumania, the Soviet Union, and the United States, to mention only a few."[49]

Thus, the editorial for the inaugural issue of the Indian feminist journal *Manushi* stated (among many other things) that "the burden of housework and childcare falls upon us. . . . And this heavy labour goes unacknowledged by society, even women themselves. When we ask a woman what she does, how often is the answer—'Oh, nothing—I'm just a housewife.' Why are we taught to trivialize ourselves and our labour?"[50] Admittedly my sources are few, but *Manushi's* sources are not, nor is the resemblance between nations, I suspect, that far-fetched.

There are resemblances back through time too, including Florence Nightingale's complaint that anyone and everyone felt free to break in on women's privacy and women's time. And here is an early feminist book, reprinted by Virago only recently, originally published in 1825 and written—or so the volume tells us—by one William Thompson. In it, not only is a woman's work rendered invisible (against Thompson's wishes), but the reason for the invisibility turns out to be surprisingly familiar. In *Appeal to One Half of the Human Race,* Thompson's introduction states unequivocally that the ideas in the book are not his but those of his associate, Anna Wheeler. He merely "endeavored to arrange" them, he says, and why? Because she herself had not the leisure to do so![51]

Rosario Morales recalls her 1950s marriage, in which, she says, her husband was supposed to take care of her:

> Take care of me? Stuff! I did the taking care of. Trust nobody to see that though. That kind of thing is real invisible, especially in the fifties. That kind of work wasn't even *there,* except you stop doing it and boy, you'd get noticed, all right. Not just shopping and cooking and dishwashing and laundry and beds and floors and bathrooms but feelings and, you know . . . mothering.[52]

In 1976 Phyllis Chesler and Emily Jane Goodman invented an advertisement:

HELP WANTED

REQUIREMENTS. Intelligence, good health, energy, patience, sociability. Skills: at least 12 different occupations. HOURS: 99.6 per week. SALARY: None. HOLIDAYS. None (will be required to remain on stand-by 24 hours a day, 7 days a week.) OPPORTUNITIES FOR ADVANCEMENT: None (limited transferability of skills acquired on the job). JOB SECURITY. None (trend is toward more layoffs, particularly as employee approaches middle age. Severance pay will depend on the discretion of the employer). FRINGE BENEFITS. Food, clothing and shelter generally provided, but any additional bonuses will depend on the financial standing and good nature of employer. No health, medical or accident insurance; no Social Security or pension plan.

They add, "Absurd? But true. This is a fairly accurate summary of the job of a full-time housewife."[53]

Giddings quotes from a Ph.D. dissertation, "The Negro Woman's College Education," written by Jeanne L. Nobel for Columbia University in 1956, in which one of Nobel's respondents wrote:

> Even though she [the Negro woman] may have a professional job, the Negro man expects her to be a buffer for him—to work eight hours a day and come home and keep house. I am sure the Negro woman feels incapable of doing this adequately. For this reason she feels that somebody has let her down. She wants college to give her information on how she can do the impossible.[54]

Such voices could go on and on, from the many countries that have no definition of unpaid family worker or statistics about such workers, the vast majority of whom are women, to the lack of recognition that such work exists at all, to the industrialized nations in which research into such work is almost nonexistent.[55]

There is some of it, though, and what there is, is a shock. According to Howe, U.S. homemakers with outside jobs worked four to eight hours a day in their homes while the time spent by full-time homemakers ranged from five to twelve hours a day. Husbands' housework, both for those women who worked outside their homes and those who did not, averaged less than an hour and a half a day. (The time judged as housework did not include coffee breaks, talking to a friend on the phone, or "waiting for the kids to come home or lying in bed listening for a sick baby's cry.") The typical total workweek of employed wives (i.e., those earning money outside the home) varied from sixty-six hours to seventy-five. The total work of these women, waged and unwaged, averaged fifteen hours more per week than their husbands'. Howe comments: "Almost two ordinary work days." According to Scott, who is citing work done in 1981, recent time-use studies made in the United States find that on the average wives do "70 per cent of work in the home, husbands 15 per cent and children the rest." That is, in terms of the time involved, "a *minimum* of forty hours a week" for a woman who does not work at a paid job outside her home (the italics are Scott's) and thirty hours if the woman does work outside the home. The "husband's contribution remains about the same whatever the family size and does not increase very much if his wife takes a job outside the home."[56]

Nor have these figures changed much over time; Jansen-Jurreit quotes figures for the United States that put the full-time housewife's workweek at fifty-two hours in 1924 and fifty-five hours in 1970. Between 1952 and 1967–68, the daily housework of gainfully employed women in the United States rose from 3.8 to 4.5 hours. According to Henley, U.S. women who worked only in the home spent about as much time on housework fifty years ago as they do now: fifty-one to fifty-six hours a week. Ehrenreich and English, using the same study as Scott does, note that "labor-saving devices," although they might make housework easier, were not in fact saving anybody time. Jansen-Jurreit mentions the growth of do-it-yourself repair in this connection and more time spent on shopping, while Scott notes that "capitalism is shifting onto the housewife work that was formerly done by paid personnel." Her description of the process: "instead of . . . phoning in her order, dropping off a shopping list, sending one of the children, or having a sales clerk explain the merchandise," the shopper must locate the goods herself, determine the price (difficult with the new scanning machines and the elimination of price tags), unload the goods herself, transport them to bus or car, travel long distances, unload them again, and store them. And, as Jansen-Jurreit notes, the more leisure time other members of the family have, the greater the tasks the housewife must perform. Oakley notes that the time men spend on work in the home is "relatively insensitive" to wives' employment for wages and that "men often say they do more in the home than they actually do."[57]

Nor do matters change strikingly as we look at other countries. Scott states that the time spent by women on housework in England has not altered during the past fifty years. In Moscow and Leningrad, says Jansen-Jurreit, there was some, but little, change from 1924 to 1965, with gainfully employed women spending 4.47 hours per workday in 1924, 3.87 hours in 1959, and 3.6 hours in 1965. (Figures do not include child care or the care of the old or ill.)[58] Here are some other figures:

Full-time housewives in twelve industrialized countries had 25 percent less leisure time than men. Women employed outside the home as well as inside it had less than that.[59]

The workday of a rural Indian woman begins "hours before the men's"; she fetches water for the family, in droughts walking as much as one to three kilometers to find it; she gathers food with "long hours of backbreaking labour"; she may "walk miles daily" to gather firewood.[60]

According to Scott, rural women in what she calls the "Third World" "gather wood, carry water, garden, store crops, process food, and work directly in crop production"—all without wages. They are listed on the official records, "if at all," as unpaid family workers.[61]

A French study puts the time expended in housework in 1975 at 30 percent more than that expended by the entire nation in paid work.[62]

In Poland the "women work in 'two shifts.' " When the women working in the textile industry in Lodz were studied in the early 1950s, they said that most of their heavy labor took place at home.[63]

A multinational study in 1975 concluded that in all countries included in the study, gainfully employed wives worked an average of 5.7 hours for house and family on their days off. On working days they devoted 3.3 hours to housework, while men contributed 1 hour. In a Czech city, "the husbands did scarcely a quarter of the housework of their wives, while in Poland, the United States and France the men's . . . time varied between 12 and 17 per cent."[64]

Another study, published in 1973, found that the husbands who offered *no* help at all to wives who worked outside the home for pay were 49 percent in Italy, 39 percent in Luxembourg, 32 percent in West Germany, 31 percent in France, 26 percent in Belgium, and a mere 24 percent in Holland (which may have something to do with Holland's shorter working hours and larger number of kindergartens and preschools than other countries, as well as the small number of Dutch women who worked outside the home at that time).[65]

Time spent on housework where household machinery was available in quantity, for example, West Germany, was not less than time so spent where it was unavailable, as in the Soviet Union.[66]

In Swedish families in which husband and wife were both gainfully employed, 67 percent of wives did all the cooking, 80 percent all the laundry, and 53 percent all the cleaning (1982 figures). According to a 1983 report by the Swedish Ministry of Labor, women spent 35 hours weekly on housework, men 7 to 8.[67]

Chinese husbands "in many agricultural communes" enjoy leisure time during their lunch hours; their wives, also workers, do food preparation and child care during this time.[68]

As for child care—certainly a very important part of The Woman Job—let us note first that the very word "father" *did not even occur* in that standard work in the professional literature of the United States, the *Manual of Child Psychology,* for 1954. Although things have certainly changed since then, in 1973 Urie Bronfenbrenner, specialist in child development, "cited research reporting that [U.S.] fathers spent on an average less than a minute to twenty minutes a day with infants of either sex." Chesler reports a 1974 study that gives the figure as 37.7 seconds to 10 minutes and 26 seconds daily, while another 1974 study estimated fathers' contacts with one-year-olds to be, on average, 15 to 20 minutes a day, and 16 minutes daily for children aged six to sixteen; and a study in 1976 reported that fathers spent an average of 15 minutes a day feeding their babies while mothers spent an average of 1.5 hours a day doing so. Nearly half these fathers never changed a diaper.[69]

In twelve European countries, "fathers scarcely took part at all" in "tasks involved in the care of small children — feeding, bathing, dressing, etc." And although there were crèches in India, Kishwar calls them "a farce"—far from workplace or residences, with neglected, ill-treated children cared for by untrained people.[70]

It's hardly surprising, looking at the above figures, to find Oakley flatly declaring that "free time" is a vacuous concept when applied to the lives of most women. She adds: "In the 1970s and 1980s, women are doing more of 'his' work than they used to, but men have made few inroads on 'hers.' This applies both to 'feminine' types of paid work and to feminine work in the home."[71]

Nor is it surprising, in light of the above, to hear that 59 percent of women surveyed in the United States, so often described by its politicians as the wealthiest country in the world, said *they had no leisure whatsoever.* The leisure of other family members, it seems, does not guarantee that of the housewife herself. As Malos puts it, "it is her work which provides the basis of other people's leisure."[72]

Not only does domestic work take large amounts of time; if paid for, it would cost a very great deal. Bernard calls "the operation and maintenance of the household" nothing less than *the largest industry in the United States* "in terms of the numbers engaged in it both as 'producers' and 'consumers.' " Oakley says the same thing about Britain's "largest industry." Estimating the cost of such an industry in hard cash, Scott quotes the Chase National Bank's 1972 figures for the United States—$275.53 a week at then-prevalent rates—and comments: "If all unpaid housework had been paid at that rate, it would have cost the country twice the national budget." Elsewhere in the same chapter she estimates that the tab for domestic labor, if financed by the U.S. government (so that the "average working man" could afford it) "would put the U.S. budget deficit to shame." Oakley sets the cost of such work for Britain as 39 percent of the British Gross National Product.[73]

As Debra Connors puts it, at such prices only the elite can afford to pay someone to "shop, transport children, cook, launder, clean or provide other consumer service." Without wives, "enormous and profit-handicapping resources would have to be devoted to catering for these . . . needs." Wives, Oakley says, take the place of servants in the modern industrial state.[74]

Or, as Scott herself sums up her chapter on women's unpaid labor: "The work women do 'in exchange for' food and lodging and sometimes pin money could not be purchased by any man." This is certainly surprising enough, but Scott goes further: "Women's unpaid labor . . . supplies services and products that no economy is prepared to pay for." And further still:

> [According to International Labor Organization data] women do two-thirds of the world's work and receive 10 percent of the world's income. When I accepted a redefinition of work that included unpaid work and assumed that all income was payment for work done, I realized that men were getting paid at a rate eighteen times that of women.[75]

Writing in the early women's liberation movement, Shulamith Firestone asked who would do women's domestic work if women were "drafted . . . into the . . . commodity economy." Our current answer is simple: women will. Women will work for pay and will do their domestic work for no pay, no regular time off, no night out that can be counted on, and (if economically dependent) she has, says Rubin, "no way, short of years of nagging or divorce, to defy her husband's authority . . . about what she may or may not do." And very likely, whether the marriage is one of the working-class ones Rubin investigated or a middle-income one, there remains the work without which children and households perish, The Woman Job. The working conditions are terrible (all my sources agree about that) and yet the job is, globally, all but inescapable. It results in longer hours and comparative poverty for those drafted into it,[76] although it is not generally considered work at all. Feminists have made women's work visible in the last two decades by some very hard political work of their own, but the problem remains: Why must this work be loaded on to women? Why can't it, for example, be shared between the sexes?

I think the answer is simple.

Who on earth would be willing to cut his income by two-thirds and double his workday? This is what men as a sex-class would have to do to relieve women of women's double workday and poverty worldwide. Perhaps more to the point, *who on earth would be willing to cut his income by 40 percent and add two hours or more to his workday?* That is roughly what the sex-class of men would have to do to make the sexes in the industrialized countries (on the average) equally rich and equally poor. Is it any wonder that most cultures on this planet regard marriage, with its unsalaried work, as the goal of a woman's life? Or that women all over the world work longer hours and are poorer than men, or that domestic work is not even considered work?[77]

Many, many feminists have maintained that women are generally underpaid at waged work because marriage has been considered a woman's "real" job. Many have also noted that women's work within the institution of marriage and the family has been made invisible by considering it part of women's nature—and so not work at all. The conclusion most of these social critics come to is that "people" must be educated to perceive that domestic work is work, that it is not natural, and that it is not necessarily women's work. That is, they assume the root of the problem to be the *ideas* that most people have about marriage and domestic work and see the solution to lie in *changing people's ideas*.

I would like to turn these causal arrows around.

I believe, like Delphy (whose ideas have been very important to me throughout this book), that it is the *objective necessity* of domestic work (that is, somebody must do it) that is the *cause of marriage*. Because domestic work must be done by somebody, and because men and nations cannot afford to pay decently for it in the paid marketplace, women must somehow be induced to perform it. Therefore, as Delphy says, we have discrimination in the labor market—low pay, ghettoized jobs, and higher unemployment—*because* such discrimination will function to "turn and return women to marriage precisely because marriage constitutes their objectively . . . least bad 'career.' " The fact that women who marry have made a *job choice* is concealed by the belief that marriage, with its attendant domestic work, is purely personal and somehow "natural" to women. This belief, of course, in and of itself constitutes part of the social pressure to marry, as do social sanctions against divorce, casual sexuality in women, celibacy, or homosexuality. If you add, as Dorothy Smith does, that "women cannot earn enough to support themselves and their children outside the marriage relationship," you can then see the nature of the circle, since "that is where the trap closes for women in marriage."[78]

After all, if very large numbers of women were to recognize that domestic work *is* work, that it was no more natural to them than it was to their husbands, if they could at the same time find a better economic deal elsewhere, they might very well refuse to enter the job of marriage at all, or refuse to stay in it, or they might demand better working conditions within it and better pay. The Wages for Housework Campaign, says Gloria Joseph, "argues that housework is free labor" and gives the figure for Canadian women's housework as "roughly one-third of the Gross National Product." She calls it (quoting the Wages for Housework Campaign) "the single largest industry in Canada."[79] So perhaps it *is* already happening. And why not provide those better working conditions and better pay?

Because—remember those estimates above—The Woman Job is a job for which no country and no large group of men (except for a small number of very elite men) can pay.

To put it bluntly, in the world as it's run right now, *they can't afford us.*

NOTES

1. Helene Moglen, *Charlotte Brontë: The Self Conceived* (New York: W. W. Norton, 1976), 174. Virginia Woolf, *A Room of One's Own* (London: Harcourt, 1929), 112. Matilda Joslyn Gage, *Women, Church, and State: The Original Exposé of Male Collaboration against the Female Sex* (Watertown, MA: Persephone Press, 1980), 195. Originally published 1873.

2. In this chapter, I have made extensive use of Hilda Scott's *Working Your Way to the Bottom: The Feminization of Poverty* (London: Pandora, 1984). Some reviewers have objected to Scott's book and the phrase "feminization of poverty" on the grounds that poverty is on the increase only among White women in the United States and that U.S. women of color have long been familiar with it. I agree, and I also find Scott's recommendations for action inadequate. Nonetheless, I believe the book to be valuable both for its wealth of statistics and because Scott emphatically places the blame for women's poverty in what she calls the "Third World" on European and United States imperialism.

3. Ibid., 19; Linda Tschirhart Sanford and Mary Ellen Donovan, *Women and Self-Esteem* (New York: Anchor/Doubleday, 1984), 201.

4. Ann Oakley, *Subject Women* (New York: Pantheon, 1981), 292.

5. Scott, *Working,* 19.

6. Ibid., 20.

7. Ibid., 19; Barbara Macdonald and Cynthia Rich, *Look Me in the Eye: Old Women, Aging, and Ageism* (San Francisco: Spinsters Ink, 1983), 105.

8. Macdonald and Rich, *Look Me,* 105.

9. Oakley, *Subject,* 292.

10. Louise Kapp Howe, *Pink Collar Workers: Inside the World of Women's Work* (New York: G. P. Putnam's Sons, 1977), 3–4; Scott, *Working,* 17. Scott adds that at the professional level the gap between men's and women's earnings is greater than it is in working-class families (33). That is, women's wages rise more slowly than men's as one crosses this class line.

11. Scott, *Working,* 8, 9.

12. Ibid., 29, 27, 26; Madhu Kishwar and Ruth Vanita, eds., *In Search of Answers: Indian Women's Voices from Manushi* (London: Zed Books, 1984), 65, 17.

13. Oakley, *Subject,* 153; Scott, *Working,* 27–28.

14. Howe, *Inside,* 6–7.

15. Ibid., 5.

16. Sanford and Donovan, *Women,* 209; Scott, *Working,* 32–33.

17. Scott, *Working*, 26, 27; Robin Morgan, ed., *Sisterhood Is Global: The International Women's Movement Anthology* (New York: Anchor, 1984), 17; Scott, *Working*, 28. In 1972 (I can't, unfortunately, find later figures), women's wages in Japan were 47.5 percent of men's. In the early 1970s, among the women in the United States whom she interviewed (women married to blue-collar men), Lillian Breslow Rubin found the median income for full-time, year-round work to be $6,000 (Rubin, *Worlds of Pain. Life In the Working Class Family* [New York: Basic Books, 1976] 236).

18. Howe, *Inside*, 9; Scott, *Working*, 62–63, 34; Howe, *Inside*, 148; Scott, *Working*, 34–35.

19. Scott, *Working*, 30–31. Howe presents statistics to the effect that in the United States in 1975 Black teenage women had "the bleak distinction of . . . the highest rate of unemployment of any group (including Black teenage males) in the nation." The unemployment rate of White teenage women in the first quarter of 1975 was 18.1 percent. For Black teenage women, the rate was *43 percent*. (Howe finds it understandably necessary at this point to emphasize that the printed figure is not a typographical error.) "A year later," she writes, "[during] economic recovery, the rate for black teenagers had barely moved" (*Inside*, 3). These are dreadful figures and I see no reason to assume that things have improved as the total economic picture has gotten worse.

20. Howe, *Inside*, 256.

21. Gloria Joseph and Jill Lewis, *Common Differences: Conflicts in Black and White Feminist Perspectives* (New York: Anchor, 1981), 129; Oakley, *Subject*, 293.

22. Scott, *Working*, 30.

23. Ibid., Oakley, *Subject*, 184, 185; Kishwar and Vanita, *In Search*, 66.

24. Scott, *Working*, 18; Phyllis Chesler, *Mothers on Trial: The Battle For Children and Custody* (New York: McGraw-Hill, 1986), 90.

25. Christine Delphy, *Close to Home: A Materialist Analysis of Women's Oppression*, translated by Diana Leonard (Amherst, MA: University of Massachusetts Press, 1984), 104. I apologize for the possible out-of-dateness of this statistic. The particular essay of Delphy's in which it appears is dated 1976. Here is another out-of-date but very interesting parallel to Delphy's figure: until 1918, the year some women got the vote in England, the Bastardy Act of 1872 fixed five shillings a week as the most a father, whatever his wealth, could be made to pay for the support of an illegitimate child (Virginia Woolf, *Three Guineas* [New York: Harcourt, 1966], 168–69). Changing this kind of law was one of the suffragists' aims in getting the vote.

26. Delphy, *Close to Home*, 20; Jessie Bernard, *The Female World* (New York: The Free Press, 1981), 208; Scott, *Working*, 14.

27. Bernard, *Female*, 208–9; Oakley *Subject*, 254–55; Barbara Smith, *Toward a Black Feminist Criticism* (Brooklyn, NY: Out and Out Books, 1977), 50; Rubin, *Worlds of Pain*, 107–8.

28. The point I wish to make here is the precariousness of an economic and

social status that depends entirely on someone else's income and position. As feminists used to say (before we entered the "postfeminist" era), *Every woman is one man away from welfare.* Insofar as a particular woman's only or major means of support is marriage, that saying is still accurate.

29. Rubin, *Worlds of Pain,* 97–98.

30. Rubin points out that wives of professional, middle-class men

> are expected to participate in their husbands' professional
> lives by cultivating an appropriate social circle, by being en-
> tertaining and charming hostesses and companions. . . .
> Husbands who require wives to perform such services must
> allow them to move more freely outside the home if they are
> to carry out their tasks properly. The working-class man has
> no need of such . . . accomplishments since his work life is
> almost wholly segregated from his family life (ibid., 98).

31. Woolf, *Three Guineas,* 39; Rubin, *Worlds of Pain,* 169.

32. Feminists have been saying for years that the majority of women work at paid jobs because they must. In the United States, for example, "one-half of all gainfully employed women are already either supporting themselves or are in sole support of a family and this is a pattern developing in all industrialized lands" (Scott, *Working,* 13). Moreover, in Britain, one-parent families increased 66 percent between 1971 and 1981, to 12.5 percent of all families (ibid., 22). In the great majority of cases, "single-parent" means actually single mother.

33. Bernard, *Female,* 109; Paula Giddings, *When and Where I Enter: The Impact of Black Women on Race and Sex in America* (New York: Morrow, 1984), 231. The percentages of women working for money are actually somewhat higher than they look. One must not assume a male labor force participation figure of 100 percent, since not all men are in the labor force from ages sixteen to sixty-five. Howe quotes figures from the 1975 *Economic Report of the President* (of the United States) to the effect that in 1973 only 87 percent of men aged twenty-five to fifty-four were actually in the labor force full-time in the United States (Howe, *Inside,* 255.) Another warning: Women's gains in the professions (or anything else, for that matter) must be compared with similar statistics *for men* in order to mean anything. It may be, for example, that women's this or that has increased only because the population in general has increased, or it may be that women's increases are exceeded by men's, or it may be that whole professions or trades have increased in numbers or decreased. Thus Jansen-Jurreit quotes U.S. Labor Department figures to the effect that from 1950 to 1960 the number of professionally qualified women in the United States rose by 41 percent. This looks like progress—until you find that in the same decade the number of similarly qualified men rose by 51 percent. She also cites a sociologist who found in 1970 in the United States that the more women who entered a particular profession, the more the income of the practitioners dropped, and also that the more

men who entered a profession, the more the income of its practitioners rose (Marie-louise Jansen-Jurreit, *Sexism: The Male Monopoly on History and Thought,* trans. Verne Moberg [New York: Farrar, Straus and Giroux, 1982], 182).

34. Oakley, *Subject,* 146–47.

35. In Ellen Malos, ed., *The Politics of Housework* (London: Alison and Busby, 1980), 153, 150.

36. Howe, *Inside,* 259.

37. In Malos, *Housework,* 149–50.

38. Woolf, *A Room of One's Own* (New York: Harcourt, 1957), 93.

39. She was defending English agricultural working women against a poem written in 1736 by Stephen Duck, an English working man, which described such women as lazy and feckless (Moira Ferguson, ed., *First Feminists: British Women Writers, 1578–1799* [Bloomington, IN: University of Indiana Press, 1985], 257).

40. Ibid., 260–61. Ferguson calls Mary Collier "the first known rural labouring woman to publish creative work." She died poor, in her own words, "in Piety, Purity, Peace and an Old Maid." Collier wrote "The Woman's Labour" in 1739. The poem ends with a complaint about working people's exploitation by the rich, whom she compares to "owners" reaping gains of honey from the bees' constant toil. Of herself, Collier wrote that she was taught to read and write by her parents when "very Young and took great delight in it; but my Mother dying, I lost my Education" (ibid., 257). That is painful reading, but we may, if we wish, find some solace in her integrity as a poet and her insistence upon her identity as a creator. Thus, she writes, of her retiring to "a Garret" in 1762, that it was ever "the poor *poet's* Fate" (ibid., italics added).

41. Howe, *Inside,* 257; Oakley, *Subject,* 16.

42. Dale Spender, *Man-Made Language* (London: Routledge, Kegan and Paul, 1980), 115; Scott, *Working,* 65. Oakley states that research on the servant class in European history is also almost nonexistent and compares women and servants as "secret agents maintaining the all-important cultural boundary between personal and public life." She notes that servants, like wives, were defined as the dependents of property owners and that servants, like wives, "were the last social group to receive enfranchisement as citizens" (Oakley, *Subject,* 182).

43. Sanford and Donovan, *Women,* 221; Smith, *Toward,* 48; Lee Comer, *Wedlocked Women* (Leeds, England: Feminist Books, 1974), 237; Phyllis Chesler, *About Men* (New York: Simon and Schuster, 1978); Ann Oakley, *Woman's Work: The Housewife, Past and Present* (New York: Pantheon, 1974), 91–104; Williams, Twort, and Bachelli in Malos, *Housework,* 114–15.

44. Mariarosa Dalla Costa and Selma James, *The Power of Women and the Subversion of the Community,* 3d ed. (Bristol, England: Falling Wall Press, 1972), 28–29. There have been many feminist arguments to the effect that pay for child-care and domestic work is as low as it is—and it is notoriously low, even in the rich United States—precisely because so many women perform the same work for no

pay at all. That is, the very existence of unpaid housewives drags down the going rate for any women who perform the same tasks for money.

45. Mary Jo Deegan and Nancy A. Brooks, eds., *Women and Disability: The Double Handicap* (New Brunswick, NJ: Transaction Books, 1985), 8, 14.

46. Macdonald and Rich, *Look Me*, 48–49.

47. In Barbara Smith, ed., *Home Girls: A Black Feminist Anthology* (New York: Kitchen Table Women of Color Press, 1983), 321.

48. Lisa Leghorn and Katherine Parker, *Woman's Worth: Sexual Economics and the World of Women* (Boston: Routledge and Kegan Paul, 1981), 185, 176–77; Petchesky in Zillah R. Eisenstein, ed., *Capitalist Patriarchy and the Case for Socialist Feminism* (New York: Monthly Review Press, 1979), 381.

49. Morgan, *Sisterhood*, 16.

50. Kishwar and Vanita, *In Search*, 242.

51. William Thompson, *Appeal of One Half the Human Race, Women, against the Pretensions of the Other Half . . .* (London: Virago, 1983), xxi, xxiii.

52. In Alma Gómez et al., eds., *Cuentos: Stories by Latinas* (New York: Kitchen Table Women of Color Press, 1983), 121.

53. Phyllis Chesler and Emily Jane Goodman, *Women, Money, and Power* (New York: Morrow, 1976), 102.

54. Giddings, *When and Where*, 251.

55. Morgan, *Sisterhood*, xix; Scott, *Working*, 40–52; Oakley, *Subject*, 183.

56. Howe, *Inside*, 188, 188–89; Scott, *Working*, 67–68.

57. Jansen-Jurreit, *Sexism*, 173; Nancy M. Henley, *Body Politics: Power, Sex, and Non-Verbal Communication* (Englewood Cliffs, NJ: Prentice-Hall, 1977), 53; Barbara Ehrenreich and Deidre English, *For Her Own Good: 150 Years of the Experts' Advice to Women* (Garden City, NY: Anchor/Doubleday, 1979), 179; Scott, *Working*, 67; Ann Oakley, *Subject Women* (New York: Pantheon, 1981), 246.

58. Scott, *Working*, 66; Jansen-Jurreit, *Sexism*, 173.

59. Leghorn and Parker, *Woman's Worth*, 193.

60. Kishwar and Vanita, *In Search*, 262.

61. Scott, *Working*, 68.

62. Ibid., 59.

63. Jansen-Jurreit, *Sexism*, 175.

64. Ibid., 172.

65. Ibid., 175.

66. Ibid., 172–73.

67. Scott, *Working*, 68.

68. Leghorn and Parker, *Woman's Worth*, 193–94.

69. Bernard, *Female*, 133; Chesler, *Mothers*, 499–500.

70. Jansen-Jurreit, *Sexism*, 174; Vanita and Kishwar, *In Search*, 67.

71. Oakley, *Subject*, 249.

72. Bernard, *Female*, 117; Malos, *Housework*, 116.

73. Bernard, *Female,* 257; Oakley, *Subject,* 163; Scott, Working, 60, 58; Oakley, *Subject,* 163.

74. Connors in Susan E. Browne et al., eds., *With the Power of Each Breath: A Disabled Woman's Anthology* (Pittsburgh: Cleis Press, 1985), 104; Oakley, *Subject,* 167. The economist J. K. Galbraith calls wives a "crypto-servant" class that is "democratically available" to the sex-class of men (ibid., 163).

75. Scott, Working, 37, 71–72, x.

76. Shulamith Firestone, *The Dialectic of Sex* (New York: Morrow, 1970), 207; Rubin, *Worlds of Pain,* 96; Morgan, *Sisterhood,* 9–10; Macdonald and Rich, *Look Me,* 43.

77. Morgan, *Sisterhood,* 9; Macdonald and Rich, *Look Me,* 43; Kishwar and Vanita, *In Search,* 13.

78. Delphy, *Close to Home,* 116; Dorothy E. Smith, *Feminism and Marxism: A Place to Begin, a Way to Go* (Vancouver: New Star, 1977), 41. If you think Delphy exaggerates, take a look at Scott's offhand quotation of Isabel Sawill of the Urban Institute: "Poor families are not the most likely to break up. *The higher a wife's earnings,* other things being equal, *the more likely it is that the couple will separate*" (Scott, *Working,* 20, italics added).

79. Joseph and Lewis, *Common Differences,* 35.

E I G H T

SEEING RED: MY LIFE IS HARDER
BECAUSE YOURS IS EASIER

Let me repeat: *they can't afford us.*

To equalize labor and wages between the sexes in the industrialized countries alone would mean a reduction in men's average wages of more than one-third and an addition to their average workload of two eight-hour days a week.

To do so for the entire world, if United Nations calculations are correct, would require that men's wages be cut by two-fifths and their workload increased by one-third.[1]

In the face of such appalling figures—and they are appalling—I find it impossible to believe that patriarchy is "caused" solely by the use of language, or by schooling, or by the social construction of sexuality, even by socialization in general, let alone by people's infantile fear of their mothers or men's natural talent for violence.[2] *Patriarchy exists because men (like women) have motives. Patriarchy benefits men.* However restricted people's options may be, however incomplete their knowledge of what options are open to them and what the consequences of their acts will be, people do know (by and large) what they like and have some notion of how to get it. Societies would not exist if this were not the case. As Christine Delphy says, first comes the fact of *exploitation;* then come various kinds of *oppression* to keep the exploited weak, miserable (and busy), and hence exploitable. Then (both logically and chronologically) comes the *ideology* that justifies the oppression and the exploitation in order to pacify the consciences of the exploiters and to muddle the common sense of the exploited, thus *mystifying* the situation of exploitation and oppression so that the exploited will accept it as natural, God-given, nobody's fault, morally correct, and inevitable.[3]

As Delphy puts it, "There is no mystery; we [women] are oppressed because we are exploited. *What we go through makes life easier for others.*"[4]

Now, terms like *exploitation* and *oppression,* however much feminists may use them nowadays, did not originate in feminist discourse. They are marxist terms, and it's to marxist discourse (very roughly speaking) that I want to turn now. If the fundamental aim of patriarchy as a system is to get a lot of work (including various kinds of services) out of one sex while constraining its equal access to such things as money, goods, services, self-determination, and leisure time, then a theory that claims to analyze the unequal distribution of the same good things between classes deserves every feminist's serious attention. This is especially true for feminists who believe, as I and many others do, that feminism goes beyond "simple reform" (Dworkin's phrase) and that liberal demands have radical implications (Eisenstein's idea).[5] I propose to at least begin to give it that attention. But here we meet with a problem.

A good many marxists detest feminists.

A good many feminists hate marxists.

It's likely, of course, that many feminists may well dislike marxist analysis because it militates against their interests as middle-class professionals. Like some gay White men who are or hope to be well-to-do, they believe themselves to be eligible for membership in the elite group—if it were not for that one mysterious and inexplicable disqualification of sex or sexuality.[6] Yet many of the feminists I found loathing the U.S. Left, new or old, or the British, have not had that sort of privilege to protect. Some are women of color, poor women, or women who once worked hard for the Left.

Thus Robin Morgan, once a dedicated member of the New Left in the United States of the 1960s, perceives her male former colleagues as the illegitimate sons of the very power structure they were supposedly trying to overthrow, men who made themselves over in the image of macho fools and insisted on "sex on demand for males," whose "ejaculatory" tactics were destructive and vicious. In an essay written in 1970 she speaks of "the puerile squabbles of a counterfeit Left that laughs at my [every woman's] pain."[7]

Kathy McAfee and Myrna Wood, also ex-members of the New Left, accuse it of respecting characteristics like the ability to argue loud, fast, and aggressively in the "I'm more revolutionary than you" style of debate, one they call "particularly appropriate to a brutally competitive capitalist society."[8]

Naomi Littlebear, another graduate of what she calls "leftist politics," speaks of the "violence and humiliation" of the connection and adds, "Please applaud my victory over those fuckers." Nor did Cherríe Moraga fare any better; she was told that "sexual issues" were "divisive to the 'larger struggle' and therefore not essential for revolution. . . . that to be concerned about the sexuality of women of color was an insult to women in the Third World." The Left, she says, has a "shaky and shabby record of commitment to women."[9]

As a young Communist, Rosario Morales writes, she lived with a man "enlightened . . . about male chauvinism and the household slavery of women and Engels on the family. But I came away with 90% of the house-work and 95% of the emotional mending and ironing."[10]

Nor do more temperate voices disagree. Malos calls the " 'normal' marxist approach to the woman question since the late twenties in the West" a matter of simply avoiding "the relationship between sex and class." Anne Snitow, Christine Stansell, and Sharon Thompson report that the "non-feminist Left has been notably tepid on questions of reproductive rights" and cite as "notorious" the incident in 1979 in which a leading U.S. socialist newspaper, *In These Times,* "called for a dialogue with the anti-abortion movement." Heidi Hartmann calls much of the Left of her experience "com-mitted antifeminists in both doctrine and practice," while Lynne Segal notes in Britain that some Left politics wanted to integrate feminism into its de-mands in the same year by simply "adding on 'women's demands' to their existing programme. . . . They do not seem to see the need for feminism to transform the whole nature of working-class politics and the left."[11] Dorothy Smith notes simply, "What you generally find among Marxists is a rejection of feminism,"[12] while Elly Bulkin quotes Rich:

> In the late sixties and early seventies many U.S. feminists, my-self included, voiced frustration and disillusionment with the Marxist Left which seemed incapable of recognizing and ad-dressing women's oppression as women. We insisted that our chains were . . . embedded in that domestic or "private" sphere where men of all classes dominate women. I believe we were right; no ideology which reduces women simply to members of the working-class or the bourgeoisie, which does not recognize how central feminism must be to the revolutionary process, can be taken seriously any longer.[13]

Marlene Dixon, another early feminist whose origins were in the Left, writes:

> Women had learned from 1964 to 1968 that to fight for or even to sympathize with women's liberation was to pay a terrible price; what little credit a woman might have earned in one of the Left organizations was wiped out in a storm of contempt and personal abuse. . . . The very recklessness and originality

of the wildcats [women's liberationists at an early conference Dixon is describing] terrified . . . [Left] women who were observing the very woman-ness, irrationality, expressiveness, emotionality and anti-intellectualism that the leftists knew provoked the most brutal reactions from the . . . men they would have to live and work with in the future.[14]

The Left's reasons for hating feminists and rejecting feminism lack the variety and fine swing of feminists' denunciations of the Left; rather the rejecters confine themselves (usually) to one charge: *feminists are bourgeois.* Nor do the actual politics of the feminists in question seem to matter, at least according to Smith, who calls the rejection "peculiarly lacking in analysis." Segal seconds her, saying Left criticisms she has met are little more than gibes about being "middle class." Thus organizing around "personal, psychological and sexual oppression" is reformist and bourgeois, and according to Malos:

> Even after the growth of the women's movement, several left organizations [in Britain] saw the main or even the only task of the women's movement as reaching women already in the paid labour force and organizing them in and around the trade unions on economic issues. . . . In this view such issues as . . . abortion or contraception were often regarded as "only of interest to bourgeois women."[15]

Although many working-class women were in fact active as feminists throughout the nineteenth century, one of my socialist feminist sources, Sheila Rowbotham, states that the nineteenth-century feminist movement was based on "middle class women who were excluded from production."[16] Kathy Kahn, author of *Hillbilly Women,* a book that is eloquent about the exploitation and labor struggles of working-class people in southern Appalachia, nonetheless quotes with no comment her interviewees' views on "women's lib": feminists are "middle class bourgeois," female chauvinists, scared of men and insecure "as women," and they ignore the plight of the poor, Black people, Chicanos, and Asian-Americans.[17] And here is the socialist Peggy Morton, who assures us that "masses of women will not relate to women's liberation because it is not relating to their needs" and proposes (instead of such ineffective feminism) the really relevant stuff, *the issues feminists don't touch:* economic independence, birth control, sexuality, day care, the male domination of unions, lack of choice in the matter of abortion, and the oppressive treatment of women by the medical profession![18] Ignorance of feminism and the automatic rejection of it could hardly go any further.

None of this is new. Marielouise Jansen-Jurreit's sketch of the European (and particularly the German) history of socialism in the nineteenth century angrily includes such antifemale stands as August Bebel's attack on the use of contraceptives—they'd not be needed in the future socialist society, in his view—and Clara Zetkin's declaration (repeated later by other radicals in other contexts) that reducing the number of births is bad because it reduces the number of revolutionary fighters. Jansen-Jurreit also notes that by the end of the nineteenth century many socialist women were complaining about the male domination of the party and its newspapers. Zetkin initiated "this fight against feminism and supporters of women's rights" in 1889, denying that socialist and bourgeois women had anything in common, as did Laura Lafargue and Marx's daughter, Eleanor Marx. The Second International Socialist Labor Congress, held in Brussels in 1891, declared that a "socialist labor congress has absolutely nothing to do with the bourgeois movement of women's rights."[19]

Turning to marxist historian Linda Gordon, we find that the split between socialism and feminism deepened in the early twentieth century "as Marxian scientific socialism began to dominate and the organized socialist movement gained a working-class constituency."[20] Nor, with some honorable exceptions, have labor unions in general been receptive to women or women's issues. Jean Gardiner notes that in 1818 in England, male spinners tried to keep women out of their trade, arguing that women's working removed them "from the home and domestic duties." In 1835 male English weavers protested against having factory machinery adapted to the use of "children and youth, and women, to the exclusion of those who ought to labor— THE MEN." Unionizing the women would have made it impossible for employers to undercut male wages by hiring women and paying them less than men (which employers had done from the beginning of the Industrial Revolution), but it would also have prevented working men's securing their wives' services at home; thus the common male solution to the problem was to ban (or attempt to ban) women's employment at any wage. This was the tenor of a letter written in 1835 by Francis Place, a British cotton spinner, which stated roundly that "the men were to blame for their own misery" by not refusing "to work . . . with girls or women as they ought to do," and "as other males had done." If only they would do so, says Place, the women "who will otherwise be degraded by factory labour, will become all that can be desired as companionable wives."[21]

In the early part of the century Owenite socialism, with its considerable feminist emphasis, had been an important presence in the English working class. According to Barbara Taylor, working-class women, "using the language of militant unionism . . . launched protests which took the 'Woman

'Question' right across the central class issues of the day, one saying publicly, 'We are only waiting for the signal to form our own lodges; and we will let them know that woman, by her own exertions and intelligence will be free.' " Another woman of that era wrote, "The men are as bad as their masters."[22]

Unsurprisingly, the "ideology of women's employment as a domestically disruptive influence" first became prominent in the 1830s in England. This period also saw the first agitation for legally limiting women's employment and "very popular anti-feminist tracts," while the succeeding half century saw a blossoming of "the ideology of women's natural and necessary restriction to the home." The idea that women have always restricted their activities to home and children, like the idea that women are new to the paid labor force, is an outgrowth of this period, not a fact but a persistent myth, according to Ann Oakley. Thus we hear again and again that "women today never had it so good and have only recently emerged from the dark ages of an exclusive preoccupation with motherhood to a new golden world of economically useful work."[23]

Some more of this history:

In England in 1846 the labor paper the *Ten Hours Advocate* (note that the working day was then *over* ten hours) stated, according to Hartmann, that "married females would be much better occupied in performing the domestic duties of a household" than working in a mill and looked forward to the day when the husband could "provide for his wife and family, without sending the former to endure the drudgery of a cotton mill."[24]

In the United States in 1854 the National Typographical Union's compositors tried to discourage the employment of women in that trade, and in 1879 the head of the Cigarmakers International Union stated, "We cannot drive the females out of the trade but we can restrict their daily quota of labor through factory laws."[25]

In 1867 the National Association of German Workingmen in Berlin (says Weinbaum) expressed antifemale sentiment and, according to Faderman, "staged a massive campaign to keep women out of jobs, arguing that working women contributed to the destruction of the family and placed that institution in 'a wretched state,' its most ideal possession—the wife and mother—being removed."[26]

Nor is more recent history more encouraging. According to Smith, unemployment, "endemic to advancing capitalism—the problem of a surplus labor population, of too many people for too few jobs" was dealt with after World War I by

the state, the trade unions, and some of the larger trusts [cooperating] . . . to reduce the problem . . . by eliminating or markedly reducing the participation of women in the labor market. For example, in Germany when men were released from the army after the war and sought jobs in an economy already severely disrupted, government and trade union action was directed against women in the labour force in general. . . . A government directive of 1919 ordered the dismissal of anyone not wholly dependent on their wage. Somehow these turned out to be women . . . In general. . . . the hostility of working-class men towards women they saw as competing for their jobs was intense. . . . In the United States during the depression [of the 1930s], the employment of women in work outside the home . . . was attacked by the state, the media and the trade unions. The American Federation of Labour . . . had a tacit agreement with the larger trusts sheltering the craft unions of white male skilled workers in exchange for *not* organizing [White] women and Blacks.[27]

In 1945 in the United States a government-initiated media campaign began to prepare the nation for women's reentry into domesticity or, for some women, the badly paying nonunionized jobs, usually in the service sector, that they had held before the war.[28] Judith Merril, a writer who "grew up in the radical thirties" in the United States and whose mother "had been a suffragette," remembers the shutting down of

the wonderful working mothers' day-care centers [after World War II as] . . . newspapers, magazines, counseling services told us firmly that children who had less than constant attention from their *very own* mothers were doomed to misery and delinquency; the greatest joy available to the "natural woman" was the pleasure of Building Her Man's Ego. . . . There was a lot of pressure; one couldn't help wondering. . . . One worried and kept trying to figure things out.[29]

Later, Dorothy Haener of the United Auto Workers Women's Department found it necessary to contradict what she called prevalent ideas that "women . . . are less organized than men because of some unspecified sex-based hostility to unionization." She blamed "the kinds of jobs most women hold . . . [because] sales and domestic workers [professions in which women are concentrated] are scattered over small units." So does Louise Howe. "As with so many other issues concerning women," she says, "the main emphasis is put on the 'special attitudes' of women. . . . on the supposed subjective factors instead of on the obvious objective ones." She then cites a 1970 U.S. study by the Industrial Conference Board that analyzed the results of 140 then-recent union elections and concluded that sex had little bearing on whether or not particular units voted for unionization or against it.[30]

As one of her most grotesque examples of unions failing women rather than women failing unions, Howe uses the beauty business, one in which women predominate—yet the union she cites is more than 97 percent male and less than 3 percent female. There were, it seems, more women in the union in the early 1970s, but the women refused to go along with a pension plan that the men wanted (according to a man Howe interviewed) because the women "weren't going to be working until they were 65. . . . So they quit." After Howe asked why the men did not attempt to compromise with the women—he had no answer—Howe elicited the information that barbers, who are men, make an average of 30 percent more than beauticians, who are women, although beauticians' work is "vastly more complicated." There are also different union contracts for barbers than there are for beauticians. "But they [barbers] are men, after all," said the man; "they have families to support." Another union Howe cites, the United Department Store Workers, upon finding out that those in their union making over $10,000 a year were "almost exclusively men," set up first a conference, and then classes for women in which the women began to discuss "some of the fears they had about moving ahead" and "trying for high commission jobs." Their worries were about

> being too competitive, about alienating men . . . [They were] afraid that the jobs weren't really open to them, that the men in the department didn't want them there and they were right. Many hadn't even been told about the tremendous difference in earnings those jobs can provide.[31]

In 1976 in the United States, says Oakley:

> 12 percent of employed women belong to trade unions and a quarter of all unions have no women members. The view prevails that women are difficult to organize because they are apathetic and/or concerned only with the next wage packet. But the male-dominated trade unions have done little to accommodate their organization and timetabling to . . . women . . . whose work also includes running homes and servicing husbands and children.

In Britain in the same year the picture looked a little better: 28.8 percent of the membership of British trade unions was female, while women made up 39 percent of the labor force. Nonetheless "far fewer women than men became shop stewards or full-time union officials."[32]

The usual view (as my sources describe it) appears to be that women ought to adapt their needs and those of their homes and children to the agendas of the male union membership—which is undoubtedly why Audrey Wise recounts with such relish an incident she observed in 1974 at the Gloucester Trades Council meeting:

> My position was that in the factory such protection as women workers had got should be retained, that we should not accept a leveling down. . . . I was being told by a male Trade Unionist the usual things, [women] "won't accept responsibility" and "the economy demands it" and "what about exports—we'll price ourselves out of the market"—and up got a woman, beautiful creature—and said "if the economy wants me to work night shift, THEN I WANT A DIFFERENT ECONOMY!" And it was said in exactly those words. And that is the consciousness we've got to get.[33]

Why men on the Left and in trade unions act so badly toward the women one might think to be their obvious allies is hardly a puzzle. As feminists have long insisted, men belonged to a privileged *sex-class*. They receive immunities and benefits from such membership, many of which partially ameliorate their position as members of an exploited *working class,* and few fail to grow attached to their privileges—which many of them think of, often quite naively in my experience, as simply their rights. Few refuse to participate in the ideological side of the battle either. As Susan Griffin notes:

> Although it has been almost always women and not men of the upper class who showed any concern for the suffering of the poor, it was a woman, Marie Antoinette, who became the symbol in male revolutionary culture for aristocratic callousness. Patricia Hearst and not her father was kidnapped.[34]

I'm afraid I agree with Delphy's analysis of many Left radicals' hatred of feminists and feminism as arising from

> hatred of all women . . . [by men] indignant to see their sexual privilege . . . held in check by the privileges (or more exactly the *protection*) of class.

Because the real power of the bourgeois man renders him unattackable, "it is easier and more rewarding to attack him through his possessions," especially since the immunities and the power of women attached to upper-class men is perceived by these supposedly radical men as illegitimate because "gender ought to outweigh class." Left women, Delphy continues, "share with their men the guilt of having class privileges but for women the left adds to this the guilt of having these privileges improperly, being women." Thus Left women feel unworthy of oppressing others or even "unworthy of being oppressed." Hence much Left theory, which finds that "even the oppression of women is not aimed at them, being a by-product of the real oppression—the oppression of men by men."[35]

In addition, Delphy notes that those who have "monopolized marxist theoretical accounts" empower themselves to approve the class consciousness of anyone else by awarding "a certificate of oppression to a group to enable it to rebel in a legitimate fashion, i.e. with the approval of the marxist establishment."[36] My intention in this book is most certainly not to claim such legitimation; I remember all too well attempting to "prove" the oppression of women in the early 1970s to male colleagues who had every reason not to believe in it and I have no desire to repeat that experience. Nonetheless there are questions that anyone reading this book has the right to ask. Feminists and the Left don't get along—but what about their theories? Do those get along? And just what theories am I talking about? Some readers of this book will of course know what I (very roughly) call marxism much better than I do, and some will not know it at all. Maybe the following will clarify what I think I know for both kinds of readers; at least I've tried to make the following as simple—and as entertaining—as I could. So, taking the points that may be relevant to the discussion that will follow them in this work, I am convinced of the following propositions:

—that Human social arrangements about who does what and who gets what (at least during the Bronze Age and later) develop out of the particular self-interest of groups of people. (Groups come into being as social groups precisely because their interests conflict.) By "interests," I mean the sort of thing described in Harris's and Maslow's account of Human desires (with obvious biological limits): more and better food rather than less; more and better protein rather than less; more pleasant sexual activity rather than less (and less or none of the unpleasant kind); more affection and admiration from those around you rather than less; more safety rather than less; more leisure rather than less; the accomplishing of work by using less energy rather than more but also the pleasures of using a healthy body rather than illness or enforced idleness, and so on[37];

—that these groups (or *classes*) are constituted by rules as to who does what and who gets what of the kind of things that can be got or, as we would say today, goods and services, but that not everyone has an equal voice in making up these rules;

—that in Human history (at least since the beginning of large-scale agriculture, which is what we usually call "civilization") one *class* has had greater access to the goodies and less of the burdens of producing them and that another *class* has had less access and more burdens;

—that the division of who does what and who gets what is made and enforced by violence and fraud (the other name for fraud being *propaganda*) practiced by the class that gets more and does less or nothing (the *ruling* class). The class that gets less and works harder is called by various names, depending on the social rules about how the goodies are to be distributed and how various people are compelled to work more or less. Without exploitation (the unequal division of the goodies), and without oppression (the various kinds of violence used by the ruling class or its employees against the other class—whose members are always much more numerous), the other class cannot be got to obey the rules (which are about who gets and how much and who works and how hard).

There is more:

First, relationships between people in *feudalism,* the economic and political structure that preceded capitalism in Europe, were directly personal and were based on "blood" relationship (an old Human social invention). Rulers ruled because they were their fathers' sons or (occasionally) their fathers' daughters. The work or loyalty given them by their "inferiors" in the feudal hierarchy was based on the same qualifications: men swore loyalty to their "superiors" (in the sense of social altitude, not personal character). Thus nobles received their lands at the hands of the reigning monarch, who received his, in turn, from God. Peasants were peasants because their fathers were peasants, and so on.[38]

Second, bit by bit, on a small scale at first and eventually on such a scale as to change Europe—and later the world—there arose between the feudal aristocracy and the feudal peasantry a "third" class. For whatever reason (and the desire to depict the United States as a classless society undoubtedly ranks high) in the United States the term "middle class" is widely used to mean a certain level of income (and perhaps a set of values and habits), but in marxist theory the *bourgeoisie* is that class of *owners* who gained ground in the towns of the later Middle Ages and whose last decisive fight with the European feudal aristocracy was the French Revolution.[39] ("Marxists use another term to designate the class 'midway between the big capitalists and the working class,' i.e., the petty bourgeoisie.")[40]

Third, this new social/economic/political set of rules as to who must do what for whom and under what conditions (what marxists call *the mode of production*) looks to be as different as is possible from the feudal hierarchy.

That is, descent is nothing, and the free market is everything. Society (supposedly) consists of individual people entering into free and open contracts with other individual people in order to exchange their labor (all that most of them own) with those people who own or have access to the tools of production because they own *capital* (hence the name *capital-ism*), while in return the *capitalists* give them a *wage* with which they then may go into the free and open market to buy whatever food, clothing, shelter, and so on they need or may fancy. Such food, clothing, or shelter is, of course, made by the labor of other individual people, who also enter into contracts in the free and open market in order to sell their ability to do work (to those who own or control the means of production) for wages with which to buy the necessities and luxuries of life. Save enough of your wages, and with thrift, judgment, foresight, intelligence, and experience (and a little bit of luck) you too may be able to enter the ranks of those who have access to enough *capital*—money that can be used to make money—to employ others to make what you (or somebody you hire) can then sell. You may also accumulate enough capital to employ it by lending it to people who need it and who will pay you *interest* on it (a fee for using it) so that you may live without producing anything at all.

What counts in capitalist society (as we all know, of course, because we live in one) is not whether you are related to this or that member of the aristocracy, but *how much you own*. As the historians I know put it, the direct person-to-person relations of feudalism have been replaced by the impersonal relations of the free market in which government exists only to ensure that everybody follows the rules (by not stealing, breaking contracts, and so on). Work hard and you will succeed. Be thriftless or stupid and you will fail. There is nobody to take the credit or the blame but yourself.

Alas! This idyllic picture (say the marxists, and I agree) is a far cry from the reality because the people who actually work to make the goods or services offered for sale in the free market (the *working class*) do not get paid the full market value of their work, i.e., the money that their goods or services bring in.

For example, turn your attention to the (entirely imaginary) Ideal Widget Company. In order to produce widgets, get them to market, and sell them, people must work on the widget assembly line, keep the books, make and broadcast the advertising, maintain the machinery that makes the widgets, drive the trucks in which the widgets are taken to market, load widgets on the trucks in the first place, unload them and move them into the stores that sell widgets, repair the machinery in the widget factory, clean the widget works and the widget stores, and so on. Let us assume that by selling one million widgets a day, at a price of one krumball each, the company takes in one million krumballs each day. (Widgets are cheap.) If each worker involved in the production of widgets received an equal share of the money that comes in every day, each would take home, let us say, twenty thousand krumballs with which to buy the evening paper, toys for the kiddies, a roast, car polish, and whatever necessities or luxuries commend themselves to the widget workers' needs and desires.

But the widget workers do not get twenty thousand krumballs each as their reward for a day of labor. Not only do some get a good deal more than others, which in itself is rather odd, but *the most any single Widget employee gets is a mere ten thousand krumballs!*

Before you decide that the company's accountants have all gone mad or that somebody's visiting child playfully threw the missing krumballs into the fire beneath the workers' communal coffeepot (thus reducing them to ashes), *look again.*

What has happened at the widget works happens every day throughout capitalist societies. When the widget works were first bought (or set up), money was necessary to construct the factory (or buy it), advertise the company's wares, maintain the machinery, pay taxes, pay employees, and so on. These necessities arise before a single widget can be exchanged (i.e., sold) for a single krumball. The money must come from somewhere. Because capitalism is a set of rules under which individual people *can* own capital—that is, money far beyond what they need to live—it is from this particular sort of person, the capital owner or *capitalist,* that the money to set up the company must come.

Now the owner of the widget works (watch that word "owner"; it's crucial) can use his own capital to set up the factory,[41] but it's also likely—especially if making widgets is an expensive business—that he will borrow all or some of it. If he does, he must pay for the use of that money. Naturally capitalists (people who live off what they own and who therefore have large amounts of spare money lying around) will not loan their money out without trying to get for it the best fee possible. They may (sometimes) forgo a high fee (interest) if you can offer them a secure opportunity to make less interest on their money rather than a risky opportunity to make more interest, but under the rules of capitalism, *money itself costs money,* and it is actually possible to live off the fees you charge for lending money out, if only you have enough money in the first place. (Thus, either the manager *or* the owner of Ideal Widget must demand as high a *profit* (more of this later) as possible, i.e., as high a *return on his investment* as he can.)

So, after Ideal Widget sells its million widgets for one million krumballs, after all its employees are paid, after its loans are paid off or reduced, after machinery is repaired when necessary, after it pays its taxes (remember that the government—which also needs money to exist—insures the peace and safety of the whole arrangement), there will remain quite a few krumballs.

They do *not* go to the employees who worked to produce widgets, keep track of widgets, truck them about, distribute them, and sell them.

These remaining krumballs (of which there are sometimes a startlingly large number) "belong" to the owner of Ideal Widget. (I'll keep to the singular pronoun simply for grammatical convenience.)

And he can do what he jolly well likes with them.

If he is a kind, generous, and sensitive capitalist, he may use some of those krumballs to make the widget factory healthy, airy, and spacious. He may build an attractive lunch room for his workers and give them frequent paid holidays. But if he spends too much on wages and accommodations for his workers, *his profits will go down* and the price he must ask for widgets will rise—unless he is maintaining Ideal Widget out of his own personal funds as a sort of expensive hobby. Then Wodget, across town, with its worse-paid workers and rotten (but cheap) working conditions, will be able to offer widgets on the market at less than Widget's prices. Thereupon customers—who also want as much return on *their* krumballs as is possible—will stop buying Widget's widgets and will start buying Wodget's widgets. And eventually, if this goes on, Ideal Widget will go out of business. Indeed, if he persists in his generous behavior, the owner (or manager) of Ideal Widget may find himself out of the owning *class* altogether and in the *class* of *workers,* people who own little or no *capital* (money-to-make-money) and who must therefore stay alive by selling their ability to do work to someone who either has capital or can borrow it from those who do.

Note, please, that *profit* is nothing more or less than that gap between what comes into a business from the sale of its products and services in the market and what goes out as expenses, including wages.

Note also, and this is crucial, that in the long run there is only one source of profit.

Profit comes from Human labor. (This is what marxists call *the labor theory of value.*) Mind you, this theory of where value—and hence profit—comes from does not include everything Human beings need or enjoy, some of which things, like sunlight, come directly from nature, but applies only to what Human beings sell and buy. Goods and services get to be goods and services because Human work creates them. If things are rare, somebody must go find them, and that is work. If they are far away from whoever wants to buy them, somebody must transport them. If they are located in the earth, someone must dig them up. Teaching is work too; nursing is work; planning or having ideas is work; singing opera is work; painting pictures is work. It's true that pieces of nature itself are sometimes bought and sold in the form of "land" or "fishing rights" or "oil" or "timber" and the like, and Human work did not produce these. What Human labor does produce, in such cases, is the right to the undisturbed enjoyment or exploitation of these things. Thus laws and police make it possible to "own" land so that the "owner" can keep others from benefiting from the use or sale of its products: crops, timber, coal, minerals, and so on. Nature produces a great deal, but if all of us presently living on this planet were to rely on nothing but what nature could produce unaided by Human labor, the vast majority of us would soon be dead. Even in the Paleolithic era (when Human beings did much less), killing animals for food, making weapons and tools, gathering food, preparing food, making containers for food and water and transporting these, as well as bringing up children and transmitting to them the knowledge of how to do these things, were, all of them, fruits of Human labor. Today the scope of Human labor is enormously wider and Human interdependence much more profound, yet those who do the work do not get a full reward for their work. Rather, a substantial chunk of that reward, in terms of goods, services, leisure, freedom, immunity from violence, and the enjoyment of luxuries—in short, the good things of this world, payable for by money, is skimmed off the top and given to those whose only qualification for enjoying it is that they happen to have attached to their persons, by way of a legal fiction that states that such an attachment is possible and must not be violated, large quantities of *capital,* the money-that-makes-money. They may own businesses without working at them or managing them or even knowing that they exist, and they need not trouble themselves about investing if they don't want to; they can hire experts to do it for them. Their undisturbed enjoyment and possession of their capital is safeguarded by the law, which asserts that one Human being may indeed "own" enormous quantities of this very peculiar abstraction. And the law is safeguarded by the police, by (an always very compromised) government, by the army, and by a system of mass-media propaganda that presents such a state of affairs as eternal, natural, and good and thus convinces everyone (or attempts to) that *private property* or *free enterprise*—meaning, in fact, *capitalism*—is sacred.[42]

But capital comes from profit.

Profit comes from labor.

Profit comes from *unpaid* labor.

Capital is thus the control of other people's unpaid labor (those missing krumballs), and *capitalists are thieves.*

If you are a little capitalist, just scraping by, say the proprietor of a small business in which you yourself work, with (if you are lucky) one or two assistants, you are a *petit bourgeois,* whose profits may extend no further than keeping yourself alive. If your grandfather was a robber baron who left his money to your father, who left it to you, you may own so much capital (in the form of investments or actual material things like land, machinery, buildings, or what-not) that you need not work at all. You may therefore spend your life in the kind of grotesque luxury that came to my notice some years ago when I read in the daily paper that Nelson Rockefeller had bought a carved antique ivory desk for three million dollars.[43]

In a society in which capital is the sine qua non of life and vast amounts of it are owned or controlled by a relatively few people (I am thinking of my junior high school lessons about "interlocking directorates" and monopolies underselling small competitors, which somehow you hear a lot less about nowadays), such people do not have only the luxuries huge amounts of money can buy. They also have—and this is much more ominous—very large amounts of power. They have such power whether they exercise it directly themselves or delegate it to those whom they employ (people who may, for example, invest their money for them or run their businesses for them). Thus giant corporations, which are considered to be people under the law—another legal fiction—can have budgets larger than those of many nations, can control national governments, and can even, as we all know, control the domestic and foreign policies of the nations whose laws are supposed to control them. Such a setup requires a good deal of propaganda to disguise the fact that the huge majority of people involved in it are being robbed, and it needs force to control them if they try to do anything about that fact. Thus, a part of the working class (which is usually given higher wages, more privileges, a more secure future, and more immunity from violence that the rest) is paid to control the rest. I've already mentioned the police and the army; teachers and entertainers are part of this group, as are writers. So are university professors and journalists and all other workers in the Idea Business. Such people do more than just control the rest of the working class, of course, and some of what they do is necessary and good, but they also act as enforcers or apologists for the capitalist status quo. This position usually leads them to identify their interests with those of the ruling class that is "above" them rather than the working class "below" them. These are the professional people who are called "middle class" in the United States today, but they are in no way identical with what Marx meant by the ruling class or the "bourgeoisie."[44] Rather they are something like middle management and they are (usually) middle-income. Confusing them with their employers serves only to disguise the existence of the very wealthy, whose control of money and power puts them in a different universe from that of their more-or-less allied employees.[45]

I've said before that the working class owns nothing (or nothing much) but its ability to work. (It does not own capital that it can exchange for the means of production.) This statement is not merely a description of the working class; it is the very definition of what it is *to be* working class. Class membership depends on what you have to do to stay alive. If you must sell your ability to work (whether that work be teaching mathematics, cutting microchips, or hauling garbage), you are part of the *working class.* If you rent out your capital instead, by investing in someone else's business (or even starting your own), you are a member of the *bourgeoisie,* that is, the ruling, or owning, class. To repeat: if you own two houses, one of which you rent in order to live off the rent, or if you own a neighborhood candy stand, which you run yourself, you are a *petit bourgeois,* or small owner. Exchanging your labor for money or loaning out your money (if you have any) is what marxists call "exchange relations" and "relations of production." Accordingly, your *class membership* depends on what *relations of production* you must enter into in order to get the money you need to live. The size of your income is not, all by itself, an unfailing index of your class membership (though it's very obviously closely related to it), and your tastes or habits are not what definitively place you in a class either. Owning your own house, or having money saved in a pension plan or a savings bank (or even having some money invested) does not necessarily make you even a petty bourgeois. The point is what you must do to get your food, your shelter, and all the other things you need to live. Here are some more bits of marxist theory:

Built into the capitalist system are those periodic economic convulsions called "the business cycle" (right-wing economists love the mildness of the term "cycle"), of which probably the best known today is the Great Depression of the 1930s. What "cured" that one was World War II. Wars have reliably ended economic downturns in the past because of the enormous amount of goods and services war simply uses up, thus ending the overproduction—or underconsumption—that is the bane of capitalism. As Joe Marcus, a New Deal economist, remembered it for Studs Terkel:

> When we got into the war . . . suddenly you've got to produce an enormous number of planes, tanks, build an eleven-million-man army, supply the British and, soon afterwards, the Russians. And the Free French. We needed an enormous jump in Production.

The U.S. playwright Garson Kanin, remembering D-Day (Terkel's book is not about economics, which makes these details all the more telling), said: "You're talking about hundreds or thousands of men. Food, water, fuel, hygienic supplies, sleeping equipment . . . We had one whole department of sixty men working on nothing but toilet paper."[46]

Still, wars end and depressions return. And although some members of the owning class may go under in such periodic bad times, the class as a whole does not. The capitalist system favors the class of owners, not this or that particular owner.

Because of the business cycle, capitalism cannot provide full employment. Worse still, capitalism cannot even allow full employment. There must be people to fire when times get bad, and people to rehire when times get better. Who gets the ax first is partly a matter of which industries or areas are doing the worst, but it's also a matter of who belongs to socially dominant or socially subordinate groups along the lines of color and gender— hence the usefulness to capitalism of racism and sexism.

Worse still, once the competition of many small businesses—the ideal form of capitalism in the view of early apologists for it, like Adam Smith— becomes *oligopoly,* a situation in which there are a few giants who dominate the field, *these giants cease to compete.* They jack up prices whether times are good or bad, they use their enormous economic power to make wars and topple governments, they move overseas to countries where labor is cheap. They also buy from or sell to other parts of themselves and pay prices that are pure bookkeeping fantasies. I was taught in junior high school—as youngsters are not taught today—how easy it is for a big business to undersell local competitors, drive them out of business, and then raise their own prices and raise them and raise them and raise them again.[47] Thus giant chains proliferate, paying wages on which no independent adult can survive. Thus huge international conglomerates (compared to which local businesses are merely pikers) behave like, and effectively are, private governments. Such are the consequences of treating corporations as if they were people and of allowing individual persons to "own" vast quantities of other people's unpaid labor. (For example, we're often told there are "no jobs" to be had when what is really meant is that there are *no profit making jobs* to be had, i.e., no jobs whose creation will enable someone to use his spare money to create more money.) Thus big business escapes the social and environmental cost of its own operations, while these costs are "exported" outside the company, to be paid for by taxpayers, the vast majority of whom are, of course, working class.

The entire activity of capitalism has only one aim: making money make more money.

In capitalist societies, people's needs are not only secondary, they are totally irrelevant unless someone can make money make more money (i.e., invest in a profit-making business) by filling those needs. Thus people who have lots of money are in luck in capitalist societies, and those who have little are out of luck. People may need dental care, medical care, shelter, leisure, food, clothes, fun, a place to live, a decent transportation system, and a hundred other things but without money, or enough money, they can't exercise what economists call "effective demand."[48] As far as the cap-italist economy is concerned, such needs do not exist and if you have them, too bad for you. Now this is very odd because everything that is for sale in capitalist economies (as in every other)—shelter, advice, paintings, food, books, vacation tours, dentistry, shoes, physiotherapy, toothbrushes, nurs-ing, ships and shoes and sealing wax, surgery, and baby clothes, you name it—has been produced by one class and one class only, and that is the working class. These are the necessary people in the world; they transport, teach, clean, cultivate, keep track of, pick, invent, move, make, store, let you know about, repair, and just plain do everything that gets done.

Capitalists do nothing.

That is, *as capitalists* they do nothing. It's entirely possible that some capitalists may—in their purely personal capacity—do actual work, like composing good music (Charles Ives was an executive officer in a bank), or repairing clocks (Louis XVI of France did this), or something else that someone can benefit from or enjoy. But in their capacity as owners of some-body else's unpaid work, they do absolutely nothing.

Now, those who plan the best way to build something or bring ideas and people together likewise do a Humanly valuable service (if that something new is something people can enjoy or use), but the frantic economic activity of Wall Street that we all know so well—which I always tune out when I'm listening to the five o'clock news because it makes my stomach hurt—is nothing more than fighting over other people's unpaid work, work that has been taken from them by a process nobody who is ethical and who under-stands it could possibly call fair or decent. U.S. foreign policy is fought about or changed, stocks go up or down, we have "national interests" here or there in some corner of the globe, more nuclear plants are built, un-employment is better or worse, the minimum wage is this or that, and so on and so forth—and all this fuss and bother has one aim only: the cross-fertilization and breeding of extremely large amounts of money.

Capitalism is about profit. Profit is its goal. Profit is its only goal. Profit makes more profit. Profit is control of others' unpaid labor. Profit is power. Profit is—by its very definition—what the working class does not get to get because it has not got that which makes profit, which is capital. (If I use "capital" and "means of production" somewhat interchangeably, that's because you can always exchange the former for the latter, and use the latter to produce the former.)

And that is why the *working* class is not the *ruling* class.

Please forgive me if you are one of the readers of this book for whom the above was a sloppy run through kindergarten. You're probably holding your head right now about the mistakes I've made. Luckily there exists a small group of theorists whose grasp of marxist thought is much better than mine, and whose writings I have been using all throughout this chapter, in fact. And it's to them that I'm now going to turn.

They are the socialist feminists.

NOTES

1. Hilda Scott, *Working Your Way to the Bottom: The Feminization of Poverty* (London: Pandora, 1984), x. To equalize work and wealth among classes and among nations would require very large readjustments also, of course.

2. These were commonplaces of the early women's liberation movement. With the rise of political reaction in the United States has come the burial of much information about feminism. I believe that ignorance is at the bottom of at least some of what I would call the "quasi-feminism" of today: the restriction of feminism to a few issues, most of them having to do with sexuality or individual male violence, the stress on women's culture as an end in itself, the transformation of feminism into a cult or even a religion, the identification of feminism with anything having to do with women and the subsequent claim that the ecology movement or the peace movement is automatically feminist because peace and the earth are somehow "feminine" or associated with "women," and so on. Similar to these, it seems to me, are attempts to cite socialization or language or pornography as *the* cause of patriarchy. Such attempts existed in the late 1960s and early 1970s, but they were more tentative then, I think, and more concerned (as we all were then) with "proving" that patriarchy existed. Since our critics always maintained that patriarchy was "natural," we labored to demonstrate that it was not; rather it was learned and men (and even women) were made patriarchal by outside forces brought to bear on them. Although the idea that patriarchy is "natural" has found a new incarnation in popularized sociobiology—i.e., men can't help underpaying women because fish do it— it seems to me that today's dangers lie elsewhere, at least in the U.S. liberal intelligentsia I know. I find in my students of the last few years—and I mean both sexes here—the assumption that sexism is wrong but that sexism means men behaving badly to women in personal interactions, particularly in the area of sexuality, so that sexism becomes entirely an individual matter. That is, a "sexist" is a male person of bad character who does and says things that are obviously and grossly evil. Such ideas are certainly an improvement over those I grew up with in the 1950s—for example, the idea that "nice" women never get raped or that girl children are somehow responsible for sexual assaults made upon them—but they leave entirely untouched the institutional nature of patriarchy and the ordinary, everyday, unspectacular behavior that upholds such institutions. Thus the "sexist" becomes a bigot and not the Everyman who benefits in many ways from patriarchy and whose ordinary, "normal," "natural," "neutral," and even "right" behavior creates and re-creates the patriarchal institution moment by moment and day after day. Many of

the young women I meet recognize *as feminist* only the anti-pornography movement, the anti-rape movement, and the fight against the rape of children; their
ignorance is otherwise abysmal and many see feminism as anti-love, anti-"romance,"
or prudish.

3. As Delphy puts it, "to say that ideology acts on reality is one thing," but
to say that ideology—language, schooling, socialization, all come under this head-
ing—*causes* reality *all by itself* leaves up in the air the very important matter of what
causes language, schooling, socialization, and so on. Ideology (says Delphy, and I
agree) cannot be the ultimate cause of anything since this "implies that ideology is
its own cause." To accept this is to fall back into a theory of culture as totally arbitrary,
i.e., that "social structure is produced by ideas, which are themselves produced by
nothing" (Christine Delphy, *Close to Home: A Materialist Analysis of Women's Oppression,* trans. Diana Leonard [Amherst, MA: University of Massachusetts Press,
1984], 173). Such a belief, which is the dominant ideology of our society, can only
describe a static situation in which patriarchy causes socialization etc., and socialization etc. causes patriarchy in an endless, unchanging loop. Some feminists have
proposed this analysis—or rather, this lack of analysis—of patriarchy.

4. Ibid., 177. Italics added.

5. Andrea Dworkin, *Right-Wing Women* (New York: Perigee, 1983), 67; Hester Eisenstein, *Contemporary Feminist Thought* (Boston: G. K. Hall, 1983), xvi.

6. Such people characteristically call for a single-issue campaign, if they are
willing to engage in public protest at all. They also tend to stress staid behavior on
the part of their own group, with "education" of employers, police, courts, neighbors, and social agencies as the remedy. All of these things are much better than
nothing—don't mistake my point—but such single-issue people typically do not
perceive the connections between their issues and others' issues. They do not easily
enter coalitions either, as they believe they can attain their own objectives, without
further analysis of their own or others' oppression, by changing the world in only
the most limited and partial ways.

I do not mean, by the way, that beliefs are always totally (or simply) determined
by one's immediate economic interests or class membership. There are always people
who are surprisingly radical for their situations, i.e., their beliefs and behavior don't
"fit" their obvious objective situations. Nonetheless class (or sex or color) has an
enormous influence, not because people are passive and stupid products of their
conditioning, but because most of us do have the sense we were born with, and
within the limits of what we know, which includes what we've been taught, we do
know where our own interests lie.

When people's situations are "split"—that is, they experience privileges derived
from one sort of identity and oppression derived from another—their thinking and
their politics usually become split too. Hence the appearance of odd groups whose
minority status (as, say, homosexual) leads them to challenge oppression in their
own case, but whose class status or skin privilege leads them to uphold oppression

in the case of others, an oppression they believe has no relation to their own. It is precisely this kind of limited perception that dooms so many minority struggles. When it becomes clear that the issues are all interconnected—and when enough people can figure out just how—then a very different kind of strategic planning becomes possible. As Elly Bulkin puts it, "The question becomes not which political priority to choose but how to choose both." This "how" goes beyond I'll-support-your-issues-if-you support mine (Elly Bulkin et al., *Yours in Struggle: Three Feminist Perspectives on Anti-Semitism and Racism* [Brooklyn, NY: Long Haul Press, 1984], 95). (More of this later.)

    7. Robin Morgan, *Going Too Far: The Personal Chronicle of a Feminist* (New York: Random House, 1977), 5, 123ff; Morgan, "Good-bye to All That," in *The World of a Woman: Feminist Dispatches 1968–1992* (New York: Norton, 1992).

    8. Edith Hoshino Altbach, ed., *From Feminism to Liberation* (Cambridge, MA: Schenkman, 1971), 31.

    9. Cherríe Moraga and Gloria Anzaldúa, eds., *This Bridge Called My Back: Writings by Radical Women of Color* (Watertown, MA: Persephone Press, 1981), 158, 13.

    10. Alma Gómez et al., eds., *Cuentos: Stories by Latinas* (New York: Kitchen Table Women of Color Press, 1983), 121.

    11. Ellen Malos, *The Politics of Housework* (London: Alison and Busby, 1980), 14; Ann Snitow et al., *Powers of Desire: The Politics of Sexuality* (New York: Monthly Review Press, 1983), 21; Hartmann in Lydia Sargent, ed., *Women and Revolution: A Discussion of the Unhappy Marriage of Marxism and Feminism* (Boston: South End Press, 1981), 31; Segal in Sheila Rowbotham et al., *Beyond the Fragments: Feminism and the Meaning of Socialism* (Boston: Alyson Publications, 1981), 184.

    12. Dorothy E. Smith, *Feminism and Marxism: A Place to Begin, a Way to Go* (Vancouver: New Star, 1977), 17. Even socialist feminists are sometimes ignorant or dismissive of feminism. For example, in a book distinguished by its serious attempt to combine feminist and socialist thinking, one contributor, Christine Riddiough, makes the astonishing statement that there is little evidence for the disintegration of the traditional family in the United States. (Divorce rates don't count, apparently.) She also describes the traditional family as the one place "people" (age, sex, and sexuality unspecified) turn for "emotional and social support" (Sargent, *Women and Revolution,* 81). We are told by Caroline Freeman, a contributor to another anthology, that "individuals' autonomy" (sex and age again unspecified) "is largely restricted to the sphere of the family" (in Malos, *Housework,* 208).

    13. Bulkin et al., *Yours,* 212.

    14. Altbach, *From Feminism to Liberation.* 1971, 56.

    15. Smith, *Feminism and Marxism,* 33; Rowbotham, *Fragments,* 186; Altbach, *From Feminism to Liberation,* 30; Malos, *Housework,* 14–15.

    16. Rowbotham, *Fragments,* 197. For example, says Oakley, "it was on the foundation of working-class women's trade union agitation, particularly in the cot-

ton towns of Lancashire, that the suffragettes built the force of their demand for the vote." She finds it "paradoxical that the reason why women in the Labour Party do not reach the top today is largely because of the strength of the trade union vote" (Ann Oakley, *Subject Women* [New York: Pantheon, 1981], 304), which is historically due, in part, to women's extensive trade union activity during the nineteenth and early twentieth centuries. Spender notes:

> Besides Sylvia Pankhurst's account of the extent to which women of *all* classes were involved in the suffragette movement, there is Annie Kenney's version (*Memories of a Militant*, 1924) which documents the diversity of backgrounds of many of the women who participated in militancy, and Teresa Billington-Greig's account (*The Militant Suffrage Movement*, 1911) which makes explicit the links between the suffrage movement and working-class women. There is also Hannah Mitchell's posthumous autobiography (*The Hard Way Up*, 1907) and Elizabeth Robins's "documentary," *The Convert* (1907), as well as numerous testimonies from working-class women in general sources such as Raeburn (1974) and Rosen (1974) and Liddington and Norris's (1978) account of the suffrage movement.

She sees the allegations that the movement was "nothing more than a bourgeois movement" as "an excuse for *not* dealing with women's ideas and experience" (Dale Spender, *Women of Ideas: What Men Have Done to Them* [London: Routledge and Kegan Paul, 1982], 571–73).

17. Kathy Kahn, *Hillbilly Women* (New York: Doubleday, 1973), 116–19. She was mistaken, but a knowledge of feminism limited solely to information in the mass media of the early 1970s might have led to just such a conclusion.

18. Malos, *Housework*, 155.

19. Marielouise Jansen-Jurriet, *Sexism: The Male Monopoly on History and Thought*, trans. Verne Moberg (New York: Farrar, Straus and Giroux, 1982), 348, 117, 120, 124.

20. Linda Gordon, *Woman's Body, Woman's Right: A Social History of Birth Control in America* (New York: Penguin, 1977), 209.

21. Imagine calling how men get work done without paying for it and how children are raised (and under what conditions) "women's" issues! (Gardiner in Sandra Allen et al., eds., *Conditions of Illusion: Papers from the Women's Movement* [Leeds, UK: Feminist Books, 1974], 252, 255, 253.)

22. Barbara Taylor, " 'The Men Are as Bad as Their Masters . . . ': Socialism, Feminism, and Sexual Antagonism in the London Tailoring Trade in the Early 1830s," *Feminist Studies* 5:1 (1979), 23.

23. Lillian Faderman, *Surpassing the Love of Men: Romantic Friendship and Love*

between Women from the Renaissance to the Present (New York: Morrow, 1981), 234; Oakley, *Subject Women*, 7, 137. Such myths of women's progress, like similar myths about Black advancement in the United States, function to disarm complaint. If things are better than they've ever been—and look how bad they were in the past!—how can you protest? Susan Koppelman notes a similar myth in literary studies, the one that U.S. women used not to write short stories—that's why you find so few of their short stories in anthologies—but now they are beginning to do so, and that's why they're not yet as expert in the form as men. In fact, says Koppelman, women preceded men writers as authors of short stories in the United States and have always written them in the same numbers women do today, as well as developing a tradition and conventions of their own (personal communication to author). Spender finds just such a myth operating in the case of the English novel: women—who did not write anything worthwhile until recently—are now only just beginning to learn how to do so. She finds, like Koppelman with the short story, that women pioneered the form and created many fine examples of it (Dale Spender, *Mothers of the Novel* [London: Pandora, 1986], 1). Such myths of progress make it possible to demand patience over and over again from each new—and hence naive—generation.

24. Sargent, *Women and Revolution*, 21.

25. Ibid.

26. Faderman, *Surpassing*, 237.

27. Smith, *Feminism*, 43–45.

28. Gordon, *Woman's Body*, 361.

29. Sargent, *Women and Revolution*, 24–25. "Love comics," comic books written for girls about the centrality of romantic love in women's lives and the lack of other interests therein, appeared at precisely this time in the United States. According to Bruce Bailey, they had "their financially spectacular beginnings in 1949" ("An Inquiry into Love Comic Books: The Token Evolution of a Popular Genre," *Journal of Popular Culture* X:1 [1976], 245). "Gothic romances," similar in theme, became successful in the United States in the reactionary 1950s. See Joanna Russ, "Somebody's Trying to Kill Me and I Think It's My Husband: The Modern Gothic," *Journal of Popular Culture* VI:4 (1973).

30. Haener quoted in Phyllis Chester and Emily Jane Goodman, *Women, Money, and Power* (New York: Morrow, 1976), 254; Louise Kapp Howe, *Pink Collar Workers: Inside the World of Women's Work* (New York: Putnam, 1977), 161, 164.

31. Ibid., 34–35, 88. Howe is doing here the same kind of demystification I found it necessary to do earlier in this book on recent accounts of "special" female psychology. Such psychology is described as if it bore no relation to women's oppression or even as if it were by itself somehow responsible for women's oppression. Similarly, gay and lesbian unhappiness has been said to be caused by homosexuality rather than the oppression visited on it. In the same way, Black people are usually poor (goes this way of thinking) because of their family structure, which causes their poverty, instead of their family structure (which is not nearly as unusual as theorists

like Daniel P. Moynihan have made out) being a means of dealing with their poverty. Similarly, poor people, color unspecified, have had their poverty blamed on their supposed inability to postpone gratification—although where anyone who is really poor is supposed to get all that much gratification not to postpone is beyond me. Never mind; blaming the victim has a long and nasty history.

32. Oakley, *Subject,* 305.

33. Allen, *Conditions,* 284.

34. Susan Griffin, *Made from This Earth: An Anthology of Writings* (London: Women's Press, 1982), 173. I would add to Griffin's example the use of Anita Bryant by many gay men as the symbol of homophobia, despite her claim that her husband, Bob Greene, pressured her into the campaign that bore her name, that he handled the business side of the campaign, and that he took with him, when he left her, the large sums of money that had been contributed to the organization of which she was nominally the head. I have seen somewhere (I'd appreciate news of its whereabouts) a photograph of Bryant standing next to an American flag and singing passionately into a microphone; behind her stands a semicircle of middle-aged White men in business suits. The picture is striking; its composition vividly embodies Bryant as the "front woman" for reactionary, White, masculine money and power.

35. Delphy, *Close to Home,* 121–27, 131–36.

36. Ibid., 149.

37. Marvin Harris, *Cultural Materialism: The Struggle for a Science of Culture* (New York: Random House, 1979), 62–63. I believe it's clear that to a degree these desires limit each other. That is, the good things listed above cease to be good things when they become physically unpleasant. Few, if any, people want to eat forty meals a day, for example.

38. In practice, they fought about it a good deal more than you might suspect from the neatness of the description.

39. My college history textbook noted the medieval European slogan "City air is free air," which meant (it said) that a peasant escaping to the growing medieval towns was safe from the feudal obligations (work and taxes) that *he* otherwise "owed" *his* feudal lord. Women were not mentioned in this connection. The same textbook sold us the French Revolution as a quest for freedom just like the American Revolution, but it did not mention that neither event was actually a working-class revolution. In the case of the French, "the people" did rise, but the bourgeoisie used their rebellion and the bourgeoisie also put them down very promptly afterward. Similarly, the American Revolution was a colonial revolution of the U.S. bourgeoisie against the old foreign monarchy conducted by many of the colonies' biggest landowners and richest men. One example is George Washington, who became a very rich man by marrying Martha Custis, a very rich widow.

40. Clara Fraser, personal communication to author, 17 May 1996.

41. You will notice that I am using the pronoun "he" in this case rather than "she" (or both). As far as the structure of capitalism is concerned, owners do not

necessarily come in one sex (nor do workers), but capitalism interacts with other social rules, which do make some very striking distinctions of this sort.

42. Very wealthy families—or rather, dynasties—don't go under. A colleague of mine spoke once about Franklin Delano Roosevelt's welfare program in the 1930s and added about the Roosevelt family, "They're still rich." Exactly.

43. A young friend of mine who made her living as a secretary once calculated that if she worked at her then-current salary without any expenses but taxes—that is, turning herself into a robot who did nothing but work eight hours a day and stood turned off in the office broom closet the rest of the time—it would take her more than three centuries to earn enough money to buy that desk. On a trip twenty-odd years ago to visit friends working in a summer camp in Maine, I had dinner in a small local restaurant. The restaurant window looked out on a lake (Maine is full of lakes) upon which was an island. On the island was a castle. I say "castle" because the ornate Gothic Thing on the island must have had a least fifty bedrooms. I was told that Nelson Rockefeller owned the castle and used it for two weeks each August (with a staff of eighty) but that it stood empty the rest of the year, save for a skeleton staff who maintained it. This is the kind of thing marxists mean when they talk of the extreme inequalities of wealth in capitalist society.

44. So common has this muddle about the middle become that even some marxists refer to teachers, journalists, etc. as "middle class." Linda Gordon briefly notes such confusion (Gordon, *Woman's Body,* xvi).

45. Sometimes employees in the Idea Biz rebel. As Juliet Mitchell puts it, "A person's physical energies can be visibly harnessed and exploited. Buying mental energies is riskier." She goes on to point out that the mental universe of a capitalist society geared to consumption, which ours is, must necessarily be "enormously much wider" than that of one geared to production, which ours used to be (Mitchell, *Woman's Estate* [New York: Random House, 1971], 28–30).

46. Studs Terkel, *Hard Times: An Oral History of the Great Depression* (New York: Pantheon, 1970), 323, 372.

47. Only last year, a family-run bakery in a neighborhood near mine was forced out of business by a chain bakery. A friend explained to me that this particular chain always locates its outlet stores by finding a viable local business of the same kind. It then drives the local company out of business—the large company can afford to carry a greater variety of merchandise and lower its prices temporarily in one store—and takes over. The small business has, in effect, done the large one's market research for it and has borne the entire cost of developing a set of customers in a particular neighborhood. The chain's actions are perfectly legal.

48. To the extent that a capitalist nation is forced into concessions, such needs do find an economic voice in welfare programs, Social Security, the minimum wage, subsidized housing, unemployment insurance, Medicare, and other programs of the same kind. Such attempts to give effectiveness to demand that hasn't the

money to be effective are usually characterized by their meagerness and their bureaucratic top-heaviness. They are almost always under Right-wing attack. The Thatcherite government in Britain and the Reagan and Bush administrations in the United States are obvious examples of such attacks.

"A SOCIALIST FEMINIST IS A WOMAN WHO GOES TO TWICE AS MANY MEETINGS"

(Barbara Ehrenreich)

They're the socialist feminists.[1]

And they're having quite a discussion about it.[2]

In fact, they are recapitulating the major issues that separate many feminists and many socialists: whether marxism sufficiently explains women's oppression without the addition of specifically feminist theory, and whether the oppression of women is or is not a by-product of the capitalists' exploitation and oppression of the working class.

Some, like Iris Young, simply say yes to both: "The marginalization of women . . . is an essential and fundamental characteristic of capitalism." So does Dorothy Smith: "Women's oppression is an integral part of capitalism." Some, like Peggy Morton, say the same thing in different words: "The structure of the family is determined by the needs of the economic system, at any given time, for a certain kind of labor power." Or here is Young again:

> Capitalism . . . [is] the first economic system whose nature dictates that not all potentially productive people be employed and which also requires a fluctuation in the proportion of the population employed. . . . Some criteria [must] be found to distinguish the core of primary workers from marginal or secondary workers. The preexistence of patriarchal ideology, coupled with the necessity that women be near small children, operated to make sex the most *natural* criterion by which to divide the workforce.[3]

Dalla Costa and James put it this way: "The community . . . is not an area of freedom and leisure auxiliary to the factory, where by chance there happen to be women who are degraded as the personal servants of men. *The community is the other half of capitalist organization.*"

Angela Weir says this: "The primary mechanism for . . . [securing the efficient reproduction of labour] was the exclusion of women from the workforce."[4]

To spell all this out: *because* capitalism must create marginal workers (to hire when times are good and to lay off when times are bad), *because* patriarchy preceded capitalism and accepting it is cheaper than fighting it, and *because* giving men a "family" wage (i.e., enough to support a wife and children) is cheaper than paying women outright for doing housework and raising children, capitalism actually *produces* and *enforces* patriarchy. The thinkers I've quoted above also maintain that this marxist analysis of women is sufficient to understand it and that patriarchy is therefore a department of capitalism, or, as they would probably put it, sexism is not the site of "primary conflict." That position belongs to the class struggle.

Others don't agree. Here are some of their comments. Juliet Mitchell: "The size of the 'absence' of women in socialist theory and practice is immense." Gloria Joseph and Jill Lewis: "[Marxist] analysis centered on the 'workplace' and only minimally and selectively dealt with the role of the family or of reproduction and childrearing." Ann Ferguson and Nancy Folbre say:

> "Reproduction of the laborer" is pictured as the physical reproduction of the adult male. The nature of the labor that wives and mothers perform is seldom explored. Furthermore, the labor time which mothers devote to their children—future workers—is never discussed.

As does Batya Weinbaum:

> How can whole areas of women's lives be theoretically "left out" of analysis of an economic structure? . . . Marx focuses on a discussion of . . . the adult male laborer. . . . The position of the father within the working class is "scientifically" designated to be synonymous with . . . all sex and age groups in the class. . . . When Marx went on to analyze the economy or the collective production of the larger society, he did so . . . abstracting away from differences based on sex and age. . . . The economic basis for cross-sex-and-age groups formed by working class individuals for survival (e.g. households) has not been analyzed.[5]

Marxism manages this sleight-of-hand, says Marielouise Jansen-Jurreit, "[by assuming] within the family a spontaneous, natural division of labor between the sexes; biological differences become grounds for the division of labor . . . on purely physiological grounds."[6]

That is, the kind of work women typically do and the institutions in which they do it are simply assumed to be *natural*.[7] Certainly this belief serves to forestall further analysis. And theories about the profitableness of women's staying in the home (from whence they can be tempted out to earn money as marginal workers when times are good and to which they can be sent back when times are bad) may be true today, as it has surely been in the past. But if they are, this does not explain why the *"family wage"* (of which more later) *had to be fought for by labor unions* and why *capitalists at first preferred employing women and children*—whom they could pay less than adult men. Since in fact labor unions did have to fight for the family wage, which capitalists, it seems, did *not* want, and had to fight also not only in the nineteenth but in the twentieth century to get capitalists to employ men instead of women and children, which, it seems, capitalists did *not* want either, it would certainly seem that the family wage was desirable not to capitalists but to someone else. If this is so, socialists' insistence that our current version of patriarchy is a by-product of capitalism is by no means certain and insisting that it is may have hidden motives.

Christine Delphy thinks so:

[Marxists] today . . . perpetuate . . . an unpardonable confusion between the principles of materialism and the analysis which Marx made of the capitalist mode of production. . . . This reduction of the former to the latter is today so widespread that most "marxists"—and plenty of others—think that capitalism "invented" exploitation, that capitalism *is* exploitation, and that exploitation *is* capitalism. . . . This *"error"* . . . *makes the antagonism between the proletarians and the capitalists*—which is one of the possible forms of exploitation—*into the principal conflict* wherever it exists; into the model for all oppression; *and finally into the very definition of exploitation*.[8]

In other words, the "error" above, which Delphy insists is politically motivated, is to make capitalism the only form of exploitation and to explain all others as produced by it. Many of the socialist feminists whose work I'm using here would not agree. Nonetheless, whether they believe the class struggle to be primary or not, none of them wants to lose sight of patriarchy and its relation to the male working class.

The answer some give (those who would not agree with Delphy, above) is that patriarchy is a matter of ideology. It is beliefs or ideas that are at stake.

Ferguson and Folbre comment: "Sex is treated [by these marxists] as a psychological, cultural, symbolic category—an element of the ideological level of society." Delphy puts it this way: "Women and their oppression are sent back to the superstructural and attributed to patriarchal 'ideology' while proletarians are the sole occupants of the economic realm." But "[attributing women's oppression] to purely ideological factors . . . implies an idealist and non-marxist definition of ideology. It treats it [ideology] as a factor which can survive in the absence of any material oppression."[9]

I agree with Delphy here, but many socialist feminists do not. Attributing working-class sexism to ideas instilled in the male working class by capitalism (because such ideas serve the interest of capitalism) does have the advantage of uniting women and men of the working class *against* patriarchy. Nonetheless such a theory also has the disadvantage for women of subsuming the struggle against patriarchy *under* that against capitalism.[10] Thus Carollee Bengelsdorf and Alice Hageman write: "Only when the fundamentals of capitalism are gone can a frontal attack on the oppression of women be launched." As does Margaret Benston: "When such [domestic] work is moved into the public sector, then the material basis for discrimination against women will be gone."[11]

Some, like Mitchell, disagree:

> The idea that women must "wait until after the revolution" [means] . . . what you are asking for now are just reforms and you can get those fairly easily. This position is a mirror reflection of how women's issues are seen within the bourgeois society itself, i.e. as not the real issue.[12]

Others, even more critical, use marxist logic to criticize such marxist positions. Weinbaum says:

> Marx's notion of change was that it came about through struggle. If he foresaw change in the . . . status of the sexes, he surely expected struggle to bring about that change. In this respect, the first wave of feminism [in the nineteenth century] was correct in what it tried to do, even when considered from a Marxist perspective. . . . But the core of . . . [this other kind of argument] was: you don't need special struggle for rights now—you need revolution. . . . One wonders why the struggle was not to limit, instead, the chores she had to perform at home—but then

one remembers how this was to be put off until private property had been overcome.[13]

Unfortunately the idea that women's oppression is materially rooted in capitalism itself leads to further difficulties. An oppression materially rooted in capitalism ought to vanish with the abolition of capitalism—but what if this has not happened in now-socialist nations? One solution is to claim that these nations were never really socialist. If they aren't (actually I tend to agree), then they can't serve as models of the relation between socialism and feminism. If they are, it's even worse; they are then obvious evidence that socialism can exist without feminism. This possibility usually embarrasses any socialist not obtuse enough, morally or intellectually, to claim that women's condition is just fine, thank you, and such people explain away such a possibility in various ways.

One solution is a transformation of women's oppression: although it was *material* before the revolution, afterward it has somehow become *ideological*. Thus Judith Stacey writes about China:

> In 1948 the party issued a new resolution encouraging women to struggle against their subordinate family status. The resolution declared that oppression of women was "an *ideological* struggle against the feudal landlords." In Maoist terms the class struggle is antagonistic, whereas contradictions among the people can be resolved through persuasion and propaganda.[14]

Bengelsdorf and Hageman agree:

> [The] first Congress of the Cuban Communist Party, in December 1975 [states] . . . that "a fundamental battle must be waged *in the realm of consciousness* because it is there that the backward *concepts* which lock us in the past continue to subsist."[15]

How was the battle waged? Like this:

> [In Cuba, after the revolution] women in general were channeled into areas and types of work historically associated with women. . . . Nor could it be expected, given *existing prejudices,* that women or their families would have readily accepted radically different types of jobs. . . . The sexual division of labor received the force of law with Resolutions 47 and 48 issued by the Ministry of Labor in 1968. The resolutions reserved some

500 job categories specifically for women and prohibited women from entering an equal number of professions.[16]

Perhaps the problem isn't purely a matter of ideology after all. Even those socialist feminists who state that it is also include—although they don't appear to notice it—straightforward accounts of the material benefits men derive from such arrangements in socialist nations: less work, more leisure, more money, and more control over a couple's income. Here is an example from Bengelsdorf and Hageman:

> Without question the major structures that guaranteed the oppression and exploitation of women have been destroyed [in Cuba]. . . . In April 1975 . . . *women worked* in their work centers and in their homes *an average of thirteen hours daily, Monday through Friday,* and *eleven and a half hours on the weekends "owing to the accumulation of domestic tasks."* Clearly, the problem has not just disappeared. . . . [Some women] have become discouraged or overcome by fatigue and left their jobs. . . . Despite that drive to increase the number of women in the work force, it is clear *there had been no corresponding effort to get men into the kitchen.* . . . The expectation held firm that women would be relieved of the "thousand unimportant trivialities" to the extent that the state could take on and collectivize these responsibilities. . . . Those tasks that remain uncollectivized *inevitably* rest in women's hands and on their shoulders.[17]

In other words, women must work a double shift because men won't and a predominantly male government won't try to make them do so.

Here are some less sympathetic descriptions of the phenomenon by Batya Weinbaum:

> Women's oppression has continued in socialist countries. Socialists explain this, inadequately, in two ways: either as a problem of inherited consciousness and ideology lagging behind structural economic changes; or as a problem of underdevelopment, forcing women to continue sacrificing equality, no matter what class takes control. . . . [In China] feminism remains within the structural division of "ideological struggle" whereas Chinese Communist literature hardly proposed that imperialism be defeated by "ideological struggle" with the Japanese. Moreover, feminism is characterized as a contradiction "among the people" . . . while the struggle between . . . the Chi-

nese Communists and the imperialists of Japan . . . is classified as a contradiction between two groups of *different* "people."[18]

Stacey writes of China:

> Even today . . . women are the first to be laid off when employment drops, and they are concentrated in the low-wage neighborhood "housewife" industries . . . urban women retain more responsibility than do their husbands for childcare and domestic chores. . . . *Because the family remains the critical income unit,* women are apt to shoulder the household responsibilities in order to free their husbands for the more lucratively awarded work-point jobs. . . . *Cadres justify the wage inequity on the grounds that women do not require further remuneration because their husbands earn sufficient wages* in the larger state-owned factories.[19]

The obvious inequities of "family" income lead one feminist critic actually to reverse Mao's logic. Quoting from *The Little Red Book* to the effect that women must be encouraged to do farm work so that the sexes both join in productive activity, and that equality between the sexes will happen only with the socialist transformation of society, Susan Cavin writes:

> It is not that farm work will liberate women; rather China needs farm work done, and women represented a "vast reserve of labor power." Sometimes this vulgar feminist streak in marxist history leads marxists to insist that women need socialism when it is truer to say that socialism needs women.[20]

And eventually, says Weinbaum,

> [in the U.S.S.R.] instead of maintaining the pre-revolutionary goal of abolishing classes, those in charge . . . contented themselves with the existence of "friendly classes." Hence those aspects which the "stage" theory puts off [revolution first, then feminism] have a tendency to become incorporated as a basic component of the resulting new order. . . . [Thus] pre-revolutionary socialists are theoretically in favor of abolishing the family, and post-revolutionary socialists declare themselves proud of the "democratic united family." . . . In the history of the Chinese revolution this was certainly the case. . . . During the United Front period . . . the Communist Party . . . reverted

> to a position of the liberation of women solely through partic-
> ipation in production, apparently forgetting that . . . [this] was
> supposed to be the first step along a . . . chain, leading to dis-
> integration of the economic basis of the family. . . . [Thus] Step
> I is that women go into production; Step II is that they will play
> a greater and greater role; Step III is . . . equality. . . . [But] what
> if men *react* to women taking their first Step I? After all, the
> bourgeoisie reacts to "slow" transitions to socialism . . . with the
> violence of fascism. . . . Socialist theory of the "gradual devel-
> opment of women's equality" obscures the possibility of an
> analogous form of reaction.

Then: "Facts, statistics and positions drawn from later years [in the Soviet Union] are also brushed aside by yet other contemporary Marxists as not representative of the golden first few years of socialism before everything went astray."[21]

I think it is clear at this point that an oppression that is material before the revolution but that becomes ideological afterward will not wash. Neither will the labeling of some kinds of privilege as a material matter for material struggle while other kinds somehow go unnoticed. But why the illogic and the inconsistencies? Perhaps there are interests at stake here "behind" (so to speak) the surface of the arguments. For example, it may be in the interest of male socialists to persuade female ones that class issues are the only ones there are, or at least the only important ones, or that women's concerns will automatically be taken care of after the revolution[22] (so that nothing much has to be done before it).[22]

There may also be female socialists who wish to get or keep male socialists as their allies; hence their similar insistence. Among the socialist feminists whose work I've studied, I've found roughly three major positions: that capitalism causes sexism and that strictly marxist analysis is therefore adequate to explain the oppression of women; that marxism doesn't treat women's oppression adequately but that patriarchy, far from being an independent system of exploitation and oppression, is purely ideological; and that patriarchy is an independent system of exploitation and oppression, the eradication of which requires independent analysis and a sex-class struggle between the sexes in which (by and large) it is in men's interest to retain patriarchy and in women's interest (by and large) to abolish it. I believe that these varied positions, when taken by socialist feminists, directly reflect their willingness to perceive the sex-class of men as enemies in the sex-class conflict and their willingness to tolerate the loss of some, or all, male support. The less willing one is to tolerate losing any male support, the more one will fail to perceive that a conflict of interests exists between men and women, the more one will insist that patriarchy is not an autonomous system, and the more one will assert that women's oppression is due only to capitalism. It is, of course, generally in the interest of revolutionary men to keep revolutionary women's support by asserting the very same things— after all, they can always change their minds afterward, whether this happens after the meeting or after the revolution.[23]

Such splits have occurred throughout history between the right wing and the left wing of feminism itself. Depending on how much particular feminists wished to keep male support or avoid losing it, their *feminism* has been more or less a radical *feminism*. That is, their emphasis on the conflict of interest between men and women and the difficulty of ending patriarchy has been more or less. The fear of divisiveness on the Left has led many socialists astray with regard to sex-class divisions. As Weinbaum puts it:

> "The laborer" does not supply himself with necessaries in order to maintain his own labor power [as Marx wrote]. More often "he" gets a wife to do so for him. . . . For individuals do not *live* in classes, although they *work* in them; they live in households. . . . *Household relations modify production relations, as well as the other way around.*[24]

Rosalind Delmar comes to the same conclusion:

> One fruitful preliminary way of approaching the problem is to analyze sexism as a structure which dominates the world of reproduction of the species and capitalism as the structure which dominates the world of production. . . . These two worlds are divided along a sex axis; the world of production is the world of men, the world of reproduction is the world of women. . . . [These] are the twin aspects of the present system— patriarchy and capitalism.[25]

Delphy sums it up: "There are (at least) two systems of oppression, each with its own material base."[26]

Now, none of the above denies that patriarchy and capitalism are *compatible* systems; they must be, as they both exist. Nor do any of the socialist feminists whose work I'm using in this chapter ignore the capitalist *uses* of patriarchy. Nonetheless, to assert that patriarchal exploitation and oppression form a separate system is a whopping great jump out of the marxist theory—it flatly contradicts it, in fact—and it also opens the very unpleasant possibility that the interests of working-class men and the interests of working-class women are in some manner genuinely in conflict. I suspect that the potential divisiveness for the Left of this idea is one reason so many marxists reject it. Any theory that carries with it the possibility of splitting the working class in two is a very serious matter. That's why I'm going to demand from socialist feminism much more than just the assertions I've quoted above.

One crucial question still remains to be answered. As Fox puts it, "The first question a feminist must ask of Marxism, and we should refuse to discuss any other issue until we get an adequate answer is, *what is women's relation to the means of production?*"[27] For if women, *by virtue of their sex and their sex alone,* have a particular relation to the means of production—that is, the the social organization of labor and who gets what for doing what—then, says Rosalind Petchesky,

> [there will be] evidence for what we suspected all along: that *working-class men, too, get something material, and not just illusory, out of patriarchy;* and that this material system of power, privilege and extra resources creates an objective tie between them and capitalist men as well as an objective division between them and "their" women.[28]

Certainly feminists have been saying for years that there is something very odd about women's work. For one thing, it isn't supposed to exist. For another, it's oddly tied up with female sexuality (or male sexual access to female bodies). Phyllis Chesler and Emily Jane Goodman put it like this:

> The low wages for women in all marketplace areas is one way of insuring a steady supply of women for prostitution—and for marriage—in a class and/or patriarchal society. . . . When women in marriages or marriagelike situations perform the work required in keeping themselves and their houses looking beautiful, and sexual and other services, it is assumed that they are doing what they *want* to do; when, done for money, the same tasks become very déclassé. . . . Women deny the *productive* labor involved in creating and maintaining homes and children. They also deny their denial by first saying they don't think of mothering as work and then that they think it is *more* valuable than money. Women are genuinely confused by a money culture that depends on their labor . . . but does not reward them for it economically.[29]

Nevertheless, of all the women whose work I've read so far, only two attempt to go beyond the bare statement that there are at least two systems of exploitation at work here: capitalism *and* patriarchy. One is Fox, whose work I'll postpone for the moment. The other is Delphy, who has actually formulated a full-dress theory of women's class position. To my mind, the crucial importance of her *Close to Home* lies in her agreeing with feminist assertions that women form a sex-class whose interests conflict in significant ways with those of the sex-class of men *and in not requiring an extra-economic, purely ideological, or psychological explanation for this fact.* What Delphy has done is to extend the marxist tools of class analysis to women's situations. I believe her work constitutes a very important bridge between socialism and feminism that—with the addition of theories about racism, the equation's indispensable third term—may yet become a body of thought that can do justice to all three exploitations at once. Like Eisenstein, I believe that a "synthesis of marxist and feminist questions requires the transformation of one by the other"; like Weinbaum, I want to "connect socialism to feminist revolution"; and like Eisenstein (again), "I think, as a feminist, there is much more to be *politically* gained by a dialogue between liberal, radical, and socialist feminists than by a dialogue between marxists and feminists."[30] Thus this book, as I'm sure is clear, is addressed (as a practical tactic) primarily to feminists who are doubtful about marxism, not to marxists who are doubtful about feminism.

It's impossible, in the confines of this work, to quote *Close to Home* as lengthily as I would like, but even a sketch of Delphy's reasoning may convey something of the impact of her work. Here at last is a demonstration, *in marxist terms,* that women constitute a class, or rather that "women-wives" (in French both meanings are conveyed by the one word *femmes*) constitute a class whose relation to production differs from that of men.

One of the first points Delphy makes is to notice the absolute illogic, in terms of class analysis, of assigning women to the class status *of their husbands,* thus using a totally different means of class assignment for women than for men. The practice, says Delphy, is suggestive in itself:

> Having made use of . . . [women's] dependent status to put women in the *same* social class as their husbands, sociologists are anxious to forget . . . that it [marriage] is the crucial criterion for allocating women to a socio-economic class. . . . Nevertheless, the fact that their dependence on their husbands is chosen as an index of class membership more frequently than their own constitutes a sign . . . that the patriarchal class system overrides the industrial one [in this instance].

She notes also:

> Women's labor may be unpaid not only when it is applied to products for use in the home, but also when it is applied to goods and services for the market. This occurs in all those sectors where the unit of production is the family (rather than the workshop or the factory), i.e. on most farms, in small retail businesses, and in small craft workshops.

And then:

> [Women's] work is only *not* paid when it is done within the family; and all the work they do within the family is not paid, whatever its nature.
>
> Housework . . . must be defined [therefore] as a certain *work relationship,* a particular relationship of production.[31]

That is:

> It is not a case of certain tasks being forbidden to women [wives] but of our being allowed to do them only in certain conditions.

It is, Delphy explains, not the "nature of [the] work" performed by women-wives that explains their relationship to production, but rather

> It is their [wives'] relation to production which explains why their work is excluded from the realm of value [i.e., unpaid]. *It is women* [wives] *as economic agents who are excluded from the exchange market, not what they produce.*

The supposed division of labor by sex, says Delphy elsewhere, does not really exist. When women keep accounts for their businessman husbands or host parties for their diplomat husbands, they are still not paid; it's "in the family" (as we would say), and the wife is only "helping out." That is, *her status as a wife keeps her from being paid.* When she washes the laundry or does the cooking or the cleaning, she is not paid either, but *in other conditions*—that is, *outside the family*—dishwashers, laundresses, and chefs *are* paid. "The fact that housework is done 'at home' flows from its being done 'for the husband' without payment."[32]

Because most women will be married at some time in their lives (Delphy quotes the statistic that fewer than 10 percent of women over the age of twenty-five never marry in "developed societies"):

> The super-exploitation of *all* women in wage-work is [therefore] determined by the domestic situation of *most* women . . . and more precisely, constitutes an economic pressure towards marriage. . . . I won't even mention the other penalties attached to spinsterhood.

Therefore:

> It is [therefore not accurate] . . . to say that the wife of a bourgeois man is herself bourgeois. . . . There is, equally . . . a confusion between women workers and the wives of workers. . . . *By pretending that women belong to their husband's class, the fact that wives belong by definition to a class other than that of their husbands, is hidden. . . . What is at issue is . . . denying the existence of a non-capitalist system of production. . . .*

To expand on the above account:

> Marriage is the institution by which unpaid work is extorted from a particular category of the population, women-wives. This work is unpaid because it does not give rise to a wage but simply to upkeep. These . . . relations of production . . . extend to include all the things women (and also children) produce within the home, and in small-scale manufacturing, shopkeeping, or farming, if the husband is a craftsman, tradesman, or farmer, or various professional services if the husband is a doctor or lawyer, etc. . . . When the same tasks are done outside the family they are paid for. The work acquires value—is remunerated—as long as the woman furnishes it to people to whom she is not related or married. . . . *The marriage contract . . . is in fact a work contract.*[33]

The marriage contract is a work contract: a crucial assertion. Furthermore— and this to me is the importance of Delphy's work—*it is a contract that yields to the same analysis as those more explicit contracts that create class.*[34] I know of no other feminist who has made these connections, although many have commented on the narrowness of a conception of "economic" that doesn't account for the work of housewives and mothers. Some go even further in describing what I have called The Woman Job and Delphy calls the work of "women-wives." One is Jessie Bernard, who uses the word "integry" (formed verbally on the model of "economy" and "polity") to describe the kind of work women do in keeping communities together, the sort of thing Rosalind Coward has called "social facilitation." Like Dale Spender, who writes of women's communicative work in *Man-Made Language,* Coward describes as one facet of this work:

> the domestic labour in routine social intercourse—"How are you? Who are you? What do you Do? Where do you live? Why the hell don't you ever say anything?" [and] the equivalent shit work in sexual intercourse—"What's upsetting you? Why don't you want to have sex? Is it something at work? Something I've said?". . . . Women function as the currency between men. Women's speech sustains men's impersonal relationships between themselves.[35]

Another phrase for the "integry" might be "social infrastructure"—the kinds of formal and informal women's organizations, networks, and groups that function to make the life of a particular community possible. Paula Giddings gives, as an example, the Black church, which she calls "the most cohesive institution in the deep South," and notes that during the civil rights struggle, "women were the most dynamic force within the church. . . . SNCC had to rely chiefly on women." In *Common Differences* Joseph notes that "intra-group survival skills were given more importance" in the lives of young Black women "than survival skills for dealing with the White society. . . . Black daughters are actually 'taught' to hold the Black community together." Similarly Willie M. Coleman describes that informal meeting place, the Black community beauty parlor as "a hell-of-a-place / to ferment / a . . . . . . revolution."[36]

There are many other accounts of the kind of networks women maintain in various communities and of the usefulness of the integry to the community as a whole. Cynthia Macdonald mentions studies of public housing projects for the elderly that reveal "creative, fluid networks of practical and emotional support among the women." The men, when they help as "handymen or chauffeurs," emphasize the businesslike impersonality of their work, for which they ask payment. It is just such understanding of women's work as part of the social infrastructure that leads Mollie Linker to describe her Eastern European Jewish mother's activity as a neighborhood leader, especially during the influenza epidemic of 1918 when the mother functioned as what we would today call a nurse and paramedic, taking care of people who were ill when everyone else was afraid to do so. She says, "I want people to know—what mothers of that era did and the respect they got."[37]

Is singing work? Paula Giddings describes the discovery made by SNCC during the civil rights struggle of

> a vital key to unity. That key, which would be used in subsequent SNCC actions, was music. *It was song, the heart of Black cultural expression, that provided the cohesive force to hold the different groups together.* Albany became known as a "singing movement" and it was the rich, darkly timbred voice of Bernice Reagon, an Albany State college student who joined SNCC, that evoked the resonance of centuries-old memories and strengths.[38]

Bernice Johnson Reagon herself says, "After a song . . . the differences between us were not so great. Somehow, making a song required an expression of that which was common to us all. . . . *This music was like an instrument, like holding a tool in your hand.*"[39]

If creating community feeling is work, then work may be something other than we're used to describing by that name, or at least something broader.[40] The ordinary definition of work in industrial capitalism is that work is what you get paid for while play is what you don't get paid for (and perhaps what you pay other people for). This definition never did fit women's unpaid work. One might replace this definition with another—play is what you like and would choose to spend your time on if you could, while work is what you don't like and wouldn't choose to do if you didn't have to— but even this definition has some problems. The definition of work as what you must do in order to live, and play as whatever commercialized amusement you rush to in order to get the taste of work out of your mouth, leaves no room for the craft work that still exists and that many people enjoy. There are also ways to "play" that, like 1950s dating, many people find hard and unpleasant and "play," like art, that is *serious play*. (It's no accident, I think, that this phrase sounds like a contradiction.) It seems to me that one of the best-kept secrets of industrial capitalism is how unutterably dull most commercialized forms of play are *when you can do nothing else*. The carrot-on-a-stick of "leisure" dangled in front of almost all of us remains luscious to so many precisely because so few get to taste more than a crumb of it.[41]

If work is indistinguishable from politics in one direction (maintaining or challenging the status quo, as in Bernard's "integry") and from affection in another (caring for a sick child or a friend), then a good many activities may really be work, even though they're usually not described that way.[42] Is giving emotional support to a husband who is tired at the end of his day work? Is sending out three hundred New Year's cards work? The feminist answer to questions like these must, I think, be yes. To take another example, are emotions work? Is the "spontaneous" and "natural" activity of smiling work? In the early years of the women's liberation movement, Shulamith Firestone's answer was yes.[43] First she noted that the dominant social group (whether that of class, color, or sex) finds the grumbling of subordinate groups unpleasant. Then:

> Oppressed groups must also appear to *like* their oppression. . . . The smile is the child/woman equivalent of the shuffle. . . . In my case I had to train myself out of that phony smile which is like a nervous tic on every teenage girl. . . . My dream action for women's liberation movement: *a smile boycott* at which declaration all women would instantly abandon their "pleasing" smiles, henceforth smiling only when something pleased *them*.[44]

Nancy Henley has called smiling "woman's badge of appeasement." She has this to say:

> Though little research has been done on smiling, it is understood as a gesture offered upwards in the status hierarchy; indeed a powerful and successful person may be said to be surrounded by a thousand suns! . . . [Such people] are likely to see serious faces only in their peers: it's no wonder that they think of their subordinates—be they "contented darkies," "beer-loving workers," "brawling hardhats" or "flighty dames"— as happy-go-lucky and carefree.[45]

And here is Bernard, citing Arlie Hochschild about all class differences (this makes four feminists altogether): "Emotions are also built into the status structure. Friendly and appreciative emotions go up and hostile emotions, down. Thus one of the most important emoluments of high status is a friendly ambience."[46]

It is precisely because women's unpaid work lies outside the usual capitalist polarity of work and play that it is useful in challenging such "commonsense" and "obvious" definitions. If anything done that supports the status quo is work and if challenging the status quo is also work (political work), then storytelling, sculpture, painting, poetry, and even music, activities supposedly free of such obligations, *are work*. If children's play rehearses children's adult roles, which it often and obviously does, then children's play is also work. If culture in general is indistinguishable from what supports things as they are, if the ties of affection and loyalty are part of a culture (or a challenge to it), then the distinction between work and play breaks down. Nothing is left to be "play," although plenty remains to be—whether detested or enjoyed, pleasant or unpleasant—work. After all, the idea that what is done in offices and factories is work while what is done in the home is "natural" (and whatever is left over can be relegated to "leisure") came into being only a few centuries ago with the rise of the very ruling class socialists are now trying to get rid of. The very recent occurrence of this division, and its origin in the interests of the bourgeoisie, should be enough to make us suspicious of it.

I would also like to propose here a more explicit counter-idea (more useful, I think, than just "like" and "don't like") that at least operates to demystify "work." That is that everything a society needs done in order for it to remain a going concern vis-à-vis itself and its neighbors, everything that a ruling class needs to have done in order that it remain a ruling class, and everything anyone needs to do to change this situation—all these activities *are work*. Keeping houses comfortable is work, bringing up children is work, keeping the powerful happy is work, women's enabling men to have conversations is work, "keeping up with the Joneses" is work, training children to have the "right" habits and personalities—so that they can work—is work, forming the "proper" sort of personality oneself and having the "proper" sort of feelings is work (if only because of the constant temptation to have the "wrong" ones), and so on. It seems to me that one of the crucial achievements of the feminism of the last twenty years is precisely to demonstrate that very large amounts of work in this world, many of them the specialties of women, are mystified by being called something other than work: "nature" for one, or even "leisure," or (for example, the case of scrubbing toilets, an activity hardly anyone would regard as natural or pleasant) mystifying the work involved by naming it not work but solely and only an expression of love.

It's all work.

Such a conclusion ought to rejoice the hearts of socialist feminists everywhere. If it's all work, then there's every possibility of extending to most Human activity the principles of analysis that most marxists have hitherto reserved for paid work and the money economy.

I think we must withstand the temptation (and I think it will be a temptation) to weaken the statement proposed above by labeling "necessary" activities as "work" and "nonsubsistence" or "luxury" activities as play. It is true that some activities stand lower in Abraham Maslow's list of Human priorities than others—for example, a modern city can undoubtedly survive a five-hour smile boycott more easily than a five-minute interruption of electricity—but if street people, in January, in a northern city, are living at subsistence level, *then everyone else is not*—and in fact, what is considered "subsistence" is clearly a matter of social, not biological definition, as Marx himself has said. Nor is providing for immediate needs "work" while providing for more distant ones (in Maslow's terms "higher" ones in the hierarchy) "play." Garbage collectors get paid for doing what they do, but so do the people who make fancy chocolates for chocolate-manufacturing firms.[47]

Nor is "play" always pleasant, nor "work" unpleasant. I need only mention the sex and dating that many teenagers, boys as well as girls, find hard work and (contrary to that) the "work" of gardening, which many people find delightful, at least in small enough doses.[48] As for thoroughly commercialized "play," it might more accurately be considered emergency repair work on people ravaged by bad conditions at work. If the working conditions were not so bad (a point often made by radicals in the 1960s), then the bad "playing conditions" might lose their appeal.

Indeed, behind the ordinary, capitalist distinctions between "work" and "play" lie another set of distinctions, not nearly so well publicized. These (which the capitalist distinctions tend to mystify) are between *what makes a profit for someone* (or is intended to do so) and *what does not make a profit for anybody.* Thus agribusiness is work, but sewing clothes for one's family is not, even though the sewing can change the standard of living of a family quite markedly and even though agribusiness may wreck the nutrition and living standards of a continent. No, it's all work. And there's a crucial corollary to *It's all work:*

  It's all economics too.

NOTES

1. I'm quoting Iris Young here in the chapter title. Barbara Ehrenreich (whom Young quotes) actually says that a socialist feminist is *a socialist* who goes to twice as many meetings (Young in Lydia Sargent, ed., *Women and Revolution: A Discussion of the Unhappy Marriage of Marxism and Feminism* [Boston: South End Press, 1981], 64). Since the socialist feminists I've been able to find are all women, and since the socialist feminists these socialist feminists cite are also all women, I've altered the word in Ehrenreich's epigram.

2. The work of the theorists I draw from in this chapter is more complex than the brief quotations I use can possibly convey. Not only that, the aim of their work—e.g., Mariarosa Dallacosta's and Selma James's—may not range them at all neatly with the "side" I've put them on in this necessarily too-short chapter. If the views of these theorists are thereby mispresented I can only ask pardon; what I intend to do here is give nonsocialist nonparticipants a sense of what's at issue and the kinds of comments likely to be heard in a discussion conducted among socialist feminists.

3. Young in Sargent, *Women and Revolution,* 58; Dorothy E. Smith, *Feminism and Marxism: A Place to Begin, a Way to Go* (Vancouver: New Star, 1977), 26; Morton

in Ellen Malos, ed., *The Politics of Housework* (London: Alison and Busby, 1980), 138, Young in Sargent, *Women and Revolution,* 58, italics added.

4. Mariarosa Dalla Costa and Selma James in Malos, *Housework,* 162, italics added; Weir in Sandra Allen et al., eds., *Conditions of Illusion: Papers from the Women's Movement* (Leeds, UK: Feminist Books, 1974), 226.

5. Juliet Mitchell, *Woman's Estate* (New York: Random House, 1971), 75; Gloria Joseph and Jill Lewis, *Common Differences: Conflicts in Black and White Feminist Perspectives* (New York: Anchor, 1981), 7; Ferguson and Folbre in Sargent, *Women and Revolution,* 317; Batya Weinbaum, *The Curious Courtship of Women's Liberation and Socialism* (Boston: South End Press, 1978), 63, 42–43, 35, 38. Again, please note that a good many of these thinkers' ideas are actually more complex and sometimes more ambiguous than I can indicate. One example is Dorothy Smith, who insists, certainly accurately, that feminism as a political analysis is incomplete because of its lack of class analysis (Smith, *Feminism,* 26) and who explicitly takes the position that the family is organized by the economic and social relations obtaining during the present stage of capitalism (ibid., 42). She also deplores the "Marxist rejection of feminism" as "peculiarly lacking in analysis" and says "there has been very little effort to understand feminism and very little attempt even to analyze and understand women's oppression in society" (ibid., 33). She then, in classic feminist fashion, goes on to analyze what it means to be dependent on someone else's wage. *Then* she calls that situation "a relation organized by capitalism" (ibid., 50) and attributes women's oppression to "that aspect of the capitalist oppression of women which directly penetrates the home" and produces "an alliance across class and among men against women" (ibid., 51).

6. Marielouise Jansen-Jurreit, *Sexism: The Male Monopoly on History and Thought,* translated by Verne Moberg (New York: Farrar, Straus and Giroux, 1982), 153.

7. Conservative views about women's work often accompany conservative views about sexuality. In the introduction to *Powers of Desire,* Ann Snitow, Christine Stansell, and Sharon Thompson state:

> The mainstream Marxist movement in Europe and the United States took its cues in sexual matters from the least challenging views of its two leading theorists. . . . A British socialist editor in 1893 spoke for many of his comrades when he rejected a request from a sex radical that he include more discussion of sex in his newspaper: "I am a radical but . . . the whole subject is nasty to me." Thus the advent of Marxian socialism represented something of a step backward in the development of a radical sexual analysis (Snitow et al., *Powers of Desire: The Politics of Sexuality* [New York: Monthly Review Press, 1983], 15).

8. Christine Delphy, *Close to Home: A Materialist Analysis of Women's Oppression*, translated by Diana Leonard (Amherst, MA: University of Massachusetts Press, 1984), 158. The history of socialism presents other questions. Weinbaum asks: "Why did early socialist and feminist movements occur at the same time. . . . Why [does] anti-feminist reaction grow linked with the rise of socialist theory and practice?" (Weinbaum, *Curious Courtship*, 63). Barbara Taylor provides, perhaps, a partial answer:

> There is a funny sense, then, in which one of the weaknesses of the early socialist movement was also one of its strengths: lacking any scientific theory of the historic role of the proletariat, they lacked also that principled basis from which to reject female claims which was later to be developed with such verve by Marxist anti-feminists (Taylor, " 'The Men Are as Bad as Their Masters . . . ': Socialism, Feminism, and Sexual Antagonism in the London Tailoring Trade in the Early 1830s," *Feminist Studies* 5:1 [1979], 34).

9. Ferguson and Folbre in Sargent, *Women and Revolution*, 317; Delphy, *Close to Home*, 177, 58.

10. The logic of such arguments is a little odd. Note the jump evident in the last sentence of the following by Margaret Coulson, Branka Magas, and Hilary Wainwright, which certainly seems to say that women's organizing is rooted in the needs of the male proletariat:

> Given . . . the relative autonomy of women's oppression and the consequent lack of any inevitable short-run unity of interests, this implies that women's self-organization is a necessary condition for the development of a vanguard that truly expresses the interests of all oppressed groups. . . . [This] is *rooted in the needs of the proletariat, both male and female* (in Malos, *Housework*, 231–32).

11. Bengelsdorf and Hageman in Zillah R. Eisenstein, ed., *Capitalist Patriarchy and the Case for Socialist Feminism* (New York: Monthly Review Press, 1979), 272; Benston in Malos, *Housework*, 126.

12. Mitchell, *Woman's Estate*, 72.

13. Weinbaum, *Curious Courtship*, 52–53.

14. In Eisenstein, *Capitalist*, 308, italics added.

15. Ibid., 290, italics added.

16. Ibid., 276, 279, italics added.

17. Ibid., 290–91, 281–88, italics added.

18. Weinbaum, *Curious Courtship*, 14, 79.

19. In Eisenstein, *Capitalist*, 327–29, italics added.

20. Susan Cavin, *Lesbian Origins* (San Francisco: Ism Press, 1985), 240–41.

21. Weinbaum, *Curious Courtship,* 74–75, 83, 62.

22. Manimala, a contributor to *Manushi*, gives an example from another part of the world of how women's issues are made secondary to "class" issues that do not in fact include them, in this case "the struggle of the landless poor" in Bodhgaya. The issue of wife-beating was brought up by her and she organized a speak-out on wife-beating in which only women were allowed to speak. Although some (the author among them) declared they "would not even drink water from the hands of a man who beat his wife," and "after this the children started bringing me news about men who beat their wives," and although "these same children began to express their resentment against it" (wife-beating) while some men "gave up wife-beating altogether," nonetheless "very few people [sic] only and consistently spoke out against it." She writes, "In general the struggle against wife-beating was not taken up in as systematic a way as was the land struggle. As a result, the wife-beating issue is now almost completely buried." Because the women's welfare depends upon the welfare of the households in which they live, their welfare depends on joining the land struggle. Because the women's welfare is opposed to the men's welfare in the matter of women's domestic behavior and male behavior that enforces it—which includes wife-battering—most men did not take up the struggle against wife-battering as they did the struggle for land, and some women were doubtful about the land struggle, many feeling "that if their men got the land, they would beat them even more." After all, the prestige and power of owning land would be added to the authority of sex, which the men already had. As the women said, "Are not women beaten and is liquor not drunk in well-off homes?" (Manimala appears to connect wife-battering with the abuse of alcohol, as many U.S. and English feminists have done.) (Madhu Kishwar and Ruth Vanita, eds., *In Search of Answers: Indian Women's Voices from Manushi* [London: Zed Books, 1984], 154–55, 161).

23. An example is cited by Gay W. Seidman:

> Before the ZANU (Zimbabwe National Union) came to power in 1980 its leaders repeatedly emphasized the party's commitment to . . . [the] emancipation of women. . . . [They] relied heavily on women's participation in the liberation struggle. [Afterward] older views of women's roles have re-emerged among the party's leadership [who] see government's goal as helping women become better mothers and citizens within the existing family structure (Seidman, "Women in Zimbabwe: Postindependence Struggles," *Feminist Studies* 10:3 [1984]).

24. Weinbaum, *Curious Courtship,* 39, italics added.

25. In Allen et al., *Conditions,* 229, 235.

26. Delphy, *Close to Home,* 179.

27. Constance Faulkner gives, as an example of the capitalist use of patriarchy, the employment of women as a marginal labor force mentioned earlier in this chapter:

> If these is any single characteristic of the American economic system on which all economists agree, it is the system's instability, that is, the business cycle. . . . In simplest terms, capitalism's instability requires inequality because upswings in economic activities require the expansion of the labor force and recessions or downturns require the opposite, a contraction of the labor force. Structural changes make similar demands. Technological changes, for example computerization or mechanization—might cause shifts in employment with temporary or permanent dislocations. Whatever the cause there is a need for a *marginal* labor force. . . . Mostly we have filled the requirement through the use of females and immigrant/minority labor. . . . After immigration in direct response to labor needs ceased, the black population tended to fill the gap. But we did not have to do it that way. In a purely economic sense, white males could have been and could still be used to fill the need for a marginal labor force—one that enters and exits [the labor market] freely, with minimal social disruption. . . . *Since . . . dominant social groups are not marginal [i.e. have too much power as groups to accede to such an event] that role had to be filled by others* (Faulkner, "The Feminist Challenge to Economics," *Frontiers*, XIII:3 [1986], 59, italics added).

Heidi Hartmann puts it this way: "Capitalist development creates the places for a hierarchy of workers, but traditional marxist categories cannot tell us who will fill which places. *Gender and racial hierarchies determine who fills the empty places*" (in Sargent, *Women and Revolution*, 18, italics added).

28. Fox [Silveira] in Delphy, *Close to Home*, 178–79, italics added; Rosalind Petchesky in Eisenstein, *Capitalist*, 379, italics added.

29. Phyllis Chesler and Emily Jane Goodman, *Women, Money, and Power* (New York: Morrow, 1976), 198, 5, 12–13, italics added. Chesler and Goodman also point out one interesting (and deliberately mystificatory) function of the fuss about women's sexual morality:

> A "good woman" is one who does whatever a man wants. But a "good" woman is also (supposed to be) a virgin, a conservative and a sexual prude. But this also makes her "uptight" or a "bad" woman. . . . One can . . . keep wonder-

ing about this, which many women do. *It keeps their minds off how little money they are making* (203, italics added).

30. Eisenstein in Sargent, *Women and Revolution*, 340–41; Weinbaum, *Curious Courtship*, 29.

31. Delphy, *Close to Home*, 39, 61, 90. Of the view that certain jobs are "natural" to women, Delphy states, "To disguise relationships between people as relations between or to things, is (or should be) a well-known characteristic of bourgeois ideology. (I refuse to give page references to the great ancestor who first taught us this)" (199). Delphy means Marx, of course. Her acerbity is one of the delights of *Close to Home*. Indeed, anthropological evidence bears her out. Maxine L. Margolis cites one study "of 186 societies from around the world" that found that in 46 percent mothers were "the primary or exclusive caretakers of infants," while in almost as many (40 percent) the *primary* care of infants was others' responsibility. In fewer than one in five were mothers the "primary or exclusive caretakers *after* infancy" (Margolis, *Mothers and Such: Views of American Women and Why They Changed* [Berkeley: University of California Press, 1984], 15).

32. Delphy, *Close to Home*, 205, 60 (italics added), 201–12. Delphy adds wryly,

> This doubtless explains why the wives of small farmers can only draw a distinction between their "household" activities and their "occupational" activities with great difficulty, and at the behest of sociologists . . . [because] the working-of-the-holding [farm] and the work-of-the-house are carried out *within the same relations of production* (90–91).

33. Ibid., 71, 168–69, 72–73 (italics added), 94–95, (italics added).

34. There are other unsuccessful attempts by socialist feminists to deal with the problem Delphy solves. Thus Eisenstein mystifies housework by asserting that "woman is a consumer. . . . As a consumer, woman is working to select, prepare and maintain the goods. . . . She is doing what is absolutely necessary for the economy—consuming" (Eisenstein, *Capitalist*, 48). In a similar vein, Sandra Harding argues that the "restriction of material causes to economic ones" is "unjustifiably reductionist" and that "economic relations" do not "exhaust the list of causal social relations." She subsequently states that there are "real, material, historically specific aspects of the division of labor by gender" that "cause the production of social persons with psychological investment in reproducing patriarchy and capital. . . . It is . . . the actual physical division of labor by gender itself, and *the consequent physical/social relations of the infant to its environment which constitute the material base*" (in Sargent, *Women and Revolution*, 143–44, 149). The relegation to women of psychological labor and the consequent detour though psychology is one method of

insisting on the importance of women's oppression without defining housekeeping and child care as work in the sense of "economics" and without defining the sexes' differential access to leisure, money, and various forms of power as the oppression needed to keep those who are exploited in their place. As I've mentioned, Mitchell takes much the same digression in *Psychoanalysis and Feminism*, i.e., she says that Marx analyzed the material basis of capitalism while Freud analyzed the ideological basis of capitalism.

35. Bernard has taken the term from Kenneth Boulding but notes, as he apparently did not, that the integry is populated largely by women. Rosalind Coward's work is *Female Desires: How They Are Sought, Bought, and Packaged* (New York: Grove Press, 1985), 140. A college administrator I know once described to me a meeting in the early 1970s in which the male staff and faculty, upset about burgeoning "women's liberation" on campus, held a meeting to decide what to do. According to her, the men found that without the presence of the women they literally could not structure a discussion. This became obvious when two of the women appeared—half an hour late—and the discussion was able, suddenly, to begin.

36. Paula Giddings, *When and Where I Enter: The Impact of Black Women on Race and Sex in America* (New York: Morrow, 1984), 284; Joseph and Lewis, *Common Differences*, 106; Coleman in Barbara Smith, ed., *Home Girls: A Black Feminist Anthology* (New York: Kitchen Table Women of Color Press, 1983), 222.

37. Barbara Macdonald and Cynthia Rich, *Look Me in the Eye: Old Women, Ageing, and Ageism* (San Francisco: Spinsters Ink, 1983), 88; Sydelle Kramer and Jenny Masur, eds., *Jewish Grandmothers* (Boston: Beacon Press, 1976), 99.

38. Giddings, *When and Where*, 283, italics added.

39. Ibid.

40. For example, the actual creation of political power is work. I do not mean the seizing of it at the top, or imagery of such seizure, in which it's assumed that all political power *is* at the top, that the "powerful" *own* power (imagined as a discrete, ownable, uncreatable sort of object), and that others can "take it away" from its present owners and then "own" it themselves. Such a concept of power is unlikely to lead to the kind of grassroots, mass-movement participation—the creation of "power" among the "powerless"—that can not only challenge the polity-as-it-is and do so effectively but that can also change the nature of power from a discrete force at the top, which is ownable, to something that is part of a new integry. It was cheering, after having written this (and rewritten it eight times) to remember Audre Lorde's *"For the master's tools will never dismantle the master's house. They may allow us temporarily to beat him at his own game, but they will never enable us to bring about genuine change"* (Audre Lorde, *Sister Outsider: Essays and Speeches* [Trumansburg, NY: Crossing Press, 1984], 112).

41. Such descriptions of work and the conditions under which it's done were

not unusual in the United States during the radical 1960s, though we hear a lot less of them now.

42. I forget which British war was supposed to have been won on the playing fields of Eton, but surely football can serve as a U.S. example.

43. When I was fifteen, I was cornered on a bus by an adult—male and White—who found my serious look unpleasant. He kept telling me to "smile" until finally, in despair, I did. He then went away.

44. Shulamith Firestone, *The Dialectic of Sex* (New York: Morrow, 1970), 90.

45. Nancy M. Henley, *Body Politics: Power, Sex, and Non-Verbal Communication* (Englewood Cliffs, NJ: Prentice-Hall, 1977), 171–72.

46. Jessie Bernard, *The Female World* (New York: The Free Press, 1981), 181.

47. Down with the owners! Up with the chocolates!

48. There is obviously no room in the industrial-capitalist distinction between "work" and "play" for craft work. Craft work involves head, hand, and (for many people) heart, while labor done in the industrial mode requires most workers to keep their heads and hearts for what they do, unpaid, on their own time. I'm not really arguing here for keeping the categories *work* and *play* but leaving the latter empty of anything; rather I think the division itself is now less than useful. What individual people like to do and what they dislike seems to me a far more reasonable and fruitful topic of inquiry, as it did to the radicals of the 1960s. Some of the material in this section came from the experience of having disabilities that made it impossible for me to do my "work"—teaching and writing—for several years; I found myself with enough income to spend "playing" a good part of that time and an absolute resentment of the necessity. (I was constantly being told by colleagues and acquaintances how "lucky" I was to be able not to "work" and how much they themselves would have liked to be idle!) I am not, by the way, recommending the goal of making all Human activity ecstatic. Unpleasant work will always be necessary to any community's survival until (and if) we reach the science-fictional state in which technology turns into magic: infinite energy and infinite choice. I do think, though, that distinguishing between what people like, what they can tolerate, and what they detest leads to much more fruitful inquiry than the very compromised ideas of "work" and "play."

IS LABOR LABOR?

It's all economics.

Even babies?

Governments think so. Here are some observations on the subject. Nawal El Saadawi says:

> Sexual freedom which allows for the birth of children, whether within wedlock or outside of it, is considered equally virtuous and desirable in a married or unmarried mother living in the Swedish society of today, for Sweden is now facing an acute shortage of people and therefore of labour.
>
> However, in countries which are faced with the problem of overpopulation, such as India and Egypt, the married mother (the unmarried mother here is, of course, completely out of bounds) is very likely to be punished if she gives birth to more than two or three children. . . . *Principles and positions seem to vary much more with the socio-economic structures of the states than they do with the religion in force.*[1]

According to Marielouise Jansen-Jurreit:

> The Soviet Union has already changed its stand on the abortion question twice since 1918. Of the other states of the Eastern bloc, five countries today are aiming for a higher birth rate. . . . Moreover, in 1966 abortion was prohibited in Rumania by a decree that stated that abortion prevented "the natural increase

of the population." Titles, orders and medals are given to mothers of large families in both Rumania and Bulgaria. . . . [2]

Linda Gordon writes:

> After World War II the U.S. government, as leader of the capitalist world, was threatened by international discontent as formerly colonial peoples demanded independence and sought economic development . . . which would have limited or even ended the continuous economic exploitation of Third World peoples by Western capitalists. *Population control . . . provided both a rationalization for the failure of capitalism to provide economic growth for the Third World masses and a proposed solution to the social stress.* . . . In Puerto Rico, model for the population controllers, where 35 per cent of women have been sterilized, abortion remains illegal, for abortion becomes too often a tool in women's own command. . . . Throughout the world, population-control programs decreasingly use diaphragms and even pills and favor IUDs and operations which are not in women's control. [3]

Here's Robin Morgan:

> *Reproductive freedom always is a first target of conservative, racist and ethnocentric forces:* in the USSR it is more difficult for a "white" Russian woman to obtain contraceptives or an abortion than for a woman in one of the ethnic republics, because the government is concerned about the darker-skinned and Asiatic population's outnumbering whites; comparably, in the US, birth-control policy has at times resulted in Afro-American, Native American, and Hispanic-American women being sterilized without their informed consent. In the international arena, the same racial and ethnic bigotries are writ large in population strategies foisted by Northern countries on Southern ones, by the "developed world" and the "developing." [4]

And Maud Pember Reeves:

> *The national preoccupation with motherhood [in Britain in the early 20th century] had its roots in the waning of national economic confidence. Since the last decades of the 19th century under the pressure of German and American industrial competition, Britain had begun*

to feel its vulnerability as a world-dominating economic power. . . .
It was because of this anxiety that the governing class acqui-
esced to the social reforms of the Liberal Government of 1906
(old age pensions, provision of school meals and school medical
inspection). And the duty of women to fulfill their natural function of motherhood efficiently and effectively became the pre-
dominant theme of much contemporary literature.[5]

Sandra Allen agrees:

*The problem of biological reproduction is clearly a matter of State
policy. . . . Decisions which affect reproduction [in Britain] are made
by an agency of the male dominated State: the National Health
Service. . . .* These are the men who make the decisions about
whether we're to have children, what contraceptive we should
use, whether or not we can have an abortion (answer: at a price)
and if and when we should be sterilised. The birth rate has been
a State concern in France for generations.[6]

Lisa Leghorn and Katherine Parker list reasons:

The number of children produced determines the number of
people that are at productive ages relative to "unproductive"
ages. *The distribution of children within races is also very important
to those in power, since it can increase disparities between groups,
strengthen the political position of minorities, etc.*[7]

Fox [Silveira] is equally emphatic:

It is commonplace to hear that one country or another, in order
to increase or decrease the size of its labor force, is restricting
or easing access to birth control or abortion, is encouraging
early or late marriages, is giving financial awards to mothers or
tax incentives to single people, and so forth. These male games
played with women's bodies are considered acceptable, even
enlightened social policy. . . . The state's real interest is in *controlling* the birthrate, up or down, depending on its needs.[8]

Few of us are apt to hear this kind of talk from our governments, our
religious leaders, or our neighbors. What we hear instead is reproduction
spoken of as a *moral matter,* particularly women's moral or religious obligation to bear children. As Ann Oakley says:

Family policies are rarely explicitly identified as such by governments. Since a crucially central ethic of family life is that families are private places, the extent of state intervention in family life must be veiled; families are to be . . . sanctuaries from, not examples of, the intrusiveness of the state.[10]

Here are some more feminist statements, this one by Cherríe Moraga:

Patriarchal systems of whatever ilk must be able to determine how and when women reproduce. For even "after the revolution," babies must be made, and until they find a way of making them without us (which is not that far off into the future) we're here for the duration. In China, for example, married couples are now being mandated by the State to limit their children to one. Abortions are not only available, but women are sometimes forced by family and friends to undergo an abortion or meet with severe economic recriminations from the State.[11]

Susan Cavin observes:

"Whosoever controls female sexuality . . . controls the reproduction of [any] society."[12]

Patricia Murphy Robinson concludes:

The control of our minds, as a sex, is an economic necessity. We think we produce children for ourselves just as we think we work for ourselves. . . .[13]

The concerns over infanticide, abortion, birth control and homosexuality . . . are mystified and made plausible through moral and religious excuses . . . when in essence their effects are economic.[14]

That is why, in the United States today, says Fox,

Doctors and courts are already asserting their right to decide what happens inside the uterus. Doctors have asked for and in some cases judges have granted them the right, against a woman's will, to confine her in a hospital or give her a Caesarian, in order to increase the fetus' chances of survival. Ironically, it was the far right and the "right-to-lifers" who began to initiate

such suits, with the goal of strengthening the individual patri-
arch's control of his wife and family; but now it looks like the
real benefit of such rulings will go to the male state, which is
extending its colonization of women to the physical occupation
of the womb itself. . . . *Not even a fully developed adult is given
the rights over another person's body that the fetus, fronting for the
patriarchy, already has been given over a woman's body.*[15]

Babies, it seems, are economics. Babies, despite the pleasure they give,
the love they inspire, and the anxieties and frustrations of caring for them,
are very much a matter of economics. Few feminists would dispute this,
yet I've found few feminist theorists who explicitly analyze reproduction *as
production*—the production of people—and it's probably significant that
those I have found come out of the socialist feminist tradition. Thus Fox
writes:

> Once we see that childbearing is an economic activity, we have
> the economic base of sexism. Women's bodies are a means of
> production. *Labor is labor.* . . . At the base of all this, I am saying,
> is pregnancy, is childbearing, nursing and childcare. *At the bot-
> tom are women's bodies manufacturing labor power.*[16]

Therefore, El Saadawi says:

> The woman's problem lies in the fact that her body, or more
> precisely, her womb, is the only receptacle within which human
> life can be reproduced. The state, in order to be in control of
> the means of reproducing human beings, and in order to submit
> those means to the interests of the economic system which hap-
> pens to be in force at the time, has been obliged to extend its
> control and subjugation to that of women's bodies. *She has
> therefore lost the real ownership of her own body, it having been
> taken over by the state.*[17]

And Christine Delphy says:

> The control of reproduction is both the cause and the means
> for the second great material oppression of women—sexual ex-
> ploitation. *Control of reproduction is the second facet of the op-
> pression of women.*[18]

If reproduction is *work*, what are its *working conditions?* Not good, say most of my sources. Note, please, that childbirth is not in and of itself the cause of women's oppression any more than the Human capacity for work is the cause of class exploitation and class oppression, or any more than Human variations in skin color and features are themselves the cause of racist exploitation and racist oppression.[19] Rather it is the domination of one group by another that makes it possible to transform biological fact (which is neutral in itself) into social, economic, or political power. Indeed, it's a conflict of interests that *creates* one socially recognized class, or sex-class, or race as distinct from another. Jansen-Jurreit, another feminist who states explicitly that pregnancy, nursing, and childbirth *are work,* has given a sketch of how the social transformation of mere biological *sex* into that social invention, *sex-class,* might have occurred:

> Underlying child rearing is a conscious or unconscious reck-
> oning of cost and benefit. . . . [Children are] allies . . . helpers
> . . . [and] through the control of their marriages, possible alli-
> ances between groups or families can be formed, and the chil-
> dren are the guarantors of old-age care. . . . This is why men as
> well as women are interested in having the optimal number of
> children that can be brought up in the particular environmental
> conditions and state of technology. But even if the increase in
> existential security through more children is fundamentally in
> the interest of both sexes, *the degree of the interest is unequal.*
> *For the women each pregnancy—and the labor time related to
> the care of a small child—means an automatic increase in the
> amount of work they do. Up until the First World War there were
> hardly any chances of survival for babies who were not nursed. . . .
> A woman who nurses totally is committed for about one and a half
> to two hours of work a day and requires about a thousand additional
> calories.* Because for the man the increase in the number of
> children does not mean the sort of extensive increase in work
> that it does for the woman, men, under the conditions of the
> majority of preindustrial societies, have a stronger interest than
> women in maximizing the number of children. . . .
> *In cattle-breeding and agrarian societies . . . the great demand for
> human labor power leads to a much higher birth rate and encourages
> the institutionalization of patriarchal structures . . . [and] the
> greater the women's reproductive burden . . .* the higher the fre-
> quency of pregnancies, the more gynecological accidents
> (mother and infant mortality), the more children are required,
> so that at least some survive. . . . The problem of population

increase . . . was not a result of the sex drive but of reproduction ideologies and concepts of morality which provided security for the economic foundations of patriarchy. . . .[20]

Fox agrees and depicts the same dynamics, if more briefly:

> With the advent of war and agriculture . . . population growth became significant to the economy. . . . In a labor intensive economy, the probability of a conflict between women and men would be high. Since pregnancy is a risk to life and health, *women would have a stronger motive to limit reproduction* and to reproduce only after careful weighing of the benefits to ourselves.[21]

Even in an ideal society, I would add, *everyone's quality of life would depend a good deal on the size and age-grading of the population, and even there the production of people will demand far more from women than from men.*[22] Even if men shared in child care, men would still not get pregnant, not carry, and not give birth. In short, as Fox [Silveira] puts it, "Women and men are in a class conflict with each other."

Charlotte Perkins Gilman put the matter bluntly in an unpublished letter about the use of women's "products," their children, in wars:

> All this talk for and against and about babies is by men. One would think the men bore the babies, nursed the babies, reared the babies. . . . The women bear and rear the children. The men kill them. Then they say: "We are running short of children— make some more."[23]

Here are some comments about the working conditions for reproduction in that wealthy country, the United States:

> Mothers, like many other forced laborers, are not given the proper tools with which to do their jobs. Most mothers do not have an adequate amount of money, education, housing and leisure to insure [a] healthy child or family development according to anybody's standards. But mothers are the first to be blamed when their poverty produces children who are self-destructive and socially dangerous.[24]

And here—although not conclusively, since the sex and age of the respondents is not specified—is a suggestive comment from columnist Ann Landers' popular U.S. advice column: "In 1976, responding to her [Ann Landers'] poll, 'Parenthood—if you had a choice would you do it again?' 70 percent of the huge numbers that answered her told her no, they would not."[25]

Nor, it seems, is the dominant culture's insistence on full-time motherhood the best thing for children. Jo Freeman notes about the United States:

> It is as though we had selected the worst features of all the ways motherhood is structured around the world and combined them. . . . Women in cultures where they were given the heaviest load of child care were more changeable in expressing warmth than those in other cultures and more likely to have hostilities not related to the behavior of the children. In fact, the greater the burden of child care assigned to these mothers, the less likely they were to be able to supply the warm care infants require. . . . Another study of forty-five cultures . . . found a relationship between a high incidence of mother-child households (as, for example, in polygyny) and the inflicting of pain on the child by the nurturant agent. And, conversely, though less markedly, a negative relationship between maternal warmth and incidence of mother-child households. . . . The two requirements we build into the role of mother—full-time care of children and sole responsibility for them—seem, in brief, to be incompatible . . . even mutually exclusive. In view of these findings it is sobering to note that in our society we seem to maximize this contradiction in the role.[26]

About pregnancy itself, Leghorn and Parker write:

> In cultures where women have minimal and token power [they include the United States] there is often very little social support for pregnancy, in the form of lessened physical demands or time off from work with pay, maternity benefits, etc. In cultures where women hold minimal power and for women from low-income backgrounds and minority racial identities in token power countries, the birth process itself often takes place under extremely arduous conditions.[27]

Morgan finds the oppression of women in the area of reproduction to be worldwide. In 1984 she gave examples:

Thirty to fifty percent of all "maternal" deaths in Latin America are due to improperly performed illegal abortions or to complications following abortion attempts. . . .

Every ten minutes in 1980, an Indian woman died of a septic abortion. . . .

Illegal abortion is the leading cause of female deaths in Caracas.

The average Soviet woman has between twelve and fourteen abortions during her lifetime because contraceptives, although legal, are extremely difficult to obtain.

In Peru, 10 to 15 percent of all women in prison were convicted for having had illegal abortions; 60 percent of the women in one Lima prison were there for having had or performed illegal abortions. . . .

Everywhere, throughout history, an individual woman's right to reproductive freedom has been used as a political pawn.[28]

She also finds familiar the way in which oppression is denied by simply asserting that it does not exist. The research not done, the concerns banished from the evening news, the figures not existing or not obtainable, the assertions that "we" don't have this or that problem or this or that kind of person "here," all are eloquent testimony to the oppression needed to control women's behavior and women's reproductive capacity.[29] Morgan writes:

When a Preface reads "No data obtainable" or "No statistics obtainable" on a given subject it means that despite intrepid efforts, we could not find or gain access to the information. Those "NDOs" and "NSOs," as our staff came to call them, form a politically revealing pattern in themselves. Again and again they arise in the categories of rape, battery, sexual harassment, incest[uous abuse] and homosexuality; these are still the "unspeakable issues" in most parts of the globe.[30]

Similar censoring occurred when the International Tribunal of Crimes against Women, which dealt largely with sexual matters, was convened in Brussels on 4–8 March 1976, attracting more than two thousand women:

Time and Newsweek decided not to print even one paragraph about the Tribunal, although they hired women reporters and photographers to cover the entire event.[31] The first question from a Time spokesman was, "What are the women wearing?"

... Indeed, the first question on the lips of most of the non-feminist media people was, "Who are the important women who are here?" We answered, "there are 1,400 [the capacity of their largest auditorium]."[32]

Here are some more glimpses of women's working conditions in the area of reproduction and the family from my own backyard, so to speak, the United States. Lenore Walker writes:

> The family has been viewed traditionally as an oasis of calm in an otherwise violent world. . . . On the contrary, it is frequently a fertile ground for often lethal aggression. Our expectations that the family will provide a refuge and a peaceful oasis from the burdens of the outside world are patently untrue. . . . Rather than being a unit of refuge, one out of every two families, I estimate, contains violence [which is] . . . almost always committed by a man against a woman.[33]

There are statistics that support this view:

> Sociologists Straus, Steinmetz and Gelles found that at least 28 per cent of all family members experience violence in their marriages. [If domestic violence is committed "almost always" by a man against a woman, then the figures should be almost the same for women alone.] When the incidence rate reaches this level, we are dealing not with a problem of individual psychology but with a serious social disorder. . . . [Domestic violence calls account for] the largest number of police fatalities . . . approximately 25 percent. . . . 40 percent if . . . injuries are included.[34]

Walker states also that four out of five batterers are violent only to their wives, that "almost all" grew up in homes where they were emotionally and physically abused—this is not true of the women they batter—and that 90 percent of the batterers in one study had been in the military, as were a high percentage of those in her own research. She also notes, as do many others, that police protection for battered women is inadequate and that mandatory arrest and charges made by the police are more effective than the usual police practice of "calming" the batterer and requiring the woman to press charges while still living with the batterer.[35]

Phyllis Chesler notes a 1984 survey in Florida to the effect that

"One in six wives [surveyed] say their husbands force them to have intercourse against their wills. One in eight say their husbands physically abuse them or threaten them with weapons. One out of 23 . . . were threatened with guns by their husbands. One in 66 had the guns actually fired at them." These findings are extrapolated from a survey of 400 married women who *did not* fit the classic description of the isolated, abused wife.[36]

Ann Jones summarizes various records of battery and abuse:

Sixty percent of night calls in Atlanta concerned domestic disputes. In Fairfax County, Virginia, one of the nation's wealthiest counties, police received 4,073 disturbance calls in 1974. During ten months in 1975–76 the Dade County Florida Citizens Dispute Settlement Center handled nearly 1,000 wife-beating cases. Seventy percent of all assault cases . . . in the emergency room at hospitals in Boston and Omaha were women who had been attacked in their homes. Eighty percent of divorce cases in Wayne County, Michigan, involved charges of abuse. Ninety-nine percent of female Legal Aid clients in Milwaukee were abused by men. . . . The same statistics began to turn up in every new account. . . . They showed all too clearly that wife-beating is a social problem of astounding dimensions.[37]

Judith Arcana writes about much less extreme events: "Mothers expect trouble from sons; many women told me that men—sons, fathers, husbands, lovers—mean 'trouble' for women."[38]

One of the forms "domestic violence" can take is that of forced sex. Judith Herman writes:

The finding [in Kinsey's study] that grown men frequently permit themselves sexual liberties with children, while grown women do not, made virtually no impact upon the public consciousness, even though this finding was repeatedly confirmed by other investigators.

Kinsey himself, though he never denied the reality of child sexual abuse, did as much as he could to minimize its importance. Some 80 percent of the women who had experienced a childhood sexual approach by an adult reported to Kinsey's investigative team that they had been frightened and upset by the incident. Kinsey cavalierly belittled these reports.[39]

Varda Burstyn says:

> After *The Burning Bed,* a television special on wife-battering, aired in October, 1984, the media, stressing the negative impact of the broadcast, reported that one viewer had set his wife on fire. *What they did not indicate was that shelters were flooded with women* (and their children), *who simply left their homes in droves; nor did they report that women's shelters are in such dire financial straits that many had to turn dozens of women away.*

She also points out:

> Theories about rape range from "individual pathology" or "deviance," to analyses that regard rape as a system of social control. . . . Feminists . . . [emphasize that rape is] supported and encouraged by a variety of myths about the victims. . . . Unless the coercion [attending it] is of an extraordinary nature . . . [the rapist] can count on a certain amount of public indifference and tolerance from the law enforcement and the judiciary.[40]

Jane Caputi, agreeing, goes so far as to claim that in the United States and England we live today in the midst of a period of intensified gynocide that began a century ago with the massive mythicization of that lively cultural metaphor, Jack the Ripper. Whether Caputi is right or not, I agree that the mass media publicity given to serial, sexual murder does work to make such violence seem unavoidable and natural. Caputi perceives the late twentieth century's escalation of male violence against women in Anglo-American culture and the myth made of it as a backlash response to feminism. Certainly the Ripper's career (at the beginning of such violence and such a myth about the glamour and even heroism of male violence against women) coincided with the high-feminist decades of the nineteenth century, just as modern glorification of the serial murder of women in the United States coincided with our two high-feminist decades.

"Glorification" may be too strong a word here, but there has certainly been considerable fascination with the sexualized murder or torture of women in our popular, commercial culture. Naomi Wolf lists as examples the Rolling Stones' song "Midnight Rambler" (a paean to the Boston Strangler), Thin Lizzy's "Killer in the House" (a rapist), Trevor Rubin's "The Ripper," Mötley Crüe's video of women as slaves in cages, Michael Jackson's "The Way You Make Me Feel" (a lone woman stalked by a gang), and Guns 'n Roses' "I Used to Love Her (But I Had to Kill Her)." As for movies in which women are threatened or stalked, I'm sure readers can think up examples for themselves.

Another working condition that bears on adult female sexuality—some writers even go so far as to consider it a sort of training—is incestuous abuse in childhood, which until recently (when those abused by it began, at least in the United States, to make the issue public) has been hushed up, not glorified. Again and again researchers find such abuse more prevalent than anyone had previously suspected. They report that the vast majority of the offenders are male and the majority (though by no means all) of the victims female, few cases are reported to the police, and even fewer convictions are obtained. Meanwhile the popular belief persists, although research does not support it, that instances of incestuous abuse are rare, that false accusations are common, and even that children are not really harmed by such behavior. Here are Diana Russell's conclusions as to the connections between incestuous abuse and male domination:

> Incestuous abuse can no longer be viewed as a problem that involves but a few sick or disturbed sex offenders. Particularly when considered along with wife rape, wife beating, and nonsexual child abuse, it reveals an intensely troubled contemporary American family. And the fact that the vast majority of this abuse is being perpetrated by males suggests that a full understanding of this problem requires seeing it within the context of severe gender and generational inequality.[41]

Unsurprisingly in Russell's study of 930 women, one-third of the women who had previously experienced incestuous sexual abuse reported that they were "very afraid" of sexual assault. Astonishingly, one-third of those who had never experienced incestuous abuse also reported that they were "very afraid" of sexual assault.[42]

Perhaps those "very afraid" of sexual assault have reason to be. It was, as far as I know, Susan Brownmiller who introduced to U.S. feminist discourse the concept of *rape as terrorism*, violence directed randomly at members of a particular group simply and only because they are members of that group. Here are some statistics:

> Of 5,058 reported sex crimes in New York City in 1975, 27.2 percent of the victims were under fourteen (20 percent female and 6.4 percent male). In a study of over 1,500 imprisoned male sex offenders, who had committed over 1,700 offenses, 998 were against children under fifteen. More than one-half of all victims of reported rape are under eighteen, and 25 percent

of this number are under twelve. . . . Dr. Frederick Green of George Washington University, Washington, D.C., found that sexually abused children "are more common among the Children's Hospital patients than broken bones and tonsillectomies."[43]

Russell reports statistics on child sexual abuse:

In our [random] . . . sample of 930 women, 648 cases of child sexual abuse before the age of eighteen were disclosed to our interviewers. Of these, only 30 cases—or 5 percent—were ever reported to the police: 4 cases of incestuous abuse and 26 cases of extrafamilial child sexual abuse. This represents 2 percent of all incest cases and 6 percent of all cases of extrafamilial child sexual abuse. These extremely low figures provide powerful evidence that reported cases are only the very tip of the iceberg.[44]

Here are some more reports from the same backyard. Mary P. Koss, a psychology professor at Kent State University, asked questions of college students, using a questionnaire that reached more than 7,000 students at 35 schools. According to Koss:

Preliminary results of the three-year study show. . . . [that] one in . . . eight women were the victims of rape, according to the prevailing legal definition. One in every 12 men admitted to having fulfilled the prevailing definition of rape or attempted rape, yet virtually none of those men identified themselves as rapists. . . . More than one third of the women raped did not discuss their experience with anyone [prior to the researchers]; more than 90 percent did not tell the police.

Furthermore:

[Although] one in eight women students had been raped and another one in four were victims of attempted rape . . . only 4 percent of all those reported the attack. Koss concluded that "at least ten times more rapes occur among college students than [are] reflected in official crime statistics." . . . Independently . . . researchers at Auburn University, Alabama, and more recently, University of South Dakota and St. Cloud State University, Minnesota, all have found that 1 in 5 women students were raped by men they knew.

Even more disturbingly:

> Koss . . . asked [the] female students if they had had sexual in-
> tercourse against their will through the use of, or threat of, force
> (the minimal legal definition of rape). Of those who answered
> yes, *only 57 percent went on to identify their experience as rape.*

Moreover:

> Koss found a core group of . . . men (4.3 percent) who use
> physical force to compel women to have intercourse, but *who
> are unlikely to see their act as rape. . . . They believe that aggression
> is normal* and women don't really mean it when they say no to
> sexual advances. . . . Barry Burkhardt, a professor of psychology
> at Auburn . . . found that 10 percent [of college men] had used
> physical force to have intercourse with a woman against her
> will, and a large majority admitted to various other kinds of
> aggression. "These are ordinary males, operating in an ordinary
> social context."[45]

According to Paula Johnson, a research psychologist at UCLA who studied 432 young people:

> It was okay to force sex if: "she gets him sexually excited"; "they
> have dated a long time"; "she says she's going to have sex with
> him, then changes her mind"; or "she'd led him on." . . . While
> only 27 percent of the females said force was acceptable if the
> young woman had led the young man on, more than half the
> males justified the use of force in that situation.
> Whatever happens sexually . . . is considered the young
> woman's doing. . . . 54 percent of the males believe that under
> some circumstances it's all right to force a young woman to
> have sex—and 43 percent of the young women agree. . . . A
> young woman's libido is judged by the tightness of her jeans,
> how deep her neckline plunges, whether she wears a bra, and
> how leggy or cheeky her shorts prove her to be . . . young men
> could wear whatever they chose without its being interpreted
> as a sexual come-on. . . . Anything that a girl took action on
> was seen as a cue for sexuality. . . . Taking any kind of initiative
> and being assertive is very likely to be mistakenly interpreted
> as a sexual sign.[46]

And here is Susan Griffin on such "working conditions" as rape, child sexual abuse, and incestuous abuse:

> We have forgotten the history of sexual abuse. Small girls bartered into marriage. Rape only a violation in the sense that a father's or a husband's property rights are violated. We tell ourselves the rape of children is a modern problem. That this form of abuse was before veiled in silence and is now spoken of everywhere only tends to support this illusion. *Not remembering, or never learning, history we can believe that rape is just one more result of abandoning civilization's fundamental values. That rape and the sexual abuse of children actually proceeds from those values and from the very institutions we see as "normal" remains inconceivable.*[47]

And here, lest you think I've forgotten the "little rapes" of street hassling that were a common feminist topic in the early 1970s but that seem to have receded before the topics of worse male violence to women, is a typical example of feminist comment from that era, this one by Gwen Linda Blair:

> If a woman objects [to street hassling] she is told that she's the one who is making a fuss, who's deviant, and/or that it's all in her head. Street hassles, in other words, are not in themselves incidents—nothing was happening until *she* started squawking. . . . It's also very difficult to confront seemingly innocuous advances such as "Nice day, isn't it?" or "Why do you look so sad?" Here "sad" means "not smiling," i.e. not displaying what is assumed to be any woman's natural expression. . . . He's asserting his right to evaluate and comment on the weather or my mental state and my duty to listen. His remarks, which would never be addressed to men, are usually simply transparent preambles to the real message ("I want to fuck you"), yet I seem irrational and "touchy" (even, sometimes, to myself, although I know it's a trap) if I protest these "harmless" remarks. . . . She feels no support from anyone on the spot. The hassler doesn't necessarily have any support, either, but he's not under attack, and the rest of the street will leave him alone.[48]

It certainly looks as if sexual access can be another kind of work, provided by women but not always controlled by them. Its working conditions can be as bad as those of women sterilized against their will, women forced to carry to term pregnancies they don't want, women forced (usually by poverty) to abort children they do want, women given unnecessary cesarean sections, women raising children in a society that gives little power and little reward to mothers, mothers not asked for their permission by the armies that take—and often kill—their sons. Whenever and wherever the conditions of work are controlled by anyone other than those who actually do the work, the workers' interests will conflict with the interest of those who control and benefit from the work but who do not themselves do it. (And I, like Delphy, refuse to name the great ancestor who taught us this!)

But why do ordinary men who are not members of a ruling elite uphold and contribute to such a state of affairs? Of course all heterosexual men benefit somewhat from a status quo in which sexual access to women is controlled, either partly or decisively, by men and in which female sexual accessibility is customarily and legally (at least in theory) made a condition of marriage. But how such men benefit from the control exercised over women's reproductive work and how much of it such men actually control isn't as clear. Feminists have given all sorts of answers as to why. Some have simply stated that all men are violent. Others have focused their attention on everything from learning, to conformity, to the influence of the mass media, to pornography, to most ordinary people's loyalty to a social system that is at least bearable and that works—at least somewhat—in their favor, to the punishment visited on nonconformists and the immunities men as a sex-class do have in a system that puts them in a dominant position vis-à-vis women, however unsatisfying the status quo may be in other ways.

My answer to such ideas is twofold. Of course, I would say first, it is true that patriarchal institutions—like any institutions—must be stabilized and sustained by learning and social sanctions, but an account of these (accurate as it may be) does not let us know what economic benefits, if any, ordinary men get from the arrangement. Men may indeed be more violent than women, but that does not in and of itself explain what they do with their muscles or their irritability. Why, for example, do they direct it—if they do—at women and not at other men or men of the ruling class? The existence of learning and social sanctions *in and of themselves* explain nothing but a totally static situation in which patriarchy produces social sanctions and propaganda, and propaganda and social sanctions produce patriarchy, without any change ever having happened in the past or being possible in the future. What we need here, I think, is another bridge between feminist and socialist theories, one that makes it clear why a big-brained, imaginative, tool-using mammal (us), one capable of understanding its own advantage to at least some degree, finds it *worth its while* (mostly his while, but sometimes hers) to do the things that keep patriarchy going. And I think there is one, a theory created by a theorist who knows both feminist and socialist theories and can connect them.

Working-class men, Fox insists, *do have a material interest in patriarchy that goes beyond the obvious ones already discussed.* More important, it is a directly economic reason, and it is built right into the class system that has existed in industrialized countries during the last two-hundred-odd years. It is our old friend, the *family wage*. Fox says:

> [The] male state is still forced to rely on the old method, indirect control of childbearing through control of individual women by individual men. *The price men have extracted from the male ruling class in return for controlling reproduction and child-care is precisely the family wage . . . and the current housework system. . . .* Poorer men, those who don't belong to the class of privileged male wage earners, do not have the economic power to individually extort housework from women or to individually control women. [Thus] women of color and poor white women are "out of control." That is, they have to be controlled [directly] by the male state, the public patriarchy. The state's cruel and floundering attempts are contradictory: Forced sterilization, birth control experiments, welfare cutbacks on the one hand, stop using abortion and birth control on the other. Men in power fear the product of "marauding hordes"; they also fear the existence of a large set of independent women who control and limit their own reproduction.

She adds:

> The ruling males want to deprive the privileged working males of [the extra wage needed to support a wife and children] and to prevent poorer men from acquiring such . . . but they want also to keep childbearing controlled. The privileged wage earning men want to be free of the burden of supporting children, but they want also to keep control of childbearing in order to keep the family wage. The poorer men do not want to take on the [economic] burden of supporting children; but they want access to the family wage, and they know that being "family men" who control their wives' childbearing is essential to that end.[49]

So far, so good. But Fox actually goes further than this and here—if I try to follow her at all—I must first digress. Socialist theory relies on particular meanings for the words *exploit* and *exploitation,* meanings you don't hear elsewhere, and to follow Fox it's necessary to understand what precisely such concepts mean. That is because the sex-class of women, though *oppressed* by the sex-class of men, as well as by the class (and sex-class) of powerful men—i.e., ruling-class men—may not actually be *exploited* by the sex-class of men in the sense that socialist theory uses the concept of *exploitation.*

In socialist theory (very roughly), *exploitation* is what happened to our unfortunate widget makers two chapters earlier. Without the production of goods or services for the paid market—that is, unless workers are paid money for their work—there cannot be *exploitation* in this sense, as the owner of the means of production can't pay his workforce less than the value of their work in the marketplace. (Nor is the work *productive* in the sense that it produces something for the market.) Without paying workers less than the value of their work, there can be no *profit* for anyone—no control over other people's unpaid labor—and therefore nobody can amass *capital.* In fact, profit results from precisely *and only* that situation in which someone has command over the unpaid labor of someone else. If everyone concerned with the actual production of widgets received enough so that their wages, altogether, made up the market value of the work they'd done, then there would be no profit, no owner, no chance for anyone to amass capital at all—and therefore no exploitation either. What you'd have, in fact, would be a worker-owned business.

Such a situation, if you extended it to entire nations—or (some say) the entire world, would be that state of affairs in which *workers owned the means of production,* in short, *socialism.* Then, no longer needing to waste enormous amounts of work and material on controlling the rebellion of the many against the few (there being no few), Human communities could produce so much collective wealth that everyone would be more or less glutted with necessities (and even luxuries), and there really would be enough for all. Then the apparatus of the national state would be no longer necessary for almost all the things we're used to it doing now, and the state, deprived of its function, would eventually disappear. And *that* condition (Marx said) would be *communism.* (And please forgive me for leaping giant theories in a single bound here.)

But *what about labor that's never been paid to begin with,* like housework for one's husband and children or the work of raising one's children? This is precisely the sort of production feminists call *domestic labor,* and Delphy calls *the patriarchal system of production.* Delphy has already pointed out— I've quoted her to this effect—that the results of such production can indeed be sold in the market in the case of family-owned businesses and that women are indeed paid for such production *when they do it outside the family.* That is, *what is produced in the patriarchal mode of production does often have an exchange value,* and its lack of exchange value when done inside the family springs from the labor contract the woman has "signed" (so to speak) *when she married.* So much I think is clear.

It's also clear, I think, that socialist theory has, in the past, generally ignored the production of goods and services within the family (in the patriarchal mode of production) and has concentrated its attention on the capitalist marketplace. (So has right-wing economics; in this particular instance, they are both equally—because identically—patriarchal.) Worse still, socialists in general (at least according to the socialist feminists whose work I've been using in this book) tend to assume that the patriarchal organization of production came into being "naturally," or that such values are created for "personal" (that is, noneconomic) reasons, or even that there is some innate, essentialist difference between *exchange values* and *use values,* so that the difference is not *by which mode of production* goods and services are produced (capitalist or patriarchal) but rather that there is a natural difference between the kind of goods and services one system produces and the kind of goods and services produced in the other system. (The whole weight of feminist thought is against this division.) What most socialists do not do is apply their own analytical tools to *both* modes of production. Rather, at best, they attribute the patriarchal mode of production to capitalism and notice (sometimes) that the patriarchal mode of production is inefficient and has a bad effect on women.

Now, feminists who aren't socialists can ignore socialist theory—many do—but I can't. The major outlines of socialist theory are too accurate and too compelling for that. Therefore, the socialist neglect of the patriarchal mode of production is a crucial problem for me and other socialist feminists. Yet there are the beginnings of a bridge between the two. As I've mentioned before, one of the crucial parts of socialist theory is that capital is the result of the control over (the ownership, in fact, of) other people's unpaid labor. The value thus obtained from the goods and services—i.e., the work—that people do that is not paid for is called "surplus value." Here is Susan Cavin with the brief suggestion of yet another bridge between the two kinds of theory:

> In *Capital,* vol. 1, Marx wrote of the close material relationship between unpaid labor and "surplus-value." Yet he never connected women's work in the home, housework, with the original and continuing source of unpaid labor, the command over which Marx defined as capital.[50]

Here is Fox, with a fuller statement of the bridge:

> [There is] a classic exploitive exchange relation between women and men. Men and not women own labor power. To own labor power is to be paid enough to obtain a housewife whom one can then exploit. With the surplus from the exploitation, men control women's access to money and thus force us to continue doing housework. When women's wages are only enough for the material necessities, we do not have the time and money men have to invest in labor power. When there are fewer jobs for women than men, women have even less time, because many of us, wage earners or not, are coerced into the "security" of marriage and are doing men's housework as well as our own. *With that housework, women reproduce men's control over the money economy.*[51]

That is, if capital is the control over unpaid labor, then there is a way in which a man does own the unpaid labor of his wife—her housework in particular—and hence he does have command over something that he can use for purposes of his own, even though he may not (although in fact he may) possess this surplus directly as money. What he may have, for one thing, is the money from his pay that a good housewife can save by managing well. He also has his (relative) leisure, his higher degree of control (on the average) of the way any disposable family income is spent, and his access (possibly) to the time necessary for job training or union activity. He also has the higher standard of living a wife can provide, as opposed to what he himself can provide for himself, a personal relationship probably sustained more by his wife's activity than his own, the higher likelihood of domestic details following his preference rather than hers, his weightier say over what the family does for recreation, and so on. This "patriarchal surplus value" is extremely unlikely to be enough to lift even one working-class man out of the class of workers, but with this "edge" (their control over a wife's unpaid labor) *men as a sex-class* can—and do—maintain themselves *as* the dominant sex-class. They can (and many do) defend their jobs against incursion by women; they can (and do) practice, or at least passively benefit from, male sexual terrorism directed at women as a group (remember Koss's survey of college students); they can sustain men's claim to the control of money, better-paying jobs, better conditions in marriage and so on; and they can make various kinds of propaganda to the effect that the patriarchal system of production is natural, good, inevitable, and necessary.

Yet, it can certainly be objected, although women's work as wives and mothers is not paid for with money, it is nonetheless recompensed in another, quite obvious way. Women are, after all, *supported by* their husbands. All women? Not quite! After all, *the family wage was never available to the majority of women* who were married to working men. Only those women married to middle-management men or the labor aristocracy benefit from it. In fact, it never affected most working men or the women married to them and it still doesn't. It is, in fact, becoming less and less of a reality all the time. Indeed, we have reached a point (at least in industrialized countries like the United States, Canada, and Britain) where "women's work" is being required of most women *in addition to paid work*—at which women are being underpaid on the grounds that they're being "supported" by the very husbands who aren't doing so because they can't do so. And even for those women whose husbands' "family wage" does allow for traditional support, such support does not ensure a wife's equal claim to a husband's wage, and it never did. We live today in a modified patriarchal setup in the industrialized countries, one which had to be fought for through the nineteenth and into the twentieth century (like the English struggle for the Married Women's Property Act). There is still folklore about women's methods of getting money out of their men; if there were not, Bernard and every woman I've ever met would not talk about it. Nor is the marriage contract one into which just any two people can enter, nor can six or eight people enter into it, nor can those who enter into it change its legal provisions to just anything they like. For example, men may not marry men nor women, women (we are fighting over that right now, a fight that would have been inconceivable thirty years ago), nor can I marry you with the legal requirement that you balance a grapefruit on your head every morning to amuse me at breakfast and then divorce you when you don't, on those grounds alone. (That is a "personal" matter only, like the standard of living provided by a husband to a wife, over which the laws have no say.) Nor is it legal, in any other contract, to require that your employee allow you to fuck her. Nor is it possible, in other contracts, to sue for the loss of *consortium* (sexual access) if the wife is injured through someone else's negligence. Nor, in any other contract will the state step in if the boss leaves no will, and divide the company's wealth among the employees after the boss's death. Such a tangle of the personal, the state-run, and the customary is the institution of marriage that it resembles no other work contract in capitalist society. Instead, marriage—which is certainly the key institution of the patriarchal mode of production—strongly resembles the *feudal* system of exploitation and oppression that existed in Europe before capitalism arose. As Freeman puts it: "Women remained serfs after men had already outgrown the state of serfdom. . . . the capitalist period marks this transition from the family phase to the individual phase generally, but . . . this transition was delayed in the case of women."[52]

The situations of a woman in Western European/North American society today and that of a peasant in Europe in, say, the tenth century, show some striking similarities. For example, a woman enters the labor pool for *certain jobs* (among them the job of wife and mother) *by being born into a certain group,* her sex, just as peasants were peasants and nobles noble, and peasants did peasants' work because they were born to it. Her job as wife and mother is the result not of *an impersonal money contract* but of a *personal relationship,* as were the relations between monarchs and subjects, liege lords and vassals. Her *status* (insofar as it's the result of her sex) is an *ascribed* one, that is, one into which she was born, just as medieval European peasants were peasants and nobles nobles because their daddies were, and that status has, as it had in feudal social systems, the most far-reaching and marked results on *her sexuality, her dress, her manner, her gait, her appearance, the way others treat her, her immunity from or susceptibility to violence,* and her *freedom, wealth, health,* and the *amount* and *kind* of her *work.*

If the feudal, personal relations between lord and peasant were a matter of exploitation and oppression—which of course they were—and if they produced wealth for one class at the expense of the other—which they most certainly did, by giving the one *class* control over the *unrecompensed work* of the other *class*—then I see no bar against applying similar terms to the patriarchal organization of production, which includes reproduction. If we do this, we are led, I think, to the inescapable conclusion *that feminism is the study of the patriarchal system of unrecompensed labor and the politics and propaganda that maintain it.* Cavin, Delphy, Fox, and Dalla Costa and James are right: housewives and mothers do produce something. Sometimes this "something" is clearly recognizable as such, as in a family business, and sometimes it is not when it is expressed, not directly in money, but in opportunities to get more money, or in things that money could buy: leisure, comfort, personal services, and control. But in no way are the arrangements that support the patriarchal organization of production either personal, natural, benevolent, inevitable, or necessary. What seems to me crucial about the ideas of the feminists I've just been discussing is that they *extend economics in general to the family* and *class analysis in particular to the patriarchal organization of production and reproduction.* That is, these feminists insist that the rules of the organization of Human societies don't suddenly change when one enters the "private" realm, and that "personal" relations can be analyzed as public institutions precisely because they *are* public institutions. By having more faith in the wide applicability of the terms of socialist analysis than many socialists do, they are effectively being *more socialist* than these and in their belief that there is no private realm—and that "private" is as much a social invention as "public"—they are also *classically feminist.*

APPENDIX

Although, like other feminists (and all reasonable Humans, I would think), I rejoice at the increase in public knowledge about the sexual abuse of children, I sometimes wonder whether the topic has become as popular as it has because it can be represented as occurring outside the family and primarily affecting little boys. In 1989, a TV program (based on an actual court case) presented the sexual abuse of children as perpetrated largely by women, connected with Satanism, occurring outside the family, and affecting (judging by what we saw) mostly little boys. The father in the particular family affected was shown as immediately believing his little son's account in contrast to the mother, who dithered and did not. Of course, the facts are that child sexual abuse is largely (though certainly not inevitably) a male crime, that it often occurs inside the family, that the men who do it are often men well respected in their community, and that many more little girls are victimized by it than are little boys. Here is some of the material about the sexual abuse of children that has been summarized in this chapter. Judith Herman writes:

> [In studies between 1970 and the present] incest follows the general pattern of child abuse in which the majority of the victims are female and the majority of the offenders are male. . . . A review of the five largest studies of parent-child incest documenting a total of 424 cases, indicates that the father was the offender in 97 percent of the cases, while the mother was the offender in only 3 percent.

> In our . . . sample of 930 women, 648 cases of child sexual abuse before the age of eighteen were disclosed to our interviewers. Of these only 30 cases—or 5 percent—were ever reported to the police: 4 cases of incestuous abuse and 26 cases of extrafamilial child sexual abuse. This represents 2 percent of all incest cases and 6 percent of all cases. . . . reported cases are only the very tip of the iceberg. . . . Of the thirty reported cases . . . only seven were known to result in convictions. . . . Of the sixty-six rapes or attempted rapes that were reported to the police, only six cases resulted in convictions. . . .

> Even if a complaint [of incest against the father] is made, which is unlikely, the chances are slight that the case will ever go to trial, still slighter that the father will be found guilty, and even slighter that, if convicted, he will be sentenced to prison. The odds . . . may be judged from a study of 250 police reports of

sexual assaults on children in New York City. In the majority of cases (75 percent) either no arrest was made (31 percent) or the accused was arraigned but never brought to trial (44 percent). Cases were dismissed for lack of corroborating evidence, or because the child, in the prosecutor's estimation, would not make a good witness, or simply to spare the child the rigors of a court appearance. . . . Twenty-three men, or *nine percent of the total,* were *sentenced to prison, the majority for one year or less.* . . . In our study, three out of the forty victims [of incest] filed charges with the police. In a similar study of clinic patients in California, seven out of thirty-eight cases (17 percent) reached the preliminary stages of court involvement. . . . In one study only six percent of over three hundred women who had had sexual experiences with adults before the age of thirteen recalled that the incident had been reported to the police. And in the state of Illinois, the Child Advocate Association of Chicago estimated that only about three percent of the approximately 22,000 cases of intrafamily sexual abuse are reported to the police each year.[53]

NOTES

1. Nawal El Saadawi, *The Hidden Face of Eve: Women in the Arab World,* translated by Sherif Hetata (Boston: Beacon Press, 1980), 64. Italics added. In citing Nawal El Saadawi by her last name throughout this book, I have followed Library of Congress usage, which insists that her last name is "Saadawi."

2. Marielouise Jansen-Jurreit, *Sexism: The Male Monopoly on History and Thought,* translated by Verne Moberg (New York: Farrar, Straus and Giroux, 1982), 350. Italics added.

3. Linda Gordon, *Woman's Body, Woman's Right: A Social History of Birth Control in America* (New York: Grossman, 1976), 392–93, 401. Italics added.

4. Robin Morgan, ed., *Sisterhood Is Global: The International Women's Movement Anthology* (New York: Anchor, 1984), 7. Italics added.

5. Maud Pember Reeves, *Round about a Pound a Week* (London: Virago, 1979), ix–x. Italics added.

6. Sandra Allen et al., eds., *Conditions of Illusion: Papers from the Women's Movement* (Leeds, England: Feminist Books, 1974), 236, 235. Italics added.

7. Lisa Leghorn and Katherine Parker, *Woman's Worth: Sexual Economics and the World of Women* (Boston: Routledge and Kegan Paul, 1981), 165. Italics added.

8. Fox [Jeanette Silveira], "Why Men Oppress Women," *Lesbian Ethics* 1:1 (1984), 47–48. Jansen-Jurreit, quoting British historian W. W. Tarn, notes that in the third and second centuries B.C.E. upper-class Greek families had only one or two children because of the fear of overpopulation. She cites such badly skewed sex ratios as 118 male children to 28 female children in the third century (among Greek families that received Milesian citizenship) and 87 sons to 28 daughters at one point in Athens. According to Delphic inscriptions from the second century, of 600 families just 1 percent reared as many as two daughters (Jansen-Jurreit, *Sexism*, 261).

9. Leghorn and Parker, *Woman's Worth*, 165.

10. Ann Oakley, *Subject Women* (New York: Pantheon, 1981), 214. Other eras—or people addressing governmental concerns rather than trying to persuade the population at large—were more frank. Margery Spring Rice's *Working-Class Wives: Their Health and Conditions,* 2d ed. (London: Virago, 1981), originally published in 1939, is an interesting example. The book bears two introductions. One, written by Barbara Wootton in 1979, notes Britain's dread in the 1930s of both overpopulation and a "shrinking population heavily weighted with the elderly" (iii). The original introduction, written by Dame Janet Campbell in 1939, spoke openly of "the contribution to national health and efficiency" such working-class wives "might make as happy wives and mothers" (xvii). Rice's earlier text opens with the statement, "The family is Nature's first group. It is biologically indispensable," a statement that blatantly contradicts Campbell's later view of the matter as one of governmental interest (13).

11. Cherríe Moraga, *Loving in the War Years* (Boston: South End Press, 1983), 109.

12. Susan Cavin, *Lesbian Origins* (San Francisco, Ism Press, 1985), 8.

13. Patricia Murphy Robinson in Carole Vance, ed., *Pleasure and Danger: Exploring Female Sexuality* (Boston: Routledge and Kegan Paul, 1984), 252.

14. Ibid., 257.

15. Silveira, "Why Men Oppress Women," 51–52.

16. Ibid., 45–44. Italics added.

17. El Saadawi, *Hidden Face*, 63.

18. Christine Delphy, *Close to Home: A Materialist Analysis of Women's Oppression,* trans. Diana Leonard (Amherst: University of Massachusetts Press, 1984), 74.

19. Spender, speaking of the social meanings of childbirth, says:

> Whether giving birth is a mark of penance or a sign of superior powers depends largely on which sex produces the meanings for society. In our society where men hold power, the capacity to give birth has been used against women—from being a reason for their exclusion from paid employment to being a sign of their disfavour in the eyes of God.

There are feminists who believe that equality between the sexes will never occur until the difference in reproductive labor between the sexes no longer exists. I think Firestone was getting at something of this kind when she denounced childbearing as "the tyranny of their [women's] reproductive biology" (Shulamith Firestone, *The Dialectic of Sex* [New York: Morrow, 1970], 206). Marge Piercy's science fiction novel, *Woman on the Edge of Time* (1976), has its utopian society form babies in artificial wombs and has both men and women nurse them as a precondition for equality between the sexes. In *The German Ideology* (1846), as Engels notes, he and Marx also considered the "first division of labor" to be that "between man and woman for child breeding." Engels does not, however, use this idea in *Origin,* in which he describes the division between men and women as occurring with the advent of civilization (Frederick Engels, *The Origin of the Family, Private Property, and the State* [New York: Pathfinder Press, 1972], 74–75). In fact, elsewhere in *The Origin of the Family* Engels writes that the division of household labor and horticultural or hunting work was "a pure and simple outgrowth of nature" that "existed only between the two sexes" (ibid., 149).

20. Jansen-Jurreit, *Sexism,* 333–35. Italics added.

21. Silveira, "Why Men Oppress Women," 37. Italics added.

22. At some times and in some places, of course, women have been forced *not* to bear children. The point is not whether childbearing has been forbidden or whether it has been enforced but that it has been forbidden or enforced by those who did not themselves have to do the work. Certainly pronatalism is not the result merely of the lack of effective contraception. In many parts of the world effective contraception has existed for centuries with chemical and mechanical means and by way of sexual practices. Gordon lists as spermicides (among other things) water in large enough quantities, citrus fruit juices, rock salt, oil, lard, lint and gum arabic (lactic acid), and tannic acid, and many recipes for pessaries ("recently . . . tested, and found effective") (Gordon, *Woman's Body,* 42–43). In Europe and England, for example, in the seventeenth century, the wives of well-to-do men sometimes endured extreme coercion in the matter of fertility. Fox [Silveira] cites one such case: Ann Fanshawe, an Englishwoman who bore twenty-one children during the twenty-three years of her marriage, her childbearing ending only by the death of her husband. She notes that Enrico Caruso was "the fifteenth child of his mother, the first to survive" (Fisher, *Women's Creation: Sexual Evolution and the Shaping of Society* [Garden City, NY: Anchor/Doubleday, 1979], 389, cited by Silveira, "Why Men Oppress Women," 44). A high infant death rate is certainly a motive for having lots of children, but I do not believe that any nonbrainwashed woman, of her own free will, would choose twenty-one or sixteen children (plus pregnancies that were not carried to term) or the misery attendant on the death of fourteen children, pregnancy after pregnancy followed by death after death.

23. Quoted in Gordon, *Woman's Body,* 145.

24. Phyllis Chesler and Emily Jane Goodman, *Women, Money, and Power* (New York: Morrow, 1976), 145.

25. David Grossvogel, *Dear Ann Landers: Our Intimate and Changing Dialogue with America's Best-Loved Confidante* (Chicago: Contemporary Books, 1987), 17.

26. Jo Freeman, ed., *Women: A Feminist Perspective*, 2d ed. (Palo Alto, CA: Mayfield, 1979), 121–25. According to Freeman, those British Victorian mothers who were faced with the same situation reacted as many women do today:

> Victorian motherhood was a male—and a middle-class— conception. The more female historians study it from the point of view of the women themselves, the less authentic it looks. It was never a genuine portrait even of the Victorian mother, let alone the mother of any other age. . . . Mothers in the home were already becoming a "social problem" a hundred years ago. They were already complaining of being boxed in (ibid., 128).

27. Leghorn and Parker, "Woman's Worth," 181.

28. Morgan, *Sisterhood Is Global,* 7.

29. I'm reminded of the first consciousness-raising meeting I ever attended, in which one woman exclaimed, "But surely there aren't any lesbians in *this* room!" (The purity of the room was maintained by a decorous silence on the part of all of us.)

30. Morgan, *Sisterhood Is Global,* xxiii.

31. The noncoverage of such an important feminist event is similar to the silence of *Time* and *Newsweek* regarding the 11 October 1987 gay rights march in Washington, D.C., in which at least six hundred thousand people participated (*Gay Community News,* 18–24 October 1987, 3).

32. Diana Russell and Nicole Van de Ven, *Crimes against Women: Proceedings of the International Tribunal* (East Palo Alto, CA: Frog in the Well Press, 1984), 3.

33. Lenore E. Walker, *The Battered Woman* (New York: Harper and Row, 1979), 42, 251–52.

34. Ibid., 42–43, 208.

35. Ibid., 212, 87, 36–37, 206, 209.

36. Phyllis Chesler, *Mothers on Trial: The Battle for Children and Custody* (New York: McGraw-Hill, 1986), 497.

37. Ann Jones, *Women Who Kill* (New York: Holt, Rinehart and Winston, 1980), 301.

38. Judith Arcana, *Every Mother's Son* (Seattle: Seal Press, 1986), 98.

39. Judith Lewis Herman, *Father-Daughter Incest* (Cambridge: Harvard University Press, 1981), 16.

40. Varda Burstyn, ed., *Women against Censorship* (Vancouver: Douglas and McIntyre, 1985), 170–71, 191. Italics added.

41. Naomi Wolf, *The Beauty Myth: How Images of Beauty Are Used against Women* (New York: Doubleday, 1992), 164; Diana E. H. Russell, *The Secret Trauma: Incest in the Lives of Girls and Women* (New York: Basic Books, 1986), 11. Herman notes also the "painful hostility between mother and daughter so frequently observed" [in studies in the United States] in families in which fathers have incestuously abused daughters. She says, "When mothers are powerless, their daughters are inevitably alienated from them" (Herman, *Incest,* 207). Some families are so violent that children are actually safer on the streets. Thus:

> A group of University of Connecticut psychologists has concluded that homelessness is actually safer for many young people than living at home. . . . According to the psychologists, 86 percent of the 195 runaways interviewed for the study were sexually and/or physically abused while at home. Of the young women surveyed, 94 percent reported abuse at home, while 64 percent were abused on the streets (*Gay Community News,* 21 August–3 September 1988, 2).

42. Russell, *Secret Trauma,* 162–63.

43. Florence Rush, *The Best Kept Secret: Sexual Abuse of Children* (New York: McGraw-Hill, 1980), 5.

44. Russell, *Secret Trauma,* 85.

45. *Ms.,* October 1985, 58, 56.

46. *Ms.,* February 1981, 23.

47. Susan Griffin, *Rape: The Politics of Consciousness,* 3d ed., (San Francisco: Harper and Row, 1986), 56. Italics added.

48. Gwen Linda Blair, "Standing on the Corner . . . " *Liberation,* July/August 1974, 6–8. My first clear (remembered) experience of sexual harassment occurred at summer camp when I was twelve. After swimming, one thirteen-year-old boy habitually amused himself by snapping at girls' bare legs with his wet towel. I protested, only to be told by my counselor that I really liked it, that the other girls liked it (they didn't), and that I could make him stop it by ignoring him (it didn't work). Later came the loud "I wanna fuck you," the quiet, out-of-the-corner-of-his-mouth "Suck my prick," and other intrusions and animal noises. I also remember male acquaintances protesting that street harassment never happened when they were around and that therefore it did not exist.

49. Fox [Silveira], "Why Men Oppress Women," 48–49, 50.

50. Cavin, *Lesbian Origins,* 239.

51. Fox, "Why Men Oppress Women," 46. Italics added.

52. Freeman, *Women: A Feminist Perspective,* 525.

53. Herman, *Incest,* 18, 167, 164. Italics added.

E L E V E N

LOOKING BACKWARD (AND FORWARD?)

If feminism, roughly speaking, is the analysis of women's unpaid work and marxism, again speaking very roughly, is the analysis of everyone's paid work, what is the historical relation of the one form of work to the other? Although capitalism began in Europe as early as the late medieval era,[1] the watershed was certainly that nineteenth-century period we call the Industrial Revolution. "The Woman Question," say Barbara Ehrenreich and Deirdre English, arose

> in the course of a historical transformation whose scale later generations have still barely grasped. It was the "industrial revolution," and even "revolution" is too pallid a word. From the Scottish highlands to the Appalachian hills, from the Rhineland to the Mississippi Valley, whole villages were emptied to feed the factory system with human labor. People were wrested from the land suddenly, by force; or more subtly by the pressure of hunger and debt—uprooted from the ancient security of family, clan, parish. A settled agrarian life which had persisted more or less for centuries was destroyed in one tenth of the time it had taken for the Roman Empire to fall. . . . The fundamental social transformation, of which even industrialization was a correlate and not a cause, was the triumph of the Market [capitalist] economy.[2]

A crucial consequence of this birth of *industrial capitalism* (which went on to change not only the industrial nations in which it began but eventually the whole world) was its opening a new possibility for large numbers of women. Rosalind Delmar says, "Capitalism raised the possibility of mass female employment for the first time." This is not to say that the vast majority of women had not worked previously or that they had not received wages for some of the work that they did. It meant something else entirely. Ehrenreich and English explain:

> It was now possible for a woman to enter the Market herself and exchange her labor for the means of survival (although at a lower rate than a man would). In Europe, in Russia, in America, wherever industry demanded more workers, there was a new wave of "single women." . . . Entering the Market as a working woman might mean low wages and miserable working conditions, loneliness and insecurity, but *it also meant the possibility—unimaginable in the Old Order—of independence from the grip of the family.*[3]

In fact, the very first workers in the new factories of England—the country that became industrialized earliest—were women and children, who could be paid less than men. In 1835,

> out of a total of 288,700 workers occupied in textile production, 46 per cent were women and a further 15 per cent were children of both sexes under the age of thirteen. . . . The majority of those migrating to the textile works were women and children, nearly 5000 between 1835 and 1837.[4]

It's important not to romanticize women's and children's independence during the early days of the Industrial Revolution. As Peggy Morton writes, there was

> a drastic increase in the exploitation of child labour in Britain in . . . 1780–1840. Even small children worked 12–18 hour days, death from over-work was common, and . . . education was almost always mythical. . . . In industrial districts [in 1864] . . . infant mortality was as high as one death in four in the first year of life, as compared to one in ten in non-industrial districts. As many as half the children died in the first five years of life in the industrial slums . . . because of the conditions under which the urban proletariat were forced to live. Girls who had worked in the mills since early childhood had a characteristic deformation of the pelvic bones which made for difficult births;

women worked until the last week of pregnancy and would return to the mills soon after giving birth for fear of losing their jobs; children were left with those too young or too old to work, were given opiates to quiet them, and often died from malnutrition resulting from the absence of the mother and the lack of suitable food.[5]

Such horribly brutal conditions certainly played an important part in the fight of male workers to keep women and children out of the factories. Nonetheless it's also important to recognize that other motives were involved as well. Engels pointed this out in his comments on the employment of women in England in the 1840s:

> Very often the fact that a married woman is working does not lead to the complete disruption of the home, but to a reversal of the normal division of labour within the family. . . . One may well imagine the righteous indignation of the workers at being virtually turned into eunuchs.

Indignant many certainly were, as various feminists have pointed out. The material is in Chapter VIII, and I won't go through it again here but will only let Heidi Hartmann sum up male workers' attempts to exclude women and children from employment: "Instead of fighting for equal wages for men and women, male workers sought the family wage, wanting to retain their wives' services at home." Batya Weinbaum elaborates:

> The working-men Engels depicts did go on to organize trade unions, to demand protective labor legislation for women and children and to regain their patriarchal position in the family, although the individual patriarch's family was no longer the locus of the productive system.[6]

From this struggle for the *family wage*—the male wage that would enable the adult male worker to support himself *and* his wife and children, a family form already achieved by the bourgeoisie—came those relatively new institutions we now call "the traditional family" and "the home" in Europe and North America. All my socialist feminist sources agree on this point. Some do so gently and with compassion for the mixed motives of the men involved, some angrily, like Fox, who points out that U.S. unions also did their best to keep men of color out of industrial jobs. Nevertheless, they all stress that the male, working-class fight for the family wage has been crucial to women's lives throughout the nineteenth and twentieth centuries. Such men, my sources say, wanted to protect children from the brutalities of work in the factories, and they may well have wanted to protect women in the same way—but they also wanted clearly and unequivocally to reserve power and privilege within the family for themselves.[7]

This "very new idea" of the family wage, as Jean Gardiner calls it, resulted in a very new ideal, what we now call the "traditional" family. As Hartmann says:

> Men sought to keep high wage jobs themselves and to raise male wages generally. They argued for wages sufficient for their wage labor alone to support their families. This "family wage" system gradually came to be the norm for stable working class families at the end of the nineteenth century and the beginning of the twentieth.

By the end of the nineteenth century in the industrialized West, says Jean Gardiner: "This ideology [of the family] was also increasingly adopted by the workers themselves. By the latter part of the 19th century it appears to have become entrenched in the organised sections of the working class."[8]

The new ideal and the new reality that it embodied can be traced in what happened to women's jobs in the countries affected as the "traditional" family created a new kind of woman: *the housewife,* the married woman all of whose work was unpaid and done in, and in the service of, her home. In 1851, early in the process, says Ann Oakley, one in four married Englishwomen with a living husband was employed outside that new institution, "the home," and the housewife was to be found overwhelmingly in the ranks of the middle class. Only in the second half of the nineteenth century did the "family" gain ground in the lives of women who were married to working-class men. Thus, by 1911 only one Englishwoman in ten married to a living husband went "out" to "work"—that is, her work was paid and performed outside her home. According to Oakley, only quite late in the nineteenth century did the British working class accept this new institution: "The idea that work outside the home for married women was a 'misfortune and disgrace' became acceptable to the [British] working classes only in the last decades of the nineteenth century."[9]

What had happened?

> Men still owned their women body and soul long after they themselves ceased to be the property of other men. Men continued to own and control female creative capacity in the family and to assume that the subordination of women in society was just and natural.[10]

Oakley takes the analysis a step further: "[The family wage] thus emerged not overnight, but gradually as *a solution engineered by male supremacy to the very substantial dislocations of the early capitalist system.*"[11]

Not that this new institution of the "traditional" family was an easy one for working-class families to adopt. Few could afford to live out such a domestic ideal. Only for the bourgeoisie (which had originated it) was what we now call the "traditional family" easy to achieve. According to Gardiner, at the end of the nineteenth century only "the highest paid skilled male factory operatives" were earning enough to support a wife and children. As Ehrenreich notes, in the United States, "The reality through most of this century is that only the more privileged male workers—those who are members of powerful unions, or of skilled crafts and professions—actually earned enough to support a family." By 1900 (as Ehrenreich describes the situation in the United States), the family wage and the family it made possible were favored by "far-seeing capitalists and middle-class reformers" because they appeared to promote social stability. Family men could be counted on to be "loyal, or at least fearful" employees. But with the increase of women, especially married women, in the workforce, the material basis of the "traditional" family had begun to disappear. Here's Ehrenreich again:

> The assumptions of the family wage system have come to out-weigh the reality. The average male wage [in the United States] is now less than that required to support a family with middle-class expectations. . . . By 1976 only 40 percent of the jobs in this country paid enough to support a family. . . . More and more high-paid "men's jobs" have vanished, perhaps for good.[12]

Statistics are similar in England. Again and again my sources either state or assume that the conjugal family is well on its way to dissolution in those countries that have a long history of industrial capitalism. Here are some more statistics: "Of British marriages made in the 1970s, more than a quarter will end in divorce at some point in the next thirty years; for American couples the figure is nearer 40 percent."[13]

Unfortunately as men leave the "family," they usually take the "family wage" with them, and women's poverty grows.[14] Varda Burstyn, writing about Canada, links the two phenomena:

> Especially over the last 30 years, even the nuclear unit itself has been coming apart. Large numbers of women—one in every six Canadian families is headed by a sole-support woman—have to rear children on economic resources equalling less than 50 percent of men's.

Ehrenreich does the same for the United States:

> In 1980 two out of three adults who fit into the federal defi-
> nition of poverty [in the United States] were women and more
> than half the families defined as poor were maintained by single
> women. . . . The fastest-growing group among America's female
> poor are single mothers. . . . Many are new recruits to poverty,
> women who had been middle-class until divorce—or deser-
> tion—severed their claim on a man's wage.[15]

Although there are some real freedoms to be found in the demise of the
"traditional" family, especially for women, poverty is not one of them. Nor
is the bleakness of life without intimacy or warmth a sort of freedom. Bell
hooks, stressing the situation of those to whom the dominant culture is
oppressive, writes:

> While there are white women activists who may experience
> family primarily as an oppressive institution. . . . many black
> women find the family the least oppressive institution. Despite
> sexism in the context of family, we may experience dignity, self-
> worth and a humanization that is not experienced in the outside
> world wherein we confront all forms of oppression. . . . Family
> ties are the only sustained support system for exploited and
> oppressed peoples. We wish to rid family life of the abusive
> dimensions created by sexist oppression without devaluing it.

Robin Morgan also makes it clear that bleakness and heartlessness are not
feminist goals:

> If the real meaning of "family" is in fact the human need to
> establish long-term relationships of trust and closeness, then
> we need none of us worry about "the family" dying out. If, on
> the other hand, "family" is restricted to . . . only . . . a hetero-
> sexual unit of production and reproduction, family as a cell of
> the State—then governmental reverence for the institution be-
> comes grimly understandable.[16]

"Liberating only in potential," says Linda Gordon, "the dissolving of family ties produces loneliness and despair." And although the death of the
family does open up newfound freedoms for some women, it provides them,
say Joseph and Lewis, only "in terms of childlessness. . . . Women have

gained a freedom not to reproduce, not the freedom to have non-oppressive and non-exploitative relationships."[17]

It seems then that the family wage—and with it the family as we know it—is on the way out, but if this is so, it's not because feminists dislike intimacy, nor is it because capitalism is devoted to women's welfare. Rather the family wage—and with it, the "traditional" family—is disappearing (all my sources agree on this) primarily *because it was always an unstable economic arrangement*, much more of an ideal for most of the working class than a workable and stable reality and very much against the immediate economic interests of capitalists. These last are having their way at the moment, and their economic support for the family wage is being withdrawn, i.e., *men's wages are shrinking*. Thus fewer and fewer can afford the luxury of a "nonworking" wife, that is, a wife all of whose work is unpaid and all of whose work takes place in and for the household in which she lives. Charnie Guettel explains why: "Increasing the labor power necessary for the subsistence of a family—and this is the major purpose in doubling the number of necessary breadwinners per family—is a way of *increasing the rate of exploitation*." Gordon explains at more length:

> *Workers are getting a smaller proportion of the value they produce than they did fifty years ago,* so that it now requires two wages to maintain the average working-class family, or to put it another way, the victories of the working class in winning a shorter working day are now being wiped out as the number of hours of labor *per family* is going up.[18]

"Per family" can mean husbands moonlighting on an extra job, or it can mean (as it obviously has so often in the past thirty years) that the extra labor is being performed by a wife who works for pay at a full-time or part-time paid job and also continues to do most of the housework and child care for the family.[19]

But why raise the rate of exploitation by employing women? For one thing, women's labor is cheaper than men's, precisely because we do live in a patriarchy. Moreover, like other groups in the population who don't have the social power to protect their economic position, most women have always been useful to capitalism as part of the "reserve army of labor," the hire-you-now, fire-you-later, pay-you-less-than-other-workers, who can be hired when the economy is in the upswing of the business cycle and thrown out of work when the economy's down. (Even though some of my sources don't believe that the statistical group of "women" is still part of the reserve army of labor, all of them do agree that *such was the case* until quite recently.)

But why increase the rate of exploitation at all? Why pay workers less and less? Why can't capitalism bring prosperity to everyone, even if it does reward some more than others? Why doesn't capitalism, damn it, *work*?

Socialist theory has an explanation for the above, which explanation involves several phenomena, the first of which is *industrialization* itself. (Again, I apologize to those for whom the following is a tedious rehearsal of the obvious.)

It seems as if industrialization, with its standardization of the labor process and its replacement of Human muscle power by machinery, should improve everybody's life, since it enormously multiplies the power of Human beings to make things.[20] But industrialization as it occurred (and still occurs) in the context of capitalism and capitalism's drive to profit making is another matter entirely.

After the Industrial Revolution (which was all about standardizing the labor process and replacing Human muscle power with machinery), any sensible capitalist would, of course, buy machinery so that his business might turn out more goods, thus increasing his sales and with them his profits. But his edge over his competitors would be only temporary. After all, the businesses that make and sell machinery are also trying to sell *their* product to as many businessmen as possible in order to maximize *their* sales and hence *their* profits. And once the competitors of our original capitalist own the same machinery that he does, everyone will have to go out and buy any new, improved machinery that may come on the market (and this will have to happen if the machine makers want to stay in business) and the whole process will simply be repeated over and over again. So far, so good. But the matter does not end there, as this shift from *labor-intensive production* (in which machinery costs form a small part of the expenses of a business and wages a large one) to *capital-intensive production* (in which expenses for plant and machines form a large part of the expenses of a business and wages to workers a small one) has other results besides increased production.

For one thing, it means *fewer jobs*. Once Widget (remember Widget?) buys widget-making machinery to replace in part the efforts of its factory employees, these employees will be laid off. They must be, if Widget is to compete effectively with Wodget, which will soon buy the same kind of machinery itself. Once Wodget does the same, a lot of former widget makers will be out of a job and will have no krumballs with which to buy widgets, no matter how much they may long for them. Some of these working people may be able, if times are good, to find jobs at, say, Dingle, Inc. (maker of dells) or Dell & Co. (maker of dingles). But eventually Dingle and Dell will mechanize too, if they can, and they too will use fewer and fewer employees.

Of course, those thrown out of work in this constantly escalating process of mechanization may eventually find work providing not goods but services, the production of which is not so easily mechanized. The fewer people it takes to produce manufactured items or even food (for agriculture too becomes competitive and is more and more mechanized), the more people will be available to work in service industries like education, entertainment, medicine, and so on. But this process can't continue forever. For although industrialization can mean increased profit in the short run—the very short run—in the long run it means less profit for *all* the companies that adopt it.

To repeat: as socialist theory makes plain, there is only one source of value in the marketplace, Human labor, and only one source of profit, *unpaid* Human labor. I had some trouble understanding this theory until I began to think of the differences between machines, which are a commodity, and Human labor, which isn't, although people in capitalist societies like ours are used to thinking of it as if it were. So here is my sketch of the differences, which those who understand the *labor theory of value* can skip and which those who don't can at least consider:

You can't cheat a machine.

But you can cheat people. That is, you can pay people less than the market value of the work they produce (you had better, if you want to make a profit because this is what profit is), but there's no way to pull off such sleight-of-hand with a machine. Machines cost what they cost, both to buy and maintain, period, and if you don't treat them properly, they will break down, and *that's the owner's problem.* If you are the owner, you can't run them for eight hours and "pay" them for six hours' work by not giving them full and proper maintenance. You can't run them faster than they're designed to run without wearing them out faster or breaking them down. If you run them part-time only (because times are bad), you will still have to give them full-time maintenance. You can't leave them out in the rain to rust when times are bad and expect them to be running properly when times get good again and you want to use them. In short, if you misuse a machine in any way or scant on its upkeep, its working life will be shortened or stopped. It will break down or wear out faster than it would otherwise, and because you are its owner you will have to invest a good deal of money in buying a new machine or getting the old one fixed.

But an owner can do all these things to his Human workforce because he is in no way responsible for its maintenance. Its maintenance is *its* problem. And if the workforce doesn't like the conditions of work—and many don't—there are always others out there who, in order to stay alive, must sell their capacity to work to someone who owns the means of production, i.e., the space, the machinery, the money for upkeep and raw materials, and so on, without which the workforce can't produce a single thing. That is why labor is a *variable* cost (to use Marx's term), while machines are not.

To repeat, if you want any profit at all (assuming that you're the owner of a business) you must *at the very least* pay this Human "machine" less than the amount its work brings in to your company, the discrepancy being what profit is. That is, you *must* run it full-time and pay it part-time wages if you want your business to survive. You can also run this "machine" longer than is healthy or comfortable for itself by lengthening its workday and paying it the same wages as before. You can speed up its work even to the point of breaking this "machine" down or shortening its lifetime by over-work. You can even, as happened often in the early nineteenth century, use up its lifetime at a horrifying rate—as long as there are (*a*) no laws against it and (*b*) more people out there whose only source of livelihood is selling their labor power. You can employ this odd "machine" part-time and pay it actually less than a subsistence wage; after all, if it starves or falls sick or has children to feed, that's not your problem either. You can also lay it off when business is bad and rehire it (or another like it) when times are good—and what happens in between to it and others like it is not your problem.

In fact, not only can you do these things, you must do them because your competitors are doing them, and if you don't do them too, your business will fail and then you may well become one of these Human "machines" yourself.

You can also (we've observed all these in action recently) promise your employees vacations and not provide them, fire people when they're close to retirement age and thus close to getting their pensions, fire them when their seniority calls for higher pay (the "revolving door" method of keeping labor costs down), insist that "part-time" work at thirty-five hours a week doesn't "deserve" medical or retirement benefits, and so on.

Here somebody might accurately object that at least in some countries businesses and even governments do take some responsibility for the welfare of their employees. What about health insurance, the eight-hour day (which used to be the seven-hour day in Manhattan in the 1960s, by the way), the minimum wage, retirement pensions, Social Security, unemployment insurance, safety requirements on the job, and all the rest? The answer is that such rights were won (where and when they were) by bitter and sometimes literally bloody struggles in the nineteenth and twentieth centuries. Such battles, many of which are still being fought—and which have to be fought over and over because they never stay won—do deserve the term "working people's struggle." That is exactly what they are.

To repeat: as industrialization intensifies, the number of jobs falls. Naturally owners' efforts to cut Human costs and thereby increase the amount of unpaid Human labor (which means profit) intensify too. If this process were to go on to infinity, we'd end up with all the goods and services in the world being provided by machines with everybody except the owners of the machines out of work, nobody but the owners able to buy anything, and no profit for anyone. But of course this is not what happens. Long, long before events reach such an impossible state, *capitalism itself changes.* Ehrenreich and English put it this way. "What occurred during the early decades of the twentieth century was no less than the creation of a new culture—the culture of *monopoly capitalism.*"[21]

Now, it may have occurred to you, reading the above argument, that capitalists could easily solve the problem of a falling rate of profit *if only they did not have to compete with one another.* After all, it's competition that keeps prices down and inspires a constant search for the newest technology, which, in turn, lowers the rate of profit. This possibility has occurred to capitalists too, of course, and there have always been attempts among them to stop competing, what used to be called (when I was in school) "a conspiracy in restraint of trade." (That's why Teddy Roosevelt's slogan was "Bust the trusts!" and why in the movie *Born Yesterday* you can hear talk of "trusts" and "cartels," words you don't hear today.)[22] It would be nice for the owners of Widget and Wodget (though not for their customers) if they could fight a falling rate of profit simply by agreeing to jack up their prices again and again, but this sort of thing is illegal, after all, and it would be highly embarrassing, to say the least, if they were caught *price fixing* (say, over an expensive dinner in a restaurant most people can't afford even to think about). Anyway, this sort of thing doesn't work when a field consists only of small producers; it's too hard to get them all to agree not to compete with each other. But it just so happens there is one set of conditions in which such an agreement works very well, and that is when a field is dominated by a few economic giants who can (because of their size and the economic power it gives them) do pretty much what they please. And *that* is "monopoly capitalism," or (as it's sometimes called) "corporate capitalism," or (more accurately) "oligopoly capitalism."

As capitalism continues to exist, it is inevitable that some businesses get bigger and some either get smaller, go under, or are bought up by yet others. Once enough small businesses in a particular field have been destroyed or bought up by others—which thereby become medium-sized businesses— and once enough of them have been ruined or bought up by others, which thereby become large businesses—well, you get the idea. (Though the process isn't nearly as orderly as I'm making it sound.) Anyway, once you have a situation in which a few economic giants dominate a field of production— there doesn't have to be just one, a few will do, and there may also be many small producers left in the field—everything changes.

Most important, these monsters *no longer compete by lowering prices.* Rather they compete *by cutting production costs* and *raising prices,* which they do in both good times and bad. They attempt to increase their share of the market and thus maximize profits by making *constant superficial changes in the style of their products* (i.e., planned obsolescence) and by huge *barrages of advertising,* which are meant to *create demand,* not just satisfy already existing demand. They prefer selling *fewer and more expensive items* to selling many cheap ones. They also regularly introduce *new or new-seeming products* (another form of planned obsolescence). Because they are international, *they relocate wherever costs are lowest,* i.e., where labor is cheapest, taxes lowest, unions and safety and ecological regulations least in evidence, and governments most easy to influence (or even buy outright). They also *profit from currency fluctuations,* and *one part of such a behemoth can set its prices wherever it wants when trading with another part of itself.* (One-third of all world trade is made up of just such transactions.)[23] They can, of course, also *allocate costs to whatever part of the company they wish,* and so on.

The above activities are not, by any stretch of the imagination, "free enterprise," although we keep hearing that they are. They amount to nothing less than *centralized world economic planning,* but *private planning* done for the profit of those few who control and are made wealthy by the multinational supergiants. So prices rise and rise, real wages fall, luxury goods proliferate, unemployment continues or rises, jobs leave the industrial countries for places without unions or decent wages or safety and ecological regulations, social welfare shrinks—and women whose grandmothers couldn't have worked for money if they'd wanted to (as well as women whose grandmothers had to and did) now find not only that they can work for pay but that they must.

So we end up with the "traditional" family falling apart, women's "right" to the double workday, women's "freedom" to go into debt (like men), to pay more and more for less and less (like men), to raise children without help (like a few men), to live alone (like men) and pay more and more for worse and worse housing (like men)—all of this together with the genuine liberations brought about by the last century and certainly by the last twenty years.

So far, so good, but there's one piece of the puzzle that still has to be put into place.

First, classical capitalism (the old kind in which many small producers compete in a market that none of them dominates) has as its heart what socialists call a basic *contradiction.* Briefly, when employees are paid less than the market value their work creates—which has to happen because otherwise there are no profits in it for anyone, and no one will invest money in an enterprise that makes no profit when there are other, profit-making ones around—*everybody's employees* (put together) *are not going to have enough money to buy everybody's products.* There may be plenty of longing on the part of a whole lot of people for a whole lot of products and services, but if there's no money to put on the line, it's not what economists call *effective demand.* Without krumballs to spend, you may desire widgets or dingles or dells as madly as you like, but you can't buy them. And because under classical capitalism, manufacturers compete in order to attract effec-tive demand to their particular widgets, more widgets get made than every-one can buy. That is, there is an overproduction of widgets (and a great many other things). What happens? Some widget manufacturers go out of business, others' profits fall, lots of widget-making workers are thrown out of work, whereupon they can no longer buy widgets (or dingles or even dells), which throws even more widget-making firms out of business *and* dingle-making and dell-making ones, whereupon they fire more employees, which results in more unemployment, still less effective demand for prod-ucts, and so on. Companies fold. Banks fail. Let overproduction pile up and you get the "down" side of the classical business cycle, an economic *de-pression.* But then something else begins to happen. With less and less ef-fective demand in existence to pay for goods and services, the sellers of goods and services *must lower their prices* in order to sell anything at all. Once prices have gone down enough, lo and behold, suddenly more people can afford widgets (which are now selling for 1/10 krumball instead of their previous price of, say, one krumball) whereupon more widget makers can be hired, and eventually business picks up. Multiply this process by a whole economy and we have *boom* times again, the "up" side of the business cycle of classical capitalism.

But with monopoly capitalism, remember, there are a few giant widget makers who dominate the field (and ditto for dingles and dells and a lot of other things). *And they don't lower prices, not even in a depression.* Rather they shift to more expensive products that they can sell to a luxury mar-ket, they hype up their advertising, they move operations to cheaper parts of the world, they change styles even more rapidly (see above), and they stay wealthy. Prices do not drop. Therefore demand does not "recover," as economists say. With enough giants dominating enough fields of the economy, *there is no "up" side to the business cycle. Good times never come.* Instead there is continual and rising unemployment and/or inflation (which amounts to cutting everybody's wages since money buys less and less), a falling standard of living, and a growing sense that something has gone mysteriously wrong. What has gone wrong, of course, is the contra-dictions involved in the very structure of production for profit. In classi-cal capitalism, this fundamental contradiction leads to the ups and very painful downs of the business cycle. With corporate capitalism not only do these economic behemoths not lower prices, *they do not even use their profits to invest in further production.* Why should they? The market is saturated already (i.e., all the people who have money to spend already have all the widgets, dingles, and dells they want). In order to produce more customers with the money to buy more products, a lot more people would have to have higher incomes—that is, there would have to be a large *redistribution of wealth*—which capitalists resist like grim death because any such redistribution would have to come out of their profits, which every capitalist business aims to make as large as possible. That is, in the long run capitalist enterprises can maximize profits only by keeping wages down (because unpaid wages *are* profits, remember?) so they must attempt to screw more and more work out of ever fewer workers by all the means I've already described. And the workers, who are also the vast majority of any company's customers, get poorer and buy less. And profits go down. Gordon puts it this way: "The Depression [of the 1930s] was not a temporary collapse but the beginning of a permanent *inability* of private corporations to provide full employment without government assistance."[24]

To repeat: companies respond to falling rates of profit by paying workers less; as men's wages shrink, wives must work at paid jobs, which provides the economic foundation for women's economic independence from the family. But although capitalism was thus historically instrumental in pulling women out of the family, that doesn't mean it's women's ally. Industrial capitalism in Europe began by forcing huge numbers of people off their land and it has always been terribly hard on all but a small elite. Since there's an enormous literature on this subject, I will add here only a few contemporary voices testifying to the effect class society has had on those born below its "upper" reaches, material I didn't go looking for but simply came across almost by accident while looking for feminist material, all (I thought then) that I would need for this book. Here is Lillian Breslow Rubin:

> "When I was young"—the phrase used by a twenty-seven-year-old sales clerk, mother of three, married ten years. "When I was young"—a phrase used repeatedly by working-class women and men well under thirty; a phrase that surprised my middle-class professional ears.

Kathy Kahn says:

> Factory workers [in textile mills] often take drugs, smoke incessantly when they are not at work, and many die at an early

age. The cause is simple: factory workers are overworked and underpaid in one of the most nerve-shattering jobs in the country. . . . Even in the newer, air-conditioned mills, there is a fine invisible cotton dust that floats through the air and accumulates in the worker's eyes, ears, nose, throat and lungs. And cotton dust, like coal dust, kills.[25]

Chrystos says:

I think about all the white women I knew in San Francisco. Women with Master's degrees & cars that daddy bought, women with straight white teeth & clear skins from hundreds of years of proper nutrition. They chose to be poor. They were quite convincing in the role of oppressed victim. I want to tell them to go down to Fillmore at Haight & tell somebody about it . . . Tell Jim my old landlord who picked cotton since he was 6. He moved here for a better life—lost his hearing & his teeth & his hair from working in the shipyards for 35 years. The constant vibration of his drill on the metal literally shook his teeth out. . . . He can't hear after years of that racket. He worked so hard for 35 years & he is still poor.[26]

Here's Rubin again:

[Industrialization] has now caught up with work in the office as well as the factory—most work continues to be steadily and systematically standardized and routinized; the skills of the vast majority of workers have been degraded [de-skilled]. So profound is this trend that generally we are unaware that the meaning of "skill" itself has been degraded as well.[27]

Michael Fabricant and Michael Kelly write:

Homeless families are the newest and, perhaps, most frightening wave of homelessness. Headed mostly by women living on AFDC, they represent the fastest growing group of homeless. . . . The present growth in homelessness began during the 1970's, which were also marked by the most acute economic crisis since the 1930's. . . . The nation also lost 30 million jobs during this period. . . . [and there was] a sharp reduction in job creation compared to the 1950's and 1960's.[28]

Even those who are not directly economically threatened can find a society governed by the profit motive a bad place to be. Feminist Elizabeth Fisher writes:

> Interpersonal relations have broken down. Everything is for sale: warmth, support and understanding from therapists or self-help books: instant riches from state lotteries; anodynes in the form of alcohol, marijuana, tranquilizers; individual salvation in a wide range of new and old religions. . . . The pathology of loneliness increases. Business and personal relations are like a constant state of war.[29]

Obviously there's a limit to a state of affairs in which fewer and fewer giant corporations screw profit out of fewer and fewer employees while selling less and less for higher and higher prices to fewer and fewer customers. Long before all the numbers in that last sentence reach zero, something quite different will have to have happened. I think it's clear that *somebody* will be planning the world's economy—somebody will have to—although who will do it and for whose benefit is another matter. Socialists want (as I do) an organization of *the relations of production* (as Marx says) not based on profit, one in which the economy is planned by all for all and in which the question of who does what and who gets what, now hidden by the ideology of "free enterprise," will be fought over openly as the fundamental political issue that it is. In short, they foresee a democracy extended to economic matters that are now supposed to arrange themselves but which are really arranged for, and by, the very, very wealthy. Such a world will undoubtedly have its problems (being real and run by Human beings), but it will avoid that punishing instability that comes from running a society for profit, a process that inevitably produces ridiculous wealth at one pole of the economic order and much poverty at the other (the wealth, of course, is what produces the poverty and vice versa). Socialists disagree about exactly how soon we can expect such a state of affairs or exactly how it will come about, but they all agree on one thing: *Don't trust capitalism*. It doesn't have your best interests at heart, even if your life—like mine—has not been grossly and obviously messed over by it . . . yet. The idea that capitalism is women's friend is not an entirely silly one—capitalism *has* been historically associated with women's freedom from the family (what Ehrenreich calls "the Old Order"), even though it has also contributed to the recent invention of the "traditional" family. That is, capitalism in its mercantile as well as its industrial phase has had two effects on women's position in capitalist societies. It's tempting, therefore, for a good many women to see capitalism as a way to freedom. Nonetheless, freedom from the restrictions of feudalism (in itself an ambiguous freedom) doesn't guarantee anything but the freedom to be oppressed in the same way men are. Whatever capitalism has done, it has not done so with anybody's interests in mind except those of a very small class of very wealthy people, a class that does not remotely include the vast, vast majority of women (or men).

But even if corporate capitalism were to disappear tomorrow, industrialization would still be with us (if we want to live at all), and it has brought with it something unprecedented in Human affairs. The enormous increase of married women and mothers in the paid work force during the last century[30] (not just in the last thirty years), women's increasing right to abortion and contraception in some parts of the world, the rise of the world gay rights movement and the world feminist movement in the last two decades—all these (along with shifts in public opinion about them, when and where such shifts have occurred) seem to me to signal a profound change in Human affairs that will persist whether or not capitalism does. I don't mean that this change is due in the future—what usually passes for prediction in economic, social, and political affairs is likely to be only a keener-than-usual perception of the present—but that it is happening right now. What we are experiencing is the Industrial Revolution's finally coming home to roost, so to speak. I mean the possible end of *kinship,* a very ancient Human invention that takes the single, bare, biological fact that children come from women's bodies and imaginatively and nonfactually translates that fact into elaborate forms of Human social organization.[31]

Kinship probably began to be modified when the first city-states rose in Asia Minor, and it was certainly weakened by that age of invention and discovery in Europe that we call the Renaissance, but industrial capitalism has smashed it, leaving us with that last vestige of it we now call the "traditional," or "nuclear," family. It has been a long process, but those of us living in the industrialized world are finally being transformed from the members of tribes and dynasties—what we used to be—to those shockingly new social inventions of the last few centuries: *citizens* and *workers.* As Marvin Harris puts it, "The entire history of state society is one convergent thrust toward the replacement of kin-organized groups by those based on the division of labor, class and other achieved statuses."[32]

In this context it becomes possible to understand some supposedly revolutionary changes of the last few decades as merely a belated catching-up with industrialization, like the change in China to the modern "conjugal" (or "nuclear") family, which has existed for some time in Europe and North America.[33] It also becomes possible to challenge ideas connected to the idea of kinship, ideas that even those of us in the feminist or gay rights movements still mistake for actualities. Here is some of this recent cutting edge of discourse from the feminist and gay rights movements:[34]

Catharine MacKinnon, a lawyer, participates in this kind of thing when she examines the legal concept of "privacy" as that realm in which women are supposed to belong—"privacy," "the home," and "women" are all connected—and decides that although privacy is something women *as women* create, it is not something that women, as women, have. That is, women create "private life" *for* men without usually having the option that men have to move between the "private" life of the household and the "public" world of work. She goes even further: as it is the oppression of women that enforces the dichotomy between public and private, it is the oppression of women by men that creates men's "privacy." Their private realm of freedom (as it's at least supposed to be) *is* women's oppression. She writes:

> Privacy is everything women as women have never been allowed to be or to have; at the same time the private is everything women have been equated with and defined in terms of *men's* ability to have. To confront the fact that we have no privacy is to confront our private degradation as the public order. . . . The very place (home, body) relations (sexual), activities (intercourse and reproduction) and feelings (intimacy, selfhood) that feminism finds central to women's subjection form the core of [legal] privacy doctrine [in the United States]. But when women are segregated in private, one at a time, a law of privacy will tend to protect the right of men "to be let alone," to oppress us one at a time.

Elsewhere she notes that when relief is denied to women's complaints of sexual harassment, the denial is always made *in terms of privacy,* a privacy that, it seems, protects men but somehow doesn't protect women. She says: " 'Personal' is the most common descriptive term for such incidents. It is usually used *as if it conclusively renders legal remedies unavailable, as if to the extent an occurrence can be described as personal the person has no legal rights.*"[35] (This logic seems to me impeccable: *insofar as* women are confined to the sphere of the private and personal and *insofar as* the private and personal are exempt from law or community regulation, so far do women have no rights at all. Other feminists have, of course, made similar statements about women's lack of leisure in the private, personal sphere and women's consequent creation of leisure *for men*.)

Here is Christine Delphy on the most fundamental concept underlying kinship, which most of us would still insist is really a matter of biological fact:

To understand patriarchy it is necessary *radically* to question the whole of patriarchal ideology. We must reject *all* its presuppositions, up to and including those which appear not to be such, but rather to be categories furnished by reality itself, e.g. the categories "women" and "men". . . . We think that gender, the respective social positions of women and men, is not constructed on the (apparently) natural category of sex (male and female) but rather that *sex has become a pertinent fact, hence a perceived category, because of the existence of gender.*

She explains:

Groups . . . [do not exist] before coming into relation with one another. On the contrary, it is their relationship which constitutes them. . . . [Thus] *Gender . . . created anatomical sex,* in the sense that the hierarchical division of humanity into two transforms an anatomical difference (which is in itself devoid of social implications) into a relevant distinction for social practice. Social practice and social practice alone transforms a physical fact (which in itself is devoid of meaning, like all physical facts) into a category of thought.[36]

Marilyn Frye spells out how the existences of "two" "sexes" is constantly enforced and re-created in everyday life:

The pressure on each of us to guess or determine the sex of everybody else both generates and is exhibited in a great pressure on each of us to *inform* everybody all the time of our sex. . . . We announce . . . [it] in a thousand ways. We deck ourselves from head to toe with garments and decorations. . . . [We use] distinct clothes, gear and accessories, hairdos, cosmetics and scents. . . . There are different styles of gait, posture, speech, humor, taste and even of perception, interest and attention. . . . The intense demand for making and for asserting what sex each person is adds up to a strenuous requirement that there *be* two distinct and sharply dimorphic sexes. . . . The apparent dimorphism of the sexes is so extreme that one can only think there is a great gulf between female and male, that the two are, essentially and fundamentally and naturally, utterly different. . . . [This requirement produces] a strong and visceral feeling . . . to the effect that sex-distinction is the most important thing in the world. . . . If one is made to feel that a thing is of prime importance but common sensory experience does not connect it with things of obvious concrete and practical importance [i.e. the culture enforces "a strong blanket rule" requiring that the "simplest and most nearly definitive physical manifestations of sex difference be hidden from view in all but the most private and intimate circumstances"] then there is . . . a strong tendency to the construction of mystical or metaphysical conceptions of its importance.[37]

In this light, Jonathan Katz analyzes the ideas of sexuality and "appropriate" or "inappropriate" dress:

All those terms [which name "transvestism"] . . . assumed the peculiarity of "cross-dressing." And all assumed without question the existence of clothes proper, exclusive to, and customary for each sex. But if no inherent link is assumed between particular clothes and a particular sex, a question arises about a phenomenon which can be called "homovestism"—the wearing of the clothes customary for the same sex to which the wearer belongs. If the link between clothes and gender is social, historical and relative, dressing in the apparel of one's own sex is seen to be quite as "peculiar," "obsessive," and problematic as "transvestism."

His ideal for the gay liberation and feminist movements is

not the liberal reform of masculinity and femininity, heterosexuality and homosexuality, but the revolutionary dissolution of all links between sex-biology and particular feelings and acts. There would then no longer be emotions or work inappropriate to either females or males. This sexual revolution would in effect abolish female and male as we now know them.[38]

And here is another crucial condition for tactical feminist advance in the future, as perceived by Nawal El Saadawi:

The state . . . in modern society has inherited much of the authority and functions which at one time were those of the father in the primitive patriarchal system. . . . The state has usurped much of the authority and rights previously exercised by the father or husband.[39]

and by Marielouise Jansen-Jurreit:

> The individual man no longer gains economic power or advantage from a family. This is why he is no longer a reliable ally of the state.[40]

If both of the above are correct, we are moving into —or are in—a situation in which patriarchy, having passed into state control, will no longer put the interests of men and women into conflict, or at least not do so as much as it has in the past. When a full-time housewife becomes an impossible luxury for all but the tiniest number of elite men, when it becomes clear enough to enough people that raising children does not guarantee a safe old age, when child care becomes a community problem, when the double workday stops being a secondary sex characteristic and elite women can "buy" their way out of childbearing as many now do out of housework (and some of the former has actually happened), maybe then the vast majority of men and women will finally have only one enemy and the same enemy: a class enemy.[41]

But there is something else long overdue in this book. Although it may seem to you as it once did to me that the above "puts it all together" quite enough, I don't think so anymore. As feminism is not complete without considering class (and vice versa), so considering both feminism and class is not itself complete without considering something else. And just as feminist politics must transform socialism (and vice versa) so it's long past time here to stop talking as if the only countries in the world affected by capitalism were those of capitalism's own early development and as if the only oppressive forces active in the world today were those deployed around sex and class. There is also—crucially and *of course*—*racism*.

NOTES

1. In support of the idea that capitalism changed women's status in Europe earlier than the nineteenth century, Mary Nelson writes of the pressure on women in towns of the European late medieval period to enter the labor force instead of marrying, cites guild rules that restricted the number of marriageable men in their membership, and notes the poverty of men employed by large manufacturers and the lowness of their wages. She asks, "What was to become of women in the cities who could not find husbands?" (in Jo Freeman, ed., *Women: A Feminist Perspective*, 2d. ed. [Palo Alto, CA: Mayfield, 1979], 461). The answers (she furnishes them) were prostitution or employment in large manufacturers' businesses or both. Freeman, like some other social historians, perceives the European witchcraft persecu-

tion as (among other things) a "backlash" response to the changing place of women. She points out that in nonindustrialized Spain the dynamic of persecution was quite different and Jews, not witches, were persecuted.

2. Barbara Ehrenreich and Deidre English, *For Her Own Good: 150 Years of the Experts' Advice to Women* (Garden City, NY: Anchor/Doubleday, 1979), 5, 9.

3. Delmar in Sandra Allen et al., eds., *Conditions of Illusion: Papers from the Women's Movement* (Leeds, UK: Feminist Books, 1974), 239; Ehrenreich and English, *For Her Own Good,* 13, italics added. According to Casey Miller and Kate Swift, the use of "Miss" and "Mrs." to distinguish unmarried women from married women began at just about this time in England. (Previously "Miss" had been used for female children and "Mrs." for adult women.) Miller and Swift attribute the change to the anonymity of the new factory towns created by the industrial revolution. In the factory, away from rural settings in which everyone knew everyone else, it was difficult to know whether women were available or not. Thus "a simple means of distinguishing married from unmarried women was needed (by men)" (Miller and Swift, *Words and Women* [Garden City, NY: Anchor/Doubleday, 1976], 89).

4. Ann Oakley, *Woman's Work: The Housewife, Past and Present* (New York: Pantheon, 1974), 37. Oakley notes that the majority of factory workers in England in the early days of the industrial revolution were "children, usually paupers, sent up in large numbers from workhouses in London and elsewhere" (ibid.).

5. Morton in Ellen Malos, ed., *The Politics of Housework* (London: Alison and Busby, 1980), 140–41. Volume I of Karl Marx's *Capital* is full of such horrors, culled from the reports of factory inspectors in England and elsewhere. Among them are the employment in the lace trade in 1860 of children of nine or ten who worked as long as twenty-two hours without stopping (Marx, *Capital,* vol. I, translated by Samuel Moore and Edward Aveling [New York: International Publishers], 1967, 243), and boys and girls as young as four who at times worked a seventeen-hour day (ibid., 463). Nor were horrible working or living conditions confined to children or to factory workers. Agricultural laboring families in Wales lived in "cabins" that were roofed with "a mass of loose and sodden thatch" and whose floors were the bare dirt. The inhabitants burned coal kneaded together with clay for heat. A doctor's report of 1865 mentions physicians attending women in labor in such cottages who found "their feet [the doctors'] sinking in the mud of the floor" and who had to "drill a hole through the wall" (an easy task, the report says) so that they might breathe (ibid., 681). In Manchester in 1875 the average age of male death in the upper middle class was thirty-eight (a shockingly low age to us), while that of the laboring class was seventeen. In Liverpool the corresponding ages were thirty-five and fifteen (ibid., 641–42).

6. Engels in Allen et al., *Conditions,* 239; Hartmann in Lydia Sargent, ed., *Women and Revolution: A Discussion of the Unhappy Marriage of Marxism and Feminism* (Boston: South End Press, 1981), 21; Batya Weinbaum, *The Curious Courtship of Women's Liberation and Socialism* (Boston: South End Press, 1978), 104.

7. Fox [Jeanette Silveira], "Why Men Oppress Women," *Lesbian Ethics* 1:1 (1984), 45. Fox calls the "sanctimonious 'working people's struggle' mantle around the union movement" simply a lie (ibid.)—I cannot agree. Certainly the desire to reserve the best-paid jobs for White men deserves that epithet, but other motives were involved, and a heterogeneous movement that spanned two centuries, and in which women were sometimes involved independently, can't be summed up that way. (Paula Giddings notes that "the only union [in the United States] that sought Black participation was the CIO" [Giddings, *When and Where I Enter: The Impact of Black Women on Race and Sex in America* (New York: Morrow, 1984), 235]).

8. Gardiner in Allen et al., *Conditions*, 256; Hartman in Sargent, *Women and Revolution*, 21; and Allen et al., *Conditions*, 254.

9. Oakley, *Woman's Work*, 44, 50.

10. Rowbotham (1973), xxxv. They would undoubtedly have added that the subordination of children to parents (or other adults) was likewise natural and just. There was a great deal of talk about children's oppression and children's freedom in the 1960s; one hears little of it today. Firestone, who was strikingly explicit on this topic, linked women's oppression with that of children, maintaining that both were privatized by the "traditional" family, both had myths made up about their happiness and special psychology, and both were marked off from adult men by stereotyped dress and behavior. Children, she says, were also specifically denied civil rights, independence, and economic freedom, were kept in jails (schools, to which they were forced to go), and were misled and kept deliberately ignorant by parents and teachers about matters that vitally concerned them (Shulamith Firestone, *The Dialectic of Sex* [New York: Morrow, 1970], 88–106). Although recent feminists have certainly fought specific abuses perpetrated against children, principally sexual and physical abuse, the kind of thing Firestone noted about children in the late 1960s has been neither challenged nor, it seems, much remembered. One exception is Morgan, another feminist who came out of the New Left in the United States of the 1960s, who wrote, "Sweden appears to be a rare country which has actually legislated *children's rights* and which has dared to define 'family' in a multitude of constructive forms" (Robin Morgan, ed., *Sisterhood Is Global: The International Women's Movement Anthology* [New York: Anchor, 1984], 13).

11. Ann Oakley, *Subject Women* (New York: Pantheon, 1981), 6–7. Italics added.

12. Gardiner in Allen et al., *Conditions*, 256, 251; Barbara Ehrenreich, *The Hearts of Men: American Dreams and the Flight from Commitment* (Garden City, NY: Anchor/Doubleday, 1983) 7, 173.

13. Oakley, *Subject*, 294, 244.

14. Also important to the dissolution of the family is the fact that children in the industrialized countries no longer bring money into the family; rather, their rearing costs money. Nor can they always be depended upon to support parents in the latter's old age. Child labor laws paralleled the invention of the family wage and

the creation of the "traditional" family. As children could no longer earn money, offspring changed from being an economic asset to being an economic burden and their custody was given to women. Carol Brown sums up this development:

> Children themselves and the labor required to rear them have changed from a valuable family asset that men wished to control to a costly family burden that men wish to avoid. . . . [Thus] women gained not so much a private right as a public obligation. . . . When the benefits [of having children] do fail, the changes in the patriarchal system have made it possible for men to cut their losses, obligating the women to the children and [thus] . . . increased the freedom of men to choose between burdens and benefits (in Sargent, *Women and Revolution*, 242, 246, 259).

Harris stated in 1977 that the cost of rearing a "middle class" child to the age of eighteen in the United States was $80,000 and that "only a minuscule portion" of this amount was returned to the parents as goods, money, or services (Harris, 1977, 282). Hartmann says essentially the same thing (in Sargent, *Women and Revolution,* 23) as do Jansen-Jurreit (Marielouise Jansen-Jurriet, *Sexism: The Male Monopoly on History and Thought,* translated by Verne Moberg [New York: Farrar, Straus and Giroux, 1982], 349) and Margolis, who estimates the cost of rearing one middle-class child at more than $250,000 (Maxine L. Margolis, *Mothers and Such: Views of American Women and Why They Changed* [Berkeley: University of California Press, 1984], 102). Phyllis Chesler's *Mothers on Trial* bears out this view, i.e., child custody still goes to fathers when the fathers want it; although uncontested custodies are almost always given to mothers, fathers win custody in three-quarters of contested cases, often on very shaky grounds (Chesler, *Mothers on Trial: The Battle for Children and Custody* [New York: McGraw-Hill, 1986], see especially 82–84). These findings substantiate the view expressed by other sources: in the countries I'm discussing here, in the nineteenth century custody went to fathers; in the twentieth it goes to mothers but not as a benefit. Rather it is mothers who have the obligation of child custody—unless the father wants it, in which case he usually gets it.

15. Varda Burstyn, ed., *Women Against Censorship* (Vancouver: Douglas and McIntyre, 1985), 8; Ehrenreich, *Hearts of Men,* 172.

16. bell hooks, *Feminist Theory from Margin to Center* (Boston: South End Press, 1984), 37; Morgan, *Sisterhood Is Global,* 13.

17. Linda Gordon, *Woman's Body, Woman's Right: A Social History of Birth Control in America* (New York: Grossman, 1976), 412; Gloria Joseph and Jill Lewis, *Common Differences: Conflicts in Black and White Feminist Perspectives* (Boston: South End Press, 1986), 250.

18. Charnie Guettel, *Marxism and Feminism* (Toronto: Canadian Women's

Educational Press, 1974), 55, italics added; Gordon, *Woman's Body*, 412, italics added.

19. With more and more women in the United States having to put in longer and longer hours at their two jobs, the paid and unpaid, it's not surprising that the U.S. mass media have been offering as their ideal of the "liberated" woman The Woman Who Does It All. White, female students of mine, probably because of mass-media propaganda and the lack of any other knowledge of feminism, have accepted this image of the ninety-hour week as *the* "feminist" goal. Never having experienced the abominableness of the 1950s, they romanticize it, following the lead of the media, as a paradise of easy happiness in which all women married effortlessly and blissfully without fear of spinsterhood and stayed married ditto without fear of divorce. They blame "feminism" for destroying this paradise for them. It is hard, sometimes, not to smack them.

20. For example, anyone who's ever done (or even just watched) hand weaving knows how tedious a process it is and how slowly it produces cloth. I vividly remember comparing the speed of just such hand work, which I'd seen done at a Folk Life festival in Seattle, with textile machinery I'd seen in the Toronto Exposition of the 1970s. To say that modern textile looms *move* faster than the Human eye can follow is nothing; textiles *shoot out from the loom* faster than the eye can follow too! The difference in productive power was so huge as to be indescribable. It simply has to be experienced to be appreciated.

21. In Mina Davis Caulfield et al., *Capitalism and the Family* (San Francisco: Agenda Publishing, 1976), 8, italics added.

22. I remember learning some of this in junior high school in the 1940s. Somehow, after that nobody seemed to get any of this in school (or explanations of the separation of church and state either). The politically reactionary atmosphere of the 1950s made many changes in the United States.

23. Robert Lekachman and Borin Van Loon, *Capitalism for Beginners* (New York: Pantheon, 1981), 54.

24. Gordon, *Woman's Body*, 338.

25. Lillian Breslow Rubin, *Worlds of Pain: Life in the Working-Class Family* (New York: Basic Books, 1976), 72; Kathy Kahn, *Hillbilly Women* (New York: Doubleday, 1973), xix–xx.

26. Chrystos in Cherríe Moraga and Gloria Anzaldúa, eds., *This Bridge Called My Back: Writings by Radical Women of Color* (Watertown, MA: Persephone Press, 1981), 68.

27. Rubin, *Worlds of Pain*, 159.

28. Michael Fabricant and Michael Kelly, "No Haven for Homeless in a Heartless Economy," *Radical America* 20:2 and 3 (March–May 1986), 26, 28.

29. Elizabeth Fisher, *Women's Creation: Sexual Evolution and the Shaping of Society* (Garden City, NY, 1979), 401.

30. Virginia Woolf wrote of "the right to earn one's living" as a right "of such immense value to the daughters of educated men that almost every word in the dictionary has been changed by it" (Woolf, *Three Guineas* [London: Harcourt, 1938], 15).

31. Kinship and the family is still presented to most people—I think I'll be brave enough to add here *in the world*—as a matter of biological fact. One example: before the invention of the microscope, biological fatherhood was impossible either to prove or observe and yet one often meets the assertion that men "discovered" the "fact" of biological fatherhood sometime way back when. Rather, fatherhood was *invented* and *asserted*. For example, in Orestes' trial in Aeschylus' *Oresteia,* Apollo (whose view was later to prevail in ancient Greek society) states that mothers are not blood kin to their children and that the only real parent is the father. This rather surprising view—after all, the visible evidence is all the other way—is clearly a political move. Half the Athenian jurors in the play accept this view (and with it, Orestes' innocence); half do not. Athena's vote breaks the tie and brings in patriliny and the new, patriarchal gods. The play was taught to me in the late 1950s as a progressive myth about replacing the blood feud with the reign of law. Nobody noticed that the play was also a myth about the creation of patriliny and patriarchy. The female Erynnis are "tamed" and their names changed to serve the new gods, who recognize fatherhood but not motherhood, who are ruled by a father (Zeus) and who, by exonerating Orestes, condemn the killing of a husband (by Orestes' mother, Clytemnestra) as a worse crime than matricide.

32. Marvin Harris, *Cultural Materialism: The Struggle for a Science of Culture* (New York: Random House, 1979), 131.

33. Katie Curtin makes this point in *Women in China* (New York: Pathfinder Press, 1975), and Judith Stacey says essentially the same thing in Zillah R. Eisenstein, ed., *Capitalist Patriarchy and the Case for Socialist Feminism* (New York: Monthly Review Press, 1979), 321, 324–25. She also notes the strictness of Chinese monogamy (e.g., adultery is punishable by law) and "a total absence of viable alternative life styles," including celibacy.

34. Others are, of course, scattered throughout this book.

35. Catharine A. MacKinnon, "Feminism, Marxism, Method, and the State: Toward Feminist Jurisprudence," *Signs* 8:4 (Summer 1983), 656–67; Catharine MacKinnon, *Sexual Harassment of Working Women: A Case of Sex Discrimination* (New Haven: Yale University Press, 1979), 83–84, italics added.

36. Christine Delphy, *Close to Home: A Materialist Analysis of Women's Oppression,* translated by Diana Leonard (Amherst: University of Massachusetts Press, 1984), 144, italics added to last sentence of first quotation.

37. Marilyn Frye, *The Politics of Reality: Essays in Feminist Theory* (Trumansburg, NY: Crossing Press, 1983), 23–28.

38. Jonathan Katz, *Gay/Lesbian Almanac: A New Documentary* (New York: Harper and Row, 1983), 146, 173.

39. Nawal El Saadawi, *The Hidden Face of Eve: Women in the Arab World*, translated by Sherif Hetata (Boston: Beacon Press, 1980), 63.

40. Jansen-Jurreit, *Sexism*, 349.

41. Such a prophecy should be no news to socialists, though some of them do appear at times to have forgotten about the absorption of the female sex into production and the socialization of housework. Marx is responsible for the above, not I.

T W E L V E

"THERE IS A VILLAGE / OVER / THAT HILL"[1]

If one can claim that marxism is incomplete without a consideration of feminism, it is certainly true that neither is complete without a consideration of racial relations. . . . Relations between races have a long and important history which is not reducible to relations between the sexes or classes. An analysis of racism thus should be undertaken prior to, or at least in conjunction with, the discussion of marxist feminist relations, thus facilitating a better understanding of how to integrate race into a theory of marxism-feminism.

—*Gloria Joseph*[2]

I am not the right person to write this chapter. What I think and feel about sexism and homophobia come out of a lifetime of having been oppressed by the one and more than forty years of having been oppressed by the other. When I think and feel about class, I do so as the granddaughter of socialist atheists and the daughter of petty civil servants who belonged, during my formative years, to an active union.[3] What I think and feel about disability issues (more of this later) comes out of a forty-three year experience with one chronic illness and more than fifteen years' experience with several others. But when I feel and think about racism, I do so absolutely and unambiguously from the oppressor's and not the oppressed's side of that ghastly institution. Because I was born White in the United States, I have been made ignorant and bigoted in ways I am only now beginning to appreciate—and everything I learn about how much my sense of safety and entitlement comes directly from my White skin privilege is apt seriously to threaten my peace of mind. As Mary Helen Washington says: "What does 'white' mean in this country? It doesn't define a person's ancestry, or culture, or language, or ethnicity. It simply defines their relationship to power and prestige."[4]

Like a great many other people, I would prefer to believe that my power and prestige aren't due to the color of my skin (and my class position) but rather that they're a tribute to the fineness of my character, the sheer brilliance of my achievements, and just possibly (on especially bad days) the charm of my personality. Being aware of unearned privilege doesn't put me in a comfortable position, morally or psychologically. And of course there are all sorts of other motivations operating that have caused me and a lot of other White people to resist acknowledging our privileges and our racism: the simple selfishness that keeps us concerned with and preoccupied with our own affairs, tiredness (who wants to become aware of more problems and the necessity of doing more work?), the comforting belief in a just universe that the very existence of racism makes impossible, and the reluctance to give up a good opinion of ourselves (we thought we'd finally made ourselves into fairly decent people) and realize that we've benefited from, and been complicitous in, a dreadful, inexcusable situation.

So I am not at all the right person to write this chapter. Nonetheless the chapter must be written, and I'm the one who must write it. As Joseph says, "It takes whiteness to give even Blackness credibility." I propose to take advantage of this very racist phenomenon to add my voice to those of other White women who are using their racist privilege of being more readily believed by other White people than women of color would be to attack racism.[5]

In doing so I want also to emphasize—with apologies to people of color, who are of course the real experts here—that much of the racism of people like myself is not the kind of obvious bigotry that I myself and many of the White feminists I know are usually quick to recognize and condemn. As Tia Cross, Freada Klein, and Barbara and Beverly Smith note, racism embraces a whole "range of behavior from subtle, nonverbal daily experience to murders by the Ku Klux Klan."[6] It is the subtler kind of racism that Barbara Smith is describing when she mentions "implied resentment at having been 'forced' to confront racism" at all and its usual accompaniment, "the illusion of being non-racist—that is, totally innocent" without "the reality of being *actively* anti-racist."[7] No more than with sexism is it necessary to make actively racist decisions or perform actively racist acts to benefit from, or insure the continuance of, racism in the United States. All it takes is the comfortably vague belief that because you feel a dim benevolence toward people of color (on which you never act), and because you *don't* insult them in public and *don't* burn crosses on their lawn, that somehow you are an exceptionally good and generous person who is doing all that can possibly be expected of you. The United States is full of such White people. I should know; I'm one of them. Along with such unexamined and barely decent beliefs, it's quite possible to believe as well that nobody's culture is as central or important or sophisticated or—well, *modern*—as ours (White people's), that of course *they* are "equal" to us (or will be when they adopt our culture and our behavior) and we don't have to take as much account of them as we do of us or pay as much attention to them, and that anyway things are getting better all the time and soon those mysteriously uncomfortable and inexplicable problems Out There (which have nothing to do with our behavior In Here) will disappear so we don't have to do a thing about them. In short, I (along with many other White people) believed about people of color exactly the same things sexism had taught *me* about me—except that racism didn't hurt me (not that I knew about, anyway), so I never concluded I had better bestir myself to do anything about it. And by falsifying my mental accounts in a way that was both blithe and dimly uncomfortable, though recognizing this state of affairs is even more so, I persuaded myself that this rather dreadful state of mind was exactly the false innocence Smith speaks about.

I wish I could write here that it was my own conscience that finally forced me out of the state of mind I've been describing, but it wasn't. Like Elly Bulkin, I have

> no illusion that I would have even begun to *act* . . . in the absence of the work of women of color. Only later did I develop some sense of how often they spoke, and in how many different ways, before I was able to hear. . . . Certainly whatever attention has been paid to racism by white feminists has resulted from over a decade's worth of women of color constantly and loudly raising that issue inside and outside the women's movement.[8]

Briefly, before I could or did even act, there had to be a long and complicated moving away from the false innocence described above. Because the shift was long and not to my credit, I may be remembering it wrong, but as far as I *can* remember, it involved changing from the fears I've mentioned above—that the universe is not just, that I'm not blameless, that I'm not automatically entitled, and that I'm not safe—to a sense that I was personally and shamefully *guilty* of racist thinking and behavior. With the feeling of shame came a fear of justified retaliation—if I were them, wow, would I be mad at me!—and a lot of anger at having to endure that fear. Then there was the anger of feeling "pushed" to change—I have enough to do, enough, enough!—and finally I think I am at least beginning to arrive at the understanding that racism is not a personal defect of character that I chose because I was a wicked person but a condition of life in these United States. Because this is so, my anger ought to be directed not at those who make this fact plain to me but at the racist institutions and the racist education that made me lazy and stupid and wicked (in this particular area) without my ever having had to be clearly aware of that fact. Because *this* is so, what's needed is not the waste of energy and time represented by guilt but the use of that energy and time in decent and responsible action. I am not talking about the megalomaniac and melodramatic action that is all too often the result of White peoples' racist assumptions that they are more central and important than people of color, just ordinary, day-to-day, unspectacular activity directed against racism. So that is what I will try to do here.

I am sure that most of the White women I have met or whose work I know in what I have been calling the feminist movement don't think of themselves as practicing racists. Nor do they think of what I have been calling "feminism" and "the women's movement" as *the White women's movement.*[9] Nonetheless they are and it is. If there is anything on which feminists of color agree, it is those two statements. Here is one of the gentlest observations, by Spring Redd:

> [In a women's community] I was always at odds with their issues . . . most of the women I was dealing with were white and middle-class. They were focusing totally on sexism. . . . I had a double problem to work with, which they did not have to work on unless they *felt* like it.[10]

Gloria Anzaldúa, who writes of "a definition of feminism that still renders most of us "invisible" and of being "the only Third World woman at readings, workshops and meetings," is more emphatic:

> During my stint in the Feminist Writers' Guild many white members would ask me why Third World women do not come to FWG meetings and readings. I should have answered, "Because their skins are not as thick as mine, because their fear of encountering racism is greater than mine. They don't enjoy being put down, ignored, not engaged in equal dialogue, being tokens. And neither do I.[11]

And here is a similar comment by Gloria Joseph:

> It is incumbent upon White women to understand that this is both a sexist and racist society and that, as social beings, they too participate in inhumane social conditions. White women's position in United States society as the benefactors of racism has allowed them to ignore their Whiteness.[12]

Here is Michele Wallace on the same subject:

When I first became a feminist, my Black friends used to cast pitying eyes upon me and say, "That's whitey's thing." I used to laugh it off. . . . The women's movement enlists the support of Black women only to lend credibility to an essentially middle-class, irrelevant movement, they asserted. Time has shown that there was . . . truth to these claims.[13]

In a poem, Lorraine Bethel ironically suggests that she will print up business cards to inform White women of her rates for showing up at events, parties, and so on as a token "Black feminist/lesbian."[14]

Jo Carillo notes, in a poem, that White women who love pictures of women of color don't react as well when they meet one in person.[15]

Again and again, these critics comment on the belief that all feminist issues are all-White feminist issues and on the flat-out ignoring of any other female experience. Joseph quotes from an unpublished paper on racism and feminism delivered by Pat Armstrong at a State University of New York conference in 1972:

The location of white women in America as the *benefactors* of racism has enabled them to ignore their whiteness. . . . White women must realize that as womanness circumscribes their whiteness (they are not white males), so their whiteness circumscribes their womanness. White feminists must come to terms with the circumscribing nature of their whiteness.[16]

And here is Bernice Carroll: "In the women's movement, I find that many of my concerns and different needs are ignored, overlooked, or rarely discussed due to the powerful myth of an all-embracing sisterhood."[17] Mitsuye Yamada says:

[A] pervasive feeling of mistrust toward the women in the movement is fairly representative of a large group of women who live in the psychological place we now call Asian Pacific America. A movement that fights sexism . . . must deal with racism, and we had hoped the leaders in the women's movement would be able to see the parallels in the lives of the women of color and themselves, and would "join" *us* in our struggle.[18]

And Tania Abdulahad avers: "White women can be challenged on their racism; they can be challenged on their ignorance and their backwardness."[19] Bell hooks writes: "The hierarchical pattern of race and sex relationships already established in American society merely took a different form under 'feminism.' "[20]

Elsewhere, hooks deplores White women's "patronizing attitude toward black women," their expectation that Black women would be "overjoyed" to join already existing White groups. She describes the "racist hostility of a group of white women" in "conference rooms, classrooms, or . . . cozy living rooms" where Black women went once and never returned and describes a feminist theory graduate class where she was met with "anger and hostility so intense I found it difficult to attend the class" when she criticized the syllabus, which contained "no material by or about black, Native American Indian, Hispanic, or Asian women."[21]

Here is Alice Walker: "White feminists are very often indistinguishable in their attitudes from any other white person in America." And here is Audre Lorde: "As white women ignore their built-in privilege of whiteness and define *woman* in terms of their own experience alone, then women of Color become the 'other,' the outsider whose experience and tradition is too 'alien' to comprehend." And Constance Carroll: "The women's movement has attempted to transcend rather than confront the racial tensions and the complexities resulting from the Black woman's involvement in the movement." No wonder Andrea Canaan warns: "The women's movement, the feminist movement, is not a middle class clique. It is not an elitist class of white women. . . . It is not white. It is not racist. It is not classist. It is not closed." No wonder also that the part of the Combahee River Collective's position statement reads:

> As Black feminists we are made constantly and painfully aware
> of how little effort white women have made to understand and
> combat their racism. . . . [This is] work for white women to do,
> but we will continue to speak to and demand accountability on
> this issue.[22]

From Barbara Smith, who laments "the absence . . . of the Black woman and her role as a member of the wedding," to Walker, who states flatly that with few exceptions "white women feminists revealed themselves as incapable . . . of comprehending Blackness and feminism in the same body, not to mention within the same imagination," to Yamada's student, who "made an effort to join some women's groups with high expectations but came away disillusioned because these groups were not receptive to the issues that were important to her as an Asian woman," to Pat Parker, who condemns the supposed leadership by the "white middle class" of the "women's movement" as "reformist and . . . counter-revolutionary," again and again feminists of color condemn the racism of White feminists.[23] Theorists and critics—all of whom are deeply concerned with feminist issues—are unanimous when it comes to this one issue. Although some, like Barbara Smith, state that there are "indeed white women worth building coalitions with," fundamentally they agree with the others. Anything less than freedom for all women, say these critics (the actual words are Smith's), is "not feminism but merely [white] female self-aggrandizement."[24] Feminists of color, as they make clear, have met a lot of the latter.

If I have quoted from feminists of color at such length on one point only, it is because I think it's crucial that White women listen to these voices. (There are many, many more instances of such judgments that could be added here.) Although I'm sure there are plenty of White women who call themselves feminists and are nonetheless actively and openly bigoted against people of color, I suspect (though I may be wrong) that a great deal of what feminists of color are pointing out and reacting to comes from White women whose racism is of the less obvious kind. Julia Perez writes:

> The worst form of racism that came at me was not from men, it was not from the whole social structure as it is . . . but from . . . feminists. Who thought that they had it so together on racism, who knew what it was like, who insulted me to my face and didn't know they were doing it.[25]

But what are these terrible things that we do? Sometimes we simply segregate White feminism and the feminism of women of color, or White women and women of color, on *our* initiative. Doris Davenport was simply told by White feminists to go away and organize Black women.[26]

Or we assume that feminism is White, and if we are suddenly informed that such is not the case, make only last-minute and hurried attempts to make it look as if we hadn't. Lorde writes:

> I stand here as a black lesbian feminist having been invited to comment within the only panel at this conference where the input of black feminists and lesbians is represented. . . . What does it mean . . . when even the two black women who did present here were literally found at the last hour? . . . Why were two phone calls to me considered a consultation? Am I the only possible source of names of black feminists?[27]

The exclusion of women of color from White events (or their last-minute inclusion) is common.

Sometimes the exclusions are more subtle and conversation somehow flows *around* the material the White feminists can't deal with or don't want to hear. Constance Carroll writes: "I have sat through meeting after meeting in which after a Black woman raises objections to certain of the movement's directions and orientations, the inevitable reverential silence sets in and then the discussion simply proceeds as before." Or, as Mitsuye Yamada notes, apparent inclusion, even attention, may mask something else. "When Third World women are asked to speak representing our racial or ethnic group, we are expected to move, charm or entertain, but not to educate in ways that are threatening to our audiences."[28]

Sometimes White feminists react not to the feminists of color who are there but to racist stereotypes they don't even know are stereotypes. Hooks writes:

> Racist stereotypes of the strong, superhuman black woman are operative myths in the minds of many white women, allowing them to ignore the extent to which black women are likely to be victimized in this society and the role white women may play in the maintenance and perpetuation of that victimization.[29]

The pressure of this sort of cumulative ignorance can be wearying. Yamada notes: "I am weary of starting from scratch each time I speak or write . . . of hearing that among the women of color, Asian women are the least political, or the least oppressed, or the most polite."[30]

When we form groups, usually we do not question our racist assumptions. Afterward, we react as if the group were somehow a "given" and racism (the assumption of total innocence again!) had to be something added on to the structure and history of the group itself. Sometimes we allocate tasks in a way that is clearly racist, as Merle Woo describes: "[There are] so many examples of groups which are 'feminist' in which women of color were given the usual least important tasks, the shitwork, and given no say in how that group is to be run." Or what seems to be generosity about inclusion may actually be an assumption of proprietorship. As hooks says: "Many white women have said to me, 'we wanted black women and other non-white women to join the movement,' totally unaware of their perception that they somehow 'own' the movement, that they are the 'hosts' inviting us as 'guests.' " This is perhaps why Moraga stated so emphatically in her talk given at the closing session of the National Women's Studies Association conference in May 1979, "We have had it with the word '*outreach*,' referring to our joining racist White women's organizations."[31]

One example of what can happen when women of color attempt to work with White feminists who believe they "own" the "women's" movement and that "women's" issues really mean White women's issues was the attempt of one of the leaders of NOW to exclude the Third World Women's Alliance, a Black feminist group, from marching in the 1970 NOW Liberation Day March with placards reading "Hands Off Angela Davis." Paula Giddings quotes Frances Beal, leader of the alliance:

> One of the leaders of NOW ran up to us [at the March] and said angrily, "Angela Davis has nothing to do with the women's liberation [sic]."
>
> "It has nothing to do with the kind of liberation you're talking about," retorted Beal, "but it has everything to do with the kind of liberation we're talking about."[32]

Another example is White feminists' lack of support for Shirley Chisholm's campaign for the U.S. presidency in 1972. Chisholm eventually resigned from the National Women's Political Caucus, an organization created in 1971 to support just such candidacies as hers. As Constance Carroll puts it:

> The Black woman sees that her numbers are few among the general membership of the women's movement, and nonexistent among its national leadership. She often is told that many of the problems she raises are problems of all Blacks and, as such, are not the special concern of the women's movement. Why, for example, should a new women's studies center with limited funds finance course offerings on Black women where there is already a Black studies center or department?[33]

In fact, as several sources point out, women of color often vanish in the view of White feminists, as if women of color were either not women or not people of color and certainly could not be both. Walker describes two encounters with this very odd view. One was at an exhibit of women painters:

> "Are there no Black women painters represented here?" one asked a white feminist.
>
> "It's a *women's* exhibit!" she replied.

Another took place at a lecture given by "Our Mother," Walker's deliberately cheeky way of referring to the heroine of the incident she tells, a young woman with a child who is teaching in academia and whose experiences bear a considerable resemblance to her own:

> WHITE STUDENT FEMINIST: "Do you think Black women artists should work in the Black community?"
> OUR MOTHER: "At least for a period in their lives . . . just to give back some of what has been received."
> WHITE STUDENT FEMINIST: "But if you say that Black women should work in the Black community, you are saying that race comes before sex. What about Black *feminists*? Should *they* be expected to work in the Black community? And if so, isn't this a betrayal of their feminism? Shouldn't they work with women?"
> OUR MOTHER: "But of course Black people come in both sexes." (Pause, while largely White audience, with sprinkle of perplexed Blacks, ponders this possibility.)[34]

Hooks spells it out:

> When black people are talked about, sexism militates against the acknowledgment of the interests of black women; when women are talked about, racism militates against a recognition of black female interests. . . . Nowhere is this more evident than in the vast body of feminist literature. . . . The racial and sexual specificity of what is being referred to is conveniently left unacknowledged or even deliberately suppressed.[35]

Gloria Hull agrees. When White feminists do this, we're doing exactly what so many White men do when they use "man" to mean us; that is, we're using "women" as a false universal. In short, to quote Woo, "Most of the time when 'universal' is used, it is just a euphemism for 'white': white themes, white significance, white culture." Or, as Bethel puts it, describing the gap of race and class that separates the White women she sees shopping at Bonwit Teller's from the old Black woman elevator operator: "It is moments / infinities of conscious pain like these that make me want to cry / kill / roll my eyes suck my teeth hand on my hip scream at so-called radical white lesbian / feminist(s) 'WHAT CHOU MEAN WE, WHITE GIRL?'"[36]

Often also, we White women, seeing ourselves as some chemically (historically?) pure version of the universal "woman," assume that women of color exist *for* our needs, whether we need to be educated or whether we need to find metaphors for our own condition. Hooks notes, "No other group in America has used black people as metaphors as extensively as white women involved in the women's movement." Lorde notes, "Oppressed peoples are always being asked to stretch a little more, to bridge the gap between blindness and humanity." Moraga speaks of the severe constraints of time and money which White feminists don't face (or don't face in such extreme form) and often can't imagine.[37]

Even when White feminists do attempt to deal with all the above, we still often act destructively because of the ignorance and thoughtlessness that have been taught us. Norma Garcia writes: "I go to conferences and I see it happening all the time. White women come and they say, 'We're open, let's talk about it, let's get it together, we have an hour.' And then you see these women of color sitting around maybe days, days, in stirred up garbage." Without a real sense of the kind of stupidity that racism promotes in White feminists, the most well-intentioned attempts will fail. Judith Moschkovich gives an example of the typical racist ignorance that is worse than simply not knowing; it is not knowing that you don't know and, worse still, *knowing wrong*. She writes: "When Anglo-American women speak of developing a new feminist or women's culture, they are still working and thinking within an Anglo-American cultural framework. This new culture would still be just as racist and ethnocentric." White women's ethnocentrism insures that they will show no reciprocity to women of color. Chrystos writes, "I was supposed to be a carpenter to prove I was a real dyke. My differences were sloughed over. None of them came to a pow wow or an AIM [American Indian Movement] fundraiser to see about *me*."[38] And Yamada describes the way her White students, during a class discussion of a new Asian American anthology, exhibited racist ignorance that stereotyping *was* stereotyping along with racist anger at having to pay attention to someone else's oppression:

> [One] blurted out that she was offended by its militant tone and that as a white person she was tired of always being blamed for the oppression of all the minorities. . . . [Several classmates agree. Asked why other militant writings used in the class hadn't offended them] they said they were not offended by any of the Black American, Chicano or Native American writings. . . . they "understood" the anger expressed by the Blacks and Chicanos and they "empathized" with the frustrations and sorrow expressed by the Native Americans. But [says one] . . . "I didn't even know the Asian Americans felt oppressed. I didn't expect their anger."[39]

Sometimes what lies behind the anger of such White women is the defensiveness that springs from guilt—but guilt is fruitless. This is a truth I owe especially to Lorde, who says: "Guilt is only another way of avoiding informed action, of buying time out of the pressing need to make clear choices, out of the approaching storm that can feed the earth as well as bend the trees." Here is Lorde's account of a fruitful ministorm of just this kind:

> They were inaugurating a program in the Education Department for these white kids going into teaching in the New York City schools . . . who were going to teach Black children. . . . I had all these white students [who] wanted to know . . . "why are our kids hating us in the classroom?" . . . I would say, "When a white kid says 2 + 2 = 4, you say 'right.' In the same class, when a Black kid stands up and says 2 + 2 = 4, you . . . say, 'Hey, that's wonderful.' But what message are you really giving?" . . . And all the fear and loathing of these young white college students would come pouring out; it had never been addressed.[40]

I do not mean to imply by the above that it's the obligation of women of color to educate us—unless that is something they particularly decide to do for their own purposes (which are not ours). Lorraine Bethel writes:

> *Dear Ms Ann Glad Cosmic Womoon*
> *We're not doing that kind of work anymore*
> *educating white women*
> *teaching Colored Herstory 101*[41]

Sometimes we not only expect to be educated but we also believe we have a right to judge the accuracy of the education provided. Hooks says of such White feminists, "And though they expected us to provide first hand accounts of black experience, they felt it was their role to decide if these experiences were authentic." Or we think it's our role to judge a whole culture, about which we typically know next to nothing. Morales gives an instance: "A room full of Anglo women who nod sympathetically and say: Latin men are soooo much worse than Anglo men. . . . It must be so hard for you to be a Latin feminist."[42] Barbara Cameron remembers a White lesbian who was taking Native American courses in college and interviewed her, lecturing Cameron after the interview about the sexism of Native Americans and demanding to know the reason therefor.[43] Judith Moschkovich writes:

> I'm sick and tired of continually hearing about the destructive
> aspects of Latin American culture, especially from women who
> don't know the culture. . . . Why is everyone so willing to ac-
> cept the very male view of Latin American culture as consisting
> simply of macho males and Catholic priests? There are scores
> of strong women living in Latin America today and our history
> is full of famous and less known strong women.

She also makes the point that Anglo culture seems less visibly sexist than
her own only because Anglo culture is less expressive than her own.[44]

Nor is it anything but racist for White women to try to "join" women of
color by insisting that they (White women) are "equally oppressed." This is
racist—and untrue—even when the White women in question are in fact
subject to other kinds of oppression. Smith writes: "When white Jewish
women of European origin claim Third World identity by saying they are not
white but Jewish [they are] refusing to acknowledge that being visibly white
in a racist society has concrete benefits and social-political repercussions."[45]

Alas, there is more. White women's racism does not vanish when they
become scholars. Women's studies (though efforts have certainly been made
in the last few years) has been found woefully lacking by many critics. A
few brief examples: Joan R. Sherman, who notes that the best place to
discover Black poets' lives and works is in manuscript materials; Jean Fagin
Yellin, who speaks of the conspicuous absence of Black women "from most
standard works in Black studies and women's studies"; Mary Berry, who
states that women's movement scholars "have been concerned, in the main,
with white women"; Rita B. Dandridge, who finds novels by Black American
women "mentioned in footnotes, tucked away in bibliographies, and
glossed over in reviews and surveys"; and Ora Williams, Thelma Williams,
Dora Wilson, and Ramona Matthewson, who find even worse difficulties in
making the works of American Black women composers available to the
public. As Lorde puts it, the statement, "How can we address the issues of
racism? No woman of color attended" is on par with "We have no one in
our department equipped to teach their work."[46]

It's important to stress here, first, that the thinkers and writers I've been
quoting share a commitment to feminism and, second, that they are not
dismissing the White women's movement or even every organization of
White women in which they've been involved. Indeed much of what I've
quoted here was spoken or written in the context of White feminist organizations and conferences, in the clear hope that White women's racism could
be challenged and changed.

During the period covered in this chapter, some White women began to challenge their own racism and the racism of other White feminists. One was Bulkin, who writes in *Yours in Struggle:*

> While it would be terrific for women to take the initiative to learn about oppressions that do not affect each of us most directly and to be active in opposing them, the unfortunate political reality is that the impetus has almost always come from those groups . . . who suffer the oppression immediately and *demand* that other women pay attention.[47]

Another example is Ellen Pence, who can write, for the benefit of other White women, "The lessons we've learned so well as women must be the basis for our understanding of ourselves as oppressive to the Third World women we work with."[48] Sarah Pearlman responds in this way to Garcia's comment earlier in this chapter:

> I know I came in here in a rush and said okay, let's get right to it, without thinking through how much pain this would expose. . . . If somebody said to me, "Okay, let's sit around for an hour and we'll talk about the Holocaust," I would go crazy.[49]

In the same way Smith can add to her condemnation of White women's claims to somehow "be" women of color a statement that the oppression those women experience as Jewish-American is nonetheless real, saying, "How we are oppressed does not have to be the same in order to qualify as real."[50]

White activists can also understand the shortcomings in their past behavior. Thus Pence writes:

> I began to see how white women ignored the need to reexamine the traditional white rigid methods of decision making, priority setting, and implementing decisions. Our idea of including women of color was to send out notices. We never came to the business table as equals. Women of color joined us on our terms.[51]

Bulkin adds:

> White women with the economic resources and institutional access to start a project seek Third World feminists to participate only when things are well under way; an issue is defined

by white women who then ask women of color to provide input within already established parameters.[52]

Minnie Bruce Pratt examines her own past behavior in detail:

> Our first community forum [in the early 1970s] had one panel out of six designated with the topic "minority women," and five of the twenty speakers for the day were Black women. This was in a day's activities which were planned, the speakers chosen, the location selected, and the publicity arranged, by three middle-class white women, me included, who had *personally* not contacted a single Black Women's organization, much less considered trying to co-plan or co-sponsor with such a group: and who had no notion of the doubts or risks that Black women in that town might have about our endeavor. Neither did we consult our common sense to discover that "minority women" in Fayetteville included substantial numbers of Thai, Vietnamese, Cambodian, Laotian, Korean and Japanese women, as well as Lumbee women and Latinas. Attendance at the forum was overwhelmingly white; we questioned our publicity instead of our perspective on power.

Elsewhere she describes saying "carelessly" that there were no Jews where she grew up and having her Jewish lover ask: "how do I know." Or:

> How *habitually* I think of my culture, my ethics, my morality, as the culmination of history, as the logical extension of what has gone before; the kind of thinking represented by . . . the word Judeo-*Christian*, as if Jewish history and lives have existed only to culminate in Christian culture.[53]

Pratt also brings up the White fears that must be faced before the journey out of racism can even begin. In particular, she addresses the fear that facing the racism in the White women's movement will destroy the unity these White feminists have just begun to enjoy or that such struggles will destroy "feminism"—as if feminists of color were not capable of constructing feminism also:

> "A loss of unity," a "disintegration" . . . [was feared by] academic feminists at the 1981 National Women's Studies Conference . . . from women activists at an organizing conference

who asked why we had to talk about homophobia and racism, couldn't we "just be women together"; from lesbians at a cultural conference who didn't want "divisive issues" raised during one of the few times they had "to be together as lesbians"; from women who felt that bringing up anti-Semitism was just adding another troublesome item on a list of political correctness.[54]

I have felt such fears myself, and yet if I've learned anything as a political person in the last twenty years, it's that movements founder not on the issues they face but on the issues they try to ignore in the interests of a false unity. For not only is it personally important to face and challenge one's own racism, and not only is such a process crucial for the women's movement—which is made up of White women's feminism *and* that of women of color—but the same process was politically crucial in the nineteenth century *and it was not done.* That is one of the most important reasons, according to some feminist thinkers, that the First Wave of feminism did not succeed. Here are some of hooks's many comments on the matter:

> Every women's movement in America from its earliest origin to the present day has been built on a racist foundation. . . . To a very grave extent women obtaining the right to vote was more a victory for racist principles than a triumph of feminist principles.

> On every occasion Sojourner Truth spoke, groups of white women protested. . . . When Sojourner Truth stood before the second annual convention of the women's rights movement in Akron, Ohio, in 1852, white women who deemed it unfitting that a black woman should speak on a public platform in their presence, screamed: "Don't let her speak! Don't let her speak! Don't let her speak!"

> While white women were rejoicing over obtaining the right to vote, a system of racial apartheid was being institutionized throughout the U.S. that would threaten the freedom of black women far more crucially than sexual imperialism.[55]

There are many, many other examples of racism in the First Wave in the United States, including much outright and shameful bigotry.[56] Giddings devotes a good deal of space to the matter. Here are some of her comments. When the Fifteenth Amendment, for manhood suffrage, was proposed in 1869:

The feminist and abolitionist camps weren't neatly divided. Leading White feminists like Lucy Stone and Julia Ward Howe did not believe the world would come to an end if Black men—whose leadership was sympathetic to woman suffrage and promised to work toward that end—were enfranchised first. On the other hand, in addition to Truth, several prominent Blacks like Charles Redmond, Robert Purvis, and his wife Harriet (Forten), leaned toward enfranchising women in tandem with or even before Black men, despite the political difficulty. . . . "In an hour like this, I repudiate the idea of expediency," Redmond had said at an earlier . . . meeting. "All I ask for myself I claim for my wife and sister."[57]

Frances Ellen Watkins Harper, the famous nineteenth-century Black poet, novelist, and abolitionist, criticized her White feminist colleagues: "The white women all go for sex, letting race occupy a minor position," she said. But for her, "Being black means that every white, including every white working-class woman, can discriminate against you."[58]

Elizabeth Cady Stanton, despite her warning that "if Black women weren't given the ballot, they would be 'fated to a triple bondage' " went so far as to use racist agitation against the proposal for manhood suffrage. Giddings describes her alliance with

> millionaire Democrat, George Train, who financed their feminist newspaper, *The Revolution*. Within its pages . . . "the dominant party . . ." wrote [Susan B.] Anthony, "have dethroned FIFTEEN MILLION WHITE WOMEN . . . and cast them under the heel of the lowest orders of manhood."

> Stanton . . . wrote . . . that giving Black men the vote was virtually a license to rape. . . . In 1866, Stanton introduced the idea that middle-class women should be enfranchised to stave off the poor, the immigrants, and the Blacks . . . whom she called "incoming pauperism, ignorance and degradation." [Thus] . . . she . . . wrote in *The Revolution*, "We prefer Bridget and Dinah at the ballot box to Patrick and Sambo."[59]

Worse still:

> Under the guiding hand of Susan B. Anthony and Elizabeth Cady Stanton, NAWSA [the National American Women's Suffrage Association] adopted a strategy of "expediency." . . . "The

government is menaced with a great danger," observed Carrie Chapman Catt in 1894. "That danger lies in the votes possessed by the males in the slums of the cities and the ignorant foreign vote." . . .

By the turn of the century, Anthony and other suffrage veterans were making way for a new generation of activists in NAWSA. Included were southern White women. . . . In 1906 a Kentucky Democrat, writing to an Ohio Republican (both national leaders in the NAWSA) . . . [wrote] "The National [Association] has always recognized the usefulness of woman suffrage as a . . . means of legally preserving White supremacy in the South. In the campaign in South Carolina we . . . never hesitated to show that the White women's vote would give supremacy to the White race. And we have also freely used the same argument to the foreign-born vote."[60]

Later, part of Anthony's strategy of expediency was to ally herself with Frances Willard, whose position on lynching may be gauged by the following:

> On a recent tour of the South, Willard . . . [had said in a published interview] "The colored race multiplies like the locusts of Egypt . . . and the grogshop is the center of power. . . . The safety of women, of childhood, of the home, is menaced in a thousand localities."[61]

In 1894:

> Susan B. Anthony asked Frederick Douglass not to attend the forthcoming NAWSA convention in Atlanta Georgia. . . . Douglass was the only man to speak on behalf of suffrage at the Seneca Falls convention in 1848. . . . At the convention in 1895, Elizabeth Cady Stanton's speech warned against the dangers of enfranchising illiterate women. . . . [Later] when a group of Black women asked her to help in organizing a branch of NAWSA, she refused—on the grounds, she said, that it would be inexpedient.

Later:

> [During a] bitter effort to make NAWSA women take a stand against segregated seating on trains . . . [Anthony refused] to

support the resolution. "We women are a helpless, disenfranchised class," she said. "Our hands are tied . . . it is not for us to go passing resolutions against railroad corporations or anybody else."[62]

After Anthony's death:

> When a huge suffrage march was organized in 1913 . . . [Black activist] Ida Wells-Barnett . . . was told that she could not march with the all-White Chicago contingent of suffragists for fear of offending southern women. For the sake of "expediency," the march for suffrage would be segregated. . . . But when the parade got under way, she was nowhere to be found. All were surprised when she suddenly appeared from behind the crowd of onlookers as the Chicago delegation made its way past her. She simply slipped into line, between two White women, and marched as she pleased.[63]

Giddings notes that "In 1914 White suffragists had not challenged the efforts of the Illinois state legislature to eliminate Black women from the voting rolls after it had enfranchised women in the state." Why? Black activist Walter White wrote to Mary Church Terrell: "Just as you say, all of them [white suffragists] are mortally afraid of the South and if they could get the Suffrage Amendment through without enfranchising colored women, they would do it in a moment."[64]

In 1919 NAWSA's Northeastern Federation of Women's Clubs, representing six thousand Blacks, applied for cooperative membership in the organization. NAWSA

> begged the federation to withdraw their application, temporarily, until the suffrage amendment was passed . . . [White suffragist Ida Husted Harper] concluded that if the Black women proceeded with their application, the entire struggle could be defeated. Couldn't they "sacrifice" the "immediate gratification" by applying at a later time?

And yet—Giddings takes considerable pleasure in pointing this out—in 1972:

> A Louis Harris–Virginia Slims poll . . . revealed that 62 percent of Black women favored "efforts to strengthen or change women's status in society," compared with only 45 percent of

White women. Even more startling, perhaps, 67 percent of Black women expressed "sympathy with efforts of women's liberation groups," compared with only 35 percent of White women![65]

Although I do not recommend eliminating racism from the White women's movement for prudential reasons only—surely the moral reasons are compelling enough—White feminists might nonetheless ponder those figures. There is another reason too, one I want to emphasize here. Staying in charge of feminism is personally comfortable and personally gratifying for White women and may avoid the struggles and problems talked about in this chapter (as well as some others), but if we do, *we will lose*. Not only will we lose allies and our moral decency—no small matter for a radical movement whose position is founded not on armies but on its claims to justice—we will lose something of even greater importance: *the ability to understand the interconnections between different kinds of oppression*. That is, we will lose any possibility of developing an accurate map of the world. And if we don't have that, we will fail, even in getting anything for ourselves.

NOTES

1. The title of Chapter XII is taken from the last lines of a poem by Jo Carillo. She calls it her "poem to land that, along with South Dakota, is a 'proposed National Sacrifice' area for energy (uranium, coal, coal gasification, etc.)." Carillo writes about White appropriation of Native American land, cultures, and people, and the dangers of radon-emitting, cancer-causing uranium mining. At one point she asks why "Navajos and other assorted types" work in the dangerous mines while the safe and more profitable trading posts are "all / worked over / by whites" (Cherríe Moraga and Gloria Anzaldúa, eds., *This Bridge Called My Back: Writings by Radical Women of Color* [Watertown, MA: Persephone Press, 1981], 65–67).

2. In Lydia Sargent, ed., *Women and Revolution: A Discussion of the Unhappy Marriage of Marxism and Feminism* (Boston: South End Press, 1981), 103.

3. The union was the teachers' union in New York City, which was quite active when I was a child. More important was the tradition of my mother's family and my parents' personal commitment. Not actually a "red diaper baby" (child brought up by socialist parents), I was nonetheless in a decidedly "pink" family. One of my aunts had traveled to Mexico in the 1930s "to live with the people" and had returned with lovely Mexican pottery and Diego Rivera prints. My elementary school friends came from cooperative, worker-owned housing (the famous Bronx Projects), which I learned about only many years later in Vivian Gornick's *The Romance of American Communism*. My father had almost joined a marxist study group

in the 1930s. His explanation to me of why the Soviet Union, our ally in World War II, suddenly became our enemy in the 1950s was pure economics. None of this constituted anything like a rigorous education in socialism, but it did make the socialism I met later in life look awfully familiar and not anything I would immediately find weird or reject out of hand.

4. Cited in Bettina Aptheker, " 'Strong Is What We Make Each Other': Unlearning Racism within Women's Studies," *Women's Studies Quarterly* 9:4 (1981), 15.

5. A fuller quotation of what Joseph actually said is:

> Adrienne Rich's recent article on feminism and racism is an exemplary one on this topic. . . . but the acclaim given to her article shows again that it takes whiteness to give . . . Blackness credibility (in Sargent, *Women and Revolution,* 105).

6. In Gloria T. Hull et al., eds., *All the Women Are White, All the Blacks Are Men, but Some of Us Are Brave: Black Women's Studies* (Old Westbury, NY: Feminist Press, 1982), 53.

7. In Elly Bulkin et al., *Yours in Struggle: Three Feminist Perspectives on Anti-Semitism and Racism* (Brooklyn, NY: Long Haul Press, 1984), 77, 71.

8. Ibid., 146, sections reversed.

9. Ten years ago I would have protested that the phrase "White women's movement" was inaccurate. Surely I was part of "the women's movement" for all "women." Nope.

10. In Barbara E. Smith, ed., *Home Girls: A Black Feminist Anthology* (New York: Kitchen Table Women of Color Press, 1983), 55.

11. Moraga and Anzaldúa, *This Bridge,* 206.

12. Gloria Joseph and Jill Lewis, *Common Differences: Conflicts in Black and White Feminist Perspectives* (New York: Anchor, 1981), 40.

13. In Hull et al., *All the Women,* 10.

14. In Lorraine Bethel and Barbara Smith, eds., *Conditions Five: The Black Women's Issue* (1979), 88.

15. In Moraga and Anzaldúa, *This Bridge,* 63.

16. In Sargent, *Women and Revolution,* 102.

17. Carroll in Hull et al., *All the Women,* 126.

18. In Moraga and Anzaldúa, *This Bridge,* 73.

19. In Smith, *Home Girls,* 301.

20. bell hooks, *Ain't I a Woman* (Boston: South End Press, 1981), 121–22.

21. Ibid., 144–45; bell hooks, *Feminist Theory from Margin to Center* (Boston: South End Press, 1984), 12, 12–13.

22. Walker in Hull et al., *All the Women,* 40; Audre Lorde, *Sister Outsider: Essays and Speeches* (Trumansburg, NY: The Crossing Press, 1984), 117, Carroll in Hull et al., *All the Women,* 122–23; Canaan in Moraga and Anzaldúa, *This Bridge,*

237; Combahee River Collective in ibid., 218. Moraga and Anzaldúa's editors' note states:

> The Combahee River Collective is a Black feminist group in Boston whose name comes from the guerilla action conceptualized and led by Harriet Tubman on June 2, 1863, in the Port Royal region of South Carolina. This action freed more than 750 slaves and is the only military campaign in American history planned and led by a woman (ibid., 210). The Collective's statement identifies the group as having met together since 1974.

23. Smith in Sargent, *Women in Revolution,* 92; Walker in Hull et al., *All the Women,* 39; Yamada in Moraga and Anzaldúa, *This Bridge,* 72; Parker in ibid., 241.

24. Smith, *Home Girls,* xxxiv; Smith in Hull et al., *All the Women,* 49.

25. Perez in Mary Bragg et al., eds., *Lesbian Psychologies: Explorations and Challenges* (Urbana: University of Illinois Press, 1987), 149.

26. Davenport in Moraga and Anzaldúa, *This Bridge,* 85.

27. Lorde, *Sister Outsider,* 110, 113. The panel was "The Personal and the Political" at the Second Sex Conference held in New York, 29 September 1979.

28. Carroll in Hull et al., *All the Women,* 123; Yamada in Moraga and Anzaldúa, *This Bridge,* 71.

29. hooks, *Feminist Theory,* 13.

30. Yamada in Moraga and Anzaldúa, *This Bridge,* 71. She goes on to say, in connection with the stereotype of Japanese women as "least political": "It is too bad not many people remember that one of the two persons in Seattle who stood up to contest the constitutionality of the Evacuation Order in 1942 was a young Japanese American woman" (ibid.).

31. Woo in Moraga and Anzaldúa, *This Bridge,* 143; hooks, *Feminist Theory,* 53; Moraga and Anzaldúa, *This Bridge,* 61.

32. Paula Giddings, *When and Where I Enter: The Impact of Black Women on Race and Sex in America* (New York: Morrow, 1984), 305. Giddings also describes how NOW dealt with minority issues in the late 1970s: Aileen Hernandez's attempts to organize a NOW minority task force, NOW's "sponsoring chapters in minority communities rather than dealing with minority issues" (a policy she finds arrogant), and the election of an all-White group of officers for the second straight year in 1979, "although a Black woman, Sharon Parker, who had headed the minority task force, was running for a national secretary position. . . . Eleanor Smeal, campaigning for reelection, failed to endorse her." Giddings adds:

> Hernandez, once the organization's president and defender, accused NOW of being too white and middle-class. In 1979 she sponsored a resolution, saying that Blacks should quit

NOW or refrain from joining the group until it confronted
its own racism and that of the larger society (ibid. 346–47).

33. Ibid., 337–40; Carroll in Hull et al., *All the Women,* 123.

34. Alice Walker, *In Search of Our Mother's Gardens: Womanist Prose* (New
York: Harcourt, 1983), 378, 375.

35. hooks, *Ain't I a Woman,* 7.

36. Woo in Moraga and Anzaldúa, *This Bridge,* 144; Bethel in Bethel and
Smith, *Conditions Five,* 85.

37. hooks, *Ain't I a Woman,* 141; Lorde, *Sister Outsider,* 132; Moraga and
Anzaldúa, *This Bridge,* 168.

38. Garcia in Bragg et al., *Lesbian Psychologies,* 149; Moschkovich in Moraga
and Anzaldúa, *This Bridge,* 83; Chrystos in ibid., 69.

39. Yamada in ibid., 35.

40. Lorde, *Sister Outsider,* 130, 95–96. Of course, there are differences of
degree. Lorde's students' racism (maybe because they *were* students and she their
teacher) seems to me a good deal less ghastly than the condescension of Anaïs Nin,
for example, who expressed in her diary her opinions of Millicent Fredericks, whom
Nin employed as a housemaid. Fredericks, a schoolteacher in Antigua, was not
allowed to teach in Europe. Gabrielle Daniels, who celebrates Fredericks in her own
"anthology of forgotten Third World women . . . *A Woman Left Behind,*" writes:

> Anaïs could not get beyond the fact of Millicent's blackness
> and poverty and suffering. The stench of the *padrona* just
> reeks about her. . . . "I would like to write the life of Milli-
> cent. But saints' lives are difficult to do. . . . A Negro is a
> concept. . . . Millicent perhaps . . . becomes a symbol of
> what they have to endure. . . . I would like to devote my life
> to the recognition of the Negro's equality, but I always feel
> ineffectual in political battles" (Moraga and Anzaldúa, *This
> Bridge,* 76).

41. Bethel in Bethel and Smith, *Conditions Five,* 88.

42. hooks, *Feminist Theory,* 11; Morales in Moraga and Anzaldúa, *This Bridge,*
54.

43. Cameron in ibid., 51.

44. Moschkovich in ibid., 82, 79.

45. Smith in Bulkin et al., *Yours in Struggle,* 75.

46. Sherman in Hull et al., *All the Women,* 252; Yellin in ibid., 223; Berry in
ibid., xv; Dandridge in ibid., 261; Williams et al. in ibid., 298; Lorde, *Sister Outsider,*
125.

47. Bulkin et al., *Yours in Struggle,* 145.

48. Pence in Hull et al., *All the Women,* 47.

49. Pearlman in Bragg et al., *Lesbian Psychologies,* 150.
50. Smith in Bulkin et al., *Yours in Struggle,* 79.
51. Pence in Hull et al., *All the Women,* 46.
52. Bulkin et al., *Yours in Struggle,* 144.
53. Pratt in ibid., 30, 18, 19. That is precisely how I was taught to think about American Indian people in the 1950s. They were either totally assimilated or somehow of the same era (and as distant and un Human) as the rocks and the fossils.

Here's Barbara Smith quoting from a review of Toni Morrison's novel *Sula* by Sara Blackburn in *The New York Times Book Review,* 30 December 1973:

> Toni Morrison is far too talented to remain only a marvelous recorder of the black side of provincial American life. If she is to maintain the large and serious audience she deserves, she is going to have to address riskier contemporary reality than this beautiful but nonetheless distanced novel. And if she does this, it seems to me that she might easily transcend that early and unintentionally limiting classification "black woman writer" (Smith, *Toward a Black Feminist Criticism* [Brooklyn, NY: Out and Out Books, 1977], 6).

It's likely, racism sometimes being as sneaky as it is, that some White readers of this book will want to defend Blackburn by saying she didn't "really" mean to put down Morrison or even that "we" can't "really" tell what Blackburn "really" meant. The review is confusing (and confused)—what, after all, is wrong with recording provincial life ("regionalism" has long been an automatic putdown of many White women writers) or Black life? Why does Blackburn call *Sula,* that very passionate book, "distanced"? And if the classification "Black woman writer" is only limiting "unintentionally" (and who intends it?), why is it still desirable that Morrison "transcend" it? Why not simply ignore it, since it is no real hindrance to her already being one of the "most serious, important and talented American novelists now working"? However I try to get Blackburn's review off the hook, in the end I agree with Smith, who says, "Blackburn unashamedly asserts that Morrison is 'too talented' to deal with mere Black folk" (ibid). That is, Morrison's subject matter, her own roots, is somehow not worthy of her talent.

54. In Bulkin et al., *Yours in Struggle,* 50.
55. hooks, *Ain't I a Woman,* 124, 171, 128, 159, 172.
56. For example, hooks writes, quoting Rayford Logan in *The Betrayal of the Negro:*

> [At the end of the nineteenth century] at the Atlanta Exposition . . . the Georgia Women's Press Club felt so strongly on the subject [of integration] that members were in favor

of withdrawing from the Federation [of women's clubs] if
colored women were admitted there (ibid., 129).

57. Giddings, *When and Where,* 68.
58. Ibid.
59. Ibid., 65, 66, 66–67.
60. Ibid., 124–26.
61. Ibid., 91
62. Ibid., 126, 127.
63. Ibid., 127–28.
64. Ibid., 159, 160.
65. Ibid., 161–62, 345.

THIRTEEN

"O.K., MUMMA, WHO THE HELL AM I?"[1]

How I cherish this collection of cables, esoesses, conjurations and fusile missiles.

—Toni Cade Bambara[2]

Because an accurate map of the world matters—no radical movement can do without one—the women whose work makes up the last chapter are particularly important for any and every radical movement in the United States. I believe their power to make such a map comes from something very particular in their lives. Look, for example, at Gloria Anzaldúa's vivid and poetic expression of it: "This task—to be a bridge, to be a fucking crossroads, for goddess' sake." Poet Donna Kate Rushin also calls herself a "bridge" who constantly finds herself mediating—that is, translating—every group to every other group and often every person to every other person.[3] And Rosario Morales says something similar:

> I am a whole circus by myself   a whole dance company with
> stance
> and posture for being in middle class homes in upper class
> buildings
> for talking to men   for speaking with blacks   for care-
> fully
> angling and directing   for choreographing my way thru the
> maze of classes
> of people and places thru the little boxes of sex   race
>   class
> nationality   sexual orientation   intellectual standing
>   political preference   the automatic contortions   the
> exhausting

camouflage with which I go thru this social space called
CAPITALIST PATRIARCHY[4]

Elsewhere Moraga and Anzaldúa explain the pervasive sense of strain as a result of attempting to handle being women of color in a White feminist movement, feminists in their own culture, and often lesbians among non-lesbians in both cultures.[5]

Such statements may at first appear to be describing the experience of being a minority *within* another minority. Yet Moraga certainly seems to be emphasizing something quite different when she writes of the "contradictions in our experience." Here's a similar statement by Tracey A. Gardner: "As a Black woman, I find myself in limbo. My experiences and concerns don't quite fit—not in the Black Liberation Movement, nor in the Women's Movement."

If the lesbian of color has no camp to retreat to (as Moraga says)[6], that is because neither the lesbian community, which is largely White and racist, nor the community of people of her color, which, like most communities, is largely heterosexist, will admit her. Barbara Smith speaks, in this context, of the "near non-existence of Black Lesbian literature" and quotes Ann Allen Shockley, fiction writer and theorist, to similar effect: "Ann Allen Shockley called the Black lesbian 'analogous to Ralph Ellison's "invisible man" . . . 'seen, but not seen.'" Anita Valerio says, "My lesbianism has become a barrier between myself and my people," and sociologist Oliva M. Espin sums up the result of her research with Latina lesbians: "Because as a Latina she is an ethnic minority person, she must be bicultural in American society. Because she is a lesbian, she must be polycultural among her own people."[7]

Perhaps it's clearer now that being in a "multiple minority" doesn't simply mean being in a small group located *within* a larger one that is, in its turn, a minority group *inside* the dominant U.S. society. What matters is, first, that *both groups are oppressed* and, second, that *the oppressions do not simply add up; they interact*—and that they do so in a particular way. That is, *membership in the groups conflicts,* and furthermore, *this conflict lies at the very heart of one's being.* That is, it is a split in identity that exists inside the person psychologically *because* it has a previous, objective existence socially and politically outside the person. Nor does this split come merely from the ordinary Human difficulties of belonging to two overlapping groups. Rather, it comes from the objective and quite impersonal fact that membership in each group somehow disqualifies one from membership in the other—but that at the same time one still belongs to both, and both have strong claims on one's loyalties precisely because both are oppressed by the dominant society. For example, as Espin notes elsewhere, "Most members of the Puerto Rican community strongly reject lesbianism." Barbara Smith, asked to describe her experience "in dealing with homophobic Black sisters," says, "There's nothing to compare with how you feel when you're cut cold by your own." And as Espin puts it: "The threat of possible rejection and stigmatization by the Latin community becomes more of a psychological burden for the Hispanic lesbian. Rejection from mainstream society does not carry the same weight."[8]

Again and again such women describe having to live out such conflicting, paradoxical, and very stressful identities. Lorde writes:

> Over and over again in the 60s I was asked to justify my existence and my work . . . because some piece of me was not acceptable. . . . [Now] I find I am constantly being encouraged to pluck out some one aspect of myself and present this as the meaningful whole, eclipsing or denying the other parts of self. But this is a destructive and fragmenting way to live.[9]

Moraga writes about being caught between identities:

> I am the daughter of a Chicana and an anglo. I think most days I am an embarrassment to both groups.[10]

Tania Abdulahad observes of a woman of color she knows:

> Because she's light [skinned] . . . she's constantly dealing with invisibility and isolation. On the one hand whites almost always assume she's white—which drives her up a wall. In situations with darker Third World people her presence and identity might be questioned.[11]

Inevitably the split in one's situation, one's group memberships, is experienced not only as stress but as a genuine split in identity, in "belongingness." This is how Morales describes her situation: "I am U.S. American. I haven't wanted to say it because if I did you'd take away the Puerto Rican."[12]

Conflicts range from the obvious, like Anita Valerio's feeling that her lesbianism led her to a barrier between herself and her people, to the subtle.[13] Spring Redd's family, Puerto Rican in culture on her mother's side but American Black on her father's side, were expected to be part of the Afro-American culture in Cambridge, Massachusetts (where there were few Puerto Ricans and none of their friends spoke Spanish).[14]

Red Jordan Arobateau writes in the short story "Nobody's People": "So what am I? White? Black? Latin? Mixed? There's always been people like me—Quadroons. . . . Not black, but black."[15]

Such political and class ambiguities abound among these writers. Here Mirtha Quintanales describes her childhood:

> Yet even though I grew up [in Cuba] having to heat my bath-water and sleep in a very lumpy bed. . . . [and] our furniture was old and dilapidated, I went to private schools, spent sum-mers at the beach. . . . [Even so] as an ethnic minority woman and a lesbian I have lived in the margins, in fear, isolated, dis-connected, silent and in pain.[16]

Other contradictions and conflicts may not be recognized until years later. Mitsuye Yamada writes of her early adulthood:

> My father reassured me that it was "all right" for me to be a pacifist [during World War II] because as a Japanese national and a "girl" *it didn't make any difference to anyone.* . . . My brother Mike, an American citizen, was suddenly expelled from the University of Cincinnati while I, "an enemy alien," was per-mitted to stay. . . . My presence on campus was not as threat-ening.[17]

Morales describes the illumination of reading Piri Thomas's *Down These Mean Streets:*

> The junkies [in the book] could be my younger brothers. The prisoners could be them. I could be the prostitute, the welfare mother, the sister and lover of junkies, the child of alcoholics. There is nothing but circumstance and good English, nothing but my mother marrying into the middle class, between me and that life. . . . [Then] I borrow the pictures from my other family, the nightmares of my Jewish ancestry, and imagine them fleeing through the streets.[18]

Chrystos, a lesbian, writes of her Menominee father:

> *He gave me all the whitest advantages*
> *square house, football school,*
> *white mother baking white bread in a white oven*

He wanted to spare me his pain
Didn't

. . . .

I don't like this man who cut off his hair
joined the government to be safe[19]

There is enormous pressure on these women (as there is on all Human beings, I suspect) to "place" themselves—that is, to choose for themselves a single identity that will be recognized by some group and to discard what doesn't "fit." The problem in their cases is that such a choice is simply not possible. All feminists of color face at least two conflicting pressures of this sort, and feminists of color who are lesbians *as well* or in the working class *as well* or who belong to some other oppressed group *as well* face even more complex pressures. What Human beings can make of such situations varies, but one of the possible responses to such situations (when circumstances permit it at all) is *creativity*. That is, it is precisely because of the impossibilities these women face every day in their ordinary lives that they have become the pioneers they are in challenging all sorts of assumptions about what constitutes group, ethnic, racial, or other kinds of "identity" and "belonging" and in making connections between the multitudinous oppressions that make up U.S. (and world) society. Mirtha Quintanales writes:

> Many of us Latinas are non-white. . . . Ask a Black or "mulatto" Puerto Rican woman what her identity is, though, and most likely she will tell you "Puerto Rican". . . . Ask a Nigerian, an Ethiopian, etc. what her identity is and she will tell you "Nigerian" or "Ethiopian" or whatever. . . . Obviously "Black Culture" is an American phenomenon.[20]

And here is Michelle Cliff, with a description of just what complexities can happen when several of these conflicting identities—well, conflict. Cliff is in London where neither her light skin nor her accent signal to the English that she is a Black Jamaican. Nor does her "ladylike" appearance or unmarried state signal anything either to the English or to her dark-skinned relatives. Cliff is also a feminist *and* an anti-imperialist *and* her cousin's education is being paid for by a U.S. company that is exploiting the mineral resources of their native island. In short, no one knows who she is totally, and her loyalties are on more sides than one:

> A cousin is visiting from M.I.T. . . . My cousin is recognizably Black and speaks with an accent. I am not and I do not—unless

I am back home, where the "twang" comes upon me. We sit
for some time in a bar in his hotel and are not served. A light-
skinned Jamaican comes over to our table. . . . an older man—a
professor at the University of London. "Don't bother with it,
you hear. They don't serve us in this bar." A run-of-the-mill
incident for all recognizably Black people in this city. But for
me it is not.

Henry's [the cousin's] eyes fill up, but he refuses to believe
our informant. "No, man, the girl is just busy." (The girl is a
fifty-year-old white woman, who may just be following orders,
but I do not mention this. I have chosen sides.) All I can manage
to say, "Jesus Christ, I hate the fucking English." Henry looks
at me. (In the family I am known as the "lady cousin." It has
to do with how I look. And the fact that I am twenty-seven and
unmarried. . . .) Our informant says—gently, but with a distinct tone of disappointment—"My dear, is that what you're
studying at the university?" . . .

You see—the whole business is very complicated.

Henry and I leave without drinks and go to meet some of his
white colleagues at a restaurant I know near Covent Garden
Opera House. . . . I tell myself, the owners are Italian *and* gay;
they *must* be halfway decent. . . . At dinner Henry joins the
white men in a sustained mockery of the waiters: their accents
and the way they walk. He whispers to me: "Why you want to
bring us to a battyman's den, lady?" (*Battyman* = *faggot* in Jamaican.) I keep quiet.[21]

Shortly afterward comes the final irony of the above incident: Cousin Henry
propositions Cousin Michelle, and she has to think up an excuse that will
neither threaten his already shaken self-esteem nor reveal that she is not
the "lady cousin" but the lesbian cousin.

What do people do when repeatedly confronted with situations in which
their identities and their loyalties cannot all be on one side? They ponder a
good deal about what constitutes identity and what situations construct it.

They also become very aware of the pain such situations can cause and
the unfairness of having to live in them. Espin writes about the women she
interviewed:

When confronted with the choice of being among Latins without coming out, or living among lesbians who are not Latin or
who are unfamiliar with Latin culture, eleven of the women
said they had chosen or would choose the second alternative.

However, this choice is not made without ambivalence. . . . A twenty-seven-year-old woman from Miami expressed not only the ambivalence, but also the pain and anger associated with choosing between different parts of herself. . . . "It is a very painful question because I feel that I am both, and I don't want to have to choose."[22]

Some of these writers make poetry out of the conflicts themselves. Anzaldúa writes:

Both cultures deny me a place in *their* universe. Between them and among others, I build my own universe, El Mundo Zurdo [The Left Handed World]. . . . I walk the tightrope with ease and grace I span abysses. . . . I walk the rope—an acrobat in equipoise, expert at the Balancing Act.[23]

But above all, the women whose work I'm quoting from solve their impossible situations not by choosing this or that identity and letting the rest go, nor by constructing their own universes *but by refusing to let any part of themselves go at all.* In a society that insists they must be one thing or another, between groups that insist they cannot bring their whole selves anywhere, *they solve the "problem" by refusing its terms.* Some of Garcia's interviewees, for example, do indeed make the choice that Garcia's interview forced upon them; they choose, even though they express pain or ambivalence. But one interviewee, says the researcher, "expressed a strong rejection" of the question itself, declaring flatly, "This is a false dichotomy."[24] It is precisely this refusal to choose that marks the politics of the radical women of color whose work I'm quoting in this chapter, and, as I see it, it is precisely their refusal to submit to such false dichotomies that is the source of the extraordinary strength and brilliance of their politics. As Byllye Avery said at a 1987 conference, "Claim every piece of who you are."[25]

Although, says Yamada, most women of color are made to feel that they must choose between their feminism and their ethnic identity: "This doesn't mean we have placed our loyalties on the side of ethnicity over womanhood. The two are not at war with one another; we shouldn't have to sign a 'loyalty oath' favoring one over the other." What Morales actually wrote earlier (I changed it) is: "I am what I am and I am U.S. American   I haven't wanted to say it because if I did you'd take away the Puerto Rican *but now I say go to hell.*"[26] Hooks states:

As a black woman interested in [the] feminist movement I am often asked whether being black is more important than being a woman: whether feminist struggle to end sexist oppression is more important than the struggle to end racism and vice-versa. All such questions are rooted in competitive either/or thinking, the belief that the self is formed in opposition to an other. . . . Rather than see anti-racist works totally compatible with working to end sexist oppression, they are often seen as two movements competing for first place.[27]

Andrea Canaan, speaking of the Black man, calls choosing between women's liberation and Black liberation "this diabolical, self-destructive game."[28] The editors of *Cuentos: Stories by Latinas,* Alma Gómez, Cherríe Moraga, and Mariana Romo-Carmona, highlight this issue in their introduction:

As Latinas living in the U.S., the issues of bilingualism and biculturalism are crucial. . . . Mixing English and Spanish in our writing and talking is a legitimate and creative response to acculturation. It doesn't mean that we are illiterate or assimilated as we are sometimes labeled by the anglo and Latin American elite.[29]

Elly Bulkin, a White lesbian radical who is also Eastern European Jewish American, says:

I think . . . of the decisions to celebrate one's identity: for those Native American women, Latinas, and Black women who could "pass" as white; for the Jewish woman whose father changed his name in the thirties so he could "make it," and raised her, ignorant of her identity, as a Christian; for the Arab-American woman, who, after internalizing her racial oppression, came only in the last few years to identify as a woman of color; for the Jewish-Latina, the Arab-Jewish woman, for any Jewish woman of color who is too often, as one Jamaican-Jewish woman has said, "a token to everybody"; for any woman of color of mixed heritage—Chinese-Korean, Native American-Black, Asian-Black, Chicana; for the Arab-American dyke who is shunned because she is a lesbian by the only other Arab woman in town, the Jewish lesbian whose family sits *shivah* [mourning for the dead] for her, the "bulldagger" whose Black community rejects her. All of the women who, told to choose between or among identities, insist on selecting all.[30]

And here is Red Jordan Arobateau:

I could choose the easy way; I too could sit back comfortable, adapting the style of the master race; or tan my skin one shade darker and perminite the strands of my hair into curls so I would belong. . . . [But] the stone that was rejected has become the cornerstone.[31]

Once someone has made the enormous creative advance of *refusing the terms* of Canaan's "diabolical self destructive game," the way is open for all sorts of advances in understanding and analysis. It then becomes possible to note, as Chrystos does, that support and understanding do not always come from the places they "should." As she writes, "I have felt less understanding between different races & from many lesbian women than I do from some straight people." It also becomes possible to notice, as Quintanales does, the oppression visited on others who belong to a group that is at the same time oppressing yours. "My lover. Working-class 'white' woman from a small town. She has no more privileges than I do. As alone as I am. She is not my enemy. World upside down."[32]

Above all, it becomes possible to identify behavior as the enemy and to find that enemy even in oneself, as Barbara Smith does when she notes that she catches herself perceiving people stereotypically or assuming that English is universally understood.[33]

None of the above is as simple (or simple-minded) as "thinking of people as individuals only" or "transcending" any kind of group identity or experience. These thinkers have not "forgotten" their marginality. Their understanding of their multiple oppressions is exquisitely sensitive, tough, active, and constant. To think otherwise is like watching the lady in pink sequins in the circus, who stands with her right foot on the back of one galloping horse, her left foot on the back of another, with the reins of fifteen more in her hands, and concluding that because she isn't falling down, she must be standing on solid ground. Marilyn Frye, like Bulkin a White feminist and a lesbian, speaks to this kind of misunderstanding when she says:

Often, in discussion about prejudice and discrimination, I hear statements like these: "I don't think of myself as heterosexual"; "I don't think of myself as white"; "I don't think of myself as a man". . . . If one is the norm, one does not have to know what one is. If one is marginal, one does not have the privilege of not noticing what one is.[34]

The women I'm speaking of here have not created their politics out of forgetting their oppressions. Neither is their politics simply a result—or a simple result—of oppression. Rather it is a creative response to a conflict built into their experience by the objective circumstances of their lives. It is these objective circumstances and their response to them that makes them the wonderful poets and social and political activists that they are. I believe (unless I'm misunderstanding her) that this is what Lorde means when she speaks of "those of us who stand outside the circle of this society's definition of acceptable women; those of us who have been forged in the crucibles of difference" and goes on to say, "Difference is that raw and powerful connection from which our personal power is forged."[35]

I do not, however much I prize these writers' work, want to romanticize the cost of such personal power. The creativity with which some Human beings can respond to oppression doesn't mean that oppression doesn't hurt them and hurt *and silence* many, many others. Oppression isn't thereby made unimportant or "all right." The cost is much, much too high. That is another clear and totally unmistakable message in their material. Again and again these thinkers speak of the pain of oppression and the particular pain of multiple oppressions, of fitting in nowhere. Once in a long while it's possible to fit in—and this "fit" is no everyday matter to those who've never experienced it before. Quintanales, a lesbian, writes:

> I remember this one party . . . so many Cuban and Puerto Rican women . . . I was so excited I wanted to cry. *Everything "felt right."*[36]

Moraga says much the same about another situation:

> There in the front row, nodding encouragement and identification, sat. . . . five avowed Latina Feminists. . . . *For once in my life every part of me was allowed to be visible and spoken for in one room at one time.*[37]

Although I don't want to romanticize these "differences," I also don't want to overemphasize the pain involved in them. What is most important for analyzing and understanding social structures is that belonging to what I shall call "conflicting minorities" *makes it impossible to ignore the interactive nature of different oppressions.* Feminist radicals of color state this over and over again. For example, Beverly Smith says:

> I think . . . what we try to do is to break things down and try to separate and compare but in reality, the way women live their lives, those separations just don't work. Women don't live their lives like, "Well, this part is race, and this is class, and this part has to do with women's identities," so it's confusing.[38]

The Combahee River Collective explicitly includes this process and the insight it provides as part of their April 1977 statement:

> In our consciousness-raising sessions . . . we have in many ways gone beyond white women's revelations because we are dealing with the implications of race and class as well as sex.[39]

When many things interact to oppress you, you can't deceive yourself that if only one change were made in society, everything would be all right. Michelle Wallace says, "Being on the bottom, we would have to do what no one else has done: we would have to fight the world." Nor can you rank oppressions as more or less crucial when, says Barbara Smith, "everything out there was kicking our behinds—race, class, sex and homophobia."[40] And also, says Smith:

> This is why Third World women are forming the leadership in the feminist movement. . . . we certainly define race and usually define class as being fundamental issues.[41]

Whereupon Beverly Smith adds, "Third world women are not in actual leadership *positions* in the women's movement in terms of policy making, etc. But we certainly have the vision."[42]

I agree. They do. And that is why a women's movement controlled by White women, a movement that does not therefore confront its own racism, is bound to fail. It's not only that U.S. racism has been and continues to be costly, dangerous, and tragic. It's also that those whose oppression is merely singular can entertain the very destructive and misleading illusion that if only one thing were changed—*their* oppression—everything would be all right. As Moraga puts it, it should be impossible not to notice the oppression of others, but oppressed groups do this all the time.[43]

How can they? I'd say that what's "wrong" with those groups whose minority membership is singular and uncomplicated (let alone those who belong to the dominant social group) is not that they're especially nasty Human beings. Rather, the problems are structural. What's wrong, for example, with affluent White gay men *as a group* (although there are certainly some honorable exceptions) is not their personal characters but their social position. Otherwise perfect candidates for privilege and power, with their consequent unconsciousnesses and immunities, they're nonetheless oppressed because of their sexual orientation. People in such a position of singular oppression either make real and active common cause with other oppressed groups—which takes extraordinary imagination and conscience, Humanly rare by definition—or they identify themselves with the ruling group/class/sex and adopt its bigotries in a vain attempt to become part of it.[46] Most of the White feminists I know are like this. I am like this. I know I am. I've been this way for decades, I didn't change spontaneously and without a constant struggle, I slide right back into being this way again. Furthermore I don't trust myself or the White feminists I know not to do so again and again. But I do trust the women of color I've been quoting in this chapter. These thinkers and activists and others like them are the moral and intellectual center of the feminist movement in the United States and they are—or they jolly well ought to be—the moral and intellectual center of the U.S. Left.

And that is why the White feminist movement must accept the leadership of feminists of color if feminism is not to fail in the United States for a second time. If such a statement sounds weird or extreme to some (no doubt White) readers of this chapter, one reason may be that so many of us have been raised on mass media whose message is that one (usually White, highly powerful, almost always male) Hero can save the universe, all by himself. The other is that most of us have been trained, very patriarchally (and very capitalistically too, if there is such a word) to confuse *leadership* with *command. Command* means having power over others or others having power over you so that when they tell you to do something you'd rather not do, however stupid or destructive, you still have to do it because otherwise they will do something to you that is even worse. *Leadership* means *knowing where to go and what to do,* and knowing where to go and what to do is crucially important for every oppressed group and every radical movement. The more people's oppression "crosses" different groups, the more likely they are to know what to do about it, provided that such a situation doesn't defeat and silence them altogether. Accepting the leadership of feminists of color, many of whom are, not accidentally, lesbians of color, means many things for White feminists. It means enduring nervousness, awkwardness, and embarrassment in order to pay attention to what such women are saying. It means supporting their work, financially and otherwise.[45] It means learning to distrust one-dimensional solutions and one-dimensional analyses. Briefly, it means spending only some of one's time with people just like oneself and spending part of it with people not like oneself so that one can learn about, prepare for, and finally enter into *coalitions,* another one of the repeated themes in the work of the women quoted in the last two chapters.

The long poem "From Sea to Shining Sea" by the Black poet June Jordan lists all the things it's not good to be in the United States—gay, Black, old, young, a pomegranate(!), a child, with or without a job, a woman, someone who lives in Queens, New York (nuclear waste is trucked through it), or Arkansas (nuclear missiles are trucked through *it*), married or unmarried, someone who wants to buy a house (because of interest rates) or rent housing (because of a decontrolled market), a Jew, a tree, a river, with or without a gun—in short, almost everyone and everything—and ends, "This is a good time / This is the best time / This is the only time to come together." Hull speaks of the "lifesaving connections among issues" and insists that all revolutionary causes and movements must be addressed if we are to "rescue the planet" and redefine power as "the human responsibility to define, transform and develop." Barbara Smith again and again emphasizes the critical necessity for coalitions, the necessity of women's bonding across racial lines, the necessity for taking risks to implement coalitions, and the strength of coalition politics because "there is no way that one oppressed group is going to topple a system all by itself."[46] The Jewish lesbian group Di Vilde Chayes[47] condemns as "divisive and strategically unsound" the idea that "all our energy must be devoted to only one of these oppressions," while Bulkin condemns what Kaye/Kantrowitz calls the "scarcity" theory of struggle, "the false assumption that ultimately one must choose which of two oppressions to confront, that one cannot choose to oppose both." In other contexts Cheryl Clarke describes how "homophobia sabotages coalitions, divides would-be comrades, and retards the mental restructuring, essential to revolution, which black people need so desperately."[48]

Here are two other statements, the first by Lewis, the second by Joseph and Lewis:

> Because people in capitalist society are organized into separate and competing groups and classes, no one segment of the women's movement represents all the interests and concerns of all women. Even among white women, different groups confront different social and economic experiences and encounter oppression and injustice in different ways. All of these . . . need to be recognized as valid oppressions to be struggled against.

> White and Black women must no longer be fooled into thinking that by pressing their personal "most severe oppression," or making a pitch that "their" oppression is the severest of oppressions, they will achieve any substantive gains. . . . Single-issue politics will result in a Pyrrhic victory at best.[49]

Perhaps the most emphatic and singly focused statement about the necessity for coalitions, and certainly the most detailed in history and psychological analysis that I have been able to find, is Bernice Johnson Reagon's "Coalition Politics: Turning the Century," which Barbara Smith used to end her anthology *Home Girls*.[50] Reagon, who (in her own words) "lived through the brilliant heat of the Civil Rights struggle," based the essay upon a speech originally given in 1981 at the West Coast Women's Music Festival in Yosemite National Forest in California.[51] Summarizing this extraordinary essay can't do it justice but perhaps I can point out here some of its themes and make it sound important and attractive enough to those readers who don't know it that they will go find it. A flat statement that coalition work is the crucial next step in U.S. politics (especially feminist politics, given Reagon's original audience), that being only with people like oneself—or pretending that such little groups are worlds in themselves—is impossible, does not convey the effect of the essay or its analysis of the process of moving from what Reagon calls "wombs" to coalition work, which is not fun and not easy. So here are some highlights:

> If you're *really* doing coalition work . . . you feel threatened to the core and if you don't, you're not really doing no coalescing.

> We've pretty much come to the end of a time when you can have a space that is "yours only" . . . we have finished with that kind of isolating. . . . It's over. Give it up.

> There is no chance that you can survive by staying *inside* the barred room [with people just like you]. . . . When those who call the shots get ready to clean house, they have easy access to you.
>
> But that space, while it lasts, should be a nurturing space where you sift out what people are saying about you and decide who you really are. . . . [If] you pretend that your room is a world . . . [that] becomes reactionary because it is totally inadequate for surviving in the world with many peoples.

> [After you let in others] it ain't home no more. . . . And what happens at that point has to do with trying to do too much in it. You don't do no coalition building in a womb . . . you generally are very soft and unshelled. . . . And you have no ability to handle what happens if you start to let in folks who are not like you.
>
> Coalition work is not work done in your home. Coalition work has to be done in the streets. And it is some of the most dangerous work you can do. And you shouldn't look for comfort. . . . You don't get fed a lot in a coalition. . . . You go to the coalition for a few hours and then you go back and take your bottle [i.e. get "fed"] wherever it is, and then you go back and

coalesce some more. . . . If you feel the strain, you may be doing some good work.[52]

Reagon explicitly warns against single-issue politics and also states explicitly that all political struggles are one:

Watch these mono-issue people. They ain't gonna do you no good. . . . Now, there were a few people who kept up with many of those issues. *They are very rare.* . . . Study with them . . . protect them. . . . They hold the key to turning the century with our principles and ideals intact. They can teach you how to cross cultures and not kill yourself.[53]

There is much more in the essay, from tracing recent radical history from the civil rights movement, to "giving away" what you do and know to people younger than you, to "allowing people to name themselves," to emphasizing the radical victories of the last forty years. With Reagon I believe that "we are at the point where in order to take the next step we've got to do it with some folk we don't care too much about." I want now to talk about some of the ways "we"—that is, White feminists like myself—can start to do coalition work without being too destructive as we do so. Or at least without being as destructive as we might be otherwise. And to do that, it is absolutely crucial for us to understand that *the women's movement does not belong to us.* We do not own it. We are not "in charge" of it. As Reagon has said (herself doing coalition work with White women): "We have just finished with that kind of isolating. There is no hiding place. There is nowhere you can go and only be with people who are like you. It's over. Give it up."[54]

NOTES

1. The title for this chapter is from Gloria Anzaldúa's title of her interview with Luisah Teish, which in turn was taken from Teish's own words in the interview (Cherríe Moraga and Gloria Anzaldúa, eds., *This Bridge Called My Back: Writings by Radical Women of Color* [Watertown, MA: Persephone Press, 1981], 221).

2. This epigraph is the first sentence of Toni Cade Bambara's foreword to *This Bridge Called My Back* (ibid., vi).

3. Ibid., 206, xxi.

4. Ibid., 92.

5. Cherríe Moraga, *Loving in the War Years* (Boston: South End Press, 1983), v; Moraga and Anzaldúa, *This Bridge,* 23.

6. Gardiner in Laura Lederer, ed., *Take Back the Night: Women on Pornography* (New York: Morrow, 1980), 114; Moraga, *Loving,* 53, italics added. In the largely White feminist anthology in which Gardner's essay appears, both her essay and its statement of being "in limbo" are themselves in limbo, i.e., Gardner is one of the few women of color included. Thus, she and her concerns are both given only token presence.

7. Barbara Smith, *Toward a Black Feminist Criticism* (Brooklyn, NY: Out and Out Books, 1977), 15; Barbara Smith, ed., *Home Girls: A Black Feminist Anthology* (New York: Kitchen Table Women of Color Press, 1983), 83; Valerio in Moraga and Anzaldúa, *This Bridge,* 44; Espin in Mary Bragg et al., eds., *Lesbian Psychologies: Explorations and Challenges* (Urbana: University of Illinois Press, 1987), 35.

8. Espin in ibid., 40; Smith in Moraga and Anzaldúa, *This Bridge,* 124; Espin in Bragg et al., *Lesbian Psychologies,* 40.

9. Audre Lorde, *Sister Outsider: Essays and Speeches* (Trumansburg, NY: Crossing Press, 1984), 143, 120.

10. Moraga, *Loving,* vi.

11. Smith, *Home Girls,* 316.

12. Moraga and Anzaldúa, *This Bridge,* 14. Moraga comments ironically on the paradox of having oppression visited on both identities when she writes, "The joys of looking like a white girl ain't so great since I realized I could be beaten on the street for being a dyke" (ibid., 29).

13. Ibid., 41, 44.

14. Smith, *Home Girls,* 53.

15. Red Jordan Arobateau, "Nobody's People," *Sinister Wisdom* 21 (1982), 41.

16. Moraga and Anzaldúa, *This Bridge,* 152.

17. Ibid., 38.

18. Ibid., 54–55.

19. Ibid., 18.

20. Ibid., 155.

21. Smith, *Home Girls,* 24.

22. Bragg et al., *Lesbian Psychologies,* 47.

23. Moraga and Anzaldúa, *This Bridge,* 209.

24. Bragg et al., *Lesbian Psychologies,* 47.

25. The conference was the National Women's Studies Association annual conference held 24–28 June 1987 at Spelman College in Atlanta, the first time an NWSA conference was held at a Black college (*off our backs* XVII:8 [1987] 2).

26. Yamada in Moraga and Anzaldúa, *This Bridge,* 73; Morales in ibid., 14, italics added.

27. bell hooks, *Feminist Theory from Margin to Center* (Boston: South End Press, 1984), 29.

28. Moraga and Anzaldúa, *This Bridge,* 235.

29. Alma Gómez et al., eds., *Cuentos: Stories by Latinas* (New York: Kitchen Table Women of Color Press, 1983), x–xi.

30. Bulkin et al., *Yours in Struggle,* 106. It was Jill Johnston, writing from the conflicting states of being a woman, a feminist, a lesbian, and a poor-white kid who'd "made it" into the artistic/journalistic "Bohemian"/intelligentsia, who said, "We are not any of us something more (or less) or other than anything that we are. We are the sum total of all we are" (Johnston, *Lesbian Nation: The Feminist Solution* [New York: Simon and Schuster, 1973], 139).

31. Arobateau, "Nobody's People," 52.

32. Chrystos in Moraga and Anzaldúa, *This Bridge,* 69; Quintanales in ibid., 148.

33. Smith, *Home Girls,* xliii.

34. Marilyn Frye, *The Politics of Reality: Essays in Feminist Theory* (Trumansbury, NY: Crossing Press, 1983), 147.

35. Lorde, *Sister Outsider,* 198, 112.

36. Barbara Kerr and Mirtha Quintanales, "The Complexity of Desire: Conversations on Sexuality and Difference," *Conditions* 8 (1982), 57, italics added.

37. Moraga and Anzaldúa, *This Bridge,* xvii, italics added.

38. Ibid., 116. For those readers who may be interested, yes, Barbara Smith and Beverly Smith are indeed related. They are twin sisters (ibid, 249).

39. Ibid., 211, 213.

40. Wallace in Gloria T. Hull et al., eds., *All the Women Are White, All the Blacks Are Men, but Some of Us Are Brave: Black Women's Studies* (Old Westbury, NY: Feminist Press, 1982), 12; Smith, *Home Girls,* xxxii.

41. Moraga and Anzaldúa, *This Bridge,* 127. The recent explosion of fiction and poetry by Black women (and even more recently by other women of color) is obviously related to this phenomenon. Nikki Giovanni writes:

> Is there any room for white men in literature? Black women on both sides of the Atlantic are keeping traditional Western literature alive. We have, in Africa, Bessie Head, who with *When Rain Clouds Gather* and *Maru* has proven herself one of the great African writers writing in the English language and, of course, Toni Morrison in the United States. Compared to what? Norman Mailer? Philip Roth? Be serious! (Mari Evans, ed., *Black Women Writers (1950–1980): A Critical Evaluation* [Garden City, NY: Anchor, 1984], 209).

In this connection Hull, Scott, and Evans write of "Alice Walker's groundbreaking course on Black women writers at Wellesley College in 1972 and how work of all sorts about Black women writers has since blossomed into a visible Black female literary renaissance" (Hull et al., *All the Women,* xxvi). Speaking of the even worse double oppression of racism and sexism against which the achievement of earlier Black women writers must be perceived, Hull writes of Alice Dunbar-Nelson:

> First of all, Dunbar-Nelson has usually been seen as the wife
> of America's first famous Black poet who incidentally "wrote
> a little" herself. . . . Furthermore, Dunbar-Nelson . . . always
> had to struggle for survival and for psychic necessities. . . .
> The notion of her as "genteel, bourgeoise" needs revision.
> Black women generally occupy an ambiguous status with
> regard to class. . . . Being Black, they have no entrenched and
> comfortable security in even their achieved class status
> (gained via breeding, education, culture, looks, etc. and not
> so much by money). And being women, their position is
> rendered doubly tangential and complex. . . . Things were
> not set up for her, a *Black woman,* to be able to make her
> living [as a writer]. . . . This had to do with the avenues of
> publication which were open to her and the circles of pres-
> tige from which she was automatically excluded. When she
> needed one most, she was not able to get a job with even
> the *Crisis* or the NAACP, or a Black newspaper or press serv-
> ice—her exceptional qualifications notwithstanding. She was
> compelled always to accept or to create low-paying employ-
> ment for herself, and to work under the most trying condi-
> tions (ibid., 192–93).

42. Moraga and Anzaldúa, *This Bridge,* 127.

43. Ibid., 30.

44. Seymour Kleinberg makes much the same point in "Where Have All the Sissies Gone?" commenting on the new fashions of "macho" dress and presentation among many gay men (*Christopher Street* 2:9 [1978]).

45. Moraga and Anzaldúa, describing the making of their anthology, say:

> We have sorely learned why so few women of color attempt
> this kind of project—no money to fall back on. . . . Both of
> us became expert jugglers of our energy and the few pennies
> in our piggybanks." (Moraga and Anzaldúa, *This Bridge* xxv).

Lorde notes:

> Even the form our creativity takes is often a class issue. . . .
> Poetry has been the major voice of poor, working class, and
> Colored women. A room of one's own may be a necessity

for writing prose, but so are reams of paper, a typewriter, and plenty of time. The actual requirements to produce the visual arts also help determine, along class lines, whose art is whose. In this day of inflated prices for material, who are our sculptors, our painters, our photographers? (Lorde, *Sister Outsider,* 116).

46. Jordan in Smith *Home Girls,* 223–29; Hull in ibid., 131; Smith in Moraga and Anzaldúa, *This Bridge,* 125, in Hull et al., *All the Women,* 49, and in Moraga and Anzaldúa, *This Bridge,* 126.

47. In Yiddish "di vilde chayes" means the wild animals. Little Eastern European Jewish American girls who didn't act like ladies would be told by their mothers to act properly and not like "vilde chayes"—i.e., wild animals who didn't comb their hair and who raced about and got their dresses dirty. Hence the group's affectionately ironic, yet fierce, name.

48. Di Vilde Chayes in Bulkin et al., *Yours in Struggle,* 140; Bulkin in ibid., 139; Clarke in Smith, *Home Girls,* 200; Parker in Moraga and Anzaldúa, *This Bridge,* 242.

49. Gloria Joseph and Jill Lewis, *Common Differences: Conflicts in Black and White Feminist Perspectives* (New York: Anchor, 1981), 51, 279.

50. Smith, *Home Girls,* 356–68.

51. Ibid., 356. Speaking of the use of music by the Student Nonviolent Coordinating Committee during the civil rights struggle in the 1950s, Giddings writes, "It was the rich, darkly timbred voice of Bernice Reagon, an Albany State College student who joined SNCC, that evoked the resonances of centuries-old memories and strengths" (Paula Giddings, *When and Where I Enter: The Impact of Black Women on Race and Sex in America* [New York: Morrow, 1984], 283).

52. Smith, *Home Girls,* 356, 357, 358, 359, 362.

53. Ibid., 363.

54. Ibid., 357.

F O U R T E E N

''COALITION WORK IS NOT DONE IN YOUR HOME''[1]

It's over. Give it up.

But how?

The process of realizing that we White women must give it up—and then finding out how to do so—and then doing it—is a long one, and it never stops, really, in a racist world. What follows here is not expertise but only a tentative beginning meant for those White women for whom it will also be a tentative beginning. All I can do here and now is to pull together some scattered ideas and experiences, almost all of which I owe to women of color, that have helped to crystallize the process for me. They have enabled me, as Minnie Bruce Pratt says, "to look seriously at what limitations we [White feminists] have placed in this 'new world' on who we feel 'close to,' who we feel 'comfortable with,' who we feel 'safe' with."[2]

First of all, *listen—and expect discomfort*. One kind is the fear miscalled "boredom," the oh-God-do-we-have-to-deal-with-that-again reaction. Barbara Smith says of this:

> For those of you who are tired of hearing about racism, imagine how much more tired *we* are of constantly experiencing it, second by literal second, how much more exhausted we are to see it constantly in your eyes. The degree to which it is hard or uncomfortable for you to have the issue raised is the degree to which you know inside yourself that you aren't dealing with the issue . . . that undermines Third World women's lives.[3]

Another kind is fear miscalled "guilt." Cherríe Moraga and Gloria Anzaldúa point out that the "guilt" White women so often talk about is a way of avoiding quite a different issue:

> Guilt is *not* a feeling. It is an intellectual mask to a feeling. Fear is a feeling—fear of losing one's power, fear of being accused, fear of a loss of status, control, knowledge. Fear is real. Perhaps this is the emotional, non-theoretical place from which serious anti-racist work among white feminists can begin.[4]

The expectation that women of color will be angry with us, that they will show that anger, and that they will be right to do so also has its roots in fear. Audre Lorde had an answer for this expectation, one that's both antiracist and feminist:

> In the male construct of brute force, we were taught that our lives depended upon the good will of patriarchal power. *The anger of others was to be avoided at all costs because there was nothing to be learned from it but pain. . . . And if we accept our powerlessness, then of course any anger can destroy us. . . .* [But] anger between peers births change, not destruction, and the discomfort and sense of loss it often causes is not fatal. . . . [5]

Yet a fourth kind of discomfort is the pain that comes with reexamining our own backgrounds and the degree to which our own cultures are implicated in racism. Pratt, a White southerner, describes her experience of this process, calling it "exhausting" and adding, "It would be a lie to say this process is comforting."[6] Pratt writes of the conflict this process produced in her:

> [It] did not . . . [move] me into a place where I joined others. Because *I* was implicated in the doing of some of these injustices, and I held myself and my people, responsible . . . I felt in a struggle with myself, *against* myself. . . . When we discover truths about our home culture, we may fear that we will lose the people who are our family, our kin, be rejected by "our own kind." . . . It is a real fear.[7]

Crucially, Pratt found the cure for this struggle "against myself" in the same tradition that implicated her so horribly and tragically in racism—for not only has every tradition its strengths (as she discovered), it also has its own radical and dissident elements. She writes:

> I found . . . a comparative and skeptical way of thinking, through my Presbyterian variety of Protestantism. . . . I also discovered a tradition of white Christian-raised women in the South, who had worked actively for social justice since at least 1849, the year a white woman in Bucktown Maryland hid Harriet Tubman during her escape from slavery. . . . From the 1840's to the 1860's Sarah and Angelina Grimké of South Carolina, living in the North, had organized both for the abolition of slavery and for women's rights, linking the two struggles.[8]

Although there's no room here for a "scholarly" proof of the following—which would require an encyclopedia anyway—I want to emphasize something of which I have become morally certain while researching this book: unless the numbers of any ethnic or regional group are vanishingly small, *there is no such group that does not have somewhere in its past, in some form, its feminists, its class struggles, its antiracist activists, and its gay resistance.* My own Eastern European Jewish background, I have increasingly found out, has all of the above.[9]

Besides tolerating our own discomfort, here are some more ways of "giving it up," whether we feel comfortable with doing so or not:

Don't use other people or their lives as metaphors. They are real and they are not you. This sort of thing includes claiming that your soul is somehow not really White, or that you were a woman of color in a previous incarnation, or adopting other people's dress, habits, religions, or rituals because they are so "interesting." It also means *letting people name themselves,* both literally and in the sense of accepting others' descriptions of their own experiences, especially when what they are describing is the way your actions impinge on their lives. You may feel utterly innocent, you may never have had the slightest intention of being racist, you may be entirely unaware of having done anything at all that could be interpreted as racist—all this is entirely irrelevant. What matters is *what you did* and when it comes to racism, they know the subject far, far better than you (or I) do. The reasonable answer to "You just did X and X is racist" is not "I'm not a racist" (which is logically irrelevant), or "No, it wasn't" (it was), or "It couldn't have been racist because I didn't mean it that way" (which means only that you're ignorant of what you did), but something like, "I'm sorry. Thank you for taking the time and trouble to confront me about this. Would it be asking too much to ask you to explain some more? I know I'm ignorant about an awful lot I ought to know." (Such responses can be practiced in front of a mirror, by the way.) After all, White feminists have been saying for years that male power to name is power, the power to identify, to judge, and to evaluate, all rolled into one. We must give up that power too. Bernice Johnson Reagon's witty comment on the White power to define who is "white" and who isn't is about just this topic:

> I had never left Georgia until after the Civil Rights movement, so . . . I knew two people. White people and Black people. When I went to New York, the white people were not the same. . . . They were too dark. I tried to make them become Black. They didn't like that at all. . . . If you had all let me run it, we would all be colored. Because I grew up in Albany, Georgia, and I knew what white people looked like, and they looked like none of them dark-skinned white folks I saw up in New York, who got mad at me when I tried to bring them over.
> . . . Respect means when somebody joins you and they need to be white, you give it to them. . . . That's called allowing people to name themselves and dealing with them from that perspective.[10]

Never start organizations or projects with only your White feminist friends as members. Pratt and Bulkin, White feminists themselves, note the destructiveness of this typical White feminist behavior. Pratt writes: "In a women's organization, when it gets started by a non-diverse group, if the diversity is not in the planning sessions, a shift later, in how and what decisions are made, is exceedingly difficult."[11] Bulkin explains why:

> [In these situations] an issue is defined by white women who then ask women of color to provide input within already established parameters. . . . The women of color function more as political symbols than as individuals.[12]

Whenever possible, answer bigotry with information. Bulkin quotes an encounter between Melanie Kaye/Kantrowitz and a Chicana who said:

> that to many Chicanas, Jewish people were just white; just *landlords;* that Jewish people came here and took land from the Indians. I said that to many Jews, Chicanos were just Catholics and she knew what the Catholics had done to the Jews [i.e., the Spanish Inquisition and the Diaspora]."[13]

Bulkin comments:

In this exchange, Kaye/Kantrowitz appears to have made some difficult decisions, the first of which was not to respond simply by labeling the ridicule as anti-Jewish. She chooses instead to . . . [reply with] information that might undercut stereotypes of Jews and with statements highlighting the similarities between biased assumptions about Jews and biased assumptions about (Chicano) Catholics.[14]

Don't be academic—or rather, don't be only academic. Barbara Smith emphatically condemns

> what I call women's studies or academic feminists: women who teach, research and publish about women, but who are not involved in any way in making radical social and political change. . . . The grassroots/community women's movement has given women's studies its life. . . . The question [of activism versus academicism] is . . . an immoral and false dichotomy. The answer lies in the emphasis and the kinds of work that will lift oppression off . . . all oppressed people. . . . If lifting this oppression is not a priority to you, then it's problematic whether you are a part of the actual feminist movement.[15]

Hull and Smith condemn women's studies for having become both more institutionalized *and* more precarious within academia, stating that its former "radical life-changing vision . . . has constantly been diminished in exchange for acceptance, respectability, and the career advancement of individuals." Hooks makes similar comments about the amount of money spent for academic conferences that could be spent on "mass outreach" instead.[16]

Feminist writer and comedian Roseanne, in her very good autobiography (yes, it's the same person), argues cogently that "the real power of women belongs to welfare mothers and women in poverty." Having had a good deal of experience with poverty herself, Roseanne says that the feminist opinion she's met so often—that these are ignorant women—is wrong and she "tried to do housewife material to prove it." Nina Baym, herself an academic, calls "feminist [literary] theory" an attempt to "address . . . an audience of prestigious male academics and . . . win its respect. It succeeds . . . only when it ignores or dismisses the earlier paths of feminist literary study . . . and grounds its own theories in those currently in vogue with the men who make theory."[17]

Expect areas of struggle and hence issues to shift constantly. When power withdraws—i.e., is driven from—one area, it will regroup in another, and such changes will change the issues important to oppressed groups. In the 1940s, as I recall, bus drivers were White men and the job had respect and status; when it was opened to more men, "somehow" it lost its status. When bank tellers were White men, the job was one of importance, responsibility, and access to advancement within the hierarchy of the bank; when such jobs were opened to White women in the 1950s, they became essentially clerical jobs carrying few of those advantages. In the last two feminist decades women have been entering law and medicine in unprecedented numbers, but how many have been admitted to the practice of corporate law or the most lucrative branches of medicine? In England in the late nineteenth and early twentieth century women won the right to study Greek and Latin only after "the classics" were no longer indicators of male class status and hence a requirement for political power. I myself once did what I sincerely hope was the worst job of teaching a class I've ever done, one supposedly about women's problems in creative writing, partly because I assumed that the issues of 1972 and the issues of 1992 would not differ so significantly that I had to find out first what had changed. "What do 'you people' want now?"—a question I've often heard from exasperated White men about "women"—is a real and crucial question, to which the answer is necessarily a constantly changing one.

Avoid trade-offs. The name of this game is Divide and Conquer. Paula Giddings and Barbara Smith have both noticed how different movements, closely related as they usually are in time, seem also to be on some kind of seesaw: as the status of one group goes up, that of another goes down. Many groups seem to be caught in the same dynamic; thus Alma Gómez, Cherríe Moraga, and Mariana Romo-Carmona note that " 'El' so-called 'Boom del escritor latinoamericano' [The boom in publishing the Latin American writer] has only meant that norteamericanos have discovered that Latin American *men* can write." Clearly, giving in to the temptation to advance "our" interests at the expense of "theirs" is destructive, but it is not oppressed groups who are responsible for setting up the temptation in the first place. Hooks writes

> "It is *no mere coincidence* that interest in white women's rights
> is kindled whenever there is mass-based anti-racist protest."[18]

Constance Carroll, who has had personal experience with these institutional ploys ("oiled by the powers that be" Bulkin says), explains how they work:

> Institutions have often met the double threat of the Black and
> women's movements by pitting the two groups against each
> other. *Everyone who has worked in compliance and affirmative*

action programs knows that this is a favorite institutional ploy. . . .
I do not know how many times I have heard avuncular remarks
to the effect that women would have to be patient since so much
money had to be spent on providing more opportunities for
minority candidates. I then hear the same administrators ad-
monishing Black groups to be patient since the women were
using up so much money. . . . I know of no institution where
the women's groups and Black groups have publicly allied to
put an end to such divisive tactics; and I know of no institution
where *significant* gains have been made for both white women
and minority women and men.[19]

And here is Susan Koppelman, White scholar and historian of U.S.
women's short stories, tracing the seesaw as it has manifested itself in literary
history in the United States:

During the decade in which women began to finally approach
. . . women's suffrage, the "Negro Renaissance" flourished in
Harlem and white liberal patrons flung themselves into . . . support for, and excursion into black culture. For the first time
black writers began to appear in the anthologies—black male
writers. . . . And then. . . . they disappeared from the anthologies after the vote was won and the confrontation between
women and the patriarchy seemed to die down.

After . . . [World War II] some black men were once again
included, as the number of women included diminished (as
they had during the twenties). But as the civil rights movement
gained momentum, the black writers disappeared again from
the white controlled anthologies. . . . Those slots allowed to
"others" were increasingly once again filled by women writers,
all white, of course.

But . . . [with the] women's liberation movement . . . in the
late sixties and early seventies, black men once again replaced
white women—along with a couple of Indians and Mexicans
(men, of course).

I think that when women [as a group] start to get upppppity
[sic] powerful white men begin to privilege and gather in their
poor and black and brown and yellow and red brothers. They
say, "Come, be men with us. We will share our privileges. The
major of which is the exploitation of women."

And the oppressed men . . . fall for it. . . .

> And the women of oppressed sub-cultures . . . fall for the appeal of group solidarity. . . .
> And the white women continue to be racist and classist and ablist and homophobic if they are straight and holier-than-thou if they are lesbian.
> So what are we going to do about it?[20]

The converse (which Koppelman has mentioned to me in conversation) is the invitation from White men to feminist White women to join them *as White,* another divide-and-conquer ploy for which many White women continue to fall. The answer, of course, as Canaan says, is that liberation is not "a fixed quantity" of which "there is only so much to go around" so that "an individual or community . . . [must be] liberated at the expense of another."[21]

Expect to fail. Don't be too hard on yourself when you do. After all, the inevitable racism of having been brought up White in the United States is not the same as personal guilt for choices made knowingly. The first does not deserve personal punishment or disrespect. Julia Perez says:

> I've seen white women who will take all kinds of disrespect and feel it's okay because it's a woman of color and "I'm so racist anyway that she has a right to treat me that way."
> *Sarah* [Pearlman]: "That's the liberal guilt."
> *Julia* [Perez]: "Right, I'm of the opinion that no one has the right to treat you in a disrespectful manner, no matter who you are.[22]

Liberal guilt is, of course, preferable to open bigotry, as the former may lead to something better while the latter won't. Moreover, it is, luckily, not necessary to be perfect, a state that is unattainable by Human beings anyway. Barbara Smith writes about her own prejudices:

> I am not writing this from a position of moral exemption. My hands are not clean, because like other non-Jews in this society I have swallowed anti-Semitism simply by living here. . . . It is neither possible nor necessary to be morally exempt in order to stand in opposition to oppression. . . . Privilege and oppression can and do exist simultaneously.[23]

Cheryl Kennedy says of her own position as a member of an interracial, intercultural relationship:

There's no way a white woman can go into an interracial, intercultural relationship and have enough information. . . . I'm
the one who's gong to blow it. . . . [I felt] really sad about the
times when I blew it. . . . And there's no way I could make it
different.[24]

What is necessary (besides trying, even after and although you fail) is to
remember that guilt and responsibility are not the same. One does not imply
the other. Bulkin describes a workshop on anti-Semitism after which one
participant mentioned

that, though everyone at the workshop agreed that silence was
unacceptable, it had also been the most common response.
Everyone laughed, recognizing in that statement our own failures . . . [and] political frailty.[25]

After all, as Gloria Joseph and Jill Lewis point out:

[Although the] White women's movement has had its own explicit forms of racism . . . it was bound to do so—given that the
movement did not begin with women who had some all-
encompassing political and historical knowledge, but with
women who responded to the forms of immediate injustices
crossing their lives.[26]

And Barbara Smith was optimistic, writing in 1982:

In my six years of being an avowed Black feminist, I have seen
much change in how white women take responsibility for their
racism, particularly within the last year. The formation of consciousness-raising groups to deal solely with this issue, study
groups and community meetings and workshops; the appearance of articles in our publications and letters in newspapers;
and the beginning of real and equal coalitions between Third
World and white women are all phenomena that have really
begun to happen.[27]

Therefore, since you do not have to be perfect, *be cranky—but always in
private.* Be upset. Be angry. Be ungrateful. Be vicious. Complain. Deplore
the impossible behavior of "all those people" you're, after all, trying to "help"
(ha!) when, after all, you don't "have" to (that's what you think), and be-
moan all the ghastly mistakes you've made and how you're giving up right

now, and nobody appreciates you, and what do your so-called allies think they're up to anyway—but do this in private with a few friends who are just like you so that you can get rid of it all and calm down—and then stop and go out and work some more. Barbara Smith, who says that for her, a Black woman, writing about racism and anti-Semitism feels like "a no-win situation," also states: "If we weren't upset about the gulfs between us, if we weren't scared of the inherent challenge to act and change that the recognition of these gulfs requires, then we wouldn't 'really [be] doing no coalescing.' "[28]

  Above all, learn, especially, how much White feminists really don't know— and then learn and learn and learn some more. As Joseph and Lewis say, learning about these cultural and situational differences is crucial for un-learning racism and learning how to do coalition work at all. In *Common Differences,* their attempt to explore the differences between Black and White women in the United States, they emphasize that "coalitions depend . . . on the *recognition of differences.*"[29] Groups of people are not the same— their histories are different, their educations, their cultures, their experiences and situation, their languages, their incomes, their food, their social cues, and the treatment they receive from institutions. The "liberal" insistence that "they" (whoever they are) are really like "us" (whoever we are) only makes these crucial differences impossible to deal with. Note: these differences must be learned, a little bit at a time, as precisely the multitude of *specific* differences that they are.[30] Here are a few differences that some women of color have taught me:

  Work. Michelle Wallace writes:

> When the middle-class white woman said "I want to work," in her head was a desk in the executive suite, while the black woman saw a bin of dirty clothes, someone else's. . . . Something similar probably happened with the poor and lower-middle-class white woman. . . . Women's Liberation, the black woman reasoned, would chain her to Ms. Anne's stove forever. None of that for her. She wanted to stay home and have her man take care of her.[31]

  Moreover, Black women's labor force participation has always been extremely high (i.e., the double shift of paid and unpaid work). Between 1973 and 1980, for example, as Sharlene Hesse-Biber points out, White women's participation in the paid labor force rose from 16.3 to 46.3 percent while Black women's rate increased from 39.7 percent *in 1890* (not a misprint) to 50.3 percent in 1976. Although some distinctions between the two groups have become small—Giddings points out their nearly identical median earnings, the common growth of female-headed households, unmarried teenage births, rising divorce rates, and higher poverty rates—some of the gap remains. Hesse-Biber writes: "By 1979 Black women were still more likely than white women to be employed in service and blue-collar positions." She also points out that although Black women professional and technical workers and managers had "somewhat higher earnings on the average" than White women, this anomaly can be explained by the White women's interrupted work histories, which the Black women simply can't afford.[32] And Patricia A. Gwartney-Gibbs and Patricia A. Taylor demonstrate that the apparent near-equity of the two groups' wages hides some important gaps:

> In 1980, if Black women had had the same average characteristics [education, hours of work, and other employment-related characteristics] as white women, their earnings would have surpassed white women's earnings [in all jobs]. . . . Black women . . . tend to be concentrated in low-skilled service and operative occupations . . . while white women tend to be concentrated in lower white collar occupations.[33]

Femininity. Different groups may mean very different things by this word. A code word among White feminists for various kinds of submission to patriarchal limitations and the artificial behavior required of White women to stay within those limits, "femininity" for other women may mean nothing more or less than respect and decent treatment. Joseph writes:

> Most Black women still do not receive the respect and treatment—mollycoddling and condescending as it sometimes is—afforded White women. So when these Black women complain about not wanting to lose their femininity, they are referring to something quite different. This difference has to be understood in an analysis of how the classic "feminine characteristics" are viewed in relation to Black women. . . . In many situations [Black women] are treated as non-females. . . . [For example] while many people would consider certain menial, laborious jobs as being "unfit for women," they fail to notice if Black women hold them.[34]

Wallace writes of her childhood, in which femininity was a state reserved for White women:

On rainy days my sister and I used to tie the short end of a scarf around our scrawny braids and let the rest of its silken mass trail to our waists. We'd pretend it was hair and that we were some lovely heroine we'd seen in the movies. There was a time when I would have called that wanting to be white, yet the real point of the game was being feminine. Being feminine *meant being white to us.*[35]

Christianity. Again, the "right" religion is not a privilege unless it's accompanied by other privileges, specifically those of race and class, as Barbara Smith notes.[36] She also emphasizes that the Christianity imposed by imperial colonizers and slave-owners was made over into something quite different by the people upon whom it was imposed.[37]

Experience of oppression. Differences here are so large—and so different in kind—that I can only sketch some of the themes that have recently emerged for me. (I still have a great deal to learn, of course.) Two that seem to me of particular importance (right now) are, first, the open, public nature of racist oppression and, second, the age at which children subject to it first understand it as the oppression practiced by one *group* of people against another. Families generally do their best to shelter their children from oppression visited via color or class, but it is the family itself that is usually the first agency to enforce sexism on children and to teach them that it is not oppression at all but "natural." Therefore the perception of racism as *group* oppression comes far, far earlier to most children than any similar perception of sexism. Barbara Smith writes that Black people aren't ever surprised by oppression since they have experienced it "from infancy on."[38]

What is actually going on here is, I think, first the undoubted fact that being White *does* provide an area in one's life—usually a very big one—in which it's not necessary to be on guard, in which one can "let go," be "ordinary" and "safe," and so on. Sexist oppression can certainly be extremely severe—it would be hard, for example, to call the repeated battering of wives or the repeated rape of girl children (and some boys) within their own families trivial. But because women do not live in a female ghetto or on the "female side of the tracks" such oppression is usually not done in public, nor is it usually perceived by others as the public act of one *group* against another *group.* Even when the topic is the rape or murder of adult women by men or women's casual sexual harassment by men at work or in the street, it's extraordinarily difficult to change public perceptions of such acts from something "personal," "private," "individual," "the woman's fault," "a lie," a fluke, an anomaly, one man's lunacy or pathology, an exception, "nature," to the systematic results of systematic oppression. It's not so much that sexist oppression can't begin early; rather the "privacy" of the family misnames and confuses such oppression, as does its identification with "nature." There is no shelter, like the family or community of color, to name it, analyze it, and warn children against it.

Still, no White woman I know or have ever heard of can say *about her sex* what these writers say about their color. To give only one example: at the age of five, Barbara Cameron had already seen one Indian man shot by police and another, old man beaten by white adolescent boys.[39] Such little children learn the public hatred of powerful others for their entire group very, very early. Their literature is full of descriptions of such childhood experiences. Lorde writes of being five years old:

> The AA subway train to Harlem. I clutch my mother's sleeve. . . . On one side . . . a woman in a fur hat staring at me. Her mouth twitches as she stares and then her gaze drops down, pulling mine with it. . . . She jerks her coat closer to her. . . . I do not see whatever terrible thing she is seeing on the seat between us—probably a roach. But she has communicated her horror to me. It must be something very bad from the way she's looking, so I pull my snowsuit closer to me away from it, too. When I look up the woman is still staring at me, her nose holes and eyes huge. And suddenly I realize there is nothing crawling up the seat between us; it's me she doesn't want her coat to touch. . . . I'm afraid to say anything to my mother because I don't know what I've done. I look at the sides of my snowpants, secretly. Is there something on them? Something's going on here I do not understand, but I will never forget it. Her eyes. The flared nostrils. The hate.[40]

Norma Garcia speaks of the same kind of early experience:

> For minority, third-world, black, Hispanic, Puerto Rican women all our relationships are interracial relationships in terms of our contact with the outside world. My first awareness that being Puerto Rican might be bad was in first grade. I remember that my teacher did not like Puerto Ricans, but I did not know what that meant. But I knew that I was Puerto Rican and she did not like Puerto Ricans, and that made me very quiet in her classroom.[41]

Having the "right" color of skin—and therefore the large part of life that is free from the oppressions of racism—also makes White women ignorant.

Bulkin recounts an incident at the 1981 National Women's Studies Conference on racism at the University of Connecticut:

> Going off campus with half a dozen women, I entered the local
> ice cream parlor immediately behind a dark-skinned Black
> woman. As she reached forward to open the restaurant door,
> she said quietly, but loud enough for me to hear, "Here I come,
> white folks!" I was momentarily startled, muttered something
> inane and hardly supportive, and realized that I was quite un-
> prepared for this particular venture into white America. The
> moment I walked through the door, my skin color did not grab
> the attention of the white person sitting over a sundae in the
> booth furthest away from where we entered. A few hours after
> I had been on a panel on racism in the lesbian community, I
> could imagine going out for an ice cream as a simple and un-
> complicated act.[42]

No wonder there is anger in Beverly Smith's reply to a Jewish man's statement that the way to stay alive "in a culture that's totally hostile to you" is to get enough money that it's "worth it for people to keep you going." Smith's answer is: "Black people don't have that. I feel anger when I hear about rich as being a survival mechanism. *Running* for Black people was a survival mechanism."[43] (Of course in medieval Europe, having money—or a reputation for it—could backfire for Jews when you found yourself, as sometimes happened, in the local Christian lord's dungeon having your teeth and fingernails extracted as a way of getting you to reveal your "treasure." Through the nineteenth century for the vast majority of Eastern European Jews, very few of whom were anything remotely recognizable as wealthy, the best survival mechanism during periods of government-sponsored massacre *was* running away and hiding in the woods—as some of my ancestors did. But as Bulkin points out, this millennium of persecution and massacre happened *in Europe*, not in the United States, and despite the Holocaust, is largely unknown in the United States today, even to many U.S. Jews, (including, at one time, me.)[44] Ignorance can run in other directions too. Barbara Smith speaks of a class taught by a friend of hers about *The Grapes of Wrath*, John Steinbeck's novel about a white family's sufferings during the 1930s depression:

> [T]he Black students refused to believe that it was about white
> people. *Refused* to believe, you know? . . . That's just incredible!
> What it shows is the class conflict, the class division that is

totally enforced in this society to keep people unaware of each other's situations, commonalities, etc.[45]

Differences between cultural codes are another area in which ignorance can be disastrous. Beverly Smith speaks about talking to White people "in your second language." More specifically, Moraga cites Gwendolyn Weindling's

> personal experience working in the white-dominated lesbian movement. She describes how any kind of emotionalism on the part of Black women is considered "angry" and "intimidating" by white women. She puts it plainly: "I've come to understand *emotionalism* as being taboo in white "cultures"—particularly white middle class or middle class cultures."[46]

Barbara Smith understands this "taboo," as I have come to do, not as a matter of emotion itself being taboo in such circles, but rather that the social codes that express it differ so markedly between groups. She quotes Melanie Kaye/Kantrowitz describing the difficulties a group of non-Jewish women had with her "style" during the process of interviewing her for a job: "Most of the women troubled by me had been sent to expensive colleges . . . they spoke with well-modulated voices, and they quaked when I raised mine. They didn't understand that with me anger is common, expressible, and not murderous. They found me 'loud' (of course) and 'emotional.' Interestingly, I got along fine with all the women of color in the group."[47]

"Loudness," intensity, and "emotionalism" are not the only differences between groups. In stressing "the importance of learning . . . one another's cultural codes," hooks writes:

> An Asian-American student, of Japanese heritage, explained her reluctance to participate in feminist organizations by calling attention to the tendency among feminist activists to speak rapidly without pause, to be quick on the uptake, always ready with a response. She had been raised to pause and think before speaking, to consider the impact of one's words, a characteristic which she felt was particularly true of Asian-Americans.

Hooks continues with the complaints of "several white women students" that

> the atmosphere in the class was "too hostile." They cited the noise level and direct confrontations . . . prior to the class starting as an example of this hostility. Our response was to explain

that what they perceived as hostility and aggression, we considered playful teasing and affectionate expressions of our pleasure at being together. . . . In their upbringing as white, middle-class females, the complaining students had been taught to identify loud and direct speech with anger. We explained . . . and encouraged them to switch codes. . . . [Then] they also learned that silence and quiet speech can in some cultures in dicate hostility and aggression.[48]

When one group (Hispanic students, let's say) indicates *respect for authority* by dropping its gaze, while another (White teachers) interprets this gesture as *guilt, slyness, or dishonesty,* there will be trouble. When another group (Black) indicates *I am listening to you; please go on* by the listener's turning away his or her face, while yet another (White like myself) believes this gesture to signal *I don't like what you're saying; please stop,* there will be trouble. When the second group indicates attentiveness by looking straight at the one talking—which signals to the one talking to *stop* talking—there will be trouble squared and endless accusations of rudeness on both sides.[49] When White women's tilted heads mean (to the women) something like *I am listening to you seriously, taking the whole conversation seriously, and my answer will be thoughtful and serious,* while to White men the same posture means something like *I am deferring to you/I am insecure/I am not an authority,* there will be trouble. When White Northwest Pacific people keep in touch by what are (I assume) to them companionable silences, while Eastern European Jewish Americans (like me), who keep in touch verbally, interpret silences as social catastrophes that must be filled by talk (or a plea of shy people to please, please not let anyone hear how socially inadequate they are), the latter will desperately keep on talking, never having received the signals to stop that they recognize, i.e., repeated interruptions, and the former, never having received the signals to begin talking, which is silence of a certain duration (I still can't tell how long the silence is supposed to last and I lived there for years), will dazedly wonder how on earth to shut the intruder up. The Northwesterners will think the Jews inexcusably pushy, loud, and rude, while the Jewish Americans will judge the Northwesterners as half-dead, muted zombies without feeling who spend most of their time staring at their feet and talking in clichés.[50] The only way to uncover these differences—and thereby become more intelligible to each other—is to take the risk of complaining and to bear the risk of others complaining about us. This is the only way we can even hope to unravel what are not even real disagreements (of which there will be plenty) but only miscommunications. If we're going to fight, let's fight about something real.

And then what? (I can hear some of my White readers saying). After I have expected discomfort and gotten it, learned not to use other people's lives as metaphors, let them "name" themselves, never started projects with only White feminists as members, answered bigotry with information (which I have worked hard to get), avoided academic jargon, patiently followed each shift in the areas of struggle (more learning), consistently avoided trade-offs, expected to fail, refrained from expressing my frustrations (except to a few friends), learned other groups' attitudes toward everything from work to class to femininity to experiences of oppression to manners and cultural codes—oh, yes, and to men—and to a vast number of things I undoubtedly don't know enough to mention—*and* connected all the issues—

Well (I imagine such a reader saying), if I'm still alive, haven't died of exhaustion, lost my job, had my kids die of inattention, still have something resembling friends and a life—what then? *What do I, who am not a saint, get out of it?* And don't tell me about the objective political necessity of coalitions, or the intellectual fact that the issues are connected, or the moral necessity of combating injustice. I know all those—I've been hearing about them for decades. I even believe you, but if you mention any of these goddamn things once more, I will deck you one.

I think this is a legitimate question, though the answer may surprise some. It is that the rewards White feminists can get from unlearning and undoing racism are selfish, personal, and enormous. This is true even though the work of doing so is hard and painful, as it has certainly been and continues to be for me. Let me try to explain.

The racism of most of the White feminists I know doesn't rest on an explicit belief in racial superiority, although it's obviously hidden in there somewhere, but rather (as does the sexism of most of the men I know) on the assumption I call the Being-in-Charge phenomenon. Of course those White women people (like those men) who are merely greedy or arrogant use this kind of Being-in-Charge as an excuse to grab stuff—that is, they translate Being-in-Charge into I-Own-Everything—but anyone with a conscience, which certainly includes virtually all of the White feminists I know, assumes, along with the assumption of Being-in-Charge, the obligation To Control (or at least To Fix) Everything.

Now this obligation is a super-Human, not a Human one, and if you take it seriously, it will kill you. It is impossible for one person To Fix Everything—which is what reasonably decent people must inevitably try to do if they believe they are in charge of everything. *This* means that the megalomania of racism (or sexism) has a hidden "down" side: *perpetual insecurity* and, for those aware enough to notice such things, *a feeling of perpetual failure.* Often the arrogance, the greed, the crushing sense of obligation, the horror and despair of never being able to succeed alone, and the accompanying impotent hatred and contempt of others, all meet in the same person. I met this combination quite often in my experience in the 1960s with many of the young White men involved in the antiwar movement. The inevitable cynicism and despair, which are the downside result of quite unconscious sexist, racist, and class arrogance, are quite common among the White men of my acquaintance right now.

Unlearning that lesson of Being-in-Charge is, I think, basic for White feminists (at least middle-management ones), not only because it allows us to work in coalitions without doing more harm than good and is therefore crucial for the success of feminism and radical politics in general, but also for our own sakes. I remember vividly and always will how my first experience of hearing feminists speak broadened the world for me. Beginning to unlearn racism has done the same, much more slowly, but also much more completely. It has immensely widened the possibilities I can imagine for myself and the world's future. It has also turned a planet full of strangers whom I thought (in the ignorant bigotry of my twenties, at least) were either parts of the landscape, frightening enemies, or mirror images of myself into a rich, many-peopled marvelousness of possible allies. Moraga writes about White women feeling "no loss, no lack, no absence when women of color are involved," but one of the benefits of unlearning racism is feeling precisely that lack, sometimes acutely. I begin to understand how right Barbara Smith is when she says that "racism distorts and lessens" the lives of White women.[51] I do not mean, of course, that women of color were put in this world to benefit White feminists (what an idea!), or that they ought to do so, or that this is their function, or even one of them, or even that such an idea ought to enter their thoughts—such beliefs are one of the more ghastly forms that White racism takes. What I do mean is that White feminists alone (and White people alone)—well, how resourceless, how *stupid* we are, when we think there is only us! Pratt puts it better, writing about her past ideas of feminist utopias: "I didn't understand what a limited, narrow space, and how short lasting, it would be, if only *my* imagination and knowledge and abilities were to go into the making and extending of it." So this is one gain for me as I change: I learn a way of looking at the world that is more accurate, complex, multi-layered, multi-dimensional, more truthful, to see the world of overlapping circles, like movement on the millpond after a fish has jumped, instead of the courthouse square with me at the middle."[52]

Precisely: overlapping, indeed interlocking, circles, everything connected and interdependent, meanings constantly widening, *and no hierarchy.*

And who else is out there? Sometimes I found the experiences of women of color to be like my own, as in Wallace's exasperated comment that "Black women have never listened to their mothers. No black woman ever pays attention to any other black woman. And so each one starts out fresh, as if no black woman had ever tried to live before";[53] or Susan Ali's wry description that "Contrary to popular belief, the Spanish Inquisition commenced the first time a Puerto Rican girl came home five minutes late. It was torture first, questioning later"; or the Combahee River Collective's account of their teenage years, "Most of us had been forced to develop our intellects at great cost to our social lives."[54] Some I found very different, like Moraga's seemingly simple phrase "La Frontera,"[55] (1987, iii) which to her means the "borderland" *between* two countries or cultures or races, the place where the two meet, while to me (a child of the dominant U.S. White culture) "the frontier" always meant the end of civilization, *beyond which there was nothing and nobody*. This is not a small difference but a genocidal one in a land whose European invaders did not perceive the ten to twelve million people living in it as Human at all and who killed so many of them that the surviving Native American population of the United States is now only 1.3 million, a tenth of what it once was.[56] And here is classicist Constance Carroll, finding enriched understanding of that classic of the dominant White culture curriculum, *Medea,* not in that culture itself but outside it, in the knowledge of her own and her Black students' situation in that culture. True, the play's chorus admits, observes Carroll, that the plight of all women is dismal, but Medea "makes some distinctions that are intrinsic to grasping one of the central issues of the play." Medea says, a "foreign woman coming among new laws / New customs . . . I am alone. I / Have no city, have no / Mother, brother, nor any of my own blood to turn to in / This extremity." It is her Black woman students, says Carroll, who really "understand and can identify with the situation of Medea."[57]

And take, for example, what White feminists have been deploring in modern, industrialized patriarchal societies for at least the last twenty years: the "splits" between public and private, "masculine" and "feminine," work and emotion, women and men, children and adults, work and play, consumption and production, objective knowledge and subjective experience, cooperativeness and competitiveness, home and the workplace, and especially the differences supposed to exist between reason and emotion. Here is Varda Burstyn, for example, about the split between education and entertainment:

> Our society divides "education" from "entertainment." To educational material we entrust the task of analysis, but we make the material so dull that those it is supposed to inform resist its messages. Because its role is to divert, entertainment is imbued with beauty, excitement and sensuality. But these precious qual-

ities become distorted and degraded when they are leeched of their emotive, poetic and social content.[58]

Mathematician and humanist Evelyn Fox Keller redefines the similar division between "objective knowledge" and mere "subjectivity" as follows: "I define objectivity as the pursuit of a maximally authentic and hence maximally reliable understanding of the world. . . . Such a pursuit is dynamic in that it actively draws on the commonalty between mind and nature as a resource for understanding." Often socialist feminists describe how these splits have come about historically. For example, Christine Delphy also comments on the "objectivity" Keller is trying to remold, writing: "The idea of a neutral science . . . is not in itself a neutral idea. . . . The idea that knowledge does not have a foundation in the social position of its producers is, on the contrary, the product of a very precise social position: the position of dominance."[59]

Unsurprisingly, it is industrial capitalism, with its division between work and the family, that has produced these splits. Ann Oakley says so, while Jonathan Katz remarks dryly about the time before industrial capitalism when "Human activity was not yet divided and organized into waged acts called 'labor,' non-waged acts called 'feeling.' " Here is a statement along the same lines from the Berkeley-Oakland Women's Union in 1974: "The split between the public and private . . . leads to a distorted view of human energy, which has to be either work or leisure."[60] And here is Rosalind Petchesky, commenting on the same phenomenon:

> "Production" and "reproduction," work and the family, far from being separate territories like the moon and the sun or the kitchen and the shop, are really intimately related modes that reverberate upon one another. . . . [The] model of separate spheres distorts reality . . . it is every bit as much of an ideological construct as are . . . "male" and "female" themselves. . . . Matters such as birth control and abortion, or definitions of "illegitimacy" are political in the highest degree. . . . There is no "private sphere."[61]

Ehrenreich and English describe some of the results of separating the personal and the public, the "family" from the "workplace":

> [The market economy, i.e., capitalism] crowd[s] into the sphere of private life as best it can . . . the personal and biological activities which remain there. For men who must cross between the two spheres daily, private life now takes on a sentimental

appeal in proportion to the coldness and impersonality of the "outside" world. They look to the home to fulfill . . . the bodily needs denied in the workplace and the human solidarity forbidden in the Market.[62]

And here are Ellen Ross and Rayna Rapp, connecting the isolation of family life from work with how we experience the "personal" today and our "sexuality" as part of it:

> The separation, with industrial capitalism, of family life from work, of consumption from production, of leisure from labor, of personal life from political life, has completely reorganized the context within which we experience sexuality. These polarities are grossly distorted and miscast as antinomies [opposites] . . . but their seeming separation creates an ideological space called "personal life," one defining characteristic of which is sexual identity.[63]

Now, I think all the statements above are true—the dominant White culture *does* split everything from everything else and make things into sets of opposites even (or especially) when they're not—but it sounds, above, as if the very problems these White feminists are reporting on, especially the split between reason and emotion, have invaded their own perceptions and their own language. They sound like people trying to do their best to make their way out of a dreadful tangle of superglue by using more superglue, i.e., their language and *its* separation of pleasure from education and thinking from feeling. I don't mean to belittle their work (which is honorable and necessary) but they are to some degree falling on their faces while trying to make their way out of a cultural education in splits/splits/splits/splits, which I share because that education was mine too. Hooks, speaking of a racist and very hostile graduate class on feminist theory she attended, later received a letter of apology from a White fellow student that said (among other things):

> I said in class one day that. . . . we, after fifteen years of education, courtesy of the ruling class, might be more entrapped than others who had not received a start in life so close to the heart of the monster. My classmate, once a close friend, sister, colleague, has not spoken to me since then. I think the possibility that we were not the best spokespeople for all women made her fear for her self-worth and for her Ph.D.[64]

Those who grew up not so close to the heart of the monster—or with their feet outside the superglue, depending on which metaphor you prefer—speak of the same things very differently. For one thing, they find them obviously foolish and have much less trouble "bridging" them. Usually they simply ignore such stuff as the nonsense it is. As Hull remarks almost casually about Toni Cade Bambara's novel *The Salt Eaters,* "[There is] TCB's belief (shared by geniuses and mystics) that all knowledge systems are really one system and that "everything is everything," that the traditional divisions are artificial and merely provide the means for alienating schisms." And here is Anita Valerio, describing her mother's story of a neighbor woman's ghost (a woman who killed herself), heard by the woman's husband crying at night:

> I say, "My that's something weird." Weird? The word is foreign
> to me as soon as I've said it. Weird? . . . Of course, I remember,
> of course I know. "Weird," only a non-Indian would say that.
> Someone who doesn't know, who hasn't been raised to see that
> life is a continuous whole from flesh to spirit, that we're not as
> easily separated as some think, I knew that.[65]

Luisah Teish flatly cites these splits, especially that between "good" and "evil," as what is causing

> the insanity in our culture. . . . We have placed morning in the
> middle of the night instead of at sunrise, put the New Year in
> the middle of winter instead of in spring, and have divided the
> beings of the Earth into rigid categories instead of recognizing
> our union and kinship as Her children.[66]

Gloria Anzaldúa writes simply: *"They lied, there is no separation between life and writing. . . . No topic is too trivial."* Chrystos, a poet whose very medium is words, nonetheless writes:

> Where are the people who cry *"I am I am"* as the gulls do? They
> rope themselves off with labels   They stand inside a box
> called their job, their clothes, their political & social opinions
> the movies or books they read   I've never believed those
> items which is why I was considered crazy I want to know the
> truth   I glimpse under that malarkey called "civilization."
> . . . I am ashamed   I am heartbroken   I still fight to
> survive   I mourn   I get up   I live a middle class life

Sometimes. . . . So I embrace anew, as my childhood spirit did, the whispers of *a world without words*.[67]

Last of all, there is no writer I know of who emphasizes the sheer wrongness of these splits as strongly as does Audre Lorde. In an essay originally published in 1977 (entitled "Poetry Is Not a Luxury") she writes:

When we view living in the European mode only as a problem to be solved, we rely solely upon our ideas to make us free, for these were what the white fathers told us were precious.

But as we come more into touch with out own ancient, non-European consciousness of living as a situation to be experienced and interacted with, we learn more and more to cherish our feelings, and to respect those hidden sources of our power from where true knowledge and, therefore, lasting action come. . . . I [do not] speak here of the sterile word play that, too often . . . cover[s] a desperate wish for imagination without insight.

Nor do Lorde's insights remain unconnected with economics and power. She continues:

The principal horror of any system which defines the good in terms of profit rather than in terms of human need, or which defines human need to the exclusion of the psychic and emotional components of that need . . . reduces work to a travesty of necessities, a duty by which we earn bread or oblivion for ourselves and those we love. . . . [This] is . . . profoundly cruel.[68]

"The erotic" she uses broadly: emotion, pleasure, "what feels right," including sexuality itself. Thus: *"The erotic is the nurturer or nursemaid of all our deepest knowledge."* Such thinking—the erotic as knowledge—not only points to the splits in living caused by industrial capitalism. It heals the splits precisely by the way it speaks of them. It is emotional *and* learned, lyrical *and* analytic, personal *and* historical, indivisibly so. Asked about such statements by Adrienne Rich in a 1979 interview, Lorde defined reason as a way of getting from one place to another but not capable of choosing what place to go to, saying, "The white fathers told us, 'I think, therefore I am,' and the Black mother within each of us—the poet—whispers in our dreams, 'I feel, therefore I can be free.' "[69]

NOTES

1. The title is from Bernice Johnson Reagon. See the conclusion of Chapter XIII.

2. Elly Bulkin et al., eds. *Yours in Struggle: Three Feminist Perspectives on Anti-Semitism and Racism* (Brooklyn, NY: Long Haul Press, 1984), 49.

3. Gloria T. Hull et al, eds., *All the Women Are White, All the Blacks Are Men, but Some of Us Are Brave: Black Women's Studies* (Old Westbury, NY: Feminist Press, 1982), 48.

4. Cherríe Moraga and Gloria Anzaldúa, eds., *This Bridge Called My Back: Writings of Radical Women of Color* (Watertown, MA: Persephone Press, 1981), 62.

5. Audre Lorde, *Sister Outsider: Essays and Speeches* (Trumansburg, NY: Crossing Press, 1984), 131, 168, italics added.

6. Bulkin et al., *Yours in Struggle,* 12. One example Pratt gives of her earlier unconsciousness as a feminist is her scheduling a feminist discussion "on religion" with "no representation . . . requested from the women of the local Jewish congregation since 'religion' meant . . . Christianity. We held the session on a Saturday because . . . Sunday was when folks went to church." Earlier she notes having often driven past the local synagogue without in the least connecting it with "religion" (ibid., 31).

7. Ibid., 35–36, 47.

8. Ibid., 44.

9. See, for example, Howard Zinn's *A People's History of the United States.* See also Sarah Schulman, "When We Were Very Young: A Walking Tour Through Radical Jewish Women's History on the Lower East Side, 1879–1919," in Melanie Kaye/Kantrowitz and Irena Klepfisz, eds., *The Tribe of Dina: A Jewish Woman's Anthology* (Montpelier, VT: Sinister Wisdom Books, 1986).

10. Barbara Smith, ed., *Home Girls: A Black Feminist Anthology* (New York: Kitchen Table Women of Color Press, 1983), 366–67.

11. Bulkin et al., *Yours in Struggle,* 51.

12. Ibid., 144.

13. Ibid., 189.

14. Ibid., 190.

15. Hull et al., *All the Women,* 50.

16. Ibid., xxi; bell hooks, *Feminist Theory from Margin to Center* (Boston: South End Press, 1984), 110. Hooks adds:

> The ability to "translate" ideas to an audience that varies in age, sex, ethnicity, degree of literacy is a skill feminist edu-cators need to develop. Concentration of feminist educators in universities encourages habitual use of an academic style that may make it impossible for teachers to communicate

effectively with individuals who are not familiar with either academic style or jargon (ibid., 111).

17. Roseanne Barr, *Roseanne: My Life as a Woman* (New York: Harper and Row, 1989), 185; Baym cited in Cheris Kramarae and Paula A. Teichler, *A Feminist Dictionary* (Boston: Pandora, 1985), 448.

18. Paula Giddings, *When and Where I Enter: The Impact of Black Women on Race and Sex in America* (New York: Morrow, 1984), 80, 340; Smith in Bulkin et al., *Yours in Struggle,* 78–79; Alma Gómez et al., eds., *Cuentos: Stories by Latinas* (New York: Kitchen Table Women of Color Press, 1983), viii; hooks, *Feminist Theory,* 52, italics added.

19. Bulkin in Bulkin et al., *Yours in Struggle,* 139; Carroll in Hull et al., *All the Women,* 125, italics added.

20. Susan Koppelman, letter to author, 20 February 1986.

21. Moraga and Anzaldúa, *This Bridge,* 235.

22. Pérez in Mary Bragg et al., eds., *Lesbian Psychologies: Explorations and Challenges* (Urbana: University of Illinois Press, 1987), 158.

23. Bulkin et al., *Yours in Struggle,* 69, 71, 76.

24. Kennedy in Bragg et al., *Lesbian Psychologies,* 157.

25. Lorde, *Sister Outsider,* 124; Bulkin et al., *Yours in Struggle,* 192.

26. Gloria Joseph and Jill Lewis, *Common Differences: Conflicts in Black and White Feminist Perspectives* (New York: Anchor, 1981), 4.

27. Hull et al., *All the Women,* 48–49.

28. Bulkin et al., *Yours in Struggle,* 68. (Smith is, of course, quoting Bernice Johnson Reagon.)

29. Joseph and Lewis, *Common Differences,* 3.

30. When I was eight years old, I thought that I could learn a foreign language—like French, for example, which I knew existed—by learning the "key" that would turn all French sentences into English sentences. I still remember my astonishment when my mother informed me that not only was each word different from English (and had to be memorized separately) but the pronunciation and grammar were different too and there were awful things called "idioms" that didn't even mean what they seemed to mean. Worse: some languages actually had different alphabets and were written up-and-down or left-to-right or even nonalphabetically, like Japanese and Chinese! The idea that "they" are really "just like us" is similar to the "key" I thought existed above. It may be the first, useful, tentative step away from the outright bigotry of "they are totally unlike us, i.e., everything bad and awful or unknowable," but it's still totally self-centered.

31. Michelle Wallace, *Black Macho and the Myth of the Superwoman* (New York: Dial, 1979), 126, 127.

32. Sharlene Hesse-Biber, "The Black Woman Worker: A Minority Group Perspective on Women at Work," *Sage* III: 1 (1986), 33, 26–27; Giddings, *When*

and Where, 353–54; Hesse-Biber, "The Black Woman Worker," 28. Hesse-Biber notes that Black women have often experienced what sociologists call the "farmer's daughter" effect, i.e., because sons could earn more than their sisters *without the same level of education,* parents tended to educate their daughters better than they did their sons (ibid., 29).

33. Patricia A. Gwartney-Gibbs and Patricia A. Taylor, "Black Women Workers' Earnings Progress in Three Industrial Sectors," *Sage* III: 1 (1986), 21 22.

34. Joseph and Lewis, *Common Differences,* 27–28.

35. Hull et al., *All the Women,* 5.

36. Bulkin et al., *Yours in Struggle,* 77–78.

37. Ibid., 78.

38. Moraga and Anzaldúa, *This Bridge,* 114.

39. Ibid., 46–47.

40. Lorde, *Sister Outsider,* 147–48.

41. Garcia in Bragg, et al., *Lesbian Psychologies,* 146.

42. Bulkin, et al., *Yours in Struggle,* 143.

43. Ibid., 116.

44. For example, in 1939 there was a proposal to allow twenty thousand war-threatened European children come the United States, two-thirds of them Jewish. One of the groups in the United States that was opposed to the bill, the American Legion, maintained that "it was traditional American policy that home life should be preserved and that the American Legion therefore strongly opposed the breaking up of families," says Bulkin (Bulkin et al., *Yours in Struggle,* 104).

45. Moraga and Anzaldúa, *This Bridge,* 117.

46. Smith in ibid., 119; Cherríe Moraga, review of Joan Gibbs and Sara Bennett, eds., *Top Rankings: A Collection of Articles on Racism and Classism in the Lesbian Community* in *Conditions* 7 (1981), 143.

47. Bulkin et al., *Yours in Struggle,* 72–73.

48. hooks, *Feminist Theory,* 56.

49. Kris Demian, personal communication with author, 1988. A former student of mine, Demian had taught in an inner-city ghetto school and told me of the training she and others received to do so, which included the interpretation of various group's cultural codes.

50. I used to ask myself what they were looking for: invisible elves under the flooring? Worse still, they never framed conversations with recognizable beginnings like "Excuse me, but could you—" or recognizable endings like "It's been nice but I have to go now. Good-bye." Instead they walked right up to me and started talking—in New York City only muggers, rapists, and mad people do that—and disappeared while I was still in midsentence, leaving me feeling rejected and baffled. As for the trouble caused by anything remotely resembling dramatic irony, which is an important part of *my* culture, *it is endless.*

An example (invented):

Northwesterner (NW) (after a long pause): "Love and hate are sometimes very close together."

New York Jew (NYJ) (me): "Does that mean if I hit you over the head with a mallet, I'm in love with you?"

I will not go into the tradition of Talmudic disputation here but only point out that the NW perceives such an answer as a personal attack, while another NYJ would appreciate it as, first, a piece of verbal wit that could be enjoyed by all, and, second, a genuine request for specificity and clarification, i.e., "What you've said is all very well and good, but I can interpret it in a way that will make it absurd. That's because it's too vague. Please be more specific, or your statement will have to include absurdities like the one I've just invented." The NYJ would smile and respond. The NW students I said things like this to (before I learned not to) looked at the floor and were distinctly not happy. None of this is a matter of morality; rather it's a problem in intelligibility. I still find Easterners understandable, but most Northwest Pacific natives still repel and baffle me. In the same way the residents of Cicely in the television comedy *Northern Exposure* find their doctor, the transplanted New York Jew Joel Fleischman, sour-tempered. He's not; it's cultural. In fact, he's warding off the shock of expected evil by loudly predicting it and getting ready for it, a procedure that made a lot of sense in czarist Russia. Jewish "pushiness" is another miscommunication; one Northwesterner complained to me of a Jewish woman at a feminist music festival who'd simply "laid down the law" to her about who was to do what. What to do? I said, "She expects you to do the same to her. When she says, 'You do X,' you say back, 'No, I do X. You do Y.' " She was misinterpreting a proposal as an order; later she tried out what I suggested and reported back to me, in great surprise, "It worked."

51. Cherríe Moraga, *Loving in the War Years* (Boston: South End Press, 1983), 57–58; Smith in Hull et al., *All the Women,* 49.

52. Pratt in Bulkin et al., *Yours in Struggle,* 30, 17.

53. Wallace, *Black Macho,* 106. Other women of color, including Black women, say otherwise. My impression is that this issue may be differentiated by class. Nonetheless, Wallace's experience, at least, does match mine and that of many White women I know.

54. Ali in Gómez et al., *Cuentos,* 76; Combahee Collective in Moraga and Anzaldúa, *This Bridge,* 214.

55. Gloria Anzaldúa, *Borderlands/La Frontera: The New Mestiza* (San Francisco: Spinsters/Aunt Lute, 1987), iii.

56. Bulkin et al., *Yours in Struggle,* 105. As for the area now called Mexico and the southwestern United States; Anzaldúa writes:

> At the beginning of the 16th century, the Spaniards and Hernán Cortés invaded Mexico and with the help of tribes that the Aztecs had subjugated, conquered it. Before the conquest

there were twenty-five million Indian people in Mexico and Yucatán. Immediately after . . . the Indian population had been reduced to under seven million. By 1650, only one-and-a-half-million pure-blooded Indians remained.

And:

> In the 1800s, Anglos migrated illegally into Texas, which was then part of Mexico, in greater and greater numbers and gradually drove the *tejanos* . . . from their lands, committing all manner of atrocities. . . . Their illegal invasion forced Mexico to fight a war to keep its Texas territory. The Battle of the Alamo, in which the Mexican forces vanquished the whites became, for the whites . . . the symbol that legitimized the white imperialist takeover (Anzaldúa, *Borderlands*, 5, 6).

57. Hull et al., *All the Women,* 124.

58. Varda Burstyn, ed., *Women against Censorship* (Vancouver: Douglas and McIntyre, 1985), 161–62.

59. Burstyn in ibid., 161; Evelyn Fox Keller, *Reflections on Gender and Science* (New Haven: Yale University Press, 1985), 116–17; Christine Delphy, *Close to Home: A Materialist Analysis of Women's Oppression,* trans. Diana Leonard (Amherst: University of Massachusetts Press, 1984), 157.

60. Ann Oakley, *Subject Women* (New York: Pantheon, 1981), 6; Jonathan Katz, *Gay/Lesbian Almanac: A New Documentary* (New York: Harper and Row, 1983), 48; Berkeley-Oakland Women's Union in Zillah R. Eisenstein, ed., *Capitalist Patriarchy and the Case for Socialist Feminism* (New York: Monthly Review Press, 1979), 358.

61. Ibid., 376–77, 81.

62. Barbara Ehrenreich and Deidre English, *For Her Own Good: 150 Years of the Experts' Advice to Women* (Garden City, NY: Anchor/Doubleday, 1978), 10–11.

63. Ann Snitow et al., eds., *Powers of Desire: The Politics of Sexuality* (New York: Monthly Review Press, 1983), 67–68.

64. hooks, *Feminist Theory,* 13.

65. Hull in Smith, *Home Girls,* 130; Valerio in Moraga and Anzaldúa, *This Bridge,* 42.

66. Teish in Smith, *Home Girls,* 348.

67. Anzaldúa in Moraga and Anzuldúa, *This Bridge;* Chrystos in ibid., 243–44, italics added.

68. Lorde, *Sister Outsider,* 37, 55.

69. Ibid., 102, 56, 38, italics added. Another multiply marginal woman, Judy Grahn (poor Southwestern White kid, lesbian, feminist, poet, and gay activist) has

written strikingly of the triumph of the State over the Tribe, the conquering of people who are fully Human by people who have been turned into machines for the purposes of a centralized state. The state in her description is Rome (in which upper-class boys were routinely beaten as part of their education), and the tribal peoples it smashed were the British Celts, led by Queen Boudica, who had earlier reduced the Roman settlement of Londinium to ashes. Her rebellion was finally crushed, says Grahn, by the "modern" Roman lines, all "iron and leather" (Judy Grahn, *Another Mother Tongue: Gay Words, Gay Worlds* [Boston: Beacon Press, 1984], 141–45).

It's probably worth noting here the peculiar historical viciousness of U.S. slavery, the peculiar viciousness of the U.S. racism that is its historical descendant, and the sexual craziness that accompanies both of them. Michele Wallace's description of the history of U.S. slavery makes many significant points. Although many poor Whites were at first kidnapped to be indentured servants in the New World and they too "suffered a harrowing middle passage," Whites could appeal to strong governments and could escape and "blend into the crowd," while Indians who escaped could simply vanish because "they knew the country." Displaced Africans could do none of these. They "were disoriented by differences in culture, language, religion, terrain . . . [and] their color made them highly visible as runaways" (Wallace, *Black Macho*, 132–33). She also notes that it took from 1640 to 1661 to establish slavery as legal in Virginia and that it was only by the 1700s that the number of Whites willing to be indentured servants dropped to the point that "slavery was well on its way to becoming a primary source of labor" (ibid., 131). Moreover:

> From the outset the primary difference between American slavery and every other kind . . . was not its barbarity [Africans had earlier been enslaved by Arabs, other Africans, the Dutch, Portuguese, Spanish and French] but the total impossibility of upward mobility for the slave. The Southern colonies and the antebellum South had no free mulatto class with established rights such as in the Caribbean islands. The slave was not allowed to work his [sic] way up . . . as he had been in the Arab and African worlds and in Ancient Greece and Rome. . . . He was permanently locked into his situation.

Perhaps most important of all for U.S. racism:

> *After the constitutional ban on slave importation,* which took effect in 1808, the market required . . . a brutal emphasis . . . upon the stud capabilities of the black man and upon the black woman's fertility. The theory of the inferiority of blacks began to be elaborated upon and to take hold. It was at this point that the black woman gained her reputation for in-

vulnerability. *She was the key to the labor supply* (ibid., 131, 137–38, italics added).

Wallace connects much U.S. racist sexual mythology to the above "market require-ments": the Black woman's supposed emotional callousness, promiscuity, and phys-ical strength (which made it all right to take away her children and "breed" her, and made it "unnecessary" for her to be protected, especially by the Black man), and the Black man's supposed spinelessness, sexual prowess, and unreliability (which made it unthinkable for him to protect her and thinkable to "breed" him too). Such hor-rible stuff—which became standard to some degree for racism directed at all people of color—can be traced directly back to the situation described in that dry phrase "the key to the labor supply."

FIFTEEN

SO . . .

Readers who find the previous chapter evasive are quite right; it is. In discussing the differences between so many feminists of color and White feminists, there is one subject that is most often misunderstood and blundered into by White feminists: *men*.

Although separatists of color most certainly do exist,[1] the strongest and most emphatic statements against separatism that I have been able to find have been made by feminists of color. Cherríe Moraga writes: "The lesbian separatist utopia? No thank you, sisters. I can't prepare myself a revolutionary packet that makes no sense when I leave the white suburbs and Watertown, Massachusetts and take the T-line to Black Roxbury."[2] The Combahee River Collective agrees,[3] as does Barbara Smith; she states explicitly that separatism is possible only to those privileged by color and class.[4] Bell hooks goes even further:

> Reactionary separatism is rooted in the conviction that male supremacy is an absolute aspect of our culture, that women have only two alternatives: accepting it or withdrawing from it to create subcultures. This position eliminates any need for revolutionary struggle and it is in no way a threat to the status quo.[5]

Although I believe that such statements misrepresent the complexity and variety of feminist separatisms (see Chapter IV), nonetheless these critics are by no means dodging the issues of autonomy and access that separatism inevitably raises. Rather they seem to see identity politics, as I now do, as crucial, inevitable, and an absolutely necessary place to begin—*but not a place to get stuck in, i.e., not a sufficient politics in and of itself.* Again and again feminists of color emphasize that their experiences of oppression are *multiple*—and that for most of the heterosexual, middle-management-level, professional-class, able-bodied, more-or-less Christian, White feminists they know, this is not the case. Beverly Smith puts it this way:

> Maybe the reason that white women got into lesbian separatism was because . . . [t]hey felt that they had to separate themselves from white men to even have a fighting chance.[6]

One enemy, one separatism. But suppose, as Barbara Smith says of the experiences of women of color, you "have experiences that have nothing to do with being female, but are nonetheless experiences of deep oppression . . . and even violence." These problems and necessities give rise to a situation in which, as Audre Lorde says,

> Black women and men have shared racist oppression and still share it. . . . Out of that shared oppression we have developed joint defenses and joint vulnerabilities to each other that are not duplicated in the white community, with the exception of the relationship between Jewish women and Jewish men.[7]

Jill Lewis, writing from her own White experience of this issue, tells of how the attitudes of White feminists like herself were formed:

> The White women . . . did not have the stakes of *racial* unity or solidarity with White men that the Black women had with Black men. The Women's Liberation Movement formed *against* the experience and consequences of White male power and *against* the kind of subjective experience of being women which this power necessitated.[9]

If, as Lewis puts it, "the advantages of 'skin privilege' . . . can blur the complexities" of all these issues, then, as Joseph and Lewis say together:

> certain White feminist modes of talking about "men" . . . had to be, in our dialogues, made specific to the economic, political, and daily realities in which White men and White women meet and interact. For Afro-American men there are *no* easily equivalent categories for the feminist rhetoric about "men."[10]

After all, as Joseph points out, "Capitalism and patriarchy do not offer to share with Black males the seat of power" in a world where "the judicial system is racist, the executive system is racist, and the legislative system is racist" as well as "the organized crime power elite." Therefore "Only a specific Black feminist analysis would reveal the character of relations between Black men and Black women."[11]

Here are only a few examples of the kind of analysis mentioned above. Paula Giddings writes:

> Where White women saw Black sexism as essentially a cruder version of that of White males, Black women saw something else. Toni Morrison contended: "For years in this country there was no one for black men to vent their rage on but black women. And for years black women accepted that rage, even regarded that acceptance as their unpleasant duty. But in so doing they frequently kicked back, and they seem never to have become the true slaves that white women see in their own history."[12]

Others view Black male sexism as an immigration/assimilation problem. Audre Lorde, for example, says bluntly, "Freedom and future for Blacks does not mean absorbing the dominant white male disease of sexism,"[13] while Michelle Wallace is even more explicit:

> Only as American blacks began to accept the standards for family life, as well as for manhood and womanhood embraced by American whites, did black men and women resent one another. . . . [but] both continued to feel a substantial group identity. . . . Over the years blacks began to lean more and more towards Americanization—in their case, another word for self-hatred.[14]

Assimilation of some Black men into the professional middle class may have something to do with what is going on. Giddings seems to think so. Citing Black sociologist Robert Staples, she describes him as "ruffled" by Ntozake Shange's play *For Colored Girls* and Wallace's *Black Macho* (both feminist works) and quotes his 1979 opinions, which seem to her both sexist and assimilationist-upwardly-mobile:

> He offered the opinion that Black men, especially middle-class Black men, disdained "strong" women . . . [and added that] such women "will not find it easy to carve out an independent

career lifestyle and maintain a stable relationship with a man."
. . . Explaining why the "best" and "brightest" Black men often
marry White women, he observed, "It could be that the most
successful Black men have values and lifestyles most in tune
with White society. . . . Among those values will exist the one
that women should be supportive and subordinate. . . . Many
Black men, including those involved with Black women, do not
believe Black women fit the model very well."[15]

Judith Arcana, the White author of *Every Mother's Son,* agrees. She says,
"Black mothers are beginning to hear this now; before, it was wives and
girlfriends who were blamed; Mama was a comfort. But Black men are
moving toward the attitude of the dominant society."[16]

If talking of some recent African American issues as "assimilation" issues
seems odd to some White readers, please bear in mind the quite recent
Black immigration of the 1920s and 1930s from the rural South to the urban
North.[17] The people who did this changed cultures and conditions as dras-
tically as any European immigrant. Thus, Renita Weems, writing about Toni
Morrison's fiction, states:

> Morrison asks us through her creation of a generation of
> women, "What happens to our children once we cross the Ma-
> son-Dixon? What have our children lost that we were too busy
> making do to lose?" Or, more specifically, "What have they
> picked up in this urban environment which sends them into
> worlds of insanity we never knew?"[18]

Offered, in Lorde's words, the "narcotic promise" of assimilation, one
they are "not allowed to fulfill,"[19] Black men live in a complex relation to
Black women, as do other men of color in relation to women of color. White
feminists must not claim to understand this relation or be surprised when
a great many feminists of color reject White versions of feminism. To give
an example, one reason Black women often talk about Black men as an
endangered species is that in a racist society, they may well be so. Sociologist
Clyde W. Franklin II quotes some appalling statistics:

> The black male life expectancy is roughly 13 years less than the
> white female, 9 years less than the black female, and 5 years
> less than the white male. . . . "There are ten percent fewer non-
> white male survivors than white male survivors by age 45 and
> by age 65 twenty percent fewer non-white survivors and by age
> 75 thirty percent fewer."

And, more than just appallingly, "Homicide is the leading cause of death among black males age 15 to 24."[20]

Franklin is another social critic who believes that Black male sexism is a problem of assimilation or attempts at assimilation:

> Before the civil rights movement, the black man's subculture reference group and the black man's peer group *both* emphasized exchanging instrumental and expressive functions among the sexes as one way to adapt to the social and economic demands of American life. . . . because of societal limitations on black men's ability to assume a traditional American male sex role. . . . Black women *and* black men knew the score . . . *role exchange was the key to black survival.* . . . This information [was] imparted . . . by the subcultural institution but it was also part of black men's peer-group socialization of its younger members. . . . Black people did not live under the illusion that they could emulate the white family.

Franklin pinpoints "the seeds of change in the black man's peer group" in the late 1960s and early 1970s,

> when increasing numbers of black men began to buy the idea that black women were largely responsible for the plight of black men because . . . they did not assume a sex role similar to the one assumed by white women. . . . When black men . . . embraced America's ideas about masculinity (e.g. competitiveness, aggressiveness, violence, sufficient distance from femininity—and this is certainly apparent in the 1980s) the decimation of black men and the destruction of the black family intensified.[21]

The result is *role strain,* that is, accepting ideals one is at the same time prevented from attaining, and (among other things) the irony of sexist scapegoating.

If the issues are thus connected in people's lives, then no theory that leaves them separated is worth much. Such connections are the only way coalitions can be formed—coalitions that will both work and last. As Elly Bulkin notes, "Done purely for others" as "bargaining chips in a larger political game," coalition work is inevitably unstable and useless. Similarly, when such work is done only to raise consciousness or "as a means of . . . assuaging guilt," it becomes a "deadended . . . form of political self-improvement" and helps nobody.[22] Connections between issues must, of course, be moral connections, but they must also be the connections that make it clear how the issues are materially related, i.e., who gets what from whom and how and why.[23] I mean by such material connections, for example, Marilyn Frye's noting that "the pressures of compulsory motherhood on white women are not just pressures to keep women down, but pressure to keep the white population up." And Pat Parker describes the function of the Klan and the Nazi groups in the United States as "tools of the governmental system" just like "our armed forces and police."[24]

Without connecting the issues it's easy to fall into the mistake of imagining that the different issues are competing with one another and that being committed to one means you can't be committed to another.[25] Bulkin writes:

> Writing about being fired from a large Southwestern state university, Melanie Kaye/Kantrowitz has described. . . . the specific "assumption that to be a strongly identified Jew *meant* being less anti-racist, as though the struggles were mutually exclusive or, worse, antagonistic."[26]

But just how to connect the issues is a more difficult matter than simply asserting that they are connected. I think by now it's clear that sexism and capitalism are economically interdependent and that capitalism, as Hilda Scott notes, cannot remain as it is without

> the enormous amount of unpaid work performed by women in the home and out of it . . . [which] is essential both to our patriarchal culture and to industrial capitalism. If it were not for the free ride these two mutually supportive interlocking systems are receiving, it would not have been necessary to disguise the economic value of women's work in the "private" sphere with so much mythology.[27]

Maxine Margolis says the same thing in slightly different terms: "The wage and salary structure of industrial capitalism was—and still is—dependent on the child care, cooking, and cleaning done gratis by housewives." And Jessie Bernard insists that it is the "integry"—populated largely by women—that keeps capitalism's contradictions from destroying capitalism.[28]

Is the same thing true of racism? Joseph states (or at least did so once) that unfortunately "the categories of marxism are sex-blind *and* race-blind" and therefore "insufficiently materialistic" to give us any help here.[29] But all socialisms are not the same, any more than feminisms or antiracisms are, and if socialist theory can be broadened to an economic analysis of the kind of labor provided by sexism (as it certainly can), then we certainly don't have to get rid of socialist theory in order to use it in ways that will analyze and account for racism. (A lot of other people have thought so too, for quite a long time, but more of this in a moment.) For now, just take a look at the "oddness" of racism—that is, its oddness from the point of view of capitalism's supposed impersonality and its reduction of all relations between people to a matter of voluntary contracts, weighted against the working class as such contracts necessarily are. One of the first things to strike me about African American women's accounts of racism (it was, of course, no surprise to them) was that *racism, like sexism, is a feudal or quasi-feudal phenomenon.*

One example: Renita Weems, quoting an interview of Toni Morrison by Thomas LeClair in *The New Republic* of 2 March 1981, speaks of Morrison's offhand description of the characters in one of her rural novels as "peasants" confronting "city values . . . there is a confrontation between old values of the tribes and new urban values." Barbara Christian, also speaking of Morrison's novels, calls the characters in one book "Southern peasants . . . reminding us that much of the Afro-American population is still under the yoke of a feudal sharecropping system." Giddings mentions the "convict lease system, always used as a pool of free southern Black labor,"[30] and the history of agricultural and domestic labor in the United States—labor most often done by Black men and Black women—repeats the story of racism as almost literally feudal in a way the oppression exercised against the White working class usually was not. In the 1930s, writes Debra Lynn Newman,

> Old-age insurance, survivors benefits and unemployment compensation were provided by the Social Security act to all occupational groups *except agricultural and domestic workers.* The National Industrial Recovery Act provided minimum wage codes for many occupations but none for these.

At that time, says Newman,

> 1930 census figures . . . [showed] that 95% of the more than two million household workers were women of all races . . . the largest occupational group of working women in the United States. Almost one-half . . . were Black women and approximately one-half of all Black working women were household workers. Nationally, white women outnumbered Black about ten to one, but in the largest occupational category Black women and white (mostly foreign born) were equally represented.[31]

She adds that arguments to include household workers in the Social Security Act "repeatedly failed" and second that "as more and more labor-protective legislation passed, private household workers were left out in the cold every time." Citing figures that three Black workers out of five "were not helped when the Depression had thrown more Blacks out of work proportionately than any other element of the population," Newman quotes Depression figures to the effect that "out of the 5,500,000 Negro workers in this country approximately two million are in agriculture and another 1,500,000 in domestic service—3,500,000 . . . dropped through the act right away. . . ."[32]

Free labor, grossly underpaid labor, the impossibility of free contract, the impossibility of leaving one's caste, the ascription of group membership by birth and appearance, the historical fact of literal enslavement—all these point to racism against African Americans as a feudal institution and are in that sense strikingly similar to sexism. And if such racism is at all similar to the racism practiced today against other people of color (which, with the historical exception of literal chattel slavery, it is) then racism is certainly as curiously "unmodern" as sexism. *Both are labor contracts signed and sealed long before the individuals subject to them were even born,* prescriptions for treatment, control of money, status, housing, medical care, and many other things completely outside the supposedly impersonal relations of capitalism.[33] The issues are not only related; they are propping each other up. In fact, it seems that on each side of the structure of capitalism, supporting it like the flying buttresses built outside medieval European cathedrals to keep the weight of the roof from demolishing the cathedral walls, are those "invisible" or "natural" or "personal" institutions of racism and sexism. Both provide a superexploited workforce that cannot be accounted for by class analysis only, *if and when such analysis is too narrowly conceived.*[34]

As Zillah Eisenstein says, speaking of big business in the United States:

> Elinor Langer in *Ms.* magazine states ". . . equality for women, coming on top of the decreasing flexibility in hiring and firing of black people that has followed the civil rights movement, would introduce an inelasticity into the labor force that their profit margins cannot bear."[35]

Nor is such a situation peculiar only to the United States; more than a century of radical analysis has linked Kipling's "white man's burden" abroad with White gentlemen's profits at home, whether such imperialism/colonialism was the open, official kind of the eighteenth and nineteenth centuries or the unnamed, unofficial economic imperialism of the twentieth. Racism has always been the justification for imperialism, its ideology, its "reason" for superexploiting not only minorities at home but whole nations abroad, an exploitation without which oligopoly capitalism—which is now international—could not continue. Radicals have been saying this for a very long time. Harry Magdoff and Paul Sweezy, to give only one example, describe imperialism as the normal result of capitalist development in which

> accumulation increasingly takes the form of conglomeration, expansion into other industries which have not yet reached the same degree of maturity, *and multinationalization*. . . . *The expansion of capital into the underdeveloped periphery on the scale desired, and in a real sense needed, by the oligopolistic corporations of the advanced countries would be totally impossible without the massive and unremitting application of the power of their states*, either individually or collectively (including through such agencies as the International Monetary Fund and World Bank). . . . This application of power takes place directly (as in Greece in the 1940s, Vietnam, and the Dominican Republic; or the recent French intervention in Zaire; or a long string of CIA-organized coups in Iran, Guatemala, Greece in 1967, Bangladesh, etc.) or . . . through arming, financing and politically supporting client regimes throughout the Third World to repress their own people. . . . The enormous apparatus of power necessary to sustain this world-wide enterprise . . . is centered in the United States and benefits from important and sometimes vital support from the other advanced capitalist countries acting as junior partners.[36]

Even without such analysis, many feminists have noted how "development" is ruinous to the infrastructure of the countries being "developed" and especially bad for the women in them. Scott speaks of the way employment in newly industrialized nations makes no provision for social services, which are "provided by the rural subsistence economy of African and Asian villages" and of the "free trade zones" created for foreign investors to which come multinational corporations looking for cheap labor, which means low wages, long hours, speed-ups, inadequate health care, workers (usually unmarried young women) living five or six in a room, and "intimidation to keep the unions away." Sulabha Brahme, quoting a committee appointed to study the status of women in India in 1975, says, "The transition to a modern economy has meant the exclusion of an increasing number of women from active participation in . . . production. . . . A considerable number continue to participate for no return and no recognition." She adds that 94 percent of women workers in India are unorganized.

Madhu Kishwar gives examples of women being thrown out of work after every technological advance, as training and higher pay go to men. Lisa Leghorn and Katherine Parker agree, calling "growth" "an accumulation of wealth for a few at the expense . . . of the many . . . extreme class stratification and debasing poverty to the overwhelming majority." Nawal El Saadawi points out that profit rules capitalist production and that "the essential needs of the vast majority of people [in the Arab countries] are a secondary matter, catered for only to the degree that will ensure the continued working of the profit machine" and that "commodities produced specifically for women . . . in the Arab countries . . . are really luxury goods." Robin Morgan sums up similar phenomena described by her contributors and gives specific examples from the Pacific Islands, Indonesia, Nepal, and India: schooling for boys but not girls, technology taking jobs from women, a "trickle down" effect that doesn't, and so on.[37]

Such connections, in theory and by way of resistance, are being made by those whose lives inevitably feel the impact of all the issues at once: women of color.[38]

How to save, in Barbara Cameron's words, a society with "arrogance rising, moon in oppression, and sun in destruction"? Those of us who aren't the CEOs of transnational corporations, their lobbyists, or the politicians they've bought, will have to work together. Such work will often take us beyond the zone in which we can understand what happens, control it—or know what to expect, at least—and stay comfortable.

Shall we (by "we" I mean feminists here, as will be clear presently) work with men? Well, yes, of course. I'm not recommending the fake sympathy that often passes for compassion, or the fear that's often disguised as concern, or the sympathy that results in ignoring oneself. What I do recommend is working with anyone who will truly work with you. Deeds, not words, as Christabel Pankhurst required of the British government. The question isn't whether "we" can trust "them" (whoever they are) but how much and in what areas.

Nonetheless, the fundamental reason for working together is that all the issues are facets of the same issue. No issue is secondary to those being hurt by it, and asking anyone to wait until "more important issues" have been attended to is a sign that the asker hasn't thought any of the issues through. Self-interest is a fine thing *because* all the issues are intimately interconnected. (If people won't listen, I think it's permissible, in the short run, to sit on them [gently] while you patiently explain what they need to know in order to realize what their long-term self-interest is, but don't use these methods for long-term results. They backfire. If someone's long-term interest is opposed to yours, that someone is your enemy and you had better regard that person in exactly that light.) If folks in the United States hadn't been conditioned by forty-odd years of Cold War politics, I'd say that the issues were *collective* issues—or, if you prefer, social issues, societal issues. Lone heroes are not capable of saving the world, Hollywood notwithstanding. Even so, some people are *placed*—that is, they exist at a social/economic/historical location—from which it's easier to understand what's happening and what can be done about it. Here are the words of three of them. Joseph and Lewis write, "There is a real feeling of hopefulness. It is a hope born out of the belief that oppressed groups will be important historical agents in bringing about the major changes needed in our society." And here, for the last word, is Bernice Johnson Reagon:

> It ain't that important what you do in a crisis. You go beyond yourself anyway, and you talk about it for years. . . . You go wishing every day was like that. Every day ain't like that, and what really counts is not what you do this weekend [the occasion of her speech] but take what this weekend has meant— try to digest it. And first thing Monday, Tuesday morning at work, before twenty-four hours go around, apply it. And then do it every day you get up and find yourself alive.[39]

NOTES

1. See, for example, Sarah Lucia Hoagland and Julia Penelope, eds., *For Lesbians Only: A Separatist Anthology* (London: Onlywomen Press, 1988).

2. Cherríe Moraga and Gloria Anzaldúa, eds., *This Bridge Called My Back: Writings by Radical Women of Color* (Watertown, MA: Persephone Press, 1981), xiii.

3. Ibid., 214.

4. Ibid., 12.

5. bell hooks, *Feminist Theory from Margin to Center* (Boston: South End Press, 1984), 33, 71.

6. Moraga and Anzaldúa, *This Bridge,* 121.

7. Ibid., 121; Audre Lord, *Sister Outsider: Essays and Speeches* (Trumansburg, NY: Crossing Press, 1984), 118.

8. Moraga and Anzaldúa, *This Bridge,* 121–22.

9. Gloria Joseph and Jill Lewis, *Common Differences: Conflicts in Black and White Feminist Perspectives* (New York: Anchor, 1981), 61–62. Barbara Smith made a remark elsewhere that, while not intended as such, might serve as a comment: "White women have a materially different relationship to . . . racism than white men. They get less out of it and often function as its pawns, whether they recognize this or not" (Gloria T. Hull et al., eds., *All the Women Are White, All the Blacks Are Men,*

but Some of Us Are Brave: Black Women's Studies [Old Westbury, NY: Feminist Press, 1982], 51). Not noticing that other women's relationship to White male power is different from one's own is indeed functioning as a pawn of the racist system, however unintentional such ignorance may be.

10. Joseph and Lewis, *Common Differences,* 44, 10.

11. In Lydia Sargent, ed., *Women and Revolution: A Discussion of the Unhappy Marriage of Marxism and Feminism* (Boston: South End Press, 1981), 101, 100, 93.

12. Paula Giddings, *When and Where I Enter: The Impact of Black Women on Race and Sex in America* (New York: Morrow, 1984), 310.

13. Lorde, *Sister Outsider,* 63.

14. Michelle Wallace, *Black Macho and the Myth of the Superwoman* (New York: Dial, 1979), 24.

15. Giddings, *When and Where,* 354–55.

16. Judith Arcana, *Every Mother's Son* (Seattle: Seal Press, 1986), 243. Arcana agrees with me about the origins of Jewish-American male mother-blaming: "Jewish men, in their rush to be accepted by Christian America, have fallen all over each other to claim the definitive [evil] mom as a Jew" (ibid.). The Christian United States, of course, usually couldn't care less, except that as all woman-blaming is popular, we now have the "Jewish American Princess" who is a combination of evils: female *and* Jewish—hardly a step toward the extinguishing of Jew-hating, needless to say.

17. Giddings, *When and Where,* 141–42, 218.

18. Weems in Barbara Smith, ed., *Home Girls: A Black Feminist Anthology* (New York: Kitchen Table Women of Color Press, 1983), 102.

19. Lorde, *Sister Outsider,* 61.

20. Franklin in Harry E. Brod, ed., *The Making of Masculinities: The New Men's Studies* (Boston: Allen and Unwin, 1987), 158, 156, 157. Franklin is quoting J. B. Stewart and J. W. Scott, "The Institutional Decimation of Black Males," *Western Journal of Black Studies* 2:2 (1978), 83.

21. Brod, *Making of Masculinities,* 165–66.

22. Elly Bulkin et al., *Yours in Struggle: Three Feminist Perspectives on Anti-Semitism and Racism* (Brooklyn, NY: Long Haul Press, 1984), 144.

23. I don't want to belittle moral and empathic connections here. They are, of course, extremely important. An example Giddings gives is the no-punches-pulled telegram drafted by the National Council of Negro Women after the Nuremberg Laws legalized the persecution of German Jews. Giddings writes:

> At a 1938 meeting, Mary Jackson McCrorey . . . passed a motion to "let our President [Roosevelt] know that we heartily recommend the action of our government towards the rehabilitation of the suffering Jews of the world, assuring him . . . that our approach is one more sympathetic than could come from any other group in this country because of our

experience in this country" (Giddings, *When and Where,* 228).

24. Marilyn Frye, *The Politics of Reality: Essays in Feminist Theory* (Trumansburg, NY: Crossing Press, 1983), 123; Parker in Moraga and Anzaldúa, *This Bridge,* 239.

25. Gloria Joseph, to give only one example of such connecting, calls racism "the incestuous child of patriarchy and capitalism" (Sargent, *Women and Revolution,* 92), and the Combahee River Collective "see[s] as our particular task the development of an integrated analysis and practice based upon the fact that the major systems of oppression are interlocking" (Smith, *Home Girls,* 272).

26. Bulkin et al., *Yours in Struggle,* 140.

27. Hilda Scott, *Working Your Way to the Bottom: The Feminization of Poverty* (London: Pandora, 1984), 57.

28. Maxine L. Margolis, *Mothers and Such: Views of American Women and Why They Changed* (Berkeley: University of California Press, 1984), 13; Jessie Bernard, *The Female World* (New York: Free Press, 1981), 36.

29. Sargent, *Women and Revolution,* 93.

30. Weems in Smith, *Home Girls,* 102; Christian in Mari Evans, ed., *Black Women Writers (1950–1980): A Critical Evaluation* (Garden City, NY: Anchor, 1984), 459; Giddings, *When and Where,* 139.

31. Debra Lynn Newman, "Black Women Workers in the Twentieth Century," *Sage* III:1 (1986), 12, 11, italics added.

32. Ibid., 12.

33. For example, it will, I hope, surprise nobody that, according to Joseph, Blacks, who number more than 10 percent of the U.S. population "own 1.2% of business equity, 1.2% of farm equity; and 0.1% of stock equity in the U.S.A.; U.S. business receipts in 1977 amounted to $2 trillion. Minority businesses accounted for 1.5% of this total" (Sargent, *Women and Revolution,* 100).

34. The question, much-vexed among socialists, of whether socialism is possible in one country or whether socialism must be worldwide to be permanent and stable, may have something to do with the feminist and antiracist question of whether socialist countries have abolished or can abolish sexism and racism. Lorde writes that "in no socialist country that I have visited have I found an absence of racism or of sexism, so the eradication of both these diseases seems to involve more than the abolition of capitalism as an institution" (Lorde, 1984, 64). An island of socialism in a sea of capitalist marketplace may find itself, even with the best will in the world (which is not always the case, of course), forced to rely on both sexism and racism as a means of exploiting enough labor to hold its own economically in a situation in that it cannot be self-sufficient and must trade outside its own borders—in a world capitalist marketplace—for resources, like minerals or industrial products, that it cannot do without. A possible analogy is the Israeli kibbutz, which,

despite an ideology of socialism and sexual equality, developed (says Scott) extreme sexual inequality between 1920 and 1950 in which "men became producers, women workers in the services" (Scott, 1984, 26). Like a small family farm, which is also forced to produce a cash crop in order to survive in an economy in which exchange values prevail (the farm cannot produce its own machinery, clothing, tools, or even its own food) the kibbutzim were forced to value work that produced cash over work that produced comfort. The second kind thus continued to be performed under conditions of hardship (like caring for infants without the luxury of hot water). Labor—and hence psychological value—had to be concentrated on production for exchange, not on production for use. Of course women got tired of doing communal housework under conditions of deprivation and preferred to work for one husband and a few children, i.e., their own families. This (very sensible) preference was then interpreted—in the absence of an economic theory that would have explained it—as a sign that the sexual division of labor was immutable and that women somehow didn't "want" "liberation." The above explanation is given by Pauline Bart (in "Biological Determinism and Sexism: Is It All in the Ovaries?" in *Biology as a Social Weapon*, edited by the Ann Arbor Science for the People Collective [Minneapolis: Burgess Publishing, 1977] 77-81.) Private households are constantly caught in the same situation. As one young woman in the United States, Suzanne Gail, noted about her husband, "Joe's work is much more necessary [than mine]—*we all live on it*" (Malos, 1980, 109, italics added). Her work—producing the labor power of her husband and of the next generation—differs from his not in importance (it is, in fact, considerably more important) but only in the fact of its not being paid. Assigning the production of exchange values to one group and that of use values to another inevitably works to the advantage of the first group. Without challenging the traditional division of labor and without analyzing the economies in which it takes place—and why—there is no way of addressing the whole problem. (A White U.S. writer, Lois Hudson, who grew up in a farm family in the dust bowl during the 1930s has described in her fiction *[Bones of Plenty]* the devaluation of women in a farm economy, in which male muscle work in the fields comes to be valued over female sustaining and enabling activities in the "house" and the cruelty of this division on girls.) All the goodwill and reeducation in the world will not solve the persistence of sexism and racism in socialist countries—at least this would be my answer to Lorde's comment above—until socialists understand the interdependence of the issues (which of course requires education and goodwill) *and until socialism is worldwide.* That doesn't mean that socialism will become worldwide in one miraculous instant and until then we must all sit down and twiddle our toes. Historical processes happen in a patchwork fashion and always have. Hence socialism in any one country is a goal worth fighting for *and* it's not going to solve everything *and* it may succeed for a while and then fail—and then succeed elsewhere and fail and recur and so on.

    35. Ibid., 350.

36. Harry Magdoff and Paul M. Sweezy, *The Deepening Crisis of U.S. Capitalism* (New York: Monthly Review Press, 1981), 86–88, italics added.

37. Scott, *Working Your Way,* 69, 50; Brahme in Madhu Kishwar and Ruth Vanita, eds., *In Search of Answers: Indian Women's Voices from Manushi* (London: Zed Books, 1984), 61; Kishwar in ibid., 17; Lisa Leghorn and Katherine Parker, *Woman's Worth: Sexual Economics and the World of Women* (Boston: Routledge and Kegan Paul, 1981), 34; Nawal El Saadawi, *The Hidden Face of Eve: Women in the Arab World,* trans. Sherif Hetata (Boston: Beacon Press, 1980), 75; Robin Morgan, ed., *Sisterhood Is Global: The International Women's Movement Anthology* (New York: Anchor, 1984), 17–18.

38. Smith, *Home Girls,* xxxvi.

39. Cameron in Moraga and Anzaldúa, *This Bridge,* 49; Joseph and Lewis, *Common Differences,* 12; Reagon in Smith, *Home Girls,* 368.

My mother, the child of poor immigrants, raised me never to waste food. As a child, I flouted this law; as an adult, I observe it. In the writing of fiction, "never waste anything" (a generalization of the same rule) can become a principle of aesthetic economy: don't waste words. Nonfiction is another matter. As I followed the process of thinking that became this book, some strands refused to be woven back into the main fabric and some slewed back—but did so too late to be included properly. Nonetheless, somebody may find a use for—or have an interest in— (to switch the metaphor) the stew that follows, made up as it is of

L E F T O V E R S

O N E

THE DAILY CORRUPTION OF THESE
SWEET SMALL BOYS

"We are slow to acknowledge the daily corruption of these sweet, small boys," says Judith Arcana,[1] but we may also, both women and men, be slow to acknowledge the pain that accompanies the privileges and immunities given, or at least promised, to the class of "men" by patriarchy. Most obvious perhaps is the contradiction between what sex-class promises all men and what is actually delivered to most of them by the facts of class or race. Allison Fell, speaking of class, put it this way:

> There's a continual tension between the reality of boring, body grinding work for the bosses, bad food, consumer leisure, bad housing, sexual alienation and the fast ways of understanding that reality. Among these would be the ideology of equal opportunity and the freedom to compete (anyone can make it if they try), the James Bond sexual performance image, and the protective, privatized bourgeois family dream. . . . So you have the *fact* of individual powerlessness and deprivation in the face of a repressive system, coupled with the *dream* of individual male power and ownership (material and sexual—the Goods). This dream is worked out at the expense of women.[2]

Michael S. Kimmel speaks also of "a profound loss of occupational autonomy" experienced by men (presumably White) in England and the United States during the last two centuries. Industrialization changed not only the nature of men's work but its conditions. Thus:

> Before the Civil War, 88% of American men were farmers or self-employed businessmen; by 1870, that figure had dropped to 2 out of 3 . . . and by 1910, less than one-third of all American men were so employed. . . . Today one-tenth of all American men are self-employed.[3]

It was this historical development that, according to Drury Sherrod, not only severed ties between men but also profoundly changed the nature of marriage, putting U.S. men in the contradictory situation of defining masculinity as freedom from ties to femininity and yet providing for these same men only women as actual intimates. Sherrod writes of industrialization's effect:

> Intimate friendships began to give way to the more superficial ties of modern working men. . . . the new marriages allowed men to rely on women for emotional support, at the same time that the changing nature of work was making it harder for men to receive that support from other men. Thus the industrial revolution set the stage for . . . the lives of most American males—marriage as best friendship.[4]

But promises that do not really apply to you and a best friendship with someone who is simultaneously a scapegoat don't promise well for anybody's peace of mind. Feminist comments on the resulting mess are many, quite a few of them dealing with the tendency of men outside what Phyllis Chesler and Emily Jane Goodman call "the propertied class within the male aristocracy" to identify themselves by sex, not class. Chesler and Goodman write: "For [such men] . . . divisions along sex lines may be their last chance to be among the oppressors rather than the oppressed." Kathy McAfee and Myrna Wood agree: "The tendency of male workers to think of themselves primarily as men (i.e. powerful) rather than as workers (i.e. members of an oppressed group) promotes a false sense of privilege and power."[5]

Part of the "masculinity" of poor men, says Chesler, is a reaction to their class status. After all:

> Remembrances of "top dogs" among poor men are remembrances of practically everyone they've known. Teachers, doc-

tors, policemen, judges, prison wardens, shop foremen, factory owners—all are remembered as "coolly" impersonal in their sadism, all as impersonally remembered as are the crime-chieftains and older gang-leaders in the neighborhoods of their childhood.

"Cool." As men talk about the "top dogs" in their lives, this adjective is an important, valued one. "Cool" denotes constant and knowledgeable activity safely disguised by corporate veils made of steel—or by poker-stiff faces; "cool" is used to describe sudden appearances, swift strikes, and equally sudden disappearances, "cool" as in cold; "cool" as in preserved forever, frozen; "cool" as in firm, unyielding, erect, and immortal.[6]

Cheryl Clarke notes about men of color that:

> Unless manhood is somehow embellished by white skin and generations of private wealth, it has little currency in racist, capitalist patriarchy. The black man, for example, is accorded native elite or colonial guard or vigilante status over black women in imperialist patriarchy. He is an overseer for the slave master. Because of his maleness . . . [he is] allowed to have his piece of turf, viz. his wife and children. That is as far as his dictatorship extends.[7]

Chesler quotes one of her interviewees:

> "I hate my job; low pay, backbreaking work. The only thing that keeps my anger under control is fucking with my wife whenever I feel the pressure building up. Afterwards, I'm less tense. . . . Things don't seem so bad. Also, I drink a little less when she gives in to me."[8]

Whatever Sherrod writes of "marriage as best friendship" (he seems to be describing a middle-class ideal that is often not a reality even there), what Chesler's interviewee describes is clearly not a best friendship—"gives in" gives a lot away. Nor is the way working-class fathers handle relations with their families (I have observed exactly the same pattern among middle-class professionals) usually consensual, according to Sennett and Cobb. Work is rationalized as being "for" the family, which sacrifice gives the husband and father a certain authority. Yet, as Sennett and Cobb remark:

Sacrifice to the husband and father may thus seem here a kind
of reciprocal "contract" with his family. But it is in fact only a
pseudo-mutual relationship: the sacrificer does not ask his family whether *they* want him to sacrifice; the very power of this
"one-way" contract lies in the fact that one person has wholly
usurped the act of giving, and so prevented the others from
asserting countervailing personal rights.[9]

Not only is this "sacrifice" unilateral and an excuse for authority; it expresses the sacrificer's unhappiness. Attempting to establish his own free
will, his hidden message is one of self-hatred. Sennett and Cobb write:

He is acting as a free man when he thinks of himself as *choosing*
to sacrifice. Having been so repeatedly denied by the social
order outside himself, now he will usurp the initiative . . . the
sacrifice of himself will become a voluntary act. . . . The outer
face of this process is a great harshness on the part of the father;
the inner face is one of self-contempt, the plea that the children
not become the same as he.

Worse still:

Again and again the fathers interviewed in Boston mixed an
ideology of self-denial with assertions of their right therefore to
tell children how to behave; yet these are not unambiguously
authoritarian parents. . . . There is a terrible paradox here. . . .
The "good home" can only be supported by long hours of labor,
only by the father's physical absence.[10]

Authoritarian yet absent, "sacrificing" yet self-hating, without the male
identity that used to be provided by independent work, such men are victims of what Brod calls "the facts of public male power and the feelings of
men's private powerlessness."[11] And, as we've seen before, it is often women
who are scapegoated for this disjunction.[12]

Even when manhood delivers some of its promised rewards—or at least
some of its immunities, which apply even to those living on the streets (e.g.,
men don't usually get raped)—there are still the costs of becoming a "man."
Some of these are exacted from very young children, as both men and
women notice. Marc Feigen Fasteau, for example, notes that masculinity
training (largely "not being like a girl") begins "as early as ages four and
five." He adds:

Beginning at about age five or six, the time children start school or nursery school, boys . . . are often subjected . . . to insistent and forceful demands to renounce "feminine," "baby" ways for tougher more manly behavior. This demand, often initiated . . . by the father, provokes a great deal of anxiety. The boy is asked in effect to switch his identification from his mother to his father, to trade her unconditional love for a world in which he must prove, by conforming to a murky and difficult standard, that he has any value at all.[13]

Judith Arcana emphasizes that this "tougher" behavior includes a great deal of physical deprivation, "the history of boys and their bodies," as she calls it:

As babies, they roll around all over each other, hug and kiss and tickle each other, stroke each other's hair and skin. This is discouraged among boys after about one year—if not before. . . . The boys are taught to give and receive a solemn handshake, often before they are two years old.[14]

Other writers I know reiterate the same themes. It's true that all of these writers are from the dominant White U.S. culture, but the European history that lies behind this culture doesn't on the face of it seem to promise much of a difference. Europe is, after all, our cultural ancestor. Nor have things changed much, according to these writers, from the 1950s. In 1959, Ruth E. Hartley was describing similar early demands "that boys conform to social notions of what is manly," that "boys are aware of what is expected of them because they are boys and restrict their interests and activities to what is suitably 'masculine' in kindergarten." That is:

More stringent demands are made on boys than on girls and at an early age when they are least able to understand either the reasons for or the nature of these demands. Moreover, these demands are frequently enforced harshly . . . [and] the desired behavior is rarely defined positively as something the child *should* do, but rather, undesirable behavior is indicated . . . as something he should *not* do or be. Indeed, a great many boys do give evidence of . . . virtual panic at being caught doing anything traditionally defined as feminine, and . . . [feel] hostility toward anything even hinting at "femininity," including females themselves.

Moreover his teachers are women—he is "under the jurisdiction of women . . . for most of his waking day," and "he is commanded to obey and learn from them."[15]

Although I question Hartley's estimate of girls' lot as an easier one (living down inferiority can be just as bad as living up to superiority), I think her estimate of little boys' anxiety is perfectly true.[16] The rest of the literature I've found echoes it. For example, Letty Cottin Pogrebin notes:

> Boys have to learn theirs [their sex roles] early, so they suffer more in childhood. One child in 3 has difficulty with school, self-esteem, friendships or family life; most of them are boys. In childhood boys also outnumber girls 2 to 1 as institution-alized mental patients.[17] At five or six years old, when "masculine" strain is severe, boys' dreams become more frightening, stressful, and nightmarish, while girls' dreams get more docile and passive in early adolescence, when "femininity" becomes important.[18]

The result of such intimidation is not only anxiety, but some very bad relations between boys, who—in a kind of solidarity of fear—mistreat each other and themselves and refuse to stop or protest mistreatment visited on them by others. Pogrebin reports:

> Even among [young male] *friends*, "sarcasm, 'put-downs,' as well as physical threats and violence are all commonplace." One boy felt impotent when his "friends" put his bike up in a tree. Another had to beg a "buddy" to let go when his "good-natured" arm-twisting became unbearably painful. "I knew I couldn't get angry or protest too much," he remembers. "I didn't want to spoil the fun."
>
> "Goody-goody," "spoil-sport," "sissy"—*fear* of such labels has propelled boys into insane initiation rites to prove themselves, ironically, *fearless*. They step off cliffs, die of exposure, allow themselves to be force-fed raw alcohol or buried alive rather than be "unmasculine" or let their "friends" down.[19]

Arcana speaks of her son, six, coming home from his first week in first grade at a new school, saying:

> I hate recess, Mom. . . . We don't play games or anything. All the big kids get the swings. And the girls won't talk to me and all the boys do is run around the playground, swooping their

arms and yelling like monsters, chasing the girls. And the girls run away and scream, but the teachers don't do anything. . . . [If the boys catch the girls] they knock 'em down or push 'em around and say they're gonna look at their underpants. . . . I run with the boys. I know it's wrong; I don't even like it. I *hate* it, Mom. But if I don't run with them, they do it to *me*—and call me GIRL! They yell GIRL, GIRL, GIRL, and chase me! [20]

Feigen Fasteau has a similar story about a friend's son, a seven-year-old who "likes a girl of the same age who lives in his apartment building" but when the girl was transferred to his school, he "got an agitated look on his face. 'It'll spoil everything,' he said." And, continues Feigen Fasteau,

It nearly has. The other boys in his class tease him and beat him up if they see him playing with her. Things got so bad that one day, when his mother came to school to walk Jeffrey and his friend back to his house so they could play together, the girl, without a word, carefully walked ten yards behind so the other boys wouldn't think Jeffrey was going to play with her. . . . In a second-grade class I visited, I asked the boys whether they played with the girls. Obviously expecting approval, they told me proudly that they didn't. One was embarrassed enough to start a fight when the other boys accused him of liking a particular girl.

A subscriber to *Ms.* . . . in a letter to the editor, described . . . a five-year-old boy . . . being teased by four other boys of about the same age. Unable to endure any more . . . he turned to the leader of the group and, with a look of pure hatred, screamed the most horrible insult he could think of: "You girl!"[21]

Another mother, Anne Wilson Schaef, reports a similar experience undergone by her son. He had been in an "alternative school" until the fourth grade, when he was, for the first time, put in a public school and subject to organized sports:

He was not aware that sports and P.E. were not supposed to be *fun*. In free school (interesting name), he played during recess and sports time and had an exuberant experience; in public school, most of the time was spent lining up, marching, and learning skills. I expressed my opinion that this . . . system was preparing [male] children to fit into a rigid and militaristic society.[22]

Boys socialized in this way certainly behave as if they were in training for something like doom or death: the nightmares, the panics, the sense of rigidity, the lack of real intimacy with each other, all point in this direction, as does Chesler's account of relations between brothers:

> Younger brothers tell me of having followed their older brothers everywhere, only to be ordered back home, laughed at, or forced into doing whatever was needed—but considered "beneath" the dignity of older boys. From younger brothers, I heard stories characterized by either *extreme* fraternal protectiveness or *extreme* fraternal brutality.

So does Pogrebin's summing up of the meaning of male achievement: "Rather than value his achievements as a measure of his competence, the boy begins to view them as amulets against failure; each success is a temporary reprieve from the downfall that must lie somewhere in the future."[23]

Against this inevitable, terrible failure ("You GIRL!") boys taunt, train, and dare each other. Feigen Fasteau remembers, from his childhood:

> For reasons no one ever articulated, the junior-high-school treehouse gang in my neighborhood provisioned itself for a war with another gang which was supposed to exist somewhere on the other side of town. We assembled supplies of rocks, wooden swords, shields, maces (pieces of garden hose with four or five nails driven through one end in different directions) and plotted raids on the other gang. . . . Somehow we never actually marched into battle. The closest we came was an intramural war waged with rock-filled snowballs. The battle stopped when a warrior's nose was broken by a direct hit. The mystery is not why it stopped but why it began. None of us had a history of violence. Only one of the kids was the kind of lunatic who just doesn't care.

As he remarks at the beginning of this account, "The message that fighting is the kind of thing boys do gets through, even if it isn't acted on."[24]

So far I have been quoting material from and about the relatively privileged: mostly White, sheltered, and "none of us had a history of violence." For them, some of the material rewards of masculinity do materialize—Feigen Fasteau, for example, is a lawyer—but even here, says Pogrebin, the impossibility of truly fulfilling the "fearless leader stereotype . . . dooms most boys and men to a deep sense of 'masculine' failure, which must then be relieved by reaffirmation of *the one manageable component of the male stereotype: superiority over women.*" The class rewards of manhood, by the way, tend to occur, says Pogrebin,

> sometime during junior high school when . . . [working-class boys who have found school too "feminine" to be interesting] experience a sudden loss of "masculine" status; academic endeavors . . . have suddenly become not "sissy" but "manly."[25]

They are also, although Pogrebin does not mention it, effectively locked into their class status by precisely this sudden change in "masculine" values.

Nor does pressure toward "masculinity" come only from peers; a good part of it, according to my sources, results from boys'—one can only call them lousy—relations with their fathers. Boys do not, it seems, like their fathers, and they do not like men. Arcana's interviewees had "troubled relations with their fathers" and "angry, sad and painful stories to tell. . . . Filled with passion when they speak of their fathers," they express "criticism and rejection . . . bitterness and denial."[26] Two themes emerge from this passion: violence and absence.

Often the violence is some kind of violence against women. Judith Arcana's son reports about his father, who now lives with his (the father's) second wife: "Michael insults Susan; he makes her feel bad. I can hear him yelling through the door, shouting at her, and I can hear the drops from her eyes falling down, and the water comes under the door she's so unhappy." Often it is violence toward sons. Steve, aged eight, says:

> "He says I can't do anything because I don't know how. Daddy has a loud voice. I'm scared when he yells. Daddy doesn't talk much when he's not yelling or making me do something. . . . Daddy is tired when he takes me and Laura out. He makes phone calls when we watch the movie. . . . I don't think Daddy has a good time at home. Daddies are like that."[27]

Sometime fathers are simply absent. Sam Julty quotes one man who said, "At the age of six I learned that my father would never kiss me again." Pogrebin reports:

> Father alienation is so severe that half the preschool children questioned in one study preferred the television to their fathers, 1 child in 10 (aged seven to eleven) said the person they are most afraid of is their father; half wish their fathers would spend more time with them; and among children of divorce, only a third said they see their fathers regularly.[28]

Chesler's responses from the men she interviewed are, to my mind, indicative of the massive denial the Steves and their like practice in adulthood—and the bizarre fashion in which that denial operates. Here are some excerpts:

> Men, upon being questioned about "castration anxiety," either report having none—or immediately start telling me about how they fear being "castrated" by mothers and wives. They rarely mention fathers or other men. . . . "Did your father ever beat you" I'll ask. And in response most men immediately discuss male violence in the abstract . . . on some other continent. . . . It was startling to hear men respond to a variety of questions about their fathers. . . . by telling me abruptly, aggressively, defensively—bizarrely—all about "sex." They said: "I'm a highly sexed man," or "I masturbate insatiably," or "I'm pretty sadistic sexually to women—but it turns me on and they have no complaints," or "I'm afraid I might be a homosexual," or "I'm a very happy homosexual, sexually speaking." . . . As if they wanted to warn me off the topic.

She adds:

> No matter how anxious or amnesiac my informants were about paternal physical violence, they were even more anxious, mute, defenseless, when I asked them, "Did your father kiss you?" . . . One thirty-year-old man said: "My father wasn't ever affectionate. He was a cold, precise person. . . . He always griped and complained about whatever I did." . . . [Another said]: "I guess I don't really know my father . . . it's very difficult for me to talk to my father."[29]

Chesler goes on to describe men's fear of other men—suppose he "turns out to be as distant or as dangerous as one's own father?" That, she says, is the classical "Oedipal" resolution of the relation between father and son:

> The son must attempt to subdue or charm his father into a more compliant intimacy through a show of physical vulnerability or affectionate, physical closeness. This is what sons are probably used to doing with their mothers.
>
> However, such a show of vulnerability or affection by a son *cannot* work with a father. It is not *supposed* to. Women may be

disarmed by . . . [this] but most men are threatened by it. They
. . . know the consequences of such overtly erotic and "trusting"
behavior toward another man. Fathers must teach their sons
never to relate to other men in such a way. . . .

Thus are adult men always comparing themselves to other
men: on the basis of penis-size and physical strength. They
always feel the need for male "truce," no matter the price. It is
a transaction they have made once before. With their fathers.[36]

Arcana, describing a "diverse" lot of sons she interviewed, "fifteen to
seventy-one . . . Black, white, Asian and Latin . . . gay and straight . . . high
school students, mobile-home salesmen, sculptors, and lawyers," describes
their longing for warmth and affection from fathers who are "warm, receptive, physically affectionate and comforting, open and honest about their
feelings and approving and accepting of their sons." They are usually disappointed, naming "distance" as a major feature of their relationship with
their fathers, although they minimize or "ignore their fathers' shortcomings
and flaws . . . speak in obvious euphemisms, or ignore . . . problems." The
conventional father-son relationship, says Arcana, requires no more. Although a minority of mothers in the group reported more positive father-
son relations, most sons

> have felt the pain, the loss and the lack; and they've had to deny
> these feelings—along with most others—and pretend that the
> standard father/son arrangement was just fine. . . . Boys and
> men bury it, cover it up, and bluff like crazy. They come to
> Mama with their grief; they take it out on their own sons and
> men with less power . . . they . . . act out violent abuse of chil-
> dren and women—as they deny their need for Daddy's love
> and support.
>
> We mothers watch young boys go from expecting to be cher-
> ished and nurtured by their fathers, to demanding that behavior
> from their fathers, to the sullen and bitter understanding that
> Dad will not come across. And . . . we see our sons come to an
> acceptance so complete that they will defend their fathers even
> against the criticism and anger they've expressed themselves.[31]

Insofar as such an upbringing occurs—and I think it is certainly to some
degree a typical one—it is clearly useful in the maintenance of competition
between men and hence in capitalism. Profound feelings of more-than-
material deprivation, and hence the desire to scapegoat someone, is very

useful in maintaining racism and sexism. *It also constitutes* mild-to-severe *child abuse,* and the personalities of the adults formed by this abuse show its mark.

One problem—which I believe still exists, despite propaganda about men's changing (gourmet cooking or the two-career yuppie marriage looks like a change in status symbols and economics, not feminism)—is that the idea of masculinity, at least as the dominant culture of the United States promotes it today, is a negative one. Wendy Chapkis remarks that "fear of effeminacy is at the heart of heterosexual masculine identity." Lillian Breslow Rubin quotes a 1975 study of four hundred college students:

> Men associate independence with negative expressiveness. While the women in our sample were able to incorporate positive expressiveness, positive instrumentalness and independence in their self-pictures, the men . . . could not. . . . This supports the theory that the . . . young boy becomes a man not by accepting masculine traits but by rejecting feminine ones.[32]

An identity that depends primarily on *not* being someone else makes for difficulties, especially without the occupational autonomy a great many men used to have. According to Feigen Fasteau, the results are pretty grim:

> The injunction that we be totally free, independent of everything but the drive to achieve, has created a nation of lonely men who are prey to impersonal substitutes for personal connection, ranging from overinvestment in gadgets to xenophobic conformity . . . to grandiose attempts to leave a permanent mark on the world.[33]

Although Feigen Fasteau's view of masculinity obviously doesn't mention its effect on those who can't overinvest in gadgets in reality because of a shortage of money, nonetheless he is certainly describing the commercial culture of the United States and the kind of ideals held up for all of us. It's not only that "70 percent of men rarely or never hug anyone" but that male friendships usually do not include anything like the intimacies common among women. Contrary to the "myth . . . that the great friendships are between men," says Feigen Fasteau of the United States, "something is missing," even though heterosexual men do, by and large, prefer men's company to women's.[34] Drury Sherrod puts it this way:

> A considerable body of research confirms the limits on self-disclosure in most close male friendships. . . . Women usually

disclose significantly more intimate information about themselves than men do, regardless of age, region of the country or
social class. When the most intimate questions are analyzed
separately, men disclose much less than women.[35]

Feigen Fasteau emphasizes this "shying away from the personal," saying:

> We talk about almost everything except how we ourselves are
> affected by people and events. Everything is discussed as
> though it were taking place out there somewhere. . . . Men also
> spend an incredible amount of time rehashing the great public
> issues of the day.[36]

With such a dearth of substance, something has to take the place of intimacy
in masculine interactions, and lacking sexual contact, which is still a strong
taboo, the principal mode left, says Feigen Fasteau, is *competition*. He calls it

> the principal mode by which men relate to each other . . . be-
> cause it is the way to demonstrate, to themselves and others,
> the key masculine qualities of unwavering toughness and the
> ability to dominate and control. The result is they inject com-
> petition into situations which don't call for it . . . [e.g.] My The-
> ory Tops Yours, disguised as a serious exchange of ideas. . . .
> Men tend to lecture at each other . . . and are often unwilling
> to listen. . . . Competition *is* the central dynamic of organized
> athletics . . . a superficially rational paradigm of total, unquali-
> fied pursuit of victory. . . . One's sense of achievement depends
> entirely on winning.

The result? "Men even try not to let it show when they feel good. . . . Happiness is a precarious, 'childish' feeling, easy to shoot down. . . . [And] what
is particularly difficult for men is seeking or accepting help from friends."[37]

Chesler agrees. About the famous phenomenon of "male bonding" she
writes, "Talking to most men about this subject is like talking to most
women about male violence; you hear that it doesn't really exist. . . . [In
fact there is] a larger picture of murderousness among men."[38]

I find her quotations on this point shocking. Here are examples:

> "Can't afford friends when you want to get things done. Power
> isn't kept by a system of friendships." . . . "I have allies and I
> have enemies, and I have my family. I have no *friends*." . . . "It's
> like two dogs circling each other. . . . I mean you check out his

economic scale. Is he manly? Is he tough? Is he great in sports?
. . . Can he help me? Can I help him? Is he gonna use me? Am
I using him? Does he know a lot of pretty women? All these
things take place in a handshake. . . . When you first meet, men
are vying to see who's going to have the top position. . . .
There's always one who's on 'top' and one who's on the 'bottom.' " . . . "I suspect that most men get together with other
men, not because of the positives, but rather to compensate for
a negative. . . . you're afraid that by being alone you may be
sexually inadequate, or you may have some other fear of inferiority. So you compensate for it." . . . "I expect people will try
to fuck me over. . . . I become angry when people not only fuck
me over but try to get close to me—to really ram it in."[39]

And here is the one quotation that I think will remain longest in my mind:
"You can become friends after a street fight, if nobody gets hurt too badly.
. . . [Then] you can team up if it's a beneficial thing to do."[40]

If nobody gets hurt too badly. And Feigen Fasteau agrees with the concept
that masculinity is founded not on being something (except for the above)
but on *not* being something—specifically anything feminine, female, or effeminate, all of which such true believers in the big M confuse with lack of
heterosexuality. One man in Feigen Fasteau's study, a corporate executive
who said "you are either dependent or independent; you can't be both,"
may have also had in mind the "ram it in" (what an expression!) quoted
earlier. Feigen Fasteau writes that:

> A major source of these inhibitions is the fear of being, or being
> thought, homosexual. Nothing is more frightening to a heter-
> osexual man in our society. It threatens, at one stroke, to take
> away every vestige of his claim to a masculine identity . . . and
> to expose him to the ostracism, ranging from polite tolerance
> to violent revulsion, of his friends and colleagues. A man can
> be labeled as homosexual . . . because of almost any sign of be-
> havior which does not fit the masculine stereotype. The touch-
> ing of another man, other than shaking hands, or, under
> emotional stress, an arm around the shoulder, is taboo. . . . Di-
> rect verbal expressions of affection or tenderness are also some-
> thing that only homosexuals and women engage in.[41]

This is a stressful way to live. The defensiveness of masculinity, its foundation in *not* being so many Human things, and the consequent necessity

of proving and reproving what one is not because the proof is, in fact, impossible, may be what leads Schaef to call masculinity a kind of *addiction* and to deplore its toll. She writes:

> The macho man is not in touch with his feelings (and he often uses chemicals to numb them), and he spends much of his time doing . . . "impression management"—trying to make others see him as he wants to be seen. . . . Because his point of reference is external, he . . . has lost his identity. . . . [He] overworks, overdrinks, and overeats. . . . He becomes a zombie, who moves through life and does not live it.[42]

Herb Goldberg agrees, listing "Basic Distrust" and "Need to Control" as the personality traits behind a drive to "success." His view of traditional masculinity very much resembles Schaef's:

> It is masculine (1) to be able to take as much pain as possible without giving in to it, (2) to hold liquor, (3) to recuperate from serious illness quickly . . . there is even something feminine just about being sick in the first place. . . . [such men] have lost touch with their bodies. . . . *Stress, self-poisoning, fatigue and emotional pain do not register.*[43]

Even "success," when some men achieve it, doesn't deliver what it promises. Marilyn French writes: "They imagine that success, or the demonstration of 'manliness,' will bring them love; instead, it often alienates those they love. They feel cheated; and they blame women." Unfortunately, success has aloneness built into it. Feigen Fasteau notes:

> Our success myths . . . are about an individual (virtually always a man) who by his lonely, independent efforts raises himself above and away from his fellow men and accomplishes great things. . . . That fulfillment of all human needs flows automatically from such success is also part of the myth.[44]

French does the same, speaking of the relation between success, competition, solitude, and their inevitable conclusion:

> The inevitable competitiveness between men who are similar . . . enforces the solitude enjoined on the hero, and, by extension, on all men. If a man cannot befriend those who are like

him, he has no place to go. To go home is to submit the self to the realm of women. . . . Beyond that, there are only animals, God and the void, the hero's true companions.[45]

More mundanely, as Sherrod quotes R. Bell, "most men today name their wife as their closest friend."[46] But it is precisely women and the feminine—the emotional, the vulnerable, the dependent—that threaten masculine identity.

In connection with this threat Chesler emphasizes men's guilt at having benefited "as a caste, from the emotional, economic, social, and political castration of women" and their fear of the rage "at [the] bottom" of such female behavior.[47] I wonder whether another dynamic may not be at work here: the fear of the "feminine" and the fear of closeness to anything that may compromise an enforced, resented, desired, and perpetually insecure identity.

And what of those who are promised "success" and *don't* get it? Bell hooks writes:

> The poor or working class man . . . is constantly concerned about the contradiction between the notion of masculinity he was taught and his inability to live up to that notion. . . . [If] he beats or rapes women, he is not exercising privilege or reaping positive rewards. . . . The ruling class male power structure . . . reaps the real material benefits. . . . As long as he is attacking women and not sexism or capitalism, he helps to maintain a system that allows him few, if any, benefits or privileges. He is an oppressor. He is an enemy to women. He is also an enemy to himself. He is also oppressed.[48]

Perhaps women are not only easy scapegoats in such a situation; it may be that rape embodies another dynamic as well. It is, after all, *sexual*. Chesler quotes one man as saying, "You have no idea how much boys and men need magazines and films in order to jerk off, how much they think about it when they're fucking." She comments:

> It is strange that men, who claim great—and greatly frustrated—sexual needs . . . [should] at the same time surround themselves with so many stimulants to "arousal". . . . I began to wonder about the meaning of a male sexual drive that needs so much arousal, so much help, so much understanding, in order that it be satisfied. . . . Many men experience some postcoital disappointment, loneliness, a vague disgust, a sense of loss—and they encounter these feelings after sex often enough to wish

that things were different, often enough to keep looking for a "change."

In fact, she adds:

> Men, upon being questioned . . . almost seem to be saying that what they enjoy most about sex with women is having it over with. . . . Men of all ages talked about a preference for "quick" fucks. . . . Married men in small towns, who economically can't *afford* to pay for prostitutes, told me that they often arrive home at noon or about four o'clock to have a "quickie" before the kids come home, or while dinner is cooking.[49]

What such men seem to be expressing by their behavior is the contradiction built into patriarchally constructed heterosexuality: the necessity for, and attraction to, something that is at the same time felt as a threat. Sam Julty says this flatly: "The aversion to being seen as feminine also expresses itself in a man's sex life. A man learns to focus his sexuality on his genitals, which inhibits a broader sensual experience." Therefore, according to Goldberg:

> The way men have continued to function sexually with this orientation is by depersonalizing the experience. . . . They are "having sex" with a "thing," "making love" to an "object," and there is no genuine awareness of their own or the woman's internal experience.[50]

Feigen Fasteau describes the contradiction between masculinity and sexuality in even more explicit and emphatic terms:

> The sex act is the only intimate contact many adult men ever have with women. . . . [but] they tend to stifle the freedom and spontaneity that make sex personal and give it meaning. . . . This . . . potential, [for intimacy and self-abandonment] in an act to which we are powerfully drawn is frightening to men who have to keep their psychic distance from women and from their own feelings. It explains some of the impersonality, often hostile, of men's remarks to or about attractive women they see on the street—"I'd like to get into her pants!" "How'd you like *that* warming your pecker?" etc. etc. It is the reason why men view sex as . . . one of the ultimate tests of their masculinity: to get this close to a woman, to the feminine in her and—because of the emotions evoked—in oneself, and still be in command.

> For men who are most heavily steeped in the masculine ideal
> . . . the sex act has a nasty edge of hostility. . . . [because] for a
> man to be dependent—in particular, dependent upon a
> woman—is a forbidden emotional state.[51]

What, then, is rape but that "nasty edge of hostility" taken to its logical extreme, the solution of the contradiction of masculinity—to be heterosexual and yet avoid losing self-control or coming into contact with dangerous femininity? This particular solution not only avoids losing control by fucking a thing and not a person, it also prevents being contaminated by the feminine by making fucking itself a domination of (and in extreme cases even the literal murder of) the woman. *Women* are chosen as victims by some of the oppressed, the marginal, and the angry among men not only because women are easier victims than men but because one kind of anger can be fused with another, and both can be connected with sexual pleasure without, as Feigen Fasteau puts it, getting anywhere near that dreadful country of "the passion of eros, the flight of imagination which fuses sexual attraction and the impulse toward intimacy."[52]

Indeed, how can a patriarchal male sexuality be designed except along these lines? Historically, patriarchies have required and they still require men to have the ability to impregnate women who range from the uninterested, to the passive, to the frightened, even to the actively hostile. Empathy, intimacy, emotionality, the natural Human impulse (as I consider it) to be aroused by a partner's arousal—all these get in the way if you're trying to design say the Rape of the Sabine Women. If patriarchal conditioning is to "take" with men at all, it must of necessity head in this direction—or patriarchy will produce no impregnations and no babies. Ideally, it is as necessary to suppress women's spontaneous sexuality as it is to distort men's *if men as a class are to dominate women as a class,* although both women and men do resist, either openly or merely through what Chesler reports as disgust, loneliness, and unfocused disappointment.[53]

But men are violent not only to women, they are also violent to each other. In a way, says Jane Caputi, who has studied male violence in England and the United States—specifically, male serial murders as glamorized by the mass media for the last century—it is finally *men* of whom men are most afraid:

> The incessant babble about male "fear of women" serves in
> many ways as a cover up for their deep and abiding fear of each
> other. That fear is . . . obscured by the solid taboo that silences
> discussion of male-on-male sex murders. . . . Why are there no
> thinly-veiled fictionalizations of the lives and times of Dean

Corll or John Wayne Gacy to match the glut of stories fearing Bundy and Berkowitz-like killers? Why no television specials on the "Trashbag Murders" [in which males were killed]? Why no "boy in danger" movies among the current glut of slasher films, stirring the imaginations and feeding the fantasies of any potential "Bluebeards" in the audience?[54]

In the United States, at least (and the U.S. commercial media go around the world today), as French puts it,

> The presentation of American life offered in movies and television is overwhelmingly violent. . . . Films and series focusing on men portray a male world of exuberant violence; moreover, it is a violence that costs nothing. . . . Hideous forms of bodily harm are shown without remorse or compunction in the characters responsible for them, without any suggestion that it might hurt to kill, that killing or harming another also kills or harms something in the self. . . . The United States has a homicide rate eight to nine times higher than that of any other major industrial country.[55]

"High" culture is not so different. Paul Lauter quotes "a colleague, Diana Hume George":

> "[The] texts made the centers of literature and humanities curricula, turn our classrooms into the 'educational' equivalents of the prime-time TV world where program after program captures and keeps its audience by feeding it myths about danger and excitement—as if such experiences were at the heart of being human. . . . We give students only a more cerebral version of tube ethics."[56]

Such experiences are also important in politics. According to Charlene Spretnak:

> In turning an anthropologist's ear to the conversation of male physicists and other energy-technologists, Laura Nader has reported that conservation is demeaned as "feminine" and solar power as "not intellectually challenging," while fission and fusion, a flirtation with danger and death, are considered glamorous and thrillingly risky, "the biggest crap game of all."[57]

Nor is such thinking recent. Here is Alice Sheldon, with an insider's view of U.S. governmental workings written in 1975:

> A few years back . . . official Washington held an air attack drill,
> a very elaborate one. The big set-piece was the whisking-away
> of the whole government to a fantastic shelter—this one was
> under a mountain—where they had all the war-rooms and red
> buttons and machinery for Retaliation Unto Cinders. . . . They
> were leaving their wives and families behind to be fried, you
> see. . . . The vision [was] of two hundred post-menopausal
> males crawling out into the lava-plain to celebrate the "saving
> of America". . . . This is pathology. Pathology of almost incon-
> ceivable luxuriance.[58]

Such stuff is easy enough, in fantasy. But what old men dream up, young men must often live out, and in such situations men are quite right to be terrified of men. Helen Michalowski, utilizing the work of Robert J. Lifton, describes the extreme of such pathology—the violence toward women and men bred of a dehumanizing terror of other men and of "femininity"—as it is deliberately induced in the United States Armed Forces.

> *Victor De Mattei, Army Paratrooper:*
> The purpose of basic training is to dehumanize a male to the
> point where he will kill on command and obey his superiors
> automatically. To do that he has to be divorced from his natural
> instincts which are essentially non-violent. I have never met
> anyone (unless he was poisoned by somebody's propaganda)
> who had a burning urge to go out and kill a total stranger. . . .
> First, you are harassed and brutalized to the point of utter ex-
> haustion. Your individuality is taken away. . . . Everyone is
> punished for one man's "failure," etc. You never have enough
> sleep or enough to eat. . . . I used to lie on my bunk at night
> and say my name to myself to make sure I existed.

> *Robert McLaine, Marine:*
> I wish somebody had a record of suicides that go on at these
> places . . . [and] the beatings that go on daily. Boys are turned
> not into men, but beasts—beasts that will fight and destroy at
> a moment's notice without any regard to what they are fighting
> or why they are fighting, but just fight.

> *Wayne Eisenhart, Marine:*
> One of the most destructive facets of bootcamp is the systematic

attack on the recruits' sexuality. . . . One is continually addressed as faggot or girl. These labels are usually screamed into
the face from a distance of two or three inches. . . . The goals
of training are always just out of reach. We would be ordered
to run five miles when no one was in shape for more than two
or were ordered to do 100 push-ups when they and we both
knew we could only do 50. . . . [Thus] one can be made to
appear weak or ineffective at any time. . . . Recruits were bru-
talized, frustrated and cajoled to a flash point of high tension.
. . . Only on . . . occasions of violent outbursts did the drill in-
structor cease his endless litany of "You dirty faggot," and "Can't
you hack it, little girls."[59]

Here is Eisenhart again describing one incident in detail:

Although [Private Green was] not effeminate by civilian standards, he was considered so in boot camp. He was continually
harassed and called girl and faggot. . . . [When Pvt. Green
dropped out during a "particularly grueling run"] the entire
platoon was ordered to run circles around him each time he
fell out. . . . He fell again . . . and four men ran from the formation and kicked and beat him. . . . He stumbled forward and
fell. Again he was pummeled. Finally four men literally carried
him on their shoulders as we ran to the base area where we
expected to rest. . . . [After the men were called "little girl fag-
gots" because they could not run as a unit, they were ordered
to do calisthenics, Private Green leading them.] As we were
made to exercise for a full hour, men became so exhausted their
stomachs cramped and they vomited. Private Green was made
to laugh at us. The DI . . . sneered, "Unless you women get with
the program, straighten out the queers, and grow some balls of
your own, you best give your soul to God 'cause your ass is
mine and so is your mother's on visiting day." With a roar, 60
to 70 enraged men engulfed Private Green, knocking him to
the ground, kicking and beating him. . . . [He] was tossed and
beaten in the air for about five minutes and was then literally
hurled onto a concrete wash rack . . . dazed and bleeding.

The results of such training are also described. Michalowski quotes from
Lifton again:

Robert McLain:
When I came back home . . . if someone irritated me, my first impulse was to kill the fucker. . . . Today there is still a lot of hate in me—a hatred that makes it difficult to form . . . relationships with anyone.

Wayne Eisenhart:
[There] is a constant fear of being harmed by someone and a constant elimination of real or fantasized adversaries in order to maintain a feeling of adequacy and security. . . . Since I was not exposed to much combat in Vietnam, I can only conclude that this process originated for me in basic training. . . . My own intrusive imagery . . . take[s] the form of daydreams. . . . brief, very violent eye-gouging, throat-ripping fantasies. . . . There is usually a woman involved and I am always dominant and inordinately violent in defeating some adversary. These brief images leave me with a feeling of power and supermasculinity.[60]

Eisenhart's experience was not unique. Robert Jay Lifton, who worked with a number of Vietnam veterans, says they

told how, when brushed by someone on the street—or simply annoyed by something another person had done—they would have an impulse to "throttle" or kill him. And they would directly associate this impulse with patterns of behavior cultivated in Vietnam: . . . with the numbing and brutalization underlying that behavior, but also with the rage beneath the numbing.[61]

He quotes one, Steve Hassna, directly:

I'd wake up in the middle of the night and throw [my wife] out of bed and throw her behind the bunker. And start screaming. She was scared of me. She finally left me. Because I would get to the point where I was so pissed off, I'd tell her, "Don't do it again; don't push me." . . . I can't relate to people no more and so I just snapped.

Hassna goes on to make precisely the connection feminists have been making for years between male socialization and this kind of behavior:

I was going like this until I realized what it was that sent me to Vietnam, indoctrinated from childbirth, the whole thing. I

THE DAILY CORRUPTION . . .

stopped having these bad dreams. Because I could see that it wasn't me that was fucked up, it was my government and my whole society that got me this way.[62]

Of course most men in the United States are not marines, or Vietnam veterans, and do not suffer such extreme consequences of having to live out the myth of masculinity. Class, for one thing, has a great deal to do with who makes up the fantasies of what it is to be a real man and who has to actually live them out—or be beaten half to death because of them. Yet all men appear to suffer to some degree from the deprivations and contradictions forced on them by current ideals of masculinity. Why then don't they do anything about it? It may be that they are like colonial administrators complaining about the malaria, who nonetheless know that "back home" they could not enjoy anything like the status, leisure, power, and standard of living they have in the colonized country. Possibly the relative benefits of masculinity outweigh the inconveniences or even the outright deprivations—or at least many men think so. Part of the answer is, of course, noted above: few men in any county are either paratroopers or shapers of national policy. Nor do all men undergo the worst excesses of growing up "masculine" or the scars this process leaves behind it. Yet the uneasy truce between men (I keep thinking of that astonishing quotation from Chesler's *About Men* about becoming friends after a street fight: *if nobody gets hurt too badly*), the loss of sensuality, the competitiveness, the constant attempt to prove something that by its very nature is unprovable, the economic contradictions that occur in the lives of the vast majority of men; all these must affect everyone to some degree. Why do they let it continue?

It may be that most men who live in patriarchal societies want to continue them because they have at least a partial out. That out is women. Women are not only useful as possible scapegoats, they provide much that the male world has made taboo. Chesler puts it this way:

> Among men . . . there are crucial and unique advantages to be gained in accepting or "resolving" the father-son relationship. If sons are adequately socialized into patriarchy, they can then "bond" with other men for economic gain. Also, they are prepared . . . for a life of "male" work; they are also able to enslave women and other men with only moderate degrees of awareness of guilt. These advantages are not spiritual or emotional ones.[63]

If such men cannot "comfort others or . . . themselves," as Chesler says, they can nonetheless get various kinds of comfort from the other sex-class precisely because of their membership in the dominant sex-class. Chesler writes:

> I wonder to what degree male hostility towards feminist aspi-
> rations is related to a male fear of being abandoned by
> women—so that men would be left totally to themselves in an
> all-male society. . . . Most men need access to on-demand trans-
> fusions of emotional and physical relief or safety; to real or
> illusory—but on-demand and male-controlled—transfusions
> of intimacy, human warmth and "maternality": access to
> women, as fashioned by men.[64]

(The relief, safety, and support need not include sexual access; I've observed just such patterns among many gay men who want access to certain kinds of help and support from women, but again *as controlled by themselves,* and without genuine or full reciprocity.) That is, men who can ignore the marine or movie killing-machine version of masculinity (or even ridicule it) none-theless have a stake in maintaining it because there is a connection between its continued existence and their privileges, and in some fashion they know this. For example, in twenty-five years of teaching I have yet to find a male student who will defend rape *as such,* but what many will do is fall silent, look bored, get angry, or protest that women "exaggerate" the subject or even that women are making the subject up because rape is impossible. Similarly, those who will directly defend conventional masculinity or the immutable and stereotypical differences between the sexes are rare (and refreshingly honest). Much more common is to have male students declare, again, that the whole thing is exaggerated, boring, stupid, out-of-date, and doesn't exist. Often they will maintain these positions to the point of fury. I have sometimes wanted to ask, "*What* are you defending?"[65] Tom Corri-gan, Bob Connell, and John Lee have an answer; as the mundane uses of a society are intimately connected with its abuses, so in the same way the

> culturally exalted form of masculinity . . . may only correspond
> to the actual characters of a small number of men. . . . There is
> a distance, and a tension, between collective ideal[s] and actual
> lives. Most men do not really act like the screen image of John
> Wayne or Humphrey Bogart; and when they try to, it is likely
> to be thought comic. . . . Yet very large numbers of men are
> complicit in sustaining the hegemonic model. There are various
> reasons: gratification through fantasy, compensation through
> displaced aggression (e.g. poofter-bashing by police and work-
> ing-class youths), and so on. *But the overwhelmingly important*

reason is that most men benefit from the subordination of women, and hegemonic masculinity is centrally connected with . . . men's dominance over women.[66]

Furthermore, as Christine Delphy puts it, sexism does not exist solely in personal relations or even personal motivations. She writes of those who

affirm, like the man in the street, and the typical oppressor, that "sexism," the ideological expression of institutionalized oppression, the surface aspects of patriarchy, constitute *all* the oppression there is. They deny the existence of the institutional *structures* which *cause* "sexism."

Men, as she puts it later, have "institutionally and materially established authority . . . without having to want it and whether or not they [themselves] are authoritarian."[67] Moreover, says Brod:

Institutional power is camouflaged, so it does not appear to be exercised by any one individual. Thus many men may appear more personally congenial farther up the economic ladder, even as they exercise the institutional power responsible for women's lower status. In contrast, men who have but their personal power are more conspicuous but actually less efficacious when exercising their power in patriarchy's service.[68]

The evidence presented here has been sketchy, and almost all of it is confined to the United States. As Rubin notes:

Partly because of the difficulties in cross-cultural research, there has been little systematic study and comparison of men's relationships with each other in this society and elsewhere. Such work on this subject as does exist is largely impressionist— work done from the outside, not the inside, therefore, work that offers little beyond what we already know from casual observation. . . . Comparisons are limited by the fact that people in different cultures not only live their external lives differently but have different internal lives as well. . . . [For example] men in Greece walk down the street arm in arm, in Tunisia they walk hand in hand. Greece and Tunisia—countries where social relations between the sexes range from highly segregated to rigidly tabooed. In such cultural contexts it's entirely possible that the relationships men form with each other are different in both tone and content from . . . men in America. Where friendly relations with women are proscribed, where else would men look for companionship, for comfort, for any of the needs for which people turn to one another?

But this says nothing about the quality of intimacy between these men . . . nothing either about whether that kind of intimacy is valued in these societies. Men may hold hands or link arms, while still being unable or unwilling, to express their inmost thought, frailties, and vulnerabilities. Or the whole issue of intimacy, as we define and value it, may be of no concern to them.[69]

Nonetheless I've found it interesting to note that in whatever way men may or may not behave toward each other and value or disvalue such behavior, there is still—in the fairly sketchy reporting of various feminists, some from the United States and therefore outsiders as well as others who are insiders—some surprising resemblances in the way these men *as a class* behave toward the class of women.

NOTES

1. Judith Arcana, *Every Mother's Son* (Seattle: Seal Press, 1986), 279.

2. Sandra Allen et al., eds., *Conditions of Illusion: Papers from the Women's Movement* (Leeds, England: Feminist Books, 1974), 65.

3. Kimmel in Harry E. Brod, ed., *The Making of Masculinities: The New Men's Studies* (Boston: Allen and Unwin, 1987), 125, 138.

4. Sherrod in ibid., 232.

5. Phyllis Chesler and Emily Jane Goodman, *Women, Money, and Power* (New York: Morrow, 1976), 5; Edith Hoshino Altbach, ed., *From Feminism to Liberation* (Cambridge, MA: Schenkman, 1971), 23.

6. Phyllis Chesler, *About Men* (New York: Simon and Schuster, 1978), 235.

7. Clark in Cherríe Moraga and Gloria Anzaldúa, eds., *This Bridge Called My Back: Writings by Radical Women of Color* (Watertown, MA: Persephone Press, 1981), 133.

8. Chesler, *About Men*, 224.

9. Richard Sennett and Jonathan Cobb, *The Hidden Injuries of Class* (New York: Knopf, 1972), 126–27.

10. Ibid., 122, 123.

11. Brod, *Making of Masculinities*, 14.

12. Some feminists in the early 1970s forgot the institutional facts of the economics of male work. I remember a colleague of mine saying bitterly that a

woman lives where her husband does and he lives where he wants. Contrast this with the remarks of Dalla Costa and James, socialist feminists of the same period:

> A housewife['s] . . . first boss is her husband's work. . . . Whatever her husband makes, that is what the family has to live on. How much clothes she buys, or whether she has to make them, whether clothes go to the laundromat or are washed by hand, whether they live in a crowded apartment or a house with enough room for the family, whether she has a washing machine . . . all of these things are decided by the kind of job her husband has. . . . Even where she lives is decided by her husband's work. The part of town that makes going to work the easiest is the part of town that you live in. And if there are no jobs in that town that are in your husband's line of work then you have to forget all your friends and all the ties of family and you go to where he can find work (Mariarosa Dalla Costa and Selma James, *The Power of Women and the Subversion of the Community*, 3d ed., [Bristol, England: Falling Wall Press, 1972], 65–66).

13. Marc Feigen Fasteau, *The Male Machine* (New York: Delta, 1975), 37, 200.

14. Arcana, *Every Mother's Son*, 35.

15. Hartley in Joseph H. Pleck and Jack Sawyer, eds., *Men and Masculinity* (Englewood Cliffs, NJ: Prentice-Hall, 1974), 7–8, 9.

16. I vividly remember a boy of about eight in a shoe store in Denver in the late 1970s being fitted for the kind of orthopedic shoes neither girls nor boys usually wear. He was screaming in real panic, "These are girls' shoes! You're giving me girls' shoes!" The shoes were, in fact, the kind neither sex of child would have voluntarily been caught dead in at that time, but his horror was directed not at their unconventionality or lack of style but at something that was to him obviously a good deal worse: the nonmasculinity of his footgear.

17. This ratio is dramatically reversed in adulthood. See Phyllis Chesler, *Women and Madness* (New York: Doubleday, 1972).

18. Letty Cottin Pogrebin, *Growing Up Free: Raising Your Child in the 80's* (New York: Grove Press, 1980), 74

19. Ibid., 326.

20. Arcana, *Every Mother's Son*, 2.

21. Feigen Fasteau, *The Male Machine*, 37.

22. Anne Wilson Schaef, *Women's Reality: An Emerging Female in a White Male Society* (New York: Harper and Row, 1985), 71.

23. Chesler, *About Men*, 237; Pogrebin, *Growing Up Free*, 63.

24. Feigen Fasteau, *The Male Machine,* 152.

25. Pogrebin, *Growing Up Free,* 42, 56, italics added.

26. Arcana, *Every Mother's Child,* 143.

27. Ibid., 7; Chesler, *About Men,* 202.

28. Sam Julty, *Men's Bodies: Men's Selves* (New York: Dell, 1979), 101; Pogrebin, *Growing Up Free,* 142.

29. Chesler, *About Men,* 215, 194, 197, 195.

30. Ibid., 209, 206–07, 214.

31. Arcana, *Every Mother's Son,* 142–43, 159–61. Arcana uses the story of Bambi (originally German) as an example of the myth of masculinity. It depicts the superiority of adult males; their absence from the lives of their sons and lack of any relationship with the sons except the occasionally tutorial (the *one*—only one!—statement of "love" in the story is taken by the son as a recompense for years of absence); and the final payoff for the whole process: Bambi's becoming an adult male himself, "silent, apparently emotionless, powerful, dominant, and solitary." He becomes, in short, part of the patriarchal hierarchy, with does on the bottom, stags next, Human hunters (capitalized) next, and "Another," presumably God, at the top (ibid., 212–14).

32. Wendy Chapkis, *Beauty Secrets: Women and the Politics of Appearance* (London: The Women's Press, 1986), 121; Lillian Breslow Rubin, *Worlds of Pain: Life in the Working-Class Family* (New York: Basic Books, 1976), 230.

33. Arcana, *Every Mother's Son,* 120; Feigen Fasteau, *The Male Machine,* 207.

34. Pogrebin, *Growing Up Free,* 263; Feigen Fasteau, *The Male Machine,* 6.

35. Sherrod in Brod, *The Making of Masculinities,* 218. Sherrod's source is B. S. Morgan, "Intimacy of Disclosure Topics and Sex Differences in Self-Disclosure," *Sex Roles* 2 (1976), 161–66.

36. Feigen Fasteau, *The Male Machine,* 7.

37. Ibid., 11, 111, 14.

38. Chesler, *About Men,* 238, 239–41.

39. Ibid., 239–41.

40. Ibid., 241.

41. Feigen Fasteau, *The Male Machine,* 14–15.

42. Schaef, *Women' Reality,* 36–37.

43. Herb Goldberg, *The New Male: From Self-Destruction to Self-Care* (New York: NAL, 1979), 41, 31–32.

44. Marilyn French, *Beyond Power: On Women, Men, and Morals* (New York: Ballantine Books, 1986), 530; Feigen Fasteau, *The Male Machine,* 205.

45. French, *Beyond Power,* 280.

46. Sherrod in Brod, *The Making of Masculinities,* 215. Sherrod's source is R. Bell, *Worlds of Friendship* (Beverly Hills: Sage, 1981).

47. Chesler, *About Men,* 212.

48. bell hooks, *Feminist Theory from Margin to Center* (Boston: South End Press, 1984), 73–74.

49. Chesler, *About Men*, 225, 227, 224.

50. Julty, *Men's Bodies*, 88; Goldberg, *The New Male*, 218.

51. Feigen Fasteau, *The Male Machine*, 20–21, 25, 24.

52. Ibid., 25.

53. Timothy Beneke, *Men on Rape: What They Have to Say about Sexual Violence* (New York: St. Martin's Press, 1982) bears out many of the conclusions reached by the other sources in this section. Some men even perceive women's "attractiveness" (i.e., the attraction they feel for certain women) as a hostile act, a taunt or challenge, or a "power" held over them. The male attitudes towards rape quoted by Beneke range from concern and revulsion, to denial, to the hostility just mentioned, to plain excitement. The book includes an extended statement by Andrea Rechtin, a rape victim advocate and feminist. Beneke's position is nearly identical with hers. At the end of the book is a list of men's organizations against rape and against male violence toward women in general.

54. Jane Caputi, *The Age of Sex Crime* (Bowling Green, OH: Bowling Green State University Popular Press, 1987), 150. Caputi points out that the historical Bluebeard, Gilles de Rais, murdered women, men, and boys. Popular European–North American legend has made his story less terrifying—to whom?—by turning him into a man who murdered only women, specifically, his wives.

55. French, *Beyond Power*, 280–81.

56. Paul Lauter, "Race and Gender in the Shaping of the American Literary Canon: A Case Study from the Twenties," *Feminist Studies* 9:3 (1983), xxv.

57. Charlene Spretnak, ed., *The Politics of Women's Spirituality: Essays on the Rise of Spiritual Power within the Feminist Movement* (New York: Anchor Press, 1968), 572.

58. Sheldon in Dorothy E. Smith and Sara J. David, eds., *Women Look at Psychiatry* (Vancouver: Press Gang Publishers, 1975), 18.

59. Helen Michalowski, "The Army Will Make a 'Man' Out of You," in Pam McAllister, ed., *Reweaving the Web of Life: Feminism and Nonviolence* (Philadelphia: New Society Publishers, 1982), 327, 328, 330. The Lifton work referred to is Robert J. Lifton, *Home from the War: Vietnam Veterans, neither Victims nor Executioners* (New York: Simon and Schuster, 1973).

60. Michalowski, "The Army," 332, 333.

61. Lifton in ibid., 333.

62. Ibid., 334.

63. Chesler, *About Men*, 106

64. Ibid., 244.

65. When I have asked, the student in question has never been able to tell me, either because he couldn't put his position into words, or because my presence

as an authority (and the possibility of a bad grade) stopped him, or even possibly because the position was in fact indefensible. The point is that an attack on *rape as an institution in the United States* is felt by many men as an attack on male privilege as such, whether or not the man in question is, or thinks of himself as, a rapist. (The attack consists, in part, of defining the issue in the way women experience what goes on, rather than the way men experience, or want to experience or define, what goes on.)

66. Brod, *The Making of Masculinities,* 92.

67. Christine Delphy, *Close to Home: A Materialist Analysis of Women's Oppression,* translated by Diana Leonard (Amherst: University of Massachusetts Press, 1984), 114.

68. Brod, *The Making of Masculinities,* 15.

69. Rubin, *Intimate Strangers,* 137–38.

SCALING THE OFFICE BUILDING

Few city dwellers expect to hack their way through untouched forest every time they go to the corner grocery or lug ropes and pitons with them every morning to reach their offices or other places of work on, say, the twentieth floor. Not at all; they expect sidewalks, roads, public transportation, and elevators, in short, what cities and towns exist to provide for everyone: *access.* What else do we pay our taxes for? But some citizens, it seems, get more access for their money than others do. Somehow these others are not included in civilization. They're not citizens. They're "special." When asked why, the answer is usually very simple: They're "sick." They're "different." They're "crippled" or "disabled" or "deformed," and that makes them "different" from the rest of "us." If "they" can't get around in the same way "we" can, then *they and their differentness are at fault and their differentness is total.* Now, ability obviously does not occur in one naturally marked-off group called "able-bodied" and another, totally separate, totally disconnected group of people called "dis-abled." Whatever the particular ability in question is, it obviously occurs among Human beings in a continuum, for example from those who can run twenty-mile marathons, to those who can run five-minute miles, to those who can run around a city block, to those who can walk across a room, to those who can walk across room with canes or walkers or braces, to those who can't walk at all. Such differences occur for each *particular* ability we're talking about. Marking one point in this continuum as separating the "able-bodied" over here, *as whole people,* not as people with particular degrees of particular abilities, from the "dis-abled" over there, also as whole people, not as people with particular degrees of particular abilities—this distinction is not one made by nature but rather one made by Human societies, one that has historical and economic roots. And it is very, very political. Thus buses are for "people in general" while buses with lifts are "special," roads are necessary for "everyone" while curb cuts aren't, and some people can have public toilets as a matter of right but others can't.

Such things have a history. According to Debra Connors, whose history of the matter I'm following here, disability is largely a social construct, which came into existence along with our old friend capitalism (in this case, in England, the mercantile capitalism that preceded industrial capitalism) and its inevitable accompaniment, unemployment. Connors writes of England:

> The Elizabethan Poor Laws differed from feudal custom in several important ways. They drew a distinction between those who were "deserving" and "not deserving" of charity. Poverty and unemployment came to be viewed as personal problems and defects of character. Receipt of charity became cause for humiliation. Newly defined as those who "could but would not work," able-bodied paupers were put to labor in workhouses. . . . Blind, old, lame people and others with "diverse maladies" were given licenses to beg. Those . . . begging without a license were publicly whipped. Overseers of the poor were appointed. . . . [and] almshouses were established for . . . "invalids." . . . *Persons who were ill or had physical impairments were legally defined as unemployable social dependents incapable of self-care.*[1]

Earlier, as Connors points out, people worked in whatever capacity they could. But as mercantile capitalism gave way to industrial capitalism, with its insistence that workers be standardized to fit the machinery that had now standardized work itself (even though machinery actually made it possible to do without Human physical strength in many instances), "disability became more fully institutionalized." After all, she continues:

> [Even though] a recent study concluded that it is no more costly to hire disabled than non-disabled workers . . . business and industrial capitalism *require* that a sector of the population be held in reserve—ready to work for minimum wages. The conditions of unemployed and disabled workers serve as a constant reminder to even the most dissatisfied active worker that *any* job may be preferable to no job at all. The presence of readily available replacements effectively holds down wages and threatens unions. Fear and blame associated with unemployment mystifies its social origins and keeps workers in their place. . . . [Thus mys-

tified,] our unemployability is a given. . . . Health offers hope for
beginning anew. . . . Illness and injury spell doom.[2]

There is other evidence that "disability" became an institution—a socially
constructed "fact"—even later in U.S. history. Anne Finger, for example,
traces the word "defective":

> Originally an adjective meaning faulty or imperfect . . . by the
> 1880's . . . people . . . had become *defective*[s]. A similar trans-
> formation took place a few decades later with the word *unfit*,
> which also moved from being an adjective to being a noun. The
> word *normal*, which comes form the Latin . . . *norma*, a square,
> until the 1830's meant standing at a right angle to the ground.
> During the 1840's it came to designate conformity to a common
> type. By the 1880's, in America, it had come to apply to people
> as well as things.

She adds:

> Compulsory sterilization laws were passed in the early 1900's.
> . . . By the 1930's . . . 41 states had laws which prohibited the
> marriage of the "insane and feeble-minded," 17 prohibited the
> marriage of people with epilepsy; four outlawed marriage for
> "confirmed drunkards." More than 20 states still have eugenics
> laws on their books.[3]

The particular kind of mystification used to make people with disabilities
into pitiful subhuman, "special," frightening people is commonplace to
those of us who have disabilities.[4] If they show, you're not Human. If they
don't (like my chronic fatigue syndrome, chronic foot pain, and back pain),
then you're not disabled. At times, I have been directly or indirectly accused
of lying, making trouble, or being rude when I insisted (as I had to) that I
needed particular conditions for sitting, lying down, or resting. My favorite
in this department is a letter from a lesbian organization I had challenged
for not accommodating people with disabilities: "But we don't consider you
disabled." Connors points out how the very existence of people who lack
certain kinds of abilities (to walk, to breathe, to talk easily, to control one's
movements) is a direct challenge to one of the most important and heavily
promoted myths of U.S. society. She writes:

> It is unpardonable in an individualist [capitalist] society to fail to
> be "self-sufficient." Our society values a false sense of indepen-

dence. . . . Yet . . . as a species, we are emphatically *interdepend-ent*. . . . A market economy . . . obscures this fact. Moreover, class relations are hidden by the ideology of individualism. We firmly believe that if we are able to purchase the goods and services we are not able to produce for ourselves, we are free of dependence. . . . Those who are able to purchase a false sense of independence [i.e., the very wealthy] are revered and are a measure by which the working class evaluates its members.[5]

Thus, she continues, access to education, work, public facilities, medical care, social support, and mobility are not seen as the right of all citizens but only of those who are "successful" and "independent"—i.e., moneyed enough to pay for them. When people can't pay for them due to what we define as "disability," *it is they or their disabilities that are held to be at fault*, not the withholding of social resources that do in fact exist and that are being withheld from particular people because they have been invented as "unemployable" and "useless" *as a class*. They are so, of course, precisely because such resources have been withheld from them. That is, they are a minority; they don't have enough money and other political resources (yet) to change the status quo. *Therefore* they are unemployable, special, sick, and not really fully Human.

There is also the terror they produce in the "nondisabled," the terror of falling through the social safety net of a society that is cruel to those who do so and the terror of death and mortality in general, a fear with which our society absolutely refuses to deal. Susan Hannaford writes: "For no access read Apartheid. Exclusion is racism. Condescension is sexism. Places I can't get into are apartheid—not just physical access, but when you get there you want to be accepted. This means just being there."[6]

Of course, "we" pity "them" (pity being the other side of contempt), and "we" wish to be charitable to "them" and "give" them things, thus reinforcing "our" goodness and "their" difference from us—but what happens to all the money raised by charities? Where does all that "wonderful money go to?" Says Hannaford:

> Not to the people who need it; the people stuck in institutions, the people who are stuck in their houses with little money and little acceptance. . . . Not to the organizations which are run by us, for us, and who desperately need money in order to bring about changes in our social position . . . [but to] charity [which is] big business. Big business makes big money. *Who said we weren't useful?*[7]

At the National Women's Studies annual conference in 1986, Linda Kool-ish delivered the plenary speech, publicly identifying herself as a woman with severe immune disregulation, a condition that affects her ability to tolerate almost everything around her. She too says:

> Like poor women and women of color, we are the so-called consumers of social services, which means that our mistreat-ment is the source of employment for many of you and our situation is identified as the source of your high taxes and the burden of social security. . . . [We are] posed on t.v. as a ques-tion of medical ethics rather than eugenics and the higher pri-ority given to military budgets over health and human services. . . . We used to see the disincentives to work that are built into the social security disability system and the denial of access to public places as solipsism or a failure of the imagination. As ignorance. Now we know better. It is a conspiracy to keep us invisible, powerless, silent.[8]

So far we've been talking about *people* with disabilities, but predictably worse conditions lie in wait for the *women* who have or acquire disabilities. To mention only one example: in a patriarchal society, women physically nurture men and are expected to do so as wives; husbands are not expected to physically nurture women. According to Gwyneth Ferguson Matthews, national statistics exist for the marriages in which one partner acquires a disability: when men become disabled, their marriages break up half the time, while for women "that figure is 99 per cent." Disabilities make women, poor as a group, even poorer; single women, poor as a group, even poorer. And yet U.S. citizens who have disabilities are not a small minority. Ac-cording to Mary Jo Deegan and Nancy A. Brooks, we number approximately one in ten. Only in 1970, they say, did the federal census attempt a count of disabled people between the ages of 16 and 64; their results were one in eleven, while in 1972 the Social Security Administration, whose standards are quite strict (as I know from my own dealings with them) and who were counting only those between the ages of 20 and 64—that is, the prime working years—found one in nine. The White House Conference on Hand-icapped Individuals counted 33 million: *one in six.*[9]

A particular coalition problem exists between women with disabilities and the feminist movement. The latter, says Anne Finger, act by and large "as if we did not exist." She adds:

> Many disabled women find . . . the reproductive rights move-ment problematic. Not only have many activists . . . talked

about the issues raised by disabled fetuses in ways that are highly exploitative and prey upon fears about disability . . . [they] have failed to address the denial of reproductive rights to disabled women and men. It [the movement] has also failed to make itself physically accessible to disabled women. . . . at a recent conference on reproductive rights I heard disabled infants referred to as "bad babies." . . . No progressive social movement should exploit an oppressed group to further its ends. . . . The right to abortion is not dependent on certain circumstances; it is our absolute and essential right to have control over our bodies. We do not need to use ableist arguments. . . . Potential parents need to consider who *they* are and what they see as *their* strengths and weaknesses as parents.[10]

In short, we are not or should not be talking about producing a perfect "product" but about what women and men wish or do not wish to undertake at any particular point in their lives.

There is much more material on disabilities and women who have disabilities, some of it by women who actually have disabilities, believe it or not. One instance of the latter is Finger's emphatic statement that our cultural terror of people who have disabilities is rooted in a denial of what we all secretly know: our Human interdependence, our bodily vulnerability and the limitations that govern all our lives. Such knowledge—which is seriously evoked by the very existence of people with "disabilities"—gives the lie to the U.S. myth of individualism, to the ideal of unlimited economic and personal growth (both of which are heavily promoted here) and to the denial of the inescapability of Human community and an equal denial of the necessity of Human limitation and Human death. Cynthia Rich puts a lot of this together, I think, connecting Human limits, age, death, patriarchy, and war, by contemplating the one sort of person who is possibly the least valued and the most feared in the United States, especially when she's poor and/or not White: the sick, possibly dying, old woman. In her sixties, Rich writes:

I . . . feel shame in talking about my bodily discomfort, aware of the stigma of "old people are always complaining." But the fact is we [Human beings] spend our lives conveying to others how we feel in our bodies. We all have a real need to communicate our bodily experience. It is the language of lovers. Babies and small children are either crying because something hurts or gurgling or giggling because something feels good. Adolescents and young adults are preoccupied with their bodies.

Women discuss their bodies endlessly [in pregnancy or men-
opause]. . . . In my sixties when my body is doing all kinds of
things . . . I am not supposed to talk about it. . . . [and] you
who are younger have been taught to hear my bodily experience
as complaining. . . . I have to ask myself, "Why am I being si-
lenced? What is the message that I have to tell you that you are
forbidden to hear?"

She traces out the message, starting with the odd and important fact that

One death was always visible in film, in art and in literature—
the agonizing death of the hero who dies gloriously in mortal
combat, usually on a battlefield. . . . [For] the escalation of ar-
maments, territorial conquests . . . to succeed, *death must be defined as a single event, not as a life process.* . . . Men in battle . . .
[die as a] noble sacrifice to spare the rest of us that fearful
moment. . . . This assumption would not be possible if the daily
deaths of ordinary people were made visible . . . and if the bravery of the old who face death every day were recognized for the
courage it demands of the human spirit. Consider . . . the bag
lady who lives on the streets . . . who not only faces death each
day because of her age, her poor health and lack of medical
care, but also . . . violent attack, rape, or murder. Contrast her
. . . with the man in the foxhole . . . who is dressed in the best
combat clothes our tax money will buy . . . [has] the best medical care and the best diet in the world, and who knows that if
he is disabled, he will be pensioned . . . and if he is killed, he
will have a military funeral. If we honor the old woman . . .
there is just no way we can glorify the guy in the foxhole. And
he is going to be a lot harder to recruit if the glory of dying has
to be shared with old women.[11]

Citing one recent (although class- and culture-limited) study "that
suggests [U.S.] men face natural death with much more anxiety than
women," Rich appears here to be agreeing with Marilyn French's analysis
of the philosophy of patriarchy, i.e., that it promises men immortality,
transcendence, lack of weakness, complete independence, power over
women and nature, and a monopoly of the Human intellect. In short, as
French says (I am choosing two brief quotations from only one theme in
a book far too monumental to quote here in detail), "Men imagine they
can turn humans into gods," and "Domination is a hysterical attempt to
emulate God."[12]

Such ideas, however, offer little help in the face of the aging and death that is the inevitable Human lot. There are other views that offer a great deal more. Here is one example only, which I found in, of all places, a murder mystery. In Tony Hillerman's *The Ghostway,* there is a phrase that's stuck with me for years. His Navajo Tribal Police detective, Jim Chee, member of a culture whose assumptions are very different from those of the patriarchal Western one, gains valuable evidence because he has been intimately familiar from childhood with the aging and death of members of his immediate family. "Chee had grown up surrounded by the old of his family, learning from them, watching them grow wise, and ill, and die."[13]

Old and wise and ill and die.

It still applies.

NOTES

1. In Susan E. Browne et al., eds., *With the Power of Each Breath: A Disabled Women's Anthology* (Pittsburgh: Cleis Press, 1985), 93–94, italics added.

2. Ibid., 95, 96–97.

3. Ibid., 295, 296.

4. Children don't automatically react this way. Over and over again, I've heard and read accounts by people with disabilities (like people with cerebral palsy or those who use wheelchairs) that children come right up to them and ask "Why do you look funny?" or "Why do you talk funny?" or "Why are you in a wheelchair?" and absorb the explanation as just one more interesting thing in a world full of adult mysteries. It's not the children but the parents who are shocked, or pull the children away, or tell them to be quiet or pretend nobody's there; in short, who teach them that the people and the subject are taboo.

5. In Browne et al., *With the Power,* 97–98.

6. Susan Hannaford, *Living Outside Inside: A Disabled Woman's Experience— Towards a Social and Political Perspective* (Berkeley: Canterbury Press, 1985), 121.

7. Ibid., 26–27, italics added.

8. *National Women's Studies Association Perspectives* 5:1 (1986), 7–8.

9. Gwyneth Ferguson Matthews, *Voices from the Shadows: Women with Disabilities Speak Out* (Toronto, Ontario: Women's Educational Press, 1983), 87; Mary Jo Deegan and Nancy A. Brooks, eds., *Women and Disability: The Double Handicap* (New Brunswick, NJ: Transaction Books, 1985), 68–69.

10. In Browne et al., *With the Power,* 297–98.

11. Barbara Macdonald and Cynthia Rich, *Look Me in the Eye: Old Women, Aging, and Ageism* (San Francisco: Spinsters Ink, 1983), 109, 110–11, italics added.

12. Ibid., 80, 88; Marilyn French, *Beyond Power: On Women, Men, and Morals* (New York: Ballantine, 1986), 352, 137.

13. Somewhere I have a note (or have been told) that Hillerman has been given the title "Friend of the Navajo Nation" by the Navajo nation. I would appreciate hearing from anyone who knows about this possibility.

T H R E E

HOME THOUGHTS FROM A (WHOLE LOT OF) BROAD(S)[1]

Only a few. Still I'd rather mention them than leave them out. What they say may be useful to some readers, although much more material is available now than it was when I began this project years ago. The story they tell is, alas, familiar.

For example, the picture of women's lives in what was then the Soviet Union as presented by Tatyana Mamonova's pioneering *Women and Russia*[2] bears many similarities to feminist depictions of the United States. One contributor, Ekaterina Alexandrova, stresses the declining quality of life for women in an economy in which militarization has taken priority over social needs and in which women must therefore marry for economic reasons, while others, Mamonova and Karelia Petrozavodsk, report that rape is common and its incidence increasing. One of two marriages ends in divorce, says Alexandrova, while both the culture and government policy penalize women who don't marry and bear children. According to Natasha Maltsova, not only is this true, but women who do marry and have children face a dual workday, while inadequate stipends are the lot of single mothers. Moreover, childbirth is badly mismanaged medically, says Maltsova.[3] If capitalism brings worse poverty (as it seems to be doing right now to a great deal of what used to be the U.S.S.R.), a lot of this could get worse. And as jobs leave the United States (international capitalism not being in the least committed to national boundaries) and fewer and fewer U.S. citizens have the money to buy back what they produce, the difference worldwide depression makes in the political climate (which includes women's "successes") is beginning to be felt there too. Even when women in the U.S.S.R.

were employed at an "exceptionally high" rate, "with almost all able-bodied women of working age in the workforce," says Hilda Scott, women were

> over-represented in traditional industries and especially in low-level white-collar work and the services. Where whole professions have become feminized, as have teaching and medicine, they have lost status, and the pay compares unfavorably with that of a skilled worker.[4]

Want to know about a country in which women are sexually harassed in the streets, in which girls are brought up without proper instruction about their own bodies, in which girls are warned to be wary of boys and men while being encouraged to dress and behave "attractively" to them, in which popular culture exalts love as the most important thing in a woman's life while the double sexual standard still exists, in which girls are not generally informed about their own sexuality, in which many wives are sexually dissatisfied and where most abortions are performed on married mothers, most of whom already have more than two children? Well, it's the United States, all right, but it's also Egypt. So reports Nawal El Saadawi, a physician dismissed from her post as Egypt's director of public health in 1972 because of the publication of her feminist book, *Woman and Sex.* Saadawi has continued to publish feminist works despite the banning of her books in her native Egypt, in Saudi Arabia, and in Libya. She published *The Hidden Face of Eve,* from which the above information is taken, in Beirut, Lebanon.[5]

In Egypt, divorce lowers women's incomes, sometimes (in this country that is poorer than the United States) to the level of "hunger" and "no home." El Saadawi's research uncovered the extreme commonness of "sexual aggression by grownup men on female children or young girls." She found in her samplings that incest occurred in from 33.7 to 45 percent of the families she studied, statistics different but not so startlingly different from Kinsey's 24 percent in 1958 in the United States (Kinsey pooh-poohed the whole topic). His estimate may have been too low, according to recent studies in the United States.[6]

Saadawi's childhood, during which she was told that her destiny was marriage and in which she was not given the same freedom of behavior as the boys in the family, resembles nothing so much as mine—down to such eerily similar details as being sharply told to keep my skirt down and my knees together because there was something mysteriously wrong with the contrary position. Like me, girls in her country were never told about their clitorises. (In the 1970s, I found out that women twenty years my junior had received the same noneducation).[7] Although the United States no longer bans sexual research—now that sexuality has been turned into a commodity, titillation and repression can coexist quite nicely—long after the Kinsey Institute's funding was threatened because of the scandalous nature of its subject matter, the 1982 Barnard feminist conference on sexuality and feminist scholarship had its funding withdrawn by the Helene Rubenstein Foundation for similar reasons.[8] Saadawi also reports on women's overloaded workday, and she finds, rather as in the United States even today, "As to be expected, the whole weight of practicing contraception in Arab societies is thrown on the shoulders of the woman," from the pills that have numerous side effects to the loop that causes cramping and bleeding.[9]

In the United States, where there is enough food for all, many women starve deliberately—we call it "trimming," "slimming," or "dieting"—and some die of it. Starvation happens elsewhere involuntarily when there is not enough food. According to Madhu Kishwar and Ruth Vanita, in most "Indian families women eat the least and the last," and among Indian cotton pickers, women eat two-thirds of the calories eaten by men, despite a fifteen-hour workday that combines (is this beginning to sound too repetitive?) domestic labor with heavy work in the fields.[10] Kishwar and Vanita, like Christine Delphy, note that the force of tradition keeps such behavior common, ordinary, and unquestioned. An editorial from *Manushi*, the Indian feminist magazine that furnishes the material for Kishwar and Vanita's book *In Search of Answers*, describes the death in September 1979 of an Indian woman who had "worked on . . . [a] canal relief project all day and then had collapsed on reaching home." Her husband maintained that she had starved to death; asked how he could say this in the face of her day's work, he replied:

> "We get very little grain and we get it very late. . . . It was *her habit* to feed me first, then the children, and not eat enough herself." Thus the traditions built into male-dominated society, which force women to see their own lives as less valuable and to think that virtue lies in self-sacrifice, mean the slow starvation of the woman when the family is living at bare subsistence level.[11]

In 1979, *Manushi* stated that marriage is supposed to be the goal of a woman's life and described the ideally feminine woman as all-giving "whatever the demand . . . and however harmful to herself." Nor is it a surprise to find out about restrictions on women's freedom of movement, the isolation of women from one another, and the sacrosanct "privacy" of the family that makes it impossible for battered women to receive help. The neighborhood men's refusal to intervene ("It was a 'family quarrel' "), the helpless indignation of neighborhood women, the assumption that the privacy of the family makes it impossible to interfere—all are very reminiscent of accounts in U.S. and British writing on the subject.[12] This "privacy" that protects men but somehow not women or children[13] is one recognized and explicitly discussed by such authors as Diana Russell (*The Politics of Rape,* 1975), Del Martin (*Battered Wives,* 1976), and Catharine MacKinnon (*Sexual Harassment of Working Women,* 1979). Even when such behavior takes place in the public workplace, MacKinnon points out, it is perceived as "personal," and its supposed personal nature is used to excuse it often by its victims as well as by its perpetrators and the courts.[14]

I do not mean to insist that women's situations in different countries are identical or that women are equally poor or equally vulnerable or equally helpless—this is emphatically not the case—but the *patterns* of patriarchal social control do seem to be remarkably similar. For example, law in the United States is not usually so blithe about murdered wives, by any means, but male reactions to women's organizing are often like those described by Sudesh Vaid, who cites a women's organization, the Ryotu Mahila Sangham, formed in the Indian village of Kodurpaka. Kankamma, its president, a young peasant woman, stated that the organization was formed "to make our lives worth living, to protect ourselves from rape and insult." One male answer was the shouted assertion that "Kankamma has brought trouble to the village. We were fine until she and the other women started their meetings."[15]

Of course, a great many things do make a difference, and the lesser social worth of women *as a group* vis-à-vis the *group* of men can manifest itself in quite different ways in different places and times. One of the topics in *Manushi,* for example, that has no specific parallel in the United States is financially motivated dowry murder. According to *Manushi,* the fight against dowry murder began in 1977–78 with an attempt to make public the supposedly "accidental" deaths of wives by fire while cooking or by supposed "suicides."[16] Yet when I read in Kishwar and Vanita that feminist groups began in India "from the mid-1970s onwards in big metropolitan centers, and more recently even in small towns and cities," it's hard for me not to see parallels with much I've observed and lived through in the United States.[17] I also react the same way when a reader of the magazine, Patna Kiran, writes that the "publication of *Manushi* has been like the breaking of a stifling silence" and that she owns and manages a press and is learning to be a compositor, although "many people malign my character" and "people try to demoralize me." Kiran hopes that her group's women's newsletter "will develop into a feminist magazine."

Again and again patriarchal techniques turn up, not as geographical specialties or parts of particular cultures only but as part of similar repertoires of social control. Before and during the French Revolution, women were among the radicals and the rioters; afterward came the Code Napoléon, which strikingly restricted women's rights. Gay W. Seidman documents a similar development in the liberation struggle in Zimbabwe showing "the party's [prerevolutionary] commitment to . . . [the] emancipation of women" and how the party-turned-government relegated women to "feminine" restriction and dependence afterward. Men battering women accounts for 70 to 80 percent of "all reported crimes every day in Peru," says Robin Morgan, but Peru is far from unique, as the "institutionalized beating of women" is "mentioned by almost every contributor to *Sisterhood is Global.*" Women's sexual and reproductive freedom, she says, is everywhere restricted, just as the "scope of physical and intellectual movement" is restricted to "the private sphere" and educational opportunities are narrowed. The husband is the authority over wife and family, to a particularly extreme degree in Latin America with the "strong support" there of the church. In supposedly egalitarian Eastern Europe in the (then) socialist countries, contraception was restricted and large families rewarded. Feminists have been working against marital rape and battery "both . . . in the United States and . . . the . . . [then] Soviet Union."[18] Sanctions against divorce, whether cultural, economic, legal, or all three, exist everywhere, and divorced women are likely to lose custody of their children.[19] Summing up contributions from fifty countries, Morgan states that even in countries with equal divorce laws, women face "economic difficulties, non-payment of child support, family disapproval [and] social stigma."[20]

Morgan is not the only researcher to mention prohibitions against women eating as well as men, even though women's nutritional needs, because of pregnancy and nursing, can sometimes be greater than men's. Morgan specifically mentions prohibitions against women eating protein in many parts of the world. Christine Delphy, investigating rural families in France, finds that customary advice on hygiene or aesthetics or morality all converge on reserving greater protein and more food, as well as luxuries like alcohol and tobacco, for adult men. Lisa Leghorn and Katherine Parker note, as contributing to women's poverty, that "cultures throughout the world" continue dietary customs that are harmful to women while better food and more of it is reserved for men.[21] A friend of mine recalls her own mother's hunger during the Great Depression of the 1930s; her husband needed food because he was the wage earner, the children because they were growing; she got what was left. And here is Barbara Macdonald to sum it all up: "Document after document, country after country, uncovered the facts of women's exploitation—their longer working hours, their unpaid labor, their greater poverty."[22]

I do not write the above to stress the relative freedom of women in the United States; quite the contrary. What is so striking (and sometimes so eerie, as in the case of women's semistarvation in rich countries in the name of "beauty") is the *continuity* of what's happening in so many places as well as the interaction between the function of the United States as "leader of the capitalist world," as Linda Gordon says, and the collusion between imperialism and world patriarchy. One example Gordon gives is the post–World War II U.S. defense against

> international discontent as formerly colonial peoples demanded independence and sought economic development through nationalist and often socialist reorganization, which would have limited or even ended the continued economic exploitation of Third World peoples by Western capitalists.

The defense/solution?

> Population control . . . provided both a rationalization for the failure of capitalism to provide economic growth for the Third World masses and a proposed solution to the social stress . . . [by making overpopulation] the main reason that economic progress in the Third World was desirable [and threatened].

She adds that the "population controllers," who "often claim to support female emancipation," nonetheless

> have not campaigned against illegitimacy legislation or for public day care or any other programs that would increase women's power to have real reproductive choice. Throughout the world, population-control programs decreasingly use diaphragms and even pills and favor IUDs and operations which are not in women's control. The population-control view of women's "emancipation" is the imposition of norms of U.S. bourgeois behavior onto women.[23]

Underpaid, segregated jobs,[24] "beauty," reproduction controlled by the medical establishment and directly or indirectly by government policies, the double workday, unpaid work, compulsory heterosexuality, compulsory self-sacrifice, less education, less leisure, less food, less authority, less safety, less physical scope, less independence—the patterns are remarkably similar again and again, in place after place.

So sticking to evidence from one country may not be so totally limiting after all.

NOTES

1. A terrible literary in-joke. Never mind.

2. Tatyana Mamonova, ed., *Women and Russia: Feminist Writing from the Soviet Union* (Boston: Beacon Press, 1984).

3. Ibid., 49, xix, 5, 41, 111, 111–16.

4. Hilda Scott, *Working Your Way to the Bottom: The Feminization of Poverty* (London: Pandora, 1984), 27.

5. Nawal El Saadawi, *The Hidden Face of Eve: Women in the Arab World,* translated by Sherif Hetata (Boston: Beacon Press, 1980). For particular references to sexual harassment, see (among other material) pp. 46–47 and 146; for sexual ignorance and the double standard, 44–47 and 84–85; for clitorodectomy and the good girl/bad girl split, 34–37; for marital dissatisfaction, 23; and for statistics on abortion, 72.

6. Ibid., 205, 20.

7. Ibid., 46, 9–10, 35.

8. See the "Notes and Letters" in *Feminist Studies Issues* 9:1 (1983) to 10:3 (1984).

9. El Saadawi, *Hidden Face,* 70–71.

10. Madhu Kishwar and Ruth Vanita, eds., *In Search of Answers: Indian Women's Voices from Manushi* (London: Zed Books, 1984), 81–82.

11. Ibid., 262. Italics added.

12. Ibid., 242, 46, 11, 216. Alfie, a contributor to *Manushi,* describes the murder of a woman at the hands of her alcoholic husband. When neighborhood men were asked why they had not intervened (his battering of her had gone on for a long time before the murder), their answer was that the incidents were a "family quarrel." When a number of women went to the local police for the dead woman's body, the police inspector stated that the deceased must have been "an immoral woman. Otherwise no sane husband would do this." Male passers-by could not understand the women's action, saying, "Why are you making a hue and cry after this? After all, it is her husband who did it." Male students in her classroom, to whom the contributor related the matter, said, "Oh, it was her husband who killed her. Then what can you do about it?" (ibid., 216).

13. Catharine A. MacKinnon writes:

> Privacy is everything women as women have never been al-
> lowed to . . . have; at the same time private is everything
> women have been equated with and defined in terms of *men's*
> ability to have. . . . When women are segregated, in private,

> one at a time, a law of privacy will tend to protect the right
> of men "to be let alone," to oppress us one at a time
> (MacKinnon, "Feminism, Marxism, Method, and the State:
> Toward Feminist Jurisprudence," *Signs* 8:4 [1983], 656–57).

14. Catharine MacKinnon, *Sexual Harassment of Working Women: A Case of Sex Discrimination* (New Haven: Yale University Press, 1979), 2, 83, 90, 162.

15. Kishwar and Vanita, eds., *In Search of Answers*, 120–21.

16. Ibid., 31. The financial motive for wife-murder, which is sometimes instigated or aided by mothers-in-law, is to get another dowry. Since the bride's family gives money or goods to the groom's family, it's possible to kill a wife, cover up the murder, and acquire another wife and with her more money or goods, and so on.

17. Ibid., 30. The introduction to *In Search of Answers* provides a possibly important glimpse into history-in-the-making, one, however, with no parallels in the United States that I know of. The editors comment that

> several communities in the South [of India], which until not
> very long ago were matrilineal and matrilocal, have been
> rapidly giving way to patrilineal and patrilocal family struc-
> tures, with increasing male dominance and concomitant fe-
> male isolation and dependence (ibid., 14).

18. Gay W. Seidman, "Women in Zimbabwe: Postindependence Struggles," *Feminist Studies* 10:3 (1984), 419–20; Robin Morgan, ed., *Sisterhood Is Global: The International Women's Movement Anthology* (New York: Anchor, 1984), 23, 9, 10.

19. Phyllis Chesler's *Mothers on Trial: The Battle for Children and Custody* (New York: McGraw-Hill, 1986) examines this process in the United States. Briefly, although custody tends to go automatically to the mother *if custody is not contested*, when the father contests custody, he usually gets it. Men's generally higher incomes are also to their advantage, both when hiring lawyers or impressing judges (most of them also male) with the greater "advantages" they can give children. Chesler also notes, as do other feminists, that child custody involves the obligations of child care but not the automatic right to keep the child; if a father contests custody after the original assignment of custody to the mother, few mothers are found "good enough" by judges to keep custody of the child.

20. Morgan, ed., *Sisterhood Is Global*, 10.

21. Ibid., 20; Christine Delphy, *Close to Home: A Materialist Analysis of Women's Oppression*, translated by Diana Leonard (Amherst: University of Massachusetts Press, 1984), 47–48; Lisa Leghorn and Katherine Parker, *Woman's Worth: Sexual Economics and the World of Women* (Boston: Routledge and Kegan Paul, 1981), 199.

22. Barbara Macdonald and Cynthia Rich, *Look Me in the Eye: Old Women, Aging and Ageism* (San Francisco: Spinsters Ink, 1983), 43.

23. Linda Gordon, *Woman's Body, Woman's Right: A Social History of Birth Control in America* (New York: Grossman, 1976), 392, 401.

24. See Scott, *Working Your Way,* 19, 27, for the United States and the then Soviet Union.

F O U R

COMPARING NOTES

When you can't bury something completely, declare it boring, selfish, and a fad. For example, Jeanne Gomoll writes about science fiction in the 1970s:

> It was not one or two or a mere scattering of women, after all, who participated in women's renaissance in science fiction. It was a great BUNCH of women: too many to discourage or ignore individually, too good to pretend to be flukes. In fact, their work was so pervasive, so obvious, so influential, and they won so many of the major awards, that their [work] demands to be considered centrally as one looks back on the late 70's and early 80's. . . . Ah ha, I thought, how could they ever suppress all THAT?![1]

Not, she continues, by criticizing the decade's feminism directly but by criticizing it in code, i.e., by attacking something that seems unrelated to it:

> For the last couple [of] years I've begun to suspect that the phrase "the me-decade" is really . . . [an] attack upon changes made by the women's movement. . . . But the ironic judgment of the men who found *themselves* cared for less well than their fathers had been, is that women who are not *selfless* must be *selfish*. . . . As time goes on, the two statements—#1: that SF was boring—or faddish—in the '70s and #2: that women's

writing and issues are boring—appear to be two separate statements and new readers are lulled into ignorance.[2]

What Gomoll is condemning is one way of rewriting history. Here's another, undoubtedly done from the best of motives: In the 1980s, in Seattle, an actress presented an evening of readings from Virginia Woolf's
diary (the version edited and published after her death by her husband,
Leonard Woolf). The performer omitted any reference to Woolf's lesbianism or her affair with Vita Sackville-West (both well-established facts in
the literary community at the time) as well as the sexual abuse Woolf suffered throughout her childhood and adolescence. When I asked her why,
after the performance, she said they were too "personal" for Woolf to
have wanted them to be known and that she wanted to present Woolf "as
an artist." Unfortunately, such a wish to spare Woolf's memory embarrassment or public shame stems from the double judgment that the facts
left out about her (her childhood abuse, her sexuality, and her madness)
had no relation to her writing *and* that these facts were and are shameful
and demeaning and therefore ought not to be talked of in public. Of
course, the whole split between "public" and "private" life, along with the
injunction to hide certain things as shameful, has always operated against
women's interests. Mind you, I think all people are prudent to keep to
themselves anything their neighbors might give them a hard time for—as
long as their behavior hurts no one else—but the assumed sanctity of the
private sphere ensures that women who make *public* complaints about the
private patriarchal order, especially in the areas of sexuality, personal violence, or economic harassment, face a triple social penalty: they will be
disbelieved and this will happen precisely because they've violated the taboo against making the "private" public. The facts so revealed (the abuse,
the rape, the sexual harassment, the battering) will somehow redound to
the shame of the victim.

Such omissions have another effect: they reinforce the idea that all women
are perfectly content with the patriarchal order. (Other means are used to
silence other groups.) In the case of the actress above, the particular false
idea being promulgated—unwittingly, I'm sure—was that a woman can
combine high artistic achievement with total fulfillment of the patriarchal
requirements for women—so why can't you? Thus, the public portrayal of
Woolf that evening was of a "normal," "feminine" woman with a sexually
happy marriage and an uneventful childhood. The performer was clearly
pleased to be able to depict a woman of achievement and purpose, a great
and serious artist. Nonetheless, when I asked her, she revealed that she had
never read or even heard of Woolf's feminist works, *A Room of One's Own*

and *Three Guineas,* or the witty, lesbian *Orlando.* That is, she did not know her subject.

Some more scattered quotations from Spender:

> Male supremacy is a carefully cultivated cultural construct. . . . This reality is too fragile for "lapses," even among men, to be allowed. It must be constantly reinforced and this is only possible by the suppression of women's meanings. So frequently are women in a position to reveal the false nature of the claims of the dominant group that there must be ways of procuring their silence. . . . Reality is constructed and sustained primarily through talk. . . . Within CR groups women have been moving towards acquiring control over their own talk, have been beginning to construct a metapatriarchal reality and have been circumventing some of the restrictions habitually imposed upon muted groups. But if that reality is to be maintained, it needs constant re-creation.[3]

Annette Kolodny writes:

> I wish the women's movement would get back to C-R; we old "war horses" (as you call us) know how valuable that process was; but no younger generation seems to have been willing to go through its pain. Something vital got lost when the C-R groups got lost as central to our movement.[4]

"In CR groups," writes Julia Penelope, "I learned that NOTHING could be assumed." Hooks also deplores the loss of C-R in feminism, noting that "as consciousness-raising groups lost their popularity new groups were not formed to fulfill similar functions." The Combahee River Collective reports on Black feminists' "feeling of craziness" before they became conscious of feminist analysis.[5]

C-R need not be formal; a lot of it is just talk between friends. Thus, Moraga describes important C-R in her life:

> Three years after graduation, in an apple-orchard in Sonoma, a friend of mine (who comes from an Italian Irish working-class family) says to me, "Cherríe, no wonder you felt like such a nut in school. Most of the people there were white and rich." It was true. All along I had felt the difference, but not until I had put

the words, "class" and "race" to the experience, did my feelings make any sense.[6]

C-R can also be reading and writing. Here's Ann Oakley with some statistical enlightenment and a warning about other silences:

> The large overlap between the sexes on all characteristics of personality and behavior is veiled by the common strategy of investigating some trait . . . in single sex groups. *When dual sex groups of subjects are taken, some "sex differences" are bound to occur for statistical reasons.* In one . . . study in which 35 categories of behavior were rated yearly for 57 females and 58 males, 7 per cent of 442 female-male differences achieved the 5 per cent level of significance. This is hardly greater than the number of "findings" that would have been expected to occur by chance.[7]

And here is some C-R from Elizabeth Janeway:

> Attacks on the old role are not only frightening to women who've spent a life at it and aren't at all sure they know how to do anything else. They also appear as personal attacks on one's own judgment and self-esteem. Self-esteem is very precious to women because it isn't easy for us to come by.[8]

Some more C-R (it's only talking, after all!) from Wendy Chapkis:

> When I was a kid, I saw an "I Love Lucy" show where Lucy and Ethel had mistaken this guest star at Ricky's club for a call girl. This woman is walking around with furs and diamonds and the men think she is the greatest thing that ever happened, doing everything she asks. Though this woman is better dressed than Lucy or Ethel ever have been and has Fred and Ricky under control (something their wives had been trying unsuccessfully to do for every episode since I'd been alive) Lucy and Ethel are treating her like dirt. I said to my mother . . . "Why is Lucy treating her so badly?" and my mother whispers "they think she's a call girl." She *whispers.* Nobody is there but us. I said, "I think that is what I want to be when I grow up."

Nonetheless, she adds:

Dressing to signal sexual intent is a dangerous act for a woman in a world of male violence. . . . Whenever a woman is on display, I feel my anger rising. She is in danger. . . . The message of the Bunny Beauty is vulnerability.

And again, Chapkis describes how she

bought myself a motorcycle, a leather jacket and boots. When astride the bike a dramatic transformation came over me. I could not for the life of me smile. For the first time in my nice girl . . . life, I felt Mean. I looked Bad. I was tough and powerful and masculine. This lasted only as long as I was dressed in my leather drag, atop my machine. And even then it folded after a few weeks. Still, leather and metal provided access to forbidden gender symbolism.[9]

In my opinion, C-R is precisely what's needed for the current feminist controversies over sexuality. If C-R could occur and continue on this topic, I believe the fights between such thinkers as Pat Califia and Andrea Dworkin (which in my opinion are not fights at all) will go the way of the old Lavender Menace,[10] not "won" or "lost" by either party but rather *understood in context and combined in theory*: what happens, how things and people fit together, and how and why people do what they do. This sort of understanding is precisely what's needed for coalition work.

The context of people's actions can be different experiences. It can also be a difference in era. Here is Martha Vicinus, quoting Judith Walkowitz's *Prostitution and Victorian Society* in a review of that book:

The British women's Freedom League, under the leadership of Teresa Billington-Greig, during the years before World War I, monitored court cases of wife-beating, child molesting, and women's crimes. . . . the heaviest sentence for wife assault was nine months, when the wife died from the effects. The most severe sentence for baby battering was four months for manslaughter; a man received three months for indecent assault on a semiparalyzed girl. As the Recorder of Sandwich, England, said, assault on a little girl was not an ordinary crime like thievery, but one which "the most respectable man might fall into."[11]

No wonder nineteenth-century British feminists were active precisely in those areas we would now call civil rights, especially eligibility for public office, the professions and the vote, i.e., a voice in making the laws under which they had to live.

Here is another example of C-R in the context of time. In a review essay on "Psychology" in the very first issue of that now venerable feminist scholarly journal *Signs,* Mary Brown Parlee wrote, "This year for the first time the *Annual Review of Psychology* contains a chapter—the shortest one in the volume—on 'The Psychology of Women.' It is not listed in the index . . . but appears under 'Special Topics.'"[12] And *that* is one reason—but only one—why we who became feminists in the 1970s were angry and active in precisely the areas *we* were at that time.

Consciousness-raising is important because bad things happen when it stops. As early as 1983, several feminist scholars who'd been active in the 1970s generously responded to a very early version of this book (its first chapter, which has since been rewritten) by documenting the political reaction they perceived occurring around them. Barbara Hillyer wrote of "the uneasy feeling that many of us have that the movement is being co-opted. I had some young students read *Sisterhood Is Powerful* and they really noticed the difference—said they wished they'd been around then." She also noted:

> Recently . . . I have noticed a new phenomenon: male professors going completely out of control and screaming (literally) at women about apparently ordinary transactions: an assistant professor states calmly that she objects to receiving a $500 "salary adjustment" when each of her male colleagues receive $4000. An office manager tells a student employee to do her filing. Why are the Department Chairman and the Dean screaming? Chairman: "I KNEW when we put you on a tenure track you'd DO THIS!" (expect equal treatment?) Dean: "NEVER tell an employee what to do *without consulting me.*" Why are these men cracking up? In both cases there is a woman who plays the admiring, feminine, dependent role for this man: another assistant professor, another dean, another (non-managerial) dean's office employee.[13]

Susan Koppelman, referring to a review of one of her books, says of another academic *feminist* critic:

> She refers to my thinking as simplistic because I discuss economic, legal, and social realities in preference to individual ego psychology. That is an old political stratagem of the "antipolitical" right. [Thus] the "scholars" who invented "The New Criticism" when it became dangerous to talk about politics ac-

cused the radical leftists of being simplistic in their discussions of literature. *When reality is so bad that to describe it accurately is to perform a revolutionary act, then people start paying arduous and jargonistic attention to individual matters.*[15]

I agree with Koppelman that far too much recent academic feminist theory has totally left behind any concern with anyone's real experience and consists largely of people theorizing from other people's theories about yet more theory, all of it in a void. For a discussion of the French feminist movement—from whose least radical wing most current academic discourse is drawn—see the "Notes and Letters" section of *Feminist Studies* 8: 3 (1982). In 1979, according to one writer, Psych et Po, the most psychoanalysis-oriented wing of French feminism, took another feminist group, the publishing house Éditions de Tierce, to court for protesting (along with eleven other feminist publishing houses at the International Women's Conference in Copenhagen) Psych et Po's attempt to establish a *legal monopoly* of the phrase "Mouvement de Libération des Femmes" (the Women's Liberation Movement) and its initials. (This is an astonishing action from anyone's point of view!) Our current "feminist" godfathers, Freud, Foucault, and Lacan, came to academia in the United States via this wing of the French feminist movement. (My sources are also Marilyn Hacker and Monique Wittig.) Much of the feminism now current in academia has few native or populist roots, which is probably the reason why its psychology is often so outré (and out-of-date), its language so difficult and meager, and why it is sometimes surprised to find that some feminist ideas actually occurred more than ten years ago, i.e., in the 1970s (or even the 1870s). There were academic mavericks in the women's movement in the 1970s (there still are), but there were also artists, welfare mothers, domestic workers, factory workers, journalists, New Leftists, and Old Socialists. Its original presence was not academic—women's studies courses were founded against very stiff opposition, much of which I remember well—but much more everyday, it throve on consciousness-raising, and its concerns were not those of the professional academic middle classes in whose world talk is king and talk about talk is emperor. It is also possible, unfortunately, to assume that the solution to problems of oppression lies *in the psychology of the oppressed or the oppressor* and be fascinated by this subject endlessly and fruitlessly without ever addressing the structural advantages of oppression to those who do the oppressing. Psychology here provides a way of changing the subject. (It is as if people attempted to solve the problems of poverty by addressing the "culture of poverty," the psychology of the poor, the psychology of the wealthy, wealthy folks' prejudices against the poor, poor folks' prejudices against the rich, "public opinion" about wealth and poverty, and so on instead of starting with the idea that in our economic system wealth creates poverty in its own interest, i.e., *class*—which, comes to think of it, lots of people in the United States have been doing rather a lot of, haven't they!)

I hope it's clear by now that consciousness-raising was never a matter of making one's life conform to already agreed-upon standards of what's feminist and what isn't. Neither was it therapy, although learning the truth about one's situation can be therapeutic. Rather, it developed theory from experience, connected experience to theory, and thereby (in a phrase Spender uses often) *made knowledge*. Why is "beauty" so important in women? Why are movies full of women being raped or stalked? Why are young men dead in war so heroic and old women living on the streets so disgusting? Why are so many people (or any people) poor? Why are some so rich? Nawal El Saadawi writes:

> The "high politics" of a country and the "great issues of society" are not related to, and are never really settled in the meeting halls, corridors and salons [of politicians]. . . . They rest, in fact, with the small events and details of the daily life of millions and millions of men and women. They depend, for example, on our capacity to ensure that peasants leave for the fields in the morning after having passed urine which is free of blood, since bilharzia has been calculated to cost an economic loss to the country equivalent to 50% of the national income. They depend on our capacity to provide each worker with a [good] breakfast . . . every morning before he or she leaves for his work, so that they can stand in front of the machine without undue fatigue. They depend on the husband not beating his peasant wife every day before she leaves for the field . . . on women employees riding on public transport without being trampled underfoot or physically assaulted, on a wife being able to refuse sex with her husband . . . on the man caring sufficiently for his children. . . . These . . . are the things that constitute society, a system, and a State. They are the elements, the material of politics. . . . Those who are involved in "politics" and yet neglect such matters do not even know what the word politics means.[15]

It is by paying attention to these ordinary things that feminists in the United States in the 1970s made politics and political theory, as well as political change, as have many other people in many other movements, both here and elsewhere. Experience alone is unintelligible. Theory alone is empty. Consciousness-raising is whatever brings the two together, formally or informally, in a classroom, a house, on the street, in an apple orchard in Sonoma. *It is research.*

NOTES

1. Jeanne Gomoll, "An Open Letter to Joanna Russ," *Aurora* 10 (winter 1986–87): 7–8.

2. Ibid.

3. Dale Spender, *Man-Made Language* (London: Routledge and Kegan Paul, 1980), 114, 119.

4. Annette Kolodny, personal communication to author, 3 February 1985.

5. Julia Penelope, "The Mystery of Lesbians: II," *Lesbian Ethics* 1:2 (1985), 30; bell hooks, *Feminist Theory from Margin to Center* (Boston: South End Press, 1984), 48; Combahee River Collective in Cherríe Moraga and Gloria Anzaldúa, eds., *This Bridge Called My Back: Writings by Radical Women of Color* (Watertown, MA: Persephone Press, 1981), 211.

6. Cherríe Moraga, *Loving in the War Years* (Boston: South End Press, 1983), 54–55.

7. Ann Oakley, *Subject Women* (New York: Pantheon, 1981), 60, italics added.

8. Elizabeth Janeway, *Between Myth and Morning: Women Awakening* (New York: Morrow, 1974), 156.

9. Wendy Chapkis, *Beauty Secrets: Women and the Politics of Appearance* (London: Women's Press, 1986), 100, 139, 146, 138.

10. Briefly, for those who may not know about it, the "lavender menace" was the "menace" of lesbians in the women's movement in the early 1970s. The idea, as I recall it, was that lesbians' very presence gave fuel to accusations that the women's movement was "just a bunch of lesbians" and that no "normal" woman could be a feminist. There was also considerable ignorant, conventional fear of lesbians. Thus, Gene Damon, beginning an essay, could warn her feminist readers that they would be "frightened when you hear what this is all about. I am social anathema, even to you brave ones, for I am a Lesbian" (in Robin Morgan, ed., *Sisterhood Is Powerful* [New York: Vintage, 1970], 297–98). When NOW (the National Organization for Women) passed its 1980 resolution declaring lesbianism to be a feminist issue, as a matter of public policy the issue died. Of course, there are still women in particular organizations, like battered women's shelters, who are asked to conceal their lesbianism, and there are still fights over whether heterosexual women or lesbians are better feminists or "real" feminists and so on. Nevertheless, as a public phenomenon the Lavender Menace is now largely history and few long-term feminists are ready to leave the room, as one nervous woman threatened to do in 1970 in a group I

attended, because there might be lesbians in it. Sexuality seems to have replaced lesbianism per se as a divisive issue. As soon as NOW published its statement declaring lesbianism a feminist issue—but not pederasty, pornography, sadomasochism, or public sex—protest began about the new exclusions. See, for example, a letter signed by 162 people, most of them women, protesting NOW's stand on these other issues, published along with the text of the NOW resolution in the "Notes and Letters" section of *Feminist Studies* 8:1 (1982).

11. Martha Vicinus, "Sexuality and Power: A Review of Current Work in the History of Sexuality," *Feminist Studies* 8:1 (1982), 144–45.

12. Mary Brown Parlee, "Review Essay: Psychology," *Signs* 1:1 (1975), 119.

13. Barbara Hillyer, personal correspondence, 25 January 1985 and 14 March 1985.

14. Susan Koppelman, personal correspondence, 25 November 1985, italics added.

15. Nawal El Saadawi, *The Hidden Face of Eve: Women in the Arab World,* translated by Sherif Hetata (Boston: Beacon Press, 1980), 182.

Bibliography

BOOKS AND PAMPHLETS

Allport, Gordon W. *The Nature of Prejudice.* Garden City, NY: Doubleday Anchor, 1958.

Anzaldúa, Gloria. *Borderlands/La Frontera: The New Mestiza.* San Francisco: Spinsters/Aunt Lute, 1987.

Arcana, Judith. *Every Mother's Son.* Seattle: Seal Press, 1986.

———. *Our Mother's Daughters.* Berkeley: Shameless Hussy Press, 1979.

Atkinson, Ti-Grace. *Amazon Odyssey.* New York: Links Books, 1974.

Barr, Roseanne. *Roseanne: My Life as a Woman.* New York: Harper and Row, 1989.

Barry, Kathleen. *Female Sexual Slavery.* New York: Prentice-Hall, 1979. Paperback, New York: Avon, 1981.

Bass, Ellen, and Laura Davis. *The Courage to Heal: A Guide for Women Survivors of Child Sexual Abuse.* New York: Harper and Row, 1988.

Baum, Charlotte, Paula Hyman, and Sonya Michel. *The Jewish Woman in America.* New York: Dial Press, 1976. Paperback, New York: NAL, 1977.

De Beauvoir, Simone. *The Second Sex.* Translated by H. M. Parshley. New York: Knopf: 1953. Paperback, New York: Bantam, 1970.

Beneke, Timothy. *Men on Rape: What They Have to Say about Sexual Violence.* New York: St. Martin's Press, 1982.

Benét, Mary Kathleen. *Secretary: An Inquiry into the Female Ghetto.* London: Sidgwick and Jackson, 1972.

Bernard, Jessie. *The Female World.* New York: Free Press, 1981.

———. *The Future of Motherhood.* New York: Dial Press, 1974. Paperback, New York: Penguin, 1975.

Bethel, Lorraine, and Barbara Smith, eds. *Conditions 5: The Black Women's Issue.* 1979.

Bleier, Ruth. *Science and Gender: A Critique of Biology and Its Theories on Women.* New York: Pergamon Press, 1984.

Brownmiller, Susan. *Against Our Will: Men, Women, and Rape.* New York: Simon and Schuster, 1975. Paperback, New York: Bantam, 1976.

————. *Femininity.* New York: Simon and Schuster, 1984.

Bulkin, Elly, Minnie Bruce Pratt, and Barbara Smith. *Yours in Struggle: Three Feminist Perspectives on Anti-Semitism and Racism.* Brooklyn, NY: Long Haul Press, 1984.

Caplan, Paula J. *The Myth of Women's Masochism.* Markham, Ontario: Fitzhenry and Whiteside, 1985. Paperback, New York: NAL, 1985.

Caputi, Jane. *The Age of Sex Crime.* Bowling Green, OH: Bowling Green State University Popular Press, 1987.

Caulfield, Mina Davis, Barbara Ehrenreich, Deidre English, David Fernback, and Eli Zaretsky. *Capitalism and the Family.* San Francisco: Agenda Publishing, 1976.

Cavin, Susan. *Lesbian Origins.* San Francisco: Ism Press, 1985.

Chapkis, Wendy. *Beauty Secrets: Women and the Politics of Appearance.* London: Women's Press, 1986.

Chesler, Phyllis. *About Men.* New York: Simon and Schuster, 1978.

————. *Mothers on Trial: The Battle for Children and Custody.* New York: McGraw-Hill, 1986.

————. *Women and Madness.* New York: Doubleday, 1972.

Chesler, Phyllis, and Emily Jane Goodman. *Women, Money, and Power.* New York: Morrow, 1976.

Chodorow, Nancy. *The Reproduction of Mothering: Psychoanalysis and the Sociology of Gender.* Berkeley: University of California Press, 1978.

Clark, Don. *Living Gay.* Millbrae, CA: Celestial Arts, 1979.

————. *Loving Someone Gay.* Millbrae, CA: Celestial Arts, 1977.

Comer, Lee. *Wedlocked Women.* Leeds, England: Feminist Books, 1974.

Coward, Rosalind. *Female Desires: How They Are Sought, Bought, and Packaged.* New York: Grove Press, 1985.

Curtin, Katie. *Women in China.* New York: Pathfinder Press, 1975.

Dalla Costa, Mariarosa, and Selma James. *The Power of Women and the Subversion of the Community.* 3d ed. Bristol, England: Falling Wall Press, 1972.

Daly, Mary. *Beyond God the Father: Toward a Philosophy of Women's Liberation.* Boston: Beacon Press, 1973. Paperback, Boston: Beacon Press, 1974.

————. *Gyn/Ecology: The Metaethics of Radical Feminism.* Boston: Beacon Press, 1978.

Davis, Elizabeth Gould. *The First Sex.* Baltimore: Putnam, 1972. Paperback, New York: Penguin, 1971.

Delphy, Christine. *Close to Home: A Materialist Analysis of Women's Oppression.* Trans. Diana Leonard. Amherst: University of Massachusetts Press, 1984.

Densmore, Dana. *Chivalry—the Iron Hand in the Velvet Glove*. Pittsburgh: KNOW, Inc., 1969 [pamphlet].

———. *Who Is Saying Men Are the Enemy?* Pittsburgh: KNOW, Inc., 1970 [pamphlet].

Dinnerstein, Dorothy. *The Mermaid and the Minotaur: Sexual Arrangements and Human Malaise*. New York: Harper and Row, 1976.

Dreifus, Claudia. *Women's Fate: Raps from a Feminist Consciousness-Raising Group* New York: Bantam, 1973.

Dunayevskaya, Raya. *Women's Liberation and the Dialectics of Revolution: Reaching for the Future*. Atlantic Highlands, NJ: Humanities Press International, 1985.

Dworkin, Andrea. *Intercourse*. New York: Free Press, 1987.

———. *Pornography: Men Possessing Women*. New York: Perigee, 1981.

———. *Right-Wing Women*. New York: Perigee, 1983.

———. *Woman Hating*. New York: Dutton, 1974.

Ehrenreich, Barbara. *The Hearts of Men: American Dreams and the Flight from Commitment*. Garden City, NY: Anchor/Doubleday, 1983. Paperback Garden City, NY: Anchor/Doubleday, 1984.

Ehrenreich, Barbara, and Deirdre English. *For Her Own Good: 150 Years of the Experts' Advice to Women*. Garden City, NY: Anchor/Doubleday, 1978. Paperback, Garden City, NY: Anchor/Doubleday, 1979.

Eichenbaum, Luise, and Susie Orbach. *What Do Women Want*. New York: Coward McCann, 1983. Paperback, New York: Berkley, 1984.

Eisenstein, Hester. *Contemporary Feminist Thought*. Boston: G. K. Hall, 1983.

Engels, Frederick. *The Origin of the Family, Private Property, and the State*. New York: Pathfinder Press, 1972.

Faderman, Lillian. *Surpassing the Love of Men: Romantic Friendship and Love between Women from the Renaissance to the Present*. New York: Morrow, 1981.

Farrell, Warren. *The Liberated Man: Beyond Masculinity: Freeing Men and Their Relationships with Women*. New York: Random House, 1975. Paperback, New York: Bantam, 1975.

Fausto-Sterling, Anne. *Myths of Gender: Biological Theories about Women and Men*. New York: Basic Books, 1985.

Feigen Fasteau, Marc. *The Male Machine*. New York: Delta, 1975.

Figes, Eva. *Patriarchal Attitudes*. New York: Stein and Day: 1970. Paperback, New York: Fawcett World Library, 1971.

Firestone, Shulamith. *The Dialectic of Sex*. New York: Morrow: 1970. Paperback, New York: Bantam, 1972.

Fisher, Elizabeth. *Woman's Creation: Sexual Evolution and the Shaping of Society*. Garden City, NY: Anchor/Doubleday, 1979.

French, Marilyn. *Beyond Power: On Women, Men, and Morals*. New York: Ballantine, 1986.

Friday, Nancy. *My Mother My Self.* New York: Delacorte Press, 1979.

Friedan, Betty. *The Feminine Mystique.* New York: Dell, 1970. Originally published 1963.

Frye, Marilyn. *The Politics of Reality: Essays in Feminist Theory.* Trumansburg, NY: Crossing Press, 1983.

Gage, Matilda Joslyn. *Women, Church, and State: The Original Exposé of Male Collaboration against the Female Sex.* Watertown, MA: Persephone Press, 1980. Originally published 1873.

Giddings, Paula. *When and Where I Enter: The Impact of Black Women on Race and Sex in America.* New York: Morrow, 1984. Paperback, New York: Bantam, 1985.

Gilligan, Carol. *In a Different Voice: Psychological Theory and Women's Development.* Cambridge: Harvard University Press, 1982.

Gilman, Charlotte Perkins. *Women and Economics.* Ed. Carl N. Degler. New York: Harper and Row, 1966.

Goldberg, Herb. *The New Male: From Self-Destruction to Self-Care.* New York: NAL, 1979.

Gordon, Linda. *Woman's Body, Woman's Right: A Social History of Birth Control in America.* New York: Grossman, 1976. Paperback, New York: Penguin, 1977.

Gould, Stephen Jay. *The Mismeasure of Man.* New York: Norton, 1981.

Grahn, Judy. *Another Mother Tongue: Gay Words, Gay Worlds.* Boston: Beacon Press, 1984.

————. *The Highest Apple: Sappho and the Lesbian Poetic Tradition.* San Francisco: Spinsters Ink, 1985.

Greer, Germaine. *The Female Eunuch.* New York: McGraw-Hill, 1971. Originally published 1970.

Griffin, Susan. *Made from This Earth: An Anthology of Writings.* London: Women's Press, 1982. Paperback, New York: Harper and Row, 1983.

————. *Pornography and Silence: Culture's Revenge against Nature.* New York: Harper and Row, 1981.

————. *Rape: The Politics of Consciousness,* 3d ed. San Francisco: Harper and Row, 1986.

Grossvogel, David. *Dear Ann Landers: Our Intimate and Changing Dialogue with America's Best-Loved Confidante.* Chicago: Contemporary Books, 1987.

Guettel, Charnie. *Marxism and Feminism.* Toronto: Canadian Women's Educational Press, 1974.

Hamilton, Cicely. *Marriage as a Trade.* London: Women's Press, 1981. Originally published 1909.

Hannaford, Susan. *Living Outside Inside: A Disabled Woman's Experience—Towards a Social and Political Perspective.* Berkeley: Canterbury Press, 1985.

Harragan, Betty Lehan. *Games Mother Never Taught You: Corporate Gamesmanship for Women.* New York: Warner, 1977.

Harris, Marvin. *Cannibals and Kings: The Origin of Cultures.* New York: Random House, 1977.

———. *Cultural Materialism: The Struggle for a Science of Culture.* New York: Random House, 1979.

Heilbrun, Carolyn. *Reinventing Womanhood.* New York: Norton, 1979.

Henley, Nancy M. *Body Politics: Power, Sex, and Non-Verbal Communication.* Englewood Cliffs, NJ: Prentice-Hall, 1977.

Herman, Judith Lewis. *Father-Daughter Incest.* Cambridge: Harvard University Press, 1981.

Hess, Katharine, Jean Langford, and Kathy Ross. *Feminismo Primero/Feminism First: An Essay on Lesbian Separatism.* Translated by Helen Weber and Fabiola Rodríguez. Seattle: Tsunami Press, 1981.

Hite, Shere. *The Hite Report: A Nationwide Study of Female Sexuality.* New York: Macmillan, 1976.

———. *The Hite Report on Male Sexuality.* New York: Ballantine, 1981.

Hoffman, Frederick J. *Freudianism and the Literary Mind.* 2d ed. Baton Rouge: Louisiana State University Press, 1957.

hooks, bell. *Ain't I a Woman.* Boston: South End Press, 1981.

———. *Feminist Theory from Margin to Center.* Boston: South End Press, 1984.

Howe, Louise Kapp. *Pink Collar Workers: Inside the World of Women's Work.* New York: Putnam, 1977. Paperback, New York: Avon, 1988.

Janeway, Elizabeth. *Between Myth and Morning: Women Awakening.* New York: Morrow, 1974.

———. *Man's World, Woman's Place: A Study in Social Mythology.* New York: Dell, 1971.

Jansen-Jurreit, Marielouise. *Sexism: The Male Monopoly on History and Thought.* Translated by Verne Moberg. New York: Farrar, Straus and Giroux, 1982.

Jeffreys, Sheila. *The Spinster and Her Enemies: Feminism and Sexuality, 1880–1930.* London: Pandora, 1985.

Johnston, Jill. *Lesbian Nation: The Feminist Solution.* New York: Simon and Schuster, 1973.

Jones, Ann. *Women Who Kill.* New York: Holt, Rinehart and Winston, 1980.

Jonston, Johanna. *Mrs. Satan: The Incredible Saga of Victoria C. Woodhull.* New York: Popular Library, 1967.

Joseph, Gloria, and Jill Lewis. *Common Differences: Conflicts in Black and White Feminist Perspectives.* New York: Anchor, 1981. Paperback, Boston: South End Press, 1986.

Julty, Sam. *Men's Bodies: Men's Selves.* New York: Dell, 1979.

Kahn, Kathy. *Hillbilly Women.* New York: Doubleday, 1973. Paperback, New York: Avon, 1974.

Katz, Jonathan Ned. *Gay American History: Lesbians and Gay Men in the U.S.A.* New York: Avon, 1976.

————. *Gay/Lesbian Almanac: A New Documentary.* New York: Harper and Row, 1983.

Keller, Evelyn Fox. *Reflections on Gender and Science.* New Haven: Yale University Press, 1985.

Klaich, Dolores. *Woman + Woman: Attitudes toward Lesbianism.* New York: William Morrow, 1975. Originally published by Simon and Schuster, 1974.

Kline, Nathan. *From Sad to Glad.* New York: Putnam, 1974.

Korda, Michael. *Male Chauvinism! How It Works.* New York: Random House, 1973.

Kramarae, Cheris, and Paula A. Treichler. *A Feminist Dictionary.* Boston: Pandora, 1985.

Lamb, Patricia Frazer, ed. *Touchstones: Letters between Two Women, 1953–1964* [Patricia Frazer Lamb and Kathryn Joyce Hohlwein]. New York: Harper and Row, 1983.

Leghorn, Lisa, and Katherine Parker. *Woman's Worth: Sexual Economics and the World of Women.* Boston: Routledge and Kegan Paul, 1981.

Lekachman, Robert, and Borin Van Loon. *Capitalism for Beginners.* New York: Pantheon, 1981.

Lewontin, R. C., Steven Rose, and Leon J. Kamin. *Not in Our Genes: Biology, Ideology, and Human Nature.* New York: Pantheon, 1984.

Lorde, Audre. *Sister Outsider: Essays and Speeches.* Trumansburg, NY: Crossing Press, 1984.

Loulan, JoAnn. *Lesbian Sex.* San Francisco: Spinsters Ink, 1984.

Macdonald, Barbara, and Cynthia Rich. *Look Me in the Eye: Old Women, Aging, and Ageism.* San Francisco: Spinsters Ink, 1983.

MacKinnon, Catharine. *Sexual Harassment of Working Women: A Case of Sex Discrimination.* New Haven: Yale University Press, 1979.

Magdoff, Harry, and Paul M. Sweezy. *The Deepening Crisis of U.S. Capitalism.* New York: Monthly Review Press, 1981.

Margolis, Maxine L. *Mothers and Such: Views of American Women and Why They Changed.* Berkeley: University of California Press, 1984.

Marine, Gene. *A Male Guide to Women's Liberation.* New York: Holt, Rinehart and Winston, 1972. Paperback, New York: Avon, 1974.

Martin, Del. *Battered Wives.* San Francisco: Glide Publications, 1976.

Martin, Del, and Phyllis Lyon. *Lesbian/Woman.* New York: Glide Publications, 1972. Paperback, New York: Bantam, 1972.

Marx, Karl. *Capital.* Vol. I. Trans. Samuel Moore and Edward Aveling. New York: International Publishers, 1967. Originally published 1867.

Maslow, Abraham. *Toward a Psychology of Being.* New York: Van Nostrand and Reinhold, 1968.

Masson, Jeffrey. *The Assault on Truth: Freud's Suppression of the Seduction Theory.* 2d ed. New York: Penguin, 1985.

Matthews, Gwyneth Ferguson. *Voices from the Shadows: Women with Disabilities Speak Out.* Toronto, Ontario: Women's Educational Press, 1983.

Mead, Margaret. *Coming of Age in Samoa: A Psychological Study of Primitive Youth for Western Civilization.* New York: Laurel, 1968. Originally published 1928.

Miller, Alice. *For Your Own Good: Hidden Cruelty in Childrearing and the Roots of Violence.* New York: Farrar, Straus and Giroux, 1983.

———. *Thou Shalt Not Be Aware: Society's Betrayal of the Child.* New York: Meridian, 1986.

Miller, Casey, and Kate Swift. *Words and Women.* Garden City, NY: Anchor/Doubleday, 1976. Paperback, Garden City, NY: Anchor Books, 1977.

Miller, Jean Baker. *Toward a New Psychology of Women.* Boston: Beacon Press, 1976.

Millett, Kate. *The Prostitution Papers.* New York: Basic Books, 1971. Paperback, New York: Avon, 1973.

———. *Sexual Politics.* New York: Doubleday, 1970. Paperback, New York: Avon, 1971.

Mitchell, Juliet. *Psychoanalysis and Feminism.* New York: Pantheon, 1974. Paperback, New York: Vintage, 1975.

———. *Woman's Estate.* New York: Random House, 1971. Paperback, New York: Vintage, 1973.

Modleski, Tania. *Loving with a Vengeance: Mass-Produced Fantasies for Women.* Hamden, CT: Archon Books, 1982. Paperback, London: Methuen, 1984.

Moers, Ellen. *Literary Women.* New York: Doubleday, 1977.

Moglen, Helene. *Charlotte Brontë: The Self Conceived.* New York, Norton, 1976.

Moraga, Cherríe. *Loving in the War Years.* Boston: South End Press, 1983.

Morgan, Robin. *Going Too Far: The Personal Chronicle of a Feminist.* New York: Random House, 1977. Paperback, New York: Vintage, 1978.

———. *The Word of a Woman: Feminist Dispatches 1968–1992.* New York: Norton, 1992.

Nicolson, Nigel. *Portrait of a Marriage.* New York: Atheneum, 1973. Paperback, New York: Bantam, 1974.

Nightingale, Florence. *Cassandra.* Old Westbury, NY: Feminist Press, 1979.

Oakley, Ann. *Subject Women.* New York: Pantheon, 1981.

———. *Woman's Work: The Housewife, Past and Present.* New York: Pantheon, 1974. Paperback, New York: Vintage Books, 1976.

Piercy, Marge. *Braided Lives.* New York: Summit Books, 1982.

———. *The Moon Is Always Female.* New York: Knopf, 1980.

Pizzey, Erin. *Scream Quietly or the Neighbors Will Hear.* New York: Penguin, 1974.

Platt, Charles. *Dream Makers: The Uncommon Men and Women Who Write Science Fiction.* Vol. II. New York: Berkley, 1983.

Pogrebin, Letty Cottin. *Growing Up Free: Raising Your Child in the 80's.* New York: Grove Press, 1980.

Radway, Janice A. *Reading the Romance: Women, Patriarchy, and Popular Literature.* Chapel Hill: University of North Carolina Press, 1984.

Reeves, Maud Pember. *Round about a Pound a Week.* London: Virago, 1979. Originally published 1913.

Rice, Margery Spring. *Working-Class Wives: Their Health and Conditions.* 2d ed. London: Virago, 1981. Originally published 1939.

Rich, Adrienne. *Blood, Bread, and Poetry: Selected Prose, 1979–1985.* New York: Norton, 1986.

———. *Of Woman Born.* New York: Norton, 1976. Paperback, New York: Bantam, 1977.

———. *On Lies, Secrets, and Silence: Selected Prose, 1966–1978.* New York: Norton, 1979.

Roback, A. A. *History of American Psychology.* New York: Library Publishers, 1952.

Rowbotham, Sheila. *Hidden from History: Rediscovering Women in History from the Seventeenth Century to the Present.* London: Pluto Press, 1973; New York: Pantheon, 1974. Paperback, New York: Vintage, 1976.

———. *Woman's Consciousness, Man's World.* Harmondsworth, England: Pelican, 1973. Paperback, Harmondsworth, England: Penguin, 1973.

———. *Women, Resistance, and Revolution.* London: Penguin, 1972; New York: Pantheon, 1973. Paperback, New York: Vintage, 1974.

Rowbotham, Sheila, Lynne Segal, and Hilary Wainwright. *Beyond the Fragments: Feminism and the Making of Socialism.* Boston: Alyson Publications, 1981.

Rubin, Lillian Breslow. *Intimate Strangers: Men and Women Together.* New York: Harper and Row, 1983.

———. *Worlds of Pain: Life in the Working-Class Family.* New York: Basic Books, 1976.

Rush, Florence. *The Best Kept Secret: Sexual Abuse of Children.* New York: McGraw-Hill, 1980.

Russ, Joanna. *The Female Man.* Boston: Beacon Press, 1986. Originally published 1975.

———. *How to Suppress Women's Writing.* Austin: University of Texas Press, 1983.

———. *Magic Mommas, Trembling Sisters, Puritans, and Perverts.* Trumansburg, NY: Crossing Press, 1985.

Russell, Diana E. H. *The Politics of Rape: The Victim's Perspective.* Briarcliff Manor, NY: Stein and Day, 1975.

———. *The Secret Trauma: Incest in the Lives of Girls and Women.* New York: Basic Books, 1986.

Russell, Diana, and Nicole Van de Ven. *Crimes against Women: Proceedings of the International Tribunal.* East Palo Alto, CA: Frog in the Well Press, 1984.

El Saadawi, Nawal. *The Hidden Face of Eve: Women in the Arab World.* Translated by Sherif Hetata. Boston: Beacon Press, 1980.

Sanford, Linda Tschirhart, and Mary Ellen Donovan. *Women and Self-Esteem.* New York: Anchor/Doubleday, 1984. Paperback, New York: Penguin, 1985.

Schaef, Anne Wilson. *When Society Becomes an Addict.* San Francisco: Harper and Row, 1987.

—————. *Women's Reality: An Emerging Female System in a White Male Society.* New York: Harper and Row, 1985.

Schreiner, Olive. *The Story of an African Farm.* New York: The Modern Library, 1927.

Scott, Hilda. *Working Your Way to the Bottom: The Feminization of Poverty.* London: Pandora, 1984.

Sennett, Richard and Jonathan Cobb. *The Hidden Injuries of Class.* New York: Knopf, 1972.

Shields, Laurie. *Displaced Homemakers: Organizing for a New Life.* New York: Mc-Graw-Hill, 1981.

Shockley, Ann Allen. *The Black and White of It.* Tallahassee, Fl.: Naiad, 1980.

Smith, Barbara. *Toward a Black Feminist Criticism.* Brooklyn, NY: Out and Out Books, 1977.

Smith, David, and Phil Evans. *Marx's Kapital for Beginners.* New York: Pantheon 1982.

Smith, Dorothy E. *Feminism and Marxism: A Place to Begin, a Way to Go.* Vancouver: New Star, 1977.

Spender, Dale. *Invisible Women: The Schooling Scandal.* London: Writers and Readers Publishing Cooperative Society, 1982.

—————. *Man-Made Language.* London: Routledge and Kegan Paul, 1980.

—————. *Mothers of the Novel.* London: Pandora, 1986.

—————. *There's Always Been a Women's Movement This Century.* London: Pandora, 1983.

—————. *Women of Ideas: What Men Have Done to Them.* London: Routledge and Kegan Paul, 1982. Paperback, London: Ark, 1983.

Stanko, Elizabeth A. *Intimate Intrusions: Women's Experience of Male Violence.* London: Routledge and Kegan Paul, 1985.

Steinem, Gloria. *Outrageous Acts and Everyday Rebellions.* New York: Holt, Rinehart and Winston, 1983. Paperback, New York: NAL, 1986.

Strasser, Susan. *Never Done: A History of American Housework.* New York: Pantheon, 1982.

Székely, Éva. *Never Too Thin.* Toronto: Women's Press, 1988.

Taylor, Debbie, Anita Desai, Toril Brekke, Manny Shirazi, Marilyn French, Zhang Jie, Jill Tweedie, Nawal El Saadawi, Germaine Greer, Elena Poniatowska, and Angela Davis. *Women: A World Report.* London: Methuen, 1985.

Tax, Meridith. *Woman and Her Mind: The Story of Daily Life.* Boston: Bread and Roses, 1970.

Terkel, Studs. *Hard Times: An Oral History of the Great Depression.* New York: Pantheon, 1970.

————. *"The Good War": An Oral History of World War Two*. New York: Ballantine, 1984.

Thompson, William. *Appeal of One Half the Human Race, Women, against the Pretensions of the Other Half, Men, to Retain Them in Political and Thence in Civil and Domestic Slavery*. London: Virago, 1983. Originally published 1825.

Trotsky, Leon. *Women and the Family*. New York: Pathfinder Press, 1970.

Vida, Ginny, ed. *Our Right to Love: A Lesbian Resource Book Produced in Cooperation with Women of the National Gay Task Force*. Englewood Cliffs, NJ: Prentice-Hall, 1978.

Walker, Alice. *In Search of Our Mother's Gardens: Womanist Prose*. New York: Harcourt, 1983. Paperback, Harvest/Harcourt, 1984.

Walker, Lenore E. *The Battered Woman*. New York: Harper and Row, 1979. Paperback, New York: Harper and Row, 1980.

Wallace, Michelle. *Black Macho and the Myth of the Superwoman*. New York: Dial, 1979.

Waring, Marilyn. *If Women Counted: A New Feminist Economics*. New York: Harper and Row, 1988.

Watts, Emily Stipes. *The Poetry of American Women from 1632 to 1945*. Austin: University of Texas Press, 1977.

Weinbaum, Batya. *The Curious Courtship of Women's Liberation and Socialism*. Boston: South End Press, 1978.

Wise, Sue, and Liz Stanley. *Georgie Porgie: Sexual Harassment in Everyday Life*. London: Pandora, 1987.

Woititz, Janet. *Adult Children of Alcoholics*. Hollywood, FL: Health Communications, 1983.

Wolf, Naomi. *The Beauty Myth: How Images of Beauty Are Used against Women*. New York: Anchor, 1992.

Wollstonecraft, Mary. *A Vindication of the Rights of Woman: With Strictures on Political and Moral Subjects*. New York: Norton, 1967.

Women's Studies: Selected New and Recent Books, 1985. New York: Harper and Row, 1985 [catalogue].

Woolf, Virginia. *A Room of One's Own*. London: Harcourt 1929. Paperback, New York: Harcourt 1957.

————. *Three Guineas*. London: Harcourt 1938. Paperback, New York: Harcourt 1966.

ANTHOLOGIES

Abel, Elizabeth, and Emily K. Abel, eds. *The Signs Reader*. Chicago: University of Chicago Press, 1983.

Adams, Elsie, and Mary Louise Briscoe, eds. *Up Against the Wall, Mother . . . : On Women's Liberation.* Beverly Hills: Glencoe Press, 1971.

Alexander, Jo, et al., eds. *Women and Aging: An Anthology by Women.* Corvallis, OR: Calyx Books, 1986.

Allen, Sandra, Lee Sanders, and Jan Wallis, eds. *Conditions of Illusion: Papers from the Women's Movement.* Leeds, England: Feminist Books, 1974.

Altbach, Edith Hoshino, ed. *From Feminism to Liberation.* Cambridge, MA: Schenkman, 1971.

Beck, Evelyn Torton, ed. *Nice Jewish Girls: A Lesbian Anthology.* Watertown, MA: Persephone Press, 1982.

Bell, Laurie, ed. *Good Girls, Bad Girls: Feminists and Sex Trade Workers Face to Face.* Seattle: Seal Press, 1987.

Benstock, Shari, ed. *Feminist Issues in Literacy Scholarship.* Bloomington, IN: Indiana University Press, 1987.

Birkby, Phyllis, et al., eds. *Amazon Expedition: A Lesbian Feminist Anthology.* Powell Road, WA: Times Change Press, 1973.

Bowles, Gloria and Renate Klein, eds. *Theories of Women's Studies.* New York: Routledge and Kegan Paul, 1983.

Bragg, Mary et al., eds. *Lesbian Psychologies: Explorations and Challenges.* Urbana: University of Illinois Press, 1987.

Brod, Harry E., ed. *The Making of Masculinities: The New Men's Studies.* Boston: Allen and Unwin, 1987.

Browne, Susan E., Debra Connors, and Nanci Stern, eds. *With the Power of Each Breath: A Disabled Women's Anthology.* Pittsburgh: Cleis Press, 1985.

Bunch, Charlotte, et al., eds. *Building Feminist Theory: Essays from* Quest, A Feminist Quarterly. New York: Longman, 1981.

Burstyn, Varda, ed. *Women against Censorship.* Vancouver: Douglas and McIntyre, 1985.

Campling, Jo, ed. *Images of Ourselves: Women with Disabilities Talking.* London: Routledge and Kegan Paul, 1981.

Cruikshank, Margaret, ed. *Lesbian Studies: Present and Future.* Old Westbury, NY: Feminist Press, 1982.

Culley, Margo, and Catherine Portuges, eds. *Gendered Subjects: The Dynamics of Feminist Teaching.* Boston: Routledge and Kegan Paul, 1985.

Curb, Rosemary, and Nancy Manahan, eds. *Lesbian Nuns: Breaking Silence.* Tallahassee, FL: Naiad Press, 1985.

Darty, Trudy, and Sandee Potter, eds. *Women-Identified Women.* Palo Alto, CA: Mayfield, 1984.

Deegan, Mary Jo, and Nancy A. Brooks, eds. *Women and Disability: The Double Handicap.* New Brunswick, NJ: Transaction Books, 1985.

Delacoste, Frédérique, and Priscilla Alexander, eds. *Sex Work: Writings by Women in the Sex Industry.* Pittsburgh: Cleis Press, 1987.

Dreifus, Claudia, ed. *Seizing Our Bodies: The Politics of Women's Health.* New York: Random House, 1977. Paperback, New York: Vintage, 1978.

Eisenstein, Zillah R., ed. *Capitalist Patriarchy and the Case for Socialist Feminism.* New York: Monthly Review Press, 1979.

Evans, Mari, ed. *Black Women Writers (1950–1980): A Critical Evaluation.* Garden City, NY: Anchor/Doubleday, 1984.

Ferguson, Moira, ed. *First Feminists: British Women Writers, 1578–1799.* Bloomington, IN: Indiana University Press, 1985.

Freeman, Jo, ed. *Women: A Feminist Perspective.* 2d ed. Palo Alto, CA: Mayfield, 1979.

Gay Left Collective, ed. *Homosexuality: Power and Politics.* London: Allison and Busby, 1980.

Gómez, Alma, Cherríe Moraga, and Mariana Romo-Carmona, eds. *Cuentos: Stories by Latinas.* New York: Kitchen Table Women of Color Press, 1983.

Gornick, Vivian, and Barbara K. Moran, eds. *Woman in Sexist Society: Studies in Power and Powerlessness.* New York: NAL, 1971. Paperback, New York: Mentor, 1972.

Grier, Barbara, and Coletta Reid, eds. *Lesbian Essays from The Ladder.* Baltimore: Diana Press, 1976.

Hoagland, Sarah Lucia, and Julia Penelope, eds. *For Lesbians Only: A Separatist Anthology.* London: Onlywomen Press, 1988.

Howe, Florence, ed. *Women and the Power to Change.* New York: McGraw-Hill, 1975.

Hull, Gloria T., Patricia Bell Scott, and Barbara Smith, eds. *All the Women Are White, All the Blacks Are Men, but Some of Us Are Brave: Black Women's Studies.* Old Westbury, NY: Feminist Press, 1982.

Jackson, Ed, and Stan Persky, eds. *Flaunting It! A Decade of Gay Journalism from the Body Politic.* Vancouver: New Star Books/Toronto: Pink Triangle Press, 1982.

Jaget, Claude, ed. *Prostitutes: Our Life.* Trans. by Anna Furse, Suzie Fleming, and Ruth Hall. Bristol, England: Falling Wall Press, 1980.

Jay, Karla, and Allen Young, eds. *Lavender Culture.* New York: Jove Publications, 1979.

———. *Out of the Closets: Voices of Gay Liberation.* New York: Douglas Book Corp., 1972.

Kampf, Louis, and Paul Lauter, eds. *The Politics of Literature: Dissenting Essays on the Teaching of English.* New York: Pantheon, 1972. Paperback, New York: Vintage, 1973.

Kaye/Kantrowitz, Melanie, and Irena Klepfisz, eds. *The Tribe of Dina: A Jewish Women's Anthology.* Montpelier, VT: Sinister Wisdom Books, 1986. Originally published *Sinister Wisdom* 29/30, 1986.

Kehoe, Monika, ed. *Historical, Literary, and Erotic Aspects of Lesbianism.* New York: Haworth Press, 1986.

Kishwar, Madhu, and Ruth Vanita, eds. *In Search of Answers: Indian Women's Voices from Manushi.* London: Zed Books, 1984.

Koppelman, Susan, ed. *Between Mothers and Daughters: Stories across a Generation.* Old Westbury, NY: Feminist Press, 1985.

————. *Old Maids: Short Stories by Nineteenth-Century U.S. Women Writers.* Boston: Pandora, 1984.

Kramer, Sydelle and Jenny Masur, eds. *Jewish Grandmothers.* Boston: Beacon Press, 1976.

Lauter, Paul, ed. *Reconstructing American Literature: Courses, Syllabi, Issues.* Old Westbury, NY: Feminist Press, 1983.

Lederer, Laura, ed. *Take Back the Night: Women on Pornography.* New York: Morrow, 1980.

Liberation Now! Writings from the Women's Liberation Movement. New York: Dell, 1971.

Linden, Robin Ruth, Darlene R. Pagano, Diana E. H. Russell, and Susan Leigh Star, eds. *Against Sadomasochism: A Radical Feminist Analysis* East Palo Alto, CA: Frog in the Well, 1982.

Malos, Ellen, ed. *The Politics of Housework.* London: Alison and Busby, 1980.

Mamonova, Tatyana, ed. *Women and Russia: Feminist Writing from the Soviet Union.* Boston: Beacon Press, 1984.

McAllister, Pam, ed. *Reweaving the Web of Life: Feminism and Nonviolence.* Philadelphia: New Society Publishers, 1982.

Millman, Marcia, and Rosabeth Moss Kanter, eds. *Another Voice: Feminist Perspectives on Social Life and Social Science.* New York: Anchor, 1975.

Mitchell, Juliet, and Ann Oakley, eds. *What Is Feminism?* New York: Pantheon, 1986.

Moraga, Cherríe, and Gloria Anzaldúa, eds. *This Bridge Called My Back: Writings by Radical Women of Color.* Watertown, MA: Persephone Press, 1981.

Morgan, Robin, ed. *Sisterhood Is Global: The International Women's Movement Anthology.* New York: Anchor, 1984.

Newhouse, Nancy R., ed. *Hers: Through Women's Eyes.* New York: Harper and Row, 1985.

Pleck, Joseph H. and Jack Sawyer, eds. *Men and Masculinity.* Englewood Cliffs, NJ: Prentice-Hall, 1974.

Robbins, Joan Hamerman, and Rachel Josefowitz Siegel, eds. *Women Changing Therapy: New Assessments, Values, and Strategies in Feminist Therapy.* New York: Harrington Park Press, 1985.

Roszak, Betty, and Theodore Roszak, eds. *Masculine/Feminine: Readings in Sexual Mythology and the Liberation of Women.* New York: Harper and Row, 1969.

Ruddick, Sara, and Pamela Daniels, eds. *Working It Out: 23 Women Writers, Artists, Scientists, and Scholars Talk about Their Lives and Work.* New York: Pantheon, 1977.

Sargent, Lydia, ed. *Women and Revolution: A Discussion of the Unhappy Marriage of Marxism and Feminism.* Boston: South End Press, 1981.

Schoenfielder, Lisa, and Barb Wieser, eds. *Shadow on a Tightrope: Writings by Women on Fat Oppression*. Iowa City: Aunt Lute, 1983.

Smith, Barbara, ed. *Home Girls: A Black Feminist Anthology*. New York: Kitchen Table Women of Color Press, 1983.

Smith, Dorothy E., and Sara J. David, eds. *Women Look at Psychiatry*. Vancouver: Press Gang Publishers, 1975.

Smith, Jeffrey D., ed. *Khatru* 3 & 4, Madison, WI: Phantasmicon Press, 1975.

Snitow, Ann, Christine Stansell, and Sharon Thompson, eds. *Powers of Desire: The Politics of Sexuality*. New York: Monthly Review Press, 1983.

Snodgrass, Jon., ed. *For Men against Sexism*. Albion, CA: Times Change Press, 1977.

Sochen, June. *The New Feminism in Twentieth-Century America*. Lexington, MA: D.C. Heath, 1971.

Spretnak, Charlene, ed. *The Politics of Women's Spirituality: Essays on the Rise of Spiritual Power within the Feminist Movement*. New York: Anchor Press, 1968.

Stanley, Penelope Julia, and Susan J. Wolfe, eds. *The Coming Out Stories*. Watertown, MA: Persephone Press, 1980.

Tanner, Leslie B., ed. *Voices from Women's Liberation*. New York: New American Library, 1971.

Thorne, Barrie, Cheris Kramarae, and Nancy Henley, eds. *Language, Gender, and Society*. Rowley, MA: Newbury House Publishers, 1983.

Tsang, Daniel, ed. *The Age of Taboo: Gay Male Sexuality, Power, and Consent*. Boston: Alyson Publications, 1981.

Vance, Carole, ed. *Pleasure and Danger: Exploring Female Sexuality*. Boston: Routledge and Kegan Paul, 1984.

Washington, Mary Helen, ed. *Black-Eyed Susans: Classic Stories by and about Black Women*. Garden City, NY:, 1975.

———. *Keeping the Faith: Writings by Contemporary Black American Women*. New York: Fawcett, 1974.

ARTICLES AND LETTERS

Alexander, Adele Logan. "Adella and Ruth: A Granddaughter's Story." *Sage* 1:2 (1984).

Allen, Paula Gunn. "Lesbians in American Indian Cultures." *Conditions* 7 (1981).

———. Review of *This Bridge Called My Back: Writings by Radical Women of Color*, eds. Cherríe Moraga and Gloria Anzaldúa. *Conditions* 8 (1972).

———. "Who Is Your Mother? Red Roots of White Feminism." *Sinister Wisdom* 43/44 (1991).

Anderson, Nancy et. al. "Responses to the NOW Resolution on Lesbian and Gay

Rights." *Feminist Studies* 8:1, 1982 ["Notes and Letters" section, signed by 21 others, and 140 not listed.]

Aptheker, Bettina. " 'Strong Is What We Make Each Other': Unlearning Racism within Women's Studies." *Women's Studies Quarterly* 9:4 (1981).

Arobateau, Red Jordan. "Nobody's People." *Sinister Wisdom* 21 (1982).

Bailey, Bruce. "An Inquiry into Love Comic Books: The Token Evolution of a Popular Genre." *Journal of Popular Culture* X:1 (1976).

Bart, Pauline. Reader's Forum letter. *Lesbian Ethics* 2:2 (1986).

Baxandall, Rosalyn, et al. "People Organize to Protest Recent NOW Resolution on Lesbian and Gay Rights." *Heresies* 3:4, issue 12 (1981).

———. "Responses to the NOW Resolution on Lesbian and Gay Rights." *Feminist Studies* 8:1 (1982).

Birtha, Becky. Review of *Freedomways* 19:4. *Conditions* 7 (1981).

Blair, Gwen Linda. "Standing on the Corner . . ." *Liberation* July/August 1974.

Brady, Maureen, and Judith McDaniel. "Lesbians in the Mainstream: Images of Lesbians in Recent Commercial Fiction." *Conditions* 6 (1980).

Bulkin, Ellie. "An Interview with Adrienne Rich, Parts 1 and 2." *Conditions* 1 and 2, 1977.

Califia, Pat. "Among Us, against Us—the New Puritans." *Advocate,* 17 April 1980.

———. "The Age of Consent: An Issue and Its Effects on the Gay Movement." *Advocate,* 30 October 1980.

———. "Feminism and Sadomasochism." *Heresies, 12* 3:4 (1981)

———. "Feminism vs. Sex: a New Conservative Wave?" *Advocate,* 21 February 1980.

———. "The Great Kiddy Porn Scare of '77 and Its Aftermath." *Advocate,* 16 October 1980.

———. Letter to the author, 15 May 1982. [Response to NOW Resolution on Lesbian and Gay Rights October/November 1980.]

———. "Queer Bashing." *Advocate,* 2 April 1981.

———. "A Secret Side of Lesbian Sexuality." *Advocate,* 12 December 1979.

———. "What Is Gay Liberation?" *Advocate,* 25 June 1981.

Chesler, Phyllis. "Voluntary Unwed Motherhood and Single Mother Adoption." Unpublished essay, 1986.

Cixous, Hélène. "The Laugh of the Medusa." Translated by Keith Cohen and Paula Cohen. In *The Signs Reader,* edited by Elizabeth Abel and Emily K. Abel. Chicago: University of Chicago Press, 1983.

Cook, Blanche Wiesen. "Female Support Networks and Political Activism: Lillian Wald, Crystal Eastman, Emma Goldman." *Chrysalis* 3 (1977).

Cosell, Hilary. "Did We Have the Wrong Dreams?" *Ladies' Home Journal,* April 1985.

Damon, Betsey. "From The Lesbian Issue Collective:" *Heresies* 1, 1977

Davis, Angela. "Reflections on the Black Woman's Role in the Community of Slaves."

In *Woman: An Issue,* edited by Lee R. Edwards, Mary Heath, and Lisa Baskin. New York: Little Brown, 1972.

Davis, Barbara Hillyer. "Disability and Mother Blaming." *Sojourner* August 1986.

Dill, Bonnie Thornton. "The Dialectics of Black Womanhood." *Signs* 4:3 (1979).

Donovan, Josephine. "The Unpublished Love Poems of Sarah Orne Jewett." *Frontiers* IV:3 (1979).

Dworkin, Andrea. "Safety, Shelter, Rules, Form, Love: The Promise of the Ultra-Right." *Ms.,* June 1979.

Ehrenreich, Barbara. "A Funny Thing Happened on the Way to Socialist Feminism." *Heresies* 9 (1980).

Enjeu, Claude, and Joana Savé. "The City: Off Limits to Women." Translated and abridged by Kathy Brown in *Liberation* 18 (July/August 1974).

Fabricant, Michael, and Michael Kelly. "No Haven for Homeless in a Heartless Economy." *Radical America* 20:2 and 3 (1986).

Faulkner, Constance. "The Feminist Challenge to Economics." *Frontiers* XIII:3 (1986).

Fisher, Berenice. "Guilt and Shame in the Women's Movement: The Radical Ideal of Action and Its Meaning for Feminist Intellectuals." *Feminist Studies* 10:2 (1984).

Fisher, Elizabeth. "If Only You'd Been a Boy." *Aphra* 4:1 (winter 1972–73).

Fox [Jeanette Silveira]. "Thoughts on the Politics of Touch." *Women's Press* 1 (1972).

———. "Why Men Oppress Women." *Lesbian Ethics* 1 (1984).

Fraser, Clara. Letter to the author. 24 April 1985.

Freeman, Jo. "The Tyranny of Structurelessness." *Ms.,* July 1973.

Garcia, Norma, et al. "The Impact of Race and Culture Differences: Challenges to Intimacy in Lesbian Relationships." In *Lesbian Psychologies: Explorations and Challenges,* edited by Mary Bragg et al. Urbana: University of Illinois Press, 1987.

Gardiner, Judith Kegan. "A Wake for Mother: The Maternal Deathbed in Women's Fiction." *Feminist Studies* 4:2 (1978).

Gomoll, Jeanne. "An Open Letter to Joanne Russ." *Aurora* 10 (winter 1986–87).

Gwartney-Gibbs, Patricia A., and Patricia A. Taylor. "Black Women Workers' Earnings Progress in Three Industrial Sectors." *Sage* III:1 (1986).

Haber, Barbara. "Is Personal Life Still a Political Issue?" *Feminist Studies* 5:3 (1979).

Hallett, Judith P. "Sappho and Her Social Context: Sense and Sensuality." *Signs* 4:3 (1979).

Haskell, Molly. "Rape Fantasy: The 2,000-Year-Old Misunderstanding." *Ms.,* V:5 (1976).

Heilbrun, Carolyn. "In Search of Authenticity." Review of *Helene Deutsch: A Psychoanalyst's Life,* by Paul Roazen, and *The Female Autograph,* edited by Donna C. Stanton. *Women's Review of Books* II:12 (1985).

Hesse-Biber, Sharlene. "The Black Woman Worker: A Minority Group Perspective on Women at Work." *Sage* III:1 (1986).

Hirsh, Elizabeth. "Writing the Self as (M)Other: Autobiographical Fictions by Joanna Russ and Rosellen Brown." Unpublished manuscript, 1984.

Hoagland, Sarah Lucia. "Lesbian Ethics: Some Thought on Power in Our Interactions." *Lesbian Ethics* 2:1 (1986).

Honig, Emily. "Burning Incense, Pledging Sisterhood: Communities of Women Workers in the Shanghai Cotton Mills, 1919–1949." *Signs* 10:4 (1985).

Hull, Gloria T. " 'Under the Days': The Buried Life and Poetry of Angelina Weld Grimké." *Conditions 5: The Black Women's Issue.* Ed. Lorraine Bethel and Barbara Smith. (1979).

Joseph, Gloria. "Black Mothers and Daughters: Traditional and New Populations." *Sage* 1:2 (1984).

Kaye/Kantrowitz, Melanie. "Culture Making: Lesbian Classics in the Year 2000?" *Sinister Wisdom* 13 (1980).

———. "Sexual Power." *Sinister Wisdom* 15 (1980).

Kerr, Barbara, and Mirtha Quintanales. "The Complexity of Desire: Conversations on Sexuality and Difference." *Conditions* 8 (1982).

Kessler-Harris, Alice. "Where Are the Organized Women Workers?" *Feminist Studies* III:1/2 (1985).

Klagsbrun, Francine. "Secrets of Long-Lasting Marriages." *Ms.* XIII: 12 June 1985.

Kleinberg, Seymour. "Where Have All the Sissies Gone?" *Christopher Street* 2:9 (1978).

Koedt, Anne. "The Myth of the Vaginal Orgasm." In *Up Against the Wall, Mother . . . ,* edited by Elsie Adams and Mary Louise Briscoe. Beverly Hills: Glencoe Press, 1971.

Koolish, Linda. "Coalition Building: Disability Caucus Plenary Speech" [NWSA Conference, 1986] *National Women's Studies Association Perspectives* 5:1 (winter 1986).

Ladner, Joyce A., and Ruby Morton Gourdine. "Intergenerational Teenage Motherhood: Some Preliminary Findings." *Sage* 1:2 (1984).

Lauter, Paul. "Race and Gender in the Shaping of the American Literary Canon: A Case Study from the Twenties." *Feminist Studies* 9:3 (1983).

Laws, Judith Long. "The Psychology of Tokenism: An Analysis." *Sex Roles* I:1 (1975).

Lee, Anna. "The Tired Old Question of Male Children." *Lesbian Ethics* 1:2 (1985).

di Leonardo, Micaela. "Warrior Virgins and Boston Marriages: Spinsterhood in History and Culture." *Feminist Issues* 5:2 (1985).

Macdonald, Barbara. "On Ageism in the Women's Movement." *Sojourner,* August 1985.

MacKinnon, Catharine A. "Feminism, Marxism, Method, and the State: An Agenda for Theory." *Signs* 7:3 (1982).

———. "Feminism, Marxism, Method, and the State: Toward Feminist Jurisprudence." *Signs* 8:4 (summer 1983).

Marcus, Jane. "Art and Anger." *Feminist Studies* 4 (1978).

Masson, Jeffrey. Letter to the author. 18 July 1984.

McAfee, Kathy, and Wood, Myrna. "Bread and Roses." *Leviathan* 1:3 (1969).

McAllister, Pam. "Wolf Whistles and Warnings." *Liberation* 18:8 (July/August 1974).

McCombs, Annie. "A Letter *Ms.* Didn't Print." *Lesbian Ethics* 1:3 (1985).

McConnell-Ginet, Sally. "Intonation in a Man's World." *Signs* 3:3 (1978).

McDaniel, Judith. "Taking Risks: The Creation of Feminist Literature." *American Voice* 17 (1989).

Meade, Marion. "The Examined Life: A Good Season for Biographies." *Ms.*, December 1984.

Michalowski, Helen. "The Army Will Make a 'Man' Out of You." In *Reweaving the Web of Life: Feminism and Nonviolence,* edited by Pam McAllister. New Society Publishers, 1982.

Miller, Jean Baker. "Psychoanalysis, Patriarchy, and Power: One Viewpoint on Women's Goals and Needs." *Chrysalis* 2 (1977).

Moraga, Cherríe. Review of *Top Rankings: A Collection of Articles on Racism and Classism in the Lesbian Community,* edited by Joan Gibbs and Sara Bennett. *Conditions* 7 (1981).

NOW [National Organization for Women] Resolution on Lesbian and Gay Rights. *Feminist Studies* 8:1 (1982).

Nardi, Bonnie A. "The Height of Her Powers: Margaret Mead's Samoa." *Feminist Studies* 10:2 (1984).

National Women's Studies Association Annual Conference, June 1987. Reported in *off our backs* XVII:8, 1987, 2.

National Women's Studies Association Perspectives 5:1 (1986).

Newman, Debra Lynn. "Black Women Workers in the Twentieth Century." *Sage* III:1 (1986).

Olafson, Erna. Review of *A History of Women's Bodies* by Edwin Shorter. *Signs* 11:1 (1985).

———. Review of *American Beauty* by Lois Banner. *Signs* 11:1 (1985).

Orenstein, Gloria Feman. "The Salon of Natalie Clifford Barney: An Interview with Berthe Cleyrergue." *Signs* 4:3 (1979).

Parlee, Mary Brown. "Review Essay: Psychology." *Signs* 1:1 (1975).

Penelope, Julia. "The Mystery of Lesbians." *Lesbian Ethics* 1:1 (1984).

———. "The Mystery of Lesbians: II." *Lesbian Ethics* 1:2 (1985).

Perloff, Marjorie. " 'Theory' and the Creative Writing Classroom." AWP [Associated Writing Programs] *Newsletter,* November/December 1987.

Petchesky, Rosalind, and Carol Joffe. "Abortion as 'Violence against Women': a Feminist Critique: Comments on MacKinnon" *Radical America* 8:2–3, 1984.

Quintanales, Mirtha N. and Barbara T. Kerr. "The Complexities of Desire." *Conditions* 8 (1972).

Rabine, Leslie W. "Romance in the Age of Electronics: Harlequin Enterprises." *Feminist Studies* II:1 (1985).

Rich, Cynthia. "Reflections on Eroticism." *Sinister Wisdom* 15 (1980).

Ringelheim, Joan. "Women and the Holocaust: A Reconsideration of Research." *Signs* 10:4 (1985).

Robinson, Lillian. "Poverty, Purpose, Pride." *Women's Review of Books* III:3, December 1985.

Rockwood, Marcia, and Mary Thom. "Teenagers in Survey Condone Forced Sex." *Ms.* [Gazette], February 1981.

Rule, Jane. "Homophobia and Romantic Love." *Conditions* 3 (1978).

Rupp, Leila J. "Imagine My Surprise: Women's Relationships in Historical Perspective." *Frontiers* V:3 (1981).

Rush, Florence. "The Freudian Cover-Up." *Chrysalis* 2 (1976).

Russ, Joanna. *"Amor Vincit Foeminam:* The Battle of the Sexes in Science Fiction." *S.-F. Studies* 20 = 7:1 (1980).

———. "Somebody's Trying to Kill Me and I Think It's My Husband: The Modern Gothic." *Journal of Popular Culture* VI:4 (1973).

Sahli, Nancy. "Smashing: Women's Relationships Before the Fall." *Chrysalis* 8 (1979).

Sayers, Dorothy. "The Human-Not-Quite-Human." In *Masculine/Feminine: Readings in Sexual Mythology and the Liberation of Women,* edited by Betty Roszak and Theodore Roszak. New York: Harper and Row, 1969.

Seidman, Gay W. "Women in Zimbabwe: Postindependence Struggles." *Feminist Studies* 10:3 (1984).

Sheldon, Alice. Letter to the author. 20 April 1985.

Shockley, Anne Allen. "A Meeting of the Sapphic Daughters." *Sinister Wisdom* 9 (1979).

———. "Red Jordan Arobateau: A Different Kind of Black Lesbian Writer." *Sinister Wisdom* 21 (1982).

Smith, Barbara. "The Convert." *Sinister Wisdom* 19 (1982).

Smith, Barbara, and Beverly Smith. " 'I Am Not Meant to Be Alone and without You Who Understand': Letters from Black Feminists, 1972–1978." *Conditions* 4 (1979).

Smith-Rosenberg, Carroll. "The Female World of Love and Ritual: Relations between Women in Nineteenth-Century America." *Signs* I:1 (1975).

Stacey, Judith. "The New Conservative Feminism." *Feminist Studies* 9:3 (fall 1983).

Stigers, Eva Stehle. "Romantic Sensuality, Poetic Sense: A Response to Hallett on Sappho." *Signs* 4:3 (1979).

Strega, Linda. "The Big Sell-Out: Lesbian Femininity." *Lesbian Ethics* 1:3 (1985).

Sturgis, Susanna J. "Breaking Silence, Breaking Faith: The Promotion of Lesbian Nuns." *Lesbian Ethics* 1:3 (1985).

Sweet, Ellen. "Date Rape: The Story of an Epidemic and Those Who Deny It." *Ms.,* October 1985.

Sylvester, Sherry. "Class Acts: Shooting Script of a Poor White Experience." *Sinister Wisdom* 24 (1983).

Taylor, Barbara. "The Men Are as Bad as Their Masters . . . : Socialism, Feminism, and Sexual Antagonism in the London Tailoring Trade in the Early 1830s." *Feminist Studies* 5:1 (1979).

Trimberger, Ellen Kay. "Women in the Old and New Left: The Evolution of a Politics of Personal Life." *Feminist Studies* 5:3 (1979).

Vance, Carole S. "Gender Systems, Ideology, and Sex Research: An Anthropological Analysis." *Feminist Studies* 6:1 (spring 1980).

Vicinus, Martha. "Sexuality and Power: A Review of Current Work in the History of Sexuality." *Feminist Studies* 8:1 (1982).

Vidal, Gore. "*Some* Jews and the Gays." *Nation,* 14 November 1981.

Wade-Gayles, Gloria. "The Truths of Our Mothers' Lives: Mother-Daughter Relationships in Black Women's Fiction." *Sage* 1:2 (1984).

Walkowitz, Judith R. "Jack the Ripper and the Myth of Male Violence." *Feminist Studies* 8:3 (1982).

Washington, Mary Helen. "How Racial Differences Helped Us Discover Our Sameness." *Ms.* X:3 (1981).

Weems, Renita. "Breaking the Silence between Mothers and Daughters." *Sage* 1:2 (1984).

Wenzel, Hélène Vivienne. "The Text as Body/Politics: An Appreciation of Monique Wittig's Writings in Context." *Feminist Studies* 7:2 (1981).

Willis, Ellen. "Betty Friedan's 'Second Stage': A Step Backward." *Nation,* 14 November 1981.

Wilson, Elizabeth. "Forbidden Love." *Feminist Studies* 10:2 (1984).

Winkler, Karen J. "Scholars Prescribe Freud's 'Talk Cure.' " *Chronicle of Higher Education,* 22 October 1986.

Yancy, Dorothy Cowser. "Dorothy Bolden, Organizer of Domestic Workers: She Was Born Poor but She Would Not Bow Down." *Sage* III:1 (1986).

Yans-McLaughlin, Virginia. "Comment on the Freeman/Mead Controversy." *Signs* 10:3 (1985).

Index

Abbott, Elizabeth, 9
Abbott, Sidney, 136
Abdulahad, Tania
 on conflicting identities, 319
 on White feminism and racism, 296
abortion
 socialism and, 236–37
 See also birth control; childbirth;
  contraceptives
About Men (Chesler), 403
Adam's Rib (Herschberger), 22
Adams, Elsie, 19
Addams, Jane
 and Mary Rozet Smith, 108–9
Afro-Americans. See Black Americans
Against Our Will (Brownmiller), 147–48
ageism, 32
 among young feminists, 4
Alarcón, Norma
 on feminist Chicanas, 89
Alexandrova, Ekaterina, 420
Ali, Susan
 on a Latina childhood, 254
Allen, Paula Gunn
 on Native Americans and lesbianism,
  105
Allen, Sandra
 on population control, 238
American Indians. See Native Americans
Anthony, Susan B., 308–10

Anzaldúa, Gloria
 on Black mother-daughter relationships,
  28
 on conflicting identities, 318, 323
 on life and writing, 357
 on racism and guilt, 337
 on White feminism and racism, 295
Appeal to One Half of the Human Race
  (William), 171
Arcana, Judith
 on the assimilation of Black men, 369
 on father-son relationships, 389, 391
 on males and trouble, 246
 on masculinity training, 385, 386
 on objectification of men by mothers,
  31
 on "sweet, small boys," 381
Armstrong, Pat
 on White feminism and racism, 295
Arobateau, Red Jordan
 on conflicting identities, 320, 324–25
Aron, Arthur
 on what couples seek in marriage, 54
Asian Pacific American women
 differences between cultural codes, 350
 mother-daughter relationships, 29–30
 and racism, 295, 299
Atkinson, Ti-Grace, 146
Avery, Byllye
 on conflicting identities, 323

Bachelli, Ann
on housewives, 169
Bacon, Francis, 72
Bambara, Toni Cade, 357
Bamberger, Joan, 19
Battered Wives (Martin), 423
Baym, Nina
on feminist literary theory, 340
Beauvoir, Simone de, 19, 24
Bebel, August, 188
Beck, Evelyn Torton
on Judaism and lesbianism, 105
Bengelsdorf, Carollee
on women's oppression and capitalism, 214–15
on women's oppression and socialism, 215
Benston, Margaret
on women's oppression and capitalism, 214
Berkeley-Oakland Woman's Union, 355
Bernard, Jessie, 21, 91, 108, 110
on housewives and monetary resources, 163–164
on marriage as a choice, 137, 142
on marriage as work, 223, 226, 257
on women in the workforce, 166
Berry, Mary, 304
Bethel, Lorraine
on White feminism and racism, 295, 303
Beyond God the Father (Daly), 106
Beyond Power (French), 106
Billington-Greig, Teresa, 433
birth control
opposition to, 188
population control, 237, 425
See also abortion; childbirth
Black Americans
and Black churches, 224
Black lesbians and homophobia, 117
children, socialization of, 30
male children and passivity, 89
male life expectancy, 369–70
obliteration of lives and histories, 8
separatist consciousness and, 87
and SNCC, 224–25
and the Social Security Act, 372–73
Black-Eyed Susans (Washington, ed.), 106
Black Macho and the Myth of the Superwoman (Wallace), 106, 368, 375

Black women
Black lesbians and homophobia, 117
and Black male violence, 368–70
and double workday/second shift, 172
homophobia of, 319
on keeping community together, 224
and lesbian separatism, 366–67
male-female relationships, 137
mother-daughter relationships, 27–29
poverty of, 155
socialization of, 28–29
on women turning to other women for emotional support, 142
Blair, Gwen Linda
sexual harassment, 251
Bleier, Ruth, 146
Blumenthal, Monica
on women as caregivers, 169
Body Politics (Henley), 69
Bogan, Louise, 64–65
Boyner, Sandra
on professionalization of academic disciplines, 71
Brady, Maureen
on lesbian existence in novels, 105–6
Brahme, Sulabha
on the status of women in India, 374
Briscoe, Mary Louise, 19
British Woman's Life, 9
Brod, Harry E., 384
on institutional power, 405
Brooks, Nancy A.
on people with disabilities, 415
Brown University speakout, sexual assault and violence at, 144–45
Brownmiller, Susan
on male violence and rape, 93, 147–48, 248–49
Bulkin, Elly
on coalitions, 370–71, 371
on conflicting identities, 324, 329
on the experience of oppression, 349
and the New Left, 186
on racism, 294, 305–6, 339–40
on trade-offs, 341
Burning Questions (Shulman), 61
Burstyn, Varda
on education vs. entertainment, 354–55
on the family wage, 269–70
on violence toward women, 247

Califia, Pat, 433
Cameron, Barbara
  on capitalism and women, 375
  on the experience of oppression, 348
  on White feminism and racism, 302
Canaan, Andrea
  on conflicting identities, 324
  on trade offs, 343
  on White feminism and racism, 297
Capital (Marx), 21, 255–56
capitalism, 265–66
  and child labor 266–67
  and disability, 169–70, 410–411
  and the economics of women, 194–203,
    211–12, 265–66, 269–80
  the family wage, 267–72
  and feudalism, 194
  and homelessness, 279
  and patriarchy, 221
  and prostitution, 220
  See also communism; economics (and
    women); socialist feminists
Caputi, Jane
  on serial murders, 247, 398–99
Carillo, Jo
  on White feminism and racism, 295
Carroll, Bernice, 354
  on White feminism and racism, 295, 297,
    299, 300
Carroll, Constance
  on trade-offs, 341–42
Cather, Willa, 109, 112
Catt, Carrie Chapman
  on White feminism and racism, 309
Cavin, Susan
  on female-female mounting among
    animals, 105
  on housewives/mothers as labor, 258
  on polyandrous marriage, 106
  on reproductive rights, 239
  on women and socialism, 217, 255–56
Chandler, Lucinda B.
  on marriage as prostitution, 131
Chapkis, Wendy
  on fear of effeminacy, 392
  on women on display, 432–33
Chesler, Phyllis, 19, 57
  on brothers, 388
  on child support, 162–63
  on father-daughter incest, 26

  on father-son relationships, 390–91,
    403–4
  on father's contact with children, 174–
    75
  "Help Wanted" advertisement, 171
  on male bonding, 393–94
  on male guilt, 396, 398
  on male sexual drive, 396–97
  on male violence, 169
  on marital rape, 245–46
  on masculinity and the workplace, 382–
    83
  on the propertied class, 382
  on risking winning, 92
  on women in the workplace, 220
Chicano Americans and feminism, 89
Chicano women. *See* Latina women
child abuse, 249, 250, 259–60
  See also male violence; rape
childbirth
  as domestic labor, 254–55, 258
  as economics, 236–60
  feminist groups obsession with, 7
  population control, 237–43
  and women's situation in the family,
    19
  working conditions of, 242–43
  See also abortion; birth control; child
    abuse; contraceptives
child labor, 266–67
Chisholm, Shirley, 300
Chodorow, Nancy, 18, 31
  on psychoanalysis, 51
  The Reproduction of Mothering, 18, 21–24,
    106
  on women's ego boundaries, 64
Christian, Barbara, 372
Chrysalis (feminist periodical), 55
Chrystos
  on class differences, 279
  on conflicting identities, 320–21, 325
  on White feminism and racism, 302
  on a world without words, 357–58
Cixous, Hélène, 64
Clarke, Cheryl
  on the manhood of Black men, 383
  on homophobia and coalitions, 329
Close to Home (Delphy), 221–23
Cliff, Michelle
  on conflicting identities, 321–22

coalition building, 336–59
 answering bigotry with information, 339–40
 areas of struggle, expecting, 340–41
 being academic, 340
 Christianity, 347
 cultural codes, differences between, 350–55
 expecting to fail, 343–46
 experience of oppression, 347–50
 how much White feminists don't know, 345–46
 organizations or projects with only White members, 339
 trade-offs, avoiding, 341–43
"Coalition Politics: Turning the Century" (Reagon), 329–31
Cobb, Jonathan
 on male sacrifice for the family, 383–84
Collier, Mary, 167–68
Combahee River Collective, 354
 on conflicting identities, 327
 on C-R (conciseness raising) groups, 431
 on lesbian separatism, 366
 position statement, 297
Comer, Lee, 169
Coming of Age in Samoa (Mead), 111
Common Differences (Joseph/Lewis), 27, 28–29, 224
communism, 184–203
 and abortion, 236–37
 feminism vs. Marxists, 185–93
 and the Left's hatred of women, 192–93
 and racism, 292
 women, oppression of, 215–22
 women and socialism, 211–28
 See also capitalism; socialist feminists
Complaints and Disorders: The Sexual Politics of Sickness (Ehrenreich/English), 21
compromise and feminist groups, 7
"Congruences among Interpretations of Psychological Test and Anamnestic Data" (Little/Schneidman), 53
Connell, Bob
 on masculinity and abuse, 404–5
Connors, Debra, 175
 on capitalism and unemployment, 412
 on disabled workers, 412–13, 413–14
conservative feminism, 5
 Reactionary Feminism, xiv

contraceptives
 opposition to, 188
 See also abortion; childbirth
Cook, Blanche Wiesen, 108
 on compulsory heterosexuality, 133–34
Corrigan, Tom
 on masculinity and abuse, 404–5
Cosell, Hilary
 on "double career" as solution, 4, 10
Costa, Mariarosa Dalla
 on housework, 169, 212, 258
Coward, Rosalind
 on keeping community together, 224
 on men as consumers of women, 139
 on women's sexuality, 141
Cross, Tia
 on racism, 293
Cuentos: Stories by Latinas (Gómez/Moraga/Romo-Carmona, eds.), 324

Daly, Mary, 1, 106
 on "femininity" as a male concept, 141
 on separatism, 88
Damon, Betsy
 on internalized homophobia, 114–15
Dandridge, Rita B., 304
Davis, Allen
 on the Jane Addams/Ellen Gates Starr relationship, 108–9
Davis, Elizabeth Gould, 19, 106
Davis, Katherine Bement
 on the percentage of bisexual women, 105
De Mattei, Victor, 400
Deegan, Mary Jo
 on people with disabilities, 415
Delmar, Rosalind
 on capitalism, 266
 on production vs. reproduction, 219
Delphy, Christine, 422, 424
 on capitalism and the patriarchy, 221, 254, 282–83
 on child support, 163
 on domestic work, 177, 258
 on exploitation and oppression, 184–85
 on the Left's hatred of women, 192–93
 on marriage and patriarchal rule, 146
 on marriage as unpaid work, 223
 on menstrual periods as a sign of inferiority, 69

on psychoanalysis, 62–63, 64
on reproductive rights, 240–41
on sexism, 405
on subjectivity vs. objectivity, 355
on women as a class, 221–23
on women and Marxism, 213, 219
on women in the workforce, 222–23
on women's sexuality, 140
Densmore, Dana
on women's self-interest, 95–96
Deutsch, Helene, 64
Di Vilde Chayes (Jewish lesbian group)
on coalitions, 329
Dialectic of Sex, The (Firestone), 19
Dickinson, Emily, 110
Dinnerstein, Dorothy, 18, 31
on "feminine carnal muting," 26
The Mermaid and the Minotaur, 18, 19–21, 106
disability and capitalism, 169–70, 411–18
Dixon, Marlene
and the New Left, 186–87
on separatism, 89
Dobkin, Mary Housepian
on the lesbianism of M. Carey Thomas, 107
domestic work. *See under* economics (and women)
Donovan, Josephine
on the Sarah Orne Jewett/Annie Fields relationship, 111–12
Donovan, Mary Ellen, 9
on marriage and loneliness, 138, 142
on questioning sexuality, 130
on women's work, 169
double workday. *See under* economics (and women)
Douglass, Frederick, 309
Down These Mean Streets (Thomas), 320
Dreifus, Claudia, 106
Dreiser, Theodore, 60
Du Bois, Barbara
on holding on to radical ideas, 71
Dworkin, Andrea, 185, 433
on acting from self-interest, 89
on the hostility of male dominance, 140
on marriage as prostitution, 131
and sex-classes, 67, 93, 133
on sexual inhibition, 129

Eckstein, Emma, 55
economic (yuppie) success
feminism and, 5–6
and feminist groups, 7
economics (and women), 154–78
Black women vs. White women, 345–46
child support, 162–63
of childbirth, 256–60
communism and, 184–203
disability and, 169–70, 411–18
domestic work, 167–78
the family wage, 267–72
housework, 164–66, 172–75
housework (financial value of), 175
housework/workforce (double workday/second shift), 166–72
monetary resources, control over, 163–64
part-time work, 164–65
poverty in the U.S., 154–56
poverty worldwide, 157
Social Security Act, 372–73
socialism and, 211–28
unemployment and, 161
unions and, 187–92
unpaid labor, 171–78, 184
wage inequities, 158, 160, 184, 220
Wages for Housework Campaign, 177
women in workforce in the U.S., 158–59
women in workforce worldwide, 159
Ehrenreich, Barbara, 21
on capitalism, 355–56
on the family wage, 269
on housework, 173
on the industrial revolution, 265, 266
Ehrlich, Clara
on feminism and economic success, 5–6
Eisenhart, Wayne, 400–401, 402
Eisenstein, Hester, 185
on big business and women, 373
on co-opting feminism, 8
on "liberal" reforms, 67
Eliot, T. S., 60
Ellis, Havelock, 128
Elshtain, Jean Bethke, 5
employment. *See* economics (and women)
Engels, Frederick, 19, 21, 267
English, Deirdre, 21
on capitalism, 355–56
on housework, 173
on the industrial revolution, 265, 266

Epstein, Barbara
  on the sex reform movement, 133
Espin, Oliva M.
  on conflicting identities, 318, 319, 322–23
Essence magazine, 137

Faber, Doris
  on the lesbianism of Lorena Hickok, 106
Fabricant, Michael
  on homelessness, 279
Faderman, Lillian, 58
  on the labor movement and women, 189
family
  central to the oppression of women, 22
  critique of, turning away from, 4
  and violence, 2, 245–46, 423
"Family as the Locus of Gender, Class, and Political Struggle, The" (Hartmann), 24
father-daughter incest, 26, 135, 246, 248
Faulkner, William, 60
Federici, Sylvia
  on female sexuality, 146
Feigen Fasteau, Marc
  on masculinity, 384–85, 387, 388, 392, 393, 394–95, 397–98
Fell, Allison
  on male power and ownership, 381
Female Eunuch, The (Greer), 19, 106
"Female Sexuality" (Freud), 58
Female World, The (Bernard), 106
"Female World of Love and Ritual, The" (Smith-Rosenberg), 106–7
Feminine Mystique, The (Friedan), 19, 24, 61, 106
"Femininity" (Freud), 58
femininity as a male concept, 141
feminism
  belittlement, caricature & dismissal of, 3, 9–11
  communism and, 184–203
  as counterculture vs. political analysis of society, 2
  and C-R (conciseness raising) groups, 431–33
  doing vs. being, 3
  economic success and, 5–6
  as middle class, 187
  and psychoanalysis, 51–58, 65–66
  and racism, 292–311

radical texts, disappearance of, 2
  See also conservative feminism;
    Reactionary Feminism; separatism
Feminism and Materialism: Women and Modes of Productivity (Kuhn/Wolpe, eds.), 24
Feminismo Primero, 92
feminist groups, negative tendencies in, 7
feminist revolution, 2
Feminist Studies, 24
feminist therapists, 3
Ferguson, Ann
  on women and socialism, 212, 214
Ferguson, Syn, 69
Fields, Annie, 111–12
Figes, Eva, 19, 106
Finger, Anne
  on women with disabilities, 415–16
  on the word "defective," 413
Firestone, Shulamith, 19
  on psychotherapy, 51–58
  on smiling/smile boycott, 34, 225–26
  on unpaid labor, 176
First Sex, The (Davis), 19, 106
Fisher, Elizabeth
  on interpersonal relations, 280
Fliess, William, 55
Folbre, Nancy
  on women and socialism, 212, 214
For Colored Girls (Shange), 368
Ford, Henry, 64
Forster, E. M., 108
Fox (Jeanette Silveira)
  on capitalism and the patriarchy, 221, 256
  on childbearing as an economic activity, 240, 242
  on housewives/mothers as labor, 258
  on reproductive rights, 238, 239–40
  on women and Marxism, 220
  on women's problems, 66
  on working-class men and the patriarchy, 253–54
Franklin, Clyde W., II
  on Black male life expectancy, 369–70
  on Black male sexism and assimilation, 370
Fraser, Clara, *xiv*, 145
  on co-opting feminism as a lifestyle, 6
Freeman, Jo, 21
  on full-time motherhood, 243
  on women as serfs, 257

Freeman, Mary E. Wilkins, 110, 112
Freewomen (publication), 143
French, Marilyn, 106
  on male competitiveness, 395–96
  on the philosophy of patriarchy, 417
  on violence in films and TV, 399
Freud, Sigmund, 18, 20–22
  address on "Femininity," 21
  feminism and, 51–58
  and masturbation, 55
Friedan, Betty, 5, 19, 24, 61, 106
  on lesbians in the women's movement,
    110
  review of *Second Stage*, 4–5
frigidity, 129–30
"From Sea to Shining Sea" (Jordan), 328–29
Frye, Marilyn
  on compulsory motherhood, 371
  on conflicting identities, 325
  on separatism, 90–92, 94
  on sex-distinction, 283–84
Furies, The (lesbian feminist paper), 146
Future of Marriage (Bernard), 21, 91

Gage, Matilda Joslyn, 1, 8, 66, 91
  on marriage, 146
  on women as unpaid labor, 154
Garcia, Norma
  on conflicting identities, 323
  on the experience of oppression, 348
  on White feminism and racism, 302
Gardiner, Jean, 188
  capitalism and family, 268, 269
  on conflicting identities, 318
Garrett, Kate, 145
Gay Academic Union conference, 35
Gay Community News, 144, 145
George, Diana Hume
  on the negative influence of TV, 399
Ghostway, The (Hillerman), 418
Giddings, Paula, 106, 172
  on the assimilation of Black men, 368–69
  on avoiding trade-offs, 341
  on Black churches, 224
  on Black female analysis, 368
  on Black women vs. White women in the
    labor force, 345–46
  on the convict lease system, 372
  on racism and the feminist movement,
    307–10, 310–11

  on singing and SNCC actions, 224–25
Gilder, George, 91
Gilligan, Carol, 18, 106
  on women's morality stresses, 92
Gilman, Charlotte Perkins, 20, 22
  on childbearing as an economic activity,
    242
Goldberg, Herb
  on male sexual drive, 397
  on masculinity, 395
Goldman, Emma
  on marriage as prostitution, 135
Gómez, Alma, 324
  on trade-offs, 341
Gomoll, Jeanne
  on the phrase "me-decade," 429–30
  on science fiction, 429
Goodman, Emily Jane
  "Help Wanted" advertisement, 171
  on the propertied class, 382
  on women in the workplace, 220
Gordon, Linda, 188
  on corporations and employment, 278
  on the family, 270
  on female sexual stimulation, 129
  on freer sexual standards, 130
  on marriage as prostitution, 131
  on population control, 237, 425
  on the sex reform movement, 133
  on two-wage households, 271
Gornick, Vivian, 19
Gould, Stephen Jay
  on scientific theories, 56, 73
Grapes of Wrath, The (Steinbeck), 349–50
Greer, Germaine, 19, 106
Griffin, Susan, 24
  on rape, child abuse and incest, 250
  on women's social concerns, 192
Guettel, Charnie
  on two-wage households, 271
Guntrip, Harry, 22
Gwartney-Gibbs, Patricia A.
  Black women vs. White women in the
    labor force, 346
Gym/Ecology (Daly), 1

Haber, Barbara
  on the critique of family, 4
Hacker, Marilyn, 435
Haener, Dorothy, 190

Hageman, Margaret
  on women's oppression and capitalism, 214
  on women's oppression and socialism, 215–16
Hallett, Judith P.
  on whether Sappho was a lesbian, 107
Hamilton, Cecily
  on marriage as a monopoly, 143
Hamod, Kay Keshod
  on psychoanalysis, 62
Hannaford, Susan
  on access, 94, 414
  on charities, 414
Hansberry, Lorraine, 112–13
Harper, Francis Ellen Watkins, 308
Harper's magazine, 55
Harris, Marvin, 70, 193
  on the division of class and labor, 281
Hartley, Ruth E.
  on masculinity training, 385
Hartmann, Heidi, 24
  on the family wage, 267, 268
  on the labor movement and women, 189
  and the New Left, 186
Haskell, Molly, 24
Hassna, Steve, 402–3
Heilbrun, Carolyn, 64
  on anti-feminist men, 93
Hemingway, Ernest, 60
Henley, Nancy
  on access, 94
  on housework, 173
  on psychoanalysis, 51, 63
  on slave psychology, 36
  on smiling as an act of appeasement, 226
  on women's dominance gestures, 69
  on women's sexuality, 141
Herman, Judith, 56
  on child abuse, 259–60
  on father-daughter incest, 135, 246
Herschberger, Ruth, 22
Hess, Katharine
  on separatism, 89
  separatism, definition of, 86
  on separatism as community base, 86–87
Hesse-Biber, Sharlene
  Black women vs. White women in the labor force, 345, 346
heterosexuality

compulsory, 26
  frigidity and prudery, 129–30
  "naturalness" of, 23
  and patriarchal rule, 146
  as a political institution, 146
  prostitution and pornography, 130–31
  sex and marriage, 128–30
  sex reform movement, 130–33
  the Woman Job, 126–46, 146–48
Hickok, Lorena, 106
Hidden Face of Eve, The (Saadawi), 421
Hillbilly Women (Kahn), 187
Hillerman, Tony, 418
Hillyer, Barbara
  on the movement being co-opted, 434
Hirschorn, Lisa
  on father-daughter incest, 135
Hirsh, Elizabeth, 63–64
Hispanic women. See Latina women
Hite, Shere
  on bisexual women, percentage of, 105
  on sexual inhibition, 129
Hite Report, The (Hite), 105, 141
Hoagland, Sarah Lucia
  on separatist consciousness, 87
Hochschild, Arlie, 226
Hollibaugh, Amber
  on women's sexuality, 141
homophobia, 114–17
  Black lesbians and, 117
  Black women's homophobia, 319
  and coalitions, 329
  internalized, 114–15
hooks, bell
  on the Black family, 270
  on Black male-female relationships, 137
  on conflicting identities, 323–24
  on C-R (conciseness raising) groups, 431
  on the differences between cultural codes, 350–51
  on lesbian separatism, 366
  on masculinity and working-class men, 396
  on trade-offs, 341
  on White feminism and racism, 296–97, 299, 301, 302, 307
  on White feminists, 28
housework. See under economics
Howe, Julia Ward, 308
Howe, Louise

on double workday/second shift, 172
on women in the workforce, 166, 190–91
on women's occupations, 158–59
Howe, Mark Anthony DeWolfe
on the Sarah Orne Jewett/Annie Fields relationship, 111–12
Hull, Gloria, 357
on White feminism and racism, 301
on women's studies, 340

Ideal Marriage (Van de Velde), 128
In a Different Voice (Gilligan), 106
In Search of Answers (Kishwar/Vanita), 422
In These Times (socialists newspaper), 186
incest, 26, 135, 246, 248, 250
Indians. *See* Native Americans
International Tribunal of Crimes Against Women, 244–45
"Is Woman's Liberation a Lesbian Plot" (Abbott/Love), 136

Jack the Ripper, mythicization of, 247
James, Alice, 112
James, Henry, 60
James, Selma
on housework, 169, 212
Janeway, Elizabeth, 19
on Freud's theories, 54
on self-esteem, 432
Jansen-Jurreit, Marielouise
on childbirth as work, 241–42
on patriarchy and the state, 285
on socialism, 173, 213
on socialism and abortion, 236–37
Jay, Karla, 35
Jeffreys, Sheila
on historical lesbian relationships, 107
on marriage as prostitution, 131
on sexual inhibition, 129
Jewett, Sarah Orne, 111–12
Jewish-American women
anti-Semitism, 305, 307, 339, 344
conflicting identities, 328, 333–34
Di Vilde Chayes, 329
differences between cultural codes, 350
and racial minorities, 305–6
Joffe, Carol
on women's sexuality, 141, 142

Johnson, Eleanor
on women's work, 170
Johnson, Paula
on rape, 250
Johnston, Jill, 116
Jones, Ann, 128
on battery and abuse, 246
Jordan, June, 320–29
Joseph, Gloria
on Black children, socialization of, 30
on Black women and men, 367–68
on capitalism and patriarchy, 368, 371
on Chodorow's *The Reproduction of Mothering*, 27–28
on coalitions, 329
on the death of the family, 270–71
on femininity, 346
on mother-daughter relationships, 27–29, 30
on oppressed groups and change, 376
on the Wages for Housework Campaign, 177
on White feminism and racism, 295, 344
on women and socialism, 212, 371
Joslyn, Matilda, 4
Judaism and lesbianism, 105
Julty, Sam
on father-son relationships, 389
Jung, Carl Gustav, 18

Kahn, Kathy, 187
on the health of factory workers, 278–79
Kanin, Garson, 200
Katz, Jonathan, 58, 128
on capitalism, 355
on gender-distinction, 284
on marriage as prostitution, 131
on questioning sexuality, 130
Kaye/Kantrowitz, Melanie, 339
on coalitions, 329
Keller, Evelyn Fox, 72
on subjectivity vs. objectivity, 355
Kelly, Michael
on homelessness, 279
Kennedy, Cheryl
on liberal guilt, 343–44
Kimmel, Michael S.
on the loss of occupational autonomy, 382
Kinsey Report, 421

I N D E X

Kiran, Patna, 423
Kishwar, Madhu
  on the status of women in India, 375,
    422
Klein, Freada
  on racism, 293
Kolodny, Annette
  on C-R (conciseness raising) groups, 431
Koolish, Linda
  on women with disabilities, 415
Koppelman, Susan, 63
  in response to a review, 434–35
  on trade-offs, 342–43
Koss, Mary P.
  on rape, 249–50
Krafft-Ebing, 128
Kuhn, Annette, 24

Ladder, The (lesbian publication), 112–13
Ladner, Joyce
  on Black women, socialization of, 28–29
Lafargue, Laura, 188
Laing, R. D., 56
Lamb, Pat, 142
Landers, Ann, 134–35, 242–43
Langer, Elinor
  on big business and women, 373
Langford, Jean
  on separatism, 89
  separatism, definition of, 86
  separatism as community base, 86–87
Latina women, 302
  conflicting identities, 319, 320, 321, 324,
    326
  and the feminist movement, 292–311
  illusion of being non-racist, 293–95
  Jewish women and, 306
  lesbians, community rejection of, 318–19
  male violence and, 144
  separatist consciousness and, 87
  token inclusion, 295, 297–301
  women's studies and, 304–6
Lauter, Paul, 399
Lawrence, D. H., 113
LeClair, Thomas, 372
Lee, Anna
  on excluding male children from
    women's events, 89
Lee, John
  on masculinity and abuse, 404–5

Leghorn, Lisa, 424
  on accumulated wealth, 375
  on population control, 238
  on social support of pregnancy, 243
  on women's work, 170
Leonardo, Micaela di, 112
Lesbian Nation (Johnston), 116
lesbianism, 104–17
  bisexuality, 105
  Boston marriages, 111–12, 126
  "crushes," 35
  Di Vilde Chayes, 329
  as a label, 136
  on historical lesbians, 107
  on historical lesbian relationships,
    107
  homophobia, internalized, 114–17
  lavender menace, 110, 433
  on lesbian existence in novels, 105–6
  in literature, 105–6
  ("not-lesbian") history, 107–12
  racism of, 318
  separatism and Black women, 366–67
  on whether Sappho was a lesbian, 107
LeSueur, Meridel, 60
Lewis, Jill
  on Black women and men, 367–68
  on coalitions, 329
  on the death of the family, 270–71
  on mother-daughter relationships, 27, 28,
    31
  on oppressed groups and change, 376
  on White feminists and racism, 344
  on women and socialism, 212
Lewis, Sinclair, 60
Liberation Now! (anthology), 19
Lifton, Robert J.
  work with veterans, 400–401, 401–2
Linker, Mollie, 224
Little Red Book, The (Mao), 217
Littlebear, Naomi
  and the New Left, 185
Lorde, Audre, 110, 113
  on the assimilation of Black men, 369
  on Black male sexism, 368
  on Black women and men, 367
  on conflicting identities, 319
  on economics and power, 358
  on the experience of oppression, 348
  on poetry, 358

on White feminism and racism, 297, 298, 302, 303, 304, 337
Love, Barbara, 136

MacDaniel, Judith
on lesbian existence in novels, 105–6
Macdonald, Barbara, 424
on ageism among young feminists, 4
on women as caregivers, 169, 224
MacKinnon, Catharine, 423
on marriage as prostitution, 131, 135
on privacy, 142–43, 282
on sexual harassment, 71–72, 141–42
on women's sexuality, 140, 141
McAfee, Kathy
on division along sex lines, 382
and the New Left, 185
McClung, Isabelle, 109
McLaine, Robert, 400, 402
Magdoff, Harry
on capitalism and imperialism, 374
Mailer, Norman, 113
male authorities
feminist groups use of, 7
"Male Homosexuality in the Rorschach" (Hooker), 53
male violence, 423
against children, 2, 249, 259–60
against women, 2
Black male violence, 368–70
Brown University speakout, 144–45
child abuse, 249, 250, 259–60
and the family, 245–46, 423
father-daughter incest, 26, 135, 246, 248, 250
media fascination with, 247–48
randomness of, 93
serial murders, 247, 398–99
sexual harassment, 71–72, 251
as women's work, 169
See also family violence; rape
Malos, Ellen, 186, 187
Maltsova, Natasha, 420
Mamonova, Tatyana, 420
Man-Made Language (Coward), 224
Man's World, Woman's Place (Janeway), 19
Manushi (Indian feminist journal), 171, 422, 423
Mao Zedong, 217
Marcus, Joe, 200

Margolis, Maxine
on capitalism, 371
Marks, Jeannette, 108, 112
marriage
abolishment of, 143
Boston marriages, 111–12, 126
as a choice, 137–38, 138–39
divorce rate, 128
polyandrous marriage, 106
as prostitution, 131–34, 135
in Russia, 420
sex and marriage, 128–30
as unpaid work, 223–24
as the Woman Job, 126–46, 146–48
Marriage as a Trade (Hamilton), 143
Martin, Del, 93, 423
Marx, Eleanor, 188
Marx, Karl, 212, 214, 255–56
Marxism, 184–203
and abortion, 236–37
feminism vs. Marxists, 185–93
and the Left's hatred of women, 192–93
and racism, 292
women, oppression of, 215–22
on women and socialism, 211–28
See also capitalism; socialist feminists
Masculine/Feminine (Roszak/Roszak), 19, 106
Maslow, Abraham, 70, 193
Masson, Jeffrey, 58
on psychoanalysis, 55–56
masturbation
Freud and, 55
women's guilt about, 139
Matthews, Gwyneth Ferguson
on people with disabilities, 415
Matthewson, Ramona, 304
Maurice (Forster), 108
Mead, Margaret, 111
Meade, Marion, 64–65
men
as the enemy, Dale Spender on, 88
father-daughter incest, 26, 135, 246, 248
masculinity training, 385–406
objectification of by mothers, 31
without women, 91
See also male violence
menstrual period as a sign of inferiority, 69
Mermaid and the Minotaur, The (Dinnerstein), 18, 19–21, 106

Merril, Judith
  on the closing of day-care centers, 190
Michalowski, Helen
  on male pathology, 400–401, 401–2
Miller, Jean Baker, 106
  on dependency, 36
Millett, Kate, 19, 24
Mitchell, Juliet, 19, 22, 106
  on separatism, 89
  on women and socialism, 212, 214
Moraga, Cherríe, 324
  on conflicting identities, 318, 319, 326
  on C-R (conciseness raising) groups, 431–
    32
  on lesbian invisibility, 114, 115
  on lesbian separatism, 366
  and the New Left, 185–86
  on racism and guilt, 337
  on reproduction and the patriarchal
    system, 239
  on trade-offs, 341
  on White feminist and racism, 299, 302
Morales, Rosario
  on conflicting identities, 317–18, 320, 323
  on woman's work, 171, 186
Moran, Barbara K., 19
Morgan, E. Noel
  on the abolishment of marriage, 143
Morgan, Robin, 19, 424
  on capitalism and women, 375
  on the family, 270
  and the New Left, 185
  on reproductive freedom, 237, 243–44
Morrison, Toni, 134, 369, 372
  on Black male violence, 368
Morton, Peggy
  on child labor, 266–67
  on women in the workforce, 166–67,
    211
Moschkovich, Judith
  on White feminism and racism, 302, 303–4
"Mother to Dinner" (Sleinger), 36
mother-daughter relationships
  and Asian-American women, 29–30
  differences between Black and White
    women, 27–29
Ms. magazine, 3–4, 373

Nader, Laura
  science and sexual roles, 399

National Women's Studies Association
    Conference (Seattle), xiv
Native Americans
  and lesbianism, 105
  obliteration of lives and histories, 8
Native American Indian women
  conflicting identities, 323–24, 328
  and the feminist movement, 292–311
  and White feminism and racism, 302
NAWSA (National American Women's
    Suffrage Association), 308–10
"Negro Woman's College Education, The"
    (Nobel), 172
New Criticism, 59–61, 65
New Feminism, The (Sochen), 106
New Republic, 372
Newman, Dedra Lynn
  on the Social Security act, 372–73
Nightingale, Florence, 171
Nobel, Jeanne L., 172
"Nobody's People" (Arobateau), 320
"Notes of a Radical Lesbian" (Shelley), 136
NOW Liberation Day March, racism at,
    300

Oakley, Ann, 24
  on capitalism, 355
  on double workday/second shift, 168–69,
    173, 175
  on the family wage, 268–69
  on housewives and monetary resources,
    164
  on marriage as a choice, 137–38
  on the poverty of women, 155–56
  on psychoanalysis, 54
  on reproduction as an obligation, 238–39
  on sex differences, 432
  on the wave of antifeminism in 1918, 9
  on women in the workforce, 166, 189,
    191
Occam, William, 49
Occupation Housewife (Znaniecki), 24
Of Woman Born (A. Rich), 21
Oline, Pam, 35
O'Niell, William
  on the Jane Adams/Mary Rozet Smith
    relationship, 108–9
Origin of the Family, Private Property, and the
    State (Engels), 19, 21
Orlando (Woolf), 19, 431

Pankhurst, Christabel, 1, 20, 95, 375
on marriage, 143
Parker, Katherine, 424
on accumulated wealth, 375
on the Klan and Nazi groups as tools of
the government, 371
on population control, 238
on social support of pregnancy, 243
on women's work, 170
Parker, Pat
on White feminism and racism, 293, 297
part-time work. *See under* economics (and
women)
Patriarchal Attitudes (Figes), 19, 106
patriarchy
capitalism and, 221
heterosexuality as primary force in
maintaining, 146
and reproduction, 239
and the state, 284–85
withdrawing support from, 8
and working-class men, 253–54
Pearlman, Sarah
on liberal guilt, 343
on White feminists and racism, 305
Peck, Ellen, 21
Pence, Ellen
on White feminists and racism, 305
Penelope, Julia
on feminist theory, 6
on the ostracism of lesbianism, 115
separatism, definition of, 87
on separatist consciousness and the
Chicano family, 87
on the women's movement and
separatism, 89
Perez, Julia
on liberal guilt, 343
on White feminism and racism, 293,
297
Perloff, Marjorie
on New Criticism, 65
Petchesky, Rosalind
on capitalism, 355
on double workday/second shift, 170
on women's sexuality, 141, 142
on women's work, 170
Petrozavodsk, Karelia, 420
Phelps, Linda
on women's sexuality, 140

Piercy, Marge, 19
on politics and art, 60
Pizzey, Erwin, 93
Place, Francis, 188
"Poetry Is Not a Luxury" (Lorde), 358
Pogrebin, Letty Cottin
on father-son relationships, 389
on masculinity, 386, 388, 389
Politics of Rape, The (Russell), 423
polyandrous marriage, 106
pornography, 130–31
*Pornography and Silence: Culture's Revenge
against Nature* (Griffin), 24
Pound, Ezra, 60
poverty. *See* economics (and women)
Pratt, Minnie Bruce
on the importance of coalitions, 336
on White feminists and racism, 306–7,
337–38, 339
Pronatalism: The Myth of Mom and Apple Pie
(Peck/Senderowitz), 21
prostitution, 130–31
marriage as, 131–34, 135
Prostitution and Victorian Society
(Walkowitz), 433
Prostitution Papers, The (Millett), 19
prudery, 129–30
psychoanalysis
feminism and, 51–58, 61–62
Purvis, Harriet, 308
Purvis, Robert, 308

Quintanales, Mirtha
on conflicting identities, 321, 325, 326
on growing up in Cuba, 320

racism, 292–311
Combahee River Collective position
statement, 297
conflicting identities, 317–31
early women's movement and, 307–10
and the feminist movement, 292–311
illusion of being non-racist, 293–96
and imperialism, 373–74
Jewish women and, 304–5
Louis Harris–Virginia Slims poll, 310–11
male violence and, 144
token inclusion, 295, 297–301
women's studies and, 304–6
See also coalition building

Radical Women, *xiv*
Radway, Janice, 18, 19, 31
  and emotional deprivation, 30, 34
  Reading the Romance, 18, 24–27
rape, 147–48, 249–50, 250–51
  of children, 2
  martial, 245–46, 247
  in Russia, 420
  sexual harassment, 71–72
  woman-woman, 105–6
  See also child abuse; family violence; male
    violence
Rapp, Rayna
  on the isolation of family from work, 356
Reactionary Feminism, *xiv*
  See also conservative feminism
Reading the Romance (Radway), 18, 24–27
Reagon, Bernice Johnson
  on coalitions, 329–31
  on oppressed groups and change, 376
  on racism, 339
  on singing and community, 225
Redd, Spring
  on Black mother-daughter relationships,
    28
  on conflicting identities, 319
  on White feminism and racism, 295
Redmond, Charles, 308
Reeves, Maud Pember
  on population control, 237–38
"Reflection on Eroticism" (C. Rich), 114
Reproduction of Mothering, The (Chodorow),
    18, 21–24, 106
Reznick, Allen
  on the lesbianism of Lillian Wald, 109
Rich, Adrienne, 19, 21, 113, 358
  on heterosexuality, 23, 133, 137, 146
  on lesbian invisibility, 114, 143
  on the McCarthy era, 60–61
  on politics and art, 59–60
  on women's self-interest, 94
  on Women's Studies, 4
Rich, Cynthia, 115
  on death and dying, 416–17
  on women as caregivers, 169
Robinson, Patricia
  on reproductive rights, 239
Romo-Carmona, Mariana, 324
  on trade-offs, 341
Room of One's Own, A (Woolf), 19, 430–31

Roosevelt, Eleanor, 107–8
Roseanne
  on working-class women, 340
Ross, Ellen
  on the isolation of family from work, 356
Ross, Kathy
  on separatism, 89
  separatism, definition of, 86
  separatism as community base, 86–87
Rossi, Alice
  on psychoanalysis, 61–62
Roszak, Betty, 19, 106
Roszak, Theodore, 19, 106
Rowbotham, Sheila, 187
Rubin, Gayle, 21
  on the effect of class society, 278
  on marriage as a choice, 137, 142
  on marriage, middle class vs. working
    class, 165
  on men relating to men, 405–6
  on monetary resources, 164
  on the sexual revolutions of the 1960s, 140
  on the standardization of skills, 279
  on working class-women, 176
Rubin, Lillian Breslow
  on fear of effeminacy, 392
Ruddick, Sara
  on sexual demands of adult life, 62
Rupp, Leila
  on Eleanor Roosevelt's lesbianism, 107–8
Rush, Florence, 56, 58
  on Freud's theories, 54–55
  on questioning sexuality, 130
Russell, Diana, 56, 423
  on incest and child abuse, 248, 249
Ryotu Mahila Sangham (Indian women's
  organization), 423

Saadawi, Nawal El
  on capitalism, 375
  on the economics of childbirth, 236, 240,
    421
  on "high politics," 436
  on patriarchy and the state, 284
  on women's overloaded workday, 422
Sackville-West, Vita, 113
  on the lesbianism of, 430
Sage, 27
Sahli, Nancy, 109
Salt Eaters, The (Bambara), 357

Sandburg, Carl, 60
Sanford, Linda Tschirhart, 9
  on marriage and loneliness, 138
  on questioning sexuality, 130
  on women's work, 169
Sappho, 107
Sartre, Jean-Paul, 22
Schaef, Anne
  on boys and organized sports, 387
  on masculinity, 395
  on questioning sexuality, 130
Schlesinger, Arthur, Jr.
  on the lesbianism of Eleanor Roosevelt, 107–8
Schreiner, Olive, 127–28
  on marriage as prostitution, 135
scientific method, 48–49
Scott, Hilda
  on double workday/second shift, 169
  on social services, 374
  on women's poverty, 156, 162
  on women's unpaid labor, 175–76, 371
  on women's work, 172–73, 173, 173–74, 421
Second Sex, The (de Beauvoir), 19, 24, 112
second shift. See under economics (and women)
Second Stage (Friedan), 4–5
"Secrets of Long-lasting Marriages" (Ms. magazine), 3–4
Segal, Lynne
  and the New Left, 186, 187
Seidman, Gay W., 424
Seizing Our Bodies (Dreifus), 106
Senderowitz, Judith, 21
Sennett, Richard
  on male sacrifice and the family, 383–84
separatism, 84–96
  active non-cooperation, 88
  as community base, 86–87
  definitions of, 86, 87
  lesbian separatism and Black women, 366–67
  lesbianism and 104–17
  male children, exclusion of, 89
serial murders, fascination with, 247–48
Servetus, Michael, 57
sex-classes, 67, 93, 133
sex reform movement, 130–33
Sexual Enlightenment of Children (Freud), 52

sexual harassment, 71–72
Sexual Harassment of Working Women (MacKinnon), 423
Sexual Politics (Millett), 24
Shange, Ntozake, 368
Sheldon, Alice
  on government and sexual roles, 400
  on nature, 72
  on psychoanalysis, 51–58
Shelley, Martha, 136
Sherman, Joan R., 304
Sherrod, Drury
  on the effects of industrialism, 382
  on male friendships, 392–93
  on marriage as friendship, 383, 396
Shockley, Ann Allen
  on Black lesbian literature, 318
Shulman, Alix Kates, 61
Signs (feminist journal), 434
Silveira, Jeanette, xiv. See also Fox (Jeanette Silveira)
Sisterhood Is Global: The International Women's Movement Anthology (Morgan, ed.), 117, 424
Sisterhood Is Powerful (Morgan, ed.), 7, 19, 434
slave psychology, 36
Sleinger, Tess, 36
smiling
  as an act of appeasement, 226
  and oppression, 225–26
  smile boycott, 34
Smith, Adam, 201
Smith, Barbara
  on Black lesbians and homophobia, 117
  on Black women's homophobia, 319
  on Christianity, 347
  on coalitions, 329
  on conflicting identities, 327
  on the differences between cultural codes, 350
  on the experience of oppression, 347, 349–50
  on housewives and monetary resources, 164
  on lesbian invisibility, 115, 116, 134
  on lesbian separatism, 366, 367
  on liberal guilt, 343
  and the New Left, 185, 187
  on trade-offs, 341, 345
  on White feminism and racism, 293, 297, 304, 336, 344

Smith, Barbara (*continued*)
  on women's studies, 340
  on women's work, 169
Smith, Beverly
  on conflicting identities, 326, 327
  on the differences between cultural codes, 350
  on racism, 293
Smith, Dorothy
  and the New Left, 186
  on women and capitalism, 211
  on women's earning power, 177
  on women in the labor market, 189–90
Smith, Mary Rozet, 108–9
Smith-Rosenberg, Carroll, 106–7, 126
Snitow, Anne, 186
Sochen, June, 106
"Social Construction of the Second Sex, The" (Freeman), 21
socialism, 184–203
  and abortion, 236–37
  feminism vs. Marxists, 185–93
  and the Left's hatred of women, 192–93
  and racism, 292
  women, oppression of, 215–22
  on women and socialism, 211–28
  See also capitalism
socialist feminists, 211–28
  economics and, 185–89
  See also communism; economics (and women)
Sociology of Women's Housework, The (Oakley), 24
Spender, Dale, *xiv*, 11
  on C-R (conciseness raising) groups, 431
  on men as the enemy, 88
  Women of Ideas, 1–2, 4, 88, 106
  on women's communicative work, 224
  on the Women's Social and Political Union, 87–88
Spretnak, Charlene
  science and sexual roles, 399
Stacey, Judith
  on conservative feminism, 5
  on women's oppression and socialism, 215, 217
Stansell, Christine, 186

Stanton, Elizabeth Cady, 308–10
Staples, Robert
  on Black men and strong women, 368–69
Starr, Ellen Gates, 108
Stoller, Robert, 110
Stone, Lucy, 308
Story of an African Farm, The (Schreiner), 127–28
Strega, Linda
  on "femininity" as a male concept, 141
Sula (Morrison), 134
Sweezy, Paul
  on capitalism and imperialism, 374

Tanner, Leslie, 19
Tax, Meredith
  on men as consumers of women, 139
Taylor, Barbara, 189
Taylor, Mary
  on women as labor, 154
Taylor, Patricia A.
  Black women vs. White women in the labor force, 346
Teish, Luisah, 28
  on the split between "good" and "evil," 357
Ten Hours Advocate (labor newspaper), 189
Terkel, Studs, 200
"That Tired Old Question of Male Children," 89
Thomas, M. Carey, 107, 112
Thomas, Piri, 323
Thompson, Sharon, 186
Thompson, William, 171
Three Guineas (Woolf), 19, 431
Touchstones (Lamb), 142
Toward a New Psychology of Women (Miller), 106
"Traffic in Women, The" (Rubin), 21
Trilling, Lionel, 60
Truth, Sojourner, 307
"2000 Year Old Misunderstanding, The" (Haskell), 24
Twort, Hazel
  on housewives, 169

"Unhappy Marriage of Marxism and Feminism, The" (Hartmann), 24

Up Against the Wall, Mother (Adams/ Briscoe), 19
Urban Research Review, 28

Vaid, Sudesh, 423
Valerio, Anita, 357
  on conflicting identities, 318, 319
Vance, Carole
  on the acceptance of heterosexual institutions, 146–47
Vanita, Ruth
  on the status of women in India, 422
Vicinus, Martha, 433
violence. *See* male violence
Viramontes, Helena Maria
  on mass media image of "happy home," 137
Voices from Women's Liberation (Tanner), 19

wage inequities. *See under* economics
Wages for Housework Campaign, 177
Wald, Lillian, 109
Walker, Alice
  definition of "womanish," 28
  on White feminism and racism, 297, 300–301
Walker, Lenore
  on the family and violence, 245
Walker, Melissa, 144
Wallace, Michelle, 106, 368
  on Black male sexism, 368
  on Black women, 353–54
  on conflicting identities, 327
  on femininity, 346–47
  on White feminism and racism, 295–96, 345
Walkowitz, Judith
  on the Freedom League, 433
Washington, Mary Helen, 106
  on race, 292
Weems, Renita
  on Black women turning to other women for emotional support, 142
  on mother-daughter relationships, 29
  on Toni Morrison, 369, 372
Weinbaum, Batya
  on the family wage, 267
  on women and Marxism, 212, 214
  on women's oppression and socialism, 216–17, 217–18, 219

Weindling, Gwendolyn
  on the differences between cultural codes, 350
Weir, Angela
  on women in the workforce, 212
Weisstein, Naomi
  on Freud, 52
  on psychoanalysis, 52–53
  on the reliability of clinical judgement, 53
Wells, Anna Mary
  on the Jeannette Marks/Mary E. Woolley relationship, 108
When and Where I Enter (Giddings), 106
"When We Dead Awaken" (A. Rich), 19
"Why Men Oppress Women" (Fox), 66
Willard, Frances
  racism of, 309
Williams, Jan
  on housewives, 169
Williams, Ora, 304
Williams, Thelma, 304
Willis, Ellen, review of *Second Stage*, 4–5
Wilson, Dora, 304
Wilson, Elizabeth
  on questioning sexuality, 130
Wise, Audrey
  on women and unions, 192
Wittig, Monique, 435
Wolf, Naomi
  on violence to women and the media, 247–48
Wollstonecraft, Mary, 112
  on marriage as prostitution, 135
Wood, Myrna
  on division along sex lines, 382
  and the New Left, 185
Woolf, Virginia, 19, 113
  on double workday, 167
  on the lesbianism of, 430–31
  on the poverty of women, 154, 165
Woolley, Mary E., 108, 112
Wolpe, Annmarie, 24
Woman Identified Woman, The (Radicalesbians), 136
Woman in Sexist Society (Gornick/ Moran), 19
Woman Job, the, 126–46, 146–48
  See also economics (and women); heterosexuality; marriage

Woman and Sex (Saadawi), 421
Woman on the Edge of Time (Piercy), 57
Woman's Estate (Mitchell), 19, 22, 89, 106
"Woman's Labor, The" (Collier), 167–68
woman-battering, 2
    See also family violence; rape; *also under* violence
"womanish," definition of, 28
Women, Church and State (Gage), 1
Women and Economics (Gilman), 20, 22
Women and Madness (Chesler), 19
Women and Russia (Mamonova), 420
Women of Ideas (Spender), 1–2, 4, 106
women's dominance gestures
    Nancy Henley on, 69
Women's Social and Political Union (WSPU), 87–88
    contributions to, 127
Women's Studies, academization of, 4
Women's Work: The Housewife, Past and Present (Oakley), 24

Woo, Merle
    on Asian-American mother-daughter relationships, 29–30
work. *See* economics (and women)
Working It Out: 23 Women Writers, Artists, Scientists, and Scholars Talk about Their Lives and Work (Ruddick/ Daniels, eds.), 62, 138–39

Yamada, Mitsuye
    on conflicting identities, 320, 323
    on racism, 295, 299
Yellin, Jean Fagin, 304
Young, Marilyn, 110
    on women and capitalism, 211
Yours in Struggle (Bulkin), 305
yuppie values and feminist groups, 7

Zetkin, Clara
    on birth control, 188
Znaniecki, Helena, 24